GAME CODING COMPLETE

THIRD EDITION

Mike "MrMike" McShaffry et al.

Charles River Media

A part of Course Technology, Cengage Learning

COURSE TECHNOLOGY
CENGAGE Learning™

Australia, Brazil, Japan, Korea, Mexico, Singapore, Spain, United Kingdom, United States

COURSE TECHNOLOGY
CENGAGE Learning™

Game Coding Complete, Third Edition
Mike "MrMike" McShaffry et al.

Publisher and General Manager, Course Technology PTR:
Stacy L. Hiquet

Associate Director of Marketing:
Sarah Panella

Content Project Manager:
Jessica McNavich

Marketing Manager:
Jordan Casey

Acquisitions Editor:
Heather Hurley

Project and Copy Editor:
Marta Justak

Technical Reviewer:
Sascha Friedmann, Vincent Magiya

PTR Editorial Services Coordinator:
Jen Blaney

Interior Layout Tech:
Bill Hartman

Cover Designer:
Kris Taylor

Indexer:
Larry Sweazy

Proofreader:
Heather Urschel

**Course Technology,
a part of Cengage Learning**
20 Channel Center Street
Boston, MA 02210
USA

For your lifelong learning solutions, visit
courseptr.com.

Visit our corporate Web site at **cengage.com**.

For product information and technology assistance, contact us at
Cengage Learning Customer & Sales Support, 1-800-354-9706

For permission to use material from this text or product, submit all requests online at **cengage.com/permissions**. Further permissions questions can be e-mailed to **permissionrequest@cengage.com**.

Microsoft, Microsoft Windows, Visual Studio, Internet Explorer, Xbox, Xbox360, and DirectX are either registered trademarks or trademarks of Microsoft Corporation in the United States and/or other countries.

3ds Max and Maya are either registered trademarks or trademarks of Autodesk, Inc. in the United States and/or other countries.

Gamecube and Wii are trademarks of Nintendo Company, Ltd. in the United States and/or other countries.

PlayStation, PlayStation 2, and PlayStation 3 are either registered trademarks or trademarks of Microsoft Corporation in the United States and/or other countries.

Photoshop is a registered trademark of Adobe Systems Incorporated in the United States and/or other countries.

Ultima and Ultima Online are either registered trademarks or trademarks of Electronic Arts, Inc. in the United States and/or other countries.

All other trademarks are the property of their respective owners.

Library of Congress Control Number: 2008939941

ISBN-13: 978-1-58450-680-5

ISBN-10: 1-58450-680-6

Cengage Learning is a leading provider of customized learning solutions with office locations around the globe, including Singapore, the United Kingdom, Australia, Mexico, Brazil, and Japan. Locate your local office at: **international.cengage.com/region**.

Cengage Learning products are represented in Canada by Nelson Education, Ltd.

Printed in the United States of America
2 3 4 5 6 7 11 10

This book and my life are dedicated to
my wife and my best friend,
Robin

KUDOS

From Blue Phoenix:

I definitely hope that it's not the last publication you make, I'm sure books can be a challenge, but you've done an amazing job. Kudos to you, the editors, publisher, and everyone who helped produce this fine book.

From CdrJ:

Overall this book is pretty much all meat. I can't recommend it highly enough, and I've praised it to my entire team. It's probably the most useful game development text on my shelf.

From Paul Jeffrey at Amazon.com

But here's a test you can take for yourself... go to www.mcshaffry.com/GameCode and see how Mike McShaffry is *still* helping folks who've read his book (or anyone who posts on the site for that matter). He's still giving *free* advice on his book's forum, when most other authors won't even respond to an email.

From Codehead on Amazon.com

This is an excellent book. The author clearly is an expert on the subject, and he has spent years developing mainstream commercial games (for example, *Ultima* series). This is a refreshing change from so many books out there written by people with some theoretical knowledge, but little practical application.

I will buy any book this guy writes in the future. Can't give a better recommendation than that.

From spotland on Amazon.com

I have studied a lot of the "standard" game coding books recently. This is the first game book I have read that I was sorry when I got to the end because there wasn't any more. I had to read it again. It is full of relevant content, peppered with real insights from someone who has obviously been there and gotten the T-shirt. Because of its breadth of scope, it has helped me fill in a lot of gaps left by some of the other texts. I have been programming in C++ for over 13 years, and I still learned a few neat tricks. One of these was directly relevant to a program I am writing—thanks for the tip!

FOREWORD

Let me start by admitting a couple of things. First, I've never written a foreword for a book before. I've written books but never a foreword. Honestly, I usually skip right over these things when I'm reading a book, so odds are that no one is ever going to read what I'm writing here anyway. That makes it safe for me to move on to admission number two: I'm not a programmer. Never have been, and I fear, never will be, despite some valiant efforts on my part (if I do say so myself). I've done okay despite not knowing a blessed thing about programming. I'm not looking for sympathy or anything, but I am here to tell you that a day doesn't go by when I don't think, "Damn, if only I knew my z-buffers from my BSP trees!" If you're already a programmer, you've got a huge leg up on me when I tried to get into the electronic game biz! (And if you're not a programmer, do as I say and not as I do—learn to program ASAP. Mike has some advice about how to do that in the pages that follow. Pay attention.)

Okay, so with those two confessions out of the way, I figure there's a fair chance any credibility I might have had is pretty well shot. Luckily for you folks, the guy who wrote this book has credibility to burn. Mike McShaffry (or "Mr. Mike" as he's known to most everyone in the game biz) is the real deal. Mike is a genuine survivor. He is a guy who can talk the talk because, Lord knows, he's walked the walk enough times to earn some talking time.

Mike's experience of game development runs the gamut in a pretty remarkable way. He was there when teams were a dozen folks, and he's been around in the era of 20, 30, and 50-person teams. He's done the start-up thing, worked for the biggest publishers in the business, worked on "traditional" games and decidedly untraditional ones—everything from *Ultima* to *Blackjack*, single player, multiplayer, online and off, and just about everything else you can imagine. When it comes to PC games, he speaks with the authority of someone who's worn just about every hat it's possible to wear—programmer, designer, project leader, director of development, studio head….

And I've had the privilege of watching him learn and grow with each new project and each new role. I was there when Mike got his first game job. I was one of the folks at Origin who interviewed him back in the Bone Ages, back in the 20th century, way back in 1990, when he applied for a programming job at Origin. (Seems like forever, doesn't it, Mike? Whew!)

He started out as "just" a programmer on *Martian Dreams,* a game I produced for Origin, but by the end of the project, he was the engine that drove that game to the finish line. The game wouldn't have happened without Mike. His drive, dedication, love of games, knack for on-the-fly design, natural leadership skills, ability to combine right brain and left brain (to say nothing of his willingness to work crazy hours), drove all of us to work that much harder and ensured that the game ended up something special (at least to those of us who worked on it together—it sure didn't sell many copies!).

I honestly don't even remember if I ever gave Mike the title "Lead Programmer" officially on *Martian Dreams,* but he sure deserved it. The guy was a machine, working longer hours than most people I've worked with (and that's saying something in the game business). He also managed to do more and better work in those hours than any human being should be allowed to. It just ain't fair to the rest of us mere mortals. When Mike was on, there was no touching him. And he was almost always on—after *Martian Dreams,* Mike did it again and again, on *Ultima VII, VIII, IX* and a bunch of others. Scary really.

In retrospect, all those hours and all the hard work that seemed so necessary, back in the days when we were all younger and more foolish than we are now, was probably an indication that Mike, like the rest of us, didn't have a clue about software development or game design or much anything else. (Okay, we had a pretty good handle on the effects of sugar and caffeine on the human body, but that's about it.) We had to work so long and so hard just to have a chance in hell of ending up with something worthwhile.

Reading this book, I couldn't help but marvel at how much Mike's learned over the years and wonder how much more Mike—and the rest of us—would have gotten done, how much better our games might have been, if we'd had the benefit of the kind of information in the pages that follow. There just wasn't anyone around back then who knew enough about games, programming practices, and software development. We were making it up as we went along.

Today, there are plenty of books out there that can teach you the typing part of programming. There are even some books that go a bit further and teach you what makes game coding different from coding a word processing program or a billing system for your local health care providers (or, as we used to call 'em, "doctors"). But even now, there just aren't many books that combine hard-core game programming advice with equally hard-core development processes, debugging, and team-building information.

Development process? Team-building? Who cares about all that? You just want to write code, right? If you're like a lot of programmers I know, that's just what you're thinking. And, man, are you wrong. There might have been a time when coders could just close their doors and type, not caring about how their work fit into the bigger picture of a game's development. Maybe that was true 10 years ago or more (probably not, but maybe…). Well, it sure isn't true anymore. With teams getting bigger all the time, with timelines stretching and budgets bloating, process and team issues are everyone's concern nowadays.

Mike gets that, something that becomes clear in the very first chapter, when he says, "Being the best developer you can be requires that you have intimate knowledge about the real demands of the industry." Amen, brother. That, in a nutshell, is what makes this book special. Most people think enthusiasm and talent are enough to get them into the game business and to ensure success once they land that all-important first gig. "I play games all the time," they say, "and I'm a kickass coder, so what more is there to know. Sign me up!"

Well, I'm here to tell you that there's plenty more to know and that's probably the single most valuable lesson this book has to offer. Games are insanely complex, and their creation involves a unique combination of art and science (some call it "magic," and they're not far wrong). Game development is demanding in a way that can only be appreciated after a stint in the trenches. At least, I used to think that was the case, but that's where Mike comes in. Having been in the trenches, he can save you the trouble and pain and scars and relationship breakups and company failures that all too often go along with game development. No matter what you may think, it isn't all glory, fame, wealth, and intense personal satisfaction (though there is a better than fair share of that last item...).

There's a ton of great stuff in Mike's book. Even if you're a nonprogrammer, you'll get something out of the introductory chapters and the section about "Professional Game Production." And I love all the insider bits found in Mike's "Tales from the Pixel Mines."

Of course, there's plenty of nuts-and-bolts stuff for folks who are already programmers but want to know what makes game programming so special (and believe me, it is). But even programmers will benefit from the other ton of stuff that often gets short shrift in the typical programming book—all that Big Picture stuff that doesn't involve code samples.

These are critical to being the most effective developer you can be, whether you're a programmer or not. This is all stuff you can't get just anywhere. You have to have lived through the process (and the pain!) a bunch of times. Or you have to find a mentor and spend years sucking his or her brain dry. Or you can stop reading this foreword and start reading this book.

What are you waiting for?

—Warren Spector

ACKNOWLEDGMENTS

Mom and Grandma Hawker
Thanks for never saying I'd never amount to anything, playing games all the time; you believed in me, and it paid off.

Dad and Lynn
Thanks for showing me I should never be afraid of hard work.

Phil Hawker
Thanks for giving me a sense of humor—I think I put it to good use here.

Warren Spector and Richard Garriott
Thanks for believing a geeky college kid could help make the games I loved to play.

Third Edition Guest Authors and Extra Help
James Clarendon, Jeff Lake, Quoc Tran, David (Rez) Graham, Chris Shelley

Third Edition Beta Testers
Sascha Friedmann, Vincent Magiya

Third Edition Publisher and Editor
Thanks to Heather Hurley for picking up the book for a third edition.
Thanks to my editor Marta Justak for making me look like a writer.

CONTRIBUTOR ACKNOWLEDGMENTS

The Cover Artist

The cover was created by my friend and co-worker Kris Taylor.
He is currently the Art Director of Red Fly Studio in Austin, Texas.

James Clarendon, Author of Chapter 11,
"Scripting With Lua"

I'd like to thank Mr. Mike for this opportunity as well as all the good times (and bad!)
we've shared in this crazy industry.

A special thanks to Edith, who has kept me sane during many of these times.

Jeff Lake, Co-author of Chapter 15,
"Collision and Simple Physics"

To Larry Lake: It's no EOR, but it's close.

David "Rez" Graham, Author of Chapter 17,
"An Introduction to Game AI"

Steph Laberis for her constant encouragement.
My father for giving me my first programming book.
My mother for never telling me to stop wasting my life playing games.
My grandfather for his sage wisdom.
And last but not least, my good friend Mike McShaffry for giving me this opportunity.

Quoc Tran, Author of Chapter 19,
"A Simple Game Editor in C#"

Dr. Bruce Naylor for inspiring me to become a game developer.
Peter Freese for giving me my first break in the industry as a programmer.
My lovely wife, whose patience and support helped me maintain my tenuous grip on sanity.

ABOUT THE AUTHOR

Mike McShaffry, aka "Mr. Mike," started programming games as soon as he could tap a keyboard—in fact, he somehow skipped seventh grade math entirely in favor of writing games in BASIC on an ancient Commodore Pet. In his single-minded pursuit of programming knowledge, he signed up for an extended stay at the University of Houston. To his surprise of himself and the Dean of Mathematics, he actually graduated five and one-half years later. Shortly after graduation, he entered the boot camp of the computer game industry: Origin Systems. He worked for Warren Spector and Richard Garriott, aka "Lord British," on *Martian Dreams*, *Ultima VII: The Black Gate*, *Ultima VIII: Pagan*, *Ultima IX: Ascension*, and *Ultima Online*.

Exactly seven years from the day he was hired, Mike arranged his escape and in 1997 formed his first company, Tornado Alley. Tornado Alley was a garage start-up whose goal was to create *No Grownups Allowed*, a massively multiplayer world for children—something that was sure to land Mike and anyone else at Tornado Alley front and center of a Congressional hearing. While *No Grownups* never left the tarmac, a kid's activity program called *Magnadoodle* by Mattel Media did, and in record development time.

The entrepreneurial bug, a ravenous and insatiable beast, finally devoured enough of Mike's remaining EA stock to motivate him to take a steady gig at Glass Eye Entertainment, working for his friend Monty Kerr, where he produced *Microsoft Casino*. Ten short months later, Monty asked Mike and his newly assembled team to start their own company called Compulsive Development, which worked exclusively with Microsoft on casual casino and card games.

Mike served as the primary coffee brew master and head of studio, and together with the rest of the Compulsive folks, 20 great people in all, produced three more casual titles for Microsoft until August 2002. Compulsive was acquired by Glass Eye Entertainment to continue work on Glass Eye's growing online casual games business.

Mike was hungry for AAA console work, and in 2003 he got what he wanted: Ion Storm's *Thief: Deadly Shadows* team called Mike in to create their third-person camera technology and work on fine-tuning character movement at the 11th hour. What started as a two-week contract turned into almost a year of labor working side-by-side with programmers who used to call Mike "boss."

While it was great to be "one of the boys" again, it couldn't last forever. Mike was recruited to start an Austin studio for Maryland-based Breakaway Games. Breakaway Austin's focus was AAA console development and high-end simulations for the U.S. military and DoD contractors. Mike and three of the BreakAway Austin team actually visited the USS Harry S. Truman, one of the U.S. Navy's CVN class Nuclear Aircraft Carriers. They flew out, landed on the carrier, spent four days and nights with the officers and crew, and got launched to go back home. Afterwards, they created *24 Blue*, a training simulator that mimics the insane environment of the deck of the carrier, jets and everything.

After BreakAway Austin, Mike founded a consulting company called MrMike. He figured that nearly 18 years in the gaming industry was enough to firmly establish that as a good identity for the company. For nearly two years, he helped small game companies choose their game technology, firm up their production practices, and pitch game ideas to industry publishers like Microsoft, EA, THQ, and others. One of his clients, Red Fly Studio, made him an offer he couldn't refuse, and he jumped back into a full-time gig.

Mike took the position of Executive Producer and helped ship *Mushroom Men: The Spore Wars*. He is currently working on *Ghostbusters* for the Wii and two unannounced titles. He still makes coffee and tries to give good advice to the programmers, artists, designers, audio guys, and producers working for him.

He still writes code when he can—most recently working with his friend Quoc creating some nifty plug-ins for Microsoft Project, called *MrMike's Addins*.

If Mike's fingers aren't tapping away at a keyboard, he's probably either "downhilling" on his mountain bike or enjoying good times with his friends in Austin, Texas.

CONTENTS

PART III: CORE GAME TECHNOLOGIES

PART IV: ADVANCED TOPICS AND BRINGING IT ALL TOGETHER	

CHAPTER 21   DEBUGGING YOUR GAME   797

INTRODUCTION

WHO IS MR. MIKE AND WHY SHOULD I CARE?

I had been playing the *Ultima* series of games by Richard Garriott since I was in high school, and I was a die-hard fan. Every game he published, I played all the way through, from *Ultima I* on the Apple][to *Ultima V* on the IBM PC. *Ultima VI* came out right as I graduated from college, and I noticed that the contact information for Origin Systems was in Austin, Texas. I was living in Houston at the time, and my wife and I were ready for a change. On a whim, I sent my resume and a letter to Richard Garriott. Weeks went by. I heard nothing.

I finally called Origin and asked the receptionist about it. When she found out that I'd sent my resume to Richard, she laughed and said that was the last thing I should have done. She gave me the name of Dallas Snell, Origin's Vice President of Product Development. I sent him my resume via Federal Express and hoped for the best. I got a call two days later, and Dallas asked me how soon I could get to Austin for an interview. I asked him if tomorrow was too soon! He told me he'd see me for the interview at 2 p.m. I was terrified. I wore a tie, but my wife smartly told me to take it off before I entered the building. It was a good thing because Dallas was dressed in shorts, flip-flops, and a Hawaiian shirt.

I didn't have a shred of game programming experience, and during my interview I was asked by a panel of Origin upper crust how I knew I could cut it at Origin. I looked around the table and saw the likes of Richard Garriott, aka Lord British, Warren Spector, Chris Roberts of *Wing Commander* fame, and six other folks. I tried not to panic. After all, I didn't know if I could cut it, did I? If I'd never actually programmed a real game before, I couldn't stand before industry luminaries and just be arrogant.

Instead, I came right out and told them that I didn't know if I could cut it. I told them that programming games was a dream I had since I could reach up and tap a keyboard. I promised them that if they hired me, and I sucked, that I'd leave Origin and not return until I earned my place there. I wanted to be a game programmer, and I'd do anything to make that dream come true. I guess they liked my answer because I got a job offer the following Monday. That was October, 1990.

I've spent the following years doing some programming but also some project management. I've worked on fantasy role-playing games, MMO's, kid's games, casual games, action stealth games, military training simulations, and platformers. I've worked on the PC, Xbox, and the Wii.

WELCOME TO THE THIRD EDITION

The first edition of this book was published in the summer of 2003, just as I was making some big transitions of my own. The first edition gave me a chance to stand back and show programmers what really goes on in the world of game development. Writing the book was a challenge but the rewards were many. I heard from programmers all around the world who enjoyed the book and found the stories, insight, and programming tips to be helpful. The second edition was almost a complete rewrite. The book went from around 700 pages to 1,110, and was more popular than the first edition.

As big as the second edition was, it didn't cover some really important topics, such as AI, multiprogramming, working with scripting languages like Lua, and how to write C# tools like your level editor. In 2008, Charles River and I and four of my friends and colleagues agreed to tackle the third edition.

What you hold in your hands is the result.

WHERE IS THE CODE? MUST I ACTUALLY TYPE?

Shortly after the publication of the first edition of this book, I made a Web site to provide resources and helpful information for readers. This site also became a great place for downloading the book's source code examples, and all manner of interesting stuff. The site has really grown since the first edition, and now it has become quite a resource center. So if you are looking for additional help, the source code, or you want to share your thoughts with other game programmers, point your browser to one of these two places:

www.mcshaffry.com/GameCode/
www.courseptr.com/downloads

I've never included a CD because the source code will get fixed and tweaked even as this book goes to press and long thereafter. Good suggestions and fixes even come from readers like you. Grab the code from my Web site (or the publisher's), and you'll be assured of getting the latest source code and information.

HOW THIS BOOK IS ORGANIZED

The book is organized into four parts:

- **Part One—Game Programming Fundamentals**: Exposes some stuff that you'll want in your game programming toolbox, like a good random number generator. It also introduces the major components of games and how they interact. After you read the chapters in this part, you'll have a good working knowledge of the real architecture that game developers use.

- **Part Two—Get Your Game Running:** It's now time to learn how to get all of the main building blocks of your game together, including the initialization and shutdown code, the main loop, game data structures, user interfaces and input device code, and sprites and fonts. You'll find your first meaty game code examples, including user interface code and your main loop. Often, many programming books just gloss over this stuff and jump right into the cool 3D code. But in reality, this is the stuff you really need to know to create a successful game, no matter what type of game you want to build.
- **Part Three—Core Game Technologies:** The tougher code examples are in this section, such as 3D programming, scripting with Lua, game audio, physics, and network game programming.
- **Part Four—Advanced Topics and Bringing It All Together:** In this section, you'll find chapters on AI, programming with threads, creating tools in C#, and bringing all the code in the book together to make a little game. You'll also see some of my best debugging tricks and an entire chapter on how it feels to be there when you release a commercial game.

Throughout the book, you'll see a few insets that are identified by the following icons:

GOTCHA

When you see this icon, you'll read about a common mistake that I'm hoping you can avoid. Mostly likely, I didn't and suffered the consequences.

BEST PRACTICE

This inset is something I do by habit, and it helps me avoid programming trouble. Usually, I learned these tips from someone else who taught me, and I'm passing on the good word.

TALES FROM THE PIXEL MINES

Working in the pixel mines is slang for working on computer games. Since I've worked in the industry since 1990 and I'm a creature of observation, I couldn't help but bring a few tall tales to the book from my game industry experiences. Some tales are taller than others, but believe it or not, they all actually happened.

WHAT YOU'LL NEED

If you're a programmer and you've had some game programming experience, you'll be able to follow along nicely. Take a moment to flip through the pages, and you'll see this book is written for programmers. Nonprogrammers could probably get something from the book, too, but there is more code in this book than noncode.

The code is written in C++, so if you are a die-hard C programmer, you'll have to at least be able to read C++ to get the most out of this book. If you don't know either language, you'll probably struggle a little with the code samples, but I'll bet you can get enough from the comments and the explanations to get your money's worth.

All of the code in this book works under Visual Studio 2003 and 2005, or at least it did when I copied it into Microsoft Word, which is how I wrote the book. I apologize ahead of time for making no attempt whatsoever to make sure the code worked in other compilers like CodeWarrior or GNU C++. I hope you'll forgive me. I figured my time would be better spent by covering as much technical ground as possible, instead of working on multicompiler-compatible code.

The code in this book also has a heavy Win32 bias. I'm a Win32 programmer, and I was a DOS programmer before that. I've had some brief forays into UNIX on the *Ultima Online* server code, but I'm hardly an expert. Much of the code in this book assumes Win32, and I didn't change the code to support cross-compiling into other operating systems for much the same reason as I chose a single compiler. It was simply better for me to cover lots of technical issues than for me to check my code under LINUX.

As far as graphics APIs are concerned, I assume you'll use DirectX 9 or later. I don't have anything against OpenGL, of course, but I'm just not an expert in the nuances. Basically, if you have a good working knowledge in C++, Win32, and a passing knowledge of DirectX, you'll be fine. You don't have to be godlike in your skill, but you should be pretty comfortable coding in these areas.

If you are a complete newbie and perhaps only know a little C++, don't feel dejected and don't return this book! I have a plan for you. Throughout this book, I'll refer to other tomes of knowledge that helped me learn how to program. They can help you, too, and you can use them in conjunction with the humble collection of knowledge you hold in your hands. With a little concentration, you can bootstrap yourself into programming prowess. I learned more about programming in C++, DirectX, and Win32 by looking at working code, of which there is plenty included in these pages for you to enjoy.

STL AND BOOST C++

This book uses STL for common data structures. If you don't know anything about STL, you'll see some good examples in this book, and I'm sure you'll be able to follow the code. I'm not attempting to teach you STL, which is something that is beyond the scope of this book. Instead, go read *The C++ Standard Library: A Tutorial and Reference* by Nicolai M. Josuttis. After you get your bearings, go read Scott Meyer's books on STL because they're fantastic.

STL is a body of code that is extremely well tested, has a widely understood API, and is available on almost every development platform. If you haven't seen it yet, stop reading right now and do a little research. You'll never have to write code for common data structures like linked lists, resizable arrays, and trees ever again. I've saved hours of grief using <list>, <vector>, and <map>.

Whatever happens, don't get caught writing your own linked-list class or tree when STL would have worked. All implementations are extremely well tested. Every bug or implementation oddity has already been exposed and discussed on the Internet. Your own code, on the other hand, is not.

While only a small portion of the Boost C++ Library is used in this book, it is an amazing resource, and like STL, it contains a wealth of well-tested code.

SOURCE CODE AND CODING STANDARDS

I despise technical books that include source code that doesn't compile. I cursed the name of every author and editor who created these books, filled with errors and broken code. I'm now doomed to join their ranks.

Microsoft Word just doesn't handle C++ source code very well. Since this book is printed in black and white, the code highlighting has to be turned off. I understand, now, why so many programming books are crawling with errors. I apologize to every author and editor I maligned. Until I wrote this book, I had no idea how difficult it was. Enough groveling! I will make a valiant effort to check and recheck the source code in this book, and I'll do what I can to set anything right if I find it broken.

Now that my conscience is at ease, you should know something about how to read the source code in this book.

Where the Code Comes from

Every line of source code has its beginning in an actual game. Of course, the code is not 100 percent verbatim. My front door would be knocked down by a wave of lawyers from Microsoft, Electronic Arts, Mattel, Eidos, and who knows what else. Instead, the code has been sufficiently tweaked to protect the intellectual property of myself and everyone who was crazy enough to employ me and my guest authors. The original code is much harder to read anyway. It usually contained optimizations and external references that I couldn't easily include in any form. Since they came from nearly 14 years of coding experience, you can imagine the wide variety of style and structure. If you want to make your own game, the source code in this book should give you a head start. You'll find some great skeletal work on which you can hang your own code. I'm even hoping that some of the code in here will save you some headaches so you can concentrate on your game.

The code in this book was written and tested on the Win32 platform under Visual Studio 2005 using the DirectX 9 application framework. Console programming is a different beast, and where it makes sense, I'll pull some advice from experts regarding a particular solution. If you're looking to use this code on a Win32 box but want to know how programming the same thing on the Xbox360, PS3, or the Wii is different, you're holding the right book.

The source code is covered under the Creative Commons Attribution Share-Alike license. You can read about this license here: http://creativecommons.org/licenses/by-sa/1.0, but basically it means that you can do what you like with the code as long as you give me and my guest authors credit and you distribute your work in exactly the same way. If you want to use this code in a commercial game, then contact me through my Web site, www.mcshaffry.com/GameCode, and I'll first try to dissuade you. If you persist, I'll be happy to accommodate you with a very affordable license.

Coding Standards and Style

Source code standards are important. I'm not necessarily a standards dictator. I can find room for other opinions on code style, and I'm happy to adopt reasonable standards when and where I must. I look at it like trying to learn a bit of the local language if you travel abroad. The locals will appreciate it, and you might even learn something.

Origin Systems didn't have company-wide coding standards. I was part of no less than three standards committees while I was there, to no avail. Every time we attempted to discuss C++ bracing style, the meeting simply broke down into a screaming match. There were many programmers at Origin who simply wouldn't adapt to anyone else's style. It got so bad that somebody wrote a little utility that would parse a source file and change the bracing style from one to the other. Madness!

Your coding standards and style exist solely to communicate useful information to other programmers, and sometimes a future version of yourself.

I use a coding style in this book extremely similar to what I use professionally. The only departures are those that make the code simpler to read. For example, the source code in the book frequently eliminates obvious error detection and handling. If I used every line of source code exactly as it appeared in real projects, this book would have to be twice as long. It was a tough trade-off, but it's better to have more examples and leave the obvious stuff out of the book.

GOTO: NOT JUST A BAD IDEA—IT WAS NONEXISTENT!

At Origin Systems, a particular programmer on *Martian Dreams* used goto at a frequency you'd find unpleasantly surprising. The new version of the Borland compiler was on everyone's desks, fresh from the presses. He'd just finished installing it and went to lunch. I went to his machine and edited the compiler executable. I changed the keyword goto to goat. When he came back from lunch, three or four of us were pouring over the Borland docs in my office. We told him that Borland's software engineers decided to eliminate goto from their implementation of C. He didn't believe us until he compiled a small test program in his newly installed compiler and received "unexpected identifier or keyword: goto" message for his trouble. We told him the truth before he reached someone at Borland's customer service department.

Using Prefixes

I see one prefix letter per identifier, and I don't under any circumstance worry about using prefixes for type, such as Win32 APIs use. Modern IDEs like Visual Studio expose the type of an identifier with a tooltip, so programmers don't have to clutter the prefix with redundant information. Here are my suggested prefixes:

- **g**: Use with global variables—g_Counter
- **m**: Use with member variables—m_Counter
- **V**: Use with virtual functions—VDraw()
- **I**: Use with Interface classes—class IDrawable

I've seen some crazy use of prefixes that attach three or more characters to the front of any identifier. It must be hard to program in Hungary. The problem with this style is that every identifier that has the same prefix looks exactly alike. That's why the prefix should be as small as possible and separated from the identifier with an underscore—it conveys useful information without overpowering the identity of the variable name. In your own code, feel free to add more prefixes to this list as you find good use for them. Just don't go overboard!

Prefixing variables for scope is an excellent use for prefixes. Programmers who change the value of something with global scope need to be slapped in the face so they can take proper precautions. Class member variables have a different scope than local variables. The "m" prefix is a clean way to differentiate locals and members when they are used in the same method, such as constructors.

Virtual functions are powerful, and therefore dangerous when used to evil ends. A prefix on virtual functions reminds programmers that they should call the parent's overloaded virtual function, and that the cost of calling the function is high.

I find it useful to apply a prefix to interface classes, ones that only define pure virtual functions and no data members, so programmers feel safe multiply inheriting from them. I avoid multiple inheritance of noninterface classes, and I advise you to do the same. The resulting code can be very confusing and hard to maintain.

Capitalization

I use capitalization to distinguish different classes of identifiers and make identifiers easier to read.

- **Variables and Parameters:** Always start with lowercase and use a capital letter for each compound word—g_BufferLength, m_BufferLength, returnValue.
- **Classes, Functions, Typedefs, and Methods:** Always start with uppercase and capitalize each compound word—SoundResource, MemoryFile.
- **Macros:** All capitals and separate compound words with underscores—SAFE_DELETE, MAX_PATH.

The first two capitalization styles help programmers distinguish between definitions of class and instances of those classes:

```
SoundResource soundResource;
MemoryFile memoryFile;
```

Macros, a source of frequent pain and suffering, should boldly state their existence in all capitals. If you want to find the definition of a macro, it's easy to search for the #define MACRO_NAME. This sets them apart from functions or methods.

Const Correct Code

I try my best to make code const correct, and the code in this book is no exception. I'm sure some of you hard-core const correct programmers will be able to throw a few thousand const keywords in where I've forgotten them. Const correctness is a pain, but it's important. Adding const to member variables, function returns, pointers, and references communicates important information to other programmers.

Strings and Localization

If you make your game for English speakers only, you're slashing your sales. Europe and Asia, especially mainland China, are hungry for quality games. Most players will put up with English, but they'd rather get their hands on a good translation in their native language. Good localization technique deserves an entire book and a master's degree in foreign cultures. Since the book has a decidedly Win32 bias, I'm going to use TCHAR as the basic character data type. It can compile with or without _UNICODE defined. Even though it is pretty unusual these days to use single-width character sets, using TCHAR makes it easier for you to port back to a single-width system if you need to. In a few years time, we can drop all this and just use a wide character set for everything.

You'll notice that CHAR and unsigned CHAR is still used in code that needs 8-bit values, specifically when dealing with graphics, sound data, or SDKs that prefer single width character sets, such as ZLib.

I tend to use std::string and std::wstring throughout the book. It is an incredibly useful string class, and while not everyone agrees, it's the one I'm most comfortable with.

In the code samples, I generally use literal strings for clarity. In a real project, every string that could possibly be seen by anyone playing the game is declared in a string table. The string table can be managed by a global class, such as your application class, and you have an easy way to swap out one language for another:

```
std::string msg = g_pApp->GetString(IDS_QUESTION_QUIT_GAME);
```

Regarding the resource constant, I don't attempt to encode the exact text of the string in the macro. It takes too long to type and muddles the code. I usually find a good abbreviation.

One final note about strings in real game code: Debug strings or names for objects are fine as literals. You can declare them at will:

```
if (impossibleError == true)
{
OutputDebugString(_T("Someone enabled the impossible error flag!"));
}
```

Commenting

Really good code comments itself, and I'm hoping the code in this book does exactly that. Good variable names and logic should obviate the need for wordy explanations. In this book, I'll sprinkle comments in the code where I think they do some good, but you'll usually find some meaty explanation immediately after the code sample.

In a real game, the meaty explanation should be inserted into the code, perhaps at the beginning of the file, so that other programmers can figure out what's going on. What seems obvious the moment you type the code degrades linearly with time to a confusing mess. For me, total confusion sets in approximately three months after I write the code. How could I possibly expect anyone else to understand it if I'm completely lost in something I wrote myself?

I always start projects with the intention of putting good comments in my code. I always end projects disappointed in other programmers and myself—we just didn't have enough time. That happens. Projects under pressure will see comments disappear because the programmers are spending 100 percent of their time coding like mad. The best policy is to start off with a lean, light commenting policy and keep it up as long as you can. If there comes a point in the project where comments are dwindling, try to make a good effort to go back in the code base after the project releases to document the code. A good friend of mine at Microsoft told me that shipping the product was a good feature. I agree.

Error Handling

There is very little error handling code in this book, so little that when I look at it, I cringe. The fact is that robust error code gets a little wordy, and I wanted to spend time on the lines of code that will teach you about making games. You can use any form of error checking you want, and I talk about some different options in the chapter on debugging.

Every hard exit in your game should have an error message that is presented to the player: "Bummer – your game is hosed because of some bug in objectdata.cpp, line 6502". Use __FILE__ and __LINE__ to identify the offending code. Unique error codes are a hassle to maintain. This data can be invaluable for the development team and customer service after the game ships. Many a patch or workaround traces its roots to a few hundred telephone calls and emails that finger a particular error code.

Memory Leak Detection

Most everywhere in the source code, you will see memory allocations use GCC_NEW:

```
m_PCMBuffer = GCC_NEW char[bytes];
```

GCC_NEW is defined in debug builds as:

```
#define GCC_NEW new(_NORMAL_BLOCK,__FILE__, __LINE__)
```

You'll learn more about this in Chapter 21, "Debugging Your Game," but suffice it to say for now that doing this helps you find memory leaks.

GAME PROGRAMMING FUNDAMENTALS

WHAT IS GAME PROGRAMMING REALLY LIKE?

In This Chapter

- The Good
- The Bad
- The Ugly
- It's All Worth It, Right?

Most programmers have no idea what it is like to work on games. The ones lucky enough to land a job in the industry are sometimes quite surprised, often pleasantly but not always. Before I talk about the code and game engine architecture, I want to let you know a little more about what you are in for.

Programming games is fundamentally different from other kinds of programming. It's not better or worse, just different. Most of the good aspects of game programming have to do with the bleeding edge challenges you run across and the fact that sometimes you actually see your name scroll across a credits screen. Games are cool, and everybody loves them. If you meet a fan at a computer game store, that person is usually really happy to meet you. You get to play with some great technology from console manufacturers like Nintendo, Microsoft, and Sony. Software development kits from companies like Emergent, Havok, Epic, Valve, and others are also a lot of fun to play with. They can give you a real boost in game development, and can bootstrap your game from nothing to something cool in record time.

The bad side of professional game programming involves the inherent unknowns that come with your work. The sweaty underbelly of this industry can be blamed mostly on insane deadlines and work hours, project management problems, ever-changing SDKs and operating systems, and intense competition. Hopefully, I can give you some perspective on the industry and at the same time show you the good, the bad, and the ugly aspects of game development. I'll try to point out some things that I've learned over the past few years. Read this chapter, and you might be able to dodge a few of these problems.

THE GOOD

Programming jobs in the games industry change fast. In fact, they've even changed since I penned the first edition of this book. Programming used to be a really broad activity because there were so many problems to solve and there were so few good and experienced programmers out there who could solve the problems. In the real early days, game programmers did everything: code, art, sound, and game design. Now you tend to see very specialized game programmers for niche areas of game technology: character movement, network communications, database, physics, and audio are just a few. When I accepted my first job in the computer game industry, my second choice was a job with American General Life Insurance. They wore ties. Their employees took drug tests. In that job I would have had the distinct privilege of working on a beta version of Microsoft's C++ compiler, programming little sales tools for insurance agents. Did I make the right decision or what?

Face it—there aren't many exciting programming jobs out there. But if you know where to look, you can still find them. The cool jobs still fall into a few categories: jobs you can't talk about, ultra high budget simulations and control software, and games. Everything else falls quickly into the "Did you put a cover sheet on your TPS report?" category.

The Job

Here's my bottom line: It's cool to work on games because they are as much art as they are science. When I wrote the first edition of this book, I put a lot of thought into why I found game programming immensely satisfying even with all of the pressures and challenges. I came to the following conclusion—I like blending the artsy side of my left brain and the engineering side of my right brain, especially when I'm in new territory. When I was on *Thief: Deadly Shadows,* I got to work on character movement—talk about a tweak fest. I had to look carefully at the character movement and understand why it "felt" wrong. I played tons of *Splinter Cell* to see how they solved some sticky problems. The "art" involved understanding how character movement was supposed to "feel." Once I had a clue, I had to convert that feeling to a piece of code that fixed the problem—that was science, mostly math. Two sides of your brain working together can solve some really cool problems. Even if you understand the science, sometimes it's up to you to tweak it, like an artist tweaks a smile on a portrait.

It's great to take a game design discussion with you to lunch. You can have a heated debate on whether the master zombie characters came from outer space or originated here on earth—the result of some tragic experiment. You get the weirdest looks, as someone screams, "Damn it, everyone knows that it's better for the zombies to come from space!"

I have the most fun coding, especially when things are going well. Game code is usually pretty difficult stuff, and you frequently have to break some new ground here and there. This is especially true when you are playing with new hardware like the latest console development kits. It's also true when you figure out how to implement a customized version of a classic algorithm so that it runs fast enough to be in a game instead of a textbook.

Probably the best part of game coding is starting from scratch and allowing everything in your libraries to be refreshed and rewritten if necessary. At the end of a project, you can't make drastic changes, and you are forced to live with some annoying hacks and hastily designed objects. When the project is done and you are starting the next one, there's nothing better than throwing off those shackles. Re-factoring, reorganizing, and rewriting an older system so that it really shines is extremely rewarding. Games probably offer more freedom than other types of programming projects because game code can have a very short shelf life. The state of the art moves pretty fast, and as a game developer, you'll be pedaling as fast as you can.

The People

If you work in the games industry, people want to know about your company and your projects. They talk to you about your job because it's high profile. They want to know when they can play your game. Every now and then, you'll find someone who played a game you worked on and enjoyed it. It's great when fans get a buzz going about a game that's still in the design phase, or they start talking about the next version before you're back from vacation. They set up Web sites devoted to your game and argue endlessly about stuff that even the development team finds minor.

BELIEVE IT, YOU HAVE FANS!

Development team t-shirts attract attention, especially from fans. I happened to be wearing an *Ultima VII* "Development Team" shirt when I walked into CompUSA to pick up a game. As I was browsing, a little nerdy guy walked up to me and started talking to me about gritty details of the game design. I'm pretty patient about this kind of thing, so I tried my best to steer the conversation to a close, where any normal human being would simply say, "Well, gee it was nice to meet you! Thanks!" and walk away. Fifteen minutes later I felt as if I wanted to chew my own arm off and give it to him, in the hopes I could make my escape!

Another category of people you come into contact with is the hopeful would-be game programmer. I enjoy meeting these folks, and I do everything I can for anyone who has talent and is willing to increase his or her skills—if I didn't, you wouldn't be reading this book! With today's mod scene and increasingly savvy hobbyists, there is also an increase in amateur developers. These developers are taking things a step beyond the more casual hobbyist level to create things that are intensely interesting. Some even graduate to cult status, or better yet, to the professional ranks. With XboxLive Community, anyone can make his own Xbox360 game, actually sell it, and make a living. The best revenge is being able to tell your parents that playing all those games actually did you some good.

The best people are those closest to you—the development team. By the end of a project, they're like your family. Certainly you've seen them more than your family, and I've even seen teammates become family. Programmers, artists, designers, audio engineers, composers, testers, and project managers make an odd mix of people. You wouldn't think that these people could all hang out and get along. But they do, most of the time anyway.

Most of your interactions in game programming are with other programmers. One big difference between the game industry and more boring jobs is that there's a significant portion of programmers who are self-taught in the game industry.

A DEMO IS BETTER THAN A RESUME

One of the best programmers I ever worked with started out as a dedicated amateur. This guy was so dedicated that he rewrote a large portion of *Ultima VII* on his own time and actually made a fantastic graphics engine that had Z-sprites before I even knew what they were. He showed us a demo that simply blew the minds of the Ultima programming team. We hired him.

That's not to say these folks are slackers by any shake of the stick. Instead, they tend to be absolutely brilliant. One difference between the self-taught hackers and the programmer with formal training is that hackers tend to design and code things before they realize that someone has already solved the problem. Sometimes, you'll catch them describing a cool data structure they just came up with, and you'll realize they are talking about a B+ tree. Their strength comes from their amazing ability to see right to the heart of a problem and fearlessly begin to solve it. One of the most brilliant programmers I ever met never graduated high school.

I wish I were a better artist. This is a skill that I admire to the point of wide-eyed wonder. Even better than admiring the raw skills, the creative insight that artists conjure up makes working with them so fantastic. Don't get me wrong—some of them are completely insane, opinionated, temperamental, and ultra-perfectionists. That description fits programmers, doesn't it? Probably the weirdest thing about working with artists on computer games is that you realize that artists and programmers are the same kind of people working with different sides of their brain.

The Tools—Software Development Kits (SDKs)

The most widely used SDK is DirectX from Microsoft. It provides APIs useful for creating game software. There are many more: SDKs for physics, SDKs for rendering 3D graphics, SDKs for audio, networking, even AI. You can't make a professional game without SDKs. You don't need all of them, but most certainly you'll use one or two. They boost your development schedule and give you some confidence that your graphics or audio system has been well tested.

When I first started writing this section, it was in my "The Ugly" section at the end of this chapter. I felt a little guilty about giving SDKs such a bad rap. After all, if they were really useless, why do I use them on every project? The truth is that SDKs give you a huge leg up. They can also be a huge pain in the butt. SDKs are widely used, so they can't appeal to the odd needs of every developer. Some of the expensive ones come with source code, which is critical for debugging problems. You can even make changes and recompile the SDK, but any customizations you perform might be invalidated by their next version. Most of the time you have to be satisfied with begging and pleading. Perhaps the SDK engineers will take pity upon you and consider your request.

The real hassle comes when you grab their latest version. You'll usually find that the new version isn't compatible with your code base, and you'll spend hours or days getting your game to compile again. Do yourself a favor and try to find SDKs that either promise to support earlier APIs or have already become stable. Anything else is madness.

The Hardware

Games run on cool hardware. Well, most games do. *Thief: Deadly Shadows* used the very latest in audio and video hardware for the PC, especially the new 5.0 EAX environmental audio system from Creative, and, of course, it also ran on the Xbox. Back in the day, the *Ultima* games pushed hardware so hard that players would usually buy a new computer every time an *Ultima* came out. Many of the big budget PC titles are created on hardware that has yet to reach any serious market penetration, which means that the hardware manufacturers are constantly sending game developers the latest greatest stuff and even a T-shirt every now and then. An established developer can still call any hardware company out there and get on their developer program. You don't exactly get truckloads of free hardware, but you do get a few bits and pieces to split among the programmers and the test group. That can save your butt if you find that your game crashes on the hottest video card—you can't fix the bug just by hoping it goes away.

The developer programs offered by hardware manufacturers are a great resource. Most of them have special developer Web sites and prerelease hardware programs. They also have dedicated engineers who can help you with a specific problem. An engineer at ATI verified a particular bug on one of the Microsoft projects I worked on, and they had a new driver ready in a few days. Of course, I was happy to have the big gorilla named Microsoft standing behind us, but you'll find that most hardware companies are really responsive when it comes to diagnosing driver problems.

The Platforms

There are a wide variety of gaming platforms, and they never stop growing. For many years, we only had to deal with consoles and desktops. Since 2001, games have popped up on handheld devices like the Nintendo DS, Sony's PSP, the iPhone, and many others.

At the time of this writing, the big consoles on the market are the Wii from Nintendo, the Xbox360 from Microsoft, and the PlayStation 3 from Sony. The most recent battle is going solidly to Nintendo, which came in third place during the PS2/GameCube/Xbox era. Since the 1950s and the very first computers, it was always software that sold the hardware, which is a fact that I feel will never

---

MY NEPHEW MADE *MUSHROOM MEN* BETTER

One thing most games go through is something called *blind playtesting*. This is when you let someone who has never seen the game come in and give it a try. Usually, this happens with some developers watching and cringing, as they see a new player have trouble with something they designed. My 10-year-old nephew, Sam, was a blind playtester for *Mushroom Men: The Spore Wars*, and actually found a pretty important bug. One of the programmers, Kain, was able to fix the bug and show Sam how his comments made the game better.

---

change. Playstation 2 won the last time because they had the best games, period. This time, the Wii is winning because of the wide appeal it has to gamers of all ages. Even my Mom is playing the Wii—it turns out she is killer at *Wii Bowling* and trounces me every time she plays.

Tables 1.1 and 1.2 list the various platforms on the market and their hardware specifications.

Table 1.1 Capabilities of Last Generation Consoles

Platform	Xbox	PS2	GameCube
CPU	733MHz	294.9MHz	485MHz
Graphics Processor	250MHz	147.5MHz	162MHz
Maximum Resolution	1920×1080	1280×1024	Up to HDTV
Memory	64MB RAM	40MB RAM	43MB RAM
Controller Ports	4	2 (4 optional)	4
Media	4x DVD-ROM (3.2–6.4GB)	5x DVD-ROM (3.2–6.4GB)	3x DVD-ROM (1.5GB)
Digital Sound	Dolby 5.1 DTS in gameplay	Dolby Pro Logic II	Dolby 5.1 for DVDs
Hardware Audio Channels	64	48	64
Hard Disk	Yes—8GB	Add-on	No
Internet	10/100 Ethernet Port	Optional modem / broadband	Optional modem / broadband
DVD Movies	Yes	Yes	No

Table 1.2 Capabilities of Next-Generation Consoles

Platform	Xbox360	PS3	Wii
CPU	3.2GHz PowerPC Xenon with three cores	3.2GHz Cell - Also has seven single-threaded special purpose processors (SPEs)	729MHz IBM Broadway
Graphics Processor	500MHz ATI	550MHz NVIDIA	243MHz ATI
Maximum Resolution	Up to 1080p HDTV	Up to 1080p HDTV	Up to 480p
Memory	512MB RAM @ 22.4Gbps	256MB RAM @ 25.6Gbps	60MB RAM @ 1.9Gbps
HDMI	Yes	Yes	No
Controller Ports	4 (wired and wireless)	7 (wired and wireless)	4 (wired and wireless)
Media	12x DVD-ROM (3.2–6.4GB)	Blu-ray (3.2–6.4GB)	Proprietary DVD (4.5GB)
Digital Sound	Dolby 5.1 DTS	Dolby 5.1 DTS	Dolby 5.1 for DVDs
Hardware Audio Channels	n/a	320 hardware, no limit with software	64
Hard Disk	Yes—20–120GB	Yes—20–120GB	No
Internet	100Mbs Ethernet	Gigabit Ethernet	Built-in wireless
DVD Movies	Yes	Yes	No
Blu-ray Movies	No	Yes	No

The best part of developing for consoles is the fact that you'll never have to worry about supporting a hellish grid of operating system and hardware configurations that are guaranteed to change at least twice during your development cycle. You do have to deal with standards compliance with the console manufacturers, which can be quite difficult if you've never had the experience.

There's a serious leap in capability from that first table to the second, isn't there? The change from the PS2 to the PS3 is nothing short of remarkable. But hardware capability doesn't mean you'll sell more—a great lesson that sometimes less is more.

When I wrote the second edition, I had a line about desktop hardware that said: "After all, you can't find CPUs topping 2Ghz in the console world...." Funny how times change—just a few years go by and that statement is completely wrong. I also wrote that consoles were always lacking behind desktops for raw processing and graphics power. That statement isn't so true in the PS3/Xbox360 era.

Desktops are still ahead when it comes to memory and hard drive storage, but they are falling behind in cool controllers, like you see with the Wii. With all the consoles being Internet-capable and having space on their hard drives, consoles even get to send updates. The lines are definitely blurring.

Still, the dizzying array of hardware and operating system combinations on desktops makes compatibility a serious problem. You'll spend a serious amount of time chasing down some crazy bug that only happens on some archaic version of Windows or on some rare video card. What a hassle!

On desktops you also have to find ways to support old legacy hardware while you make your game look good on the bleeding-edge gear. The CPU delta can be nearly 10:1, and the graphics delta is worse. Old video cards might not have programmable pipelines at all. That means your games need tons of configurable options so that players with crappy computers can turn off everything to get some decent frame-rate. Let the flamethrowers turn on multichannel MP3 decompression, full dynamic lighting and shadows, full-screen graphics effects like motion blur and bloom, ultra-high texture and model density, stereo 1600×1200×32 displays, and quasi-telepathic AI. Each of these options deserves separate testing paths on all the hardware configurations.

It makes you glad you can send patches over the Internet.

The Show

The game industry throws awesome tradeshows and parties. Find out for yourself and register for the Electronic Entertainment Expo (E3), usually held in Los Angeles in May. Other great shows include the Tokyo Game Show and Games Convention, traditionally held in Leipzig, Germany and drawing over 200,000 visitors in 2008. Sometimes, you have to be part of the industry to get registered, so if you don't have a game job, then launch a game review Web site and call yourself "press." Everybody else does. When you get there, play every game you can and dork around with the latest console gear. The show floor is where the game companies pull out all the stops to attract attention. You've got to go see for yourself. It's unbelievable.

If you want to learn about game development, go to the Game Developer's Conference in San Francisco, which is held in March. It's brutally expensive, but you'll find the cream of the game development crop telling willing crowds some of their secrets. Before you sign up for any of the workshops, roundtables, or sessions, it's a good idea to do a Google search on the speakers and get an idea of what they've worked on recently. Choose the sessions that have speakers with the most game industry experience and subject matter you're ready to hear—some of them are fairly advanced.

SNEAKING AROUND IS DEFINITELY A BEST PRACTICE

Throughout this book, I'll be including a number of "best practice" tips from my years of experience as a developer. I couldn't resist including this one for your first "best practice" dose. It can be a lot of fun to snag party invitations from the in-crowd, and talk your way into the "by invitation only" areas. A friend of mine who worked for Dell was able to get into virtually every private area of the show just by showing up, flashing his Dell credentials, and talking like he was someone important. Almost everyone bought it. It's all good fun.

THE BAD

Every job has its good parts and bad parts. Game programming is no different. First, game programming is hard, sometimes to the point of being frustrating. Many before me have argued that programming games is the most challenging form of programming there is. Bad things are a matter of perspective; some people find these things challenging while others find them burdensome. You'll have to judge for yourself.

Game Programming Is Freaking Hard

It's not uncommon for a game programmer to do something completely new and try to hit a deadline at the same time. I'm not talking about a modification of a data structure to fit a certain problem; I'm talking about applying experimental and theoretical designs to a production system that meets deadlines. On *Ultima VII*, one programmer wrote a 32-bit memory management system that was based on a little known Intel 486 processor flag and hand-coded assembly, since there were no 32-bit compilers. On *Ultima VIII*, one of the low-level engineers wrote a multithreaded real-time multitasker two years before Win32 went beta. On *Ultima IX*, the graphics programmer figured out how to make a software rasterizer appear to pump 32,000 textured polygons per second on a first generation Pentium. Everyone knows what *Ultima Online* did—found a way to get every *Ultima* fan playing in Britannia all at the same time. I can't even begin to talk about the innovation that had to happen there just to get this system to work.

It would be one thing if this stuff were all research, where results come when they may and the pressure is bearable. A game project is different because the schedule is relentless. For all the media press about how late games are, I'm surprised that you see some of them at all, given the level of difficulty.

Bits and Pieces

Games are built from more than code. Go find any PC game you bought recently and take a look at the directory where you installed it. You'll find the expected EXE and DLL files, with a few INIs or TXT files, too. You'll also find gigabytes of

RICHARD GARRIOTT USES JEDI MIND TRICKS

Technology isn't the only thing that makes game programming hard. Game designers will push you farther than you ever thought you could go. I remember very well a conversation the senior staff at Origin had with Richard Garriott about the world design for *Ultima IX*. The team was pushing for a simple design that was reminiscent of the old *Ultima* games—the outdoor map was separate from the city maps. This was a simple design because each map could be loaded at once and no complicated map streaming would be required. Richard didn't go for it. He wanted a seamless map like *Ultima VII*. This was a much harder problem. We knew going into the meeting that if we couldn't convince Richard to use a simpler world design we'd have a hard time making our deadlines. We steeled ourselves with resolve, and armed with our charts and graphs and grim schedule predictions, we entered the conference room. Two hours later, we all walked out of the room completely convinced that Richard was right, a seamless map was the way to go. I wish I knew how he does that!

other stuff with file extensions that don't necessarily map to any program you've ever seen. These other files hold art, models, levels, sounds, music, scripts, and game data. This data didn't just fall out of the ether. Every texture was once a BMP or TIF file. Every sound was once a WAV, probably converted to MP3 or OGG. Each model and game level had its own file, too, perhaps stored in a 3ds Max file. Even a small game will collect hundreds, if not thousands, of these bits and pieces, all of which need to be catalogued and organized into a manageable database of sorts.

LOSING FILES IS EASIER THAN YOU THINK

Logistically, these things can be a nightmare to manage. I worked on a project where an artist wiped every file he'd worked on without even knowing it. Art files would get changed on the network, but wouldn't get copied into the build, or even worse, the artist would change the name of a file, and it would get lost forever. When you have thousands of files to look though, it's sometimes easier to just repaint it. Luckily, there are some tools out there to help manage this problem. The situation is certainly better than when I started, when I think our best file management scheme was a pad of paper.

Very few software projects share this problem. The only thing that comes close is a Web site, and there just aren't that many assets. After all, they have to get sent over the Internet so there can't be that many. Certainly not enough to fill up a DVD, and a compressed one at that.

That's Not a Bug—That's a Feature

Actual bug: I was walking along and the trees turned into shovels and my character turned into a pair of boots and then the game crashed.

You certainly won't see a bug report like that working on a database application. Seriously, some of these reports convince you beyond any shadow of doubt that some testers are certifiably crazy.

You might wonder why I put something so amusing in the "bad" section of working on games. There are plenty of funny bugs; stuff goes wrong in a game and has a bizarre result. Luckily, Quality Assurance (QA) should find it because it will be funnier for you as a developer than it will be for a player whose crashed game just lost a few hard hours of play.

Beyond the funny bugs, there's a dark side.

One bad thing is just the sheer volume of bugs. Games tend to be rushed into testing and the QA department does what they are paid to do and writes up every problem they observe. I think they hope that eventually the producers will get the point and stop sending proto-ware into the test department. They hope in vain because the pressure to call the game "testable" is usually too much for the project management to bear. It's too bad that there tends to be no solid definition of "testable" unless you work in QA. From their point of view, it's pretty obvious.

The heavy bug volume weighs on everyone, developers and testers alike. They end up creating a logistical nightmare. The graphical reports that get spit out by the bug database are watched like the stock market; only this time, a steep

YOU WON'T BE ABLE TO FIX EVERY BUG

There's nothing like having the rug pulled out from underneath you because a bug that you intended to fix is marked "won't fix" by the team leadership. You might even have the code fixed on your machine, ready to check in for the next build. Instead, you get to undo the change. The final straw is when some critic on the Internet bashes the programmers for writing buggy code, and even points out the very bug that you intended to fix. Most programmers I know are perfectionists and take a lot of pride in their work, and because of that they lose sleep over bugs. As evil as this seems, making those decisions is as tough as knowing your code has a bug you aren't allowed to fix. Believe me, I've done that a few thousand times.

upward curve tends to have a negative effect on team morale. The worst part by far is what happens when the team can't quite keep the bug count under control, which is most of the time. The project leadership gathers together in a locked office and "fixes" bugs without ever touching the project. The bug simply becomes a feature, maybe a weird screwed-up annoying feature, but a feature all the same.

The Tools

Richard Garriott, aka Lord British and creator of the *Ultima* RPG series, once said that the computer game industry is a lot like the movie industry. He also said that at the beginning of every game project we start by inventing new cameras, film and processing techniques, and projectors. He said that 10 years ago, and while there is great middleware out there for sound and graphics and even complete turnkey game engines like *Unreal 3*, many game projects end up writing their own development tools from scratch.

Other games use a simpler strategy, a wise choice if you don't need 20 people building seamless maps and levels. The basic game level is assembled in a modeling tool like 3ds Max. A special editing tool usually loads that level and drops in special actions, dynamic object generators, and characters, almost as if you were playing the game. If you are developing a smaller game with a small team, there's no need to have a complicated, multiperson aware tool. In fact, with a little work you can make 3ds Max act like your level editor—just don't try this on an AAA title.

There are a number of game engines on the market from Emergent, Epic, Crytek, id, Valve, Vicious Cycle, Trinigy, and others. The days of creating custom level and mission editors may be over, but you'll still have to write quite a bit of custom tools and code to make your game unique. So, worry not, the job of the game programmer is safe for a long time.

TALES FROM THE PIXEL MINES

BEFORE WE MADE THE GAME, WE MADE THE TOOLS

Most games have level or mission editors. When we developed the *Ultima* games, we spent the first year or so of development writing the game editor—a tool that could import graphics, sounds, and models from all the art and modeling software like Photoshop, Lightwave, 3ds Max, Maya, and others. *Ultima IX*'s level editor was fully networked and used TCP/IP to communicate peer/peer to all the designers and programmers running it. They could even edit the same map at the same time, since smaller portions of the map could be locked out for changes. The editor could launch into game mode at the press of a button, so the designers could test their work. *Ultima Online*'s editor was much more like the game than *Ultima IX*. *UO* already had a client/server system up and running, and it used a special god client to change the map levels and add new assets to the game.

THE UGLY

There are plenty of factors that make game coding a fluid and unpredictable task. The design of the game frequently changes drastically during development, motivated by many factors inside and outside the development team. Mounting schedule slippage and production pressure leads to the legendary "crunch mode" so prevalent on many game projects. Dependant software tools like DirectX change constantly, challenging software teams to keep up. Unlike many software projects, games frequently must support a wide variety of operating systems, graphics APIs, and platforms.

Hitting a Moving Target

Most industry software projects are carefully designed and planned. Systems analysts study customer requirements, case studies of previous versions of the software, and prospective architectures for months before the first line of code is ever written. *Ultima VIII's* architecture was planned by seven programmers in a single afternoon on a whiteboard.

Architecture notwithstanding, you can't design "fun." Fun is a "tweakable" thing, not something that exists in a design document. You hope like hell that the original design will result in a fun game, but the first playable version frequently leaves you with the distinct impression that the game needs some more chili powder and a little more time on the stove.

Sometimes, the entire design is reworked. *Ultima IX's* architecture and game design changed no less than three times in development. I was there for two of them, and didn't stick around for the third. When a game is in development for multiple years, it's easy for new hardware technology to blaze past you. In *Ultima IX's* case, 3D accelerated video cards were just coming into their own as we were putting the finishing touches on what had to be the finest software rasterizer anyone ever wrote. It never saw the light of day.

TALES FROM THE PIXEL MINES

SOMETIMES YOUR GAME IS JUST PLAIN BORING

Ultima VIII's map design had a hub-and-spoke model. The hub was an underground dungeon that connected every other map. We released the game to QA, and word came back that it was completely boring. The culprit was a sparse central map that wasn't much more than an underground maze with a few bad guys hanging out here and there. It wasn't good enough. Two designers worked day and night to rework the central map. Puzzles, traps, monsters, and other trickery finally added a little spice. The central map ended up being one of the best parts of the whole game.

Crunch Mode (and Crunch Meals)

Every now and then you end up at a technological dead-end and have to start completely over. I was brought into the late stages of a Mattel project that was supposed to be in the test phase in about two weeks. I took one look at the code and realized, to my horror, that the entire graphics engine was using Windows GDI. Unless someone out there knew something I didn't, the GDI in 1999 couldn't texture map polygons. In less than five weeks, the entire project was rebuilt from scratch, including a basic 2D vector animation tool.

Those five weeks were really more like 15 weeks. The tiny development team worked late into each night and dragged themselves back each morning. There were no weekends. There were no days off. I'd estimate that we worked 90-hour workweeks on that project. You might think that unreasonable, and that nobody should have to work like that. That project was only five weeks. It was nothing compared to the pixel mines of Origin Systems circa 1992. Back then, Origin had something called the "100 Club." The price of entry was working 100 hours in a single workweek. The last time I counted, there were only 168 hours in seven days, so the folks in the 100 Club were either working or sleeping.

TALES FROM THE PIXEL MINES

THE INFAMOUS ORIGIN HOSTEL

To facilitate a grueling schedule, the teams built bunk beds in the kitchen. Company kitchens are no place for bedding. My office was unfortunately located right across the hall, and I observed the kitchen/bedroom getting higher occupancy than the homeless shelter in downtown Austin. After about a week, I began to detect an odor emanating from across the hall. It seemed that the brilliant organizers of Hotel Origin never hired a maid service, and that an unplanned biology experiment was reporting its initial results via colorless but odorous gasses. Origin management soon liquidated the experiment.

It's not uncommon for companies insisting on long hours from salaried employees to provide meals. These "crunch meals" are usually ordered out and delivered to the team. Origin was able to get a local deli to bill them instead of requiring a credit card, so they began to order from them almost every night. Months went by, and everyone on the development team knew every item on the menu by heart, and knew exactly which bits of food were most likely to survive delivery intact. Fifteen years later, I can still tell you what's on the menu at Jason's Deli, and even though the food is good, I rarely eat there.

At the ripe old age of 38, I signed on to full-fledged crunch mode at Ion Storm to help finish *Thief: Deadly Shadows*. Let me tell you something, the older you get, the harder it is to stay awake and code. I actually cheated a little and came in early, but the long hours still were pretty tiring, especially after the fourth month. Good grief—when will this industry ever learn?

Bah Humbug

Computer games are a seasonal business. They sell like crap in the summer, and profits soar at Christmas time. Of course, they only soar for your project if you're not still working on it. This puts a significant amount of pressure on development teams. Sometimes, the pressure begins before the team begins working. Every game contract I signed stipulated specific release dates simply to make sure the boxes would have enough lead time to get built, shipped, and on store shelves.

This lead time varies from publisher to publisher. A big company like Microsoft has a huge manufacturing pipeline that includes everything from the latest version of *Halo* to their latest version of *Office*. I once worked on a game that shipped the same month as Windows XP. I'll bet that if you were standing on the assembly line you'd be hard pressed to notice the brief flash of dark green as 50,000 boxes of my game whizzed by. You shouldn't be surprised to see a publisher like Microsoft require you to finish your title by September at the latest in order to make the shelves by the holiday season.

Other publishers are more nimble, and they might be more accommodating if you've got a AAA title coming in hot and steep as late as November. You won't get the best sales if you release after Thanksgiving, but even getting out the week before Christmas is better than missing the season altogether. It's always best to have everything in the can before October if you want to see your game under Christmas trees.

Basically, Christmas is only merry if your game is done.

Operating System Hell

Microsoft Excel doesn't need to support full-screen modes, and it certainly doesn't need to worry about whether the installed video card has 2.0 shaders. That's one of the reasons that games get some special dispensations from Microsoft to qualify for logo compliance. Logo compliance means that your game exposes certain features and passes quality assurance tests from Microsoft. When your game passes muster, you are allowed to display the Windows logo on the box—something that is good for any game but especially important for mass-market games.

The Microsoft projects we developed had to pass QA testing for Windows 98, Windows ME, Windows 2000, and all versions of Windows XP. By 2002, Microsoft wasn't supporting Windows 95 anymore, which was a good thing. It was hard enough building an old box for our Windows 98 test machine. The OS that required the most tweaking was Windows XP, mostly because of the new requirement that the *Program Files* directory was essentially read/only for nonadministrator accounts. Most games store their dynamic data files close to the executable, which will fail under Windows XP Home. These drastic changes to Windows XP motivated many game companies to drop support for all Windows 9x platforms by the end of 2004. For a big company, Microsoft can move pretty fast, and as a game programmer, you have to keep up.

The hell doesn't even stop there—some programmers choose to write graphics engines that work under DirectX and OpenGL. Some graphics middleware supports this natively, so you don't have to worry about it. Why would you bother? Performance.

Most video cards have DirectX and OpenGL drivers, but it's not guaranteed that you'll achieve equal performance or graphics quality under both. The performance differences are directly proportional to the effort put into the drivers, and there are cases where the OpenGL driver beats DirectX soundly. Of course, there are mirror cases as well, where DirectX is the way to go. Even better, the quality of the drivers changes from operating system to operating system. The result of all this is a huge increase in effort on your side. Even if you choose one particular graphics API, you still have to support a wide array of operating systems. This increase in effort simply widens the market for your game. It doesn't make your game fun or provide a deeper experience. It just keeps it from misbehaving on someone's computer.

I almost forgot, what about Linux? What about Mac? They are still tiny slivers of the gaming market. Linux is growing, and there are people out there with Mac computers. The question about writing a cross-platform game for these operating systems is more logistical and financial than technological. Most game projects can be ported to similar platforms with a tolerable dose of programming hell.

Moving games to very dissimilar platforms can be nigh impossible, such as a direct port of a PC game to a console. The lack of a keyboard or game controller, different screen resolution, and smaller secondary storage preclude some games from ever appearing on consoles. That doesn't even begin to address the inherent design concerns that differ sharply from consoles to desktops.

Fluid Nature of Employment

The game industry, for all its size and billions of dollars of annual revenue, is not the most stable employment opportunity out there. You can almost guarantee that if you get a job in the industry you'll be working with a completely different set of people every two years or so, and perhaps even more often than that.

Every year at the Origin Christmas party, employees were asked to stand up as a group. Everyone who had worked there less than a year was asked to sit down, followed by second and third year employees. This process was repeated until only a handful of people were left. This was usually by the fourth or fifth year. In my sixth year, I became the twelfth most senior person in the company by time of service, and Origin had hundreds of employees. This is fairly common throughout the industry.

The stresses of incredibly short schedules and cancelled projects have chased many of my friends out of the industry altogether. Whole studios, including two of my own, take root for a while and then evaporate or get bought. Your boss today will not be your boss tomorrow, especially if your boss attempts to do something crazy, like start his own game studio!

IT'S ALL WORTH IT, RIGHT?

There's something odd about human psychology. After a particularly scary or painful experience, some of us will say to ourselves, "Hey, that wasn't so bad. Let's do it again!" People that make games do this all the time. The job is incredibly difficult and can drive you completely mad. Your tools and supported operating systems change more often than you'd like. Some days you delete more code than you write.

Taking three steps forward and five steps back is a good recipe for long hours, and you'll get an "all you can eat" buffet of overtime. It will get so bad that you'll feel guilty when you leave work before 7 p.m. on a Sunday night. When crunch mode is over, and you get back to a normal 60-hour workweek, you'll wonder what to do with all the extra time on your hands.

Why bother? Is it possible that that boring job at American General Life Insurance was a better option for me? Not a chance. There are plenty of good things, but there's one that beats them all: After all the work, lost weekends, and screaming matches with producers and testers, your game finally appears on the retail shelves somewhere. A few weeks after it ships, you start looking. You make excuses to go to Wal-Mart, GameStop, and Best Buy and wander the software section. Eventually, you see it. Your game. In a box. On the shelf.

There's nothing like it. As you hold it in your hands, someone walks up to you and says, "Hey, I was thinking of buying that game. Is it any good?" You smile and hand him the box, "Yeah, it's damn good."

WHAT'S IN A GAME?

In This Chapter

There are tons of reasons programmers get attracted to games: graphics, physics, AI, networking, and more. Looking at all of the awesome games that have been released over the past few years, such as *Halo 3*, *Grand Theft Auto IV*, *Gears of War 2*, and others, you might first think that all of the major technology advances have been in the area of graphics or physics programming. There is certainly more than meets the eye, and after seeing for myself how some games glue major subsystems together, I often wonder how they even function.

When building a game, programmers will typically start with a DirectX sample, import some of their own miserable programmer art, put an environment map or a bump map on everything in sight, and shout "Eureka! The graphics system is finished! We'll be shipping our game by next weekend!"

By the time the next weekend rolls around, the same newbie game programmers will have a long laundry list of things that need to be done, and there are a number of subtle things that they will have completely missed—like how to manage memory and game processes properly. These hidden systems are usually the heart of every game, and you're never aware of them when you play games because you're not supposed to be aware of them.

This book is about more than just the visible parts, It is primarily about how to glue all these parts together in a way that won't drive you and your programming colleagues insane. This chapter takes the first step, and it shows you a high-level view of how commercial games are (or should be) architected.

After you finish this chapter, you'll have a good understanding of the main components of game code and how they fit together. The rest of this book digs into the details of these systems and how they are built.

The important lesson to learn here is that you'll be able to build much better games if you really understand the architecture, the components, and how everything fits together. In other words, think and plan before you start coding, because a great foundation can hold a big game, where a crappy one simply can't hold up to the strain. We all hear this good advice over and over, but it's easy to neglect because it takes a lot longer to get something up and running. Think of this like you would approach building a house. Don't be like the guy down the street who just starts putting up walls without really thinking through the kinds of components that he'll really need to do the job right.

GAME ARCHITECTURE

There are as many ways to assemble the subsystems of a game as there are game programmers. Being a game programmer, I'll give you my opinion of what the subsystems are, what they do, and how they communicate. You'll probably do things differently, and that's perfectly fine by me, especially since what I'm going to present is geared toward understandability, not necessarily efficiency. Once you understand something, you can find your own path to making it run pegged at

60Hz or better, but you sure can't get something to run that fast if you have no idea what's going on.

I can't say this enough—you don't have to do things my way—but since my way is the easiest for me to describe, it makes some sense that I'll preach a little of my own opinions. As you read this chapter, think first about what problems I'm solving with this system and at least grab hold of the subsystems and what they do on their own. If you come up with a better way to build this mousetrap, call me, and I'll hire you.

Let's start at the top level and work our way down. You can take every subsystem in a game and classify it as belonging to one of three primary categories: the application layer, the game logic layer, and the game view layer (see Figure 2.1). The application layer deals with the hardware and the operating system. The game logic layer manages your game state and how it changes over time. The game view layer presents the game state with graphics and sound.

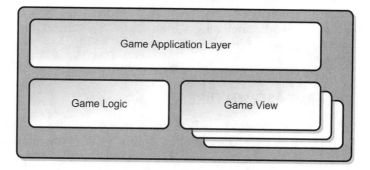

FIGURE 2.1 High-level game architecture.

If you think this architecture sounds familiar (and you're familiar with MFC's document/view architecture), you're exactly right, but don't burn this book in disgust just yet. While I loathe programming in MFC as much as the next person, there is amazing flexibility in separating a game into these three independent systems. Another popular design pattern, the Model-View-Controller, seeks to separate the logic of a system from the interface used to present or request changes to data. The architecture I propose encapsulates that and adds a layer for hardware or operating system specific subsystems.

The application layer concerns itself with the machine your game runs on. If you were going to port your game from Windows to Mac, or from the PlayStation 3 to Xbox360, you would rewrite most of the code in the application layer, but hopefully not much else. In this area you'll find code that deals with hardware devices like the mouse or a gamepad, operating system services such as network communications or threading, and operations such as initialization and shutdown of your game.

The game logic layer is your game, completely separated from the machine your game runs on or how it is presented to the player. In a perfect world, you could simply recompile all the source code related to your game logic, and it would run on any platform or operating system. In this area, you'll find subsystems for managing your game's world state, communicating state changes to other systems, and accepting input commands from other systems. You'll also find systems that enforce rules of your game system's universe. A good example of this is a physics system, which is the authority on how game objects move and interact.

The third and last system component is the game view. This system is responsible for presenting the game state and translating input into game commands that are then sent to the game logic. What's interesting about the game view is that it can have different implementations, and you can have as many views attached to your game as your computer can handle. One type of game view is for your players; it draws the game state on the screen, sends audio to the speakers, and accepts input through the user interface. Another type is the view for the artificial intelligence (AI) agent, and a third might be a view for a remote player over a network. They all get the same state changes from the game logic—they just do different things.

APPLYING THE GAME ARCHITECTURE

It might seem weird to you at first that the code for the AI would communicate through the same pathways and in exactly the same manner as a human being. Let me give you a more concrete example. Let's design a racing game using the game logic and game view architecture, and we'll also create two views: one for a human player and one for an AI driver who will race with you on the track.

The game logic for a racing game will have the data that describes cars and tracks, and all the minute properties of each. For the car, you'll have data that describes how weight is distributed, engine performance, tire performance, fuel efficiency, and things like that. The track will have data that describes its shape and the properties of the surface all along the route. You'll also have a physics system that can calculate what happens to cars in various states of acceleration and steering, how they respond to the track, change in input controls, or even collisions with each other.

For inputs, the game logic cares about only four things for each car: steering, acceleration, braking, and perhaps the emergency brake. If your cars have guns on them, like we all wish, you would also have an input for whether the fire trigger is down. That's it; the game logic needs nothing else as input to get the cars moving around the track.

Outputs from the game logic will be state changes and events. This includes each car's position and orientation, and the position and orientation of the wheels in relation to the car's body. If the game supports damage, you'll also have damage statistics as an output. If your cars have guns, a state change could also be whether the weapon is firing and how much ammo is left. Another important game state, especially the way I play racing games, is collision events. Every time a collision happens, the game logic sends an event with all the collision data. Events and state changes are sent to game views.

The game view for the human has a lot of work to do to present the view of the game state. It has to draw the scene from various points of view, send audio to the speakers, spawn particle effects—especially when bad drivers like myself are scraping down the guardrails—and rumble the force feedback controls. The view also reads the state of the game controller, and translates that into game logic commands. A good example of this is to notice the right trigger pressed to full throttle, and it sends the "Accelerator at 100%" command to the game view, or changes in the left thumbstick to "Steer left at 50%." These commands are sent back to the game logic as requests to change the game state.

Imagine what happens when a player mashes the A button on the controller— the normal control for the emergency brake in my favorite racing game. The human view interprets this as a request to hit the emergency brake on my Ferrari, and sends a "player hit emergency brake" message to the game logic. The game logic evaluates the request, sets the m_bIsEmergencyBrakeOn to true, and sends a state update back to the human view. The human view responds to this message by playing a sound effect of the tires squealing or maybe showing something on the screen, like the car spinning into the nearest guardrail. Another example is the throttle setting. Pressing the right trigger usually controls the throttle. If I press it to 82% of its range, the view interprets this as a command to set the accelerator to 82% and sends a "throttle to 82%" request to the game logic. The game logic determines that the rear tires have broken loose by looking at the car, its weight, the tires, the track condition, and other factors. It sends a message back to the game view that the rear tires are spinning, and the game view could then respond by playing a sound effect.

You can see that a game controller's thumbstick or button state doesn't affect the game state directly. Instead, the controller's state is interpreted by the game view and converted into commands, which are sent to the game logic by an event. The game logic receives events generated by the view and uses those commands, along with its physics simulation, to figure out what is happening in the game universe. The state changes in the game world get sent back to the view, so it can draw polygons, play sound effects, and rumble the controller.

The game view for the AI is a little different. It will receive the same game state events received by the human game view, such as which track the race is occurring on, the weather conditions, and the constantly updated positions, orientations, and velocity of cars on the track. It will take this information and recalculate what commands to send into the game logic. For example, in response to the "Go" event from the game logic, the AI might send an "Accelerator at 100%" command back to the game logic. While negotiating a turn, it might send "Steer left at 50%" to the game logic.

You should be aware that the commands sent from the human view and the AI view to the game logic are exactly the same. While it might take a little more thinking to convince yourself that the inputs to the game view, namely the game status and game events, are exactly the same, I assure you it is true.

I mentioned before that this game architecture is flexible. You've probably already surmised that a particular game logic can have any number of views, both human and AI. It is a trivial matter to swap a human player, or even all human players, with AI players. But wait, it gets better.

You could create a special VCR game view that does nothing but record game events into a buffer and play them back. In a sense, the game logic is entirely short circuited, but since the game state changes and events are exactly the same, they can be presented in the VCR view with very little recoding. Of course, if you want a "rewind" feature, you've got some extra work to do because the game events don't necessarily go equally back in time as they go forward!

You could also create a special game view that forwards game status and events to a remote player across the Internet. Think about that: the game logic doesn't have to care whether the players are local or separated by thousands of miles. The remote view should be pretty smart about collecting game states and events, compressing them into as few bytes as possible, and shipping them via TCP or UDP to the remote player. The game commands received from the remote player should go through a verification filter, of course. You can never be too sure about remote players, or remote game logics, for that matter.

One thing to note—players with different views can be advantaged or disadvantaged. For example, those who play on 4:3 screens can't see quite as much as those playing on 16:9 screens. Taken a step further, you can easily see that any differences in view definitions can give any consumer of that view a huge edge, or take it away. Be cautious with your view definitions, whether it has to do with something obvious like screen size, or the types of events the view receives from the game logic.

I hope I've convinced you that this architecture is a good way to go. I'll be quite honest and tell you that it isn't an easy architecture to code, especially at first. You'll go through a phase where you are sure there is an easier way, and you'll want to abandon this event-driven architecture where game logic is completely separate from the view. Please be patient and resist the urge. Given some time, you'll never go back to a simpler, but less flexible design.

APPLICATION LAYER

The contents of the application layer are divided further into different areas that deal with devices, the operating system, and your game's lifetime (see Figure 2.2).

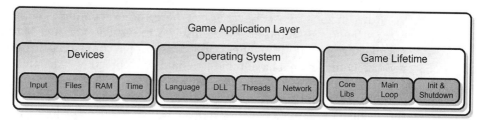

FIGURE 2.2 A closer look at the application layer.

Reading Input

Games have an amazing variety of user input devices: keyboard, mouse, gamepad, joystick, dance pad, steering wheel, and my personal favorite, the guitar. Reading these devices is almost always completely dependent on calls to the operating system and device drivers. The state of these devices should always be translated into game commands. Some of these commands might be sent back to the game logic, such as "fire missile," while others might be handled by the game view, such as "show me my inventory." Either way, you'll likely write an entire subsystem to read these devices and interpret them as commands.

This same system should also be configurable. I play console shooters with an inverted Y-axis, but many people like it the other way around, even though I'll never understand why. If you have a system that reads devices as input and sends game commands as output, you can create the system to read a configuration file to match controls with commands. Then all you have to do is modify this data file, and you'll have completely configurable controls.

One thing is critical: You can't simply change the game state directly when you read user input. Every bit of game sample code out there does this; you can see where games make direct changes to data simply because the W key was pressed. This is a vastly inflexible system and will haunt you later, I guarantee it.

File Systems and Resource Caching

File systems include DVD-ROM, hard disk, or removable memory cards. Code in this subsystem will generally be responsible for managing game resource files and loading and saving the game state. Managing resource files can be pretty complicated—much more so than simply opening a JPG or an MP3 file.

A resource cache is one of those hidden systems I told you about. An open world game like *Grand Theft Auto* has gigabytes of art and sound, and the system only has a fraction of the memory needed to load everything. Imagine the problem of getting a crowd of people out of a burning building. Left to their own devices, the crowd will panic, attempt to force themselves through every available exit, and only a small fraction of the people will escape alive.

Now imagine another scenario, where the evacuation is completely organized. The crowd would divide themselves into single file lines, each line going out the nearest exit. If the lines don't cross, people could almost run. It would be very likely that even a large building could be completely evacuated.

This analogy works well for game resources. The burning building is your optical media, and the doors are the limited bandwidth you have for streaming this media. The bits on the disk represent the crowd. Your job is to figure out a way to get as many of the bits from the optical media into memory in the shortest possible time. That's not the entire problem, though. A resource cache is exactly what the name implies—commonly used assets like the graphics for the HUD are always in memory, and rarely used assets like the cinematic endgame are only in memory while it's playing, and most likely only a piece of it at that.

The resource cache manages assets like these in a way that fools the game into thinking that they are always in memory. If everything works well, the game will never have to wait for anything, since the resource cache should be smart enough to predict which assets will be used and load them before they are needed.

Every now and then, the cache might miscalculate and suffer a cache miss. Depending on the resource, the game might be able to continue without it until it has been loaded, such as the graphics for an object in the far distance. In that case, the graphic can fade in once it is safely in memory. In other cases, the game isn't so lucky, such as a missing audio file for a character's lines. Since they are synched to the facial animations, the game has to wait until the audio is loaded before the character can begin speaking.

So it's not enough to write a little cache that knows whether resources exist in memory at the moment they are needed. It has to be clever, predicting the future to some extent and even providing the game with a backup in case the cache suffers a miss.

Luckily, I've included an entire chapter on the subject of file systems and the resource cache. This just might be one of the most under-discussed topics in game development.

Managing Memory

Managing memory is a critical system for AAA games, but is largely ignored by most game developers until they run out of it. Simply put, the default memory manager that comes with the default C-runtime libraries is completely unsuitable for most game applications. Many game data structures are relatively tiny things, and they belong in different areas of memory, such as RAM or video memory. A general memory manager tries to be all things to all applications, where you will know every detail about how your game needs and uses memory. Generally, you'll write your own memory manager to handle allocations of various sizes and persistence, and more importantly to track budgets.

BEST PRACTICE

VIRTUAL MEMORY—CAN BE GOOD, CAN BE BAD

Windows can use virtual memory, and when a game runs out of physical memory, the OS will automatically begin to use virtual memory. Sometimes, Windows games can get away with this, but it is a little like playing Russian Roulette—at some point, the game will slow to a crawl. A console game is completely different. For example, if your game allocates a single byte larger than the available memory, it will crash. Every game programmer should be as careful about memory as console programmers. Your game will run faster and will simply be more fun. Create some way to track every byte of memory, which subsystem is using it, and when any one of these areas exceeds its memory budget. Your game will be better for it.

Initialization, the Main Loop, and Shutdown

Most Windows software waits for the user to do something before any code is executed. If the mouse isn't moving and the keyboard isn't being hammered, an application like Excel is completely idle. This is good because you can have a bunch of applications up and running without a large CPU overhead. Games are completely different. Games are simulations that have a life of their own. Without player input, they'll happily send some horrific creature over to start pounding on your character's skull. That will probably motivate a few button presses.

The system that controls this ongoing activity is the main loop, and it has three major components: grabbing and queuing player input, ticking the game logic, and presenting the game state to all the game views, which means rendering the screen, playing sounds, or sending game state changes over the Internet.

At the highest level, your game application layer creates and loads your game logic, creates and attaches game views to that logic, and then gives all these systems some CPU time so they can do their jobs. You'll learn more about this in Chapter 5, "Game Initialization," and Chapter 6, "The Main Loop."

Other Application Layer Code

There are lots of other important subsystems in the application layer, including the following:

- The system clock
- String handling
- Dynamically loaded libraries (DLLs)
- Threads and thread synchronization
- Network communications
- Initialization
- Main loop
- Shutdown

The system clock is critical for games. Without it, you have no way to synchronize game animations and audio, move objects at a known speed, or simply be able to time your credits so that people have enough time to read them. Almost every game subsystem will care about time: physics, animations, user interface, sound, and so on.

Game programming becomes more global year after year, and generally games that sell well in one language will also sell well if they are translated or *localized*. If you structure your game correctly and factor all user-presented strings into external files, you'll find it a lot easier to translate your game into a similar language. Note that I said "similar language." Although it is possible to structure a game to be in completely different languages like English and Japanese, remember that you don't just have a technology barrier to multilingual gaming. You also have a culture barrier—not every game is one that can cross cultures easily.

Most operating systems have a way to dynamically swap code in and out of memory at runtime. This is critical for conserving valuable memory space or replacing a subsystem entirely. You might use a DLL to swap a DirectX for an OpenGL renderer, for example.

Today's multicore desktops and consoles make multithreaded and multicore programming a must. I actually remember a time when games didn't use threads—instead everything ran in a single execution path. It was easier in some ways, but harder in others. Threads are used for audio streaming data, AI, and if you are clever, even physics. I've read in other places that shall remain nameless that suggest you can use threads for everything. Don't believe this for a minute; if every subsystem had to be thread safe, you'd spend most of your CPU time waiting for thread synchronization.

Network communications is another service provided by the operating system. This network code will generally provide your game with a way to make a network connection with another computer and a way to read and write data from the network stream. The definition of what actually gets sent and how received data is interpreted is actually coded in the game view and game logic layer. I'll talk more about that shortly.

The last group in the application layer is responsible for your game's life cycle: initialization, the main loop, and shutdown. I've also included in this group your core libraries that standardize basic data structures and templates, as well as your script interpreter.

Initialization can be something of a nightmare. Many game subsystems have complicated interrelations, and they tend to depend on one another. We'll discuss details of the initialization sequence in Chapter 5.

Most games use scripting languages. Whether it is UnrealScript, Python, LUA, or something a game team creates from scratch, these systems and the scripts they run are critical components for today's commercial game development. You'll learn more about scripting languages, and Lua in particular, in Chapter 11.

GAME LOGIC

The game logic (see Figure 2.3) is the heart and soul of your game. It defines the game universe, what things are in the universe, and how they interact. It also defines how the game state can be changed by external stimulus, such as a human player pressing a gamepad key or an AI process taking action to kill you. Let's take a closer look at all of the components of the game logic system.

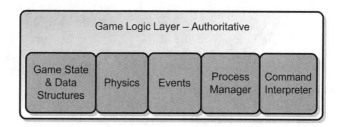

FIGURE 2.3 Game logic and its subsystems.

Game State and Data Structures

Every game will have a container for game objects. Simple games can use a list structure, but more complicated games will need something more flexible and optimized for quick local searching or streaming. Your game engine must be able to traverse the object data structures quickly to change an object's state, and yet it must be able to hold a flexible array of properties for each object. These two requirements are frequently at odds with each other; one is quick to search, the other is easy to extend.

Ultima used a simple two-dimensional array of object lists. It was easy to find objects within a given range of a map location, and each grid square was small enough to have a quickly traversable list of objects. *Thief: Deadly Shadows*, on the other hand, used a simple list of objects, but it was heavily tangled by internal pointers. If two objects needed to know about each other, such as an elevator button and the elevator door, they were linked by the game editor. This solution actually worked quite well and is commonly used.

Object properties, such as hit points, engine horsepower, and wacky things like that, tend to be stored in custom data structures whose efficiency can be anything from fantastic to dismal. *Ultima Online* used text strings to define properties on objects, which had the benefit of easy and flexible development at some cost in memory storage. *Thief: Deadly Shadows* had an extremely complicated property system that was actually object oriented; you could define object properties for an archetype, like a barrel, but overload existing properties or even create totally new ones for a particular barrel that was placed only once in the game universe. The system was memory efficient since it never copied property data, but it ran at some extra cost in CPU time because the property system was essentially a tree structure. There are trade-offs no matter how you do it.

It's easy to confuse the game logic representation of an object with the visual representation of an object. The game logic holds the object state, such as the amount of damage an object has—probably stored in an integer. The visual representation, managed by the game view, holds model data and textures that convey the state visually to the player, such as a bloody arm stump. A bloody arm stump texture is completely different from m_damage = 30.

You might feel that it would be better to store all of these things in a single C++ object—how much damage had been done and whether the arm texture is healthy or bloody. You'd be wrong. In this architecture, there are two C++ objects—one belongs to the game logic, and is usually called an *actor*. The other belongs to the renderer, and is called a *textured skeletal mesh*. When the game actor changes, the game logic broadcasts an event. The renderer reacts to this event by changing the texture. More on this later.

I wish I had more time in this book to exhaustively go over game data structures, but to be honest, they are extremely custom and are finely tuned to suit the requirements of a particular game. My suggestion to you is to make sure that you have an excellent knowledge of classic data structures such as linked lists, hash lists, trees, B-trees, and all those other things you learn in classic data structures texts. Games absolutely use these structures, or perhaps abuse them, to get the results they need.

Physics and Collision

Physics falls under the general category of "rules of your game universe," and is solidly a member of your game logic. It defines everything from how objects move when they fall under gravity to what they do when they tumble around.

You certainly don't need a complicated physics system to have a fun game, but you can bet your bottom dollar that a bad physics system will completely remove the fun from any game. There's a great game concept that says that when something is completely abstract, it's easy to ignore unrealistic representations of things. When you inject reality into a game, even small errors create complaints from your players. You can prove this to yourself by looking at the movements of a stick figure on one of those Flash games on the Internet, and compare it to the best human animations in a game like *Gears of War*. You'll forgive the stick figure for moving in weird ways because it is so abstract, but you'll be upset with the *Gears* character for the smallest mistake in shoulder animation—(one of the hardest things to animate by the way) because the character looks so realistic.

This concept has to do with human psychology and how we observe things. It comes into serious play when you create any game technology that approaches reality, as physics systems do. You'll spend a staggering amount of time making the tiniest tweaks to your system to remove the smallest movement problems because the smallest mistake in reality is glaring.

Events

When the game logic makes changes in the game state, such as creating or moving an object, a number of game systems will respond. Here's an example. Imagine that one object in your game is a portable radio. The graphics system will need to create polygons and textures so you can see the radio. The sound system will create a sound effect so your radio will play some great music—perhaps a little Jimi Hendrix. AI processes might respond to the presence of the object. In this case, they might just chill out and enjoy the sublime guitar from our boy Jimi. All three of these subsystems—the graphics system, the audio system, and even the AI system—need to know that this radio exists and what it is doing. These systems are notified through events. Just like a Windows application hears about a WM_MOUSEMOVE event, your game systems can listen and react to a game event for practically any change in game state or input from a player. There are also global game events, such as events to inform subsystems that a new level has been loaded or the game is being saved.

Many games create an event system that defines these events and the data that accompanies them. Different subsystems register with the event manager to listen for events that they'll react to. A good example of this is the sound system; it might register to listen for object collision events so that it can play the appropriate sound effect when two objects are smashed together.

Event-based architectures tend to make your game system clean and efficient. Instead of making API calls to four or five subsystems when an object collision is detected, the code simply sends an event to the event manager, and all the subsystems that registered to receive event notifications of this type will get notified in turn.

The event code is the glue that holds this entire game architecture together. The application layer holds the event registry, subsystems register to listen to events they care about, and other subsystems send events as needed. These events get sent to only the subsystems that have subscribed to them.

Chapter 10, "Game Event Management," will dig into this system and show you how it works.

Process Manager

Any simulation of a game world is usually composed of discrete bits of very simple code, such as a bit of code to move an object along a linear path or parse a Lua script. These bits of code can be combined to act on a single game object, which will have the effect of combining these state changes. These bits of code are usually organized into classes, and they can be instantiated for any game object. If you were to create a "move along this path" class and a "run Lua script" class, and instantiated them both on one object, you'd create an interesting and complicated interaction from two simple pieces of code.

This is the heart of another important game subsystem: the process manager. It keeps a list of processes and gives each one a little CPU time by calling it once every game loop. A great example of this is a pathfind process. It acts to move an object from one place to another and when the destination is reached, it simply terminates and ceases acting on the object.

LEARNING OUR LESSONS FROM *ULTIMA VII*

After *Ultima VII*, all of the programmers met in the courtyard of Origin Systems with a plan to redesign the *Ultima* technology for *Ultima VIII*. We had a nice sunny day, a whiteboard, and real motivation to make a much better system. We realized that any code that operated on an object or group of objects for a period of time could be encapsulated in a cooperative process, and it could even be responsible for its own lifetime. When its job was done, it would kill itself off. The best thing of all was that the entire thing could be managed from a single class that contained a list of every running process. This technology eventually evolved to become almost as useful and complex as a simple operating system, managing both cooperative and real-time processes.

On *Ultima*, we found it very useful to allow processes to have dependencies on one another, where one process would wait for another to complete before starting. A good example of this is something you might use for a Molotov cocktail: one process tracks the parabolic movement of any game object until it collides with something, and another process manages a fireball explosion. Your game can string these processes together to create some amazingly cool effects.

You'll learn more about this system in Chapter 6, "Controlling the Main Loop."

Command Interpreter

A game logic needs to respond to external commands. For a human playing a racing game, these commands will send input to the game logic's representation of the car: acceleration, braking, and steering. An AI process will do exactly the same thing. External entities, such as a human holding a gamepad or an AI process using a command-based interface, can communicate to the game logic *with exactly the same commands.*

You might ask why this is necessary. In any racing game, there should be someplace in the code that says something like "If button A is down, set emergency brake" or something like that. I know it seems like a lot of extra work, but that breaks the separation between game logic and game views that I have found to be so important when creating games.

What should happen is this: The game view presents an interface to the human player that changes the "Button A is pressed" state into a game command, "Set Emergency Brake." That game command is then sent to the game logic, but here's the rub: the code that actually sets the emergency brake state on the data structure representing the car is actually in the game logic. This code only sets the emergency brake in response to a command—not through a direct tweak to the `m_bIsEmergencyBrakeOn` member of a class somewhere.

I can hear you whining about this, and I'm not even sitting near you. Let me try to show you how cool this is before you call me a complete freak.

If your game logic can accept commands through an event-based interface instead of direct API calls to game logic classes, you can create a programming language for your own game, just like you see in so many games that have heavy mod hooks like *Unreal* and *Doom*. The command interpreter you use for your game will probably have an ultra efficient low level, but there's nothing keeping you from coding a higher level interface that accepts console input. Then you could actually type "SET CAR 2 EMERGENCY BRAKE" or something like that, and guess what will happen? Car two will lock up the tires and go spinning out of control, all at your command.

UNREAL'S COMMAND CONSOLE

Ion Storm's core code base was basically *Unreal Warfare*, a modified version of *Unreal 2*, and thus had an amazing console command system that could be used to control almost anything. You could do almost anything: add or remove properties, move them, make AIs blind, deaf, dumb, or even all three. The console system could even take input from a file, creating a weird meta-programming language for our game. Believe me it was nice to have—because even if your game doesn't have a rigorous separation between game logic and game view, you can still create a command interpreter that provides a very low-level way to tweak your game while it is running.

GAME VIEW FOR THE HUMAN PLAYER

A game view is a collection of systems that communicates with the game logic to present the game to a particular kind of observer. This observer can be a human being with a controller of some kind like a keyboard or a dance pad, but it can also be an AI agent, whose view of the game state will determine the AI process's next course of action.

The game view for a human being has a lot of work to do (see Figure 2.4). It must respond to game events and figure out how to draw the scene, send output to the speakers, translate controller input into game commands, and more. Let's look at the main areas.

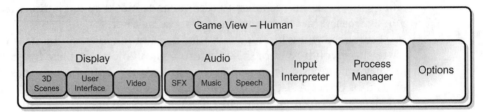

FIGURE 2.4 Subsystems that create a game view for a human player.

Graphics Display

The display renders the objects that make up a game scene, the user interface layer on top of the scene, and perhaps even streaming video. The renderer should draw the screen as fast as it possibly can. The display is one of the biggest suckers of CPU budget in a game, and should therefore scale well with the capabilities of a wide range of CPUs and GPUs (graphics processing unit). For PC games, it should also perform well under different hardware configurations. Generally, lower-end CPUs will cut expensive features, such as full screen effects, in order to run at the best frame rate they can.

Video cards will draw all the polygons you stuff into the GPU, even if it takes them forever. Forever, by the way, is defined as anything more than 50ms, giving you a frame rate of 20fps. The real problem a 3D engine has is choosing which polygons to draw to make the most compelling scene.

Consider the problem of a flight simulator like Microsoft Flight Simulator X. When the plane is on the ground, the display looks a lot like every other 3D game out there. You see a few buildings, a few other planes, and a runway. You might also see some scenery in the distance like a mountain range or a city skyline (see Figure 2.5).

Once the plane is up in the air, you have a different story altogether. You've increased the viewable surface by a few orders of magnitude, and therefore you've increased the potential viewable set of polygons. Players who attempt a naive approach of simply drawing all the polygons will learn quickly that they can't get their plane more than 150 feet off the ground. The frame rate will fall in inverse geometric proportion to the altitude of the plane, because that's how many more polygons you have to draw to achieve a realistic look.

The actual approach to this problem uses different levels of detail to draw areas of terrain and objects, depending on their distance from the viewer. On some flight simulators, you can catch this happening. Simply begin a slow descent

FIGURE 2.5 Microsoft Flight Simulator X.

and watch as the terrain suddenly becomes better looking; the green patches will increase in detail and eventually become individual trees until you crash into them. One of the trickier parts of most 3D engines is getting the levels of detail to transition smoothly, avoiding the "popping" effect.

Another problem is avoiding overdraw. If your game is in a complex interior environment or deep in the concrete canyons of New York City, you'll achieve the fastest frame rate if you only draw the polygons that you can see. Again the naive approach is to simply draw all of the polygons in the view frustum, omitting any that are facing away from the camera. This solution will most likely result in a disastrous frame rate in certain areas but not others, even if the camera is pointed straight at an interior wall. When the game is bogging down like this, it is drawing an enormous number of polygons behind the wall, only to be covered up by the bigger polygons close to the camera. What a waste!

You'll need some advanced tools to help you analyze your level and calculate what areas can be seen given a particular viewing location. Umbra Software has technologies to do this either offline or on the fly, but many games can use a simple portal technique. Competitive games are all pushing the envelope for the illusion of extremely complicated worlds. The trick is to create these worlds so that your environments behave well with whatever culling technique is best for your renderer. Add to that mix of technology some nice levels of detail, and you can get a game that looks good when objects are close up or far away.

Since 3D engines are only capable of drawing so much scenery per frame, an amazing amount of effort must go into creating the right level of design. Any environment that is too dense must be fixed, or the frame rate will suffer along with your reviews.

YOUR ARTISTS NEED TO KNOW WHAT YOUR ENGINE CAN DO

The most common mistake made on 3D games is not communicating with the artists about what the graphics engine can and can't do. Remember that the world environment is just a backdrop, and you'll still need to add interactive objects, characters, special effects, and a little bit of user interface before you can call it a day. All these things, especially the characters, will drag your performance into the ground if the background art is too aggressive. Try to establish CPU budgets for drawing the background, objects, characters, and special effects early on and hold your environment artists and level designers to it like glue. Measure the CPU time spent preparing and rendering these objects and display it for all to see.

Audio

Audio is one of my favorite areas of game development, and I've been lucky enough to work with some of the best audio engineers and composers in the business. Game audio can generally be split up into three major areas: sound effects, music, and speech.

Sound effects are pretty easy things to get running in a game. You simply load a WAV file and send it into DirectX with volume and looping parameters. Almost every sound system is capable of simulating the 3D position of the object relative to the listener. You just provide the position of the object, and the 3D sound system will do the rest.

Music can be really easy or really hard. Technically, it's not really different from sound effects, unless you want to get into complicated mixing of different tunes to reflect what's going on in the game. Anyone who's played *Halo* knows how effective this can be; the distinctive combat music tells you you'd better reload your shotgun.

Speech is much trickier—not just technically, but keeping track of all the bits and pieces recorded in the studio and matching them with a 3D lip-synched character. This usually involves anything from a total hack, to a carefully hand-tweaked database of mouth positions for each speech file, to a tool that can automatically generate this data.

You'll see a good introduction to game audio in Chapter 12, "Game Audio."

User Interface Presentation

The user interface for a game doesn't look like the standard Windows GDI. Game interfaces have a creative flair, and they should. This means that the user interface code needs to be baked fresh every time, especially since every health meter and HUD is different for every game.

The irony of this is that games still need things like a button control, so players can easily click "OK" for whatever thing the game is asking about. These controls aren't hard to write, but if you're like me, you hate rewriting something that already exists and is well understood by both coders and players. You'll probably roll your own, and hopefully keep that code around from game to game so you won't have to rewrite it ever again. Another option is licensing ScaleForm GFx, which lets your artists create your entire UI in Flash and import the results directly into your game.

I'll cover these topics more in Chapter 9, "User Interface Programming."

Process Manager

Having a little déjà vu? You aren't crazy, because you saw this same heading under the game logic group just a few pages back. It turns out that game views can use their own process manager to handle everything from button animations to streaming audio and video. Keep this in the back of your mind as you read about the process manager in Chapter 6. You'll use it all over your game.

Options

Most games have some user-configurable options like sound effects volume, whether your controls are Y-inverted or not, and whether you like to run your game in 4:3 or in 16:9 widescreen. These options are useful to stick in something simple like an INI file so that anyone can easily tweak it, especially during development.

Multiplayer Games

One thing you might not have considered—this event-based, logic/view architecture makes it simple to have a multiplayer game. All you need to do is attach more human views to the same game logic. Okay, I'll come clean. It's a little more trouble than that because each view needs to share what is likely a single display from the application layer, figure out how to iterate the additional controls, and so on. That stuff is fairly easy compared to getting the overall architecture built to support multiple players, especially if it wasn't designed to do so from the very beginning.

GAME VIEWS FOR AI AGENTS

A great argument for the harsh breakdown between game logic and game views is that humans and AI processes can interact with the game logic through exactly the same event-based interface. An AI agent's view of a game generally has the components shown in Figure 2.6.

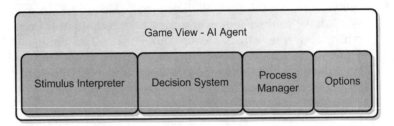

FIGURE 2.6 An AI agent's view of the game.

The stimulus interpreter receives the exact same events that all other game views receive: object movement, collisions, and so on. It's up to the AI programmer to determine how the AI will react to each event the AI agent receives. It would be easy enough for an AI process to ignore certain events or react to events that are filtered by the human view, and this would certainly affect what the AI process would do.

For example, AI agents might react to sound effects, which are the result of game events such as objects colliding, footsteps, or noisy objects like radios being activated. If an AI is supposed to be deaf, it merely filters the sound events. If an AI is supposed to be blind, it filters any event about the visible state of an object. You can set the nature of an AI agent's behavior completely by controlling what stimuli the AI agent receives.

The second part of an AI view is the decision system. This is a completely custom written subsystem that translates stimuli into actions. Your AI agent might be able to send commands into the game your human can't, giving them extra abilities such as opening locked doors. The reverse is also true, and the combination of AI stimulus filters and command sets can have a great effect on how smart your AI agents are.

If your AI needs to solve difficult problems, such as how to navigate a complicated environment or make the next move in a chess match, then you might need a process manager just as in the game logic and game view. You might use this to have AI spread its evaluation of stimuli and decisions over time, amortizing the cost of these expensive calculations over many frames.

Finally, you'll certainly want a list of AI options that you can tweak through a simple text file. The stimulus filter and decision set options are certainly enough to warrant a large options file, but more importantly, your AI options can be extremely useful for AI tuning during development. Even if you eventually hard code the AI parameters, you'll certainly want an instantly "tweakable" version while your game is in development.

NETWORKED GAME ARCHITECTURE

If you implement the game architecture that I've been beating you with since the beginning of this chapter, you can write two additional classes and transform your single player game into a networked, multiplayer game. That might seem like an insane boast, but it is completely true. Look at Figure 2.7 to get another look at how game views interact with the game logic.

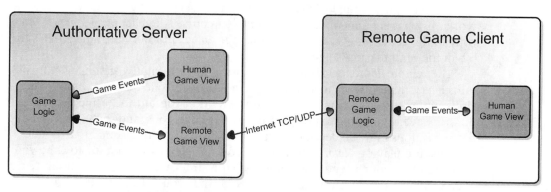

FIGURE 2.7 Client/server networked game architecture.

You'll see the same game logic/game view architecture, but there is a new implementation of the game logic and a new implementation of the game view. Both are needed to create remote versions of their single player brethren.

Remote Game View

On the server machine, the remote player should appear just like an AI agent. The remote view receives game events from the game logic and responds with commands back to the game logic. What happens inside the remote view is completely different from the AI agent view or the human view.

Game events received from the game logic are packaged up and sent via TCP or UDP to a client computer across the network. Since game events on a local machine can be somewhat bloated, there should be some processing of the event data before it is sent out. First, redundant messages should be removed from the message stream. It makes no sense to send two object move events when the only one that matters is the last one. Second, multiple events should be sent together as one packet. If the packet is large enough, it should be compressed to save bandwidth.

The remote game view also receives IP traffic from the remote machine, namely the game commands that result from the controller input. One difference in the remote game view is that it should never trust this command data entirely. The game logic should be smart enough to do some sanity checking on impossible commands, but the remote view can take a front-line approach and attempt to short-circuit any hacking attempts, such as detecting badly formed packets or packets that come in with an unusual frequency. Once the game commands have gone through some kind of anti-hacking filter, they are sent on to the game logic.

Remote Game Logic

In this model, the game logic is an authoritative server; its game state is the final word on what is happening in the game. Of course, the client machines need a copy of the game state and a way to manage delays in Internet traffic. This is the job of the remote game logic.

The remote game logic is quite similar to the authoritative game logic. It contains everything it needs to simulate the game, even code that can simulate decisions when it must. It has two components that the authoritative game logic doesn't have: something to predict authoritative decisions, and something to handle corrections in those decisions. This is easier to see with a concrete example.

Imagine playing *Halo*, and imagine you are about to shoot an RPG at your best friend. If your friend is playing over the Internet and has a bad lag, your friend's machine might not get the message that you fired the RPG until a few hundred milliseconds after you fired it. If you could watch both screens at the same time, you'd see your RPG rocketing over to blow up your friend, but your friend wouldn't see anything at all, for just a short time.

Some 500ms later, your friend's machine gets the message that you fired an RPG. Since there was no way to predict this message, it must show the fired RPG, but begin to move the rocket fast enough to "catch up" to the rocket on the authoritative server, or *host*.

That's why playing shooter games is impossible when you have bad lag and you're not running the host! That's also why no one will play with you when you run the host over a slow connection, because it gives you an unfair advantage. The remote machines simply don't get the messages fast enough.

What this means to the remote game logic is that it has to make corrections in its game state, perhaps breaking the "rules" in order to get things back in sync. In the previous example, the rule that had to be bent a bit was the acceleration and speed of an RPG. If you've ever seen an RPG turn a corner and kill you dead, you've experienced this firsthand.

Other than that, the remote game logic interacts with the game view in pretty much exactly the same way as the authoritative view; it sends the game view events and changes in game state, and accepts game commands from the view. Those commands are then packaged and forwarded on to the server machine, specifically the remote game view mentioned in the previous section.

YOU NEED MULTIPLAYER? GIVE ME A FEW HOURS...

We designed our last card game for Microsoft using a rigorous implementation of the game logic/game view system. When we started working on the game, Microsoft wanted us to code it such that we could create a multiplayer version of the game in as short a time as possible. Believe me, it wasn't easy, and all the programmers had to take some time to learn how to deal with this very different architecture. After we shipped the project, I was curious how well we'd done in creating something that was multiplayer-aware, even though we'd never actually used the feature. One of our programmers spent about two days and had our card game playing over the Internet. If that's not proof, I don't know what is.

DO I HAVE TO USE DIRECTX?

If your platform of choice is the PC, you have to consider whether to use DirectX in your game or try an alternative API for graphics, sound, and input.

Just to be perfectly clear, this section has nothing to do with how to draw a shaded polygon under Direct3D. This section is going to enlighten you about why you would choose something like OpenGL over Direct3D. Believe it or not, the choice isn't clear-cut no matter what your religious beliefs.

ALL ROADS LEAD TO ROME

It's not possible for me to be more tired of the religious nature of the OpenGL/DirectX debate. Any good programmer should understand what's under the hood of every API if you have to make a choice between them. Disregarding DirectX simply because Microsoft made it is asinine.

Design Philosophy of DirectX

DirectX was designed to sit between the application and the hardware. If the hardware was capable of performing an action itself, DirectX would call the driver and be done with it. If the hardware wasn't there, DirectX would emulate the call in software. Clearly, that would be much slower.

One thing that was gained by this design philosophy was a single API for every hardware combination that supported DirectX. Back in the old days (that would be the early 1990s), programmers weren't so lucky. A great example was all the work that needed to be done for sound systems. Origin supported Adlib, Roland, and SoundBlaster with separate bits of code. Graphics were similar; the old EGA graphics standard was completely different than Hercules. What a pain!

Of course, DirectX isn't the simplest API to learn. COM is a weird thing to look at if you aren't used to it. It also seems weird to have 50 lines of code to initialize a 3D rendering surface when OpenGL does it so much easier. Herein lies one basis for religious argument: old-time C versus newfangled COM. Get over it long enough to understand it.

DirectX exposes a lot more about what the hardware is capable of doing. Those CAPS bits can tell you if your video card can support nothing, hardware transform and lighting (T&L), or the latest shaders. Perhaps that means you'll load up denser geometry or simply bring up a dialog box telling some loser that he needs a better video card. Your customer service people will thank you if you decide to leave the word "loser" out of the error message.

Direct3D or OpenGL

I'm not going to preach to you about why DirectX is unusable and why OpenGL is God's gift. Instead, I hope to give you enough knowledge about how and why you would judge one against the other with the goal of making the best choice for your game, your team, and the good people that will throw money at you to play your latest game. I'm sure to get lovely emails about this section. Bring it on. I'm going to take a weirder tack on this argument anyway. Both APIs will get you a nice-looking game. There are plenty of middleware rendering engines that support both. What does that tell you? It tells me that while there may be interesting bits and pieces here and there that are unique, the basic job of pushing triangles to the video card is essentially equivalent.

You don't have control over the quality of the driver. I'm sure we could find OpenGL drivers that suck, and we can certainly find Direct3D drivers that never should have seen the light of day. Given that unfortunate reality, you should choose the API that has the best drivers for all the people who will play your game.

If you have a hard-core title like *Half Life 2*, you're pretty safe in choosing OpenGL, since the drivers for high-end cards tend to have a high quality. Of course, the Direct3D drivers for these same cards are going to be equally good, since they're high-end cards after all. Your choice gets murkier if your game has a wider appeal and perhaps runs on older machines. It's a safe bet that there are more video cards out there that have Direct3D drivers than OpenGL drivers, and that on the low-end cards the Direct3D drivers are going to be better.

Why is this true? The video card companies making low-end cards had to make a choice, too, and allocate resources to write drivers. They generally chose Direct3D first and got that driver out the door and on the install disk. The OpenGL driver might come later on the Web site, if they had time and resources to do it. Again, this points to the fact that a hard-core audience will likely have OpenGL drivers on a rocking video card, because they sought it out.

The mass market went where they were told: Direct3D. I guess that's where you should go, too, if you are doing a game with mass-market appeal. Hard-core games can make whatever choice they like.

DirectSound or What?

For years, I never looked farther than RAD Game Tools, Inc. for sound and video technology. The Miles Sound System includes full source code, has a flat license fee, and works on every platform in existence today. The Bink Video tools are cross platform and support all the latest consoles, Win32, and Macintosh. Check out the latest at www.radgametools.com. It doesn't hurt that RAD has been in business since 1988 and has licensed their technology for thousands of games. They are probably the most used middleware company in the industry.

Miles can use DirectSound as a lower layer. This is quite convenient if you want to do some odd thing that Miles can't. One nail in the coffin for DirectSound is that it doesn't include the ability to decode MP3 files. Part of your license fee for Miles pays for a license to decode MP3s, which are a fantastic alternative to storing bloated WAV files or weird-sounding MIDIs. You could use OGG files, which are completely open source and unencumbered by an expensive license—in fact, the audio chapter shows you how to do this. There is one great thing Miles gets you—and that's streaming. You don't have to load the entire sound file in memory at once if you don't want to, and believe me, Miles makes this easy. Bottom line, do yourself a favor and get Miles for your game.

Other audio technologies, like FMod or WWise, take playing sound buffers to the next step and allow tighter control over sound in your game: how sounds are mixed, which sounds have higher priority, and what tunable parameters your game can tweak to make different effects in real time. WWise is more expensive than Miles, but is more capable. FMod is a good choice since it is free for noncommercial software development.

DirectInput or Roll Your Own

DirectInput encapsulates the translation of hardware-generated messages to something your game can use directly. This mapping isn't exactly rocket science, and most programmers can code the most used portions of DirectInput with their eyes closed. The weirder input devices, like the force feedback joysticks that look like an implement of torture, plug right into DirectInput. DirectInput also abstracts the device so that you can write one body of code for your game, whether or not your players have the weirdest joystick on the block.

OTHER BITS AND PIECES

There are tons of other bits and pieces to coding games, many of which you'll discover throughout this book. These things defy classification, but they are every bit as important to games as a good random number generator.

Beyond that, you'll find some things important to game coding such as how to convince Microsoft Windows to become a good platform for your game—a more difficult task than you'd think. Microsoft makes almost all of its income from the sales of business software like Microsoft Office, and the operating system reflects that. Sure, DirectX is supposed to be the hard-core interface for game coders, but you'll find that it's something of a black sheep even within Microsoft. Don't get me wrong, it works and works surprisingly well, but you can't ever forget that you are forcing a primarily business software platform to become a game platform, and sometimes you'll run into dead-ends.

Debugging games is much more difficult than other software, mostly because there's a lot going on in real time, and there are gigabytes of data files that can harbor nasty bugs. Combine that with the menagerie of game hardware like video cards, audio cards, user input devices, and even operating systems, and it's a wonder that games work as well as they do. It's no secret that games are considered to be the most unstable software on the market, and it reflects the difficulty of the problem.

Now that you know what's in a game, let's discuss how game code needs a certain style.

FURTHER READING

Design Patterns: Elements of Reusable Object-Oriented Software, Erich Gamma, Richard Helm, and Ralph E. Johnson

Antipatterns: Refactoring Software, Architectures, and Projects in Crisis, William J. Brown, Raphael C. Malveau, and Thomas J. Mowbray

Modern C++ Design: Generic Programming and Design Patterns Applied, Andrei Alexandrescu

3

CODING TIDBITS AND STYLE THAT WILL SAVE YOU

In This Chapter

- Smart Design Practices
- Smart Pointers and Naked Pointers
- Using Memory Correctly
- Mike's Grab Bag of Useful Stuff
- Developing the Style That's Right for You
- Further Reading

When you pick up a game programming book, the last thing you probably want to do is read about programming style and coding techniques. You want to dive right in and learn how to code 3D graphics or AI. As cool as that stuff is, I want to show you some useful things you'll use throughout your entire code base. I'll also show you some things to avoid in your code—much of which is geared toward working with other programmers. Your code should communicate clearly to other programmers at every opportunity. Something I've learned over the years is that the distance between exuberance and experience is paved with mistakes. If you can avoid a few of those mistakes, you'll be a happier programmer.

In the first edition of this book, this chapter was called "Dumb Stuff All Game Programmers Should Know." It turned out that this stuff wasn't so dumb or obvious. My goal in this chapter is to set the foundation for the coding techniques that I'll be presenting throughout this book. I've developed this style over the years watching really smart people, and it worked for me so I've kept it around.

As you read this chapter, keep in mind that when it comes to programming style, every programmer can be very different. For example, the techniques you use to program games on a PC platform, where you have more robust tools and plenty of memory to work with, might be different from the techniques you use to program on a platform such as the PS3. Using C, C++, or C# also makes a huge difference in style. In other words, not every problem has a single solution and no single style fits all situations. Also, every programmer and programming team is different. They'll sometimes never agree on even trivial things. I don't expect you'll agree with everything I present in this chapter, nor this book.

Let me put it this way. If you find something you really hate, it means you have opinions different than mine, and you've formed those opinions through firsthand experience. That's great! It means you're a programmer, and you and I can debate endlessly on the Web about the best way to do things. Just remember, neither of us is wrong—just different and opinionated.

We'll start by looking at design practices that you should consider when writing a game, and then we'll move on and look at specific programming techniques such as working with pointers, memory management, how to avoid memory leaks, and other goodies. In the last part of this chapter, I'll provide you with a few coding tools taken from my own personal toolbox.

SMART DESIGN PRACTICES

Isaac Asimov's Foundation series invented an interesting discipline called *psychohistory*, a social science that could predict societal trends and macro events with great certainty. Each historian in the story was required to contribute new formulas and extend the science. As a programmer, your job is similar. Every new module or class that you create gives you the opportunity to extend the capabilities and usefulness of the code base. But to do this effectively, you must learn how to think ahead and design code with the goal of keeping it in use for many projects and many years.

Designing good code in an object-oriented language can be more difficult than in a procedural language like C or PASCAL. Why? The power and flexibility of an object-oriented language like C++, for example, allows you to create extremely complicated systems that appear quite simple. This is both good and bad; it's easy to get yourself into trouble without realizing it. A great example of this is the C++ constructor. Some programmers create code in a constructor that can fail—maybe they tried to read data from an initialization file and the file doesn't exist. A failed constructor doesn't return any kind of error code, so the badly constructed object still exists and might get used again. While you can use structured exception handling to catch a failure in a constructor, it is a much better practice to write constructors that can't fail. Another example is the misuse of virtual functions. For example, a naive programmer might make every method in the class virtual, thinking that future expandability for everything is good. Well, he'd be wrong. On some platforms, virtual functions can be very expensive. A well thought through design is more important than blind application of object-oriented programming constructs.

You can make your work much more efficient by improving how you design your software. With a few keystrokes, you can create interesting adaptations of existing systems. There's nothing like having such command and control over a body of code. It makes you more artist than programmer.

A different programmer might view your masterpiece entirely differently, however. For example, intricate relationships inside a class hierarchy could be difficult or impossible to understand without your personal guidance. Documentation, usually written in haste, is almost always inadequate or even misleading.

To help you avoid some of the common design practice pitfalls, I'm going to spend some time in this chapter up-front discussing how you can do the following:

- Avoid hidden code that performs nontrivial operations.
- Keep your class hierarchies as flat as possible.
- Be aware of the difference between inheritance and containment.
- Avoid abusing virtual functions.
- Use interface classes and factories.
- Use streams in addition to constructors to initialize objects.

Avoiding Hidden Code and Nontrivial Operations

Copy constructors, operator overloads, and destructors are all party to the "nasty" hidden code problems that plague game developers. This kind of code can cause you a lot of problems when you least expect them. The best example is a destructor because you never actually call it explicitly. It is called when the memory for an object is being deallocated or the object goes out of scope. If you do something really crazy in a destructor, like attach it to a remote computer and download a few megabytes of MP3 files, your teammates are going have you drawn and quartered.

My advice is that you should try to avoid copy constructors and operator overloads that perform nontrivial operations. If something looks simple, it should be simple and not something deceptive. For example, most programmers would assume that if they encountered some code that contained a simple equals sign or multiplication symbol that it would not invoke a complicated formula—like a Taylor series. They would assume that the code under the hood would be as straightforward as it looked—a basic assignment or calculation between similar data types like `floats` or `doubles`.

Game programmers love playing with neat technology, and sometimes their sense of elegance drives them to push nontrivial algorithms and calculations into C++ constructs, such as copy constructors or overloaded operators. They like it because the high level code performs complicated actions in a few lines of code, and on the surface, it seems like the right design choice. Don't be fooled.

Any operation with some meat to it should be called explicitly. This might annoy your sense of cleanliness if you are the kind of programmer that likes to use C++ constructs at each and every opportunity. Of course, there are exceptions. One is when every operation on a particular class is comparatively expensive, such as a 4×4 matrix class. Overloaded operators are perfectly fine for classes like this because the clarity of the resulting code is especially important and useful.

Sometimes, you want to go a step further and make copy constructors and assignment operators private, which keeps programmers from assuming the object can be duplicated in the system. You can use the Boost `noncopyable` class to achieve this. Just inherit from it, and your class will be protected. A good example of this is an object in your resource cache, such as an ambient sound track that could be tens of megabytes. You clearly want to disable making blind copies of this thing, because an unwary programmer might believe all he's doing is copying a tiny sound buffer.

A recurring theme I'll present throughout this book is that you should always try to avoid surprises. Most programmers don't like surprises because most surprises are bad ones. Don't add to the problem by tucking some crazy piece of code away in a destructor or similar mechanism.

Class Hierarchies: Keep Them Flat

One of the most common mistakes game programmers make is that they either over-design or under-design their classes and class hierarchies. Getting your class structure well designed for your particular needs takes real practice.

We created so many classes in *Ultima VII* that we ran out of good names to use. The compiler was so taxed by the end of the project that we couldn't add any more variables to the namespace or risk crashing the compiler. We were forced to use global variables to store more than one piece of data by encoding it in the high and low words rather than creating two new variables. By the end of the

---

EVERYTHING IN MODERATION

My first project at Origin developed with C++ was *Ultima VII*. This project turned out to be a poster child for insane C++. I was so impressed by the power of constructors, virtual functions, inheritance, and everything else that once I got the basics down I went nuts and made sure to use at least three C++ constructs on every line of code. What a horrible mistake! Some *Ultima VII* classes were seven or eight levels of inheritance deep. Some classes added only one data member to the parent—our impotent attempt at extending base classes.

---

project, I was terrified of adding any new code, because the compiler would most likely crash.

On the opposite end of the spectrum, a common problem found in C++ programs is the Blob class, as described in the excellent book *Antipatterns* by Brown et al. This is a class that has a little bit of everything in it, and comes from the reluctance on the programmer's part to make new, tightly focused classes. In the source code that accompanies this book, the GameCodeApp class is probably the one that comes closest to this, but if you study it a bit you can find some easy ways to factor it.

When I was working on *Ultima VII*, we actually had a class called KitchenSink and sure enough it had a little bit of everything. I'll admit to creating such a class on one of the *Microsoft Casino* projects; it would have made intelligent programmers sick to their stomachs. My class was supposed to encapsulate the data and methods of a screen, but it ended up looking a little like MFC's old CWnd class. It was huge, unwieldy, and simply threw everything into one gigantic bucket of semicolons and braces.

I try always to use a flat class hierarchy. Whenever possible, it starts with an interface class and has at most two or three levels of inheritance. This class design is usually much easier to work with and understand. Any change in the base class propagates to a smaller number of child classes, and the entire architecture is something normal humans can follow.

Try to learn from my mistakes. Good class architecture is *not* like a Swiss Army Knife; it should be more like a well-balanced throwing knife.

Inheritance Versus Containment

Game programmers love to debate the topics of inheritance and containment. Inheritance is used when an object is evolved from another object, or when a child object *is* a version of the parent object. Containment is used when an object is composed of multiple discrete components, or when an aggregate object *has* a version of the contained object.

A good example of this relationship is found in user interface code. A screen class might have the methods and data to contain multiple controls such as buttons or check boxes. The classes that implement buttons and check boxes probably inherit from a base control class.

When you make a choice about inheritance or containment, your goal is to communicate the right message to other programmers. The resulting assembly code is almost exactly the same, barring the oddities of virtual function tables. This means that the CPU doesn't give a damn if you inherit or contain. Your fellow programmers will care, so try to be careful and clear.

Virtual Functions Gone Bad

Virtual functions are powerful creatures that are often abused. Programmers often create virtual functions when they don't need them, or they create long chains of overloaded virtual functions that make it difficult to maintain base classes. I did this for a while when I first learned how to program with C++.

Take a look at MFC's class hierarchy. Most of the classes in the hierarchy contain virtual functions, which are overloaded by inherited classes or by new classes created by application programmers. Imagine for a moment the massive effort involved if some assumptions at the top of the hierarchy were changed. This isn't a problem for MFC because it's a stable code base, but your game code isn't a stable code base. Not yet.

An insidious bug is often one that is created innocently by a programmer mucking around in a base class. A seemingly benign change to a virtual function can have unexpected results. Some programmers might count on the oddities of the behavior of the base class that, if they were fixed, would actually break any child classes. Maybe one of these days someone will write an IDE that graphically shows the code that will be affected by any change to a virtual function. Without this aid, any programmer changing a base class must learn (the hard way) for himself what hell he is about to unleash. One of the best examples of this is changing the parameter list of a virtual function. If you're unlucky enough to change only an inherited class and not the base class, the compiler won't bother to warn you at all; it will simply break the virtual chain, and you'll have a brand new virtual function. It won't ever be called by anything, of course.

BEST PRACTICE

LET THE COMPILER HELP YOU

If you ever change the nature of anything that is currently in wide use, virtual functions included, I suggest you actually change its name. The compiler will find each and every use of the code, and you'll be forced to look at how the original was put to use. It's up to you if you want to keep the new name. I suggest you do, even if it means changing every source file.

From one point of view, a programmer overloads a virtual function because the child class has more processing to accomplish in the same "chain of thought." This concept is incredibly useful, and I've used it for nearly 10 years. It's funny that I never thought how wrong it could be.

An overloaded virtual function changes the behavior of an object and gains control over whether to invoke the original behavior. If the new object doesn't invoke the original function at all, the object is essentially different from the original. What makes this problem even worse is that everything about the object screams to programmers that it is just an extension of the original. *If you have a different object, make a different object.* Consider containing the original class instead of inheriting from it. It's much clearer in the code when you explicitly refer to a method attached to a contained object rather than calling a virtual function.

What happens to code reuse? Yes, have some. I hate duplicating code. I'm a lazy typist, and I'm very unlucky when it comes to cutting and pasting code. I create bugs like crazy.

Try to look at classes and their relationships like appliances and electrical cords. Always seek to minimize the length of the extension cords, minimize the appliances that plug into one another, and don't make a nasty tangle that you have to figure out every time you want to turn something on. This metaphor is put into practice with a flat class hierarchy—one where you don't have to open 12 source files to see all the code for a particular class.

Use Interface Classes

Interface classes are those that contain nothing but pure virtual functions. They form the top level in any class hierarchy. Here's an example:

```
class IAnimation
{
public:
   virtual void VAdvance(const int deltaMilliseconds) = 0;
   virtual bool const VAtEnd() const = 0;
   virtual int const VGetPosition() const = 0;
};


typedef std::list<IAnimation *> AnimationList;
```

This sample interface class defines simple behavior common for a timed animation. We could add other methods, such as one to tell how long the animation will run or whether the animation loops; that's purely up to you. The point is that any system that contains a list of objects inheriting and implementing the IAnimation interface can animate them with a few lines of code:

```
AnimationList::iterator end = animList.end();
for(AnimationList::iterator itr = animList.begin(); itr != end; ++itr)
{
    (*itr).VAdvance( delta );
}
```

Interface classes are a great way to enforce design standards. A programmer writing engine code can create systems that expect a certain interface. Any programmer creating objects that inherit from and implement the interface can be confident that the object will work with the engine code.

Another great benefit of using interface classes is they reduce compile time dependencies. The interfaces can be defined in a single #include file, or a very small number of them, and because they hide all the disgusting guts of implementation classes, there's very little for the compiler to do but register the class and move on.

Consider Using Factories

Games tend to build complex objects constructing groups of objects, such as controls or sprites, and storing them in lists or other collections. A common way to do this is to have the constructor of one object, say a certain implementation of a screen class, "new up" all the sprites and controls. In many cases, many types of screens are used in a game, all having different objects inheriting from the same parents.

In the book *Design Patterns: Elements of Reusable Object-Oriented Software* by Erich Gamma et al., one of the object creation patterns is called a *factory*. An abstract factory can define the interface for creating objects. Different implementations of the abstract factory carry out the concrete tasks of constructing objects with multiple parts. Think of it this way—a constructor creates a single object. A factory creates and assembles these objects into a working mechanism.

Imagine an abstract factory that builds screens. The fictional game engine in this example could define screens as components that have screen elements, a background, and a logic class that accepts control messages. Here's an example:

```
class SaveGameScreenFactory : public IScreenFactory
{
public:
    SaveGameScreenFactory();

    virtual IScreenElements * const BuildScreenElements() const;
    virtual ScreenBackground * const BuildScreenBackground() const;
    virtual IScreenLogic * const BuildScreenLogic() const;
};
```

The code that builds screens will call the methods of the ISCreenFactory inter-face, each one returning the different objects that make the screen, including screen elements like controls, a background, or the logic that runs the screen. As all interface classes tend to enforce design standards, factories tend to enforce orderly construction of complicated objects. Factories are great for screens, anima-tions, AI, or any nontrivial game object.

What's more, factories can help you construct these mechanisms at the right time. One of the neatest things about the factory design pattern is a delayed instantiation feature. You could create factory objects, push them into a queue, and delay calling the "BuildXYZ" methods until you were ready. In the screen example, you might not have enough memory to instantiate a screen object until the active one is destroyed. The factory object is tiny, perhaps a few tens of bytes, and can easily exist in memory until you are ready to fire it.

Use Streams to Initialize Objects

Any persistent object in your game should implement a method that takes a stream as a parameter and reads the stream to initialize the object. If the game is loaded from a file, objects can use the stream as a source of parameters. Here's an example to consider:

```
class AnimationPath
{
public:
   AnimationPath();
   Initialize (std::vector<AnimationPathPoint> const & srcPath);
   Initialize (InputStream & stream);
   //Of course, lots more code follows.
};
```

This class has a default constructor and two ways to initialize it. The first is through a classic parameter list, in this case, a list of AnimationPathPoints. The sec-ond initializes the class through a stream object. This is cool because you can ini-tialize objects from a disk, a memory stream, or even the network. If you want to load game objects from a disk, as you would in a saved game, this is exactly how you do it.

Some programmers try to do stream initialization inside an object's construc-tor. If you find the first edition of this book you'll see that I used to do that too:

```
AnimationPath (InputStream & stream);
```

That was a horrible idea, and I'm not too big to admit it either. Thanks for the kind "corrections" posted on the Web site. The unkind ones I'll happily forget!

Here's why this is a bad idea—a bad stream will cause your constructor to fail, and you'll end up with a bad object. You can never trust the content of a stream. It could be coming from a bad disk file or hacked network packets. Ergo, construct objects with a default constructor you can rely on and create initialization methods for streams.

BEST
PRACTICE

EXERCISE YOUR LOAD/SAVE SYSTEM

Test your stream constructors by loading and saving your game automatically in the DEBUG build at regular intervals. It will have the added side effect of making sure programmers keep the load/save code pretty fast.

SMART POINTERS AND NAKED POINTERS

All smart pointers wear clothing.

If you declare a pointer to another object, you've just used a naked pointer. Pointers are used to refer to another object, but they don't convey enough information. Anything declared on the heap must be referenced by at least one other object, or it can never be freed, causing a memory leak. It is common for an object on the heap to be referred to multiple times by other objects in the code. A good example of this is a game object like a clock. A pointer to the clock will exist in the game object list, the physics system, the graphics system, and even the sound system.

If you use naked pointers, you must remember which objects implicitly own other objects. An object that owns other objects controls their existence. Imagine a ship object that owns everything on the ship. When the ship sinks, everything else is destroyed along with it. If you use naked pointers to create these relationships, you have to remember who owns who. This can be a confusing or even impossible task. You'll find that using naked pointers will quickly paint you into a corner.

Smart pointers, on the other hand, hold extra information along with the address of the distant object. This information can count references, record permanent or temporary ownership, or perform other useful tasks. In a sense, an object controlled by a smart pointer "knows" about every reference to itself. The horrible nest of naked pointers evaporates, leaving a simple and foolproof mechanism for handling your dynamic objects.

Reference Counting

Reference counting stores an integer value that counts how many other objects are currently referring to the object in question. Reference counting is a common mechanism in memory management. DirectX objects implement the COM based

IUnknown interface, which uses reference counting. Two methods that are central to this task are AddRef() and Release(). The following code shows how this works:

```
MySound *sound = new MySound;
sound->AddRef();                       // reference count is now 1
```

After you construct a reference counted object, you call the AddRef() method to increase the integer reference counter by one. When the pointer variable goes out of scope, by normal scoping rules or by the destruction of the container class, you must call Release(). Release() will decrement the reference counter and destroy the object if the counter drops to zero. A shared object can have multiple references safely without fear of the object being destroyed, leaving bad pointers all over the place.

USE AddRef() AND Release() WITH CAUTION

Good reference counting mechanisms automatically delete the object when the reference count becomes zero. If the API leaves the explicit destruction of the object to you, it's easy to create memory leaks—all you have to do is forget to call Release(). You can also cause problems if you forget to call AddRef() when you create the object. It's likely that the object will get destroyed unexpectedly, not having enough reference counts.

Anytime you assign a pointer variable to the address of the reference counted object, you'll do the same thing. This includes any calls inside a local loop:

```
for (int i=0; i<m_howMany; ++i)
{
    MySound *s = GoGrabASoundPointer(i);
    s->AddRef();

    DangerousFunction();

    if (s->IsPlaying())
    {
        DoSomethingElse();
    }

    s->Release();
}
```

This kind of code exists all over the place in games. The call to `DangerousFunction()` goes deep and performs some game logic that might attempt to destroy the instance of the `MySound` object. Don't forget that in a release build the deallocated memory retains the same values until it is reused. It's quite possible that the loop will work just fine even though the `MySound` pointer is pointing to unallocated memory. What's more likely to occur is a terrible corruption of memory.

Reference counting keeps the sound object around until `Release()` is called at the bottom of the loop. If there was only one reference to the sound before the loop started, the call to `AddRef()` will add one to the sound's reference count, making two references. `DangerousFunction()` does something that destroys the sound, but through a call to `Release()`. As far as `DangerousFunction()` is concerned, the sound is gone forever. It still exists because one more reference to it, through `MySound *s`, kept the reference count from dropping to zero inside the loop. The final call to `Release()` causes the destruction of the sound.

Boost C++'s shared_ptr

If you think calling `AddRef()` and `Release()` all over the place might be a serious pain in the rear, you're right. It's really easy to forget an `AddRef()` or a `Release()` call, and your memory leak will be almost impossible to find. It turns out that there are plenty of C++ templates out there that implement reference counting in a way that handles the counter manipulation automatically. One of the best examples is the `shared_ptr` template class in the Boost C++ library, found at www.boost.org.

Here's an example of how to use this template:

```cpp
#include <boost\config.hpp>
#include <boost\shared_ptr.hpp>

using boost::shared_ptr;

class IPrintable
{
public:
    virtual void VPrint()=0;
};

class CPrintable : public IPrintable
{
    char *m_Name;
public:
    CPrintable(char *name)    { m_Name = name; printf("create %s\n",m_Name); }
    virtual ~CPrintable()     { printf("delete %s\n",m_Name); }
    void VPrint()             { printf("print %s\n",m_Name); }
};
```

```cpp
shared_ptr<CPrintable> CreateAnObject(char *name)
{
   return shared_ptr<CPrintable>(new CPrintable(name));
}


void ProcessObject(shared_ptr<CPrintable> o)
{
   printf("(print from a function) ");
   o->VPrint();
}


void TestSharedPointers(void)
{
   shared_ptr<CPrintable> ptr1(new CPrintable("1"));    // create object 1
   shared_ptr<CPrintable> ptr2(new CPrintable("2"));    // create object 2

   ptr1 = ptr2;                      // destroy object 1
   ptr2 = CreateAnObject("3");       // used as a return value
   ProcessObject(ptr1);              // call a function

   // BAD USEAGE EXAMPLES....
   //
   CPrintable o1("bad");
   //ptr1 = &o1;       // Syntax error! It's on the stack....
   //
   CPrintable *o2 = new CPrintable("bad2");
   //ptr1 = o2;        // Syntax error! Use the next line to do this...

   ptr1 = shared_ptr<CPrintable>(o2);

   // You can even use shared_ptr on ints!

   shared_ptr<int> a(new int);
   shared_ptr<int> b(new int);

   *a = 5;
   *b = 6;

   const int *q = a.get();   // use this for reading in multithreaded code

   // this is especially cool - you can also use it in lists.
   std::list< shared_ptr<int> > intList;
   std::list< shared_ptr<IPrintable> > printableList;
```

```
for (int i=0; i<100; ++i)
{
    intList.push_back(shared_ptr<int>(new int(rand())));
    printableList.push_back(shared_ptr<IPrintable>(new CPrintable("list")));
}

// No leaks!!!! Isn't that cool...
}
```

The template classes use overloaded assignment operators and copy operators to keep track of how many references point to the allocated data. As long as the `shared_ptr` object is in scope and you behave yourself by avoiding the bad usage cases, you won't leak memory, and you won't have to worry about objects getting destroyed while you are still referencing them from somewhere else.

This smart pointer even works in multithreaded environments, as long as you follow a few rules. First, don't write directly to the data. You can access the data through const operations such as the `.get()` method. As you can also see, the template works fine even if it is inside an STL container such as `std::list`. A similar smart pointer, `std::auto_ptr`, cannot be used in STL structures.

BEST PRACTICE

BE CAREFUL USING THREADS AND SHARING MEMORY

Don't ignore multithreaded access to shared memory blocks. You might think that the chances of two threads accessing the shared data are exceedingly low and convince yourself that you don't need to go to the trouble of adding multithreaded protection. You'd be wrong, every time.

There are a couple of safety tips with smart pointers.

- You can't have two different objects manage smart pointers for each other.
- When you create a smart pointer, you have to make sure it is created straight from a raw pointer `new` operator.

I'll show you examples of each of these abuses. If two objects have smart pointers to each other, neither one will ever be destroyed—it may take your brain a moment to get this—since each one has a reference to the other.

```
class CJelly;
class CPeanutButter
{
public:
    shared_ptr<CJelly> m_pJelly;
    CPeanutButter(CJelly *pJelly) { m_pJelly.reset(pJelly); }
};
```

```
class CJelly
{
public:
    shared_ptr<CPeanutButter> m_pPeanutButter;
    CJelly();
};

CJelly::CJelly()
{
    m_pPeanutButter.reset(new CPeanutButter(this));
}

void PleaseLeakMyMemory()
{
    shared_ptr<CJelly> pJelly(new CJelly);
}
```

If you follow the code you'll find that CJelly has two references, one from the free function and the other from CPeanutButter. The CPeanutButter class only has one reference, but it can't ever be decremented because the CJelly smart pointer will end up with a single reference count. Basically, because they point to each other, it's almost like two stubborn gentlemen saying, "No, sir, after you" and "Please, I insist" when trying to go through a single door—because they point to each other, they will never be destroyed.

The solution to this is usually some kind of "owned" pointer or "weak referenced" pointer, where one object is deemed the de-factor owner, and therefore won't use the multiply referenced shared_ptr mechanism. In the Boost library, the weak_ptr template is used exactly for this purpose.

The other gotcha is constructing two smart pointers to manage a single object:

```
int *z = new int;
shared_ptr<int> bad1(z);
shared_ptr<int> bad2(z);
```

Remember that smart pointers work with a reference count, and each of the smart pointer objects only has one reference. If either of them goes out of scope, the memory for the object will be deallocated, and the other smart pointer will point to garbage.

USING MEMORY CORRECTLY

Did you ever hear the joke about the programmer trying to beat the Devil in a coding contest? Part of his solution involved overcoming a memory limitation by storing a few bytes in a chain of sound waves between the microphone and the speaker. That's an interesting idea, and I'll bet we would have tried that one on *Ultima VII* had someone on our team thought of it.

Memory comes in very different shapes, sizes, and speeds. If you know what you're doing, you can write programs that make efficient use of these different memory blocks. If you believe that it doesn't matter how you use memory, you're in for a real shock. This includes assuming that the standard memory manager for your operating system is efficient; it usually isn't, and you'll have to think about writing your own.

Understanding the Different Kinds of Memory

The system RAM is the main warehouse for storage, as long as the system has power. Video RAM or VRAM is usually much smaller and is specifically used for storing objects that will be used by the video card. Some platforms, such as Xbox and Xbox360, have a unified memory architecture that makes no distinctions between RAM and VRAM. Desktop PCs run operating systems like Windows Vista, and have virtual memory that mimics much larger memory space by swapping blocks of little-used RAM to your hard disk. If you're not careful, a simple memcpy() could cause the hard drive to seek, which to a computer is like waiting for the sun to cool off.

System RAM

Your system RAM is a series of memory sticks that are installed on the motherboard. Memory is actually stored in nine bits per byte, with the extra bit used to catch memory parity errors. Depending on the OS, you get to play with a certain addressable range of memory. The operating system keeps some to itself. Of the parts you get to play with, it is divided into three parts when your application loads:

- **Global memory**: This memory never changes size. It is allocated when your program loads and stores global variables, text strings, and virtual function tables.
- **Stack**: This memory grows as your code calls deeper into core code, and it shrinks as the code returns. The stack is used for parameters in function calls and local variables. The stack has a fixed size that can be changed with compiler settings.
- **Heap**: This memory grows and shrinks with dynamic memory allocation. It is used for persistent objects and dynamic data structures.

Old-timers used to call global memory the DATA segment, harkening back to the days when there used to be near memory and far memory. It was called that because programmers used different pointers to get to it. What a disgusting practice! Everything is much cleaner these days because each pointer is a full 32 bits.

(Don't worry, I'm not going to bore you with the "When I went to school I used to load programs from a linear access tape cassette" story.)

Your compiler and linker will attempt to optimize the location of anything you put into the global memory space based on the type of variable. This includes constant text strings. Many compilers, including Visual Studio, will attempt to store text strings only once to save space:

```
const char *error1 = "Error";
const char *error2 = "Error";

int main()
{
   printf ("%x\n", (int)error1);
   // How quaint. A printf.
   printf ("%x\n", (int)error2);
   return 0;
}
```

This code yields interesting results. You'll notice that under Visual C++, the two pointers point to the same text string in the global address space. Even better than that, the text string is one that was already global and stuck in the CRT libraries. It's as if we wasted our time typing "Error." This trick only works for constant text strings, since the compiler knows they can never change. Everything else gets its own space. If you want the compiler to consolidate equivalent text strings, they must be constant text strings.

Don't make the mistake of counting on some kind of rational order to the global addresses. You can't count on anything the compiler or linker will do, especially if you are considering crossing platforms.

On most operating systems, the stack starts at high addresses and grows toward lower addresses. C and C++ parameters get pushed onto the stack from right to left—the last parameter is the first to get pushed onto the stack in a function call. Local parameters get pushed onto the stack in their order of appearance:

```
void testStack(int x, int y)
{
   int a = 1;
   int b = 2;

   printf("&x= %-10x &y= %-10x\n", &x, &y);
   printf("&a= %-10x &b= %-10x\n", &a, &b);
}
```

This code produces the following output:

```
&x= 12fdf0      &y= 12fdf4
&a= 12fde0      &b= 12fdd4
```

Stack addresses grow downward to smaller memory addresses. Thus, it should be clear that the order in which the parameters and local variables were pushed was y, x, a, and b. Which turns out to be exactly the order in which you read them—a good mnemonic. The next time you're debugging some assembler code, you'll be glad to understand this, especially if you are setting your instruction pointer by hand.

C++ allows a high degree of control over the local scope. Every time you enclose code in a set of braces, you open a local scope with its own local variables:

```
int main()
{
   int a = 0;

   {              // start a local scope here...
     int a = 1;
     printf("%d\n", a);
   }

   printf("%d\n", a);
}
```

This code compiles and runs just fine. The two integer variables are completely separate entities. I've written this example to make a clear point, but I'd never actually write code like this. Doing something like this in Texas is likely to get you shot. The real usefulness of this kind of code is for use with C++ objects that perform useful tasks when they are destroyed—you can control the exact moment a destructor is called by closing a local scope.

Video Memory (VRAM)

Video RAM is the memory installed on your video card, unless we're talking about an Xbox. Xbox hardware has unified memory architecture or UMI, so there's no difference between system RAM and VRAM. It would be nice if the rest of the world worked that way. Other hardware such as the Intel architectures must send any data between VRAM and system RAM over a bus. The PS2 has even more different kinds of memory. There are quite a few bus architectures and speeds out there, and it is wise to understand how reading and writing data across the bus affects your game's speed.

As long as the CPU doesn't have to read from VRAM, everything clicks along pretty fast. If you need to grab a piece of VRAM for something, the bits have to be sent across the bus to system RAM. Depending on your architecture, your CPU and GPU must argue for a moment about timing, stream the bits, and go their separate ways. While this painful process is occurring, your game has come to a complete halt.

This problem was pretty horrific back in the days of fixed function pipelines when anything not supported by the video card had to be done with the CPU, such as the first attempts at motion blur. With programmable pipelines, you can create shaders that can run directly on the bits stored in VRAM, making this kind of graphical effect extremely efficient.

The hard disk can't write straight to VRAM, so every time a new texture is needed you'll need to stop the presses, so to speak. The smart approach is to limit any communication needed between the CPU and the video card. If you are going to send anything to it, it is best to send it in batches.

If you've been paying attention, you'll realize that the GPU in your video card is simply painting the screen using the components in VRAM. If it ever has to stop and ask system RAM for something, your game won't run as fast as it could.

TALES FROM THE PIXEL MINES

MR. MIKE'S FIRST TEXTURE MANAGER

The first texture manager I ever wrote was for *Ultima IX*. (That was before the game was called *Ultima: Ascension*.) I wrote the texture manager for 3DFx's Glide API, and I had all of an hour to do it. We wanted to show some Origin execs what *Ultima* looked like running under hardware acceleration. Not being the programmer extraordinaire, and I only had a day to work, my algorithm had to be pretty simple. I chose a variant of LRU, but since I didn't have time to write the code to sort and organize the textures, I simply threw out every texture in VRAM the moment there wasn't any additional space. I think this code got some nomination for the dumbest texture manager ever written, but it actually worked. The player would walk around for 90 seconds or so before the hard disk lit up and everything came to a halt for two seconds. I'm pretty sure someone rewrote it before *U9* shipped. At least, I hope someone rewrote it!

Optimizing Memory Access

Every access to system RAM uses a CPU cache. If the desired memory location is already in the cache, the contents of the memory location are presented to the CPU extremely quickly. If, on the other hand, the memory is not in the cache, a new block of system RAM must be fetched into the cache. This takes a lot longer than you'd think.

A good test bed for this problem uses multidimensional arrays. C++ defines its arrays in row major order. This ordering puts the members of the right-most index next to each other in memory.

TestData[0][0][0] and TestData[0][0][1] are stored in adjacent memory locations.

> ### ROW ORDER OR COLUMN ORDER?
>
> Not every language defines arrays in row order. Some versions of PASCAL define arrays in column order. Don't make assumptions unless you like writing slow code.

If you access an array in the wrong order, it will create a worst-case CPU cache scenario. Here's an example of two functions that access the same array and do the same task. One will run much faster than the other:

```
const int g_n = 250;
float TestData[g_n][g_n][g_n];

inline void column_ordered()
{
    for (int k=0; k<g_n; k++)              // K
        for (int j=0; j<g_n; j++)          // J
            for (int i=0; i<g_n; i++)      // I
                TestData[i][j][k] = 0.0f;
}

inline void row_ordered()
{
    for (int i=0; i<g_n; i++)              // I
        for (int j=0; j<g_n; j++)          // J
            for (int k=0; k<g_n; k++)      // K
                TestData[i][j][k] = 0.0f;
}
```

The timed output of running both functions on my test machine showed that accessing the array in row order was nearly nine times faster:

```
Column Ordered=2817 ms    Row Ordered=298 ms    Delta=2519 ms
```

Any code that accesses any largish data structure can benefit from this technique. If you have a multistep process that affects a large data set, try to arrange your code to perform as much work as possible in smaller memory blocks. You'll optimize the use of the L2 cache and make a much faster piece of code. While you surely won't have any piece of runtime game code do something this crazy, you might very well have a game editor or production tool that does.

Memory Alignment

The CPU reads and writes memory-aligned data much faster than other data. Any N-byte data type is memory aligned if the starting address is evenly divisible by N. For example, a 32-bit integer is memory aligned on a 32-bit architecture if the starting address is 0x04000000. The same 32-bit integer is unaligned if the starting address is 0x04000002, since the memory address is not evenly divisible by 4 bytes.

You can perform a little experiment in memory alignment and how it affects access time by using example code like this:

```
#pragma pack(push, 1)
struct ReallySlowStruct
{
   char c : 6;
    __int64 d : 64;
   int b : 32;
   char a : 8;
};

struct SlowStruct
{
   char c;
   __int64 d;
   int b;
   char a;
};

struct FastStruct
{
   __int64 d;
   int b;
   char a;
   char c;
   char unused[2];
};

#pragma pack(pop)
```

I wrote a piece of code to perform some operations on the member variables in each structure. The difference in times is as follows:

```
Really slow=417 ms
Slow=222 ms
Fast=192 ms
```

Your penalty for using the SlowStruct over FastStruct is about 14 percent on my test machine. The penalty for using ReallySlowStruct is code that runs twice as slowly.

The first structure isn't even aligned properly on bit boundaries, hence the name ReallySlowStruct. The definition of the 6-bit char variable throws the entire structure out of alignment. The second structure, SlowStruct, is also out of alignment, but at least the byte boundaries are aligned. The last structure, FastStruct, is completely aligned for each member. The last member, unused, ensures that the structure fills out to an 8-byte boundary in case someone declares an array of FastStruct.

Notice the #pragma pack(push, 1) at the top of the source example? It's accompanied by a #pragma pack(pop) at the bottom. Without them, the compiler, depending on your project settings, will choose to spread out the member variables and place each one on an optimal byte boundary. When the member variables are spread out like that, the CPU can access each member quickly, but all that unused space can add up. If the compiler were left to optimize SlowStruct by adding unused bytes, each structure would be 24 bytes instead of just 14. Seven extra bytes are padded after the first char variable, and the remaining bytes are added at the end. This ensures that the entire structure always starts on an 8-byte boundary. That's about 40 percent of wasted space, all due to a careless ordering of member variables.

Don't let the compiler waste precious memory space. Put some of your brain cells to work and align your own member variables. You don't get many opportunities to save memory and optimize CPU at the same time.

Virtual Memory

Virtual memory increases the addressable memory space by caching unused memory blocks to the hard disk. The scheme depends on the fact that even though you might have a 500MB data structure, you aren't going to be playing with the whole thing at the same time. The unused bits are saved off to your hard disk until you need them again. You should be cheering and wincing at the same time. Cheering because every programmer likes having a big memory playground, and wincing because anything involving the hard disk wastes a lot of time.

Just to see how bad it can get, I took the code from the array access example and modified it to iterate through a three-dimensional array 500 elements cubed.

The total size of the array would be 476MB, much bigger than the installed memory on the test machine. A data structure bigger than available memory is sometimes called *out-of-core*. I ran the `column_ordered()` function and went to lunch. When I got back about 30 minutes later, the test program was still chugging away. The hard drive was seeking like mad, and I began to wonder whether my hard disk would give out. I became impatient and re-ran the example and timed just one iteration of the inner loop. It took 379.75 seconds to run the inner loop. The entire thing would have taken over 50 hours to run. I'm glad I didn't wait. Any game written badly can suffer the same fate, and as you can see, the difference between running quickly and paging constantly to your hard disk can be as small as a single byte.

Remember that the original array, 250 elements cubed, ran the test code in 298ms when the fast `row_ordered()` function was used. The large array is only eight times bigger, giving an expectation that the same code should have run in 2384ms, or just under two-and-a-half seconds.

Compare 2384ms with 50 hours, and you'll see how virtual memory can work against you if your code accesses virtual memory incorrectly.

CACHE MISSES CAN COST YOU DEARLY

Any time a cache is used inefficiently, you can degrade the overall performance of your game by many orders of magnitude. This is commonly called "thrashing the cache" and is your worst nightmare. If your game is thrashing cache, you might be able to solve the problem by reordering some code, but most likely you will need to reduce the size of the data.

Writing Your Own Memory Manager

Most games extend the provided memory management system. The biggest reasons to do this are performance, efficiency, and improved debugging. Default memory managers in the C runtime are designed to run fairly well in a wide range of memory allocation scenarios. They tend to break down under the load of computer games, though, where allocations and deallocations of relatively tiny memory blocks can be fast and furious.

A standard memory manager, like the one in the C runtime, must support multithreading. Each time the memory manager's data structures are accessed or changed, they must be protected with critical sections, allowing only one thread to allocate or deallocate memory at a time. All this extra code is time consuming, especially if you use `malloc` and `free` very frequently. Most games are multithreaded to support sound systems, but don't necessarily need a multithreaded

THE INFAMOUS VOODOO MEMORY MANAGER

Ultima VII: The Black Gate had a legendary memory manager: The VooDoo Memory Management System. It was written by a programmer who used to work on guided missile systems for the Department of Defense, a brilliant and dedicated engineer. *U7* ran in good old DOS back in the days when protected mode was the neat new thing. VooDoo was a true 32-bit memory system for a 16-bit operating system, and the only problem with it was you had to read and write to the memory locations with assembly code, since the Borland compiler didn't understand 32-bit pointers. It was done this way because *U7* couldn't really exist in a 16-bit memory space—there were atomic data structures larger than 64KB. For all its hoopla, VooDoo was actually pretty simple, and it only provided the most basic memory management features. The fact that it was actually called VooDoo was a testament to the fact that it actually worked; it wasn't exactly supported by the operating system or the Borland compilers.

VooDoo MM for *Ultima VII* is a great example of writing a simple memory manager to solve a specific problem. It didn't support multithreading, it assumed that memory blocks were large, and finally it wasn't written to support a high number or frequency of allocations.

memory manager for every part of the game. A single threaded memory manager that you write yourself might be a good solution.

Simple memory managers can use a doubly-linked list as the basis for keeping track of allocated and free memory blocks. The C runtime uses a more complicated system to reduce the algorithmic complexity of searching through the allocated and free blocks that could be as small as a single byte. Your memory blocks might be either more regularly shaped, fewer in number, or both. This creates an opportunity to design a simpler, more efficient system.

Default memory managers must assume that deallocations happen approximately as often as allocations, and they might happen in any order and at any time. Their data structures have to keep track of a large number of blocks of available and used memory. Any time a piece of memory changes state from used to available, the data structures must be quickly traversed. When blocks become available again, the memory manager must detect adjacent available blocks and merge them to make a larger block. Finding free memory of an appropriate size to minimize wasted space can be extremely tricky. Since default memory managers solve these problems to a large extent, their performance isn't as high as another memory manager that can make more assumptions about how and when memory allocations occur.

If your game can allocate and deallocate most of its dynamic memory space at once, you can write a memory manager based on a data structure no more complicated than a singly-linked list. You'd never use something this simple in a more general case, of course, because a singly-linked list has O(n) algorithmic complexity. That would cripple any memory management system used in the general case.

A good reason to extend a memory manager is to add some debugging features. Two features that are common include adding additional bytes before and after the allocation to track memory corruption or to track memory leaks. The C runtime adds only one byte before and after an allocated block, which might be fine to catch those pesky x+1 and x-1 errors, but doesn't help for much else. If the memory corruption seems pretty random, and most of them sure seem that way, you can increase your odds of catching the culprit by writing a custom manager that adds more bytes to the beginning and ending of each block. In practice, the extra space is set to a small number, even one byte, in the release build.

DIFFERENT BUILD OPTIONS WILL CHANGE RUNTIME BEHAVIOR

Anything you do differently from the debug and release builds can change the behavior of bugs from one build target to another. Murphy's Law dictates that the bug will only appear in the build target that is hardest, or even impossible, to debug.

Another common extension to memory managers is leak detection. It is a common practice to redefine the new operator to add __FILE__ and __LINE__ information to each allocated memory block in debug mode. When the memory manager is shut down, all the unfreed blocks are printed out in the output window in the debugger. This should give you a good place to start when you need to track down a memory leak.

If you decide to write your own memory manager, keep the following points in mind:

- **Data structures:** Choose the data structure that matches your memory allocation scenario. If you traverse a large number of free and available blocks very frequently, choose a hash table or tree-based structure. If you hardly ever traverse it to find free blocks, you could get away with a list. Store the data structure separately from the memory pool; any corruption will keep your memory manager's data structure intact.

- **Single/multithreaded access:** Don't forget to add appropriate code to protect your memory manager from multithreaded access if you need it. Eliminate the protections if you are sure that access to the memory manager will only happen from a single thread, and you'll gain some performance.

- **Debug and testing:** Allocate a little additional memory before and after the block to detect memory corruption. Add caller information to the debug memory blocks; at a minimum, you should use __FILE__ and __LINE__ to track where the allocation occurred.

One of the best reasons to extend the C runtime memory manager is to write a better system to manage small memory blocks. The memory managers supplied in the C runtime or MFC library are not meant for tiny allocations. You can prove it to yourself by allocating two integers and subtracting their memory addresses as shown here:

```
int *a = new int;
int *b = new int;

int delta1 = ((int)b - (int)a) - sizeof(int);
```

The wasted space for the C runtime library was 28 bytes for a release build and 60 bytes for the debug build under Visual Studio. Even with the release build, an integer takes eight times as much memory space as it would if it weren't dynamically allocated.

Most games overload the new operator to allocate small blocks of memory from a reserved pool set aside for smaller allocations. Memory allocations that are larger than a set number of bytes can still use the C runtime. I recommend that you start with 128 bytes as the largest block your small allocator will handle and tweak the size until you are happy with the performance.

MIKE'S GRAB BAG OF USEFUL STUFF

Before we leave this chapter, I want to arm you with some lifesaving snippets of code. Some code defies classification. It gets thrown into a toolbox with all the other interesting things that simply won't die. I try to dust them off and use them on every project, and I'm never disappointed. I'll start with a great random number generator, show you a template class you can't live without, and end with a neat algorithm to traverse any set in random order without visiting the same member twice.

An Excellent Random Number Generator

There are as many good algorithms for generating random numbers as there are pages in this book. Most programmers will soon discover that the ANSI rand() function is completely inadequate because it can only generate a single stream of random numbers. Most games need multiple discrete streams of random numbers.

Unless your game comes with a little piece of hardware that uses the radioactive decay of cesium to generate random numbers, your random number generator is only pseudo-random. A pseudo-random number sequence can certainly appear random, achieving a relatively flat distribution curve over the generation of billions of numbers mapped to a small domain, like the set of numbers between 1 and 100. Given the same starting assumption, commonly called a *seed*, the sequence will be exactly the same. A truly random sequence could never repeat like that.

This might seem bad because you might feel that a hacker could manipulate the seed to affect the outcome of the game. In practice, all you have to do is regenerate the seed every now and then using some random element that would be difficult or impossible to duplicate. In truth, a completely predictable random number generator is something you will give your left leg for when writing test tools or a game replay system.

EVEN OLD CODE CAN BE USEFUL

Every *Ultima* from *Ultima I* to *Ultima VIII* used the same random number generator, originally written in 6502 assembler. In 1997, this generator was the oldest piece of continuously used code at Origin Systems. Finally, this RNG showed its age and had to be replaced. Kudos to Richard Garriott (aka Lord British) for making the longest-lived piece of code Origin ever used.

Here's a cool little class to keep track of your random numbers. You'll want to make sure you save this code and stuff it into your own toolbox. The RNG core is called a *Mersenne Twister pseudorandom number generator*, and it was originally developed by Takuji Nishimura and Makoto Matsumoto:

```
class CRandom
{
    unsigned int        rseed;
    unsigned long mt[CMATH_N];   // the array for the state vector
    int mti;                     // mti==N+1 means mt[N] is not initialized

public:
    CRandom(void);

    unsigned int Random( unsigned int n );
    void SetRandomSeed(unsigned int n);
    unsigned int GetRandomSeed(void);
    void Randomize(void);
};
```

The original code has been modified to include a few useful bits, one of which is to allow this class to save and reload its random number seed, which can be used to replay random number sequences by simply storing the seed. Here's an example of how you can use the class:

```
CRandom r;
r.Randomize();
unsigned int num = r.Random(100);    // returns a number from 0-99, inclusive
```

You should use a few instantiations of this class in your game, each one generating random numbers for a different part of your game. Here's why: Let's say you want to generate some random taunts from AI characters. If you use a different random number sequence from the sequence that generates the contents of treasure chests, you can be sure that if the player turns off character audio, the same RNG sequence will result for the treasure chests, which nicely compartmentalizes your game. In other words, your game becomes predictable and testable.

TALES FROM THE PIXEL MINES

YOUR RANDOM NUMBER GENERATOR CAN BREAK AUTOMATION

I was working on an automation system for some Microsoft games, and the thing would just not work right. The goal of the system was to be able to record game sessions and play them back. The system was great for testers and programmers alike. It's hard, and boring, to play a few million hands of blackjack. Our programming team realized that since the same RNG was being called for every system of the game, small aberrations would occur as calls to the RNG went out-of-sync. This was especially true for random character audio, since the timing of character audio was completely dependent on another thread, which was impossible to synchronize. When we used one CRandom class for each subsystem of the game, the problem disappeared.

Supporting Optional Variables with Optional<T>

A really favorite template of mine is one that encapsulates optional variables. Every variable stores values, but they don't store whether the current value is valid. Optional variables store this information to indicate if the variable is valid or initialized. Think about it, how many times have you had to use a special return value to signify some kind of error case?

Take a look at this code, and you'll see what I'm talking about:

```
bool DumbCalculate1(int &spline)
{
   // imagine some code here....
   //
   // The return value is the error, and the value of spline is invalid return
   false;
}


#define ERROR_IN_DUMBCALCULATE (-8675309)
int DumbCalculate2()
{
   // imagine some code here....
   //
   // The return value is a "special" value, we hope could never be actually
   // calculated
   return ERROR_IN_DUMBCALCULATE;
}


int _tmain(void)
{
   //////////////////////////////////////////////////////////////
   // Dumb way #1 - use a return error code,
   // and a reference to get to your data.
   //
   int dumbAnswer1;
   if (DumbCalculate1(dumbAnswer1))
   {
      // do my business...
   }


   //////////////////////////////////////////////////////////////
   // Dumb way #2 - use a "special" return value to signify an error
   int dumbAnswer2 = DumbCalculate2();
   if (dumbAnswer2 != ERROR_IN_DUMBCALCULATE)
   {
      // do my business...
   }
}
```

There are two evil practices in this code. The first practice, "Dumb Way #1," requires that you use a separate return value for success or failure. This causes problems because you can't use the return value DumbCalculate1() function as the parameter to another function because the return value is an error code:

```
AnotherFunction(DumbCalculate1());       // whoops. Can't do this!
```

The second practice I've seen that drives me up the wall is using a "special" return value to signify an error. This is illustrated in the DumbCalculate2() call. In many cases, the value chosen for the error case is a legal value, although it may be one that will "almost never" happen. If those chances are one in a million and your game sells a million copies, how many times per day do you think someone is going to get on the phone and call your friendly customer service people? Too many.

Here's the code for optional<T>, a template class that solves this problem.

```cpp
class optional_empty { };

template <unsigned long size>
class optional_base
{
public:
    // Default - invalid.

    optional_base() : m_bValid(false) { }
    optional_base & operator = (optional_base const & t);
    optional_base(optional_base const & other)
      : m_bValid(other.m_bValid)  { }

    //utility functions
    bool const valid() const     { return m_bValid; }
    bool const invalid() const   { return !m_bValid; }

protected:
    bool m_bValid;
    char m_data[size];  // storage space for T
};

template <class T>
class optional : public optional_base<sizeof(T)>
{
public:
    // Default - invalid.

    optional()    {    }
    optional(T const & t)  { construct(t); m_bValid = (true);   }
    optional(optional_empty const &) {    }

    optional & operator = (T const & t);
    optional(optional const & other);

    optional & operator = (optional const & other);
```

```
    bool const operator == (optional const & other) const;
    bool const operator < (optional const & other) const
    ~optional() { if (m_bValid) destroy(); }

    // Accessors.

    T const & operator * () const     { assert(m_bValid); return * GetT(); }
    T & operator * ()                 { assert(m_bValid); return * GetT(); }
    T const * const operator -> () const { assert(m_bValid); return GetT(); }
    T * const operator -> ()     { assert(m_bValid); return GetT(); }

    //This clears the value of this optional variable and makes it invalid once
    // again.
    void clear();

    //utility functions
    bool const valid() const     { return m_bValid; }
    bool const invalid() const   { return !m_bValid; }

private:

    T const * const GetT() const
       { return reinterpret_cast<T const * const>(m_data); }
    T * const GetT()
       { return reinterpret_cast<T * const>(m_data);}
    void construct(T const & t)  { new (GetT()) T(t); }
    void destroy() { GetT()->~T(); }
};
```

As you can see, it's not as simple as storing a Boolean value along with your data. The extra work in this class handles comparing optional objects with each other and getting to the data the object represents.

Here's an example of how to use optional<T>:

```
#include "stdafx.h"
#include "optional.h"

optional<int> Calculate()
{
    optional<int> spline;
    spline = 10;            // you assign values to optionals like this...
    spline = optional_empty();   // or you could give them the empty value
    spline.clear();         // or you could clear them to make them invalid

    return spline;
}
```

```
int main(void)
{
    optional<int> answer = Calculate();
    if (answer.valid())
    {
        // do my business...
    }
    return 0;
}
```

BEST
PRACTICE

-1 IS A FINE NUMBER

I personally don't see why so many programmers have it out for the value (-1). Everyone seems to use that to stand for some error case. I think (-1) is a fine upstanding number, and I refuse to abuse it. Use optional<T> *and join me in saving (-1) from further abuse.*

If you are familiar with Boost C++, you'll know that it has an optional template too. But to be honest, it does something I don't like very much, namely overloading the ! operator to indicate the validity of the object. Imagine this code in Boost:

```
optional<bool> bIsFullScreen;
    // imagine code here…
if (!!bIsFullScreen)
{

}
```

Yes, that's no typo. The !! operator works just fine with Boost's optional template. While it is something of a matter of taste, I personally think this is unsightly and certainly confusing.

Pseudo-Random Traversal of a Set

Have you ever wondered how the "random" button on your CD player worked? It will play every song on your CD at random without playing the same song twice. That's a really useful solution for making sure players in your games see the widest variety of features like objects, effects, or characters before they have the chance of seeing the same ones again.

The following code uses a mathematical feature of prime numbers and quadratic equations. The algorithm requires a prime number larger than the ordinal value of the set you want to traverse. If your set has 10 members, your prime number would be 11. Of course, the algorithm doesn't generate prime numbers; instead, it just keeps a select set of prime numbers around in a lookup table. If you need bigger primes, there's a convenient Web site for you to check out at www.rsok.com/~jrm/printprimes.html.

Here's how it works. A skip value is calculated by choosing three random values greater than zero. These values become the coefficients of the quadratic, and the domain value (x) is set to the ordinal value of the set:

```
Skip = RandomA * (members * members) + RandomB * members + RandomC
```

Armed with this skip value, you can use this piece of code to traverse the entire set exactly once, in a pseudo random order:

```
nextMember += skip;
nextMember %= prime;
```

The value of skip is so much larger than the number of members of your set that the chosen value seems to skip around at random. Of course, this code is inside a while loop to catch the case where the value chosen is larger than your set but still smaller than the prime number. Here's the class definition:

```
class PrimeSearch
{
    static int prime_array[];

    int skip;
    int currentPosition;
    int maxElements;
    int *currentPrime;
    int searches;

    CRandom r;

public:
    PrimeSearch(int elements);
    int GetNext(bool restart=false);
    bool Done() { return (searches==*currentPrime); }
    void Restart() { currentPosition=0; searches=0; }
};
```

I'll show you a trivial example to make a point.

```
void FadeToBlack(Screen *screen)
{
    int w = screen.GetWidth();
    int h = screen.GetHeight();

    int pixels = w * h;

    PrimeSearch search(pixels);

    int p;
    while((p=search.GetNext())!=-1)
    {
        int x = p % w;
        int y = h / p;
        screen.SetPixel(x, y, BLACK);
    }
}
```

The example sets random pixels to black until the entire screen is erased. I should warn you now that this code is completely stupid, for two reasons. First, you wouldn't set one pixel at a time. Second, you would likely use a pixel shader to do this. (I told you the example was trivial.) Use PrimeSearch for other cool things like spawning creatures, weapons, and other random stuff.

DEVELOPING THE STYLE THAT'S RIGHT FOR YOU

Throughout this chapter I've tried to point out a number of coding techniques and pitfalls that I've learned over the years. I've tried to focus on the ones that seem to cause the most problems and offer the best results. Of course, keep in mind that there is no single best approach or one magic solution for coding a game.

I wish I had more pages because there are tons of programming gems and even game programming gems out there. Most of it you'll beg or borrow from your colleagues. Some of it you'll create yourself after you solve a challenging problem.

However you find them, don't forget to share.

FURTHER READING

Beyond the C++ Standard Library. An Introduction to Boost, Björn Karlsson

C++ Templates: The Complete Guide, Nicolai M. Josuttis und David Vandevoorde

Effective C++, Scott Meyers

More Effective C++, Scott Meyers

Effective STL, Scott Meyers

Exceptional C++, Herb Sutter

More Exceptional C++, Herb Sutter

Modern C++ Design: Applied Generic and Design Patterns, Andrei Alexandrescu

Standard C++ IOStreams and Locales, Angelika Langer

The C++ Programming Language, Bjarne Stroustrup

Thinking in C++ Vol. 1, Bruce Eckel

Thinking in C++ Vol. 2, Bruce Eckel and Chuck Allison

BUILDING YOUR GAME

In This Chapter

Do you ever freeze up just before starting a new project? I do, and I'm not afraid to admit it. I get hung up thinking about the perfect directory structure, where the art and sound data should be stored, how the build process should work, and mostly how I will keep my new game from becoming a horrible mess. By the end of a project, it usually turns out to be a mess anyway! So I'm always thankful I plan out a directory structure, employ good version control tools, and incorporate automation scripts that all keep entropy just low enough for a human like me to be able to keep track of what I'm doing.

In this chapter, I'm going to tell you everything you need to know to get your game projects organized from the start, and how to configure project files and use version control tools effectively. This is an area where many game developers try to cut corners, so my advice is to invest a little time and ensure that your projects go together smoothly and stay that way. Hopefully, they'll stay organized right to the day you ship.

As you read through this chapter, you might feel that you are getting an education in software engineering. Try not to feel overwhelmed. These techniques are very critical to the process of successfully developing games, and they are used by real game developers.

A Little Motivation

Games are much more than source code. A typical game includes raw and optimized art and sound data, map levels, event scripts, test tools, and more. Don't forget the project documentation—both the docs that ship with your project, such as the user guide, and the internal documents, such as the technical design document, design document, and test plans.

There are two essential problems that all these files create. First, the sheer number of game files for art, sound, music, and other assets need to have some rational organization—there can be hundreds of thousands of these files. Games like *Age of Empires* easily have hundreds of thousands of asset files in production. With this many files, it can be really easy to lose track of one, or a few hundred. The second problem is the difficulty of ensuring that sensitive debug builds and other internal files are kept separate from the stuff that will be shipped to consumers. The last thing you need is to release your debug build, with all its symbols, to the public at large. The best setup lets you segregate your release files from everything else so you can burn a single directory tree to a DVD without worrying about culling a weird list of files. Over the last few years, I've settled on a project organization that solves these two problems.

The process of building a project should be as automatic as possible. You should be able to automatically build your game every night so that you can check your latest work. A game that can't build every day is in big trouble. Even dumb producers know this, so if you want an easy way to get a project snuffed, just make it impossible to fulfill a build request at a moment's notice.

The directory structure, project settings, and development scripts you use should make building, publishing, and rebuilding any previously published build a snap. If your source code repository supports branching, you'll be ahead of the game because you can support multiple lines of development simultaneously. I'll explain a little later what this is and why using branches is important.

Everyone does things differently, but the project organization, build scripts, and build process you'll learn in this chapter are hard to beat. I figure that if they're good enough for Microsoft, and they got our projects out the door on time, I'll keep them.

CREATING A PROJECT

This might sound a little hokey, but every project I work on has its own code word. I picked this up from Microsoft, and I love it. You should let your project team choose the code word, but try to make sure that the name chosen is somewhat cryptic. It's actually really convenient if you end up at the bar with a bunch of software developers from other companies. You can talk all day about finishing a build for "Slickrock" or that "Rainman" needs another programmer. Cloak and dagger aside, there's a real utilitarian reason to use short code words for projects.

You can use this code word for your top-level project directory and the SLN file that builds your game and tools. It is an easy step from there to create a standard build script that can find your SLN file, build the game, and even test it. If you work in a studio with multiple projects, a master build server can easily build every project in development every night and take very little maintenance to add or subtract projects.

Beyond that, a code word for a project has one other use. If you end up making multiple versions of the same product, you can use different code words to refer to them instead of version numbers. You are ready to start your project, so choose a code word and create your top-level directory. May whatever gods you believe in have mercy on your soul:

```
mkdir <codeword>
```

Build Configurations

Every project should have two build targets at a minimum: debug and release. The release build will enable optimizations critical for a product the customer will actually use. Many projects also have a profile build, which usually disables enough optimizations to allow for debugging but disables code inside #ifdef DEBUG constructs to allow it to actually run in real time. It's a good idea to have all three targets because they serve different purposes. Mostly, programmers will run and develop with a profile build target, and they will use the debug target only when something really nasty is in their bug list.

DON'T GO TOO LONG BETWEEN BUILDS

Try to keep all your build targets alive and working every day. If you ignore any build configuration, especially the release build, it could take a very long time to figure out why it's not working properly. Build it nightly, if you can, and make sure any problems get handled the very next day.

Create a Bullet-Proof Directory Structure

Over the years of developing complex projects, I've experimented with different directory structures trying to find the ideal structure. I've learned that it is important to have a good working directory structure from the start. It will help you work your way through all of the stages of developing a project—from writing your first lines of source code to testing and debugging your project. You also need to keep in mind that you'll likely need to share aspects of your project with others during the development process, even if you are the only one writing all the source code. For example, you might need to hire an independent testing team to work over your game. If you organize your project well, you'll be able to share files when necessary with a minimum of hassle.

Keeping all of this in mind, here's my recommended directory structure where should store each project you develop, including your game engine:

- *Docs*
- *Media*
- *Source*
- *Obj*
- *Bin*
- *Test*

The *Docs* directory is a reference for the development team. It should have an organized hierarchy to store both design documents and technical specifications. I always put a copy of the contract exhibits and milestone acceptance criteria in it for my team, since these documents specify our obligations to the publisher. (You don't want to ever forget who is paying the bills!) While I'm developing a project, it's not unusual to find detailed character scripts, initial user interface designs, and other works in progress in the *Docs* directory.

The *Media* directory is going to store all your art and sound assets in their raw, naked form. This directory is likely going to get huge, so make sure the source control system is configured to filter it out for people who don't care about it. I say "raw and naked" not just because I enjoy putting it in print—these assets are those *not* used by the game directly, but those that are used by artists, designers, or sound engineers while they are working on them. Think of it as the same kind of directory that programmers use for their code. When the assets get imported or packed into game files that are used by the game directly, they'll be inside the *Bin* directory where all the distributable stuff lives. One more thing, this directory will be a huge, complicated hierarchy that will most likely be created to appease the whims of artists or sound engineers, so don't expect to have much control over it.

The source code lives in the *Source* directory. It should be organized by the programmers in whatever manner they see fit. The project's solution file or make-file should also reside in the *Source* directory, and be named according to the code word for the project. The rest of the source code should be organized into other directories below *Source*.

When a project is being built, each build target will place temporary files into the *Obj* directory. On most projects, you'll have at least an *Obj\Debug* directory to hold the debug build and an *Obj\Release* directory to hold the release build. You may have other build targets, and if you do, put them in their own directory.

VISUAL STUDIO DEFAULTS AREN'T ALWAYS SO GREAT

Visual Studio does a really bad thing by assuming that software engineers want their build targets to clutter up the Source *directory. I find this annoying, since I don't want a single byte of the* Source *directory to change when I build my project. Why, you ask? First, I like to be able to copy the entire* Source *directory for publishing or backup without worrying about large temporary files. Secondly, I can compare two different* Source *directories from version to version to see only the deltas in the source code, instead of wading through hundreds of useless .OBJ, .SBR, and other files. Thirdly, I know I can always delete the* Obj *directory to force a new build of the entire project. I also know that I never have to back up or publish the* Obj *directory.*

The *Bin* directory should hold the release build and every game data file that is used to create your project. You should be able to send the contents of the *Bin* directory to a separate testing group or to someone in the press, and they'd have everything they would need to run and test the game. You also want to ensure that they don't get anything you want to keep to yourself, such as confidential project documentation or your crown jewels—the source code. Generally, you'll place release executables and DLLs in *Bin*, and store all your game data and config files in *Bin/Data*. If you take the time to set up a directory that stores the files that you may be providing to others from time to time, you'll likely avoid sending out your source code or internal project design documents.

The *Test* directory should hold the debug and profile targets of the game and special files only for the test team. It usually contains test scripts, files that unlock cheats, and test utilities. Some games have a logging feature that writes diagnostic, warning, and error messages to a text file—the *Test* directory is a great place for them. Most importantly, it should contain the release notes for the latest build. The release notes are a list of features that work, or don't work, in the latest build. They also contain quick instructions about anything the test team needs to know, such as how to expose a certain feature or a part of your game that needs special attention. As you are developing your project, I strongly encourage you to keep the release notes up-to-date. If you hand your game over to a testing team, they won't have to pull out their hair trying to figure out how to get your project to work. You'll discover that Visual Studio has to be convinced to use this directory structure, and it takes a little work to create projects under this standard. Visual Studio assumes that everything in the project lives underneath the directory that stores the solution file. It may be a pain to get Visual Studio to conform to this structure, but trust me, it is worth it.

C# PROJECTS ARE TOUGHER TO REORGANIZE

While you can tweak the directory structure of C++ projects under Visual Studio, C# projects are tougher. There is a way to reconfigure the solution files to make my recommended directory structure work, but it isn't exactly supported by Microsoft. Perhaps Microsoft will in their great wisdom figure this out someday, but don't hold your breath. For more on this topic, visit the companion Web site for this book.

The directory structure is useful because it caters to all the different people and groups that need access to your game development files. The development team gets access to the whole thing. Executives and press looking for the odd demo can copy the *Bin* directory whenever they want. The test group grabs *Bin* and *Test*, and they have everything they need.

If you store the build targets in the *Source* directory, like Visual Studio wants you to, you'll have to write complicated batch files to extract the build target, clean temporary files, and match game data with executables. Those batch files are a pain to maintain, and are a frequent source of bad builds. If you pound Visual Studio for a little while to get a better directory structure started, you won't have to worry about a nasty batch file during the life of your product.

Where to Put Your Game Engine and Tools

In case it wasn't clear, your game engine should get its own directory, with the same directory structure in parallel with your game. On one project I worked on, our game engine had a pretty uncreative code name: Engine. It was stored in an *Engine* directory with *Source*, *Docs*, *Obj*, and *Lib*, instead of *Bin*, since the output of the build was a library. There was some debate about separating the #include files into an *Inc* directory at the top level. That's a winner of an idea because it allows the game engine to be published with only the #include files and the library. The source code would remain safely in our hands.

Tools are a little fuzzier, and depend somewhat on whether the tool in question is one that is a custom tool for the project or something that everyone on every project uses. As you might expect, a tool for one project would go into the source tree for the project, and one that everyone uses would go into the same directory hierarchy as your shared game engine. If neither seems to fit, such as a one-off tool to convert some wacky file format to another, and it would never need to change or undergo any further development, perhaps you should install it into a special directory tree for those oddballs. Basically, the rule of thumb is that any directory tree should be under the same kind of development: rapid, slow, or completely static.

If your game needs any open source or third-party libraries to build, I suggest putting them in a *3rdParty* directory inside your *Source* directory. This makes it easy to keep all the right versions of those things with your code base, and it is convenient for other programmers who need to grab your code and work with it. After all, it might be tough to find an old version of something if your source code requires it.

Setting Visual Studio Build Options

I mentioned that you have to coax Visual Studio to move its intermediate and output files outside the directory that stores the solution file. To do this, open your solution, right-click the solution in your solution explorer, and select Properties. Click the "General" group under Configuration Properties (see Figure 4.1), and you'll be able to select the *Output* and *Intermediate* directories.

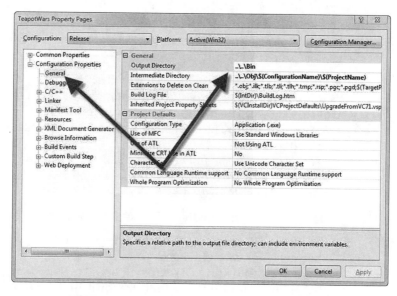

FIGURE 4.1 Visual Studio 2005 Configuration properties.

The Intermediate directory is set to where you want all of your .OBJ and other intermediate build files to be saved. Visual Studio has defined the macro $(ConfigurationName) to separate intermediate files in directories with the configuration name, such as *Debug* or *Release*. I also like to add the macro $(Project-Name), just in case I have two Visual Studio project files that happen to have the same name. In these property settings, you can use the $(IntDir) macro to identify the entire path defined in the *Intermediate* directory setting, so you can find it useful for things like placing other build-specific files like your build log.

The *Output* directory is where the linked result, such as your .EXE file, will go. You should set that to your *Bin* directory for the Release configuration and the *Test* directory for other configurations. The $(OutDir) macro can then be used to store any build output file you want to live in your *Output* directories.

Under the linker settings, you set the output filename to $(OutDir)/$(Project-Name)d.exe for the debug build, $(OutDir)/$(ProjectName)p.exe for the profile build, and $(OutDir)/$(ProjectName).exe for the release build. The names you give to the output files will set the $(TargetName) and $(TargetPath) macros, which comes in handy to keep things like the PCH files named to match their executable counterparts.

RENAME YOUR BUILD TARGETS SO THEY CAN EXIST IN THE SAME DIRECTORY

You can distinguish the debug, profile, and release files by adding a "d" or a "p" to the end of any final build target. You could also use the $(ConfigurationName) macro if want absolute clarity. If for any reason the files need to coexist in the same directory, you don't have to worry about copying them or creating temporary names.

With the target directories set right, Visual Studio has some macros you can use in your project settings.

- **$(IntDir):** The path to intermediate files
- **$(OutDir):** The path to the output directory (..\Bin\ or ..\Test\)
- **$(TargetDir):** The path to the primary output file
- **$(TargetName):** The name of the primary output file of the build without the extension
- **$(TargetPath):** The fully qualified path and filename for the output file
- **$(ConfigurationName):** Set to the name of your current configuration, such as Debug or Release

Use these macros for the following settings for all build configurations:

- **Debugging/Debugging Command:** $(TargetPath) will call the right executable for each build target
- **Debugging/Working Directory:** Should always be ..\..\Bin
- **C/C++/Precompiled Headers/Precompiled Header File:** $(IntDir) $(ProjectName)$(ConfigurationName).pch

- **C/C++/Output Files:** $(IntDir) for the ASM list location, object filename, and program database filename
- **Linker/Debug Settings/Generate Program Database File:** $(IntDir)$(TargetName).pdb
- **Linker/Debug Settings/Map File:** $(IntDir)$(TargetName).map

SOME NOTES ABOUT CHANGING DEFAULT DIRECTORIES IN VISUAL STUDIO

There are plenty of third-party tools that work with Visual Studio. Most of them make the same assumptions about project default directories that Visual Studio does. They'll still work with my suggested directory structure, but you'll have to tweak the search directories for source code and symbol files.

The macros also help to keep the differences between the build targets to a minimum. For example, $(IntDir) can stand for ..\Obj\Debug or ..\Obj\Release because they are the same in all build targets, and they don't disappear when you choose "All Configurations" in the project settings dialog.

Multiplatform Projects

If you happen to be lucky enough, or unlucky enough, to work on a multiplatform project, you'll need to tweak the previous solution just a little. Multiplatform projects usually have files that are common to all platforms and platform-specific files, too. The general idea is to keep all the common files together and create parallel directories for the platform-dependent stuff.

You'll need to install the platform-specific SDK before Visual Studio will recognize the new project platform. Your platform SDK will usually have instructions for this if it is compatible with Visual Studio, but most of the console manufacturers have SDKs that are compatible, so even if you are working on the Nintendo Wii you can still use Visual Studio to do your work.

Once the platform SDK is installed, you add the platform to your solution by opening the Configuration Manager from the Build menu. Then for each project, drop down the platform choice and choose New. You should be able to select the new platform (see Figure 4.2).

You can use the $(PlatformName) macro in your properties settings to keep platform-specific intermediate and output files nice and neat.

As far as how you should change your directory structure, here's an example of how to set up a Win32/Xbox360/Wii multiplatform structure.

Take a look at Figure 4.3. The project root is *C:\Projects\GameCode3\Dev*. That directory stores the familiar *Bin, Media, Obj, Source,* and *Test* directories I mentioned earlier. There are two accommodations for platform-dependent files and directories. First, the *Bin* directory has a special platform-dependent directory for

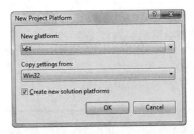

FIGURE 4.2 Adding a new platform configuration to your project.

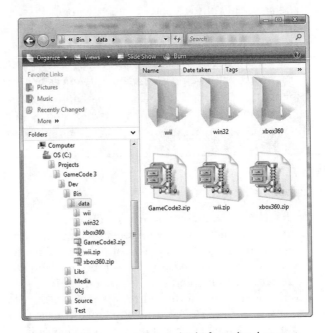

FIGURE 4.3 How to organize multiplatform development.

each platform. These directories will hold executables and DLLs. The *Bin\data* directory holds both the common files and platform-dependent files, named for what they contain. GameCode3.zip stores cooked game assets common to all platforms, and there are platform-specific files as well. Basically, you follow the same rules as before—make it easy to find and filter your files based on what you want—in this case, by platform.

During development you'll want the convenience of having all the platforms side-by-side, which keeps you from making tons of copies of the common files for every platform. You'll need to make a small change to your deployment script, in order to strip unwanted platform files from platform-specific builds, such as those that would get burned to an installation disk. After all, there's no reason to have a Win32 version of your game on the Wii, is there?

Source Code Repositories and Version Control

In comparing game development with other kinds of software development projects, what really stands out is the sheer number of parts required. Even for a small game, you may have many tens of thousands of source files for code, sound, art, world layout, scripts, and more. You may also have to cook files for your game engine or platform. Most sound effects come from a source WAV, and are usually converted to OGG or MP3. Textures may have a source PSD if they were created in Photoshop and have a companion JPG or PNG after it's been flattened and compressed. Models have a MAX file (if you use 3ds Max) and have multiple source textures. You might also have HTML files for online help or strategy guides. The list goes on and on. Even small games have hundreds, if not thousands, of individual files that all have to be created, checked, fixed, rechecked, tracked, and installed into the game. Big games will frequently have hundreds of thousands of files.

TALES FROM THE PIXEL MINES

THE FLAME

When I first arrived at Origin Systems, I noticed some odd labels taped to people's monitors. One said, "The Flame of the Map" and another "The Flame of Conversation." I thought these phrases were Origin's version of Employee of the Month, but I was wrong. This was source control in the days of SneakerNet, when Origin didn't even have a local area network. If someone wanted to work on something, they physically walked to the machine that was the "Flame of Such and Such" and copied the relevant files onto a floppy disk, stole the flame label, and went back to their machine. Then they became the "Flame." When a build was assembled for QA, everyone carried his or her floppy disks to the build computer and copied all the flames to one place. Believe it or not, this system worked fairly well.

Many years later, I was working on a small project and one afternoon a panicked teammate informed me that our development server went down and no one could work. We were only two days away from a milestone, and the team thought we were doomed. "Nonsense!" I said, as I created a full list of our development files and posted them outside my office. I reintroduced our team to SneakerNet—and they used a pencil to "check out" a file from the list and a diskette to move the latest copy of the file from my desktop to theirs where they could work on it.

We made our milestone, and no files were lost or destroyed. Sometimes an old way of doing something isn't so bad after all.

Back in the old days, the source files for a big project were typically spread all over the place. Some files were stored on a network (if you knew where to look), but most were scattered in various places on desktop computers, never to be seen again after the project finished. Unfortunately, these files were frequently lost or destroyed while the project was in production. The artist or programmer would have to grudgingly re-create their work, a hateful task at best.

Source control management is a common process used by game development teams everywhere. Game development is simply too hard and too risky to manage without it. Nonprogrammers find source control systems unwieldy and will complain for a while, but they will get used to it pretty quickly. Even 3ds Max has plug-ins for source control systems so everyone on the team can use it.

Outside of source control, many companies choose to track these bits and pieces with the help of a database, showing what state the asset is in and whether it is ready to be installed in the game. Source control repositories can help you manage who is working on something, but they aren't that good at tracking whether something is "good enough" to be in the game. For that, you don't need anything more than an Excel spreadsheet to keep a list of each file, who touched it last, what's in the file, and why it is important to your game. You could also write a little PHP/MySQL portal site and put a complete content management intranet up on your local network to track files.

To help you put your own version control process in place, I'll introduce you to some of the more popular version control tools that professional game developers use in their practice. I'll also tell you which ones to avoid. Of course, keep in mind that there is no perfect, one-size-fits-all tool or solution. The important thing is that you put some type of process together and that you do it at the beginning of any project.

Visual SourceSafe from Microsoft

Visual SourceSafe is the source repository distributed with Microsoft's Visual Studio, and it is an excellent example of, "You get what you pay for." What attracts most people to this product is an easy-to-use GUI interface and an extremely simple setup. You can be up and running on SourceSafe in 10 minutes if you don't type slowly.

The biggest problem with SourceSafe is how it stores the source repository. If you dig a bit into the shared files where the repository is stored, you'll find a data directory with a huge tree of files with odd names like AAAAAAB.AAA and AAACCAA.AAB. The contents of these files are clear text, or nearly, so this wacky naming scheme couldn't have been for security reasons. If anyone out there knows why they did it this way, drop me an email. I'm completely stumped.

Each file stores a reverse delta of previous revisions of a file in the repository. Every revision of a file will create a new SourceSafe file with one of those wacky names. For those of you paying attention, you'll remember that many of these files will be pretty small, given that some source changes could be as simple as a single character change. The amount of network drive space taken up by Source-Safe is pretty unacceptable in my humble opinion.

There's also a serious problem with speed. Even small projects get to be a few hundred files in size, and large projects can be tens, or even hundreds of thousands of files. Because SourceSafe stores its data files in the repository directory structure, access time for opening and closing all these files is quite long and programmers can wait forever while simply checking to see if they have the most recent files. SourceSafe doesn't support branching (see my discussion on branching a little later), unless you make a complete copy of the entire tree you are branching. Ludicrous!

Forget attempting to access SourceSafe remotely. Searching thousands of files over a pokey Internet connection is murder. Don't even try it over a T1 line. Finally, SourceSafe's file index database can break down, and even the little analyzer utility will throw up its hands and tell you to start over. I've finished projects under a corrupted database before, but it just happened that the corruption was affecting a previous version of a file that I didn't need. I was lucky.

SourceSafe also has a habit of corrupting itself, making your entire repository a useless pile of unfathomable files. This is especially true when you store large binary assets like sounds, textures, and video.

If I haven't convinced you to try something other than SourceSafe, let me just say it: Don't use it. I've heard rumors that Microsoft doesn't use it, so why should you?

Subversion and TortoiseSVN

Subversion is a free source repository available at http://subversion.tigris.org. It uses a command-line interface, which can give some nonprogrammers some heartburn when using it. Luckily, you can also download TortoiseSVN, a GUI that integrates with Windows Explorer. It is available at http://tortoisesvn.tigris.org. Both are free, are easy to set up and administer, and are a great choice for a development team on a budget.

The system stores the file state on the local machine, which makes it trivial to work on files even if you have no network access. You just work on them and tell the Subversion server when you are ready to commit them to the server. If anyone else made modifications with you in parallel, the system will let you merge the changes.

Complaints about the system generally fall into the speed and scalability category. If you are working on a large game with a huge directory structure and tens of thousands of assets, you would be wise to consider something else, such as Perforce.

I developed this edition of the book, and all the source code in it, under Subversion. So if you are reading this now and can play with the source code, I guess Subversion worked just fine.

Perforce by Perforce Software

My favorite product in this category is Perforce. I've used this product for years, and it's never let me down. For any of you lucky enough to move from Source-Safe to Perforce, the first thing you'll notice is its speed. It's damn fast.

Perforce uses a client/server architecture and a Btrieve-based database for storing the repository. Btrieve is an extremely efficient data storage and retrieval engine that powers Pervasive's SQL software. That architecture simply blows the pants off anything that uses the network directory hierarchy. More than storing the current status of each version of each file, it even stores the status of each file for everyone who has a client connection. That's why most SourceSafe slaves freak out when they use Perforce the first time; it's so fast they don't believe it's actually doing anything. Of course, this makes remote access as fast as it can possibly be.

DON'T FORGET TO ASK PERFORCE'S PERMISSION

Since Perforce "knows" the status of any file on your system, you have to be careful if you change a file while you are away from your network connection and you can't connect to the Perforce server to "check out" a file. Since Perforce knows nothing of the change, it will simply complain later that a local file is marked read/write, so while it won't blow away your changes, it also doesn't go out of its way to remind you that you've done anything. SourceSafe actually does local data/time comparisons, so it will tell you that the local file is different than the network copy. Subversion stores your local file status locally, so it is much faster than SourceSafe.

Perforce has a nice GUI for anyone who doesn't want to use the command line. The GUI will perform about 99 percent of the tasks you ever need to perform, so you can leave the command line to someone who knows what they're doing. Even better, Perforce integrates with Windows Explorer, and you can edit and submit files just by right-clicking them. Artists love that kind of thing.

The branching mechanisms are extremely efficient. If you make a branch from your main line of development to a test line, Perforce only keeps the deltas from branch to branch. Network space is saved, and remerging branches is also very fast. Subversion and others make a completely new copy of the branch, taking up enormous network storage space.

You'll find almost as many third-party tools that work with Perforce as with some of the free repositories. Free downloads are available, including tools that perform graphical merges, C++ APIs, conversion tools from other products like SourceSafe, Subversion, and tons of others.

PERFORCE + VISUAL SOURCESAFE = CHAOS

When I worked for Ion Storm, the programmers used Perforce, but everyone else used Visual SourceSafe. What a fiasco! The content tree that stored art, game levels, and sounds would always be a little "off" from the source code in Perforce. If you even had to check in a change that required a parallel change to content, you had to practically halt the entire team and tell everyone to do this massive refresh from the network. This was simply horrible and wasted an amazing amount of time. Don't screw around—make sure that you get source code control licenses for everyone on your development team: programmers, artists, and everyone else that touches your game.

AlienBrain from Avid

For those of you with really serious asset tracking problems and equally serious budgets, there's a pretty good solution out there that will track your source code and other assets: AlienBrain from Avid. They have a huge client list that looks like a who's who of the computer game industry. Their software integrates with nearly every tool out there: CodeWarrior, Visual Studio, 3ds Max, Maya, Photoshop, and many others.

AlienBrain is somewhat more expensive than Perforce, but has some features Perforce doesn't have. AlienBrain is used by game developers, filmmakers, and big iron simulations developers that have needs to track much more than source code. They've also made some serious strides in the last few versions to improve performance and bring better branching to their software that better matches other software. They also have some excellent production pipeline helpers in their software, so files can be reviewed and approved after they are checked in.

Programmers and "build gurus" will like the fact that AlienBrain has sophisticated branching and pinning mechanisms just like the more advanced source code repositories on the market. (I'll discuss the importance of branching a little later in this chapter.) Artists and other contributors will actually use this product, unlike others that are mainly designed to integrate well with Visual Studio and not creative applications such as Photoshop and 3D Studio Max. One of the big drawbacks of other products is their rather naive treatment of nontext files. AlienBrain was written with these files in mind. They have some great features to track peer review in art files, for example.

Using Source Control Branches

I freely admit that up until 2001 I didn't use branching. I also admit that I didn't really know what it was for, but it also wasn't my fault. I blame Microsoft. Their Visual SourceSafe tool is distributed with Visual Studio, and some engineers use it without question. Microsoft software, like Office, has hundreds of thousands of source files and many hundreds of engineers. SourceSafe was never designed to handle repositories of that size.

Branching is a process where an entire source code repository is copied so that parallel development can proceed unhindered on both copies simultaneously. Sometimes the copies are merged back into one tree. It is equally possible that after being branched, the branched versions diverge entirely and are never merged. Why is branching so important? Branches of any code imply a fundamental change in the development of that code. You might branch source code to create a new game. You might also branch source code to perform some heavy research. Sometimes a fundamental change, such as swapping out one rendering engine for another or coding a new object culling mechanism is too dangerous to attempt in the main line of code. If you make a new branch, you'll wall off your precious main code line, have a nice sandbox to play in, and get the benefits of source control for every source file.

SourceSafe's branching mechanism, and I use that term loosely, makes a complete copy of the entire source tree. That's slow and fat. Most decent repositories keep track of only the deltas from branch to branch. This approach is much faster, and it doesn't penalize you for branching the code.

Here are the branches I use and why:

- **Main:** Normal development branch
- **Research:** A "playground" branch where anything goes, including trashing it entirely
- **Gold:** The branch submitted for milestone approvals or release

The Research and Gold branches originate from the Main branch. Changes in these branches may or may not be merged with the Main branch, depending on what happens to the code. The Main branch supports the main development effort; almost all of your development effort will happen in the Main branch.

The Research branch supports experimental efforts. It's a great place to make some core API changes, swap in new middleware, or make any other crazy change without damaging the main line or slowing development there. The Gold branch is the stable branch that has your last, or next, milestone submission. Programmers can code fast and furious in the main line while minor tweaks and bug fixes needed for milestone approval are tucked into the Gold branch.

Perhaps the best evidence for branching code can be found in how a team works under research and release scenarios. Consider a programming team about to reach a major milestone. The milestone is attached to a big chunk of cash, which is only paid out if the milestone is approved. Say this team is old-fashioned and doesn't know anything about branching.

Just before the build, the lead programmer runs around and makes everyone on the team promise not to check on any code while the build is compiling. Everyone promises to keep their work to themselves, and everyone continues to work on their own machines.

Most likely the build doesn't even compile the first time. One of the programmers might have forgotten to check in some new files, or simply gotten sloppy and checked in work that didn't compile. By the time the lead programmer figures out who can fix the build, the programmer at fault may have already started work on other things, which now may have to be reverted to get the build working again. This is a big waste of time. While all of this is going on, another programmer is frustrated because he can't begin making major changes to the AI code since it might need a tweak to make the build work too. Getting the build to become stable with everyone working in one branch basically shuts everyone down until the build is complete, which can take more than a day in some cases.

But the problems don't stop there. Let's assume the completed build is going to be tested by a remote test team, and the build takes hours to upload to their FTP site. By the time the build is uploaded and then grabbed by the test team, it could be two days. If the test team finds a problem that halts testing, the whole process starts again with the whole development team hobbled until testing gives the green light. This whole process could take two to three days or more.

If you don't think this is that bad, you are probably working without branches and have trained yourself to enjoy this little hellish scenario. You've probably developed coping mechanisms that you call "process" instead of what they are, which is crazy. I used to do the same thing because I thought branches were too much trouble and too confusing. Until I tried them myself.

Let's look at the same scenario from the perspective of a team that uses branches.

The lead programmer walks around and makes sure the team has all the milestone changes checked in. She goes to the build machine and launches a milestone build. The first thing that happens is the Gold branch gets refreshed with the very latest of everything in the Main branch. The build finishes with the same failure as before—compile errors due to missing files. The programmer responsible simply checks in the missing files into both the Main branch and the Gold branch, and everything continues without delay. The AI programmer mentioned previously continues working without worry, since all of his changes will happen in the Main branch, safely away from the Gold branch.

The finished build is checked and sent to the testing group via the same FTP site, and it still takes almost eight hours. When the build gets just as hosed as before, the lead programmer makes a small tweak directly in the Gold branch to get it working, and she uploads a small patch. The test team gets to work and reports a few issues, which are then fixed directly in the Gold branch and merged back into the Main branch. When the milestone is approved, the Gold branch has the latest and greatest version of the game, and the development team never lost a second during the entire process. They even have the bug fixes that were made in the Gold branch.

Every minute of lost development time means your game is a little less fun, or a little less polished than it could be. Given the above—which team do you think is going to make the best game? My money and Metacritic are going with the team that used branches.

SILVER, GOLD, AND LIVE

A friend of mine who worked at Microsoft was in the Build lab for Microsoft Office. At the time, they used three branches: a Main, a Silver, and a Gold. The teams would publish from Main to Silver when a milestone was about to be delivered, but because of the vast number and speed of changes that happened even in the Silver branch, they also published Silver to Gold when a real "version" was ready to go into final testing.

This same strategy is also used by my friends working on online games—they usually have three branches too: Main, Gold, and Live. Sometimes, you have to make a change directly in the Live branch to fix a critical issue right on the live servers and then propagate that change back to the Gold and Main branches.

BUILDING THE GAME: A BLACK ART?

You can't build a testable version of your game by simply grabbing the latest source code and launching the compiler. Most games have multiple gigabytes of data, install programs, multiple languages, special tools, and all manner of components that have nothing at all to do with the executable. All of these components come together in one way or another during the build. Every shred of code and data must make it onto the install image on one or more CDs or on the network for the test team. Frequently, these components don't come together without a fight. Building the game is something of a black art, assigned to the most senior code shamans.

Ultima VIII had a build process that was truly insane. It went something like this:

1. Grab the latest source code: editor, game, and game scripts.
2. Build the game editor.
3. Run the game editor and execute a special command that nuked the local game data files and grab the latest ones from the shared network drive.
4. Build the game.
5. Run the UNK compiler (*Ultima*'s game scripting language) to compile and link the game scripts for English. Don't ask me what UNK stands for, I really can't remember....

6. Run the UNK compiler twice more and compile the French and German game scripts.
7. Run the game and test it. Watch it break and loop back to Step 1 until the game finally works.
8. Copy the game and all the game data into a *temp* directory.
9. Compress the game data files.
10. Build the install program.
11. Copy the English, French, and German install images to 24 floppy disks.
12. Copy the CD-ROM image to the network. (The only CD burner was on the first floor.)
13. Go to the first floor media lab and make three copies of each install: 72 floppy disks and three CDs. And hope like hell there are enough floppy disks.

Before you ask, I'll just tell you that the fact that the build process for *Ultima VIII* had 13 steps never sat very well with me. Each step generally failed at least twice for some dumb reason, which made building *Ultima VIII* no less than a four hour process—on a good day.

The build was actually fairly automated with batch files. The game editor even accepted command line parameters to perform the task of grabbing the latest map and other game data. Even so, building *Ultima VIII* was so difficult and fraught with error that I was the only person who ever successfully built a testable version of the game. That wasn't an accomplishment, it was a failure.

On one of my trips to Microsoft, I learned something about how they build Office. The build process is completely automatic. The build lab for Office has a fleet of servers that build every version of Office in every language, and they never stop. The moment a build is complete, they start again, constantly looking for compile errors introduced by someone in the last few minutes. Office is a huge piece of software. If Microsoft can automate a build as big and complex as this, surely you can automate yours.

Automate Your Builds

My experience has taught me that every project can and should have an automatic build. No exceptions. It's far easier (and safer) to maintain build scripts that automate the process instead of relying on a build master, whose knowledge is so arcane he might better be called a witchdoctor. My suggestion is that you should try to create Microsoft's build lab in miniature on your own project. Here is what's needed:

- A build machine, or even multiple machines, if your project is big enough
- Good tools for automatic building, both from third-party sources or made yourself
- Invest time creating and maintain automation scripts

The Build Machine

Don't try to save a buck and use a programmer's development box as your build machine. Programmers are always downloading funky software, making operating system patches, and installing third-party development tools that suit their needs and style. A build machine should be a pristine environment that has known versions and updates for each piece of software: the operating system, compiler, internal tools, SDKs, install program, and anything else used to build the game.

BEST PRACTICE

AFTER YOU GO GOLD, BACK UP YOUR BUILD MACHINE

A complete backup of the build machine is good insurance. The physical machine itself, preserved for eternity, is even better. If you need to build an old project, the backup of the build machine will have the right versions of the compiler, operating system, and other tools. New versions and patches come out often, and a project just 12 months old can be impossible to build, even if the source code is readily available in the source code repository. Just try to build something 10 or 12 years old, and you'll see what I mean. If anyone out there has a good copy of Turbo Pascal and IBM DOS 3.3, let me know!

The build machine should be extremely fast, have loads of RAM, and have a high performance hard disk, preferably multiple hard disks with high RPM and configured with at least RAID 0 for ultimate speed. Compiling is RAM- and hard disk-intensive, so try to get the penny-pinchers to buy a nice system. If you ever used the argument about how much money your company could save by buying fast computers for the programmers, imagine how easy it would be to buy a nice build machine. The entire test team might have to wait on a build. How much is that worth?

Automated Build Scripts

Automated builds have been around as long as there have been makefiles and command-line compilers. I admit that I've never been good at the cryptic syntax of makefiles, which is one reason I put off automating builds. If you use Visual Studio, you might consider using the prebuild or postbuild settings to run some custom batch files or makefiles. I wouldn't, and here's why: You'll force your programmers to run the build scripts every time they build. That's probably wasteful at best, completely incorrect at worst.

Prebuild and postbuild steps should run batch files, makefiles, or other utilities that are required every time the project is built. Build scripts tend to be a little different and skew toward getting the build ready for the test department or burning to DVD. As an example, the build script will always grab the latest code from the source repository and rebuild the entire project from scratch. If you forced your programmers to do that for every compile, they'd lynch you.

Batch files and makefiles are perfectly fine solutions for any build script you need. You can also write great batch files or shell scripts, since Visual Studio builds can be run from the command line. There are some better tools for those like myself who like GUIs, such as Visual Build Pro from Kinook Software (see Figure 4.4).

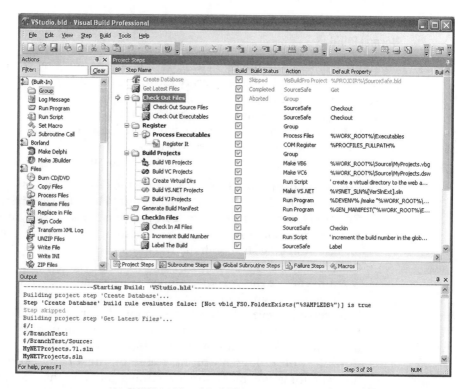

FIGURE 4.4 Visual Build from Kinook Software.

This tool is better than batch files or makefiles. The clean GUI helps you understand and maintain a complicated build process with multiple tools and failure steps. The build script is hierarchical, each group possibly taking different steps if a component of the build fails. Visual Build also integrates cleanly with a wide variety of development tools and source code repositories.

Every internal tool you create should have a command-line interface. Whether the tool creates radiosity maps for your levels, calculates visibility sets, analyzes map data, or runs a proprietary compression technology, it must be able to take input from the command line, or you won't be able to automate your build process.

CREATING BUILD SCRIPTS

You'll want to create a few build scripts for your project. Most builds will simply grab the latest code, build it, and copy the results somewhere on the network. The milestone build is a little more complicated and involves branching and merging the source code repository.

Normal Build

The normal build script builds a clean version of the game and copies the results somewhere useful. It is run as a part of the milestone build process, but it can also run automatically at regular intervals. I suggest you run a normal build at least once per day, preferably in the wee hours of the morning, to check the code on the network for any errors. The normal build script is also useful for building ad-hoc versions of the game for the test team.

The normal build script performs the following steps:

- **Clean the build machine.** If you use the directory structure I suggest at the beginning of this chapter, you can just delete the *Obj* directory.
- **Get the latest source code and game media.** I used to recommend cleaning everything and starting from nothing, but on most games this simply takes too long. Just grab the recent files.
- **Grab the latest version number and label the build.** You can decide when to change the version number—each build or even each night. You can use the version number to specify the ultimate destination on your build server, so every build you've ever made can be available. Visual Build Pro has a utility to grab or even change the version number of Visual Studio resource files, but it's pretty easy to write one yourself.
- **Compile and link every build target: debug, profile, and release.** The project settings will make sure everything goes into the right place.
- **Run automatic test scripts.** If you have automated testing, have the build machine run the test scripts to see if the build is a good one. This is more reliable than a bleary-eyed programmer attempting to test the game at 4 a.m.
- **Process and copy the build results.** The destination directory should use the code name of the project and the version number to distinguish it from other projects or other versions of the same project. For example, version 2.0.8.25 of the Rainman project might go into *E:\Builds\Rainman\2.0.8.25*. The nightly build of the same project might go into *E:\Builds\Rainman\ Nightly*.

A nightly build process is actually trivial to set up if you have your automated build working—just set up a scheduled task on the build machine. For Windows Vista, you can create a scheduled task by going into the Control Panel, run Administrative Tools, and run the Task Scheduler. The wizard will take you

SCRIPTS CAN'T UPDATE THEMSELVES WHILE THEY ARE RUNNING

If you're paying attention, you'll realize that the build scripts themselves should be checked to make sure they haven't changed. If the build script is running, how can it clean itself off the build machine and get itself from the source code repository? It can't, at least not easily. If you standardize your projects with a single directory structure, it's better to create a master build script that works for any project. Project-specific build commands are put into a special build script that lives in the same directory as the project files. The master build script should only change when the build process for every project is changed—something that should be extremely rare.

through the steps of defining when and how often to run it. If you happen to be a Linux person, look up the cron command. Usually, it's a good idea to copy the results of the build to your network where everyone can grab it.

Milestone Build

Milestone builds add more steps to the beginning and end of the build since they involve branching the code. They also involve an approval process that takes days or weeks instead of minutes, so the build process has an "open," a "create," and a "close" script to manage the branches and make sure that any changes that happen during approval get back into the main code line.

Every project should have a Main branch and a Gold branch. Every source code repository does this a little differently. When a milestone build is launched, the first thing that happens is the Gold branch gets a fresh copy of the Main branch. The branches are synchronized without merging, which means that the entire Main branch is simply copied to the Gold branch, making them identical. The build machine runs the build scripts from the Gold branch to make the milestone build. This implies that the Main and Gold branch can exist on the same machine at the same time. This is true.

Most source code repositories allow a great degree of freedom for each client to configure how they view the contents of the repository. It's pretty easy to configure the client to put all the Main branches of every project into a *D:\Projects\Main* directory and all the Gold branches into *D:\Projects\Gold*. The build scripts can even use a branch macro to figure out which branch needs building.

After the milestone build is assembled, it should be packaged and sent to testing. In our case, this meant Zip'ing up the entire build and putting it on our FTP site so Microsoft's Test department could grab it.

NO BUILD AUTOMATION = MADNESS

At Origin Systems, we didn't do anything special for milestone builds on the *Ultima* projects. Some unlucky programmer, usually me, launched the build on his desktop machine and after plenty of cursing and a few hours, the new version was ready to test. The other programmers kept adding features and bugs as fast as the test team could sign off old features. New code and features would break existing code—stuff the test team approved. The bugs would pile up, and it was difficult to figure out if the project was making any progress. To minimize the pain of this process, it was usually done in the middle of the night when most of the developers had gone home.

The projects I've been on since then were entirely different, mostly due to ditching SourceSafe and using branches. Our source code repository, Perforce, had excellent branching and merging capabilities. The programming team resisted at first, but quickly saw that milestone builds were linked directly to their paychecks. A few milestones later everyone wondered how we ever developed projects without branching.

OLD ADVICE TURNED OUT TO BE DUMB ADVICE

In the first and second editions of this book, I advised readers to use monolithic ZIP or RAR files to package their entire build and FTP that one file. This turns out to be a horrible idea. I was working on a project that had to upload a multigigabyte file, and when the FTP failed seven hours into the upload, we had to start all over. Instead, use RAR/PAR files. Most Rar tools can split a monolithic Rar file into smaller components, each of which may only be a few hundred megabytes. The PAR files can be used to actually rebuild a corrupted file on the receiving end, saving both parties a ton of time.

Teams almost never submit milestone builds that are approved with no changes. Most of the time, testing will require some changes, both major and minor. Any of these changes should happen in your Gold branch. You can then rebuild the Gold branch and resubmit to your testing group. This process continues until the test team is satisfied. The Gold branch is then merged to the Main branch. This is usually an automatic process, but sometimes merge conflicts force a human to stare at the changes and merge them.

The two additional scripts you'll need to build and manage your changes in a multibranch environment are "Open" and "Close." Here's an outline of what you'll want in the "begin" script:

- Get the latest files in the Main branch.
- Unlock the Gold branch and revert any modified files.
- Force integrate from Main to Gold.
- Submit the Gold branch.

You may notice a command to "unlock" the Gold branch. More on that in a moment. Take a look at the "close" script:

- Get the latest files in the Gold branch.
- Integrate from Gold to Main.
- Resolve all changes.
- Submit the Main and the Gold branch.
- Lock the Gold branch from all changes.

The integration commands are expected, but if you look at the last two lines of the Close phase, you'll see that the Gold branch is locked so that no one can change it. The Open phase unlocks the files and reverts any changes. Why bother? This makes absolutely sure that the Gold branch is only open for changes during milestone approval. If no milestone build is in test, there should be no reason to change the Gold branch.

TALES FROM THE PIXEL MINES

BUILDS WERE TOUGH ON *THIEF: DEADLY SHADOWS*

On *Thief: Deadly Shadows*, there was an unfortunate problem in the build process that no automation could possibly fix. Since the project was really large and there was no automated testing, the test team would only get new builds every couple of days. It would take them that long just to be sure they could send the latest version to the entire test team. The problem was that the new build was launched at fairly random times, and the development team was never given any notice. Now, I know what you're thinking. If every submission to the source repository were individually checked, then a new build should be able to launch at any time without error. Wrong! The builds took days to perform because there was little, if any, integration testing on the part of programmers. They simply tested their own stuff in quick, isolated tests. This rarely caught the odd problems due to integration flaws, and these problems accumulated between builds. The solution? Give the developers a little notice—at least a few hours—and get them to run some more serious integration tests of their own before the build. That, and for goodness sake, create some automated testing and run it nightly.

This has an added side effect: Anyone who wants the latest approved milestone build can simply grab the code in the Gold branch and build the game. This is especially useful if the odd executive or representative of the press wants to see a demo. Even if the last build is missing from the network, you can always re-create it by building the Gold branch.

MULTIPLE PROJECTS AND SHARED CODE

It's difficult to share code between multiple projects if the shared code is still under rapid development. Two different teams will eventually be in different stages of development because it is unlikely they both will have the same project schedule. Eventually, one team will need to make a change to the shared code that no one else wants.

There are a couple of different cases you should consider:

- One team needs to put a "hack" in the shared code to make a milestone quickly, and the other team wants to code the "real" solution.
- One team is close to shipping and has started a total code lockdown. No one can change anything. The other team needs to make modifications to the shared code to continue development.

How do you deal with this sticky problem? Branching, of course.

In the case of the scenario where two project teams need to share a common game engine, the game engine has three branches:

- **Main:** The normal development branch
- **Gold_Project_A:** The Gold branch for the first project
- **Gold_Project_B:** The Gold branch for the second project

While both projects are in normal development, they both make changes to the shared engine code in the Main branch. If either project goes into a milestone approval phase, they fix milestone blockers in the Gold branch for their project. Since they each get their own Gold branch, both projects can be in approval simultaneously without worrying about each other. If they happen to be broken in exactly the same way, you can always make the change in the Main branch and integrate that single change forward to both Gold branches, it's totally up to you. After their milestone has been approved, the changes get merged back into the main line. When either project hits code lockdown, meaning that only a few high priority changes are being made to the code, the project stays in the Gold branch until it ships.

All this work assumes the two teams are motivated to share the game engine and continually contribute to its improvement. There might be a case for one project permanently branching the shared code, in which case, it should get its own code line apart from the Main branch of the original shared code. If the changes are minor, and they should be, it's trivial to merge any two arbitrary code lines, as long as they originated from an original source. Even if you got unlucky and the changes were overhauls, the difficulty of the merge is preferable to making huge changes in your main code line while trying to satisfy a milestone. Best to leave this activity in its own branch.

SOME PARTING ADVICE

This chapter has likely shown you that there is a lot of drudgery on any software project, and games are no exception. Back in the dark ages, I built game projects by typing in commands at the command prompt and checking boxes on a sheet of paper. Since most of this work happened way after midnight, I made tons of mistakes. Some of these mistakes wasted time in copious amounts—mostly because the test team had a broken build on their hands, courtesy of a decaffeinated or just exhausted Mike McShaffry.

Without using branching techniques, all the programmers had to tiptoe around their code during a build. Moving targets are much harder to hit. Programmers take a long time to get in a good zone. If you break anyone's concentration by halting progress to do a build, you lose valuable time.

My parting advice: Always automate the monkey work, give the test team a good build every time, and never ever get in the way of a developer in the zone.

GET YOUR GAME RUNNING

GAME INITIALIZATION AND SHUTDOWN

In This Chapter

- Initialization 101
- Some C++ Initialization Pitfalls
- The Game's Application Layer
- Stick the Landing: A Nice Clean Exit
- Getting In and Getting Out

There are a million little details about writing games that no one talks about. Lots of books and Web sites can teach you how to draw textured polygons in Direct3D. But when it comes to figuring out your initialization sequence, you'll find little discussion. Most programmers hack something together over time that eventually turns into a horrible mess.

I've written this chapter to show you the ins and outs of the entire initialization sequence. As you check out the code in this chapter, keep in mind that the solutions provided shouldn't be used verbatim because your game might be very different and require a different solution. Hopefully, you'll gain an understanding of my approach and be able to adapt it to your particular situation. Truly elegant solutions and algorithms never just fall out of the sky. They usually come to you after seeing some code that falls slightly short of what you need, and you push it the rest of the way yourself.

Every piece of software, including games, has initialization, the core or main loop, and cleanup. Initialization prepares your canvas for painting pixels. The main loop accepts and translates user input, changes the game state, and renders the game state until the loop is broken. This loop is broken by a user quitting the game or some kind of failure. The cleanup code releases key system resources, closes files, and exits back to the operating system.

This chapter deals with initialization and shutdown. Chapter 6, "Controlling the Main Loop," will dig a little deeper and show you how to control the main loop of your game.

INITIALIZATION 101

Initializing games involves performing setup tasks in a particular order, especially on Windows platforms. Initialization tasks for Windows games are a superset of console games due to a more unpredictable hardware and OS configuration. There are some tasks you must perform before creating your window, and others that must have a valid window handle or HWND, and therefore happen after you create your window. Initialization tasks for a Windows game should happen in this order:

- Check system resources: hard drive space, memory, input and output devices.
- Check the CPU speed.
- Initialize your main random number generator (this was covered in Chapter 3).
- Load programmer's options for debugging purposes.
- Initialize your memory cache.
- Create your window.
- Initialize the audio system.

- Load the player's game options and saved game files.
- Create your drawing surface.
- Perform initialization for game systems: physics, AI, and so on.

SOME C++ INITIALIZATION PITFALLS

Before we work through our initialization checklist, let's get some critical initialization pitfalls out of the way, starting with the misuse of C++ constructors. I've heard that power corrupts, and absolute power corrupts absolutely. You might get some disagreement from Electronic Art's executives on this point. I'll prove it to you by showing you some problems with going too far using C++ constructors to perform initialization. It turns out that C++ constructors are horrible at initializing game objects, especially if you declare your C++ objects globally.

Programming in C++ gives you plenty of options for initializing objects and subsystems. Since the constructor runs when an object comes into scope, you might believe that you can write your initialization code like this:

```
// Main.cpp – initialization using globals
//
DataFiles g_DataFiles;
AudioSystem g_AudioSystem;
VideoSystem g_VideoSystem;

int main(void)
{
    BOOL done = false;
    while (! done)
    {
        // imagine a cool main loop here
    }
    return 0;
}
```

The global objects in this source code example are all complicated objects that could encapsulate some game subsystems. The fledgling game programmer might briefly enjoy the elegant look of this code, but that love affair will be quite short lived. When any of these initialization tasks fail, and they will, there's no easy way to recover.

I'm not talking about using exception handling as a recovery mechanism. Rather, I'm suggesting that any problem with initialization should give the player a chance to do something about it, such as wiping the peanut butter off the DVD. To do this, you need a user interface of some kind, and depending on where the failure happens, your user interface might not be initialized yet.

Global objects under C++ are initialized before the entry point, in this case main(void). One problem with this is ordering; you can't control the order in which global objects are instantiated. Sometimes the objects are instantiated in the order of the link, but you can't count on that being the case with all compilers, and even if it were predictable, you shouldn't count on it. What makes this problem worse is that since C++ constructors have no return value, you are forced to do something ugly to find out if anything went wrong. One option, if you can call it that, is to check a member variable of the class to see if the initialization completed properly:

```cpp
// Main.cpp – initialization using globals
//

DataFiles g_DataFiles;
AudioSystem g_AudioSystem;
VideoSystem g_VideoSystem;

int main(void)
{
    // check all the global objects for initialization failure
    if (! g_DataFiles.Initialized() ||
        ! g_AudioSystem.Initialized() ||
        ! g_VideoSystem.Initialized() )
    {
        printf("Something went horribly wrong. Please return this game to the "
            "store in a fit of anger and write scathing posts to every Web site "
            "you can about the company that would hire such idiots.");

        return (1);
    }

    BOOL done = false;
    while (! done)
    {
        // imagine a cool main loop here
    }
    return (0);
}
```

This code is suddenly looking less elegant. But wait, there's more! The wise programmer will inform his game players about what has gone wrong so they can have some possibility of fixing the problem. The simpler alternative of failing and dropping back to the operating system with some lame error message is sure to provoke a strong reaction.

If you want to inform the player, you might want to do it with a simple dialog box. This assumes that you've already initialized the systems that make the dialog box function: video, user interface, data files that contain the button art, font system, and so on. This is certainly not always possible. What if your nosey game player hacked into the art data files and screwed them up? You won't have any button art to display your nice dialog box telling hackers they've screwed themselves. You have no choice but to use the system UI, such as the standard message box under Windows. It's better than nothing.

BEST

PRACTICE

INITIALIZE YOUR STRING SUBSYSTEM EARLY

Initialize your text cache, or whatever you use to store text strings, very early. You can present any errors about initialization failures in the right language. If the initialization of the text cache fails, present an error with a number. It's easier for foreign language speakers almost anywhere in the world to use the number to find a solution from a customer service person or a Web site.

There are some good reasons to use global objects. One of the best ones is to trap the general exception handler; your code then has control over how the game will handle failures during initialization. Make sure that any global object you create cannot fail on construction.

Global object pointers are much better than global objects. Singleton objects, such as the instantiation of the class that handles the audio system or perhaps your application object, are naturally global, and if you're like me, you hate passing pointers or references to these objects in every single method call from your entry point to the lowest level code. Declare global pointers to these objects, initialize them when you're good and ready, and free them under your complete control. Here's an example of a more secure way to initialize:

```
// Main.cpp — initialization using pointers to global objects
//


// A useful macro
#define SAFE_DELETE(p)    { if (p) { delete (p); (p)=NULL; } }

DataFiles *gp_DataFiles = NULL;
AudioSystem *gp_AudioSystem = NULL;
VideoSystem *gp_VideoSystem = NULL;

int main(void)
{
   gp_DataFiles = new DataFiles;
   if ( (NULL==gp_DataFiles) || (!gp_DataFiles->Initialized() ) )
```

```
{
    // Please excuse the naked text strings! They are better for
    // examples, but in practice I'd use a text cache for
    // localization. Not everyone speaks English, you know.

    _stprintf("The data files are somehow screwed. "
        "Try to reinstall before you "
        "freak out and return the game.");
    return (1);
}

gp_AudioSystem = new AudioSystem;
if ( (NULL==gp_AudioSystem) || (!gp_AudioSystem ->Initialized() ) )
{
    _stprintf("The audio system is somehow screwed. "
        "Reboot and try running the "
        "game again. That almost always works. ");
    return (1);
}

gp_VideoSystem = new VideoSystem;
if ( (NULL==gp_VideoSystem) || (!gp_VideoSystem ->Initialized() ) )
{
    _stprintf("The video system is screwed. Go get a real video "
        "card before you even think of trying to run this game.");
    return (1);
}

BOOL done = false;
while (! done)
{
    // imagine a cool main loop here
}

SAFE_DELETE(gp_VideoSystem);        // AVOID DEADLOCK!!!
SAFE_DELETE(gp_AudioSystem);
SAFE_DELETE(gp_DataFiles);
return (0);
}
```

Note that the objects are released in the reverse order in which they are instantiated. This is no mistake, and it is a great practice whenever you need to grab a bunch of resources of different kinds in order to do something. In multithreaded operating systems with limited resources, you can avoid deadlock by allocating and deallocating your resources in this way.

Deadlock is a nasty situation whereby two processes are attempting to gain access to the same resources at the same time, but cannot because they each have access to the resource the other process needs to continue. Deadlock can even happen in a single-threaded program, if other programs are attempting to gain access to the same limited resources. Computers are very patient, and will happily wait until the sun explodes. Get in the habit of programming with that problem in mind, even if your code will never run on an operating system where that will be a problem. It's a great habit, and you'll avoid some nasty bugs.

Exception Handling

Sometimes you have no choice but to write code in a C++ constructor that has the possibility of failing. Certainly if you wrap the creation of some DirectX objects in a nice class, you'll have plenty of places you'd wish a constructor could return an HRESULT. Instead of rewriting all your code to cripple the constructor and replace it with the ubiquitous Init() method that returns success or failure, use exception handling as shown here.

```cpp
// A useful macro
#define SAFE_DELETE(p)        { if (p) { delete (p); (p)=NULL; } }

DataFiles::DataFiles()
{
    // Imagine some code up here…
    {
        // blah blah blah
    }
    if (somethingWentWrong)
    {
        // Throw anything you want, I'm throwing a custom class that
        // defines errors, so don't go looking in MSDN for the ErrorCode
        // class; it's something you would define yourself!
        throw ErrorCode(EC_DATAFILES_PROBLEM);
    }
}


DataFiles *gp_DataFiles = NULL;
AudioSystem *gp_AudioSystem = NULL;
VideoSystem *gp_VideoSystem = NULL;


int main(void)
{
    BOOL returnCode = 0;
```

```
try
{
    // initialize everything in this try block
    gp_DataFiles = new DataFiles;
    gp_AudioSystem = new AudioSystem;
    gp_VideoSystem = new VideoSystem;

    BOOL done = false;
    while (! done)
    {
        // imagine a cool main loop here
    }
}

catch(ErrorCode e)
{
    e.InformUser();    // ErrorCode can inform the user itself
    returnCode = 1;
}

SAFE_DELETE(gp_VideoSystem);        // AVOID DEADLOCK!!!
SAFE_DELETE(gp_AudioSystem);
SAFE_DELETE(gp_DataFiles);

return (returnCode);
}
```

That code is looking much nicer, and it's beginning to appeal to my sense of elegance. Any problem in initialization will throw an exception, jumping past the main loop entirely. The ErrorCode class, the design of which I'll leave as an exercise for the reader, simply reports the error back to the user in the best way possible, given what systems are up and running. Perhaps the only thing it can do is send a text string out to stdout, or maybe it can bring up a nice dialog box using your game's graphics. After the error is reported to the player, a useful macro frees the global objects that have been constructed. Finally, a return code is sent back to the operating system.

THE GAME'S APPLICATION LAYER

We're now ready to work our way through the initialization checklist. We'll create the class for your application layer, a very Win32-specific thing. The application layer would be completely rewritten for different operating systems, such as Linux or consoles like the Wii. The application layer class is instantiated as a global singleton object, and is referred to throughout your code through a pointer. It is constructed globally too, since it has to be there from the entry point to the program termination.

WinMain

The place where all Windows applications start is _tWinMain. I've decided to use the DirectX Framework for rendering, mostly because it handles all of the pain and suffering of dealing with running a DirectX-based application under Windows. Take a quick look at the code in one of the source files in the DirectX Framework, DXUT.cpp, sometime, and you'll see exactly what I mean! The following code can be found in *Source\GameCode.cpp*:

```
INT WINAPI wWinMain(HINSTANCE hInstance,
                    HINSTANCE hPrevInstance,
                    LPWSTR    lpCmdLine,
                    int       nCmdShow)
{
    // Set up checks for memory leaks.
    int tmpDbgFlag = _CrtSetDbgFlag(_CRTDBG_REPORT_FLAG);
    // always perform a leak check just before app exits.
    tmpDbgFlag |= _CRTDBG_LEAK_CHECK_DF;
    _CrtSetDbgFlag(tmpDbgFlag);

    DXUTSetCallbackD3D9DeviceCreated( GameCodeApp::OnCreateDevice );
    DXUTSetCallbackD3D9DeviceDestroyed( GameCodeApp::OnDestroyDevice );
    DXUTSetCallbackMsgProc( GameCodeApp::MsgProc );
    DXUTSetCallbackD3D9DeviceReset( GameCodeApp::OnResetDevice );
    DXUTSetCallbackD3D9DeviceLost( GameCodeApp::OnLostDevice );
    DXUTSetCallbackD3D9FrameRender( GameCodeApp::OnRender );
    DXUTSetCallbackFrameMove( GameCodeApp::OnUpdateGame );

    // Show the cursor and clip it when in full screen
    DXUTSetCursorSettings( true, true );

    // Perform application initialization
    if (!g_pApp->InitInstance (hInstance, lpCmdLine))
    {
        return FALSE;
    }

    DXUTMainLoop();
    DXUTShutdown();
```

```
//_CRTDBG_LEAK_CHECK_DF is used at program initialization
// to force a leak check just before program exit. This
// is important because some classes may dynamically
// allocate memory in globally constructed objects.
//
//_CrtDumpMemoryLeaks();    // Reports leaks to stderr

    return g_pApp->GetExitCode();
}
```

These calls to the DXUTSetCallbackEtc functions allow the DirectX Framework to notify the application about device changes, user input, and Windows messages. You should always handle the callbacks for device reset/lost, or your game won't be able to withstand things like fast user task switching under Windows.

The calls to the _CrtDumpMemory functions set up your game to detect memory leaks, something discussed at length in Chapter 21, "Debugging Your Game."

The global object to our game application is g_pApp. This points to a global object that stores the game's application layer. Let's take a look at the base class, GameCodeApp.

The Application Layer: GameCodeApp

The game's application layer handles operating system-specific tasks, including interfacing with the hardware and operating system, handling the application life cycle including initialization, managing access to localized strings, and initializing the game logic. This class is meant to be inherited by a game-specific application class that will extend it and define some game-specific things, such as title, but also implementations for creating the game logic and game views and loading the initial state of the game.

The class acts as a container for other important members that manage the application layer:

- A handle to the language DLL, m_LangDll, which contains nothing but a string resource so the game can easily be localized into other languages.
- A font handler, which uses the operating system to load fonts that can be rendered by the graphics system.
- The game logic implementation.
- A data structure that holds game options, usually read from an INI file.
- The resource cache, which is responsible for loading textures, meshes, and sounds from a resource file.
- The script manager, in this case, a LUA script manager.
- The main event manager, which allows all the different game subsystems to communicate with each other.
- The network communications manager.

All of these members are initialized in GameCodeApp::InitInstance().

InitInstance(): Checking System Resources

InitInstance():Checking System Resources is especially important for Windows games, but console developers don't get off scot-free. Permanent storage, whether it is a hard disk or a memory card, should be checked for enough space to store game data before the player begins. Windows and console games that support special hardware, like steering wheels or other input devices, must check for their existence and fall back to another option, like the gamepad, if nothing is found. System RAM and VRAM checks or calculating the CPU speed is clearly a job for the Windows programmer.

The code inside InitInstance is particularly sensitive to order, so be careful if you decide to change this method. You should also keep your exit code in sync, or rather reverse sync, with the order of initialization. Always release systems and resources in the reverse order in which you requested or created them.

Here's what this method does:

- Detects multiple instances of the application.
- Loads the language DLL.
- Checks secondary storage space, RAM, and VRAM.
- Parses command lines.
- Loads the game's resource cache.
- Creates the script state manager.
- Creates the game's event manager.
- Uses the script manager to load initial game options.
- Initializes DirectX and creates the window for the application.
- Creates the game logic and game views.
- Creates the display devices.

```
char const * const kpLangDllName = "Lang" APP_SUFX ".dll";

bool GameCodeApp::InitInstance(HINSTANCE hInstance, LPTSTR lpCmdLine)
{
    // Check for existing instance of the same window
    //
#ifndef _DEBUG
    // Note - it can be really useful to debug network code to have
    // more than one instance of the game up at one time - so
    // feel free to comment these lines in or out as you wish!
    if (!IsOnlyInstance(VGetGameTitle()))
        return false;
#endif

    // We don't need a mouse cursor by default, let the game turn it on
    SetCursor( NULL );
```

```
// Load the string table from the language resource dll
// Note: Only load it from same dir as exe ...
char appPath[MAX_PATH+1] = {0};

memset( appPath, 0, sizeof(appPath) );
GetModuleFileNameA( NULL, appPath, MAX_PATH );
char const * pSep = strrchr( appPath, _T('\\') );

if ( pSep == NULL )
   strcpy( appPath, kpLangDllName );
else
   strcpy( appPath + (pSep - appPath) + 1, kpLangDllName );

m_LangDll = LoadLibraryA(appPath);
if (!m_LangDll)
{
   TCHAR msg[4096];
   _stprintf( msg, _T("Error 6502: %s not found.\n"
"Please reinstall from your original CD."), kpLangDllName );
   MessageBox(NULL, msg, _T("Error 6502"), MB_OK);
   return false;
}

// Check for adequate machine resources.
bool resourceCheck = false;
while (!resourceCheck)
{
   try
   {
      const DWORD physicalRAM = 512 * MEGABYTE;
      const DWORD virtualRAM = 1024 * MEGABYTE;
      CheckMemory(physicalRAM, virtualRAM);

      const int diskSpace = 10 * MEGABYTE;
      CheckHardDisk(diskSpace);

      const int minCpuSpeed = 1300;    // 1.3Ghz
      extern int GetCPUSpeed();
      int thisCPU = GetCPUSpeed();
      if (thisCPU < minCpuSpeed)
         throw GameCodeError(GCERR_INIT_CPU_TOO_SLOW);
   }
```

```
      catch (GameCodeError err)
      {
         if (err.Handle()==ERROR_RETRY)
            continue;
         else
            return false;
      }

      resourceCheck = true;
}

m_hInstance = hInstance;

m_pOptions = new GameOptions("m_pOptions->ini");
ParseCommandLine(lpCmdLine);

// Initialize the Resource Cache
//
m_ResCache =
   new ResCache(30, new ResourceZipFile(_T("data\\GameCode3.zip")));
if (!m_ResCache->Init())
{
   return false;
}

// Rez up the Lua State manager now, and run the initial script.
m_pLuaStateManager = new LuaStateManager();
if (!m_pLuaStateManager)
{
   return false;
}

// event manager should be created next so that subsystems
// can hook in as desired.
m_pEventManager = new EventManager("GameCodeApp Event Mgr", true );
if (!m_pEventManager)
{
   return false;
}

// Now that the event manager and the Lua State manager
// are init'd, let's run the initialization file.
const bool bLuaInitSuccess =
   m_pLuaStateManager->Init( "data\\Scripts\\init.lua" );
```

```
if ( false == bLuaInitSuccess )
{
   return false;
}

if (!m_pOptions->m_gameHost.empty())
{
   ClientSocketManager *pClient =
      new ClientSocketManager(
         m_pOptions->m_gameHost, m_pOptions->m_listenPort);
   if (!pClient->Connect())
   {
      assert(0 && _T("Couldn't attach to game server."));
      return false;
   }
   m_pBaseSocketManager = pClient;
}
else if (m_pOptions->m_listenPort != -1)
{
   BaseSocketManager *pServer = new BaseSocketManager();
   if (!pServer->Init())
      return false;

   pServer->AddSocket(
      new GameServerListenSocket(m_pOptions->m_listenPort));
   m_pBaseSocketManager = pServer;
}

// Initialize the sample framework and create the Win32 window and
// Direct3D device for the application. Calling each of these
// functions is optional, but they allow you to set several options
// which control the behavior of the framework.

m_pDialogResourceManager = new CDXUTDialogResourceManager();
DXUTInit( true, true, lpCmdLine, true );

HICON icon = VGetIcon();
DXUTCreateWindow( VGetGameTitle(), hInstance, icon );
if (!GetHwnd())
{
   return FALSE;
}
SetWindowText(GetHwnd(), VGetGameTitle());
```

```
   // initialize game options - including finding the profiles directory
   _tcscpy(m_saveGameDirectory,
      GetSaveGameDirectory(GetHwnd(), VGetGameAppDirectory()));

   // You usually must have an HWND to initialize your game views...
   m_pGame = VCreateGameAndView();
   if (!m_pGame)
      return false;

   DXUTCreateDevice( true, SCREEN_WIDTH, SCREEN_HEIGHT );

   // initialize the font system
   m_pFontHandler = new FontHandler();

   m_bIsRunning = true;
   return TRUE;
}
```

As I mentioned before, this code is very sensitive to order. You have to make sure that everything is initialized before some other subsystem needs it to exist. Inevitably, you'll find yourself in a catch-22 situation, and you'll see that two subsystems depend on each other's existence. The way out is to create one in a hobbled state, initialize the other, and then notify the first that the other exists. It may seem a little weird, but you'll probably run into this more than once.

One thing you might notice is the try/catch loop around the resource checking code—this is a good thing for those Win32 apps that give the player a chance to free up some resources if the game needs them. Perhaps they'll just have to risk the boss walking in while they are playing the latest version of *World of Warcraft* with no Excel to hide the evidence.

The next sections tell you more about how to do these tasks and why each is important.

Checking for Multiple Instances of Your Game

If your game takes a moment to get around to creating a window, a player might get a little impatient and double-click the game's icon a few times. If you don't take the precaution of handling this problem, you'll find that users can quickly create a few dozen instances of your game, none of which will properly initialize. You should create a splash screen to help minimize this problem, but it's still a good idea to detect an existing instance of your game.

```
bool IsOnlyInstance(LPCTSTR gameTitle)
{
   // Find the window.  If active, set and return false
   // Only one game instance may have this mutex at a time...

   HANDLE handle = CreateMutex(NULL, TRUE, gameTitle);

   // Does anyone else think 'ERROR_SUCCESS' is a bit of a dichotomy?
   if (GetLastError() != ERROR_SUCCESS)
   {
      HWND hWnd = FindWindow(gameTitle, NULL);
      if (hWnd)
      {
         // An instance of your game is already running.
         ShowWindow(hWnd, SW_SHOWNORMAL);
         SetFocus(hWnd);
         SetForegroundWindow(hWnd);
         SetActiveWindow(hWnd);
         return false;
      }
   }
   return true;
}
```

The Win32 `CreateMutex()` API is used to gate only one instance of your game to the window detection code, the `FindWindow()` API. You call it with your game's title, which uniquely identifies your game. A mutex is a process synchronization mechanism and is common to any multitasking operating system. It is guaranteed to create one mutex with the identifier `gameTitle` for all processes running on the system. If it can't be created, then another process has already created it.

Checking Hard Drive Space

Most PC games need a bit of free hard disk space for saving games, caching data from the DVD-ROM drive, and other temporary needs. Here's a bit of code you can use to find out if your player has enough free space for those tasks:

```
void CheckHardDisk(const DWORDLONG diskSpaceNeeded)
{
   // Check for enough free disk space on the current disk.
   int const drive = _getdrive();
   struct _diskfree_t diskfree;

   _getdiskfree(drive, &diskfree);
```

```
unsigned __int64 const neededClusters =
  diskSpaceNeeded /
  ( diskfree.sectors_per_cluster * diskfree.bytes_per_sector );

if (diskfree.avail_clusters < neededClusters)
{
  // if you get here you don't have enough disk space!
  throw GameCodeError(GCERR_INIT_NOT_ENOUGH_DISK_SPACE);
}
}
```

If you want to check free disk space, you'll use the _getdrive() and _getdisk-free() utility functions, which work on any ANSI-compatible system. The return value from the _getdiskfree() function is in clusters, not in bytes, so you have to do a little math on the results.

Checking Memory

Checking for system RAM under Windows is a little trickier; sadly, you need to leave ANSI compatibility behind. You should check the total physical memory installed, as well as the available virtual memory, using Win32 calls. Virtual memory is a great thing to have on your side as long as you use it wisely. You can think of it as having a near infinite bank account, with a very slow bank. If your game uses virtual memory in the wrong way, it will slow to a crawl. You might as well grab a pencil and sketch a storyboard of the next few minutes of your game; you'll see it faster.

```
void CheckMemory(
  const DWORDLONG physicalRAMNeeded, const DWORDLONG virtualRAMNeeded)
{
  MEMORYSTATUSEX status;
  GlobalMemoryStatusEx(&status);
  if (status.ullTotalPhys < (physicalRAMNeeded))
  {
    // you don't have enough physical memory. Tell the player to go get a
    // real computer and give this one to his mother.
    throw GameCodeError(GCERR_INIT_NOT_ENOUGH_PHYS_RAM);
  }

  // Check for enough free memory.
  if (status.ullAvailVirtual < virtualRAMNeeded)
  {
    // you don't have enough virtual memory available.
    // Tell the player to shut down the copy of Visual Studio running in the
    // background, or whatever seems to be sucking the memory dry.
```

```
      throw GameCodeError(GCERR_INIT_NOT_ENOUGH_VIRT_RAM);
   }

   char *buff = GCC_NEW char[virtualRAMNeeded];
   if (buff)
      delete[] buff;
   else
   {
      // The system lied to you. When you attempted to grab a block as big
      // as you need the system failed to do so. Something else is eating
      // memory in the background; tell them to shut down all other apps
      // and concentrate on your game.

      throw GameCodeError(GCERR_INIT_NOT_ENOUGH_CONTIG_RAM);
   }
}
```

This function relies on the `GlobalMemoryStatusEx()` function, which returns the current state of the physical and virtual memory system. In addition to that, this function allocates and immediately releases a huge block of memory. This has the effect of making Windows clean up any garbage that has accumulated in the memory manager, and double-checks that you can allocate a contiguous block as large as you need. If the call succeeds, you've essentially run the equivalent of a Zamboni machine through your system's memory, getting it ready for your game to hit the ice. Console programmers should nuke that bit of code—it simply isn't needed in a system that only runs one application at a time.

Calculating CPU Speed

You'd think that grabbing the CPU speed from a Wintel box would be as easy as reading the system information. There's a great bit of code written by Michael Lyons at Microsoft that does the job nicely.

```
#define SLEEPTIME 0

//========================================================================
// define static variables
//========================================================================
static int    s_milliseconds;
static __int64    s_ticks;

static int    s_milliseconds0;
static __int64    s_ticks0;
```

```
//==========================================================================
// StartTimingCPU
//
// Call this function to start timing the CPU. It takes the CPU tick
// count and the current time and stores it. Then, while you do other
// things, and the OS task switches, the counters continue to count, and
// when you call UpdateCPUTime, the measured speed is accurate.
//
//==========================================================================
int StartTimingCPU()
{
   //
   // detect ability to get info
   //
   __asm
   {
      pushfd                     ; push extended flags
      pop       eax              ; store eflags into eax
      mov       ebx, eax         ; save EBX for testing later
      xor       eax, (1<<21)     ; switch bit 21
      push      eax              ; push eflags
      popfd                      ; pop them again
      pushfd                     ; push extended flags
      pop       eax              ; store eflags into eax
      cmp       eax, ebx         ; see if bit 21 has changed
      jz        no_cpuid         ; make sure it's now on
   }

   //
   // make ourselves high priority just for the time between
   // when we measure the time and the CPU ticks
   //
   DWORD dwPriorityClass = GetPriorityClass(GetCurrentProcess());
   int dwThreadPriority = GetThreadPriority(GetCurrentThread());
   SetPriorityClass(GetCurrentProcess(), REALTIME_PRIORITY_CLASS);
   SetThreadPriority(GetCurrentThread(), THREAD_PRIORITY_TIME_CRITICAL);

   //
   // start timing
   //
   s_milliseconds0 = (int)timeGetTime();
```

```
    __asm
    {
        lea       ecx, s_ticks0         ; get the offset
        mov       dword ptr [ecx], 0    ; zero the memory
        mov       dword ptr [ecx+4], 0  ;
        rdtsc                           ; read time-stamp counter
        mov       [ecx], eax            ; store the negative
        mov       [ecx+4], edx          ; in the variable
    }

    //
    // restore thread priority
    //
    SetThreadPriority(GetCurrentThread(), dwThreadPriority);
    SetPriorityClass(GetCurrentProcess(), dwPriorityClass);

    return 0;

no_cpuid:
    return -1;
}


//==========================================================================
// UpdateCPUTime
//
// This function stops timing the CPU by adjusting the timers to account
// for the amount of elapsed time and the number of CPU cycles taked
// during the timing period.
//==========================================================================
void UpdateCPUTime()
{
    //
    // make ourselves high priority just for the time between
    // when we measure the time and the CPU ticks
    //
    DWORD dwPriorityClass = GetPriorityClass(GetCurrentProcess());
    int dwThreadPriority = GetThreadPriority(GetCurrentThread());
    SetPriorityClass(GetCurrentProcess(), REALTIME_PRIORITY_CLASS);
    SetThreadPriority(GetCurrentThread(), THREAD_PRIORITY_TIME_CRITICAL);

    //
    // get the times
    //
```

```
    s_milliseconds   = -s_milliseconds0;
    s_ticks          = -s_ticks0;

    s_milliseconds   += (int)timeGetTime();

    __asm
    {
       lea      ecx, s_ticks       ; get the offset
       rdtsc                       ; read time-stamp counter
       add      [ecx], eax         ; add the tick count
       adc      [ecx+4], edx       ;
    }

    //
    // restore thread priority
    //
    SetThreadPriority(GetCurrentThread(), dwThreadPriority);
    SetPriorityClass(GetCurrentProcess(), dwPriorityClass);

    return;
}


//==========================================================================
// CalcCPUSpeed
//
// This function takes the measured values and returns a speed that
// represents a common possible CPU speed.
//==========================================================================
int CalcCPUSpeed()
{
    //
    // get the actual cpu speed in MHz, and
    // then find the one in the CPU speed list
    // that is closest
    //
    const struct tagCPUSPEEDS
    {
       float    fSpeed;
       int      iSpeed;
    } cpu_speeds[] =
    {
       //
       // valid CPU speeds that are not integrally divisible by
       // 16.67 MHz
       //
```

```
      {  60.00f,     60 },
      {  75.00f,     75 },
      {  90.00f,     90 },
      { 120.00f,    120 },
      { 180.00f,    180 },
};

//
// find the closest one
//
float   fSpeed=((float)s_ticks)/((float)s_milliseconds*1000.0f);
int   iSpeed=cpu_speeds[0].iSpeed;
float   fDiff=(float)fabs(fSpeed-cpu_speeds[0].fSpeed);

for (int i=1 ; i<sizeof(cpu_speeds)/sizeof(cpu_speeds[0]) ; i++)
{
    float fTmpDiff = (float)fabs(fSpeed-cpu_speeds[i].fSpeed);

    if (fTmpDiff < fDiff)
    {
        iSpeed=cpu_speeds[i].iSpeed;
        fDiff=fTmpDiff;
    }
}

//
// now, calculate the nearest multiple of fIncr
// speed
//

//
// now, if the closest one is not within one incr, calculate
// the nearest multiple of fIncr speed and see if that's
// closer
//
const float fIncr=16.6666666666666666666667f;
const int iIncr=4267; // fIncr << 8

//if (fDiff > fIncr)
{
    //
    // get the number of fIncr quantums the speed is
    //
```

```
    int   iQuantums   = (int)((fSpeed / fIncr) + 0.5f);
    float  fQuantumSpeed  = (float)iQuantums * fIncr;
    float  fTmpDiff   = (float)fabs(fQuantumSpeed - fSpeed);

    if (fTmpDiff < fDiff)
    {
            iSpeed = (iQuantums * iIncr) >> 8;
       fDiff=fTmpDiff;
    }
  }

  return iSpeed;
}


//===========================================================================
// GetCPUSpeed
//
// Gets the CPU speed by timing it for 1 second.
//===========================================================================
int GetCPUSpeed()
{
   static int CPU_SPEED = 0;

   if(CPU_SPEED!=0)
   {
      //This will assure that the 0.5 second delay happens only once
      return CPU_SPEED;
   }

   if (StartTimingCPU())
      return 0;

   //This will lock the application for 1 second
   do
   {
      UpdateCPUTime();
      Sleep(SLEEPTIME);
   } while (s_milliseconds < 1000);

   CPU_SPEED = CalcCPUSpeed();
   return CPU_SPEED;
}
```

The only thing you have to do is call `GetCPUSpeed()`. The first call will start the timer, which takes a few seconds to run. The longer it runs, the more accurate the timing, but there's no reason to run it any longer than two seconds, and one second will provide a pretty accurate count. You can use the results of this calculation to turn off certain CPU-sucking activities like decompressing MP3 files or drawing detailed animations. It's not completely crazy to save the value in a game options setting, so you don't have to calculate it each time your game runs.

What About Estimating VRAM?

There are now five different ways to grab the amount of video memory on your system. What is making this more complicated is that some video cards can access memory on the motherboard, called *shared memory*. This memory is usually accessed at a slower rate than dedicated video memory. Sometimes, the shared memory is counted as video memory, which might not be what you want. The following APIs are available to any system running Windows XP or later:

- DirectX 7's `GetAvailableVidMem()`: Usually gives good results, but can sometimes give you wrong results on cards that can use shared memory.
- Windows Management Interface (WMI): Gives similar results to the DirectX 7 call.
- DxDiag: Uses both DirectX 7 and WMI to give you a better result than either would alone.
- D3D9's `GetAvailableTextureMemory()`: Gives you the total amount of texture memory, which might include shared memory and won't count any VRAM already used by textures and display surfaces.

Depressing, isn't it? It's almost like someone at Microsoft just doesn't want us to find out easily how much memory is on the video card.

The last method is only available to users of Windows Vista or later operating systems. It uses the `CreateDXGIFactory` API, which you must call via `GetProcAddress()`. It will return the amount of dedicated VRAM, the amount of shared memory available, and the amount of dedicated system memory. It is the best of the 4 methods, but it is not available on XP.

All of these methods are implemented in a DirectX Sample called *VideoMemory* if you have the March 2008 drop of DirectX or later.

Do You Have a Dirtbag on Your Hands?

If you are lucky (or probably unlucky) enough to be working on a mass-market title, you have to support computers that should really be at the business end of a boat's anchor chain. Everyone wants a game to look really good, but when you have to support machines that have only 15 percent of the CPU speed as the top-end rigs, then something has to give. Choose a benchmark for your game that makes sense to determine what makes a computer a dirtbag and what doesn't. Whatever you use, it is important to set your standards and determine if the computer the player is using is at the shallow end of the wading pool.

WHAT TO DO WITH YOUR DIRTBAG

Once you figure out what computer is at the bottom end, you should set your game defaults for new players accordingly. A good start would be to turn off any CPU-intensive activities like decompressing MP3 streams, scaling back skeletal detail, animations, and physics, or reducing the cycles you spend on AI. If the player decides to bring up the options screen and turn some of these features back on, my suggestion is to let him do it if it's possible. Maybe he'll be inclined to retire his old machine.

Initialize Your Resource Cache

I covered general memory management in Chapter 3 and resource caching is covered in Chapter 7, "Loading and Caching Game Data." Initializing the resource cache will be a gateway to getting your game data from the media into memory. The size of your resource cache is totally up to your game design and the bottom-end hardware you intend to support. It's a good idea to figure out if your player's computer is a dirtbag or flamethrower and set your resource cache memory accordingly.

NO ROOM EVEN FOR THE BASICS?

You can't impress a player with fantastic graphics until you reserve a nice spot in system and video memory for your textures, models, and animations. If your resource cache allocation fails, you can't even bring up a nice dialog box telling a loser player they are low on memory. The game should fail as elegantly as possible, and maybe print out a coupon for some memory sticks.

In this book, we'll use Zip files to store game resources. It's reasonably speedy, especially if no decompression is necessary. In the `InitInstance()` function you saw the following line:

```
new ResCache(30, new ResourceZipFile(_T("data\\GameCode3.zip")));
```

This creates the `ResCache` object and initializes the resource cache to 30 megabytes. It also creates an object that implements the `IResource` interface.

Choosing the size of your resource cache has everything to do with what kind of computer you expect your players to have. Players of the latest game from Crytek are going to have way more memory than my mother-in-law's computer—an old laptop I gave her about four years ago. After you choose the size of your cache, you should be cautious about how that memory is being used as you stuff in more textures, sounds, animations, and everything else. Once you run out, your game will stop performing like it should as it suffers cache misses. Console programmers have a harsher climate—if they run one byte over, their game will simply crash.

Your Script Manager and the Events System

The next section of the initialization sequence creates the script parser and event system. The *Game Coding Complete* source code uses Lua, which is popular and fairly easy to learn.

```
m_pLuaStateManager = new LuaStateManager();
   m_pEventManager = new EventManager("GameCodeApp Event Mgr", true );
   const bool bLuaInitSuccess;
bLuaInitSuccess = m_pLuaStateManager->Init( "data\\Scripts\\init.lua" );
```

Once it is created, you could actually use a Lua initialization script to control the rest of the initialization sequence. This can be a fantastic idea, as the script doesn't add very much additional time to the initialization sequence. What the programmer gets in return is the capability to change the initialization sequence without recompiling the game. The only other way to do this would be to throw some crazy options on the command line, which can be unwieldy, even in a trivial case. A Lua script has control mechanisms for evaluating expressions and looping—something you'll come to enjoy very quickly.

Initialize DirectX and Create Your Window

Win32 programmers can't put off the task of creating their window any longer. Creating a game window is easy enough, especially since the DirectX Framework does the whole thing for you. Here's the code that does this job inside InitInstance:

```
m_pDialogResourceManager = GCC_NEW CDXUTDialogResourceManager();
DXUTInit( true, true, lpCmdLine, true );
DXUTCreateWindow( VGetGameTitle(), hInstance, VGetIcon());
if (!GetHwnd())
{
   return FALSE;
}
SetWindowText(GetHwnd(), VGetGameTitle());
```

The dialog resource manager is a DirectX Framework object that manages user interface controls like buttons and sliders. If you are rolling your own user interface, you don't need it. Notice the calls to the virtual methods `VGetGameTitle()` and `VGetIcon()`. They are overloaded to provide this game-specific information to the `GameCodeApp` base class. You'll see exactly how to do this in Chapter 19, when we create a game of *Teapot Wars* with this code.

Create Your Game Logic and Game View

After the game window is ready, you can create the game logic and all the views that attach to the game logic. This is done by calling `VCreateGameAndView()`, which is a pure virtual function in the `GameCodeApp` class. Here's an example of what it might look like in the inherited class:

```
BaseGame *BreakoutGameApp::VCreateGameAndView()
{
   BaseGame *game = NULL;
   game = new TeapotWarsGame(*m_pOptions);
   shared_ptr<IGameView> gameView(GCC_NEW TeapotWarsGameView());
   game->VAddView(gameView);

   return game;
}
```

Create the DirectX D3D Device

This is one of those catch-22 initialization problems—the game device needs to exist before you load your game because loading the game will likely require the device. This is certainly true if you call into any DirectX methods for loading meshes and whatnot.

If you are using the DirectX Framework, you can create your device with this single line of code:

```
DXUTCreateDevice( true, SCREEN_WIDTH, SCREEN_HEIGHT );
```

Load Your User Options and Save Game

Finding the right directory for user-settable game options used to be easy. A programmer would simply store user data files close to the EXE and use the `GetModuleFileName` API. Starting with Windows XP Home, the `Program Files` directory is off limits by default, and applications are not allowed to write directly to this directory tree. Instead, applications must write user data to the *C:\Documents and Settings\{User name}\Application Data* directory for XP and *C:\Users\{User*

Name}\Application Data directory for Vista. Not only can this directory be completely different from one version of Windows to another, but some users store these on a drive other than the C: drive. You can use a special API to deal with this problem: SHGetSpecialFolderPath(). Windows XP Pro is more forgiving, and doesn't limit access to these directories by default. XP Home was designed this way to keep the casual, home user from stomping though the Program Files directory in a ham-fisted attempt to solve various problems.

If it were that easy, I wouldn't have to show you the next code block. If you open Windows Explorer to your application data directory, you'll see plenty of companies who play by the rules, writing application data in the spot that will keep Windows XP from freaking out. Usually, a software developer will create a hierarchy, starting with their company name, maybe adding their division, then the product, and finally the version. A Microsoft product I worked on used this path:

```
GAME_APP_DIRECTORY = "Microsoft\\Microsoft Games\\Bicycle Casino\\2.0";
```

GAME_APP_DIRECTORY = YOUR REGISTRY KEY

The value for your GAME_APP_DIRECTORY *is also a great value for a registry key. Don't forget to add the version number at the end. You might as well hope for a gravy train: 2.0, 3.0, 4.0, and so on.*

It's up to you to make sure you create the directory if it doesn't exist. This can be a hassle, since you have to walk down the directory tree, creating all the way down:

```
const TCHAR *GetSaveGameDirectory(HWND hWnd, const TCHAR *gameAppDirectory)
{
   HRESULT hr;

   static TCHAR m_SaveGameDirectory[MAX_PATH];
   TCHAR userDataPath[MAX_PATH];

   hr = SHGetSpecialFolderPath(hWnd, userDataPath, CSIDL_APPDATA, true);

   _tcscpy_s(m_SaveGameDirectory, userDataPath);
   _tcscat_s(m_SaveGameDirectory, _T("\\"));
   _tcscat_s(m_SaveGameDirectory, gameAppDirectory);

   // Does our directory exist?
   if (0xffffffff == GetFileAttributes(m_SaveGameDirectory))
   {
```

```
// Nope - we have to go make a new directory to store application data.
//
// On Win32 systems you could call SHCreateDirectoryEx to create an
// entire directory tree, but this code is included for ease of
// portability to other systems without that.
//
//
TCHAR current[MAX_PATH];
TCHAR myAppData[MAX_PATH];

_tcscpy_s(current, userDataPath);
_tcscpy_s(myAppData, gameAppDirectory);

TCHAR token[MAX_PATH];
token[0] = 0;

do {
   TCHAR *left = _tcschr(myAppData, '\\');
   if (left==NULL)
   {
      _tcscpy_s(token, myAppData);
      myAppData[0] = 0;
   }
   else
   {
      _tcsncpy_s(token, myAppData, left-myAppData);
      token[left-myAppData] = 0;
      _tcscpy_s(myAppData, left+1);
   }

   if (_tcslen(token))
   {
      _tcscat_s(current, _T("\\"));
      _tcscat_s(current, token);
      if (false == CreateDirectory(current, NULL))
      {
         int error = GetLastError();
         if (error != ERROR_ALREADY_EXISTS)
         {
            return false;
         }
      }
   }
}
```

```
        } while (_tcslen(myAppData));
    }

    _tcscat_s(m_SaveGameDirectory, _T("\\"));
    return m_SaveGameDirectory;
}
```

This code parses each element of the directory path, and for each one, it will make sure each subdirectory exists using `GetFileAttributes()`. If any directory needs to be created, `CreateDirectory()` is called. On Win32 systems, you can also shorten this code by calling `SHCreateDirectoryEx()`, which can create a directory tree. I've left the old school system in there for those of you who might have to port this code—every little bet helps. Finally, the value of `m_SaveGameDirectory` is set to the name of that directory—drive letter and all, and then returned to the calling function.

DEVELOPERS HAVE DIFFERENT NEEDS THAN YOUR PLAYERS

Make sure that you have two different game options files—one for users and one for developers. For example, it can be very convenient to have some way to override the full-screen option in the user settings to open in windowed mode for a debug session. Debugging a full screen application with a single monitor is sure to send you on a killing spree.

STICK THE LANDING: A NICE CLEAN EXIT

Your game won't run forever. Even the best games will take a back seat to food and water, regardless of what Microsoft's XBox ads seem to imply. There may be a temptation to simply call `exit(0)` and be done with it. This isn't a wise choice because your DirectX drivers might be left in a bad state, and it can be difficult to tell if your game is leaking resources.

DirectX drivers sometimes handle hard exits badly, causing your video card to be in a state that might require a reboot to restart your game. Rebooting used to be a normal thing, and every gamer was used to multiple reboots every day, but those days are long gone. Players who find that your game requires a reboot after they're done will get pretty annoyed, and most likely will return your game. If you don't have a decent exit mechanism, you'll also find it impossible to determine where your game is leaking memory or other resources. After all, a hard exit is basically a huge memory leak. A tight exit mechanism will show you a single byte of leaked memory before returning control to the operating system. This is important for all games, Win32 or console.

ALWAYS FIX LEAKS, FAST

Games should never leak memory. Period. The reality of it is that some Win32 calls leak re-sources, and you just have to live with it. That's no reason your game code should be sloppy; hold yourself to a higher standard, and you won't get a reputation for crappy software.

How Do I Get Out of Here?

There are two ways to stop a game from executing without yanking the power or causing some kind of exception:

- The player quits the game on purpose.
- The system shuts the application down (Win32).

If the player chooses to stop playing, the first thing you should do is ask the player if he or she wants to save their game. The last thing someone needs is to lose six hours of progress only to hit the wrong button by accident. One standard detects if the current state of the game has changed since the last time the user saved, and only if the state is different does the system ask if the player wants to save his or her game. It is equally annoying to save your game, select quit, and have the idiot application ask if the game needs saving all over again.

Console programmers can stop here and simply run their exit code, destroy-ing all the game systems generally in the reverse order in which they were cre-ated. Windows programmers, as usual, don't get off nearly that easy.

When the Win32 OS decides your game has to shut down, it sends a different message. Win32 apps should intercept the WM_SYSCOMMAND message and look for SC_CLOSE in the wParam. This is what Win32 sends to applications that are being closed, perhaps against their will. This can happen if the machine is shut down or if the player hits Alt-F4.

The problem with this message is that Alt-F4 should act just like your normal exit, asking you if you want to quit. If you can save to a temporary location and load that state the next time the player starts, your players will thank you. Most likely, they were just getting to the boss encounter and the batteries on their lap-top finally ran out of motivated electrons.

You have to double-check for multiple entries into this code with a Boolean variable. If your players hit Alt-F4 and bring up a dialog box in your game asking if they want to quit, nothing is keeping them from hitting Alt-F4 again. If your players are like the folks at Microsoft's test labs, they'll hit it about 50 times. Your game is still pumping messages, so the WM_SYSCOMMAND will get through every time a player presses Alt-F4. Make sure you handle that by filtering it out.

If your game is minimized, you have to do something to catch the player's attention. If your game runs in full-screen mode and you've tabbed away to another app, your game will act just as if it is minimized. If your player uses the system menu by right-clicking on the game in the start bar, your game should exhibit standard Windows behavior and flash. This is what well-behaved Windows applications do when they are minimized but require some attention from a human being.

```
void GameCodeApp::FlashWhileMinimized()
{
   // Flash the application on the taskbar
   // until it's restored.
   if ( ! GetHwnd() )
      return;

   // Blink the application if we are minimized,
   // waiting until we are no longer minimized
   if (IsIconic(GetHwnd()) )
   {
      // Make sure the app is up when creating a new screen
      // this should be the case most of the time, but when
      // we close the app down, minimized, and a confirmation
      // dialog appears, we need to restore
      DWORD now = timeGetTime();
      DWORD then = now;
      MSG msg;

      FlashWindow( GetHwnd(), true );

      for (;;)
      {
         if ( PeekMessage( &msg, NULL, 0, 0, 0 ) )
         {
            if ( msg.message != WM_SYSCOMMAND || msg.wParam != SC_CLOSE )
            {
               TranslateMessage(&msg);
               DispatchMessage(&msg);
            }

            // Are we done?
            if ( ! IsIconic(GetHwnd()) )
            {
               FlashWindow( GetHwnd(), false );
               break;
            }
         }
         else
```

```
        {
            now = timeGetTime();
            DWORD timeSpan = now > then ? (now - then) : (then - now);
            if ( timeSpan > 1000 )
            {
                then = now;
                FlashWindow( GetHwnd(), true );
            }
        }
    }
  }
}
```

Doing this is a little tricky. You basically have to run your own message pump in a tight loop and swallow the WM_SYSCOMMAND/SC_CLOSE messages until your game isn't minimized anymore, all the while calling FlashWindow() at regular time intervals.

Forcing Modal Dialog Boxes to Close

When your game is closed by something external, such as a power down or selecting "End Process" in the Windows Task Manager, you might have some tricky cleanup to do if you are inside one of your modal dialogs we'll be discussing in Chapter 8, "Programming Input Devices." Since you are running a special version of the message pump, the "real" message pump won't get the message.

The solution lies in forcing the modal dialog to close with its default answer and then resending the WM_SYSCOMMAND with the SC_CLOSE parameter back into the message pump. If you happen to have nested dialogs up, this will still work because each dialog will get a forced close, until the normal message pump can process the close message.

Here's the pseudo-code for the code inside the SC_CLOSE message handler:

```
If (you want to prompt the user)
{
    If (m_bQuitRequested)
        Return early — user is spamming Alt-F4

    Set your m_bQuitRequested = true
    Call the model dialog box: "Are you sure you want to quit?"
    If (user said no)
    {
        Abort the quit request — return here.
    }
}
```

```
// By here we are quitting the game, by request or by force.
Set you m_bQutting = true
If (a modal dialog box is up)
{
    Force the dialog to close with a default answer
    Repost the WM_SYSCOMMAND message again to close the game
    Set m_bQuitRequested = false
}
```

You'll want to take a closer look at the source code to see more, but this code will allow the game to bring up a quit dialog even if the player hits Alt-F4 or another app, like an install program, and attempts to shut down your game by force.

Shutting Down the Game

With some exceptions, you should shut down or deallocate game systems in the reverse order of which they were created. This is a good rule of thumb to use whenever you are grabbing and releasing multiple resources that depend on each other. Each data structure should be traversed and freed. Take care that any code that is run inside destructors has the resources it needs to properly execute. It's pretty easy to imagine a situation where the careless programmer has uninitialized something in the wrong order and a destructor somewhere fails catastrophically. Be extremely aware of your dependencies, and where multiple dependencies exist, lean on a reference counting mechanism to hold on to resources until they really aren't needed anymore.

The message pump, GameCodeApp::MsgProc, will receive a WM_CLOSE message when it is time for you to shut down your game, and you'll handle it by calling the nonstatic GameCodeApp::OnClose method:

```
case WM_CLOSE:
{
    result = g_pApp->OnClose();
    break;
}
```

The application layer will delete things in the reverse order in which they were created. The creation order was resource cache first, the game window second, and the game logic object third. We'll release them in the reverse order.

```
LRESULT GameCodeApp::OnClose()
{
    // release all the game systems in reverse order from which they were
    // created
```

```
    SAFE_DELETE(m_pGame);
    SAFE_DELETE(m_pFontHandler);
    DestroyWindow(GetHwnd());
    SAFE_DELETE(m_pBaseSocketManager);
    SAFE_DELETE(m_pEventManager);
    SAFE_DELETE(m_pLuaStateManager);
    SAFE_DELETE(m_ResCache);
    SAFE_DELETE(m_pOptions);
    return 0;
}
```

If you extended the GameCodeApp application layer into your own class, you'll want to do exactly the same thing with the custom objects there and release them in the reverse order. When the game logic is deleted, it will run a destructor that releases its objects, including its process manager and all the views attached to it.

After the WM_CLOSE message is processed, the main message pump exits and control will eventually return to the WinMain function, which calls DXUTShutdown() to release the DirectX Framework.

What About Consoles?

This book has a decidedly Windows bent, mostly because most of you out there use Windows as your programming platform. But that doesn't mean you can't be exposed to some discussion about how to perform certain tasks with the constraints imposed by console platforms—and shutdown is no exception.

Consoles run one program at a time, and essentially don't have to worry about being left in a weird state. The shutdown solution used on *Thief: Deadly Shadows* could have been documented in a single page—we simply rebooted the machine. Is this a good idea or not?

From the player's point of view, it's a great idea. Shutdown doesn't have to take any time whatsoever, simply unrolling the data structures and cleaning up allocated memory. It just exits—and BAM—you are back to the launch window.

From a programmer's point of view, it is easier, but you don't have to clean up your mess, so to speak. A lazy programmer can create systems that are so entangled they can't be torn down in an orderly manner, and that's clearly a bad thing. If something can't be torn down during runtime, you have no choice but to allow it to exist whether it is being actively used or not, and console resources are so tight you still want every byte.

I propose a dual solution—the release build should reboot, exit the game all at once, and take as little time as possible. This is for the player's convenience. The debug build should attempt a clean exit, and any problems with a clean exit should be addressed before they become a cancer in the rest of your system.

GETTING IN AND GETTING OUT

Games have a lot of moving parts and use every bit of hardware in the system. Getting all the green lights turned on in the right order can be a real pain, as you saw in initialization. It's really easy to have dependent systems, so much so that you have "chicken and egg" problems—where more than one system has to be first in the initialization chain. I don't think I've ever worked on a game where we didn't have to hack something horribly to make initialization work correctly. Start with a good organization and hopefully your problems in this area will be minimal at best.

Shutting down cleanly is critical under Windows, not only to make sure system resources like video memory are released, but it also helps the engineering team to know that the underlying technologies can be torn down in an orderly manner. It doesn't guarantee good technology, but it is a good sign of clean code.

Now you have a good grounding in the wrapper for your game—getting in and getting back out again. The next chapter discusses the main loop for your game: reading input, processing game logic, and watching it all happen with a view.

CONTROLLING THE MAIN LOOP

In This Chapter

- Inside the Main Loop
- A Base Class for Game Actors and Game Logic
- Can I Make a Game Yet?

As you learned in Chapter 5, "Game Initialization and Shutdown," initialization brings your game's application layer and many of the subsystems online. In this chapter, you'll learn about the main loop. It accepts and translates user input, changes the game state, and renders the game state until the loop is broken. This loop is broken by a user input or some kind of failure. When the main loop exits, your game shuts down.

The code in this chapter is written to integrate with the DirectX Framework, which handles many nasty problems, such as detecting when a player switches screen resolutions or Alt-Tabs to another full-screen application. If you code on other platforms, you'll likely be spared these issues. Windows can run multiple applications simultaneously, and the user can change hardware configurations, like screen size, while your game is running. On consoles you can't do that, and you avoid all of those hellish little problems.

In this chapter, you'll also see a neat system to control hundreds of independent game tasks that need a little CPU time every game loop—everything from AI to sound effects to button animations. It uses a light cooperative multitasker—technology that actually hearkens back before Windows 3.1, but it's an elegant and simple solution to a tricky problem in game programming. This simple version doesn't handle preemptive multitasking; you'll get a chance to learn all about that in Chapter 18, "Introduction to Multicore Programming." Walk first, run later.

INSIDE THE MAIN LOOP

The main difference between games and most other applications is that games are constantly busy doing something in the background. Most Windows applications will do absolutely nothing until you move the mouse or mash keys on the keyboard. You can't even do that if you coded a game of chess (even the chess AI should be thinking in the background while the player thinks of his next move). The main loop of a game should accomplish two tasks until the player quits the game or deactivates the window:

- Update your game logic.
- Render and present the scene.

We'll start by taking an example of a classic Win32 message pump and build it up until it works for games. Taken straight from an old DirectX sample, the simplest game message pump looks like this:

```
while( msg.message!=WM_QUIT )
{
    if( PeekMessage( &msg, NULL, 0U, 0U, PM_REMOVE ) )
    {
```

```
        TranslateMessage( &msg );
        DispatchMessage( &msg );
    }
    else
        MyRender();
}
```

Assume for a moment that the `MyRender()` method does nothing more than render and present the frame. You'll also have to assume that any game logic update occurs only as a result of messages appearing in the message queue. The problem with this message pump is that if there are no messages in the queue, there's nothing in the code to change the game state. If you changed the game state only as a result of receiving messages, you would only see animations happen if you moved the mouse or Windows happened to send your application a message. Either way, you can't count on Windows to control the processing of your main loop; you want complete control over that.

Windows provides a message that seems like a good solution to this problem: `WM_TIMER`. This Win32 message can be sent at definite intervals. Using the Win32 `SetTimer()` API, you can cause your application to receive these `WM_TIMER` messages, or you can specify a callback function. For programmers like me who remember the old Windows 3.1 days, `WM_TIMER` was the only way games could get a semblance of background processing. Windows 3.1 was a cooperative multitasking system, which meant that the only way your application got CPU time was if it had a message to process and no other app was hogging the message pump. The biggest problem with using `WM_TIMER` is resolution. Even though you specify `WM_TIMER` calls down to the millisecond, the timer doesn't actually have millisecond accuracy, and you are not guaranteed to be called in the exact intervals your game will require.

Rendering and Presenting the Display

The DirectX 10 Framework provides a pretty good routine to render and present the display. It is called from the `DXUTMainLoop()` function when the game is not processing messages, in exactly the way the `MyRender()` function was mentioned in the previous chapter. The function is `DXUTRender3DEnvironment9()` inside *Source\DX10\DXUT.cpp*. Let's pick it apart so you can understand what's going on. Since I don't have permission to reprint this method, you should launch Visual Studio and load either a DirectX sample or the *Game Coding Complete* source code and follow along.

The first thing you should notice about this function is how much can go wrong, and that it can pretty much go wrong after nearly every single line of code. The reason for this is a quirk of Win32 games—players have an annoying tendency to actually have other applications up, like MSN Messenger or something, while playing your game! Any kind of task switching, or user switching under XP or Vista, can cause DirectX to lose its display surfaces or devices.

The first part calls `Sleep()` to relinquish time back to other applications if your game is minimized or not in focus; this is just part of being a nice Win32 application and even silly Win32 tools that have similar message pumps should do this. You might decide to tweak the amount of time you sleep. Your mileage with the sleep values in the framework could vary from game to game.

The next big section handles the situation where the device has been lost, which is what would happen if you set the desktop to a new bit depth. Since your game probably loaded all manner of textures and formatted them to run as fast as possible on the old bit depth, you'll probably have to reload all your textures. This is the reason why you see `VOnRestore()` calls all over the source code in this book; it separates the two tasks of creating the object in memory and formatting—or restoring—it for fast display.

After all that homework, the code handles issues related to timers and timing. This is the section of code that starts with `DXUTGetGlobalTimer()->GetTimeValues()`. Almost every game needs to track how many milliseconds have elapsed since the last frame so that animations and object movement can be kept in sync with reality. The alternative is to ignore time altogether and just render things based on each frame that renders, but that would mean that faster computers would literally play the game faster—not in the "gamer" sense but in an actual sense. If you keep track of time, then objects on faster computers will still fall to the ground at the same rate as slower computers, but the faster computers will look smooth as silk.

The next section of code retrieves and calls the application's frame move callback function. This callback is set to `GameCodeApp::OnUpdateGame()`, which controls the game logic and how the game state changes over each pass of the main loop. Control passes to the game logic's `VOnUpdate()` method, which will update all the running game processes and send updates to all the game views attached to the game logic.

The next bit of code retrieves and calls the application's frame render callback, which will call `VOnRender()` methods of views attached to the game. After the rendering is complete, the screen must be presented, which is when things can go awry. Back in the good old days, this was called "slamming" because the back buffer was copied byte-by-byte to the front buffer in one memory copy. Now this is handled by a simple pointer change in the video hardware, and is generally called "flipping" because nothing is really copied at all. If the call to `Present()` fails, the D3D device is considered lost and will have to be re-created.

After all that, the frame counter is updated, and a little status bit is checked to see if the game should exit after one frame. This is actually a quite handy thing to have, whether you write your own frame counter or use the one in the framework, because you can use it to smoke test your game. An amazing amount of code runs when you initialize, update, and render your game, and any problems during this process could be written out to a log file for later analysis. This is a great thing to do, and it can be an important part of a simple smoke test where you can be somewhat sure that the game can at least get to the first frame.

Your Callback Functions for Updating and Rendering

Luckily, the DirectX Framework has done most of the major work for you, even to the point of splitting updates in your game logic from the rendering of the game. This matches well with the architecture I'm pushing in this book. If you recall the _tWinMain() implementation from the previous chapter, among the code were these two calls:

```
DXUTSetCallbackD3D9FrameMove( GameCodeApp::OnUpdateGame );
DXUTSetCallbackD3D9FrameRender( GameCodeApp::OnRender );
```

The first is a callback where you can update your game, and the second is a callback where your game can render. Let's take a look at the implementation of those two methods:

```
void CALLBACK GameCodeApp::OnUpdateGame(
IDirect3DDevice9* pd3dDevice, double fTime, float fElapsedTime )
{
   if (g_pApp->HasModalDialog())
      // don't update the game if a modal dialog is up.
      return;

   if (g_pApp->m_bQuitting)
   {
      PostMessage(g_pApp->GetHwnd(), WM_CLOSE, 0, 0);
      return;
   }

   if (g_pApp->m_pGame)
   {
      // allow event queue to process for up to 20 ms
      safeTickEventManager( 20 );
      g_pApp->m_pGame->VOnUpdate(fTime, fElapsedTime);
   }
}
```

This method updates your game logic, but only if there isn't a modal dialog box up and if the application isn't quitting.

This code implies that you shouldn't perform any quit mechanism while you are pumping messages. Quitting takes a good amount of time, and a player worried about getting caught playing your game while he is supposed to be doing something else can press Alt-F4 to close your game about 20 times in a single second. If you send all those quit messages into the message pump, you've got to filter them out, which is why we check to see if we're actually quitting so we can post a `WM_CLOSE` message. The user interface control that receives the quit button click event or the hot key event should simply set a Boolean variable to true, which will be checked after the last message in the queue has been handled.

This function is a member of `GameCodeApp`, but since this method is a callback, it must be declared static, which means we have to use the global `g_pApp` pointer to get to the instance of the `GameCodeApp` class. The same is true for the `GameCodeApp::OnRender` call:

```
void CALLBACK GameCodeApp::OnRender(
    IDirect3DDevice9* pd3dDevice, double fTime, float fElapsedTime )
{
    BaseGame *pGame = g_pApp->m_pGame;
    for(GameViewList::iterator i=pGame->m_gameViews.begin(),
    end=pGame->m_gameViews.end(); i!=end; ++i)
    {
        (*i)->VOnRender(fTime, fElapsedTime);
    }
    g_pApp->m_pGame->VRenderDiagnostics();
}
```

This method simply iterates through all the views attached to the game logic, `g_pApp->m_pGame`, and calls `VOnRender()` for each one. After that, the game logic calls a special method for rendering debug information, `VRenderDiagnostics()`. This is a convenience for programmers who would rather not adhere to the separation between logic and view just to draw some debug lines on the screen.

A good example of how I use `VRenderDiagnostics()` is drawing physics information, such as mesh wireframe of any objects moving on the screen. The physics system is purely a game logic object, and the renderer really belongs to the game view. If you wanted to religiously follow the separation of game logic and game view, you'd have to do something like have the game logic create special "line" objects and send messages to the game view that it needs to draw these lines.

That's just dumb, in my opinion. A game logic should be able to use the application layer—in this case DirectX's renderer—to draw debug data onto the screen. Yes, it breaks the rules, but yes, you should do it.

Game Logic

Game logic could include AI, physics, character position and speed, and so on. Games tend to handle an enormous amount of seemingly autonomous entities that come to life, stomp around the game world, and die off. Each of these game objects can affect the life cycle of other objects, such as a missile colliding with and destroying an enemy vehicle, and itself. Back in the dark ages, circa 1991, each major subsystem of the game had a handler function:

```
void MyGame::VOnUpdate(float fTime, float fElapsedTime)
{
   CalculateAI(fElapsedTime);
   DetectTriggerFire(fElapsedTime);
   ReticulateSplines(fElapsedTime);
   RunPhysicsSimulation(fElapsedTime);
   MoveKinematicObjects(fElapsedTime);
   ProcessIncomingCommands(fElapsedTime);
}
```

Each of these subsystems was called in a simple linear fashion. The internals of each function were completely customized, but generally they manipulated lists of objects and ran some code on each one, sometimes changing the members of the lists in the process.

This design wasn't very flexible, and it got a little ugly. Perhaps the ReticulateSplines() call needs to happen at a different frequency than once per main loop. Back in the old days, you'd just call it more than once, in different places in the list. A more general system is required, one that is based on cooperative multitasking.

Cooperative multitasking is a mechanism where each process gets a little CPU time in a round-robin fashion. It's called *cooperative* because each process is responsible for releasing control back to the calling entity. If a process goes into an infinite loop, the entire system will hang. The trade-off for that weakness is that the system is simple to design and extremely efficient.

Imagine a simple base class called CProcess with a single virtual method, VOnUpdate():

```
class CProcess
{
public:
   virtual void VOnUpdate(const int deltaMilliseconds);
};
```

You could create objects inheriting from this class and stick them in a master process list. Every game loop, your code could traverse this list and call VOnUpdate() for each object:

```
typedef std::list<CProcess*> ProcessList;
ProcessList g_ProcessList;

void UpdateProcesses(int deltaMilliseconds)
{
   ProcessList::iterator i = m_ProcessList.begin();
   ProcessList::iterator end = m_ProcessList.end();
```

```
   while ( i != end )
   {
      CProcess* p = *i;
      p->VOnUpdate( deltaMilliseconds );
      ++i;
   }
}
```

The contents of the VOnUpdate() overload could be anything. It could move the object on a spline, it could monitor the contents of a buffer stream and update it accordingly, and it could run some AI code. It could monitor user interface objects like screens and buttons. If everything in your game was run by a process, you could actually get away with a main function that looked like this:

```
void main()
{
   if (CreateProcesses())
   {
      RunProcesses();
   }
   ShutdownProcesses();
}
```

It may sound crazy, but *Ultima VIII's* main looked almost exactly like that, give or take a few lines.

There are a few wrinkles to this wonderful design that you should know. If creating a system to handle your main loop were as easy as all that, I wouldn't bother devoting so much time to it. The first big problem comes when one process's VOnUpdate() can destroy other processes, or even worse cause a recursive call to indirectly cause itself to be destroyed. Think of the likely code for a hand grenade exploding. The VOnUpdate() would likely query the game object lists for every object in a certain range, and then cause all those objects to be destroyed in a nice fireball. The grenade object would be included in the list of objects in range, wouldn't it?

The solution to this problem involves some kind of reference counting system or maybe a smart pointer. The shared_ptr template class in Chapter 3, "Coding Tidbits and Style That Will Save You," solves this problem well, and it will be used in the next section.

A Simple Cooperative Multitasker

A good process class should contain some additional data members and methods to make it interesting and flexible. There are as many ways to create this class as there are programmers, but this should give you a good start. There are three classes in this nugget of code:

- shared_ptr: A smart pointer class from the Boost C++ library. This class was presented in Chapter 3. If you can't remember what a smart pointer is, you'd better go back now and review.
- class CProcess: A base class for processes. You'll inherit from this class and redefine the VOnUpdate() method.
- class CProcessManager: This is a container and manager for running all your cooperative processes.

Here's the definition for CProcess:

```cpp
class CProcess : boost::noncopyable
{
    friend class CProcessManager;

protected:
    int      m_iType;       // type of process running
    bool     m_bKill;        // tells manager to kill and remove
    bool     m_bActive;
    bool     m_bPaused;
    bool     m_bInitialUpdate;   // initial update?
    shared_ptr<CProcess>  m_pNext;   // dependant process

private:
    unsigned int    m_uProcessFlags;

public:
    CProcess(int ntype, unsigned int uOrder = 0);
    virtual ~CProcess();

public:
    bool IsDead(void) const { return(m_bKill);};

    int GetType(void) const { return(m_iType); };
    void SetType(const int t) { m_iType = t; };

    bool IsActive(void) const { return m_bActive; };
    void SetActive(const bool b) { m_bActive = b; };
    bool IsAttached()const;
    void SetAttached(const bool wantAttached);

    bool IsPaused(void) const { return m_bPaused; };
```

```
    bool IsInitialized()const { return ! m_bInitialUpdate; };

    shared_ptr<CProcess> const GetNext(void) const { return(m_pNext);}
    void SetNext(shared_ptr<CProcess> nnext);

    // Overloadables
    virtual void    VOnUpdate(const int deltaMilliseconds);
    virtual void    VOnInitialize(){};
    virtual void VKill();
    virtual void VTogglePause() {m_bPaused = !m_bPaused;}
};

inline void CProcess::VOnUpdate( const int deltaMilliseconds )
{
    if ( m_bInitialUpdate )
    {
        OnInitialize();
        m_bInitialUpdate = false;
    }
}
```

Most of the methods are self-explanatory. There are four virtual methods that you should overload. VOnInitialize() is where you will place any initialization code. It's a better practice to place initialization code here since you can actually mark the process dead before it even runs.

VOnUpdate() is the method that gets ticked each pass through the main loop, so this is where you'll actually make changes to whatever game object you are controlling, such as moving an elevator. If the process ends, such as when a door finishes opening, you'll call VKill() from within VOnUpdate(), which will mark the process dead. The CProcessManager class will handle all dead processes after all active processes have been handled. If you have any special bits of code that should run when the process is marked dead, you can overload VKill() and do it there.

The last overloadable method is VTogglePause(). This is overloadable so you can run custom code if the process is paused or restarted, such as you might do if the process is controlling a sound effect and you need to notify DirectSound.

Note the use of the shared_ptr class throughout. This is an excellent example of using smart pointers in a class that uses an STL list. Any reference to a shared_ptr <CProcess> object is managed by the smart pointer class, ensuring that the process object will remain in memory as long as there is a valid reference to it. The moment the last reference is cleared or reassigned, the process memory is finally freed. That's why the CProcessManager has a list of shared_ptr <CProcess> instead of a list of CProcess pointers.

One method that might need explanation is `SetNext()`. It sets a process dependency such that one process will wait for another to finish, which can be great for creating complicated sequences of events in code where one process would depend on another to complete before beginning. With `SetNext()` it is possible to create code that looks like this:

```
CWalkProcess *walk = new CWalkProcess(george, door);
CAnimProcess *openDoor = new CAnimProcess(OPEN_DOOR, avatar, door);
CAnimProcess *drawSword = new CAnimProcess(DRAW_WEAPON, avatar, sword);
CCombatProcess *goBerserk = CCombatProcess(BERSERK, avatar);

walk->SetNext(openDoor)->SetNext(drawSword)->SetNext(goBerserk);
processManager->Attach(walk);
```

This code begins a sequence of events that starts object George walking to the door, opening it, drawing his sword, and going berserk. This kind of system makes it very simple to "stage direct" and chain multiple processes to perform interesting actions on your game world.

A SERIOUSLY NASTY BUG ON *ULTIMA VIII*

One of the trickiest bugs I ever had to find had to do with a special kind of process in *Ultima VIII*. *Ultima VIII* processes could attach their `OnUpdate()` calls to a real-time interrupt, which was pretty cool. Animations and other events could happen smoothly without worrying about the exact CPU speed of the machine. The process table was getting corrupted somehow, and no one was sure how to find it as the bug occurred completely randomly—or so we thought. After tons of QA time and late nights, we eventually found that jumping from map to map made the problem happen relatively frequently. We were able to track the bug down to the code that removed processes from the main process list. It turned out that the real-time processes were accessing the process list at the same moment that the list was being changed. Thank goodness we weren't on multiple processors; we never would have found it.

Here is the definition of the `CProcessManager` class:

```
// ProcessList is a list of smart CProcess pointers.
typedef std::list<shared_ptr<CProcess> > ProcessList;
```

```
class CProcessManager
{
public:
    // call this to attach a process to the process manager
    void Attach( shared_ptr<CProcess> pProcess );

    bool HasProcesses();
    bool IsProcessActive( int nType );

    void UpdateProcesses(int deltaMilliseconds);
    ~CProcessManager();

protected:
    ProcessList    m_ProcessList;

private:
    void Detach( shared_ptr<CProcess> pProcess );
};
```

When you create a Cprocess, you'll need to call Attach() to actually attach it to the process manager. The process manager class has a few bookkeeping methods, such as HasProcesses() and IsProcessActive(), which can be useful if you want to query the state of the process manager or whether a particular kind of process is active.

The ~CProcessManager() destructor does exactly what you would expect—it runs through the list of processes and calls Detach() for each, which removes the process from the list and sets its attachment state to false.

The UpdateProcesses() method is the real meat of this class:

```
void CProcessManager::UpdateProcesses(int deltaMilliseconds)
{
    ProcessList::iterator i = m_ProcessList.begin();
    ProcessList::iterator end = m_ProcessList.end();

    shared_ptr<CProcess> pNext;

    while ( i != end )
    {
        shared_ptr<CProcess> p( *i );

        if ( p->IsDead() )
        {
            // Check for a child process and add if exists
            pNext = p->GetNext();
```

```
        if ( pNext )
        {
            p->SetNext(shared_ptr<CProcess>((CProcess *)NULL));
            Attach( pNext );
        }
        Detach( p );
    }
    else if ( p->IsActive() && !p->IsPaused() )
    {
        p->OnUpdate( deltaMilliseconds );
    }
    ++i;
  }
}
```

Recall that nearly 100 percent of the game code could be inside various overloads of `CProcess::OnUpdate()`. This game code can, and will, cause game processes and objects to be deleted, all the more reason that this system uses smart pointers.

This method iterates through the processes in the process list from beginning to end in a round-robin fashion. One thing to beware of is that all of your processes must be able to be processed quickly in a single pass without causing your frame rate to stall. If you can't and you must amortize the cost of all your processes across multiple passes of your main loop, you shouldn't start back at the beginning of the list!

TALES FROM THE PIXEL MINES

ROUND ROBIN SCHEDULING GONE BAD

This system was used extensively to control the login servers of *Ultima Online.* When it was initially deployed, customer service began to receive complaints that some users were waiting more than five minutes for the login process to finish, and that didn't agree with the login server metrics, which measured over 2,000 logins per minute and an average login time of 15 seconds or so. The problem was identified after a little digging. I had bailed early from serving all the processes in the list in an attempt to poll network sockets and database activity, and in so doing, I left a few processes at the end of the list completely out in the cold.

Examples of Classes that Inherit from CProcess

A very simple example of a useful process using this cooperative design is a wait process. This process is useful for inserting timed delays, such as the fuse on an explosive. Here's how it works:

```
class CWaitProcess : public CProcess
{
protected:
   unsigned int m_uStart;
   unsigned int m_uStop;

public:
   CWaitProcess(CProcess* pParent, unsigned int iNumMill );

   virtual void VOnUpdate(const int deltaMilliseconds);
};

CWaitProcess::CWaitProcess(CProcess* pParent, unsigned int iNumMill ) :
   CProcess( PROC_WAIT, 0, pParent ),
   m_uStart( 0 ),
   m_uStop( iNumMill )
{
}

void CWaitProcess::VOnUpdate( const int deltaMilliseconds )
{
   CProcess::VOnUpdate( deltaMilliseconds );

   if ( m_bActive )
   {
     m_uStart += deltaMilliseconds;

      if ( m_uStart >= m_uStop )
        VKill();
   }
}
```

Here's how you create an instance of CWaitProcess:

```
shared_ptr<CProcess> wait(new CWaitProcess(3000));
processManager.Attach(wait);
```

Take note of two things. First, you don't just "new up" a `CWaitProcess` and attach it to the `CProcessManager`. You have to use the `shared_ptr` template to manage `CProcess` objects. This fixes problems when processes get deleted, but other objects may still point to them. Second, you must call the `Attach()` method of `CProcessManager` to attach the new process to the process manager.

As the main loop is processed and `CProcessManager::UpdateProcesses()` is called, the `CWaitProcess` counts the elapsed time, and once it has passed the wait period, it calls `VKill()`. By itself it's a little underwhelming—it just uses up a little CPU time and goes away. But if you define another process, such as `CKaboomProcess`, things get a little more interesting. You can then create a nuclear explosion with a three-second fuse without a physics degree:

```
// The wait process will stay alive for three seconds
Shared_ptr<CProcess> wait(new CWaitProcess(3000));
processManager.Attach(wait);

// The CKaboomProcess will wait for the CWaitProcess
//   Note — kaboom will be attached automatically
Shared_ptr<CProcess> kaboom(new CKaboomProcess());
wait->SetNext(kaboom);
```

The `CProcess::SetNext()` method sets up a simple dependency between the `CWaitProcess` and the `CKaboomProcess`. `CKaboomProcess` will remain inactive until the `CWaitProcess` is killed.

More Uses of `CProcess` Derivatives

Every updatable game object can inherit from `CProcess`. User interface objects such as buttons, edit boxes, or menus can inherit from `CProcess`. Audio objects such as sound effects, speech, or music make great use of this design because of the dependency and timing features.

A BASE CLASS FOR GAME ACTORS AND GAME LOGIC

Game logic is certainly something that will be completely custom for your game, but any game logic has a few common components, and it's helpful to explain them here. The `CProcessManager` lives inside the game logic, and now you can see how a base game logic class is built. First, take a look at the interface class for `IGameLogic`:

```
typedef unsigned int ActorId;
class IGameLogic
```

```
{
public:
   virtual shared_ptr<IActor> VGetActor(const ActorId id)=0;
   virtual void VAddActor(shared_ptr<IActor> actor, struct ActorParams *p)=0;
   virtual void VMoveActor(const ActorId id, Mat4x4 const &mat)=0;
   virtual void VRemoveActor(ActorId id)=0;

   virtual bool VLoadGame(std::string gameName)=0;

   virtual void VOnUpdate(float time, float elapsedTime)=0;
   virtual void VChangeState(enum BaseGameState newState)=0;
};
```

Most of the methods in the `IGameLogic` interface deal with game actors. Game actors are a general term for any object in a game that can change state—anything from a car in a racing game to a candle in an action/adventure title. The `IActor` interface class and some unusual implementations of `IActor` are discussed in Chapter 19, "A Game of Teapot Wars."

There's a method for loading the game, `VLoadGame()`, which in this context creates the initial game state. Not every game needs to save, but it wouldn't be a bad idea to consider adding that to increase this interface definition.

The remaining two pure virtuals are for updating your game, and they handle a change in game state. In this context, game states are things like initialization, running, paused, and so on.

Now that you've seen the interface class, take a look at `BaseGameLogic`, an implementation of the `IGame` interface:

```
typedef std::map<ActorId, shared_ptr<IActor> > ActorMap;

enum BaseGameState
{
   BGS_Initializing,
   BGS_LoadingGameEnvironment,
   BGS_WaitingForPlayers,
   BGS_Running
};

class BaseGameLogic : public IGameLogic
{
   // This is only to gain access to the view list
   friend class GameCodeApp;

protected:
   CProcessManager *m_pProcessManager;
```

```
    CRandom m_random;        // our RNG
    GameViewList m_gameViews;    // views attached to our game

    ActorMap m_ActorList;
    ActorId m_LastActorId;

    BaseGameState m_State;
    int m_ExpectedPlayers;       // how many players are expected

public:

    BaseGameLogic(struct GameOptions const &optionss);
    virtual ~BaseGameLogic();

    void TogglePause(bool active);
    void SetPlayer(GameViewType type, GameViewId viewId, ActorId aid);

    virtual void VAddView(shared_ptr<IGameView> pView);

    virtual void VAddActor(shared_ptr<IActor> actor, ActorParams *p);
    virtual shared_ptr<IActor> VGetActor(const ActorId id);
    virtual void VRemoveActor(ActorId id);
    virtual void VMoveActor(const ActorId id, Mat4x4 const &mat);
    virtual bool VLoadGame(std::string gameName) { return true; }

    virtual void VOnUpdate(float time, float elapsedTime);
    virtual void VChangeState(BaseGameState newState);

    virtual void VRenderDiagnostics() { };
};
```

This game logic class has a few components that you've been introduced to already: a process manager, a random number generator, and a list of game views attached to the logic.

Actor management is accomplished with an STL map that makes it easy and efficient to find any actor in the game given its ID. The implementations of the actor management methods like VAddActor() simply manage the contents of the STL map.

The heavy lifting in this class is done by VOnUpdate():

```
void BaseGameLogic::VOnUpdate(float time, float elapsedTime)
{
    int deltaMilliseconds = int(elapsedTime * 1000.0f);
```

```
switch(m_State)
{
    case BGS_Initializing:
        // If we get to here we're ready to attach players
        VChangeState(BGS_LoadingGameEnvironment);
        break;

    case BGS_LoadingGameEnvironment:
        if (g_pApp->VLoadGame())
        {
            VChangeState(BGS_WaitingForPlayers);
        }
        else
        {
            assert(0 && _T("The game failed to load."));
            g_pApp->AbortGame();
        }
        break;

    case BGS_WaitingForPlayers:
        if (m_ExpectedPlayers == m_gameViews.size() )
        {
            VChangeState(BGS_Running);
        }
        break;

    case BGS_Running:
        m_pProcessManager->UpdateProcesses(deltaMilliseconds);
        break;

    default:
        assert(0 && _T("Unrecognized state."));
        // Not a bad idea to throw an exception here to
        // catch this in a release build...
    }

    GameViewList::iterator i=m_gameViews.begin();
    GameViewList::iterator end=m_gameViews.end()
    while (i != end)
    {
        (*i)->VOnUpdate( deltaMilliseconds );
    ++I;
    }
}
```

This method is a simple state machine that runs different bits of code for each possible state. Initialization in this class is trivial, it just sets the state to BGS_WaitingForPlayers. This state waits for players to join the game until the number of views attached to the game equals the number of expected players and then changes the state to BGS_Running. During the running state, the game calls the UpdateProcesses() method of the CProcessManager attached to the game logic.

For all states, the game logic calls VOnUpdate() for each view attached to the game logic so they can update their states in preparation for rendering.

CAN I MAKE A GAME YET?

By now you've learned a lot about some of the hidden superstructure of game code, most notably about GameCodeApp, BaseGame, CProcess, and CProcessManager. You've probably figured out that most of the subsystems discussed so far can benefit from cooperative multitasking: animated objects, user interface code, and more. If you're like me, you've already played with writing your own games, and you're itching to put everything together in a tight little game engine. But there are quite a few important bits and pieces you should know before you strike out on your own.

You probably never thought about how game engines stuff a few gigabytes of game art and sounds through a much smaller memory space. Read the next chapter and find out.

LOADING AND CACHING GAME DATA

In This Chapter

- Game Resources: Formats and Storage Requirements
- Resource Files
- The Resource Cache
- I'm Out of Cache

Once you get a nice 3D model or sound, how do you actually get it into your game? Most game books present code examples where the game loads .X, WAV, or MP3 files directly. This doesn't work in real games. Real games have tens of thousands of these files and other bits of data. They might not fit into memory at the same time either. When you see a detailed environment in *Gears of War*, you can bet that it fills memory nearly to the last bit, and the act of walking into another room or building needs some way of kicking out the old and bringing in the new. So how does this really work? Take a look at Figure 7.1.

Games usually pack selected bits of game data into a single file, often called a *resource file*. By the way, just in case I haven't mentioned it, I tend to use the terms *game assets* and *game resources* to mean the same thing—they are all *game data*. Art, sounds, 3D meshes, and map levels are all game assets. These files usually map one-to-one with an entire game level. When you see a loading screen, you are likely witnessing the game reading one of the resource files.

Each game resource you use must be converted to the smallest possible format, taking care to keep quality at the right level. This is pretty easy for sounds,

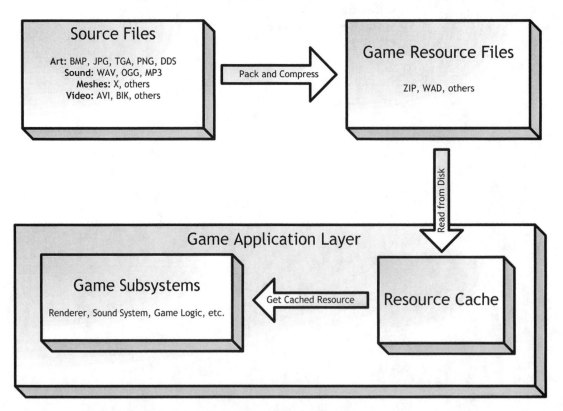

FIGURE 7.1 This is how data flows from game resource files to your game subsystems.

since you can easily predict the quality and size delta of a 44KHz stereo WAV versus an 11KHZ mono WAV stream. Textures are trickier to work with, on the other hand, because the best storage format is completely dependent on its use in the game and what it looks like.

These conversions are also dependent on the hardware platform. You can count on the fact that the Sony PS3 and the Microsoft Xbox360 will want sounds and textures presented in two completely different formats. This process will result in different resource files for each platform you support.

Later in this chapter, I'll show you how you can use Zip files as resource files, packing all your game assets into one neat file.

If your game is more of an open world design, your technology has to be more complicated and manage resources streaming from DVD into memory and out again as the player moves through the game world. That subject is beyond the scope of this book to present a detailed solution, but you will be introduced to the technology behind open world games.

GAME RESOURCES: FORMATS AND STORAGE REQUIREMENTS

Modern games have gigabytes of data. A single layer DVD can hold 4.7GB, and a single layer of a Blu-ray disc can hold up to 25GB. For PC games, you can browse the install directories and get an idea of what they store and how much storage they need. I'll go over the big stuff, give you an idea of how the data is stored, what formats you can use, how you can compress it, and what that does to the final product. I'll cover the following game data file types:

- **3D Object Meshes and Environments:** This usually requires a few tens of megabytes, and stores all the geometry for your game.
- **3D Mesh/Object Animation Data:** This is much smaller than you'd think, but lots of in-game cinematics can blow this up to many tens of megabytes.
- **Map/Level Data:** This is a catchall for components like trigger events, object types, scripts, and others. Together, they take up very little space, and are usually easy to compress.
- **Sprite and Texture Data:** These get pretty big very fast, and can take many hundreds of megabytes.
- **Sound, Music, and Recorded Dialogue:** Recorded dialogue usually takes more space on games than any other data category, especially when the games have a strong story component.
- **Video and Prerendered Cinematics:** Minute-per-minute, these components take up the most space, so they are used sparingly in most games. They are essentially the combination of sprite animation and stereo sound.

3D Object Meshes and Environments

3D object and environment geometry takes up a lot less space than you'd think. A 3D mesh, whether it is for an object, a character, or an environment, is a collection of points in 3D space with accompanying data that describes how these points are organized into polygons, and how the polygons should be rendered.

The points in 3D space are called *vertices*. They are stored as three floating-point numbers that represent the location of the point (X,Y,Z) from the origin. Individual triangles in this mesh are defined by three or more indices into the point list. Here's an example of the mesh for a misshapen cube:

```
Vec3 TestObject::g_SquashedCubeVerts[] =
{
    Vec3( 0.5,0.5,-0.25),        // Vertex 0.
    Vec3(-0.5,0.5,-0.25),        // Vertex 1.
    Vec3(-0.5,0.5,0.5),          // And so on.
    Vec3(0.75,0.5,0.5),
    Vec3(0.75,-0.5,-0.5),
    Vec3(-0.5,-0.5,-0.5),
    Vec3(-0.5,-0.3,0.5),
    Vec3(0.5,-0.3,0.5)
};

WORD TestObject::g_TestObjectIndices[][3] =
{
    { 0,1,2 },   { 0,2,3 },   { 0,4,5 },
    { 0,5,1 },   { 1,5,6 },   { 1,6,2 },
    { 2,6,7 },   { 2,7,3 },   { 3,7,4 },
    { 3,4,0 },   { 4,7,6 },   { 4,6,5 }
};
```

Feel free to plot it out on graph paper if you want, or you can take my word for it. The eight vertices are stored in an array, and the triangles are defined by groups of three indices into that array. A cube has eight points in space and six faces, but those faces are each comprised of two triangles. Twelve groups of three indices each are needed to define 12 triangles that make a cube.

If you have some experience with 3D programming, you might know that there are ways to save some space here. Instead of storing each triangle as a group of three points, you can store a list of connected triangles with fewer indices. These data structures are called *triangle lists* or *triangle fans*. Either of these stores the first triangle with three indices, and each following triangle with only one additional index. This technique is a little like drawing a shape without picking up your pencil, since each extra triangle requires only one additional vertex rather than an entire set of three vertices. This way you can store *n* triangles with only *n+2* indices instead of *n*3* vertices—quite a savings.

Let's assume you have an object with 2,000 vertices: 300 triangles stored in 100 triangle groups. Take a look at Table 7.1 to see how much space this data takes.

Table 7.1 Raw Geometry Sizes

Object	Members	Size
Vertices	2,000 points @ (3 floating-point numbers × 4 bytes each)	24,000 bytes
Each triangle group	300 triangles @ (302 indices × 2 bytes each)	604 bytes
All triangle groups	100 groups @ 604 bytes = 60,400 bytes Vertices @ 24,000 bytes + Triangles @ 60,400 bytes	84,400 bytes

It looks like you can store the raw geometry in about 82KB. But wait, there's a little more data to consider. The above data doesn't tell you anything about how to texture the object. Renderers will assume that each triangle group has the same material and textures. For each group, you'll need to store some additional data.

A material describing the diffuse map is going to define the color of an object and how it reflects light. The size of the material can vary depending on what the renderer can handle. The renderer can also apply one or more textures to the object. This data can vary in size. If the object is unaffected by lighting and has a solid color, it will require only a few bytes. If the object is affected by lighting, and has a base texture, a decal texture, a normal map, a specular map, an environment map, and stores color information for ambient, diffuse, and specular lighting, then it could require almost 100 bytes per vertex. This information is stored for each index in each triangle group.

Let's look at two cases, shown in Table 7.2. The first has a simple textured, colored object, and the second has an additional 64 bytes per index in each triangle group to store material and lighting data.

Table 7.2 Storing Simple Versus Complicated Objects

Object	Members	Size
Simple textured and lit object (30 bytes per vertex):	302 indices per group × 100 groups @ 30 bytes	906,000 bytes
Complicated material info (80 bytes per vertex):	302 indices per group × 100 groups @ 80 bytes	2,416,000 bytes

Notice the staggering difference. The more complicated object is quite a bit larger. So what have you learned? The complexity of the geometry can be made much smaller if your 3D models make good use of triangle strips and fans, but most of the savings comes from being frugal with complicated material models.

One thing you should note: The actual textures are stored separately from the mesh data, and we haven't even talked about those yet. They are much larger, too.

Animation Data

Animations are stored as changes in position and orientation over time. You already know that a position in 3D space takes 12 bytes—4 bytes each for X, Y, and Z coordinates. Orientation is usually stored as a 12-byte or 16-byte data structure, depending on the rendering engine. This is the difference between storing the orientation as angles of yaw, pitch, and roll (Euler angles), or a mathematical entity known as a *quaternion*, which is a 4-vector (X, Y, Z, W). (You'll learn all about the quarternion in Chapter 13, "3D Basics.") For now, we'll assume the orientation takes 12 bytes.

One way to store animations is by recording a stream of position and orientation data at fast intervals, say 30 times per second. For each second and each object, we have the following:

12 bytes for position + 12 bytes for orientation = 24 bytes per sample

30 samples per second × 24 bytes per sample = 720 bytes/second

An object like a character is represented by a lot of discrete objects. Assuming we have even a simple character with only 30 separate movable parts (called *bones*), this gets pretty big very fast:

720 bytes/second × 30 bones = 21,600 bytes per second

Of course, there are ways to cheat. Games never store this much data for animations—it is like storing an uncompressed TGA file for every frame of an entire movie. First, most motions don't need 30 samples per second to look good. Actually, even complicated motions can usually get by with 15 samples per second or less. Your mileage may vary with different motions, so your code might need to store different motions sampled at different rates. One thing you can be sure of, not every animation can look good with the same sampling rate, so your engine should be sophisticated enough to use animation data at different sampling rates.

Sometimes objects don't need to change position and orientation; they might just rotate or move. This implies you could store a stream of changes in position or orientation when they happen, and store nothing at all but a time delay when the object is still. Reversing an animation is a complicated thing, since you'd have to start at a known position and reapply the position and orientation deltas, but that's usually not a problem. Every second or so, you should store the full position and orientation information. These snapshots are usually called *keyframes*. They can be very useful for jumping quickly to somewhere in the middle of an animation, and they can also reduce small errors that can accumulate.

Finally, since the position and orientation changes are small, you can usually get away with storing them in something other than floating-point numbers. You can convert them to 2-byte integers, for example. These compression techniques can dramatically reduce the size of animation data down to a few tens of kilobytes per second for an animated character. The animation data for a main character like Garrett in *Thief: Deadly Shadows* that can use different weapons, climb on walls, crouch, crawl, and perform other activities should be in the 5MB to 7MB range.

Assuming that your game has a big storyline and you want to store lots of in-game cinematics, you can estimate the size of your in-game movies, minus the audio like this:

- Assume average of two characters moving simultaneously per cinematic
- Each cinematic averages 30 seconds
- 50KB per second (25KB per character per second) × 30 seconds = 1.53MB

Don't get too excited yet; the animation data is the least of your problems. Just wait until you see how much storage your digital audio is going to take.

Map/Level Data

Most game object data is stored in a proprietary format, which is often determined by the type of data and the whim of the programmer. There is no standard format for storing game object data, AI scripts, dialogue, and other components. This data is usually packed in a binary format for the game, but during development it is usually stored in a format that is easy to work with, such as XML. There's a good public domain XML parser called *Xerces*, and you can find it at http://xml.apache.org/xerces-c/.

Either way, this data is usually the least of your problems as far as storage is concerned. Your textures, audio, and animation data will overshadow this stuff by a long, long way.

Texture Data

Left to their own devices, artists would hand you every texture they create in a TIF or TGA file. The uncompressed 32-bit art would look exactly like the artist envisioned. When you consider that a raw 32-bit 1024 × 768 bitmap tips the scales at just over 3MB, you'll quickly decide to use a more efficient format.

As always, you'll generally need to trade quality for size. Load time will also need to be considered. The best games choose the right format and size for each asset. You'll be better at doing this if you understand how bitmaps, textures, and audio files are stored and processed, and what happens to them under different compression scenarios.

Bitmap Color Depth

Different bitmap formats allocate a certain number of bits for red, green, blue, and alpha channels. Some formats are indexed, meaning that the pixel data is actually an index into a color table that stores the actual RGBA values. Here's a list of the most common formats:

- **32-bit (8888 RGBA):** The least compact way to store bitmaps, but retains the most information.
- **24-bit (888 RGB):** This format is common for storing backgrounds that have too much color data to be represented in either 8-bit indexed or 16-bit formats, and have no need for an alpha channel.
- **24-bit (565 RGB, 8 A):** This format is great for making nice-looking bitmaps with a good alpha channel. Green gets an extra bit because the human eye is more sensitive to changes in green than red or blue.
- **16-bit (565 RGB):** This compact format is used for storing bitmaps with more varieties of color and no alpha channel.
- **16-bit (555 RGB, 1 A):** This compact format leaves one bit for translucency, which is essentially a chroma key.
- **8-bit indexed:** A compact way to store bitmaps that have large areas of subtly shaded colors; some of the indexes can be reserved for different levels of translucency.

Many renderers, including DirectX, support a wide variety of pixel depth in each red, blue, green, and alpha channel.

BEST
PRACTICE

SUPPORT TOOLS YOUR CONTENT CREATORS WILL ACTUALLY USE

Avoid writing oddball tools to try to save a few bits here and there. Try to write your game so that your content creators, such as artists, can use the same art formats used by popular art tools like Photoshop. They will be able to easily manipulate their work in a common and well-known tool, and your game will look exactly the way the artists intend it to look. You'll also be able to find artists who can work on your game if you stick to the standard formats and tools.

Which Is Better: 24-, 16-, or 8-Bit Art?

It's virtually impossible to choose a single format to store every bitmap in your game and have all your bitmaps come through looking great. In fact, I can assure you that some of your bitmaps will end up looking like they should be in your laundry pile.

Figure 7.2 shows three different bitmaps that were created by drawing a grayscale image in Photoshop. The bitmap on the far left uses 8 bits per channel, the center bitmap is stored using 5 bits per channel, while the one on the right is stored using 4 bits. If you attempt to store a subtly shaded image using too few colors you'll see results closer to the right bitmap, which looks crummy.

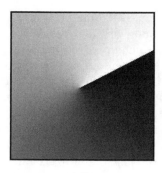

FIGURE 7.2 Grayscale banding patterns for 24-bit, 16-bit, and 8-bit depths.

If you can use 8 bits for each channel, you'll see the best result, but you'll trade this quality for a much larger size. Needless to say, if your artist storms into your office and wonders why her beautiful bitmaps are banded all to hell, you've likely forced them into a bad color space.

Using Lossy Compression

A discussion of art storage wouldn't be complete without taking a look at the effects of using a lossy compression scheme such as JPG. The compression algorithm tweaks some values in the original art to achieve a higher compression ratio, hence the term "lossy." It's not a mistake that if you spell-check the word lossy you get "lousy" as one of your choices. Beyond a certain threshold, the art degrades too much to get past your QA department, and it certainly won't get past the artist that spent so much time creating it.

Perhaps the best approach is to get artists to decide how they'll save their own bitmaps using the highest lossiness they can stand. It still won't be enough, I guarantee you, because they are much more sensitive to subtle differences than a consumer, but it's a start.

Data Sizes for Textures

Texture storage is one of the big budget areas for games. They take up the most space second only to audio and streaming video. Character textures for games like *Gears of War* can be as large as 2048 × 2048. They also have multiple layered maps for specular and emissive effects that weigh in at 512 × 512 or 1024 × 1024. This starts to add up extremely quickly.

An uncompressed 1024 × 1024 texture is going to take 2MB to 4MB in memory, depending on whether it is a 16-bit or 32-bit texture. Most of your level geometry and game objects won't need that kind of density; they'll usually use different textures in layers to create interesting effects.

A single object, such as a wall, might have a 16-bit 512×512 texture on it taking 1MB of memory, but add to that a couple of 128×128 decals, a 128×128 normal map, and you start eating up some memory. This one object with these three textures will take almost 2MB of texture memory. Your game might have a few hundred objects of various detail, eating your memory faster than you expect. The Nintendo Wii only has 64MB RAM in the first place, which means you have to budget your textures more than almost any other game asset.

Even the best video cards don't perform well when you have to swap textures in and out of video memory. If your game is expected to run well on a 512MB video card, you'd better be careful and take that into account when building levels. A few hundred objects and 10 characters will chew up that 512MB in a real hurry, and you'll have to scramble to fix the problem. Believe me, you won't be able to ask your customers to simply buy new video cards, unless of course you are Valve and are publishing the latest *Half-Life*.

Finally, most textures need some additional storage for their mip-maps. A textured object with a mip-map will look good no matter what the camera distance is. If you've ever seen a really cheap 3D game where the object textures flashed or scintillated all the time, it's because the game didn't use mip-mapped textures. A mip-map precalculates the image of a texture at different distances. For example, a 128×128 texture that is fully mip-mapped has a 64×64, 32×32, 16×16, 8×8, 4×4, 2×2, and a 1×1 version of itself. The renderer will choose one or more of these mip-maps to render the final pixels on the polygon. This creates a smooth textured effect, no matter how the camera is moving.

A full mip-map for a texture takes 33 percent more space as the texture does by itself. So don't forget to save that texture space for your mip-maps. One interesting bit—games almost always pregenerate their mip-maps and store them in the resource file rather than generating them on the fly. The reason is that it is faster to load them than generate them, and improving loading speed can be a much bigger problem than media storage.

Sound and Music Data

Sound formats in digital audio are commonly stored in either mono or stereo, sampled at different frequencies, and accurate to either 8 or 16 bits per sample. The effect of mono or stereo on the resulting playback and storage size is obvious. Stereo sound takes twice as much space to store but provides left and right channel waveforms. The different frequencies and bit depths have an interesting and quite drastic effect on the sound.

Digital audio is created by sampling a waveform and converting it into discrete 8- or 16-bit values that approximate the original waveform. This works because the human ear has a relatively narrow range of sensitivity: 20Hz to 20,000Hz. It's no surprise that the common frequencies for storing WAV files are 44KHz, 22KHz, and 11KHz.

It turns out that telephone conversations are 8-bit values sampled at 8KHz, after the original waveform has been filtered to remove frequencies higher than 3.4MHz. Music on CDs is first filtered to remove sounds higher than 22KHz, and then sampled at 16-bit 44KHz. Just to summarize, Table 7.3 shows how you would use the different frequencies in digital audio.

Use lower sampling rates for digital audio in your game to simulate telephone conversations or talking over shortwave radio.

Table 7.3 Using Different Audio Frequencies with Digital Formats

Format	Quality	Size per Second	Size per Minute
44.1KHz 16-bit stereo WAV	CD quality	172KB/second	10MB/minute
128Kbps stereo MP3	Near CD quality	17KB/second	1MB/minute
22.05KHz 16-bit stereo WAV	FM Radio	86KB/second	5MB/minute
64Kbps stereo MP3	FM Radio	9KB/second	540KB/minute
11.025KHz 16-bit mono WAV	AM Radio	43KB/second	2.5MB/minute
11.025KHz 8-bit mono WAV	Telephone	21KB/second	1.25MB/minute

Video and Prerendered Cinematics

Animated sequences in games go as far back as *Pac Man*, where after every few levels you'd see a little cartoon featuring the little yellow guy and his friends. The cartoons had little or nothing to do with the game, but they were fun to watch and gave players a reward. One of the first companies to use large amounts of video footage in games was Origin Systems in the *Wing Commander* series. More than giving players a reward, they actually told a story. Epic cinematics are not only common in today's games, they are expected.

There are two techniques worth considering for incorporating cinematic sequences. Some games like *Wing Commander III* will shoot live video segments and simply play them back. The file is usually an enormous AVI file that would fill up a good portion of your optical media. That file is usually compressed into something more usable by the game.

The second approach uses the game engine itself. Most games create their animated sequences in 3ds Max or Maya and export the animations and camera motion. The animations can be played back by loading a relatively tiny animation file and pumping the animations through the rendering engine. The only media you have to store beyond that is the sound. If you have tons of cinematic sequences, doing them in-game like this is the way to go. Lots of story-heavy games are going this direction because it is simply impossible to store that much prerendered video.

The biggest difference your players will notice is in the look of the cinematic. If an animation uses the engine, your players won't be mentally pulled out of the game world. The in-game cut-scenes will also flow perfectly between the action and the narrative, as compared to the prerendered cut-scenes, which usually force some sort of slight delay and interruption as the game engine switches back and forth between in-game action and retrieving the cut-scene from the disc or hard drive. If the player has customized the look of their character, that customization is still visible in the cinematic because it is being rendered on the fly. As a technologist, the biggest difference you'll notice is the smaller resulting cinematic data files. The animation data is tiny compared to digital video. You should make sure the AI characters hold for the cinematic moment and attack you only after it is over!

Sometimes you'll want to show a cinematic that simply can't be rendered in real time by your graphics engine—perhaps something you need Maya to chew on for a few hours in a huge render farm. In that case, you'll need to understand a little about streaming video and compression.

Streaming Video and Compression

Each video frame in your cinematic should pass through compression only once. Every compression pass will degrade the art quality. Prove this to yourself by compressing a piece of video two or three times, and you'll see how bad it gets even with the second pass.

Compression settings for streaming video can get complicated. Predicting how a setting will change the output is also tricky. Getting a grasp of how it works will help you understand which settings will work best for your footage. Video compression uses two main strategies to take a 5GB two-minute movie and boil it down into a 10MB or so file. Just because the resolution drops doesn't mean you have to watch a postage stamp-sized piece of video. Most playback APIs will allow a stretching parameter for the height, width, or both.

BEST PRACTICE

USB HARD DRIVES AND FEDEX

If you need to move a large dataset like uncompressed video from one network to another, use a stand-alone Ethernet or high-speed USB-capable hard drive. It might make security conscious IT guys freak out, but it's a useful alternative to burning a stack of DVDs or worse, trying to send a few hundred gigabytes over the Internet. This is modern day "Sneakernet."

Don't waste your time backing up uncompressed video files. Instead, make sure that you have everything you need to re-create them, such as a 3ds Max scene file or even raw videotape. Make sure the source is backed up and the final compressed files are backed up.

The first strategy for compressing video is to simply remove unneeded information by reducing the resolution or interlacing the video. Reducing resolution from 800×600 to 400×300 would shave 3GB from a 4GB movie, a savings of 75 percent. An interlaced video alternates drawing the even and odd scanlines every other frame. This is exactly how television works; the electron gun completes a round trip from the top of the screen to the bottom and back at 60Hz, but it only draws every other scanline. The activated phosphors on the inside of the picture tube persist longer than 1/30th of a second after they've been hit with the electron gun, and can therefore be refreshed or changed at that rate without noticeable degradation in the picture. Interlacing the video will drop the data set down to one-half of its original size. Using interlacing and resolution reduction can make a huge difference in your video size, even before the compression system kicks in.

Video compression can be lossless, but in practice you should always take advantage of the compression ratios even a small amount of lossiness can give you. If you're planning on streaming the video from optical media, you'll probably be forced to accept some lossiness simply to get your peak and average data rates down low enough for your minimum specification CD-ROMs. In any case, you'll want to check the maximum bit rate you can live with if the video stream is going to live on optical media. Most compression utilities give you the option of entering your maximum bit rate. The resulting compression will attempt to satisfy your bit-rate limitations while keeping the resulting video as accurate to the original as possible. Table 7.4 shows the ideal bit rate that should be used for different CD-ROM, DVD, and Blu-ray speeds.

Table 7.4 Matching Bit Rates with CD-ROM/DVD Speeds

Technology	Bit Rate	Technology	Bit Rate
1x CD	150 Kbps	16x DVD	2.21 Mbps
1x DVD	1,385 Kbps	1x Blu-ray	36 Mbps
32x CD	4,800 Kbps	8x Blu-ray	288 Mbps

BEST PRACTICE

SAVE VIDEO COMPRESSION SETTINGS—THEY'RE HARD TO REMEMBER!

Getting the video compression settings just right can be a black art, and can be difficult to reproduce later. Make sure that you record these settings in a convenient place so you can get to them again.

RESOURCE FILES

When I wrote the first edition of this book in 2003, many hard disks rotated as fast as 7,200rpm. By the second edition, the fast drives were already up to 15,000rpm. At the writing of the third edition, there is talk of a 20,000rpm hard disk, but I'm not so sure I want to sit anywhere near that thing. For a 15,000rpm device, the CPU must wait an average of 2ms for a desired piece of data to be located in the right position to be read, assuming the read/write head doesn't have to seek to a new track. For a modern day processor operating at 2GHz or more, this time is interminable. It's a good thing processors aren't conscious because they'd go mad waiting for hard disks all the time. Seeking time is much slower. The head must accelerate, move, stop, and become stable enough to accurately read the magnetic media. For a CPU, that wait is an eternity.

Optical media is even worse. Their physical organization is a continuous spiral from the inside of the disc to the outside, and the read laser must traverse this spiral at a constant linear velocity. This means that not only does the laser read head have to seek to an approximate location instead of an exact location, but also the rotational velocity of the disc must change to the right speed before reading can begin. If the approximate location was wrong, the head will re-seek. All this mechanical movement makes optical media much slower that their magnetic brethren.

The only thing slower than reading data from a hard drive or optical media is to have an intern actually type the data in manually from the keyboard.

Needless to say, you want to treat data in your files like I treat baubles in stores like Pier One. I do everything in my power to stay away from these establishments (my wife loves them) until I have a big list of things to buy. When I can't put it off any longer, I make my shopping trip a surgical strike. I go in, get my stuff, and get out as fast as I can. When your game needs to grab data from the hard drive or optical media, it should follow the same philosophy.

The best solution would completely compartmentalize game assets into a single block of data that could be read in one operation with a minimum of movement of the read/write head. Everything needed for a screen or a level would be completely covered by this single read. This is usually impractical because some

BEST
PRACTICE

KNOW YOUR HARDWARE

Knowing how hardware works is critical to writing any kind of software. You don't have to be a guru writing device drivers to crack the books and learn exactly how everything works and how you can take advantage of it. This same lesson applies to the operating system and how the hardware APIs work under the hood. This knowledge separates armchair game programmers from professional game programmers.

common data would have to be duplicated in each block. A fine compromise factors the common data in one block and the data specific for each level or screen in their own blocks. When the game loads, it is likely you'll notice two seeks—one for the common data block and one for the level specific block. You should make sure the common data stays in memory, even if new levels are loaded.

Packaging Resources into a Single File

It's a serious mistake to store every game asset, such as a texture or sound effect, in its own file. Separating thousands of assets in their own files wastes valuable storage space and makes it impossible to get your load times faster.

Hard drives are logically organized into blocks or clusters that have surprisingly large sizes. Most hard drives in the gigabit range have cluster sizes of 16KB–32KB. File systems like FAT32 and NTFS were written to store a maximum of one file per cluster to enable optimal storage of the directory structure. This means that if you have 500 sound effect files, each 1/2 second long and recorded at 44KHz mono, you'll have 5.13MB of wasted space on the hard disk:

0.5 seconds * 44KHz mono = 22,000 bytes

32,768 bytes minimum cluster size – 22,000 bytes in each file = 10,768 bytes wasted per file

10,768 bytes wasted in each file * 500 files = 5.13MB wasted space

You can easily get around this problem by packing your game assets into a single file. If you've ever played with DOOM level editors, you're familiar with WAD files; they are a perfect example of this technique. These packed file formats are file systems in miniature, although most are read only. *Ultima VIII* and *Ultima IX* had a read/write version (FLX files) that had multiuser locking capabilities for development. Almost every game on the market uses some custom packing scheme for more reasons than saving hard drive space.

Other Benefits of Packaging Resources

The biggest advantage of combining your resources by far is load time optimization. Opening files is an extremely slow operation on most operating systems, and Windows is no exception. At worst, you'll incur the cost of an extra hard disk seek to read the directory structure to find the physical location of the file.

Another advantage is security. You can use a proprietary logical organization of the file that will hamper armchair hackers from getting to your art and sounds. While this security is quite light and serious hackers will usually break it before the sun sets the first day your game is on the shelves, it's better than nothing.

HARD DRIVE TICKING? MAYBE YOU SHOULD LISTEN

During PC development, keep your ear tuned to the sounds your hard drive makes while you play your game. At worst, you should hear a "tick" every few seconds or so as new data is cached in. This would be common in a game like Ultima IX, *where the player could walk anywhere on an enormous outdoor map. At best, your game will have a level design that grabs all the data in one read.*

A great trick is to keep indexes or file headers in memory while the file is open. These are usually placed at the beginning of a file, and on large files the index might be a considerable physical distance away from your data. Read the index once and keep it around to save yourself that extra seek.

Data Compression and Performance

Compression is a double-edged sword. Every game scrambles to store as much content on the distribution media and the hard drive as possible. Compression can achieve some impressive space ratios for storing text, graphics, and sound at the cost of increasing the load on the CPU and your RAM budget to decompress everything. The actual compression ratios you'll get from using different utilities are completely dependent on the algorithm and the data to be compressed. Use algorithms like Zlib or LZH for general compression that can't afford lossiness. Use JPG or MPEG compression for anything that can stand lossiness, such as graphics and sound.

Consider the cost of decompressing MP3 files for music, speech, or sound effects. On the upper end, each stream of 128KB stereo MP3 can suck about 25MHz from your CPU budget, depending on your processor. If you design your audio system to handle 16 simultaneous streams, a 2GHz desktop will only have 1.6GHz left, losing 400MHz to decompressing audio.

KEEP AN EYE ON YOUR MESSAGE QUEUE DURING CALLBACKS

If your decompressor API uses a callback, it is quite likely that the decompression will forward Windows system messages into your message pump. This can create a real nightmare since mouse clicks or hot keys can cause new art and sounds to be recursively sent into the decompression system. Callbacks are necessary for providing user feedback like a progress bar, but they also wreak havoc with your message pump. If this is happening to your application, trap the offending messages and hold them in a temporary queue until the primary decompression is finished.

Zlib: Open Source Compression

If you need a lossless compression/decompression system for your game, a good choice that has stood the test of time is Zlib, which can be found at www.gzip.org/zlib/. It's free, open source, legally unencumbered, and simple to integrate into almost any platform. Typical compression ratios with Zlib are 2:1 to 5:1, depending on the data stream.

Zlib was written by Jean-Loup Gailly and Mark Adler and is an abstraction of the DEFLATE compression algorithm. A Zip file uses Zlib to compress many files into a single file. An overview of the basic structure of a Zip file is shown in Figure 7.3. I'll show you the basic structure first, and then we'll look at the code that can read it.

Zip files store their table of contents, or file directory, at the end of the file. If you read the file, the `TZipDirHeader` at the very end of the file contains data members such as a special signature and the number of files stored in the Zip file. Just before the `TZipDirHeader`, there is an array of structures, one for each file, that

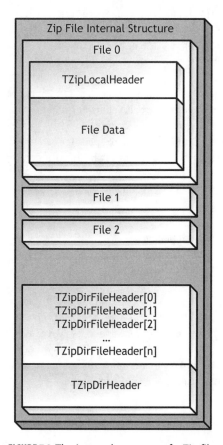

FIGURE 7.3 The internal structure of a Zip file.

stores data members such as the name of the file, the type of compression, and the size of the file before and after compression. Each file in the Zip file has a local header stored just before the compressed file data. It stores much of the same data as the TZipDirFileHeader structure.

One fine example of reading a Zip file comes from Javier Arevalo. I've modified it only slightly to work well with the rest of the source code in this book. The basic premise of the solution is to open a Zip file, read the directory into memory, and use it to index the rest of the file. Here is the definition for the ZipFile class:

```
// This maps a path to a zip content id
typedef std::map<std::string, int> ZipContentsMap;

class ZipFile
{
public:
    ZipFile() { m_nEntries=0; m_pFile=NULL; m_pDirData=NULL; }
    ~ZipFile() { End(); fclose(m_pFile); }

    bool Init(const _TCHAR *resFileName);
    void End();

    int GetNumFiles()const { return m_nEntries; }
    void GetFilename(int i, char *pszDest) const;
    int GetFileLen(int i) const;
    bool ReadFile(int i, void *pBuf);
    optional<int> Find(const char *path) const;

    ZipContentsMap m_ZipContentsMap;

private:
    struct TZipDirHeader;
    struct TZipDirFileHeader;
    struct TZipLocalHeader;

    FILE *m_pFile;        // Zip file
    char *m_pDirData;     // Raw data buffer.
    int  m_nEntries;      // Number of entries.

    // Pointers to the dir entries in pDirData.
    const TZipDirFileHeader **m_papDir;
};
```

```cpp
// --------------------------------------------------------------------
// Basic types.
// --------------------------------------------------------------------
typedef unsigned long dword;
typedef unsigned short word;
typedef unsigned char byte;


// --------------------------------------------------------------------
// ZIP file structures. Note these have to be packed.
// --------------------------------------------------------------------

#pragma pack(1)
// --------------------------------------------------------------------
struct ZipFile::TZipLocalHeader
{
   enum
   {
      SIGNATURE = 0x04034b50
   };
   dword    sig;
   word     version;
   word     flag;
   word     compression;      // COMP_xxxx
   word     modTime;
   word     modDate;
   dword    crc32;
   dword    cSize;
   dword    ucSize;
   word     fnameLen;         // Filename string follows header.
   word     xtraLen;          // Extra field follows filename.
};

struct ZipFile::TZipDirHeader
{
   enum {  SIGNATURE = 0x06054b50  };
   dword    sig;
   word     nDisk;
   word     nStartDisk;
   word     nDirEntries;
   word     totalDirEntries;
   dword    dirSize;
   dword    dirOffset;
   word     cmntLen;
};
```

```
// -----------------------------------------------------------------
struct ZipFile::TZipDirFileHeader
{
   enum { SIGNATURE   = 0x02014b50 };
   dword   sig;
   word    verMade;
   word    verNeeded;
   word    flag;
   word    compression;        // COMP_xxxx
   word    modTime;
   word    modDate;
   dword   crc32;
   dword   cSize;              // Compressed size
   dword   ucSize;             // Uncompressed size
   word    fnameLen;           // Filename string follows header.
   word    xtraLen;            // Extra field follows filename.
   word    cmntLen;            // Comment field follows extra field.
   word    diskStart;
   word    intAttr;
   dword   extAttr;
   dword   hdrOffset;

   char *GetName    () const { return (char *)(this + 1);   }
   char *GetExtra   () const { return GetName() + fnameLen; }
   char *GetComment() const { return GetExtra() + xtraLen; }
};
// -----------------------------------------------------------------
#pragma pack()
```

You should notice a couple of interesting things about the definition of these structures. First, there is a #pragma pack around the code. This disables anything the C++ compiler might do to optimize the memory speed of these structures, usually by spreading them out so that each member variable is on a 4-byte boundary. Anytime you define a structure that will be stored onto a disk or in a stream, you should pack them. Another thing is the definition of a special signature for each structure. The sig member of each structure is set to a known, constant value, and it is written out to disk. When it is read back in, if the signatures don't match the known constant value, you can be sure you have a corrupted file. It won't catch everything, but it is a good defense.

When a Zip file is opened, the class reads the TZipDirHeader structure at the end of the file. If the signatures match, the file position is set to the beginning of the array of TZipDirFileHeader structures. Note that there is a length of this array already stored in the TZipDirHeader. This is important because there's actually a little extra data stored in between each TZipDirFileHeader. It is variable length data and contains the filenames, comments, and other extras.

Enough memory is allocated to store the directory, and it is read in one chunk. The data is then processed a bit. All the signatures are checked, the UNIX slashes are converted to backslashes, and the pointers to each entry in the directory are set for quick access. The filenames are also stored in an STL map for quick lookup.

The ReadFile method takes the index number of the file you want to read and a pointer to the memory you've preallocated. Prior to calling this method, you'll call GetFileLen to find the size of the buffer and allocate enough memory to hold the file. It reads and decompresses the entire file at once in a blocking call, which could be bad if you have a large compressed file inside the Zip file. If you want to decompress something larger asynchronously, you'll need to extend this class.

One thing is a matter of taste for Win32 programmers: Under UNIX operating systems filenames are case sensitive, which means that you could have two filenames in the same directory that differ only in case. The same thing is true of Zip files, and while it is not exactly perfect form to convert all filenames to lowercase before you compare names, it sure makes it easier on you and the development team. An artist might name a file "Allbricks.bmp" and a programmer might expect it to be named "allbricks.bmp." If you don't force the names to lowercase, the class will think the file doesn't exist.

With this class, you can iterate through all of the files packed in the Zip, find their names, read and decompress the file data, and use the data in your game. Here's an example:

```
char *buffer = NULL;
ZipFile zipFile;
if (zipFile.Init(resFileName))
{
   optional<int> index = zipFile.Find(path);
   if (index.valid())
   {
      int size = zipFile->GetFileLen(*index);
      buffer = new char[size];
      if (buffer)
      {
         zipFile.ReadFile(*index, buffer);
      }
   }
}
return buffer;
```

This is about as easy as it gets: After the Zip file is initialized, you find the index to the name of the file inside the Zip, grab the size, allocate the memory buffer, and read the bits.

Zip files are a good choice for the base file type of a general purpose resource file—something you can open once and read sounds, textures, meshes, and pretty much everything else. It's a common practice to load all of the resources you'll use for a given level in a single Zip file. Even doing this, you might soon discover that the Zip file for any one level is much bigger than your available memory. Some resources, like the sounds for your character's footsteps, will be around all the time. Others are used more rarely, like a special sound effect for a machine that is only activated once.

This problem calls for a cache, and luckily you're about to find out how one works.

THE RESOURCE CACHE

Resource files need a resource cache. If your game has a tiny set of graphics and sounds small enough to exist completely in memory for the life of your game, you don't need a cache. It's still a good idea to use resource files to pack everything into one file; you'll save disk space and speed up your game's load time.

Most games are bigger. If your game is going to ship on a DVD, you'll have almost five gigabytes to play around in, and on Blu-ray over 25GB. Optical media will certainly be larger than the RAM you have. What you need is a resource cache—a piece of technology that will sit on top of your resource files and manage the memory and the process of loading resources when you need them. Even better, a resource cache should be able to predict resource requirements before you need them.

Resource caches work on similar principles as any other memory cache. Most of the bits you'll need to display the next frame or play the next set of sounds are probably ones you've used recently. As the game progresses from one state to the next, new resources are cached in. They might be needed, for example, to play sound effects for the first time. Since memory isn't available in infinite quantities, eventually your game will run out of memory, and you'll have to throw something out of the cache.

Caches have two degenerate cases: cache misses and thrashing. A cache miss occurs when a game asks for the data associated with a resource and it isn't there. The game has to wait while the hard drive or the optical media wakes up and reads the data. A cache miss is bad, but thrashing is fatal.

Cache thrashing occurs when your game consistently needs more resource data than can fit in the available memory space. The cache is forced to throw out resources that are still frequently referenced by the game. The disk drives spin up and run constantly, and your game goes into semi-permanent hibernation.

The only way to avoid thrashing is to decrease the memory needed or increase the memory requirements. On console platforms, you don't get to ask for more RAM—it is what it is. On PC projects, it's rare that you'll get the go-ahead to increase the memory requirements, so you're left with slimming down the game data. You'll probably have to use smaller textures, fewer sounds, or cut entire sections out of your levels to get things to fit.

Most of the interesting work in resource cache systems involves predictive analysis of your game data in an attempt to avoid cache misses. There are some tricks to reduce this problem, some of which reach into your level design by adding pinch points such as doors, elevators, or elbow hallways. Some games with open maps, like flight simulators, can't do this. They have to work a lot harder. I'll show you a very simple resource cache so you can get your bearings. Then I'll discuss why this problem generally gets its own programmer, and a good one.

For the sake of simplicity, I'm going to assume that the cache only handles one resource file. It's easy enough to make the modifications to track resources across multiple files. You'll need to attach a file identifier of some sort to each resource to track which resources came from which file. There's no need to create a monolithic file that holds all the game assets. You should just break them up into manageable chunks. Perhaps you'll put assets for a given level into one resource file, and assets common to all levels in another. It's totally up to you.

Resources might not exist in memory if they've never been loaded or if they've been thrown out to make room for other resources. You need a way to reference them whether they are loaded or not. You need a mechanism to uniquely identify each resource. This enables the cache to match a particular resource identifier with its data. For our simple resource system, we'll assume that resources have unique names. You might need something a little more robust, such as a hash or GUID.

YOU MIGHT HAVE MULTIPLE RESOURCE CACHES IN YOUR GAME

Different assets in your game require different resource caching. Level data, such as object geometry and textures, should be loaded in one chunk when the level is loaded. Audio and cinematics can be streamed in as needed. Most user interface screens should be loaded before they are needed, since you don't want players to wait while you cache something in. If you are going to load something, make sure you load it when the player isn't going to notice. Some games just load everything they need when you begin playing and never hit the disk for anything else at all, so a resource cache isn't something every game uses.

Since the resource cache also manages memory, it's convenient to store the size of the resource where it can be accessed quickly. These two members are stored together in a structure:

```
class Resource
{
public:
    std::string m_name;
```

```
Resource(std::string name)
    { m_name=name; }
virtual ResHandle *VCreateHandle (
    const char *buffer, unsigned int size, ResCache *pResCache);
};


ResHandle *Resource::VCreateHandle(
    const char *buffer, unsigned int size, ResCache *pResCache)
{
    return GCC_NEW ResHandle(*this, (char *)buffer, size, pResCache);
}
```

Two phases are involved in using a resource cache: creating the resource and using it. When you create a resource, you are simply creating an identifier for the resource. It doesn't really do much of anything. The heavy lifting happens when you send the resource into the resource cache to gain access to the bits or a resource handle. Since the handle is managed by a shared_ptr, the bits are guaranteed to be good as long as you need them. Here's an example of how to use the Resource class to grab a handle and get to the bits:

```
Resource resource("Brick.bmp");
shared_ptr<ResHandle> texture = g_pApp->m_ResCache->GetHandle(&resource);
int size = texture->GetSize();
char *brickBitmap = (char *) texture->Buffer();
```

Now you're ready to see how the resource cache is coded. You've already seen how a resource is defined through the Resource structure. There are a few other parts of a resource cache, and I'll go over each one in detail:

- IResourceFile interface and ResourceZipFile, the resource file
- ResHandle, a handle to track loaded resources
- ResCache, a simple resource cache

IResourceFile Interface

A resource file should be able to be opened, closed, and provide the application programmer access to resources. Here's a simple interface that defines just that:

```
class IResourceFile
{
public:
    virtual bool VOpen()=0;
    virtual int VGetResourceSize(const Resource &r)=0;
```

```
   virtual int VGetResource(const Resource &r, char *buffer)=0;
   virtual ~IResourceFile() { }
};
```

There are only three pure virtual functions to implement. I told you it was simple. The implementation of VOpen() should open the file and return success or failure based on the file's existence and integrity. VGetResourceSize() should return the size of the resource based on the name of the resource, and VGetResource() should read the resource from the file.

The accompanying source code implements the IResourceFile interface with a ZipFile interior, so all of the resources in *Game Coding Complete* source code can be stored in a Zip file and read at will. This is a great example of using interfaces to hide the technical implementation of something while maintaining a consistent API. If you wanted to, you could implement this interface using a completely different file structure, like CAB or WAD.

ResHandle: Tracking Loaded Resources

For the cache to do its work, it must keep track of all the loaded resources. A useful class, ResHandle, encapsulates the resource identifier with the loaded resource data:

```
class ResHandle
{
   friend class ResCache;

protected:
   Resource m_resource;
   char *m_buffer;
   unsigned int m_size;
   ResCache *m_pResCache;

public:
   ResHandle ( Resource & resource,
               char *buffer,
               unsigned int size,
               ResCache *pResCache);
   virtual ~ResHandle();
   virtual int VLoad(IResourceFile *file)
      { return file->VGetResource(m_resource, m_buffer); }

   unsigned int Size() const { return m_size; }
   char *Buffer() const { return m_buffer; }
};
```

```
ResHandle::ResHandle(
    Resource & resource, char *buffer, unsigned int size, ResCache *pResCache)
    : m_resource(resource)
{
    m_buffer = buffer;
    m_size = size;
    m_pResCache = pResCache;
}

ResHandle::~ResHandle()
{
    if (m_buffer) delete [] m_buffer;
    m_pResCache->MemoryHasBeenFreed(m_size);
}
```

When the cache loads a resource, it dynamically creates a ResHandle, allocates a buffer of the right size, and reads the resource from the resource file. The ResHandle class exists in memory as long as the resource caches it in, or as long as any consumer of the bits keeps a shared_ptr to a ResHandle object. The ResHandle also tracks the size of the memory block. If the resource cache gets full, the resource handle is discarded and removed from the resource cache.

The destructor of ResHandle makes a call to a ResCache member, MemoryHasBeen-Freed(). ResHandle objects are always managed through a shared_ptr, and can therefore be actively in use at the moment the cache tries to free them. This is fine, but when the ResHandle object goes out of scope, it needs to inform the resource cache that it is time to adjust the amount of memory actually in use.

There's a useful side effect of holding a pointer to the resource cache in the ResHandle—it is possible to have multiple resource caches in your game. One may control a specific type of resource, such as sound effects, whereas another may control level geometry and textures.

ResCache: A Simple Resource Cache

Since most of the players are already on the stage, it's time to bring out the ResCache class, an ultra simple resource cache.

While the resource is in memory, a pointer to the ResHandle exists in two data structures. The first, a linked list, is managed such that the nodes appear in the order in which the resource was last used. Every time a resource is used, it is moved to the front the list, so we can find the most and least recently used resources.

The second data structure, an STL map, provides a way to quickly find resource data with the unique resource identifier:

```
// LRU (least recently used)
typedef std::list< shared_ptr <ResHandle > > ResHandleList;

// maps identifiers to data
typedef std::map<std::string, shared_ptr < ResHandle  > > ResHandleMap;

class ResCache
{
protected:
    ResHandleList m_lru;            // LRU (least recently used) list
    ResHandleMap m_resources;       // STL map for fast resource lookup
    IResourceFile *m_file;          // Object that implements IResourceFile

    unsigned int   m_cacheSize;    // total memory size
    unsigned int   m_allocated;    // total memory allocated

    shared_ptr<ResHandle> Find(Resource * r);
    const void *Update(shared_ptr<ResHandle> handle);
    shared_ptr<ResHandle> Load(Resource * r);
    void Free(shared_ptr<ResHandle> gonner);

    bool MakeRoom(unsigned int size);
    char *Allocate(unsigned int size);
    void FreeOneResource();
    void MemoryHasBeenFreed(unsigned int size);

public:
    ResCache(const unsigned int sizeInMb, IResourceFile *resFile);
    ~ResCache();

    bool Init() {  return m_file->VOpen(); }
    shared_ptr<ResHandle> GetHandle(Resource * r);

    void Flush(void);
};
```

The first two members of the class have already been introduced; they are the least recently used (LRU) list and the STL map. There is a pointer to the resource file and two unsigned integers that track the maximum size of the cache and the current size of the cache.

The m_file member points to an object that implements the IResourceFile interface.

The two unsigned integers, m_cacheSize and m_allocated, keep track of the cache size and how much of it is currently being used.

The constructor is pretty basic. It simply sets a few member variables. The destructor frees every resource in the cache by making repeated calls to FreeOneResource until there's nothing left in the cache.

```
ResCache::ResCache(const unsigned int sizeInMb, IResourceFile *resFile )
{
   m_cacheSize = sizeInMb * 1024 * 1024;        // total memory size
   m_allocated = 0;                             // total memory allocated
   m_file = resFile;
}


ResCache::~ResCache()
{
   while (!m_lru.empty())
   {
      FreeOneResource();
   }
   SAFE_DELETE(m_file);
}
```

To get the bits for a resource, you call GetHandle():

```
shared_ptr<ResHandle> ResCache::GetHandle(Resource * r)
{
   shared_ptr<ResHandle> handle(Find(r));
   if (handle==NULL)
      handle = Load(r);
   else
      Update(handle);
   return handle;
}
```

ResCache::GetHandle() is brain-dead simple: If the resource is already loaded in the cache, update it. If it's not there, you have to take a cache miss and load the resource from the file.

The process of finding, updating, and loading resources is easy.

- ResCache::Find() uses an STL map, m_resources, to locate the right ResHandle given a Resource.
- ResCache::Update() removes a ResHandle from the LRU list and promotes it to the front, making sure that the LRU is always sorted properly.
- ResCache::Free() finds a resource by its handle and removes it from the cache.

The other members, `Load()`, `Allocate()`, `MakeRoom()`, and `FreeOneResource()`, are the core of how the cache works:

```
shared_ptr<ResHandle> ResCache::Load(Resource *r)
{
   int size = m_file->VGetResourceSize(*r);
   char *buffer = Allocate(size);
   if (buffer==NULL)
   {
      return shared_ptr<ResHandle>();        // ResCache is out of memory!
   }

   // Create a new resource and add it to the lru list and map
   shared_ptr<ResHandle> handle (r->VCreateHandle(buffer, size, this));
   handle->VLoad(m_file);

   m_lru.push_front(handle);
   m_resources[r->m_name] = handle;

   return handle;
}
```

The `Load()` method grabs the size of the resource from the resource file and calls `Allocate()` to make room in the cache. If the memory allocation is successful, the handle is created with a call to `Resource::VCreateHandle()`. This requires a bit of explanation.

A resource handle might only need to track a buffer and a size, as you have seen in the `ResHandle` class. Different kinds of resources may need additional kinds of data, such as a sound resource, which may want to track additional things such as what kind of sound compression is used in the buffer or its length in milliseconds.

Different kinds of resources can be created using the `VCreateHandle()` virtual—by inheriting from both the `Resource` and `ResHandle` classes. You'll learn more about this in Chapter 12, which discusses using the resource system to create sound resources.

Next up is the `Allocate()` method, which makes more room in the cache when it is needed.

```
char *ResCache::Allocate(unsigned int size)
{
   if (!MakeRoom(size))
      return NULL;
```

```
    char *mem = new char[size];
    if (mem)
        m_allocated += size;

    return mem;
}
```

Allocate() is called from the Load() method when a resource is loaded. It calls MakeRoom() if there isn't enough room in the cache, and updates the member variable to keep track of all of the allocated resources.

```
bool ResCache::MakeRoom(unsigned int size)
{
    if (size > m_cacheSize)
    {
        return false;
    }

    // return null if there's no possible way to allocate the memory
    while (size > (m_cacheSize - m_allocated))
    {
        // The cache is empty, and there's still not enough room.
        if (m_lru.empty())
            return false;

        FreeOneResource();
    }

    return true;
}
```

After the initial sanity check, the while loop in MakeRoom() performs the work of removing enough resources from the cache to load the new resource by calling FreeOneResource(). If there's already enough room, the loop is skipped.

```
void ResCache::FreeOneResource()
{
    ResHandleList::iterator gonner = m_lru.end();
    gonner--;

    shared_ptr<ResHandle> handle = *gonner;

    m_lru.pop_back();
    m_resources.erase(handle->m_resource.m_name);
}
```

`ResCache::FreeOneResource()` removes the oldest resource and updates the cache data members. Note that the memory used by the cache isn't actually modified here—that's because any active shared_ptr<ResHandle> in use will need the bits until it actually goes out of scope.

Here's an example of how this class is used. You construct the cache with a size in mind, in our case 3MB, and an object that implements the IResourceFile interface. You then call Init() to allocate the cache and open the file.

```
ResourceZipFile zipFile("data\\GameCode3.zip");
ResCache resCache (3, zipFile);
if (m_ResCache.Init())
{
    Resource resource("Brick.bmp");
    shared_ptr<ResHandle> texture = g_pApp->m_ResCache->GetHandle(&resource);
    int size = texture->GetSize();
    char *brickBitmap = (char *) texture->Buffer();
    // do something cool with brickBitmap !
}
```

If you want to use this in a real game, you've got more work to do. First, there's hardly a line of defensive or debugging code in ResCache. Resource caches are a significant source of bugs and other mayhem. Data corruption from buggy cache code or something else trashing the cache internals will cause your game to simply freak out.

A functional cache will need to be aware of more than one resource file. It's not reasonable to assume that a game can stuff every resource into a single file, especially since it makes it impossible for teams to work on different parts of the game simultaneously. Associate a filename or number with each resource, and store an array of open resource files in ResCache.

That brings us to the idea of making the cache multithreading compliant. Why not have the cache defrag itself if there's some extra time in the main loop, or perhaps allow a reader in a different thread to fill the cache with resources that might

WRITE A CUSTOM MEMORY MANAGER

Consider implementing your own memory allocator. Many resource caches allocate one contiguous block of memory when they initialize and manage the block internally. Some even have garbage collection, where the resources are moved around as the internal block becomes fragmented. A garbage collection scheme is an interesting problem, but it is extremely difficult to implement a good one that doesn't make the game stutter. Ultima VIII used a scheme like this.

be used in the near future? With the generation of consoles after the PS2 and Xbox, this is one of the areas in game programming getting tons of attention. The new multiprocessor systems have tons of CPU horsepower, and resource management will surely get its own thread. The problem is going to be synchronization and keeping all the CPUs from stalling.

It's also not unusual to use separate resource caches for different kinds of resources like textures, objects, or cinematics. This is especially true for textures, since they can exist in two different kinds of memory: video memory or system memory. A good texture cache needs to take that into account.

Caching Resources into DirectX, et al.

Luckily for you, DirectX objects like sound effects, textures, and even meshes can all load from a memory stream. For example, you can load a DirectX texture using the D3DXCreateTextureFromFileInMemory() API, which means loading a texture from your resource cache is pretty easy:

```
Resource resource(m_params.m_Texture);
shared_ptr<ResHandle> texture = g_pApp->m_ResCache->GetHandle(&resource);
if ( FAILED (
    D3DXCreateTextureFromFileInMemory(
        DXUTGetD3D9Device(),
        texture->Buffer(),
        texture->Size(),
        &m_pTexture ) ) )
{
    return E_FAIL;
}
```

There are some SDKs out there that don't let you do this. They require you to send filenames into their APIs, and they take complete control of loading their own data. While it's unfortunate, it simply means you can't use the resource cache for those parts of your game.

World Design and Cache Prediction

Perhaps you've just finished a supercharged version of ResCache—good for you. You're not done yet. If you load resources the moment you need them, you'll probably suffer a wildly fluctuating frame rate. The moment your game asks for resources outside of the cache, the flickering hard disk light will be the most exciting thing your players will be able to watch.

First, classify your game design into one of the following categories:

- **Load Everything at Once:** This is for any game that caches resources on a screen-by-screen basis or level-by-level. Each screen of *Myst* is a good example, as well as *Grim Fandango*. Most fighting games work under this model for each event.
- **Load Only at Pinch Points:** Almost every shooter utilizes this design, where resources are cached in during elevator rides or in small barren hallways.
- **Load Constantly:** This is for open-map games where players can go anywhere they like. Examples include flight simulators, racing games, massively multiplayer games, and action/adventure games like *Grand Theft Auto: Vice City*.

The first scheme trades one huge loading pause for lightning fast action during the game. These games have small levels or arenas that can fit entirely in memory. Thus, there's never a cache miss. The game designers can count on every CPU cycle spent on the game world instead of loading resources. The downside is that since your entire playing area has to fit entirely in memory, it can't be that big.

Shooters like *Halo* on the Xbox360 load resources at pinch points. The designers add buffer zones between the action where relatively little is happening in the game. Elevators and hallways with a few elbow turns are perfect examples of this technique. The CPU spends almost no time rendering the tiny environment in these areas, and it uses the leftover cycles to load the next hot zone. In elevators, players can't change their minds in the middle of the trip until the elevator gets to the right floor, which happens to be timed to open exactly when the next area is loaded. Elbow hallways are constructed so that the loading time will always be less than the maximum running speed of the player. The more loading is needed, the longer the hallway will be.

One thing you may notice is that with each of these designs, the ResCache needs to load in the background while the rest of the game continues to run. This turns out to be pretty tricky stuff.

BUFFER ZONES IN YOUR GAME AFFECT PACING AND PLAYER TENSION

These buffer zones will exist in many places throughout the game, providing the player with a brief moment to load weapons and rest happy trigger fingers. The designers at Bungie took advantage of this and placed a few surprise encounters in these buffer zones, something that always made me freak out when I was playing Halo.

Even better, the folks at Bungie were wise enough to use the hallways to set the tone for the next fight with Covenant forces or The Flood. Sometimes it was as simple as painting the walls with enemy blood or playing some gruesome sound effects.

GAMERS DON'T WANT TO READ, THEY WANT TO PLAY

Don't make the player read a bunch of text in between levels just to give yourself time to cache resources. Players figure this out right away, and want to click past the text they've read five or six times. They won't be able to do so since you've got to spend a few more seconds loading resources, and they'll click like mad and curse your name. If you're lucky, the worst thing they'll do is return your game. Don't open any suspicious packages you receive in the mail.

Open-mapped games such as flight simulators, racing games, fantasy role-playing games, or action/adventure games have a much tougher problem. The maps are huge, relatively open, and the game designers have little or no control over where the player will go next. Players also expect an incredible level of detail in these games. They want to read the headlines in newspapers or see individual leaves on the trees, while tall buildings across the river are in plain view. Players like that alternate reality. One of the best games that uses this open world design is *Grand Theft Auto*.

Modern operating systems have more options for multithreading, especially for caching in game areas while the CPU has some extra time. They use the player's direction of travel to predict the most likely areas that will be needed shortly, and add those resources to a list that is loaded on an ad hoc basis as the cache gets some time to do extra work. This is especially beneficial if the game designers can give the cache some hints, such as the destination of a path or the existence of pinch points, such as a tunnel. These map elements almost serve as pinch points like the hallways in *Halo*, although players can always turn around and go the other direction.

BATCH YOUR CACHE READS IF YOU CAN

Create your cache to load multiple resources at one time, and sort your cache reads in the order in which they appear in the file. This will minimize any seeking activity on the part of the drive's read head. If your resource file is organized properly, the resources used together will appear next to each other in the file. It will then be probable that resource loads will be accomplished in a single read block with as few seeks as possible.

If you want to find out how your resources are being used, you should instrument your build. That means you should create a debug build with special code that creates a log file every time a resource is used. Use this log as a secondary data file to your resource file creator, and you'll be able to sequence the file to your game's best advantage.

In open world games, the maximum map density should always leave a little CPU time to perform some cache chores. Denser areas will spend most of their

CPU time on game tasks for rendering, sound, and AI. Sparse areas will spend more time preparing the cache for denser areas about to reach the display. The trick is to balance these areas carefully, guiding the player through pinch points where it's possible, and never overloading the cache.

If the CPU can't keep up with cache requests and other game tasks, you'll probably suffer a cache miss and risk the player detecting a stutter in the game. Not all is lost, however, since a cache miss is a good opportunity to catch up on the entire list of resources that will be needed all at once. This should be considered a worst case scenario, because if your game does this all the time, it will frustrate players. If you do this in a first-person shooter, you'll end up with a lot of bad reviews.

A better solution is a fallback mechanism for some resources that suffer a cache miss. Flight simulators and other open architecture games can sometimes get away with keeping the uncached resource hidden until the cache can load it. Imagine a flight simulator game that caches in architecture as the plane gets close. If the game attempts to draw a building that hasn't been cached in, then the building simply won't show up. Think for a moment what is more important to the player: a piece of architecture that will likely show up in 100ms or so anyway, or a frustrating pause in the action?

BEST PRACTICE

NOT ALL RESOURCES ARE EQUALLY IMPORTANT

It's a good idea to associate a priority with each resource. Some resources are so important to the game that it must suffer a cache miss rather than fail to render it. This is critical for sound effects, which must sometimes be timed exactly with visual events such as explosions.

The really tough open-map problems are those games that add a level of detail on top of an open-map design. This approach is common with flight simulators and action adventure games. Each map segment has multiple levels of detail for static and dynamic objects. It's not a horrible problem to figure out how to create different levels of detail for each segment. The problem is how to switch from one level of detail to another without the player noticing. This is much easier in action/adventure games where the player is on the ground and most objects are obscured from view when they flip to a new level of detail.

Flight simulators don't have that luxury. Of all the games on the market, flight simulators spend more time on caching continuous levels of detail than any other nonrendering task. Players want the experience of flying high enough to see the mountains on the horizon and diving low enough to see individual trees and ground clutter whiz by at Mach 1.

This subject is way beyond the scope of this book, but I won't leave you hanging. There is some amazing work done in this area, not the least of which was published in *Level of Detail for 3D Graphics* by D. Luebke, M. Reddy, J. Cohen, A. Varshney, B. Watson, and R. Huebner. They also have a Web site at http://lodbook.com.

I'm Out of Cache

Smart game programmers realize early on that some problems are harder than others. If you thought that creating a good flight simulator was a piece of cake, I'd tell you that the part that's tricky isn't simulating the airplane, but simulating the ground. The newbie game programmer could spend all his time creating a great flight model, and when he started the enormous task of representing undulating terrain with smooth detail levels, he would fold like laundry.

Games need enormous amounts of data to suspend disbelief on the part of players. No one, not even Epic, can set their system RAM requirements to hold the entire contents of even one disk of current day optical media. It's also not enough to simply assume that a game will load resources as needed and the game designers can do what they want. That is a tragic road traveled by many games that never shipped. Most games that suffer fatal frame rate issues ignored their cache constraints.

It's up to programmers to code the best cache they can and figure out a way to get game level designers, artists, and sound engineers to plan the density of game areas carefully. If everyone succeeds in his task, you get a smooth game that plays well. If you succeed, you'll get a game that can almost predict the future.

8

PROGRAMMING INPUT DEVICES

In This Chapter

- Getting the Device State
- Using DirectInput
- A Few Safety Tips
- Working with the Mouse (and Joystick)
- Working with a Game Controller
- Working with the Keyboard
- What, No Dance Pad?

Even though user interface programming seems easy, it's actually quite tricky, which is ironic since most game companies assign the user interface code to their greenest programmers. It's a simple matter under almost any platform to read a keyboard, mouse, or gamepad. Most programmers take this input, like the X,Y coordinate of a mouse, and use it to directly modify the game state, such as where the player is looking in a first-person shooter. This technique works, all too well, until you want to do something like switch out that mouse for a USB gamepad, or perhaps change how the controls are interpreted by the game. Maybe your player wants to switch the up/down or Y-axis of the camera controls from normal to inverted, like I prefer.

The framework presented in this book puts reading the hardware input devices squarely inside the application layer, which is the layer that handles any and all operating system or machine-dependent code. Once the application layer handles the raw input, it is handed off to the game view layer, usually a game view written specifically for a human player, to interpret the raw input and translate it into a command for your game. This chapter deals with the hardware and the raw messages, and you'll learn how these messages are handled in a game view in the next chapter on user interface programming.

First, we'll play with the hardware.

GETTING THE DEVICE STATE

No matter what type of device you use—keyboard, mouse, joystick, and so on—you'll need to understand the techniques and subtleties of getting and controlling the state of your input devices. We'll start by working at the lowest level, and then we'll work our way up the input device food chain. The interfaces to input devices are completely dependent on the platforms you use, and to some extent any middleware you might be using. Many 3D graphics engines also provide APIs to all the input hardware. Regardless of the API used or devices they control, there are two schemes for processing user input:

- **Polling:** This method is a little old-fashioned but still very popular. It requires an application to query each device to find out its state. Your code should react to the state accordingly, usually comparing it against a previous state and calling an input handler if anything changed. This is how DirectInput works.
- **Callbacks or messages:** This method is more common in advanced game engines that handle the low level stuff for you. Here you just register input device callbacks based on which devices you care about, and when they change state, your callback will get control. They poll at the low level just like DirectX, but state changes are detected for you, which will launch your callback.

Meaningful changes in hardware state should be translated into a game event, whether you use a polling method or callback method. With a little work, you can structure your code to do this.

Of course, every platform operates a little differently, but the code looks very similar; mouse buttons still go up and down, and the entire device moves on a two-dimensional plane. It's not crazy to assume that most device-handling code reflects the nature of the specific device.

- **Buttons:** They will have up and down states. The down state might have an analog component. Most game controllers support button pressure as an 8-bit value.
- **One-axis controllers:** They will have a single analog state, with zero representing the unpressed state. Game controllers usually have analog triggers for use in features such as accelerators in driving games.
- **Two-axis controllers:** A mouse and joystick are 2D controllers. Their status can be represented as integers or floating-point numbers. When using these devices, you shouldn't assume anything about their coordinate space. The coordinate (0,0) might represent the upper left-hand corner of the screen, or it might represent the device center.

Game controllers, even complicated ones, are built from assemblies of these three component types. The tricked-out joysticks that the flight simulator fans go for are simply buttons and triggers attached to a 2D controller. To support such a device, you need to write a custom handler function for each component. Depending on the way your handler functions get the device status, you might have to factor the device status for each component out of a larger data structure. Eventually, you'll call your handler functions and change the game state.

CHOOSE CONTROLS WITH FIDELITY IN MIND

When you choose a control scheme for your game, be mindful of the fidelity of each control. For example, a gamepad thumbstick has a low fidelity because the entire movement from one extreme to another is only a few centimeters. The mouse, on the other hand, has a very high fidelity since its movement is perhaps 10 times as far. This is a fundamental difference between games that use the gamepad, where targets are large and few in number, versus games that require a mouse, where targets require speed and precision, such as a headshot. If you attempt to force a gamepad thumbstick into the same role as a mouse control, your players will be extremely frustrated and likely will stop playing your game. For games that are gamepad based, the players using gamepads will certainly need a little help aiming, as do most console shooters such as *Halo*. The players still need a high degree of skill, and its design cleverly balances the movement of the AI, the aiming help, and the control scheme to be fun.

You can create some interface classes for each kind of device that takes as input the translated events that you received from messages, callbacks, or even polling. You can write these any way you want, but here are some examples to help you get started:

```
class IKeyboardHandler
{
    virtual bool VOnKeyDown(unsigned int const kcode)=0;
    virtual bool VOnKeyUp(unsigned int const kcode)=0;
};


class IMouseHandler
{
    virtual bool VOnLMouseDown(int const x, int const y)=0;
    virtual bool VOnLMouseUp  (int const x, int const y)=0;
    virtual bool VOnRMouseDown(int const x, int const y)=0;
    virtual bool VOnRMouseUp  (int const x, int const y)=0;
    virtual bool VOnMouseMove (int const x, int const y)=0;
};


class IJoystickHandler
{
    virtual bool VOnButtonDown(int const button, int const pressure)=0;
    virtual bool VOnButtonUp(int const button)=0;
    virtual bool VOnJoystick(float const x, float const y)=0;
};


class IGamepadHandler
{
    virtual bool VOnTrigger(bool const left, float const pressure)=0;
    virtual bool VOnButtonDown(int const button, int const pressure)=0;
    virtual bool VOnButtonUp(int const button)=0;
    virtual bool VOnDirectionalPad(int directionFlags)=0;
    virtual bool VOnThumbstick(int const stickNum, float const x,
                  float const y)=0;
};
```

Each function represents an action taken by a control when something happens to an input device. Here's how the return values work: If the message is handled, the functions return true; otherwise, they return false.

You'll implement these interfaces in control classes to convert input from devices to commands that can change the game state. Control objects in your game are guaranteed to receive device input in a standard and predictable way.

Thus, it should be a simple matter to modify and change the interface of your game by attaching new control objects that care about any device you've installed.

The interface classes described previously are simple examples, and they should be coded to fit the unique needs of your game. You can easily remove or add functions at will, and not every game will use input exactly the same way.

BEST
PRACTICE

MAP CONTROLS DIRECTLY TO CONTROLLED OBJECTS

Don't add parameters to distinguish between multiple joysticks or gamepads. A better solution is to create controls that map directly to the object they are controlling. For example, if multiple gamepads control multiple human drivers, the control code shouldn't need to be aware of any other driver but the one it is controlling. You could set all this up in a factory that creates the driver and the controller and informs the input device code where to send the input from each gamepad.

If you follow a modular design, your game objects can be controlled via the same interface, whether the source of that control is a gamepad or an AI character. For example, the AI character could send commands like "brake 75%" or "steer 45%" into a car controller, where the human player touches a few gamepad keys, generating translated events that eventually result in exactly the same calls, but to a different car.

This design should always exist in any game where AI characters and humans are essentially interchangeable. If humans and AI characters use completely different interfaces to game objects, it becomes difficult to port a single player game to multiplayer. You'll soon discover that none of the "plugs" fit.

You'll see in Chapter 9, "User Interface Programming," how to attach a mouse handler and keyboard handler to a game view class, and you'll also see in Chapter 14, "3D Scenes," how to implement a user interface using both the mouse and the keyboard to move about a 3D scene.

USING DIRECTINPUT

DirectInput is the DirectX API for input devices such as the mouse, keyboard, joystick, game controllers, and force feedback devices. DirectX sits in between your application and a physical device like a video or sound card. For video and sound systems, many things are handled directly by the hardware, such as a video card's ability to texture map a polygon. If the hardware doesn't have that feature, it is simulated in software. This architecture is usually called a *hardware abstraction layer*, or HAL. While there is nothing for DirectInput to hardware accelerate, it does provide an important service, which is to expose the capabilities of the user input hardware. For example, a USB game controller might have a rumble or force feedback feature. If it does, DirectInput will give your game a way to detect it and use it to make your game more interesting.

Windows can certainly grab user input with DirectInput. Mouse and keyboard messages are well understood by a Win32 programmer the moment they create their first Win32 application. You might not be aware that the Win32 Multimedia Platform SDK has everything you need to accept messages from your joystick. You don't even need DirectInput for that, so why bother? Straight Win32 code does not expose every feature of all varieties of joysticks or PC game controller pads. For example, you can grab input from a Logitech PC gamepad without DirectInput with this code:

```
bool CheckForJoystick(HWND hWnd)
{
   JOYINFO joyinfo;
   UINT wNumDevs, wDeviceID;
   BOOL bDev1Attached, bDev2Attached;
   if((wNumDevs = joyGetNumDevs()) == 0)
      return false;
   bDev1Attached = joyGetPos(JOYSTICKID1,&joyinfo) != JOYERR_UNPLUGGED;
   bDev2Attached = joyGetPos(JOYSTICKID2,&joyinfo) != JOYERR_UNPLUGGED;
   if(bDev1Attached)
      joySetCapture(hWnd, JOYSTICKID1, 1000/30, true);
   if (bDev2Attached)
      joySetCapture(hWnd, JOYSTICKID2, 1000/30, true);

   return true;
}
```

After this code runs, Windows will begin sending messages to your game such as MM_JOY1MOVE and MM_JOY2BUTTONDOWN. You might feel that this simple code is preferable to the much larger initialization and required polling needed by Direct-Input, but DirectInput gives you access to the entire device—all the buttons, the rumble, force feedback, and so on. The Windows Multimedia Platform SDK only gives you the most basic access to joystick messages.

Beyond this, another feature of DirectInput that's pretty useful is called *action mapping*. This is a concept that binds actions to virtual controls. Instead of looking at the X-axis of the joystick to find the direction of a car's steering wheel, Direct-Input can map the action of steering the car to a virtual control. The actual controls can be mapped to the virtual controls at the whim of the player, and are the basis for providing a completely configurable control system. Hardcore gamers really love this. If you are making a hardcore game, you'll need configurable controls. DirectInput isn't the only way to make that work, however, but it does buy you a few other things like a standard way to tweak the force feedback system.

BEST PRACTICE

REMAPPABLE CONTROLS ARE EXPECTED BY YOUR PLAYERS

Whether you use DirectInput or not, this action-mapping idea is something every game should have, even if you have to code it yourself. If you can easily switch your controls from right-handed to left-handed, or from normal camera movement to inverted camera movement, you'll automatically get more people to play your game. Actually, you'll keep people from throwing your game in the garbage. Players expect a customizable interface, and you'll never convince someone to "learn" your control scheme, no matter how much fun your game is. Even more importantly, PC gamepads from different manufacturers may map input completely differently—for example, one may switch the thumbsticks from left-handed to right-handed or give you negative values when you expect positive values. A configurable input scheme lets you easily remap these wacky values to a standard your game will use.

Mass market games that don't use any advanced features of joysticks or don't have insanely configurable controls can work just fine with Windows messages and the Windows Multimedia Platform SDK. You don't have to learn to use DirectInput to make games, and Windows messages are easy and familiar. There are plenty of DirectInput samples in the DirectX SDK for you to look at, so I'm not going to waste your time or any trees on the subject. What I want to work on is the fact that there's plenty to talk about in terms of user interface code, regardless of the API you use.

A FEW SAFETY TIPS

I've probably spent more of my programming time on user interface tasks than almost anything else. The design for the early *Ultima* games loaded tons of control on the mouse—the idea being that the player could play the whole game without ever touching the keyboard. As good an idea as it seemed at the time, this was a horrible idea because it ignored simple physiology and the nature of the hardware. Remember that any input scheme should be designed around how players physically manipulate the device, and that they tend to do this for hours at a time.

If it ain't broke, don't fix it. There are plenty of standard conventions for input devices, from Microsoft Windows to *Quake*. When you sit down to write your interface code, consider your control scheme carefully and make a conscious decision whether you want to stay with a well-known convention or go in a totally new direction. You take a risk with going rogue on user interface controls, but it can pay off too. After all, before the shooter-style game was popular, how many games used the mouse as a model for a human neck? This idea worked well in a case like this for two reasons: It solved a new problem, and the solution was intuitive.

IF IT AIN'T BROKE, DON'T FIX IT

If you're solving an interface problem that has a standard solution and you choose a radically different approach, you take a risk of annoying players. If you think their annoyance will transition into wonder and words of praise as they discover (and figure out) your novel solution, then by all means give it a try. Make sure that you test your idea first with some colleagues you trust. They'll tell you if your idea belongs on the garbage heap. After your colleagues, try the idea out on real players. Be careful with interfaces, though. A friend of mine once judged the many entrants into the Indie Games Festival (www.indiegames.com) and he said the biggest mistake he saw that killed promising entrants was poor interface controls. He was amazed to see entries with incredible 3D graphics not make the cut because they were simply too hard to control. What's worse, even game professionals get caught in this problem. The big retail buyers will give your game just a few minutes, and if they can't figure out your control scheme, they won't buy your game. Believe me, if someone like Walmart or Best Buy doesn't buy your game, you are destined for the great bargain bin in the sky. In short, don't be afraid to use a good idea just because it's already been done.

Be cautious with overloading simple controls with complicated results. Context sensitivity in controls can be tough to deal with as a player. It's easy to make the mistake of loading too much control onto too little a device. The *Ultima* games generally went a little too far, I think, in how they used the mouse. A design goal for the games was to have every conceivable action be possible from the mouse, so every click and double-click was used for something. In fact, the same command would do different things if you clicked on a person, a door, or a monster. I'm sometimes surprised that we never implemented a special action for the "shave and a haircut, two bits" click.

Give the player some feedback. One thing I think the *Ultima* games did well was how they used the pointer or cursor. The cursor would change shape to give the player feedback about what things were and whether they could be activated by a mouse command. This is especially useful when your screens are very densely populated. When the mouse pointer changes shape to signify that the player can perform an action, players immediately understand that they can use the pointer to explore the screen. In *Thief: Deadly Shadows*, the gamepad controls did very different things when the player was shooting an arrow or picking a lock. The very first tutorial mission exposed these differences with specific tasks the player had to complete during the tutorial mission, and the screens were very different for both modes. The last game I was on, *Mushroom Men: The Spore Wars* for the Wii, brought the changing icon back to tell the player what special power was possible on any object being pointed to by the Wii Remote.

Players won't use it if they don't know about it. A great term in games is "discoverability." It describes how easy it is for a player to figure things out on his own. Power-user moves are sometimes hidden on purpose, such as a special button combo in a fighting game, and that's a fine thing to hide. A special shortcut to page through equipped weapons is different—it is something that more advanced players will use to shorten the time between their desire to do something and having it actually happening. Make sure that you expose anything like this in a tutorial or in hints during loading screens. Documenting it isn't good enough—players usually never read documentation.

Watch and learn. When you finish any work on any kind of interface, bring some people in and watch them try to use it. Stand behind them and give them a task to perform, but don't give them any hints. An interface should be self evident to players, and they should be able to figure it out in 30 seconds or less on their own. A really good tip: Watch what your impromptu testers do first, and most likely they'll all do something similar. If they struggle with your solution, consider carefully whether your design will work.

Avoid pixel perfect accuracy. It's a serious mistake to assume that players of all ages can target a screen area with pixel perfect accuracy. Even with a high-fidelity control like a mouse, this task is very difficult; on a very low-fidelity control like the Wii Remote, this is simply impossible. An example of this might be a small click target on a draggable item or a small drop point on the screen. Anything that will change as a result of a pointing device and a click should have a little buffer zone widening the available target area. On *Thief: Deadly Shadows*, these "sloppy" targeting areas would sometimes overlap on-screen, and the code had to choose which item was the most likely one targeted. The solution was to choose the closest one to the screen, but that doesn't necessarily work all the time.

Anyone who has attempted to cast spells in the original version of *Ultima VIII* will agree. The reagents that made some of the spells work had to be placed exactly. This requirement made spell casting frustrating and arbitrary.

TARGETING IS ALWAYS A LITTLE SLOPPY

The *Ultima VII* mouse code detected objects on the screen by performing pixel collision testing with the mouse (x,y) position and the images that made up the objects in the world. Most of these sprites were chroma-keyed, and therefore had spots of the transparent color all through them. This was especially true of things like jail cell bars and fences. *Ultima VII's* pixel collision code ignored the transparent color, allowing players to click through fences and jail cell bars to examine objects on the other side. That was a good feature, and it was used in many places to advance the story. The problem it created, however, was that sometimes the transparent colored pixels actually made it harder for players to click on an object. For example, double-clicking the door of the jail cell was difficult. If you use an approach like this, take some care in designing which objects are active, and which are simply scenery, and make sure you make this clear to your players.

This is an extremely important issue with casual games or kids' games. Very young players or older gamers enjoy games that include buffer zones in the interface because they are easier to play.

A FINE USE OF A PIECE OF TAPE

With *Ultima VIII,* the left mouse button served as the "walk/run" button. As long as you held it down, the Avatar character would run in the direction of the mouse pointer. *Ultima* games require a lot of running; your character will run across an entire continent only to discover that the thingamajig that will open the gate of *whosiz* is back in the city you just left, so you go running off again. By the time I'd played through the game the umpteenth time, my index finger was so tired of running I started using tape to hold the mouse button down. One thing people do in a lot of FPS games when playing online is set them to "always run" mode. I wish we'd had done that with *Ultima VIII.*

WORKING WITH THE MOUSE (AND JOYSTICK)

I'm not going to talk about basic topics like grabbing WM_MOUSEMOVE and pulling screen coordinates out of the LPARAM. Many books have been written to cover these programming techniques. If you need a primer on Win32 and GDI, I suggest you read Charles Petzold's classic book: *Programming Windows: The Definitive Guide to the Win32 API.*

Capturing the Mouse

I'm always surprised that Win32 documentation doesn't make inside jokes about capturing the mouse. At least we can still laugh at it. If you've never programmed a user interface before, you probably don't know what capturing the mouse means or why any programmer in his right mind would want to do this. Catching a mouse isn't probably something that's high on your list.

To see what you've been missing, go to a Windows machine right now and bring up a dialog box. Move the mouse over a button, hopefully not one that will erase your hard drive, and click the left mouse button and hold it down. You should see the button graphic depress. Move the mouse pointer away from the button, and you'll notice the button graphic pop back up again. Until you release the left mouse button, you can move the mouse all you want, but only the button on the dialog will get the messages. If you don't believe me, open up Microsoft Spy++ and see for yourself. Microsoft Spy++ is a tool that you use to figure out which Windows messages are going to which window, and it's a great debugging tool if you are coding a GUI application. Here's a quick tutorial:

1. If you are running Visual Studio, select Spy++ from the Tools menu. You can also launch it from the Tools section of the Visual Studio area of your Start menu.
2. Close the open default window and select Find Window from the main menu or press Ctrl-F.
3. You'll then see a little dialog box that looks like the one shown in Figure 8.1.
4. Click and drag the little finder tool to the window or button you are interested in, and then click the Messages radio button at the bottom of the dialog. You'll get a new window in Spy++ that shows you every message sent to the object.

FIGURE 8.1 The Find Window with Spy++.

Perform the previous experiment again, but this time use Spy++ to monitor the Windows messages sent to the button. You'll find that as soon as you click on the button, every mouse action will be displayed, even if the pointer is far away from the button in question. That might be interesting, but why is it important? If a user interface uses the boundaries of an object like a button to determine whether it should receive mouse events, capturing the mouse is critical. Imagine a scenario where you can't capture mouse events:

1. The mouse button goes down over an active button.
2. The button receives the event and draws itself in the down position.
3. The mouse moves away from the button, outside its border.
4. The button stops receiving any events from the mouse since the mouse isn't directly over the button.
5. The mouse button is released.

The result is that the button will still be drawn in the down position, awaiting a button release event that will never happen. If the mouse events are captured, the button will continue to receive mouse events until the button is released.

To better understand this, take a look at a code snippet that shows some code you can use to capture the mouse and draw lines:

```
LRESULT APIENTRY MainWndProc(HWND hwndMain, UINT uMsg, WPARAM wParam,
                             LPARAM lParam)
{
    static POINTS ptsBegin;          // beginning point

    switch (uMsg)
    {
        case WM_LBUTTONDOWN:
            // Capture mouse input.
            SetCapture(hwndMain);
            bIsCaptured = true;
            ptsBegin = MAKEPOINTS(lParam);
            return 0;

        case WM_MOUSEMOVE:
            // When moving the mouse, the user must hold down
            // the left mouse button to draw lines.
            if (wParam & MK_LBUTTON)
            {
                // imaginary code - you write this function
                pseudocode::ErasePreviousLine();

                // Convert the current cursor coordinates to a
                // POINTS structure, and then draw a new line.
                ptsEnd = MAKEPOINTS(lParam);

                // also imaginary
                pseudocode::DrawLine(ptsEnd.x, ptsEnd.y);
            }
            break;

        case WM_LBUTTONUP:
            // The user has finished drawing the line. Reset the
            // previous line flag, release the mouse cursor, and
            // release the mouse capture.
```

```
        fPrevLine = FALSE;
        bIsCaptured = false;
        ReleaseCapture();
        break;
    }


    case WM_ACTIVATEAPP:
    {
        if (wParam == TRUE)
        {
            // got focus again - regain our mouse capture
            if (bIsCaptured)
                SetCapture(hwndMain);
        }
        break;
    }
    return 0;
}
```

If you were to write functions for erasing and drawing lines, you'd have a nice rubber band line-drawing mechanism, which mouse capturing makes possible. By using it, your lines will continue to follow the mouse, even if you leave the window's client area.

One thing to note: If your application loses focus, you'll also lose the mouse capture, which can be handled easily by listening to the WM_ACTIVATEAPP message.

Making a Mouse Drag Work

You might wonder why a mouse drag is so important. Drags are important because they are prerequisites to much of the user interface code in a lot of PC games. When you select a group of combatants in RTS games like *Command & Conquer*, for example, you drag out a rectangle. When you play *Freecell* in Windows, you use the mouse to drag cards around. It is quite likely that you'll have to code a mouse drag at some point.

Dragging the mouse adds a little complexity to the process of capturing it. Most user interface code distinguishes a single click, double-click, and drag as three separate actions, and therefore will call different game code. Dragging also relates to the notion of legality; it's not always possible that anything in your game can be dragged to anywhere. If a drag fails, you'll need a way to set things back to the way they were. This issue might seem moot when you consider that dragging usually affects the look of the game—the dragged object needs to appear like it is really moving around, and it shouldn't leave a copy of itself in its original location. That might confuse the player big-time.

The code to support dragging requires three phases:

- Detect and initiate a drag event.
- Handle the mouse movement and draw objects accordingly.
- Detect the release and finalize the drag.

The actions that define a drag are typically a mouse press (button down) followed by a mouse movement, but life in the mouse drag game is not always that simple. Also, during a double-click event, a slight amount of mouse movement might occur, perhaps only a single pixel coordinate. Your code must interpret these different cases.

In Windows, a drag event is only allowed on objects that are already selected, which is why drags usually follow on the second "click and hold" of the mouse button. The first click of the left mouse button always selects objects. Many games differ from that standard, but it's one of the easier actions to code since only selected objects are draggable.

Since a drag event involves multiple trips around the main loop, you must assume that every mouse button down event could be the beginning of a drag event. I guess an event is assumed draggable until proven innocent. In your mouse button down handler, you need to look at the mouse coordinates and determine if they are over a draggable object. If the object is draggable, you must create a temporary reference to it that you can find a few game loops later. Since this is the first button down event, you can't tell if it's a bona fide drag event just yet.

The only thing that will make the drag event real is the movement of the mouse, but only movement outside of a tiny buffer zone. On an 800 × 600 screen, a good choice is five pixels in either the x or y coordinate. This is large enough to indicate that the drag was real, but small enough that small shakes in the mouse during a double-click won't unintentionally initiate a drag. If you were to create a drag on a Wii game, you'd want a much sloppier buffer zone since the Wii Remote pointer can shake quite a bit. If you can set this buffer size while the game is running, like with a hack or a cheat, you'll be able to tune this to suit a majority of players quickly.

Here's the code that performs this dirty work of the drag:

```
// Place this code at the top of your mouse movement handler
if (m_aboutToDrag)
{
    CPoint offset = currentPoint - dragStartingPoint;
    if (abs(offset.x) > DRAG_THRESHOLD || abs(offset.y) > DRAG_THRESHOLD)
    {
        // We have a real drag event!
        bool dragOK =
            pseudocode::InitiateDrag(draggedObject, dragStartingPoint);
```

```
        SetCapture( GetWindow()->m_hWnd );
        m_dragging = TRUE;
    }
}
```

The call to `pseudocode::InitiateDrag()` is something you write yourself. Its job is to set the game state to remove the original object from the display and draw the dragged object in some obvious form, such as a transparent ghost object.

Until the mouse button is released, the mouse movement handler will continue to get mouse movement commands, even those that are outside the client area of your window if you are running in windowed mode. Make sure that your draw routines don't freak out when they see these odd coordinates.

While the drag is active, you must direct all the mouse input to the control that initiated the drag. Other controls should essentially ignore the input. The best way to do this is to keep a pointer to the control that initiated the drag and send all input directly to it, essentially bypassing any code that sends messages to your control list. It's a little like masking all the controls in your control list, rendering them deaf to all incoming messages until the drag is complete.

What must go down, must finally come up again. When the mouse button is released, your drag is complete, but the drag location might not be in a legal spot, so you might have to reset your game back to the state before the drag started, like this:

```
// Place this code at the top of your mouse button up handler
if ( m_dragging )
{
    ReleaseCapture();
    m_bDragging = false;

    if (!pseudocode::FinishDrag(point))
    {
        pseudocode::AbortDrag(dragStartingPoint);
    }
}
```

This bit of code would exist in your handler for a mouse button up event. The call to `ReleaseCapture()` makes sure that mouse events get sent to all their normal places again. `pseudocode::FinishDrag()` is a function you'd write yourself. It should detect if the destination of the drag was legal, and perform the right game state manipulations to make it so. If the drag is illegal, the object has to snap back to its previous location as if the drag never occurred. This function can be trickier to write than you'd think, since you can't necessarily use game state information to send the object back to where it came from.

GAME EDITORS ARE ALL POWERFUL

In *Ultima VII* and *Ultima VIII,* we created a complicated system to keep track of object movement, specifically whether or not an object could legally move from one place to another. It was possible for a game designer to use the all-powerful game editor to force objects into any location, whether it was legal or not. If these objects were dragged to another illegal location by the player, the object had to be forced back into place. Otherwise, the object would exist in limbo. What we learned was that the drag code could access the game state at a low enough level to run the abort code.

You can have exactly the same problem with modern games that use modern physics systems. These days when you place an object like a candle inside a table or something, the physics system essentially removes the candle completely from the collision detector, causing it to fall through the table and plummet downward, perhaps forever. This can make dragging objects with real physics somewhat painful. The best course of action is to require the world editor to place dynamic objects in proper positions where they can be moved by the player later.

WORKING WITH A GAME CONTROLLER

Working on Ion Storm's *Thief: Deadly Shadows* game was my first experience with console development, and my first experience with writing code for a gamepad. It was much more of an eye opener than I thought it would be. Until I actually had one of these things in my hot little hands and the code saturating my over-caffeinated brain, I thought these devices were little more than a collection of buttons and joysticks. Boy, was I wrong!

Having played tons of console games, I already had a pretty good feel for a good control scheme, but I'd never had the chance to write one myself. The basics of the gamepad interface code are really quite the same as a mouse, keyboard, or joystick, but subtle differences between interface design and interpreting the device inputs warrant some additional explanation. I'll talk a little about dead zones, normalizing input, input acceleration, and the design impact of one-stick versus two-stick control schemes.

Dead Zones

A dead zone is any area of a control interface that has no input effect. This keeps small errors in hand movement from adversely affecting game input. You know you need a dead zone in a control when you watch players make mistakes because the controls were too sensitive and interpreted their input in a way that they didn't expect.

A great example of this was on the *Thief: Deadly Shadows* camera control for the Xbox gamepad. It used a two-stick control scheme like *Halo* or *Splinter Cell*, which meant that the character moved with the left thumbstick and the camera moved with the right thumbstick.

The first iteration of the camera movement code was pretty simple; the right thumbstick controlled the camera. Up/down movement caused the camera to pitch, left/right movement caused the camera to yaw. But when I went to QA and watched them play, I noticed something really strange happening. As the QA person would spin the camera left or right, the camera would also pitch a few degrees up or down. This happened every time in QA, but not with me as I tested the code.

I watched QA play more to try to figure out what was happening, and I realized that when they were actually playing the game they'd jam the left thumbstick left or right to see if something was behind them, and it was a pretty fast movement. Once the thumbstick hit the extreme position, it would stop, of course, but it would usually also be in a slightly up or down angle as well as all the way left or right. In my tests, I wasn't jamming the controller, and thus I never had the slight up/down position. Even though it was small, the up/down error in the thumbstick movement always resulted in the camera pitching up/down, just as I wrote the code.

Figure 8.2 shows the movement area of a thumbstick controller on a gamepad. By convention, gamepads, joysticks, and other two-axis controllers usually have raw output ranges from [-1.0f, 1.0f], and the neutral position returns a raw output value of (0.0f, 0.0f). Every now and then, you might find a control device returning odd values, like integers from [0,255] or something like that. If you ever see this happening, it's a good idea to remap the output range back to [-1.0f, 1.0f]. Standardizing these ranges helps keep the code that interprets these values nice and clean.

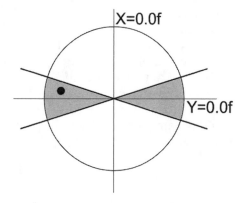

FIGURE 8.2 Dealing with a dead zone for pitch control.

If the thumbstick were positioned at the location of the black spot, you'd expect an X,Y value of (-0.80, 0.15) or thereabouts. That small positive Y input would be the cause of my previous trouble; the camera would slowly pitch until it was looking straight up or down, depending on the control scheme.

You might not think this is a serious problem—until you watch players play the game. Many first-person shooter players like to twitch-look—where they snap the thumbstick quickly to the left or right and pause for a second or two. If there's no dead zone, the camera will always begin to pitch a little up or down, depending on how the player is holding the gamepad. At some point the player has to stop and correct the camera pitch, usually with a snort of disgust. Many players and game critics complain about bad cameras, but it seems that what they are really complaining about is bad camera *control*.

The answer to my problem, and yours if you are coding thumbstick controls, is a dead zone for pitch control. The dead zone is represented by the darkened area in Figure 8.2. Inside this area, all Y values are forced to zero. The values of our block spot become (-0.80, 0.0), and our camera pitch stays mercifully still.

You might be wondering why the dead zone has a bowtie shape instead of just a simple dead area all the way across the middle of the circle. There's a really good reason: when the thumbstick is close to the center, and being moved about with a fine degree of control, the player is probably doing something like aiming a sniper rifle. A dead zone in this situation would be really annoying, since any up/down movement would require the player to push the thumbstick all the way out of the dead zone. That would make it almost impossible to aim properly.

The dead zone shape also doesn't have to be exactly what you see in Figure 8.2. Depending on your game and how people play it, you might change the shape by making the angle shallower or even pull the left and right dead areas away from the center, giving the player complete control over camera pitch until the thumbstick is closer to the extreme right or left side. The only way to figure out the perfect shape is by watching a lot of people play your game and seeing what they do that frustrates them. Controls that are too sensitive or too sluggish will frustrate players, and you'll want to find a middle ground that pleases a majority of people.

There's one additional trick to this solution. Think about what happens when the thumbstick moves away from the dead zone into the active, clear zone. One thing players expect in all control schemes is continuous, predictive movement. This means that you can't just force the Y value to zero in the dead zone and use regular values everywhere else; you have to smoothly interpolate the Y values outside of the dead zone from 0.0 to 1.0, or the player will notice a pop in the movement of the camera pitch. The code to do this is not nearly as bad as you might think:

```
float Interpolate(float normalizedValue, float begin, float end)
{
   // first check input values
   assert(normalizedValue>=0.0f);
   assert(normalizedValue<=1.0f);
   assert(end>begin);

   return ( normalizedValue * (end - begin) ) + begin;
}

void MapYDeadZone(Vec3 &input, float deadZone)
{
   if (deadZone>=1.0f)
      return;

   // The dead zone is assumed to be zero close to the origin
   // so we have to interpolate to find the right dead zone for
   // our current value of X.
   float actualDeadZone = Interpolate(fabs(input.x), 0.0f, deadZone);

   if (fabs(input.y) < actualDeadZone)
   {
      input.y = 0.0f;
      return;
   }

   // Y is outside of the dead zone, but we still need to
   // interpolate it so we don't see any popping.

   // Map Y values [actualDeadZone, 1.0f] to [0.0f, 1.0f]
   float normalizedY = (input.y - actualDeadZone) / (1.0f - actualDeadZone);
   input.y = normalizedY;
}
```

Normalizing Input

Even though the game controller thumbsticks have a circular area of movement, the inputs for X and Y only reach 1.0 at the very top, bottom, left, and right of the circle. In other words, X and Y are mapped to a Cartesian space, not a circular space. Take a look at Figure 8.3, and you'll see what I mean.

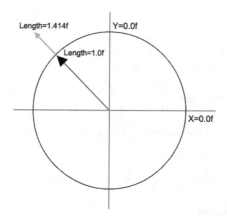

FIGURE 8.3 Normalized input from a two-axis controller.

Imagine what happens when a player pushes a control diagonally up and to the left. On some controllers, you'll get values for X and Y that are close to their maximum range and probably look something like (-0.95f, 0.95). The reason for this is how the controllers are built. Remember the two-axis controller I mentioned earlier? X and Y are both analog electrical devices called *potentiometers*. They measure electrical resistance along an analog dial, and are used for things like volume controls on stereos and, of course, joysticks and thumbsticks. On two-axis controllers like these, you have two potentiometers: one for each axis.

You can see from Figure 8.3 that the Y potentiometer can reach 1.0 or -1.0 if you push the controller all the way up or down. You can get the same values for the X potentiometer. You might think that all you need to do to calculate the input speed is find the length of the combined vector. That's just classic geometry, the Pythagorean Theorem.

$$a^2 + b^2 = c^2$$
$$\sqrt{a^2 + b^2} = \pm c$$
$$\sqrt{1^2 + 1^2} = \pm\sqrt{2} = \pm 1.414$$

This length is represented by the gray arrow in Figure 8.3. The problem is that the new input vector is 1.414f units long, and if you feed it right into the game, you'll be able to move diagonally quite a bit faster than in the cardinal directions. The direction of the new vector is correct, but it is too long.

For character movement, the forward/back motion of the character is mapped to the up/down movement of the thumbstick, and the left/right motion of the character is mapped to the left/right movement of the thumbstick. Usually, the speed of the character is controlled by how far the thumbstick is pushed. If you push the thumbstick all the way forward, the character will run forward as fast as it can.

But look at what happens when you want the character to run and turn left at the same time, as Figure 8.3 would suggest. Since I have to move the controller to the left, I automatically increase the length of the X input while the Y value stays at 1.0f, and the character begins to run too fast.

The solution to this problem is actually pretty simple: The speed of the character is mapped to the length of the X/Y 2D vector, not the value of the Y control alone, and you have to cap the speed at 1.0f. All you do is take the capped length and multiply it by the maximum speed:

```
int speed = maxSpeed * min(1.0f, sqrt((x * x) + (y * y)));
```

Of course, you may have different maximum speeds for going forward and back, or even side to side.

You might not realize it, but you also want to use this normalizing scheme on keyboard input. Consider the classic WASD scheme used by most first-person shooters on the PC. W and S move the player forward and back. A and D strafe the player from side to side. If you press W and A together, your character should move diagonally forward and to the left. If you don't normalize the input, your character will move faster diagonally than in the cardinal directions, because the combined forward and left inputs add together to create a longer vector, just as it does on the gamepad.

One Stick, Two Stick, Red Stick, Blue Stick

It's never a bad thing to invoke Dr. Seuss, is it? One of the huge design decisions you'll make in your game is whether to follow a one-stick or two-stick control scheme. You'll attract different players for either one, and depending on your level design, you might be much better off going with one over the other.

A one-stick design lets the player control the character movement with one thumbstick, and the camera is usually controlled completely by the computer. There might be a camera control, but it is usually relegated to the D-pad instead of the other thumbstick. Lots of games do this, such as racing games like *Project Gotham 4* on the Xbox360 and *Mario Galaxies* on the Wii. It's generally seen by game designers and players as the easiest interface to control.

The two-stick design puts complete control of camera movement in the other thumbstick. This is done in games like *Halo*, *Thief: Deadly Shadows*, and *Gears of War*. This control scheme is harder to learn and is generally reserved for a hard-core audience.

How do you decide which one to use for your game? The best thing to do in my mind is try to compare your game design to others that have succeeded with a particular control scheme. We chose the control scheme in *Thief* by looking at

Halo and *Splinter Cell,* and decided that the gameplay was quite close to those two products. We also realized that because the game was first and third person, the same control interface would work exactly the same way in both modes.

Ramping Control Values

Ramping is another way of saying *accelerating.* The raw control values are usually not sent directly into things like camera rotation because the movement can be quite jarring. You can jam a thumbstick control from the center to the edge of the control area extremely quickly, perhaps less than 80ms. If you take a little extra time to accelerate the movement of whatever it is you are controlling, you'll get a smoother acceleration, which adds a finer degree of control and looks much better to boot.

The input parameters for this calculation are the current elapsed time, the current speed, the maximum speed, and the number of seconds you want to accelerate.

```
// Ramp the acceleration by the elapsed time.
float numberOfSeconds = 2.0f;
m_currentSpeed += m_maxSpeed * ( (elapsedTime*elapsedTime) / numberOfSeconds);
if (m_currentSpeed > m_maxSpeed)
    m_currentSpeed = m_maxSpeed;
```

The elapsed time should be a floating-point number measuring the number of seconds it has been since the last time this code was called. It turns out that humans have a keen sense of how things should accelerate, probably because we watch things fall under the acceleration of gravity all the time. If those things are coconuts and we happen to be standing beneath them, this skill becomes quite life saving. Whenever you accelerate anything related to a control in your game, always accelerate it with a time squared component so that it will "feel" more natural.

WORKING WITH THE KEYBOARD

There are many ways to grab keyboard input from Win32. They each have their good and bad points, and to make the right choice, you need to know how deep you need to pry into keyboard input data. Before we discuss these various approaches, let's get a few vocabulary words out of the way so that we're talking the same language:

- **Character code:** Describes the ASCII or UNICODE character that is the return value of the C function, getchar().

- **Virtual scan code:** Macros defined in Winuser.h that describe the components of data sent in the wParam value of WM_CHAR, WM_KEYDOWN, and WM_KEYUP messages.
- **OEM scan code:** The scan codes provided by OEMs. They are useless unless you care about coding something specific for a particular keyboard manufacturer.

Those definitions will resonate even more once you've seen some data, so let's pry open the keyboard and do a little snooping.

Mike's Keyboard Snooper

I wrote a small program to break out all of the different values for Windows keyboard messages, and as you'll see shortly, this tool really uncovers some weird things that take place with Windows. Taken with the definitions we just discussed, however, you'll soon see that the different values will make a little more sense. Each line in the tables below contains the values of wParam and lParam for Windows keyboard messages. I typed the following sequence of keys, 1 2 a b, to produce the first table. Look closely at the different values that are produced for the different Windows messages:

```
WM_KEYDOWN, WM_CHAR, WM_KEYUP, and so on:
WM_KEYDOWN   Code:49 '1'   Repeat:1   Oem: 2   Ext'd:0   IsAlt:0   WasDown:0   Rel'd:0
WM_CHAR      Code:49 '1'   Repeat:1   Oem: 2   Ext'd:0   IsAlt:0   WasDown:0   Rel'd:0
WM_KEYUP     Code:49 '1'   Repeat:1   Oem: 2   Ext'd:0   IsAlt:0   WasDown:0   Rel'd:1
WM_KEYDOWN   Code:50 '2'   Repeat:1   Oem: 3   Ext'd:0   IsAlt:0   WasDown:0   Rel'd:0
WM_CHAR      Code:50 '2'   Repeat:1   Oem: 3   Ext'd:0   IsAlt:0   WasDown:0   Rel'd:0
WM_KEYUP     Code:50 '2'   Repeat:1   Oem: 3   Ext'd:0   IsAlt:0   WasDown:0   Rel'd:1
WM_KEYDOWN   Code:65 'A'   Repeat:1   Oem:30   Ext'd:0   IsAlt:0   WasDown:0   Rel'd:0
WM_CHAR      Code:97 'a'   Repeat:1   Oem:30   Ext'd:0   IsAlt:0   WasDown:0   Rel'd:0
WM_KEYUP     Code:65 'A'   Repeat:1   Oem:30   Ext'd:0   IsAlt:0   WasDown:0   Rel'd:1
WM_KEYDOWN   Code:66 'B'   Repeat:1   Oem:48   Ext'd:0   IsAlt:0   WasDown:0   Rel'd:0
WM_CHAR      Code:98 'b'   Repeat:1   Oem:48   Ext'd:0   IsAlt:0   WasDown:0   Rel'd:0
WM_KEYUP     Code:66 'B'   Repeat:1   Oem:48   Ext'd:0   IsAlt:0   WasDown:0   Rel'd:1
```

You'll first notice that the message pipe gets the sequence of WM_KEYDOWN, WM_CHAR, and WM_KEYUP for each key pressed and released. The next thing you'll notice is that the code returned by WM_CHAR is different from the other messages when characters are lowercase.

This should give you a clue that you can use WM_CHAR for simple character input when all you care about is getting the right character code. What happens if a key is held down? Let's find out. The next table shows the output I received by first pressing and holding an "a" and then the left Shift key:

```
WM_KEYDOWN   Code:65 'A'   Repeat:1   Oem:30   Ext'd:0   IsAlt:0   WasDown:0   Rel'd:1
WM_CHAR      Code:97 'a'   Repeat:1   Oem:30   Ext'd:0   IsAlt:0   WasDown:0   Rel'd:1
WM_KEYDOWN   Code:65 'A'   Repeat:1   Oem:30   Ext'd:0   IsAlt:0   WasDown:0   Rel'd:1
WM_CHAR      Code:97 'a'   Repeat:1   Oem:30   Ext'd:0   IsAlt:0   WasDown:0   Rel'd:1
WM_KEYDOWN   Code:65 'A'   Repeat:1   Oem:30   Ext'd:0   IsAlt:0   WasDown:0   Rel'd:1
WM_CHAR      Code:97 'a'   Repeat:1   Oem:30   Ext'd:0   IsAlt:0   WasDown:0   Rel'd:1
WM_KEYDOWN   Code:65 'A'   Repeat:1   Oem:30   Ext'd:0   IsAlt:0   WasDown:0   Rel'd:1
WM_CHAR      Code:97 'a'   Repeat:1   Oem:30   Ext'd:0   IsAlt:0   WasDown:0   Rel'd:1
WM_KEYDOWN   Code:65 'A'   Repeat:1   Oem:30   Ext'd:0   IsAlt:0   WasDown:0   Rel'd:1
WM_CHAR      Code:97 'a'   Repeat:1   Oem:30   Ext'd:0   IsAlt:0   WasDown:0   Rel'd:1
WM_KEYUP     Code:65 'A'   Repeat:1   Oem:30   Ext'd:0   IsAlt:0   WasDown:0   Rel'd:1
WM_KEYDOWN   Code:16 '_'   Repeat:1   Oem:42   Ext'd:0   IsAlt:0   WasDown:0   Rel'd:0
WM_KEYDOWN   Code:16 '_'   Repeat:1   Oem:42   Ext'd:0   IsAlt:0   WasDown:0   Rel'd:1
WM_KEYDOWN   Code:16 '_'   Repeat:1   Oem:42   Ext'd:0   IsAlt:0   WasDown:0   Rel'd:1
WM_KEYDOWN   Code:16 '_'   Repeat:1   Oem:42   Ext'd:0   IsAlt:0   WasDown:0   Rel'd:1
WM_KEYDOWN   Code:16 '_'   Repeat:1   Oem:42   Ext'd:0   IsAlt:0   WasDown:0   Rel'd:1
WM_KEYUP     Code:16 '_'   Repeat:1   Oem:42   Ext'd:0   IsAlt:0   WasDown:0   Rel'd:1
```

It seems that I can't count on the repeat value as shown here. It is completely dependent on your equipment manufacturer and keyboard driver software. You may get repeat values and you may not. You need to make sure your code will work either way.

For the next sequence, I held the left Shift key and typed the same original sequence—1 2 a b:

```
WM_KEYDOWN   Code:16 '_'   Repeat:1   Oem:42   Ext'd:0   IsAlt:0   WasDown:0   Rel'd:0
WM_KEYDOWN   Code:16 '_'   Repeat:1   Oem:42   Ext'd:0   IsAlt:0   WasDown:0   Rel'd:1
WM_KEYDOWN   Code:16 '_'   Repeat:1   Oem:42   Ext'd:0   IsAlt:0   WasDown:0   Rel'd:1
WM_KEYDOWN   Code:16 '_'   Repeat:1   Oem:42   Ext'd:0   IsAlt:0   WasDown:0   Rel'd:1
WM_KEYDOWN   Code:16 '_'   Repeat:1   Oem:42   Ext'd:0   IsAlt:0   WasDown:0   Rel'd:1
WM_KEYDOWN   Code:49 '1'   Repeat:1   Oem: 2   Ext'd:0   IsAlt:0   WasDown:0   Rel'd:0
WM_CHAR      Code:33 '!'   Repeat:1   Oem: 2   Ext'd:0   IsAlt:0   WasDown:0   Rel'd:0
WM_KEYUP     Code:49 '1'   Repeat:1   Oem: 2   Ext'd:0   IsAlt:0   WasDown:0   Rel'd:1
WM_KEYDOWN   Code:50 '2'   Repeat:1   Oem: 3   Ext'd:0   IsAlt:0   WasDown:0   Rel'd:0
WM_CHAR      Code:64 '@'   Repeat:1   Oem: 3   Ext'd:0   IsAlt:0   WasDown:0   Rel'd:0
WM_KEYUP     Code:50 '2'   Repeat:1   Oem: 3   Ext'd:0   IsAlt:0   WasDown:0   Rel'd:1
WM_KEYDOWN   Code:65 'A'   Repeat:1   Oem:30   Ext'd:0   IsAlt:0   WasDown:0   Rel'd:0
WM_CHAR      Code:65 'A'   Repeat:1   Oem:30   Ext'd:0   IsAlt:0   WasDown:0   Rel'd:0
WM_KEYUP     Code:65 'A'   Repeat:1   Oem:30   Ext'd:0   IsAlt:0   WasDown:0   Rel'd:1
WM_KEYDOWN   Code:66 'B'   Repeat:1   Oem:48   Ext'd:0   IsAlt:0   WasDown:0   Rel'd:0
WM_CHAR      Code:66 'B'   Repeat:1   Oem:48   Ext'd:0   IsAlt:0   WasDown:0   Rel'd:0
WM_KEYUP     Code:66 'B'   Repeat:1   Oem:48   Ext'd:0   IsAlt:0   WasDown:0   Rel'd:1
WM_KEYUP     Code:16 '_'   Repeat:1   Oem:42   Ext'd:0   IsAlt:0   WasDown:0   Rel'd:1
```

There's nothing too surprising here; the Shift key will repeat until the next key is pressed. Note that the repeats on the Shift key don't continue. Just as in the first sequence, only the WM_CHAR message gives you your expected character.

You should realize by now that if you want to use keys on the keyboard for hot keys, you can use the WM_KEYDOWN message and you won't have to care if the Shift key (or even the Caps Lock key) is pressed. Pressing the Caps Lock key gives you this output:

```
WM_KEYDOWN Code: 20 '_'  Repeat:1  Oem:58  Ext'd:0  IsAlt:0  WasDown:0  Rel'd:0
WM_KEYUP   Code: 20 '_'  Repeat:1  Oem:58  Ext'd:0  IsAlt:0  WasDown:0  Rel'd:1
```

The messages that come through for WM_CHAR will operate as if the Shift key were pressed down.

Let's try some function keys, including F1, F2, F3, and the shifted versions also:

```
WM_KEYDOWN Code:112 'p'  Repeat:1  Oem:59  Ext'd:0  IsAlt:0  WasDown:0  Rel'd:0
WM_KEYUP   Code:112 'p'  Repeat:1  Oem:59  Ext'd:0  IsAlt:0  WasDown:0  Rel'd:1
WM_KEYDOWN Code:113 'q'  Repeat:1  Oem:60  Ext'd:0  IsAlt:0  WasDown:0  Rel'd:0
WM_KEYUP   Code:113 'q'  Repeat:1  Oem:60  Ext'd:0  IsAlt:0  WasDown:0  Rel'd:1
WM_KEYDOWN Code:114 'r'  Repeat:1  Oem:61  Ext'd:0  IsAlt:0  WasDown:0  Rel'd:0
WM_KEYUP   Code:114 'r'  Repeat:1  Oem:61  Ext'd:0  IsAlt:0  WasDown:0  Rel'd:1
WM_KEYDOWN Code: 16 '_'  Repeat:1  Oem:42  Ext'd:0  IsAlt:0  WasDown:0  Rel'd:0
WM_KEYDOWN Code:112 'p'  Repeat:1  Oem:59  Ext'd:0  IsAlt:0  WasDown:0  Rel'd:0
WM_KEYUP   Code:112 'p'  Repeat:1  Oem:59  Ext'd:0  IsAlt:0  WasDown:0  Rel'd:1
WM_KEYDOWN Code:113 'q'  Repeat:1  Oem:60  Ext'd:0  IsAlt:0  WasDown:0  Rel'd:0
WM_KEYUP   Code:113 'q'  Repeat:1  Oem:60  Ext'd:0  IsAlt:0  WasDown:0  Rel'd:1
WM_KEYDOWN Code:114 'r'  Repeat:1  Oem:61  Ext'd:0  IsAlt:0  WasDown:0  Rel'd:0
WM_KEYUP   Code:114 'r'  Repeat:1  Oem:61  Ext'd:0  IsAlt:0  WasDown:0  Rel'd:1
WM_KEYUP   Code: 16 '_'  Repeat:1  Oem:42  Ext'd:0  IsAlt:0  WasDown:0  Rel'd:1
```

There's a distinct lack of WM_CHAR messages, isn't there? Also, notice that the code returned by the F1 key is the same as the lowercase "p" character. So, what does "p" look like?

```
WM_KEYDOWN Code: 80 'P'  Repeat:1  Oem:25  Ext'd:0  IsAlt:0  WasDown:0  Rel'd:0
WM_CHAR    Code:112 'p'  Repeat:1  Oem:25  Ext'd:0  IsAlt:0  WasDown:0  Rel'd:0
WM_KEYUP   Code: 80 'P'  Repeat:1  Oem:25  Ext'd:0  IsAlt:0  WasDown:0  Rel'd:1
```

Isn't that interesting? The virtual scan code for "p" as encoded for WM_CHAR is exactly the same as the code for WM_KEYUP and WM_KEYDOWN. This funky design leads to some buggy misinterpretations of these two messages if you are looking at nothing but the virtual scan code. I've seen some games where you could use the function keys to enter your character name!

FUNCTION KEYS REQUIRE SPECIAL HANDLING

You can't use WM_CHAR to grab function key input or any other keyboard key not associated with a typeable character. It is confusing that the ASCII value for the lowercase "p" character is also the VK_F1. If you were beginning to suspect that you couldn't use the wParam value from all these messages in the same way, you're right.

If you want to figure out the difference between keys, you should use the OEM scan code.

There's a Win32 helper function to translate it into something useful:

```
// grab bits 16-23 from LPARAM
unsigned int oemScan = int(lParam & (0xff << 16))>>16;
UINT vk = MapVirtualKey(oemScan, 1);
if (vk == VK_F1)
{
    // we've got someone pressing the F1 key!
}
```

The VK_F1 is a #define in WinUser.h, where you'll find definitions for every other virtual key you'll need: VK_ESCAPE, VK_TAB, VK_SPACE, and so on.

Processing different keyboard inputs seems messy, doesn't it? Hold on, it gets better. The next sequence shows the left Shift key, right Shift key, left Ctrl key, and right Ctrl key:

```
WM_KEYDOWN Code: 16 '_'  Repeat:1  Oem:42  Ext'd:0  IsAlt:0  WasDown:0  Rel'd:0
WM_KEYUP   Code: 16 '_'  Repeat:1  Oem:42  Ext'd:0  IsAlt:0  WasDown:0  Rel'd:1
WM_KEYDOWN Code: 16 '_'  Repeat:1  Oem:54  Ext'd:0  IsAlt:0  WasDown:0  Rel'd:0
WM_KEYUP   Code: 16 '_'  Repeat:1  Oem:54  Ext'd:0  IsAlt:0  WasDown:0  Rel'd:1
WM_KEYDOWN Code: 17 '_'  Repeat:1  Oem:29  Ext'd:0  IsAlt:0  WasDown:0  Rel'd:0
WM_KEYUP   Code: 17 '_'  Repeat:1  Oem:29  Ext'd:0  IsAlt:0  WasDown:0  Rel'd:1
WM_KEYDOWN Code: 17 '_'  Repeat:1  Oem:29  Ext'd:1  IsAlt:0  WasDown:0  Rel'd:0
WM_KEYUP   Code: 17 '_'  Repeat:1  Oem:29  Ext'd:1  IsAlt:0  WasDown:0  Rel'd:1
```

The only way to distinguish the left Shift key from the right Shift key is to look at the OEM scan code. On the other hand, the only way to distinguish the left Ctrl key from the right Ctrl key is to look at the extended key bit to see if it is set for the right Ctrl key. This insane cobbler of aggregate design is the best example of what happens if you have a mandate to create new technology while supporting stuff as old as my high school diploma (or is that my grade school one?).

YOU MIGHT NEED YOUR OWN KEYBOARD HANDLER

BEST PRACTICE

To get around the problems of processing keyboard inputs that look the same as I've outlined in this section, you'll want to write your own handler for accepting the WM_KEYDOWN and WM_KEYUP messages. If your game is going to have a complicated enough interface to distinguish between left and right Ctrl or Shift keys, and will use these keys in combination with others, you've got an interesting road ahead. My best advice is to try to keep things as simple as possible. It's a bad idea to assign different actions to both Ctrl or Shift keys anyway. If your game only needs some hot keys and no fancy combinations, WM_KEYDOWN will work fine all by itself.

Here's a summary of how to get the right data out of these keyboard messages:

- WM_CHAR: Use this message only if your game cares about printable characters: no function keys, Ctrl keys, or Shift keys as a single input.
- WM_KEYDOWN/WM_KEYUP: Grabs each key as you press it, but makes no distinction between upper- and lowercase characters. Use this to grab function key input and compare the OEM scan codes with MapVirtualKey(). You won't get upper- and lowercase characters without tracking the status of the Shift keys yourself.

It's almost like this system was engineered by a Congressional conference committee.

GetAsyncKeyState() and Other Evils

There's a Win32 function that will return the status of any key. It's tempting to use, especially given the morass of weirdness you have to deal with going a more traditional route with Windows keyboard messages. Unfortunately, there's a dark side to these functions and other functions that poll the state of device hardware outside of the message loop.

Most testing scripts or replay features pump recorded messages into the normal message pump, making sure that actual hardware messages are shunted away. Polling functions like GetAsyncKeyState() aren't easily trapped in the same way. They also make debugging and testing more difficult, since timing of keyboard input could be crucial to re-creating a weird bug.

There are other polled functions that can cause the same issues. One of them is the polled device status functions in DirectInput, such as IDirectInputDevice:: GetDeviceState(). The only way I'd consider using these functions is if I wrote my own mini-message pump, where polled device status was converted into messages sent into my game logic. That, of course, is a lot more work.

Handling the Alt Key Under Windows

If I use the same program to monitor keyboard messages related to pressing the right and left Alt keys, I get nothing. No output at all. Windows keeps the Alt key for itself and uses it to send special commands to your application. You should listen to WM_SYSCOMMAND to find out what's going on. You could use the polling functions to find out if the Alt keys have been pressed, but not only does that go against some recent advice, but it's not considered "polite" Windows behavior. Microsoft has guidelines that well-behaved applications should follow, including games. The Alt key is reserved for commands sent to Windows. Users will not expect your game to launch missiles when all they want to do is switch over to Excel and try to look busy for the boss.

WHAT, NO DANCE PAD?

I freely admit that I'm a *Dance Dance Revolution* junkie and anyone who knows me is probably wondering why I didn't spend a few pages on dance pad controls. At first blush, you might say that the dance pad is programmed exactly the same way as the game controller—it has buttons that get pressed just like the controller you hold in your hand.

Now that you've read this chapter, you probably realize that the programming for a dance pad is quite different, simply because the player is using his feet and not his hands. You still use the same code to get button down and up messages. But think for a moment about how your feet are different from your hands. They move slower, for one thing—at least mine do. You have two feet moving on four buttons, which is different than a handheld controller where only your right thumb can hit those four buttons. Tuning for timing is probably really different, too, especially since there is a vast skill difference between people like my Mom and the kids in the arcades who can move so fast you can't even see their feet.

Input devices are physiological, and you can't ever forget that when defining how your game gets mouse movement events or thumbstick events. One is controlled with the arm and wrist, the other the thumb. This one fact is a key issue when working with input devices.

Here's my best example. Why do you think the WASD control scheme became so popular in first-person shooters on the PC? I'll take an educated guess—fine movements like aiming, firing, and looking are mapped to the mouse, which is usually in a player's right hand. The movement keys, which are W,A,S, and D, are easily controllable with the player's left hand. The physical nature of the keyboard, mouse, and the fact that most people are right-handed made this interface so popular.

USER INTERFACE PROGRAMMING

In This Chapter

- The Human's Game View
- A WASD Movement Controller
- Screen Elements
- A Custom MessageBox Dialog
- Modal Dialog Boxes
- Controls
- Control Identification
- Hit Testing and Focus Order
- Control State
- More Control Properties
- Some Final User Interface Tips

After exploring input devices in the previous chapter, we're ready to move a little deeper and see what happens when the raw input messages are passed from the application layer to your game.

Games usually have a small set of user interface components, and they are almost always custom coded. Windows games don't use GDI to create their menus, dialogs, or radar screens. These special controls are always home grown. Sure, the number of controls you can attach to dialog boxes and screens is overwhelming, but most games don't need rich text editors, grid controls, OLE containers, property pages, and so on. Rather, the lack of control over position, animation, and sounds usually compels game programmers to roll their own simple user interface.

These simple interfaces break the job into two parts: controls and containers for controls. Some user interface designs, such as Windows, don't distinguish between controls and control containers. Everything in the Win32 GDI has an HWND. This might seem a little weird because it would be unlikely that a button in your game would have other little buttons attached to it.

Instead of proposing any specific design, it's best to discuss some of the implementation issues and features any game will need in a user interface. I'll talk about the human game view, then screens and dialog boxes, and end up with a discussion about controls.

If you've seen any of DirectX Foundation, you've probably noticed that Microsoft implemented an entire GUI system that uses the DirectX rendering pipeline and yet has most of the functionality of traditional Windows controls. This is pretty nice, and it's a great place to start, but it does have its drawbacks. I'll show you how you can integrate this GUI system with the game logic/game view architecture in this book, and I will suggest some future directions.

THE HUMAN'S GAME VIEW

Recall from Chapter 2, "What's in a Game?" that the game interface should be completely separate from the game logic. A game view receives game events, such as "object was created" or "object was moved," and does whatever it needs to present this new game state. In return, the view is responsible for sending any commands back to the game logic, such as "request throw grenade." It would be up to the game logic to determine whether this was a valid request.

I'm about to show you a base class that creates a game view for a human player. As you might expect, it's pretty heavy on user interface. I think it's a good idea to take somewhat of a top-down approach, showing you major components and how they fit together.

```
typedef std::list<shared_ptr<IScreenElement> > ScreenElementList;

class HumanView : public IGameView
{
protected:
   GameViewId        m_ViewId;
   optional<ActorId> m_ActorId;

   // this CProcessManager is for things like button animations, etc.
   CProcessManager *m_pProcessManager;

   DWORD m_currTick;       // time right now
   DWORD m_lastDraw;       // last time the game rendered
   bool m_runFullSpeed;    // set to true if you want to run full speed

   ID3DXFont*              m_pFont;
   ID3DXSprite*            m_pTextSprite;

   virtual void VRenderText(CDXUTTextHelper &txtHelper) { };

public:
   // Implement the IGameView interface
   virtual HRESULT VOnRestore();
   virtual void VOnRender(double fTime, float fElapsedTime );
   virtual void VOnLostDevice();
   virtual GameViewType VGetType() { return GameView_Human; }
   virtual GameViewId VGetId() const { return m_ViewId; }

   virtual void VOnAttach(GameViewId vid, optional<ActorId> aid)
   {
      m_ViewId = vid;
      m_ActorId = aid;
   }

   virtual LRESULT CALLBACK VOnMsgProc( AppMsg msg );
   virtual void VOnUpdate( int deltaMilliseconds );

   // Virtual methods to control the layering of interface elements
   virtual void VPushElement(shared_ptr<IScreenElement> pScreen);
   virtual void VPopElement();

   ~HumanView();
   HumanView();
```

```
ScreenElementList m_ScreenElements;

// Interface sensitive objects
shared_ptr<IMouseHandler> m_MouseHandler;
shared_ptr<IKeyboardHandler> m_KeyboardHandler;

// Audio
bool InitAudio();
};
```

Let's take a quick look at the data members of this class.

The first two members store the view ID and the actor ID, if it exists. This makes it easy for the game logic to determine if a view is attached to a particular actor in the game universe.

The CProcessManager was presented in Chapter 6, "Controlling the Main Loop." This class is a convenient manager for anything that takes multiple game loops to accomplish, such as playing a sound effect or running an animation.

The next three members deal with drawing time and frame rate. They keep track of when the view was rendered last and whether or not to limit the frame rate. There's no reason to draw the 3D scene any more than 60 times per second, or 60Hz. This leaves more time for your game to do other things like spend CPU time on physics or AI.

The next two members are specific to DirectX—sorry about that. I'm sure all you OpenGL fans can easily swap in your own equivalents. They, and the virtual method VRenderText(), help you draw text to the screen.

The next set of virtual methods completes the implementation of the IGameView interface originally discussed back in Chapter 2. You'll see what each of these methods is responsible for shortly.

The next two virtual methods, VPushElement() and VPopElement(), control the ordering and layering of screen interface elements.

The next data member is an STL list of pointers to objects that implement the IScreenElement interface. A screen element is a strictly user interface thing, and is a container for user interface controls like buttons and text edit boxes. You could have a number of these components attached to do different things, and because they are separate entities, you could hide or show them individually. A good example of this kind of behavior is modular toolbars in the Window GUI.

The last two members are a generic mouse handler and a keyboard handler. You'll create mouse and keyboard handlers to interpret device messages into game commands.

Let's take a look at some of the more interesting bits of the HumanView class, starting with the VOnRender() method. The render method is responsible for rendering the view at either a clamped maximum refresh rate or at full speed, depending on the value of the local variables.

```
void HumanView::VOnRender(double fTime, float fElapsedTime )
{
   m_currTick = timeGetTime();

   // early out — we've already drawn in this tick
   if (m_currTick == m_lastDraw)
      return;

   HRESULT hr;

   // It is time to draw ?
   if( m_runFullSpeed ||
      ( (m_currTick - m_lastDraw) > SCREEN_REFRESH_RATE) )
   {
       // Clear the render target and the zbuffer
      V( DXUTGetD3D9Device()->Clear((0, NULL, D3DCLEAR_TARGET |
         D3DCLEAR_ZBUFFER, D3DCOLOR_ARGB(0, 45, 50, 170), 1.0f, 0) );

       // Render the scene
       if( SUCCEEDED( DXUTGetD3D9Device()->BeginScene() ) )
      {
          CDXUTTextHelper txtHelper( m_pFont, m_pTextSprite, 15 );
          VRenderText(txtHelper);
          m_ScreenElements.sort(
            SortBy_SharedPtr_Content<IScreenElement>());

          for(ScreenElementList::iterator i=m_ScreenElements.begin();
             i!=m_ScreenElements.end(); ++i)
          {
            if ( (*i)->VIsVisible() )
            {
               (*i)->VOnRender(fTime, fElapsedTime);
            }
          }

          // record the last successful paint
          m_lastDraw = m_currTick;
      }
      V( DXUTGetD3D9Device()->EndScene() );
   }
}
```

If the view is ready to draw, it calls the `IDirect3DDevice9::Clear()` routine to wipe the rendering surface of the last frame. If your game is guaranteed to over-draw every pixel, you don't need this call. Then the `IDirect3DDevice9::Begin-Scene()` API is called to get the Direct3D device ready for rendering. The `VRenderText()` method is next, which will render any text applied directly to the screen. In this class, the method has a null implementation. In Chapter 20, "A Game of Teapot Wars," a human view class will overload this to display some debug text.

The `for` loop iterates through the screen layers one-by-one, and if it is visible, it calls `IScreenElement::VOnRender()`. This implies that the only thing the view really draws for itself is the text in `VRenderText()`, and that's exactly correct. Everything else should be drawn because it belongs to the list of screens. The last thing that happens is a call to the end scene API of DirectX.

Notice that the screen list is drawn from the beginning of the list to the end of the list. That's important because screens can draw on top of one another in layers, such as when a modal dialog box draws on top of everything else in your game.

```
HRESULT HumanView::VOnRestore()
{

HRESULT hr = S_OK;
   if( !m_pFont )
   {
      // Initialize the font
      D3DXCreateFont( DXUTGetD3D9Device(), 15, 0, FW_BOLD, 1, FALSE,
                      DEFAULT_CHARSET, OUT_DEFAULT_PRECIS, DEFAULT_QUALITY,
                      DEFAULT_PITCH | FF_DONTCARE, L"Arial", &m_pFont );
   }
   else
   {
      V_RETURN( m_pFont->OnResetDevice() );
   }

   if (!m_pTextSprite)
   {
      // Create a sprite to help batch calls when drawing many lines of text
      V_RETURN( D3DXCreateSprite( DXUTGetD3D9Device(), &m_pTextSprite ) );
   }
   else
   {
      V_RETURN( m_pTextSprite->OnResetDevice() );
   }
```

```
for(ScreenElementList::iterator i=m_ScreenElements.begin();
    i!=m_ScreenElements.end(); ++i)
{
   V_RETURN ( (*i)->VOnRestore() );
}

return hr;
}

void HumanView::VOnLostDevice()
{
   if( m_pFont )
      m_pFont->OnLostDevice();
   SAFE_RELEASE( m_pTextSprite );
}
```

The HumanView::VOnRestore() method is responsible for re-creating anything that might be lost while the game is running. Also remember that VOnRestore() gets called just after the class is instantiated, so this chain is just as useful for initialization as it is restoring lost objects. These objects include the font, the text sprite, and calling all of the attached screens. The HumanView::VOnLostDevice() method will be called prior to VOnRestore(), so it is used to chain the "on lost device" event to other objects, or simply release the objects so they'll be re-created in the call to VOnRestore(). This is a common theme in DirectX applications on the PC, since any number of things can get in the way of a game, such as a change of video resolution or even Alt-Tabbing away to another application that makes exclusive use of DirectX objects.

The view is called once per frame by the application layer so that it can perform nonrendering update tasks. The VOnUpdate() chain is called as quickly as the game loops and is used to update any object attached to the human view. In this case, the process manager is updated, as well as any of the screen elements attached to the human view. As you will see in Chapter 14, "3D Scenes," this includes updating the objects in the 3D scene, which is itself a screen element.

```
void HumanView::VOnUpdate( int deltaMilliseconds )
{
   m_pProcessManager->UpdateProcesses(deltaMilliseconds);
   for(ScreenElementList::iterator i=m_ScreenElements.begin();
       i!=m_ScreenElements.end(); ++i)
   {
       (*i)->VOnUpdate(deltaMilliseconds);
   }
}
```

This code deserves a little clarity, perhaps, since there are a number of potentially confusing things about it. A game object that exists in the game universe and is affected by game rules, like physics, belongs to the game logic. Whenever the game object moves or changes state, events are generated that eventually make their way to the game views, where they update their internal representations of these objects. You've all seen crates in games—you can knock them downstairs and break them open.

There is a different set of objects that only exist visually and have no real effect on the world themselves, such as particle effects. The VOnUpdate() that belongs to the human view is what updates these objects. Since the game logic knows nothing about them, they are completely contained in the human view and need some way to update them if they are animating.

Another example of something the human perceives, but the game logic does not, is the audio system. Background music and ambient sound effects have no effect on the game logic per se, and therefore can safely belong to the human view. The audio system is actually managed as a CProcess object that is attached to the CProcessManager contained in the human view.

But wait—you might ask, didn't *Thief: Deadly Shadows* have systems that allowed the AI characters to respond to sounds? Well, yes and no. The AI in *Thief* didn't respond directly to what was being sent out of the sound card, but rather it responded to collision events detected by the game logic. These collision events were sent by the game logic and were separately consumed by both the sound manager *and* the AI manager. The sound manager looked at the type of collision and determined which sound effect was most suitable. The AI manager looked at the proximity and severity of the collision to determine if it was past the AI's motivational threshold. So the AIs actually responded to collision events, not sounds.

The real meat of the human view is processing device messages from the application layer. Somewhere in the application layer of all Windows games is the main message processor, where you get WM_CHAR, WM_MOUSEMOVE, and all those messages. Any conceivable message that the game views would want to see should be translated into the generic message form and passed on to all the game views. The following is a code fragment from GameCodeApp::MsgProc(), which is the main message handling callback that was set up with DXUTSetCallbackMsgProc(GameCodeApp::MsgProc).

```
switch (uMsg)
{
    case WM_KEYDOWN:
    case WM_KEYUP:
    case WM_MOUSEMOVE:
    case WM_LBUTTONDOWN:
    case WM_LBUTTONUP:
    case WM_RBUTTONDOWN:
    case WM_RBUTTONUP:
```

```
case MM_JOY1BUTTONDOWN:
case MM_JOY1BUTTONUP:
case MM_JOY1MOVE:
case MM_JOY1ZMOVE:
case MM_JOY2BUTTONDOWN:
case MM_JOY2BUTTONUP:
case MM_JOY2MOVE:
case MM_JOY2ZMOVE:
{
    // translate the windows message into the 'generic' message.
    AppMsg msg;
    msg.m_hWnd = hWnd;
    msg.m_uMsg = uMsg;
    msg.m_wParam = wParam;
    msg.m_lParam = lParam;

    for ( GameViewList::reverse_iterator i=m_gameViews.rbegin();
          i!=m_gameViews.rend(); ++i)
    {
        if ( (*i)->VOnMsgProc( msg ) )
        {
            return true;
        }
    }
}
break;
}
```

I completely admit that I'm cheating by taking the Win32 message parameters and sticking them into a structure. Call me lazy; I can live with that. I'll give you the task of completely generalizing these messages.

If a game view returns true from VOnMsgProc(), it means that it has completely consumed the message, and no other view should see it. In practice this makes perfect sense, since there's only one keyboard, one mouse, and one human operating these devices at once.

This architecture will still work with a multiple player, split-screen type of game—here's how. The HumanView class can contain multiple screens, but instead of being layered, they will sit side by side. The HumanView class will still grab input from all the devices and translate it into game commands, just as you are about to see, but in this case, each device will be treated as input for a different player.

Back to the implementation of HumanView::VOnMsgProc(). Its job is to iterate through the list of screens attached to it, forward the message on to the visible ones, and if they don't eat the message, then ask the mouse and keyboard handler if they can consume it.

```cpp
LRESULT CALLBACK HumanView::VOnMsgProc( AppMsg msg )
{
    // Iterate through the screen layers first
    // In reverse order since we'll send input messages to the
    // screen on top
    for(ScreenElementList::reverse_iterator i=m_ScreenElements.rbegin();
        i!=m_ScreenElements.rend(); ++i)
    {
        if ( (*i)->VIsVisible() )
        {
            if ( (*i)->VOnMsgProc( msg ) )
            {
                return 1;
            }
        }
    }

    LRESULT result = 0;
    switch (msg.m_uMsg)
    {
        case WM_KEYDOWN:
            if (m_Console.IsActive())
            {
                // Let the console eat this.
            }
            else if (m_KeyboardHandler)
            {
                result = m_KeyboardHandler->VOnKeyDown(
                    static_cast<const BYTE>(msg.m_wParam));
            }
            break;

        case WM_KEYUP:
            if (m_Console.IsActive())
            {
                // Let the console eat this.
            }
            else if (m_KeyboardHandler)
            {
                result = m_KeyboardHandler->VOnKeyUp(
                    static_cast<const BYTE>(msg.m_wParam));
            }
            break;
```

```
case WM_MOUSEMOVE:
   if (m_MouseHandler)
     result = m_MouseHandler->VOnMouseMove(
         CPoint(LOWORD(msg.m_lParam), HIWORD(msg.m_lParam)));
   break;

case WM_LBUTTONDOWN:
   if (m_MouseHandler)
   {
      SetCapture(msg.m_hWnd);

      result = m_MouseHandler->VOnLButtonDown(
         CPoint(LOWORD(msg.m_lParam), HIWORD(msg.m_lParam)));
   }
   break;

case WM_LBUTTONUP:
   if (m_MouseHandler)
   {
      SetCapture(NULL);
      result = m_MouseHandler->VOnLButtonUp(
         CPoint(LOWORD(msg.m_lParam), HIWORD(msg.m_lParam)));
   }
   break;

case WM_RBUTTONDOWN:
   if (m_MouseHandler)
   {
      SetCapture(msg.m_hWnd);
      result = m_MouseHandler->VOnRButtonDown(
         CPoint(LOWORD(msg.m_lParam), HIWORD(msg.m_lParam)));
   }
   break;

case WM_RBUTTONUP:
   if (m_MouseHandler)
   {
      SetCapture(NULL);
      result = m_MouseHandler->VOnRButtonUp(
         CPoint(LOWORD(msg.m_lParam), HIWORD(msg.m_lParam)));
   }
   break;
```

```
        case WM_CHAR:
            if (m_Console.IsActive())
            {
                const unsigned int oemScan =
                    int( msg.m_lParam & ( 0xff << 16 ) ) >> 16;
                m_Console.HandleKeyboardInput(
                    msg.m_wParam, MapVirtualKey( oemScan, 1 ), true );
            }
            else
            {
                //See if it was the console key.
                if (('~'==msg.m_wParam) || ('`'==msg.m_wParam))
                {
                    m_Console.SetActive(true);
                }
            }
            break;

        default:
            return 0;
    }

    return 0;
}
```

Did you notice that I used a reverse iterator for the screens? Here's why: If you draw them using a normal forward iterator, the screen on top is going to the be the last one drawn. User input should always be processed in order of the screens from top to bottom, which in this case would be the reverse order.

If none of the screen elements in the list processed the message, we can ask the input device handlers, in this case m_KeyboardHandler and m_MouseHandler, to process the messages. Of course, you could always write and add your own input device handler, perhaps for a dance pad or gamepad—if you do, here's where you would hook it in.

Notice that the existence of the handler is always checked before the message is sent to it. There's nothing that says you have to have a keyboard for every game you'll make with this code, so it's a good idea to check it.

A WASD Movement Controller

You might be wondering how you use this system to create a WASD movement controller, since this interface requires the use of a mouse and a keyboard combined. At the beginning of the chapter, you read about the IMouseHandler and

IKeyboardHandler interface classes. You can use these to create a single controller class that can respond to both devices:

```cpp
class MovementController : public IMouseHandler, public IKeyboardHandler
{
protected:
   Mat4x4  m_matFromWorld;
   Mat4x4   m_matToWorld;
   Mat4x4  m_matPosition;

   CPoint     m_lastMousePos;
   BYTE       m_bKey[256];            // Which keys are up and down

   // Orientation Controls
   float      m_fTargetYaw;
   float      m_fTargetPitch;
   float      m_fYaw;
   float      m_fPitch;
   float      m_fPitchOnDown;
   float      m_fYawOnDown;
   float      m_maxSpeed;
   float      m_currentSpeed;

   shared_ptr<SceneNode> m_object;

public:
   MovementController(shared_ptr<SceneNode> object,
                      float initialYaw, float    initialPitch);
   void SetObject(shared_ptr<SceneNode> newObject);
   void OnUpdate(DWORD const elapsedMs);

public:
   bool VOnMouseMove(const CPoint &mousePos);
   bool VOnLButtonDown(const CPoint &mousePos) { return false; }
   bool VOnLButtonUp(const CPoint &mousePos) { return false; }
   bool VOnRButtonDown(const CPoint &) { return false; }
   bool VOnRButtonUp(const CPoint &) { return false; }

   bool VOnKeyDown(const BYTE c) { m_bKey[c] = true; return true; }
   bool VOnKeyUp(const BYTE c) { m_bKey[c] = false; return true; }

   const Mat4x4 *GetToWorld() { return &m_matToWorld; }
   const Mat4x4 *GetFromWorld() { return &m_matFromWorld; }
};
```

I'm giving you something of a sneak peak into Chapter 13, "3D Basics," with the introduction of the Mat4x4 member variables. I won't explain them in detail here, but suffice it to say that these members track where an object is in relation to the game world and how it is oriented.

Since this WASD controller doesn't have any weapons fire, we'll simply return false from the mouse button up and down handlers. Notice that the VOnKeyUp() and VOnKeyDown() methods simply set members of a Boolean array to be true or false to match the state of the key. Now, take a look at VOnMouseMove():

```
bool MovementController::VOnMouseMove(const CPoint &mousePos)
{
   if(m_lastMousePos!=mousePos)
   {
      m_fTargetYaw = m_fTargetYaw + (m_lastMousePos.x - mousePos.x);
      m_fTargetPitch = m_fTargetPitch + (mousePos.y - m_lastMousePos.y);
      m_lastMousePos = mousePos;
   }
   return true;
}
```

This method was probably simpler than you expected. All it does is set the target yaw and pitch of the controller to match the mouse movement. Here's the real meat of the controller, OnUpdate():

```
void MovementController::OnUpdate(DWORD const deltaMilliseconds)
{
   if (m_bKey['W'] || m_bKey['S'])
   {
      // code here will calculate movement forward & backward
   }

   if (m_bKey['A'] || m_bKey['D'])
   {
      // code here will calculate movement left & right
   }

   {
      // code here will set object rotation based on
      // previously calculated pitch and yaw values.

      // then, the movements forward, backward, left or
      // right will be used to send a movement command
      // to the game logic, which will evaluate them
      // for legality and actually move the object
   }
}
```

The full code of this routine requires some deeper knowledge of 3D transformations. To avoid sending you into convulsions, I'll postpone those discussions until Chapter 13.

SCREEN ELEMENTS

You've seen how the human view works; its big job is managing the list of screen elements, drawing them, sending them input, and managing a couple of things like the audio system and the process manager. The audio system is discussed in detail in Chapter 12, "Game Audio," and you should remember the process manager from Chapter 6, "The Main Loop."

A screen element is anything that draws and accepts input. It could be anything from a button to your rendered 3D world. In Chapter 14, "3D Scenes," we create a screen element that can draw 3D objects and accept mouse and keyboard input to move the camera through the 3D world. In this chapter, we'll concentrate on user interface components like buttons and dialog boxes.

Screen elements can be hierarchical—for example, a dialog box can have buttons attached to it. A scroll bar has lots of moving parts: a background, two buttons, and a movable bit in the middle to represent where the scrolled data is positioned.

Screen elements in various configurations create the user interface for your game, such as a menu, inventory screen, scoreboard, radar, or dialog box. Some run on top of the main game screen, such as a radar or minimap, but others might completely overlay the main view and even pause the game, such as an options

BEST
PRACTICE

SCREENS NEED TRANSITION MANAGEMENT

If your game has multiple screens, and even simple games have many, it's wise to manage them and the transitions between them in a high-level API. This might seem a little strange to Windows programmers, but it's a little like programming multiple applications for the same window, and you can freely move from one screen to another by selecting the right controls.

If your screens are fairly small "memory-wise," consider preloading them. Any transitions that happen will be blazingly fast, and players like responsive transitions. If your screens have tons of controls, graphics, and sounds, you won't necessarily be able to preload them because of memory constraints, but you might consider loading a small transition screen to give your players something to look at while you load your bigger screens. Lots of console games do this, and they usually display a bit of the next mission in the background while a nice animation plays showing the load progress. The animation during the load is important, because all console manufacturers require animations during loading screens beyond some small threshold, such as 10 seconds.

screen. Throughout this chapter, I'll generally refer to a screen as something that contains a list of screen elements, and a control as the leaf nodes of this hierarchy. A screen is simply a container for controls, and it knows how to parse user input messages from the application layer and translate them into game messages.

Lots of kids' games and mass market titles use a screen architecture like the one shown in Figure 9.1 throughout the entire game. When the right controls are activated in the right order, the current screen is replaced by a new one with different controls.

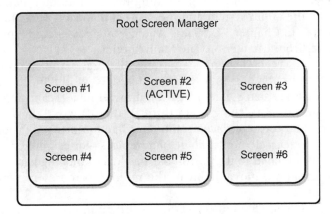

FIGURE 9.1 Screens need a screen manager.

Other games use multiple screens to set up the characters or missions. When everything is set up for the player, the game transitions to the game screen where most, if not all, of the game is played. Almost every console game uses this model. Let's look at a simple interface design for a screen:

```
struct AppMsg
{
    HWND m_hWnd;
    UINT m_uMsg;
    WPARAM m_wParam;
    LPARAM m_lParam;
};

class IScreenElement
{
public:
    virtual HRESULT VOnRestore() = 0;
    virtual HRESULT VOnRender(double fTime, float fElapsedTime) = 0;
    virtual void VOnUpdate(int deltaMilliseconds) = 0;
    virtual int VGetZOrder() const = 0;
```

```
virtual void VSetZOrder(int const zOrder) = 0;
virtual bool VIsVisible() const = 0;
virtual void VSetVisible(bool visible) = 0;

virtual LRESULT CALLBACK VOnMsgProc( AppMsg msg )=0;

virtual ~IScreenElement() { };
virtual bool const operator <(IScreenElement const &other)
   { return VGetZOrder() < other.VGetZOrder(); }
};
```

This interface shows that a screen knows how to restore itself when it needs to be rebuilt, render itself when it's time to draw, how it should be ordered in the master draw list, and whether it is visible. You'll also notice a familiar method that will accept device input. In this case, you can see our custom AppMsg that you saw earlier in this chapter.

A Custom MessageBox Dialog

The best way to show you how this works is by example. Let's create a simple message box that your game can call instead of the MessageBox API. The code for this uses the DirectX GUI framework that is defined in DXUTgui.h. Word to the wise: The DirectX GUI framework is a great start for a game interface, but it does make some assumptions about how you want to load textures and some other quirks. On the other hand, it sure keeps you from having to write a text edit control from scratch. If you simply hate DirectX and you are sufficiently motivated, just surgically remove the DirectX components and roll your own.

This message box class conforms pretty well with the Win32 MessageBox API. You send in a text message and what kind of buttons you want, and the dialog will store the ID of the control that was pressed:

```
class CMessageBox : public IScreenElement
{
protected:
   int         m_PosX, m_PosY;
   int         m_Width, m_Height;
   CDXUTDialog m_UI;    // DirectX dialog
   int m_ButtonId;
   optional<int>       m_Result;

public:
   CMessageBox(std::wstring msg, std::wstring title, int buttonFlags=MB_OK);
```

```
// IScreenElement Implementation
virtual HRESULT VOnRestore();
virtual HRESULT VOnRender(double fTime, float fElapsedTime);
virtual int VGetZOrder() const { return 0; }
virtual void VSetZOrder(int const zOrder) { }
virtual bool VIsVisible() const { return true; }
virtual void VSetVisible(bool visible) { }

virtual LRESULT CALLBACK VOnMsgProc( AppMsg msg );
static void CALLBACK OnGUIEvent(
    UINT nEvent, int nControlID, CDXUTControl* pControl );
};
```

The class design is pretty simple. It contains DirectX's CDXUTDialog, and has a few member variables to keep track of the size, position, and dialog result. The constructor sets the callback routine and creates controls for the static text message and the buttons:

```
CMessageBox::CMessageBox(std::wstring msg, std::wstring title, int buttonFlags)
{
   // Initialize dialogs
   m_UI.Init( &g_pApp->g_DialogResourceManager );
   m_UI.SetCallback( OnGUIEvent );

   // Find the dimensions of the message
    RECT rc;
   SetRect( &rc, 0,0,0,0);
   m_UI.CalcTextRect( msg.c_str(),
                      m_UI.GetDefaultElement(DXUT_CONTROL_STATIC,0), &rc );
   int msgWidth = rc.right - rc.left;
   int msgHeight = rc.bottom - rc.top;

   int numButtons = 2;
   if ( (buttonFlags == MB_ABORTRETRYIGNORE) ||
        (buttonFlags == MB_CANCELTRYCONTINUE) ||
        (buttonFlags == MB_CANCELTRYCONTINUE) )
   {
      numButtons = 3;
   }
   else if (buttonFlags == MB_OK)
   {
      numButtons = 1;
   }
```

```
int btnWidth = 125;
int btnHeight = 22;

int border = 35;
m_Width = std::max(msgWidth + 2 * border, btnWidth + 2 * border);
m_Height = msgHeight + (numButtons * (btnHeight+border) ) + (2 * border);

m_PosX = (DXUTGetD3D9BackBufferSurfaceDesc()->Width-m_Width)/2;
m_PosY = (DXUTGetD3D9BackBufferSurfaceDesc()->Height-m_Height)/2;
m_UI.SetLocation( m_PosX, m_PosY );

m_UI.SetSize( m_Width, m_Height );
m_UI.SetBackgroundColors(g_Gray40);

int iY = border;
int iX = (m_Width - msgWidth) / 2;

m_UI.AddStatic( 0, msg.c_str(), iX, iY, msgWidth, msgHeight);

iX = (m_Width - btnWidth) / 2;
iY = m_Height - btnHeight - border;

buttonFlags &= 0xF;
if ( (buttonFlags == MB_ABORTRETRYIGNORE) ||
     (buttonFlags == MB_CANCELTRYCONTINUE) )
{
  // The message box contains three push buttons:
  // Cancel, Try Again, Continue.
  // This is the new standard over Abort,Retry,Ignore

  m_UI.AddButton( IDCONTINUE, g_pApp->GetString(IDS_CONTINUE).c_str(),
                  iX, iY - (2*border), btnWidth, btnHeight );
  m_UI.AddButton( IDTRYAGAIN, g_pApp->GetString(IDS_TRYAGAIN).c_str(),
                  iX, iY - border, btnWidth, btnHeight );
  m_UI.AddButton( IDCANCEL, g_pApp->GetString(IDS_CANCEL).c_str(),
                  iX, iY, btnWidth, btnHeight );
}
else if (buttonFlags == MB_OKCANCEL)
{
  //The message box contains two push buttons: OK and Cancel.
  m_UI.AddButton( IDOK, g_pApp->GetString(IDS_OK).c_str(),
                  iX, iY - border, btnWidth, btnHeight );
  m_UI.AddButton( IDCANCEL, g_pApp->GetString(IDS_CANCEL).c_str(),
                  iX, iY, btnWidth, btnHeight );
}
```

```
        else if (buttonFlags == MB_RETRYCANCEL)
        {
            //The message box contains two push buttons: Retry and Cancel.
            m_UI.AddButton( IDRETRY, g_pApp->GetString(IDS_RETRY).c_str(),
                            iX, iY - border, btnWidth, btnHeight );
            m_UI.AddButton( IDCANCEL, g_pApp->GetString(IDS_CANCEL).c_str(),
                            iX, iY, btnWidth, btnHeight );
        }
        else if (buttonFlags == MB_YESNO)
        {
            //The message box contains two push buttons: Yes and No.
            m_UI.AddButton( IDYES, g_pApp->GetString(IDS_YES).c_str(),
                            iX, iY - border, btnWidth, btnHeight );
            m_UI.AddButton( IDNO, g_pApp->GetString(IDS_NO).c_str(),
                            iX, iY, btnWidth, btnHeight );
        }
        else if (buttonFlags == MB_YESNOCANCEL)
        {
            //The message box contains three push buttons: Yes, No, and Cancel.
            m_UI.AddButton( IDYES, g_pApp->GetString(IDS_YES).c_str(),
                            iX, iY - (2*border), btnWidth, btnHeight );
            m_UI.AddButton( IDNO, g_pApp->GetString(IDS_NO).c_str(),
                            iX, iY - border, btnWidth, btnHeight );
            m_UI.AddButton( IDCANCEL, g_pApp->GetString(IDS_CANCEL).c_str(),
                            iX, iY, btnWidth, btnHeight );
        }
        else //if (buttonFlags & MB_OK)
        {
            // The message box contains one push button: OK. This is the default.
            m_UI.AddButton( IDOK, g_pApp->GetString(IDS_OK).c_str(),
                            iX, iY, btnWidth, btnHeight );
        }
    }
}
```

First, a callback function is set. On every game user interface I've ever worked on, there's some mechanism for a control to send a message to the screen that it has been clicked on or otherwise messed with. The OnGuiEvent() will trap those events so we can see which button was clicked.

The next bit of code figures out how big the text message is, and it assumes that carriage returns have already been inserted into the message. This is a pretty good idea since you might want a fine control of message formatting, such as adding paragraphs to longer sections of text. Sticking your own newline characters into the message outside of the message box is a good way to do this.

After that, we start laying out the controls and positioning the dialog in the center of the screen. The idea here is to find the number of buttons we're going to add, place them in a vertical stack at the bottom of the dialog box, and add up all the space we're going to need to make sure there's enough room to have the buttons and the text. Also, everything should be centered, which is done by subtracting the inner width from the outer width and dividing by two:

```
m_PosX = (DXUTGetD3D9BackBufferSurfaceDesc()->Width-m_Width)/2;
m_PosY = (DXUTGetD3D9BackBufferSurfaceDesc()->Height-m_Height)/2;
```

If you subtract the width of the dialog from the width of the screen and divide by two, you've got the X position that will center the dialog. Switch all the parameters for heights, and you'll have the correct Y position. You see that kind of thing a lot, and it works a hell of a lot better than hard-coded positions and widths. Now we're ready to add controls to the dialog member; you'll see that in the calls to AddStatic() for the message text and AddButton() for the buttons.

One thing you should notice right away in the call to add buttons is no hard-coded text:

```
m_UI.AddButton( IDOK, g_pApp->GetString(IDS_OK).c_str(),
                      iX, iY - border, btnWidth, btnHeight );
```

I mentioned this back in the application layer discussion. Instead of seeing the naked text, "OK," you see a call into the application layer to grab a string identified by IDOK. The application layer is responsible for grabbing text for anything that will be presented to the player because you might have multiple foreign language versions of your game. You could create this text grabber in any number of ways, but for PC games I prefer using a string table. The cool thing about string tables is that you can stick them in a DLL and swap them out for whatever language you are running in, and you never have to worry about it.

In the event of a device restoration event like a full-screen/windowed mode swap, it's a good idea to tell the DirectX dialog how big it is and where it is on the screen, which you can do through the VOnRestore API:

```
HRESULT CMessageBox::VOnRestore()
{
    m_UI.SetLocation( m_PosX, m_PosY );
    m_UI.SetSize( m_Width, m_Height );
    return S_OK;
}
```

The render method for our screen class simply calls `CDXUTDialog::OnRender`. If you create your own GUI system, this is where you'd iterate through the list of controls and draw them:

```
HRESULT CMessageBox::VOnRender(double fTime, float fElapsedTime)
{
    m_UI.OnRender( fElapsedTime );
    return S_OK;
};
```

You feed Win32 messages to the DirectX GUI controls through the `VOnMsg-Proc()` method. If you create your own GUI, you'd have to iterate through your controls and have them process messages. A good example of that would be to highlight the control if the mouse moved over it or change the graphic to depress the control if the mouse went down over the control's area:

```
LRESULT CALLBACK CMessageBox::VOnMsgProc( AppMsg msg )
{
    return m_UI.MsgProc( msg.m_hWnd, msg.m_uMsg, msg.m_wParam, msg.m_lParam );
}
```

The only thing left to handle is the processing of the control messages. In the case of a message box, the only thing you need to do is send the button result back to a place so that you can grab it later. We'll do that by posting a custom Win32 message into the message pump:

```
void CALLBACK CMessageBox::OnGUIEvent( UINT nEvent, int nControlID,
                                        CDXUTControl* pControl )
{
    PostMessage(g_pApp->GetHwnd(), MSG_END_MODAL, 0, nControlID);
}
```

This might seem confusing at first. Why not just set the member variable in the dialog box class that holds the last button the player selected? The answer lies in how you have to go about creating a modal dialog box in Win32 games, which is our very next subject.

MODAL DIALOG BOXES

Modal dialog boxes usually present the player with a question, such as "Do you really want to quit?" In most cases, the game stops while the dialog box is displayed so the player can answer the question (see Figure 9.2). The answer is usually immediately accepted by the game.

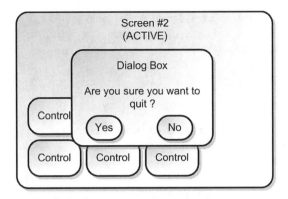

FIGURE 9.2 A modal dialog box.

This might seem easy to code, but it's actually fraught with pain and suffering. Why? Let's look at the anatomy of the "quit" dialog. The code to bring up a message box in Win32 looks like this:

```
int answer = MessageBox(_T("Do you really want to quit?"),
                        _T("Question"), MB_YESNO | MB_ICONEXCLAMATION);
```

When this code is executed, a message box appears over the active window and stays there until one of the buttons is pressed. The window disappears, and the button ID is sent back to the calling code. If you haven't thought about this before, you should realize that the regular message pump can't be working, but clearly some message pump is active, or the controls would never get their mouse and mouse buttons messages. How does this work? The trick is to create another message pump that runs in a tight loop and manage that within a method that handles the life cycle of a modal dialog box:

```
#define QUIT_NO_PROMPT MAKELPARAM(-1,-1)
#define MSG_END_MODAL (WM_USER+100)

int GameCodeApp::Modal(
    shared_ptr<IScreenElement> pModalScreen, int defaultAnswer)
{
    // If we're going to display a dialog box, we need a human view
    // to interact with.
    HumanView *pView;
    for(GameViewList::iterator i=m_pGame->m_gameViews.begin();
        i!=m_pGame->m_gameViews.end(); ++i)
    {
        if ((*i)->VGetType()==GameView_Human)
        {
```

```
            shared_ptr<IGameView> pIGameView(*i);
            pView = static_cast<HumanView *>(&*pIGameView);
    }
}

if (!pView)
{
    // Whoops! There's no human view attached.
    return defaultAnswer;
}

assert(GetHwnd() != NULL && _T("Main Window is NULL!"));
if ( ( GetHwnd() != NULL ) && IsIconic(GetHwnd()) )
{
    FlashWhileMinimized();
}

if (m_HasModalDialog & 0x10000000)
{
    assert(0 && "Too Many nested dialogs!");
    return defaultAnswer;
}

m_HasModalDialog <<= 1;
m_HasModalDialog |= 1;

pView->VPushElement(pModalScreen);

LPARAM lParam = 0;
int result = PumpUntilMessage(MSG_END_MODAL, NULL, &lParam);
if (lParam != 0)
    result = (int)lParam;

pView->VPopScreen();
m_HasModalDialog >>= 1;

return result;
}
```

The first thing that `GameCodeApp::Modal()` method does is find an appropriate game view to handle the message. You can imagine a case where you have nothing but AI processes attached to the game, and they couldn't care less about a dialog box asking them if they want to quit. Only a human view can see the dialog and react to it, so we iterate through the list of game views and find a view that belongs to the human view type. If we don't find one, we return a default answer.

If the entire game is running in a window, and that window is minimized, the player will never see the dialog box. The player needs a clue, and the standard Windows application behavior is to flash the window until the player maximizes the window again, which is what `FlashWhileMinimized()` accomplishes.

The next thing you see is a dirty trick, and I love it. You can imagine a situation where you have a modal dialog on the screen, such as something to manage a player inventory, and the player hits Alt-F4 and wants to close the game. This requires an ability to nest modal dialog boxes, which in turn means you need some way to detect this nesting and if it has gone too deep. This is required because the modal dialogs are managed by the game application. I use a simple bit field to do this, shifting the bits each time we nest deeper.

The next thing that happens is we push the modal screen onto the view we found earlier, and we call a special method that acts as a surrogate Win32 message pump for the modal dialog:

```
int GameCodeApp::PumpUntilMessage (UINT msgEnd, WPARAM* pWParam, LPARAM* pLParam)
{
    int currentTime = timeGetTime();
    MSG msg;
    for ( ;; )
    {
        if ( PeekMessage( &msg, NULL, 0, 0, PM_NOREMOVE ) )
        {
            if ( PeekMessage( &msg, NULL, 0, 0, 0 ) )
            {
                if ( msg.message != WM_SYSCOMMAND ||
                    msg.wParam != SC_CLOSE )
                {
                    TranslateMessage(&msg);
                    DispatchMessage(&msg);
                }

                // Are we done?
                if ( ! IsIconic(GetHwnd()) )
                {
                    FlashWindow( GetHwnd(), false );
                    break;
                }
            }
        }
    }
```

```
        else
        {
            // Update the game views, but nothing else!
            // Remember this is a modal screen.
            if (m_pGame)
            {
                int timeNow = timeGetTime();
                int deltaMilliseconds = timeNow - currentTime;
                for(GameViewList::iterator i=m_pGame->m_gameViews.begin();
                    i!=m_pGame->m_gameViews.end(); ++i)
                {
                    (*i)->VOnUpdate( deltaMilliseconds );
                }
                currentTime = timeNow;
                DXUTRender3DEnvironment();
            }
        }
    }
    if (pLParam)
        *pLParam = msg.lParam;
    if (pWParam)
        *pWParam = msg.wParam;

    return 0;
}
```

The `PumpUntilMessage` function works similarly to the message pump in your main loop, but it is a special one meant for modal dialog boxes. One message, `WM_CLOSE`, gets special treatment since it must terminate the dialog and begin the game close process. Other than close, the loop continues until the target message is seen in the message queue. I define this custom message myself:

```
#define MSG_END_MODAL   ( WM_USER + 100 )
```

If there are no messages in the queue, the pump calls the right code to make the game views update and render. Without this, you wouldn't be able to see anything, especially if you drag another window over your game.

As soon as the modal dialog wants to kill itself off, it will send the `MSG_END_MODAL` into the message queue, and the `PumpUntilMessage` method will exit back out to the `Modal` method we saw earlier. `MSG_END_MODAL` is a special user-defined message, and Win32 gives you a special message range starting at `WM_USER`. I usually like to start defining application specific windows messages at `WM_USER+100`, instead of starting right at `WM_USER`, since I'll be able to tell them apart in the message queue.

The trick to this is getting the answer back to the calling code, which is done with the parameters to the MSG_END_MODAL. In this case, we look at the ID of the control that was clicked on. Recall CMessageBox::OnGUIEvent():

```
void CALLBACK CMessageBox::OnGUIEvent(
UINT nEvent, int nControlID, CDXUTControl* pControl, void *pUserContext )
{
    PostMessage(g_pApp->GetHwnd(), MSG_END_MODAL, 0, nControlID);
}
```

This posts MSG_END_MODAL to the message queue, which is what the PumpUntilMessage method was looking for all along. This breaks the tight loop, and the GameCodeApp::Modal() method can extract the answer the player gave to the modal dialog box.

CONTROLS

Controls have lots of permutations, but most of them share similar properties. I've seen push buttons, radio buttons, check boxes, combo boxes, edit boxes, expandable menus, and all sorts of stuff. I've also coded quite a few of them, I'm sad to say.

Luckily, the DirectX Framework has already implemented most of the standard GUI controls for you:

- CDXUTButton: A simple push button, like "OK" or "Cancel"
- CDXUTStatic: A static text control, for putting non-active text on a dialog
- CDXUTCheckBox: A check box control for selecting on/off status for different items
- CDXUTRadioButton: A radio button control for selecting one thing out of many choices
- CDXUTComboBox: A combo box uses one line, but can drop down a list box of choices
- CDXUTSlider: A simple slider to do things like volume controls
- CDXUTEditBox: A text edit box, for doing things like entering your name or a console command
- CDXUTIMEEditBox: A foreign language edit box
- CDXUTListBox: A list of choices displayed with a scroll bar
- CDXUTScrollBar: A vertical or horizontal scroll bar

You can attach any of these controls to a CDXUTDialog object to create your own user interface, and as you saw in the CMessageBox example in the previous section, these interfaces can be modal or modeless.

The tough thing about implementing a new kind of control in your game isn't how to draw a little "x" in the check box. If you want to learn how to do that, you can trace through the source code in the CDXUTCheckBox and find out how it works. Rather, the tough thing is knowing what features your controls will need beyond these simple implementations. You also need to be aware of the important "gotchas" you'll need to avoid. Let's start with the easy stuff first.

- **Identification:** How is the control distinguished from others on the same screen?
- **Hit Testing/Focus Order:** Which control gets messages, especially if they overlap graphically?
- **State:** What states should controls support?

I suggest you approach the first problem from a device-centric point of view. Each device is going to send input to a game, some of which will be mapped to the same game functions. In other words, you might be able to select a button with the mouse to perform some game action, like firing a missile. You might also use a hot key to do the same thing.

CONTROL IDENTIFICATION

Every control needs an identifier—something the game uses to distinguish it from the other controls on the screen. The easiest way to do this is define an enum, and when the controls are created, they retain the unique identifier they were assigned in their construction:

```
enum MAINSCREEN_CONTROL_IDS
{
   CID_EXIT,
   CID_EXIT_DESKTOP,
   CID_PREVIOUS_SCREEN,
   CID_MAIN_MENU,
   CID_OPTIONS
};

void CALLBACK CGameScreen::OnGUIEvent( UINT nEvent, int nControlID, MyControl*
                                       pControl )
 {
   switch(pControl->GetID())
   {
      case CID_EXIT:
         // exit this screen
         break;
```

```
    case CID_EXIT_DESKTOP:
        // exit to the desktop
        break;

    // etc. etc.
    }
}
```

This is very similar to the way Win32 sends messages from controls to windows via the WM_COMMAND message, but simplified. The only problem with defining control IDs in this manner is keeping them straight, especially if you create screen classes that inherit from other screen classes, each with its own set of controls.

FLATTEN YOUR SCREEN CLASS HIERARCHIES

There's almost no end to the religious arguments about creating new screens by inheriting from existing screen classes. Object-oriented coding techniques make it easy to extend one class into another, but there is a risk of confusion and error when the new class is so different from the original that it might as well be a completely new class. This is why it's better to define functionality in terms of interfaces and helper functions, and flatten your class hierarchy into functional nuggets. A deep inheritance tree complicates the problems of changing something in a base class without adversely affecting many classes that inherit from it.

Some games define controls in terms of text strings, assigning each control a unique string. But there is a downside to using strings to identify controls—you have to do multiple string compares every time a control sends a message to your string class. You'll learn about a more efficient and interesting solution for this problem in Chapter 10, "Game Event Management." It does make things easier to debug, but there's nothing stopping you from including a string member in the debug build of the class. You can solve this problem by writing a bit of debug code that detects multiple controls with the same ID. Your code should simply assert so you can go find the problem and redefine the offending identifier.

HIT TESTING AND FOCUS ORDER

There are two ways controls know they are the center of your attention. The first way is via a hit test. This is where you use a pointer or a cursor and position it over the control by an analog device such as a mouse. This method is prevalent in PC games, and especially games that have a large number of controls on the screen.

The second method uses a focus order. Only one control has the focus at any one time, and each control can get the focus by an appropriate movement of the input device. If the right key or button is pressed, the control with focus sends a message to the parent screen. This is how most console games are designed, and it clearly limits the number and density of controls on each screen.

Hit testing usually falls into three categories: rectangular hit testing, polygonal hit testing, and bitmap collision testing. The rectangle hit test is brain-dead simple. You just make sure your hit test includes the entire rectangle, not just the inside. If a rectangle's coordinates were (15,4) and (30,35), then a hit should be registered both at (15,4) and (30,35).

The hit test for a 2D polygon is not too complicated. The following algorithm was adapted from Graphics Gems, and assumes the polygon is closed. This adaptation uses a point structure and STL to clarify the original algorithm. It will work on any arbitrary polygons, convex or concave:

```cpp
#include <vector>
struct Point
{
    int x, y;
    Point() { x = y = 0; }
    Point(int _x, int _y) { x = _x; y = _y; }
};

typedef std::vector<Point> Polygon;

bool PointInPoly( Point const &test, const Polygon & polygon)
{
    Point newPoint, oldPoint;
    Point left, right;

    bool inside=false;

    size_t points = polygon.size();

    // The polygon must at least be a triangle
    if (points < 3)
            return false;

    oldPoint = polygon[points-1];

    for (unsigned int i=0 ; i < points; i++)
    {
        newPoint = polygon[i];
```

```
      if (newPoint.x > oldPoint.x)
      {
         left = oldPoint;
         right = newPoint;
      }
      else
      {
         left = newPoint;
         right = oldPoint;
      }

      // A point exactly on the left side of the polygon
      // will not intersect - as if it were "open"
      if ((newPoint.x < test.x) == (test.x <= oldPoint.x)
         && (test.y-left.y) * (right.x-left.x)
            < (right.y-left.y) * (test.x-left.x) )
      {
         inside=!inside;
      }

      oldPoint = newPoint;
   }
   return(inside);
}
```

Bitmap collision is easy. You simply compare the pixel value at the (x,y) coordinate with your definition of the transparent color.

CONTROL STATE

Controls have four states: active, highlighted, pressed, and disabled, as shown in Figure 9.3. An active control is able to receive events, but it isn't the center of attention. When the control gets the focus or passes a hit test from the pointing

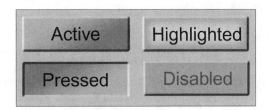

FIGURE 9.3 Four control states used with controls.

device, its state changes to highlighted. It's common for highlighted controls to have separate art or even a looping animation that plays as long as it has focus.

When the player presses a button on the mouse or controller, the control state changes state to the pressed state. The art for this state usually depicts the control in a visually pressed state so that the player can tell what's going on. If the cursor moves away from the control, it will change state to active again, giving the player a clue that if the activation button is released, nothing will happen.

Disabled controls are usually drawn darkened or grayed out, giving the impression that no one is home. I know that Windows does this all over the place, but there is one thing about it that really bothers me: I can never tell *why* the control is disabled. Its fine to have a disabled state, but make sure that the player can figure out why it's disabled, or you'll just cause a lot of frustration.

BEST PRACTICE

USE THE MOUSE CURSOR FOR USER FEEDBACK

If your interface uses a mouse, change the mouse cursor to something different, like a hand icon, when you are over an active control. This approach will give the player another clue that something will happen when he or she clicks the button. Use the Win32 LoadCursor() *API to grab a handle to the right mouse cursor and call* SetCursor() *with the cursor handle. If you want a good package to create animated mouse pointers, try Microangelo by Impact Software at www.impactsoftware.com.*

Don't get confused about the control states mentioned here and control activation. Control activation results in a command message that propagates through to the screen's OnControl() function. For a standard push button control, this only happens if the mouse button is pressed and released over the button's hit area.

MORE CONTROL PROPERTIES

There are some additional properties you can attach to controls, mostly to give the player a more flexible and informative interface.

Hot Keys

An excellent property to attach to any control on a PC game is a hot key. As players become more familiar with the game, they'll want to ditch the mouse control in favor of pressing a single key on the keyboard. It's faster, which makes hardcore players really happy. You can distinguish between a hot key command and a normal keyboard input by checking the keyboard focus. The focus is something your screen class keeps track of itself, since it is an object that moves from control to control. Let's assume that you have a bunch of button controls on a game screen, as well as a chat window. Normally, every key down and up event will get sent to the controls to see if any of their hot keys match. If they do match, the OnControl() method of the screen will get called. The only way to enable the chat window is to click it with the mouse or provide a hot key for it that will set the keyboard focus for the screen.

As long as the keyboard focus points to the chat control, every keyboard event will be sent there, and hot keys are essentially disabled. Usually, the focus is released when the edit control decides it's done with keyboard input, such as when the Enter key is pressed. The focus can also be taken away by the screen, for example, if a different control were to be activated by the mouse.

Tooltips

Tooltips are usually controlled by the containing screen, since it has to be aware of moving the tooltip around as different controls are highlighted. Tooltips are trickier than you'd think, because there's much more to enabling them than creating a bit of text on your screen for each control.

For one thing, every tooltip needs to have a good position relative to the control it describes. You can't just assume that every tooltip will look right if you place it in the same relative position to every control. If you decide that every tooltip will be placed in the upper-right area of every control, what happens when a control is already at the upper-right border of the screen? Also, you'll want to make sure that tooltips don't cover other important information on the screen when they appear. You don't want to annoy the heck out of your users.

TOOLTIPS DON'T DO MUCH GOOD OFF-SCREEN

Even if you provide a placement hint, such as above or beside a control, you'll still need to tweak the placement of the tooltip to make sure it doesn't clip on the screen edge. Also, make sure that screens can erase tooltips prematurely, such as when a dialog box appears or when a drag begins.

Context-Sensitive Help

Context-sensitive help is useful if you have a complicated game with lots of controls. If the player presses a hot key to launch the help window when a control is highlighted, the help system can bring up help text that describes what the control will do. An easy way to do this is to associate an identifier with each control that has context-sensitive help. In one game, this identifier was the name of the HTML file associated with that control. When the screen gets the hot key event for help, it first finds any highlighted control and asks it if it has an associated help file.

Dragging

Controls can initiate a drag event or accept drag events. Drag initiation is simply a Boolean value that is used to indicate if a drag event can start on top of the control or not. Drag acceptance is a little more complicated. Most drag events have a source type, as discussed at the beginning of this chapter. Some controls might accept drags of different types, given only particular game states. An example of this might be dragging items around in a fantasy role-playing game. A character in the game might not be able to accept a dragged object because he's already carrying too much, and thus not be a legal target for the drag event.

Sounds and Animation

Most controls have a sound effect that launches when the button changes state. Some games associate a single sound effect for every button, but it's not crazy to give each control its own sound effect. Animation frames for buttons and other controls are usually associated with the highlighted state. Instead of a single bitmap, you should use a bitmap series that loops while the control is highlighted. You'll find out more about animations and animating processes in Chapter 10.

SOME FINAL USER INTERFACE TIPS

As parting advice, there are a few random, but important, tips I can give you on user interface work.

- All rectangular interfaces are boring.
- Localization can make a mess of your UI.
- UI code is easy to write, but making a good UI is a black art.

If your interface code doesn't use polygonal hit testing or bitmap collision, you are destined to have legions of square buttons and other controls populating your interface. That's not only a dull and uncreative look, but your artists will probably strangle you before you ever finish your game. Artists need the freedom to grow organic shapes in the interface, and will resist all those vertical and horizontal lines.

Localization is a huge subject, but a significant part of that subject is interface design. You may hear things like, "make all your buttons 50 percent wider for German text," as the be-all end-all for localization. While that statement is certainly true, there's a lot more to it than that. It's difficult to achieve an excellent interface using nothing but icons, instead of clear text labels. We attempted that on one of the casino games we developed, and we were completely stymied with the problem of choosing an international icon for features like blackjack insurance and placing a repeat bet on a roulette table. The fact is that international symbols are used and recognized for men and women's bathrooms and locating baggage claim, but they are only recognized because they are advertised much more aggressively than the unique features you use in your games. If you use icons, more power to you, but you'd better provide some tooltips to go along with them.

A truly international application has to conform with much more than left-to-right, top-to-bottom blocks of text. Asian and Middle Eastern languages don't always follow Western European "sensibility." All you can really count on is being able to print text to a definable rectangle. If you have to print lots of text, consider using a well-known format like HTML and be done with it.

When you design your user interface, know your audience. Older players are more comfortable with menus and labeled buttons. Younger players enjoy the experience of exploring a graphical environment with their mouse and clicking where they see highlights. This is extremely problematic if you are a youngish programmer writing games for little kids or your parents. They simply don't think the same way you do, and nothing you do in your interface code will change that. Mimic proven solutions if you can, but always get a random sample of your target audience by taking your interface design for a test drive.

There's nothing more humbling than when you stand behind someone playing your game and silently watch them struggle with the simplest task. You want to scream at the top of your lungs, "Simpleton! How do you find enough neurons to respirate?" In a calmer moment, perhaps you'll realize that the one with missing neurons looks back at you from mirrors.

CORE GAME TECHNOLOGIES

GAME EVENT MANAGEMENT

In This Chapter

- Game Events
- What Game Events Are Important?
- Distinguishing Events from Processes
- Further Reading

Y ou're about to learn that this chapter might be the most important one in the book. After all, game events touch every aspect of a game. From reading the previous chapters of this book, I'm hoping that you've learned that the data flow or communication between all the different subsystems in a game can get extremely complicated. Consider this example: a game script creates an object, such as a ticking time bomb. The script inserts the time bomb into the game object list and the physics system so it can exist in the game world. The bomb object might then interact with the game audio system to kick off a sound effect, likely a ticking sound. The graphics system will need to know about the bomb so it can be drawn. The user interface will need to be informed, too, if the player has any hope of defusing it! Finally, you might have AI characters that need to react appropriately, such as running away in a panic, and you'll also need to schedule future explosion events.

A naive programmer might code this complicated system by using a series of API calls to various subsystems of the game engine. This approach could get extremely messy, and could require a morass of #includes at the top of every CPP file. I'm sure that you have come across code like this before. Each system would have to know about the public API of every other system that it interacted with. I've worked on a number of games that were built this way, and each experience was pretty horrible. Whenever even a trivial modification was made to a subsystem, it seemed that the whole game would have to be recompiled.

In this chapter, you'll learn that you can solve the problems of communications between game subsystems and how they interact with game objects by using a general purpose game event system and incorporating scripting languages into your development efforts. We'll start first by exploring game events, and then we'll build a basic event manager that you can use as a building block for your own games.

GAME EVENTS

Whenever some authoritative system in your game makes something important happen, such as moving a game object, it signifies an event. Your game must then notify all the appropriate subsystems that the event has occurred so that they can handle the event in their own way. A good example of an authoritative system is the physics system, which is responsible for moving dynamic objects. An example of a subsystem that consumes events is the game renderer. It needs to know about the new position and orientation of every moving object so that it can render them in their new position.

The physics system could try to keep track of all the systems that need to know about moving objects, such as the renderer, and call each system's API to tell each one that an object has moved. If there are a number of systems that need to know about moving objects, the physics system must call into each one, probably using a slightly different API and parameter list. Yuck!

Fortunately, there's a much better way to do this. Instead of calling each system every time an object moves, the physics system could create a game event and send it into a system that knows how to distribute the event to any subsystem that wants to listen. One side effect of this solution is that it cleans up the relationship between game subsystems. Mostly, they don't care about anything but themselves and the event management system.

A system such as an audio system already knows what events it should listen to. In this case, it would listen to "object collided" or "object destroyed." On the other hand, there might be tons of other messages that the audio system could safely ignore, such as an event that signals the end of an animation.

In a well-designed game, each subsystem should be responsible for subscribing to and handling game events as they pass through the system. The game event system is global to the application, and therefore makes a good candidate to sit in the application layer. It manages all communications going on between the game logic and game views. If the game logic moves an object, an event is sent, and all the game views will receive it. If a game view wants to send a command to the game logic, it does so through the event system. The game event system is the glue that holds the entire game logic and game view architecture together.

The game event system is organized into three basic parts:

- Events and event data
- Event listeners
- Event Manager

Events and event data are generated by authoritative systems when an action of any significance occurs, and they are sent into the Event Manager, sometimes also called a *listener registry*. The Event Manager matches each event with all the subsystems that have subscribed to the event, and calls each event listener in turn so it can handle the event in its own way.

Events and Event Data

A classic problem in computer games is how to define types of data or objects. The easiest way to define different types of elements, such as event types, is to put them all into a single enumeration like this:

```
Enum EventType
{
   Event_Object_Moved,
   Event_Object_Created,
   Event_Object Destroyed,
   Event_Guard_Picked_Nose,
   // and on and on....
};
```

With this type of solution, each subsystem in your game would likely need this enumeration because each probably generates one or more of these events. In coding this approach, you would need to have every system #include this enumeration. Then, every time you add to it or change it, your entire game would need to be recompiled, clearly a bad thing.

BUILD TIMES ON *THIEF: DEADLY SHADOWS*

When I was working on *Thief: Deadly Shadows* at Ion Storm, we had a few systems like this, including the event system. Each event type was defined in a huge enumeration, and creating a new event or deleting a deprecated one caused us to recompile everything, and I mean everything. *Thief: Deadly Shadows* had nine build targets: PC Game, Xbox Game, and Editor, with each having Debug, Profile, and Release build flavors. Even on a fast desktop workstation, it would take us 15 minutes or more to build just one, and building everything took more than an hour. Screams of anguish could be heard when someone checked in one of these core header files without sending a warning email with plenty of advance notice. The moment someone had to get code off the net, that person might as well go take a prolonged break. Believe me, we didn't want the break either because it would just turn a 12-hour day into a 13-hour day.

Fortunately, there's a better way to do this, at the cost of a little CPU time. Instead of creating a massive enumeration in a core header file, you can create a unique hash from a string and use that as your unique identifier. It's fast, only hits the CPU when you generate the hash, and saves your team from the terrible monolithic enumeration that everyone has to reference:

```
class HashedString
{
public:
    explicit HashedString ( char const * const pIdentStr )
        : m_ident( hash_name(pIdentStr) ),
          m_identStr(pIdentStr)
    {}

    unsigned long getIdent() const
    {
        return reinterpret_cast<unsigned long>(m_ident);
    }
```

```
char const * const getStr() const { return m_identStr;    }

bool operator< ( EventType const & o ) const
{
  bool r = ( getIdent() < o.getIdent() );
  return r;
}

bool operator== ( EventType const & o ) const
{
  bool r = ( getIdent() == o.getIdent() );
  return r;
}

static void * hash_name( char const *  pIdentStr );

private:

  // note: m_ident is stored as a void* not an int, so that in
  // the debugger it will show up as hex-values instead of
  // integer values. This is a bit more representative of what
  // we're doing here and makes it easy to allow external code
  // to assign event types as desired.

  void *        m_ident;
  char const * m_identStr;

};

void * HashedString::hash_name( char const * pIdentStr )
{
  // largest prime smaller than 65536
  unsigned long BASE = 65521L;

  // NMAX is the largest n such that
  // 255n(n+1)/2 + (n+1)(BASE-1) <= 2^32-1
  unsigned long NMAX = 5552;

  #define DO1(buf,i)   {s1 += tolower(buf[i]); s2 += s1;}
  #define DO2(buf,i)   DO1(buf,i); DO1(buf,i+1);
  #define DO4(buf,i)   DO2(buf,i); DO2(buf,i+2);
  #define DO8(buf,i)   DO4(buf,i); DO4(buf,i+4);
  #define DO16(buf)    DO8(buf,0); DO8(buf,8);
```

```
   if (pIdentStr == NULL)
      return NULL;

   if ( strcmp( pIdentStr, kpWildcardEventType ) == 0 )
      return 0;

unsigned long s1 = 0;
unsigned long s2 = 0;

for ( size_t len = strlen( pIdentStr ); len > 0 ; )
{
   unsigned long k = len < NMAX ? len : NMAX;
   len -= k;
   while (k >= 16)
   {
      DO16(pIdentStr);
      pIdentStr += 16;
      k -= 16;
   }

   if (k != 0) do
   {
      s1 += *pIdentStr++;
      s2 += s1;
   } while (--k);

   s1 %= BASE;
   s2 %= BASE;
}

#pragma warning(push)
#pragma warning(disable : 4312)

return reinterpret_cast<void *>( (s2 << 16) | s1 );

#pragma warning(pop)
#undef DO1
#undef DO2
#undef DO4
#undef DO8
#undef DO16
}
```

The code to compute the hash is loosely based upon the Adler-32 checksum by Mark Adler and published as part of the Zlib compression library sources. For those of you who are a little rusty on what a hash is and what it is used for, it is basically a way to boil down a complicated or large data structure, such as an arbitrary string, to a unique ID code. The ID code represents the data in as unique a way as possible. It's like having a unique key to unlock a particular door—you don't have to carry around everything behind the door, as long as you have the key.

Hashes are not guaranteed to be unique. It is possible that the hash_name method will return the same hash for two different strings, although this is extremely rare. If you ever use a hash, your code should handle this problem, which is called *hash collision*—the situation where two different data items hash to the same value.

In the event system you are about to see, each event is assigned a name in a std::string, and it is this string value that is hashed. If two different strings came up with the same hash, the Event Manager would complain and require the programmer to choose a different string.

You'll also notice that the strings are always converted to lowercase before they are sent into the hash function. Programmers can hardly agree on anything, and capitalization of strings is no exception. Converting the strings to lowercase also serves to cut down on the permutations of the different strings that can be hashed, which will also lower the chance for two strings to have the same hash.

Note that there is a special string, kpWildcardEventType, which can be used to represent all event types. Sometimes it's useful for the Event Manager system to use an event type wildcard.

BEST PRACTICE

USE CASE INSENSITIVE COMPARES ON ANY PROGRAMMER-DEFINED STRINGS

Anytime you compare strings in your game, don't make your comparison algorithm case sensitive. It's simply too easy for a bleary-eyed programmer to forget to capitalize in the right place or remember to always type strings in lowercase. In systems like this one, the string is turned into a hash, which is essentially impossible to match back to your original string, and therefore tough to debug if something is mistyped. You can head these problems off easily by just deciding ahead of time that strings are always converted to lowercase. The pain and suffering you save may be your own.

Now you have an easy way to create as many event types as you want. Here's how to create events and data that can ride along with the event:

```
typedef HashedString EventType;
class IEventData
{
public:
    virtual const EventType & VGetEventType( void ) const = 0;
    virtual float VGetTimeStamp() const = 0;
    virtual void VSerialize(std::ostrstream &out) const = 0;
};


typedef boost::shared_ptr<IEventData> IEventDataPtr;


class BaseEventData : public IEventData
{
public:
    explicit BaseEventData( const float timeStamp = 0.0f )
        : m_TimeStamp( timeStamp ) { }
    virtual ~BaseEventData()    { }
    virtual const EventType & VGetEventType( void ) const = 0;
    float VGetTimeStamp( void ) const { return m_TimeStamp; }
    virtual void VSerialize(std::ostrstream &out) const { }

protected:
    const float m_TimeStamp;
};
```

BEST PRACTICE

CHOOSE YOUR STREAM IMPLEMENTATION CAREFULLY

Did you note the use of std::ostrstream *in the previous code snippet? This was chosen to make the stream human readable, which can be very useful during development, but a big mistake for any shipping game. For one thing, a human-readable stream is trivial to hack. More importantly, the stream is large and takes much longer to load and parse than a binary stream. Try using* std::ostream *instead or your own custom stream class.*

An event encapsulates the event type, the event data, and the time the event occurred. Event data is defined by you, the programmer, and you are free to create ad-hoc data that will accompany your event. It's a little easier to see what's going on with a concrete example. Assume for a moment that every dynamic object in your game, sometimes called an *actor*, has a unique identifier you can use to track it. If an actor is ever destroyed, this Actor ID would get sent along with an event so other subsystems could remove the actor from their lists. The event data class for an "actor destroyed" event would look like this:

```
typedef unsigned int ActorId;

struct EvtData_Destroy_Actor : public BaseEventData
{
   static const EventType sk_EventType;
   virtual const EventType & VGetEventType( void ) const
      { return sk_EventType;   }

   explicit EvtData_Destroy_Actor( ActorId id )
      : m_id( id )   {       }

   explicit EvtData_Destroy_Actor( std::istrstream & in )
      {   in >> m_id;   }

   virtual ~EvtData_Destroy_Actor() {}

   virtual void VSerialize(std::ostrstream &out) const
      {   out << m_id;   }

   ActorId m_id;
};


const EventType EvtData_Destroy_Actor::sk_EventType( "destroy_actor" );
```

The event data inherits from the `BaseEventData` so it can be wired into the event system. When an actor is destroyed, its `ActorId` is sent along with the event.

The "destroy_actor" string is what is sent into the `EventType` for hashing. You still don't know how to actually create or send the event yet. First, you need to know about the event listener class.

The Event Listener

Events and event data need to go somewhere, and they always go to event listeners. Any class or subsystem in your game can listen for events. All you have to do is inherit from and implement the pure virtual functions of the `IEventListener` interface:

```
class IEventListener
{
public:

   explicit IEventListener() {}
   virtual ~IEventListener() {}
```

```
// Returns ascii-text name for this listener, used mostly for
// debugging
virtual char const * GetName(void) = 0;

// Return 'false' to indicate that this listener did NOT
// consume the event, (and it should continue to be
// propogated )
//
// return 'true' to indicate that this listener consumed the
//event, ( and it should NOT continue to be propagated )
virtual bool HandleEvent( Event const & event ) = 0
{
    // Note: while HandleEvent() MUST be implemented in all
    // derivative classes, (as this function is pure-virtual
    // and thus the hook for IEventListener being an
    // interface definition) a base implementation is
    // provided here to make it easier to wire up do-nothing
    // stubs that can easily be wired to log the
    // unhandled-event (once logging is available)

    // HandleEvent() functioning should be kept as brief as
    // possible as multiple events will need to be evaluated
    // per-frame in many cases.
    return true;
}
};
```

There are only two pure virtuals to implement: one to return a name for the listener and the other, HandleEvent(), to handle the event. Notice that the pure virtual does have a default implementation, which is a little used C++ construct known as *pure virtual with a body*. You must still implement the pure virtual in any derived class you want to instantiate, but if you want to call the default implementation you can do so explicitly by naming the abstract class in the call. In this case, the default implementation simply returns true, indicating the event was handled.

Here's an example of an event listener that listens to all events:

```
class EventSnooper : public IEventListener
{
public:
    explicit EventSnooper( char const * const kpLogFileName = NULL);
    ~EventSnooper();
    char const * GetName(void) { return "Snoop" };
    bool HandleEvent( Event const & event );
```

```
private:
   FILE *m_hOutFile;
   char m_msgBuf[4090];
};
```

This event listener looks at each event that comes in, and constructs a debug message that will be sent to a log file and the debugger's output window. The constructor opens the log file in the same directory as the executable—a handy place to put it:

```
EventSnooper::EventSnooper( char const * const kpLogFileName )
   : m_hOutFile(INVALID_HANDLE_VALUE)
{
   if ( kpLogFileName )
   {
      // compute the path to our current exe and use it as the
      // basis for the log file ...

      char fullPathName[MAX_PATH];
      memset( fullPathName, 0, sizeof(fullPathName) );
      GetModuleFileNameA( NULL, fullPathName, MAX_PATH );

      // normalize path separators, take note of the last
      // separator found as we go ... if any

      char * pSep = NULL;
      for ( size_t i = 0, j = strlen(fullPathName); i < j ; i++ )
      {
         if ( fullPathName[i] == '\\' )
         {
            fullPathName[i] = '/';

            pSep = & fullPathName[i];
         }
      }

      if ( pSep != NULL )
      {
         strcpy( pSep + 1, kpLogFileName );
      }
      else
      {
         strcpy( fullPathName, kpLogFileName );
      }
```

```
         m_hOutFile = fopen(fullPathName, "w+");
   }
}

EventSnooper::~EventSnooper()
{
   if ( m_hOutFile)
   {
      fclose( m_hOutFile );
      m_hOutFile = NULL;
   }
}

bool EventSnooper::HandleEvent( Event const & event )
{
#ifdef _DEBUG
   memset( m_msgBuf, 0, sizeof(m_msgBuf));

#pragma warning( push )
#pragma warning( disable : 4313 )

   _snprintf( m_msgBuf, sizeof(m_msgBuf)-1,
"Event Snoop : event %08lx time %g : type %08lx [%s] : \n",
            & event,
            event.getTime(),
            event.getType().getIdent(),
            event.getType().getStr(),
            0 );

#pragma warning( pop )

   OutputDebugStringA( m_msgBuf );

   if ( m_hOutFile != NULL )
   {
      fwrite( m_msgBuf, (DWORD) strlen(m_msgBuf), 1, m_hOutFile );
   }
#endif

   return false;
}
```

You now know how to create an event and write a class that listens for events, but you still lack a crucial piece of this puzzle. The Event Manager is the nexus of events in your game. It receives them from practically anywhere, and sends them out to classes that have implemented the listener interface.

The Event Manager

As you might expect, the Event Manager is more complicated than the events or the listeners. It has a tough job matching events with listeners and doing it in a manner that is pretty fast. First, you'll see the IEventManager interface. The Event Manager class is set up to be a global singleton, and it manages its own global pointer. This is pretty useful, since virtually every system in your game will need access to the Event Manager object. There are also some helper functions that clean up access to the Event Manager.

The interface defines the following methods:

- VAddListener: Matches a listener with an event type, so anytime the event type is sent, the listener will be notified.
- VDelListener: Removes a listener.
- VTrigger: Immediately fires an event to listeners that care about it.
- VQueueEvent: Puts an event in a queue to be fired later.
- VAbortEvent: Removes an event from the queue.
- VTick: Processes the events in the queue. This is called every game loop.
- VValidateType: Determines if an event type is legal.

```
typedef boost::shared_ptr<IEventListener>    EventListenerPtr;

class IEventManager
{
public:
    enum eConstants {   kINFINITE = 0xffffffff   };
    explicit IEventManager( char const * const pName, bool setAsGlobal );
    virtual ~IEventManager();

    // Register a handler for a specific event type, implicitly
    // the event type will be added to the known event types if
    // not already known.
    //
    // The function will return false on failure for any
    // reason. The only really anticipated failure reason is if
    // the input event type is bad ( e.g.: known-ident number
    // with different signature text, or signature text is empty )
```

```
virtual bool VAddListener
    ( EventListenerPtr const & inHandler, EventType const & inType ) = 0;

// Remove a listener/type pairing from the internal tables
//
// Returns false if the pairing was not found.

virtual bool VDelListener
    ( EventListenerPtr const & inHandler, EventType const & inType ) = 0;

// Fire off event - synchronous - do it NOW kind of thing -
// analogous to Win32 SendMessage() API.
//
// returns true if the event was consumed, false if not. Note
// that it is acceptable for all event listeners to act on an
// event and not consume it, this return signature exists to
// allow complete propogation of that shred of information
// from the internals of this system to outside uesrs.

virtual bool VTrigger ( IEventData const & inEvent ) const = 0;

// Fire off event - asynchronous - do it WHEN the event
// system VTick() method is called, normally at a judicious
// time during game-loop processing.
//
// returns true if the message was added to the processing
// queue, false otherwise.

virtual bool VQueueEvent ( IEventDataPtr const & inEvent ) = 0;

// Find the next-available instance of the named event type
// and remove it from the processing queue.
//
// This may be done up to the point that it is actively being
// processed ...  e.g.: is safe to happen during event
// processing itself.
//
// if 'allOfType' is input true, then all events of that type
// are cleared from the input queue.
//
// returns true if the event was found and removed, false
// otherwise
virtual bool VAbortEvent
    ( EventType const & inType, bool allOfType = false ) = 0;
```

```
// Allow for processing of any queued messages, optionally
// specify a processing time limit so that the event
// processing does not take too long. Note the danger of
// using this artificial limiter is that all messages may not
// in fact get processed.
//
// returns true if all messages ready for processing were
// completed, false otherwise (e.g. timeout )

virtual bool VTick ( unsigned long maxMillis = kINFINITE ) = 0;

// --- information lookup functions ---

// Validate an event type, this does NOT add it to the
// internal registry, only verifies that it is legal (
// e.g. either the ident number is not yet assigned, or it is
// assigned to matching signature text, and the signature
// text is not empty ).

virtual bool VValidateType( EventType const & inType ) const = 0;

private:

// internal use only accessor for the static methods in the
// helper to use to get the active global instance.

static IEventManager * Get();

// These methods are declared friends in order to get access to the
// Get() method. Since there is no other private entity declared
// in this class this does not break encapsulation, but does allow
// us to do this without requiring macros or other older-style
// mechanims.

friend bool safeAddListener
    ( EventListenerPtr const & inHandler, EventType const & inType );
friend bool safeDelListener
    ( EventListenerPtr const & inHandler, EventType const & inType );
friend bool safeTriggerEvent( IEventData const & inEvent );
friend bool safeQueEvent( IEventDataPtr const & inEvent );
friend bool safeAbortEvent
    ( EventType const & inType, bool allOfType = false );
```

```
        friend bool safeTickEventManager
            ( unsigned long maxMillis = IEventManager::kINFINITE );
        friend bool safeValidateEventType( EventType const & inType );
    };


    bool safeAddListener( EventListenerPtr const & inHandler, EventType const &
                          inType )
    {
       assert(IEventManager::Get() && _T("No event manager!"));
       return IEventManager::Get()->VAddListener( inHandler, inType );
    }


    bool safeDelListener( EventListenerPtr const & inHandler, EventType const &
                          inType )
    {
       assert(IEventManager::Get() && _T("No event manager!"));
       return IEventManager::Get()->VDelListener( inHandler, inType );
    }


    bool safeTriggerEvent( IEventData const & inEvent )
    {
       assert(IEventManager::Get() && _T("No event manager!"));
       return IEventManager::Get()->VTrigger( inEvent );
    }


    bool safeQueEvent( IEventDataPtr const & inEvent )
    {
       assert(IEventManager::Get() && _T("No event manager!"));
       return IEventManager::Get()->VQueueEvent( inEvent );
    }


    bool safeAbortEvent( EventType const & inType, bool allOfType /*= false*/ )
    {
       assert(IEventManager::Get() && _T("No event manager!"));
       return IEventManager::Get()->VAbortEvent( inType, allOfType );
    }


    bool safeTickEventManager( unsigned long maxMillis /*= kINFINITE*/ )
    {
       assert(IEventManager::Get() && _T("No event manager!"));
       return IEventManager::Get()->VTick( maxMillis );
    }
```

```
bool safeValidateEventType( EventType const & inType )
{
    assert(IEventManager::Get() && _T("No event manager!"));
    return IEventManager::Get()->VValidateType( inType );
}
```

You can take a look at the comments above each method to see what it is supposed to do. The implementation of `IEventManager` manages two sets of objects: event data and listeners. As events are sent into the system, the Event Manager matches them up with subscribed listeners and calls each listener's `HandleEvent` method with events they care about.

There are two ways to send events—by queue and by trigger. By *queue* means the event will sit in line with other events until the game processes `IEventManager::VTick()`. By *trigger* means the event will be sent immediately—almost like calling each listener's `HandleEvent` directly from your calling code.

The `SafeBlahBlah` free functions make your code a lot cleaner, and make it easy to remember that the Event Manager might not be created when some subsystems attempt to send events. If this ever happens, you should always assert and figure out what is wrong with your initialization chain. The Event Manager should be one of the very first systems initialized in your application layer.

Remember the `EventSnooper` class from the last few pages? Here's how you would use the `safeAddListener` free function to attach it to your global Event Manager:

```
EventListenerPtr snoop(new EventSnooper("event.log"));
safeAddListener( snoop, EventType( kpWildcardEventType ) );
```

Now you're ready to see how an Event Manager class implements the interface:

```
typedef std::vector<EventListenerPtr> EventListenerList;
typedef std::vector<EventType>        EventTypeList;

class EventManager : public IEventManager
{
public:

    explicit EventManager( char const * const pName, bool setAsGlobal );
    ~EventManager();

    bool VAddListener ( EventListenerPtr const & inListener,
                 EventType const & inType );
    bool VDelListener ( EventListenerPtr const & inListener,
                 EventType const & inType );
```

```
        bool VTrigger ( Event const & inEvent ) const;
        bool VQueueEvent ( EventPtr const & inEvent );
        bool VAbortEvent ( EventType const & inType, bool allOfType );
        bool VTick ( unsigned long maxMillis );
        bool VValidateType( EventType const & inType ) const;

        // --- more information lookup functions ---

        // Get the list of listeners associated with a specific event type.
        EventListenerList GetListenerList ( EventType const & eventType ) const;

        // Get the list of known event types.
        EventTypeList GetTypeList ( void ) const;

private:

        // one global instance
        typedef std::set< EventType >  EventTypeSet;

        // insert result into event type set
        typedef std::pair< EventTypeSet::iterator, bool >       EventTypeSetIRes;

        // one list per event type ( stored in the map )
        typedef std::list< EventListenerPtr > EventListenerTable;

        // mapping of event ident to listener list
        typedef std::map< unsigned int, EventListenerTable >   EventListenerMap;

        // entry in the event listener map
        typedef std::pair< unsigned int, EventListenerTable >  EventListenerMapEnt;

        // insert result into listener map
        typedef std::pair< EventListenerMap::iterator, bool >  EventListenerMapIRes;

        // queue of pending- or processing-events
        typedef std::list< EventPtr >  EventQueue;

        enum eConstants     { kNumQueues = 2 };

        // list of registered event types
        EventTypeSet      m_typeList;

        // mapping of event types to listeners
        EventListenerMap m_registry;
```

```
// double buffered event processing queue (prevents infinite cycles)
EventQueue        m_queues[kNumQueues];

// which queue is actively processing, en-queing events
// goes to the opposing queue
int               m_activeQueue;
```

```
};
```

There's quite a bit here so let me break it down into four manageable chunks. First, we have the simple constructor and destructor. Second, we have the primary use methods. You'll use them to register listeners and send events. Third, we have the information lookup methods that will help us determine if an event is legal or gain access to the lists of listeners and event types. Fourth, we have the definition of the data types and the data members themselves, which are all declared private. Let's go over the data types first and then the public methods.

The private `typedefs` define data types that are used by the Event Manager. All of them use STL, and here's what each of them defines:

- `EventTypeSet`: An STL set that holds the unique event types that the Event Manager can handle. When an event listener tells the Event Manager it wants to be notified of an event type, the event type is added to a set if it wasn't already there.
- `EventTypeSetIRes`: An STL pair that can hold the result of an insertion into an `EventTypeSet`.
- `EventListnerTable`: An STL list of pointers to event listener objects.
- `EventListenerMap`: An STL map that relates a list of listener objects to a specific event identifier.
- `EventListnerMapEnt`: An STL pair that can hold the result of a search in the `EventListenerMap`.
- `EventListenerMapIRes`: An STL pair that can hold the result of an insertion into an `EventListenerMap`.
- `EventQueue`: An STL list of events that are queued and ready to distribute to listeners' objects.

You'll see these data types used throughout the Event Manager code.

There are only four data members of the `EventManager` class. First, there is the `EventTypeSet`, and it stores all the event types that have been registered with the Event Manager. Second, the `EventListenerMap` relates a list of listeners with a specific event. The Event Manager uses it to find all the listener objects that care about a particular event. Finally, we have the `EventQueue` and the integer that tracks which queue is active. You'll notice there are actually two queues. When the system processes events, it is possible that new events will be generated. Those new events go into the "other" queue. This makes it easy to just process the events that were generated during the last loop of the game code, saving the newest events for the next time around. There's also the very possible situation where a single event queue could create an infinite loop where one listener spawns an event that is handled by itself—a single loop wouldn't ever finish!

The constructor and destructor are pretty bare bones:

```
EventManager::EventManager(char const * const pName, bool setAsGlobal )
   : IEventManager( pName, setAsGlobal ),  m_activeQueue(0)
{
}

EventManager::~EventManager()
{
    m_activeQueue = 0;
}
```

Here's the code for adding a new listener. Listeners and event types are registered with a single call. If either one is new to the system, it is validated and entered into the lookup data structures:

```
bool EventManager::VAddListener (
      EventListenerPtr const & inListener, EventType const & inType )
{
   if ( ! VValidateType( inType ) )
      return false;

   // check / update type list
   EventTypeSet::iterator evIt = m_typeList.find( inType );

   // find listener map entry, create one if no table already
   // exists for this entry ...

   EventListenerMap::iterator elmIt =
      m_registry.find( inType.getHashValue() );

   if ( elmIt == m_registry.end() )
   {
      EventListenerMapIRes elmIRes = m_registry.insert(
         EventListenerMapEnt( inType.getHashValue(), EventListenerTable() ) );

      // whoops, could not insert into map!?!?
      if ( elmIRes.second == false )
         return false;

      // should not be possible, how did we insert and create
      // an empty table!?!?!
```

```
    if ( elmIRes.first == m_registry.end() )
      return false;

    // store it so we can update the mapped list next ...
    elmIt = elmIRes.first;
  }


  // update the mapped list of listeners, walk the existing
  // list (if any entries) to prevent duplicate addition of
  // listeners. This is a bit more costly at registration time
  // but will prevent the hard-to-notice duplicate event
  // propogation sequences that would happen if double-entries
  // were allowed.

  // note: use reference to make following code more simple
  EventListenerTable & evlTable = (*elmIt).second;

  for ( EventListenerTable::iterator it = evlTable.begin(),
        itEnd = evlTable.end(); it != itEnd ; it++ )
  {
    bool bListenerMatch = ( *it == inListener );

    if ( bListenerMatch )
      return false;
  }

  // okay, event type validated, event listener validated,
  // event listener not already in map, add it

  evlTable.push_back( inListener );
  return true;
}
```

First, the event type is validated. You don't want an illegal event type in the event set. An event would be illegal if, by some chance, the hash for the event type had already been added and the two event type strings were different. This might happen about as often as me winning the Texas lottery. Yes, I buy tickets.

If the event type has never been seen before, it is added to the event type list. Likewise for the listener. If it has never been seen before, it is inserted into the event listener table. The last thing that happens is the existing list of mapped listeners/event types is checked to make sure you aren't adding a duplicate relationship between this listener and this event type. If you allowed duplicates in this mapping, the listener would get multiple events when only one was sent.

Here's how you remove a listener:

```
bool EventManager::VDelListener (
   EventListenerPtr const & inListener, EventType const & inType )
{
   if ( ! VValidateType( inType ) )
      return false;

   bool rc = false;

   // brute force method, iterate through all existing mapping
   // entries looking for the matching listener and remove it.

   for ( EventListenerMap::iterator it = m_registry.begin(),
         itEnd = m_registry.end(); it != itEnd; it++ )
   {
      unsigned int const    kEventId = it->first;
      EventListenerTable & table    = it->second;

      for ( EventListenerTable::iterator it2 = table.begin(),
            it2End = table.end(); it2 != it2End; it2++ )
      {
         if ( *it2 == inListener )
         {
            // found match, remove from table,
            table.erase( it2 );

            // update return code
            rc = true;

            // and early-quit the inner loop as addListener()
            // code ensures that each listener can only
            // appear in one event's processing list once.
            break;
         }
      }
   }

   return rc;
}
```

This is an ugly nested for loop, but there's really no reason to do anything more complicated. Removing a listener should be a relatively rare event, which implies that listeners tend to be tied to subsystems, like an audio system, and not individual objects, like a particular AI character. You don't want the event system to have a giant list of listeners to iterate through every time an event is sent, and you want the systems, such as the AI system, to be responsible for managing objects under their control. A manager for a subsystem can use whatever evaluation is best for the objects it manages—whether that's a list, a tree, a hash table, or whatever. Here's a good rule of thumb to follow: Any listener that cares about messages important to game objects like AI characters should be tied to the system manager, not a class representing each object.

While the situation may be unusual, you may want to fire an event and have all listeners respond to it immediately and not use the event queue. In all honesty, this method would break the paradigm of remote event handling, as you will see done in Chapter 16, "Network Programming Primer," but just in case you need it, here's the VTrigger() method:

```
bool EventManager::VTrigger ( IEventData const & inEvent ) const
{
   if ( ! VValidateType( inEvent.VGetEventType() ) )
      return false;

   EventListenerMap::const_iterator itWC = m_registry.find( 0 );

   if ( itWC != m_registry.end() )
   {
      EventListenerTable const & table = itWC->second;

      bool processed = false;

      for ( EventListenerTable::const_iterator it2 = table.begin(),
            it2End = table.end(); it2 != it2End; it2++ )
      {
         (*it2)->HandleEvent( inEvent );
      }
   }

   EventListenerMap::const_iterator it =
      m_registry.find( inEvent.VGetEventType().getHashValue() );

   if ( it == m_registry.end() )
      return false;

   EventListenerTable const & table = it->second;

   bool processed = false;
```

```
for ( EventListenerTable::const_iterator it2 = table.begin(),
    it2End = table.end(); it2 != it2End; it2++ )
{
    EventListenerPtr listener = *it2;
    if ( listener->HandleEvent( inEvent ) )
    {
        // only set to true, if processing eats the messages
        processed = true;
    }
}

return processed;
}
```

You should notice there are two nearly identical sections of code. Both seem to find an event listener table, iterate through them, and call HandleEvent for every listener in the table. Some listeners care about all events, such as the snooper listener you saw earlier. Other listeners care only for particular events. The first section of code handles those listeners that care about all event types, and the second section handles the listeners that care about specific events.

Queuing events is also possible with the VQueueEvent method:

```
bool EventManager::VQueueEvent ( IEventDataPtr const & inEvent )
{
    assert ( m_activeQueue >= 0 );
    assert ( m_activeQueue < kNumQueues );

    if ( ! VValidateType( inEvent->VGetEventType() ) )
        return false;

    EventListenerMap::const_iterator it =
        m_registry.find( inEvent->VGetEventType().getHashValue() );

    if ( it == m_registry.end() )
    {
        // if global listener is not active, then abort queue add
        EventListenerMap::const_iterator itWC = m_registry.find( 0 );

        if ( itWC == m_registry.end() )
        {
            // no listeners for this event, skipit
            return false;
        }
    }
```

```
m_queues[m_activeQueue].push_back( inEvent );

return true;
}
```

That one is pretty simple. It just validates the event, makes sure there's a listener out there that cares about the event, and inserts it into the event queue. You might be curious about the different effects of firing an event now versus queueing it up until the next game loop. It's similar to the Win32 `SendMessage` and `PostMessage` idea, whenever you can use the queue. It does tend to even out your game loops, pushing events created in the current game loop in the queue for processing the next time around.

A much smarter event processor might be able to do things like collapse events or even remove events if they are meaningless. A good example of this is two "object moved" events for the same object. Clearly, only the last one is meaningful, so one could be ignored. Also, if this system were sending, or marshalling, events across the Internet for a multiplayer game, it would also be pretty smart about compressing and packaging multiple events into a single squirt of data. This would be much more efficient than one event at a time. Those examples could really only be done if messages were queued instead of processed as they were generated.

Of course, you could change your mind about a queued message, and want to take it back, like some of those emails I sent to my boss:

```
bool EventManager::VAbortEvent ( EventType const & inType, bool allOfType )
{
    assert ( m_activeQueue >= 0 );
    assert ( m_activeQueue < kNumQueues );

    if ( ! VValidateType( inType ) )
        return false;

    EventListenerMap::iterator it = m_registry.find( inType.getHashValue() );

    if ( it == m_registry.end() )
        return false; // no listeners for this event, skipit

    bool rc = false;

    EventQueue &evtQueue = m_queues[m_activeQueue];
```

```
for ( EventQueue::iterator it = evtQueue.begin(),
        itEnd = evtQueue.end(); it != itEnd; it++ )
{
    if ( (*it)->VGetEventType() == inType )
    {
        it = evtQueue.erase(it);
        rc = true;
        if ( !allOfType )
            break;
    }
    else
    {
        ++it;
    }
}
return rc;
}
```

The VAbortEvent() method is a simple case of looking in the active queue for the event of a given type and erasing it. Note that this method can erase the first event in the queue of a given type or all events of a given type, depending on the value of the second parameter. You could use this method to remove redundant messages from the queue, such as two "move object" events for the same object.

All those queued messages have to be processed sometime. Somewhere in the game's main loop the Event Manager's VTick() method should be called, and the queued messages will get distributed like so many pieces of mail:

```
bool EventManager::VTick ( unsigned long maxMillis )
{
    unsigned long curMs = GetTickCount();
    unsigned long maxMs =
        ( maxMillis == IEventManager::kINFINITE ) ?
            IEventManager::kINFINITE   : (curMs + maxMillis );

    EventListenerMap::const_iterator itWC = m_registry.find( 0 );

    // swap active queues, make sure new queue is empty after the swap ...

    int queueToProcess = m_activeQueue;
    m_activeQueue = ( m_activeQueue + 1 ) % kNumQueues;
    m_queues[m_activeQueue].clear();
```

```
// now process as many events as we can ( possibly time limited ) ...
// always do AT LEAST one event, if ANY are available ...

while ( m_queues[queueToProcess].size() > 0 )
{
   IEventDataPtr event = m_queues[queueToProcess].front();
   m_queues[queueToProcess].pop_front();

   EventType const & eventType = event->VGetEventType();

   EventListenerMap::const_iterator itListeners =
      m_registry.find( eventType.getHashValue() );

   if ( itWC != m_registry.end() )
   {
      EventListenerTable const & table = itWC->second;
      bool processed = false;

      for ( EventListenerTable::const_iterator
            it2 = table.begin(), it2End = table.end();
            it2 != it2End; it2++ )
      {
         (*it2)->HandleEvent( *event );
      }
   }

   // no listerners currently for this event type, skip it
   if ( itListeners == m_registry.end() )
      continue;

   unsigned int const kEventId = itListeners->first;
   EventListenerTable const & table = itListeners->second;

   for ( EventListenerTable::const_iterator
         it = table.begin(), end = table.end();
         it != end ; it++ )
   {
      if ( (*it)->HandleEvent( *event ) )
      {
         break;
      }
   }
}
```

```
   curMs = GetTickCount();

   if ( maxMillis != IEventManager::kINFINITE )
   {
      if ( curMs >= maxMs )
      {
         // time ran about, abort processing loop
         break;
      }
   }
}


// if any events left to process, push them onto the active
// queue.
//
// Note: to preserve sequencing, go bottom-up on the
// remainder, inserting them at the head of the active
// queue...

bool queueFlushed = ( m_queues[queueToProcess].size() == 0 );

if ( !queueFlushed )
{
   while ( m_queues[queueToProcess].size() > 0 )
   {
      IEventDataPtr event = m_queues[queueToProcess].back();
      m_queues[queueToProcess].pop_back();
      m_queues[m_activeQueue].push_front( event );
   }
}

// all done, this pass
return queueFlushed;
}
```

The Vick() method takes queued messages and sends them to the listener objects via their HandleEvent() method. There are actually two queues. This is almost like double buffering in a renderer. Sometimes handling events creates new events; in fact, it happens all the time. Colliding with an object might cause it to move and collide with another object. If you always added events to a single queue, you might never run out of events to process. This problem is handled easily with two queues: one for the events being actively processed and the other for new events.

The code is very much like what you saw in the VTrigger() method, with one more difference than the fact the events are being pulled from one of the queues. It also can be called with a maximum time allowed. If the amount of time is exceeded, the method exits, even if there are messages still in the queue.

This can be pretty useful for smoothing out some frame rate stutter if you attempt to handle too many events in one game loop. If your game events start to pile up, and your queue always seems to stay full, perhaps you'd better work on a little optimization.

The next set of methods gives you information about the Event Manager: what event types are legal, what listeners are attached to the Event Manager, and what event types have been registered by all the listeners:

```
bool EventManager::VValidateType(   EventType const & inType ) const
{
   if ( 0 == inType.getStr().length() )
      return false;

   if ( ( inType.getHashValue() == 0 ) &&
        (strcmp(inType.getStr().c_str(),kpWildcardEventType) != 0) )
      return false;

   EventTypeSet::const_iterator evIt =   m_typeList.find( inType );

   if ( evIt == m_typeList.end() )
   {
      assert( 0 && "Failed validation of an event type; it was probably not
                  registered with the EventManager!" );
      return false;
   }

   return true;
}
```

The first check for a legal event type is if the string description of the event type is non-null. Every event type has to have a name or the EventType::hash_name method won't work. The next check requires that the calculated identity of the string is either non-zero or the string is the wildcard string.

If those checks pass, the manager checks all the event types that are currently registered. If it is found, hopefully, it is because two listeners are both listening for the same event type. This would happen quite often, especially with events such as "object_moved." Lots of game subsystems, and therefore listener objects, would care about that kind of event. If the strings for two event types that happened to share the same hash calculated by EventType::hash_name are different, then the new event is declared illegal, and you can officially call yourself horribly unlucky. Choose a new name for your event and get on with your life.

The last two methods return lists of listeners and event types registered with the Event Manager:

```
EventListenerList EventManager::getListenerList
    ( EventType const & eventType ) const
{
    // invalid event type, so sad
    if ( ! VValidateType( eventType ) )
        return EventListenerList();

    EventListenerMap::const_iterator itListeners =
        m_registry.find( eventType.getHashValue() );

    // no listerners currently for this event type, so sad
    if ( itListeners == m_registry.end() )
        return EventListenerList();

    EventListenerTable const & table = itListeners->second;

    // there was, but is not now, any listerners currently for
    // this event type, so sad
    if ( table.size() == 0 )
        return EventListenerList();

    EventListenerList result;
    result.reserve( table.size() );

    for ( EventListenerTable::const_iterator it = table.begin(),
        end = table.end(); it != end ; it++ )
    {
        result.push_back( *it );
    }

    return result;
}

EventTypeList EventManager::getTypeList ( void ) const
{
    // no entries, so sad
    if ( m_typeList.size() == 0 )
        return EventTypeList();
```

```
EventTypeList result;
result.reserve( m_typeList.size() );

for ( EventTypeSet::const_iterator it = m_typeList.begin(),
       itEnd = m_typeList.end(); it != itEnd; it++ )
{
   result.push_back( it->first );
}

return result;
}
```

Further Work

One thing you might notice is the Event Manager currently doesn't have serialization support. This is one homework assignment I'll give you—perhaps you'll consider using boost::serialization to implement it. The event system will likely have events queued every game loop, and these events will probably need a way to be saved and reloaded at any time. Another bit of useful work you can do to make these classes more useful for prime time game development is much better error checking and the implementation of exceptions. Currently, the asserts in the code will help you find bugs during development, but in a release build will happily allow the code to continue to run with bad data.

WHAT GAME EVENTS ARE IMPORTANT?

It's a little something of a cop-out, but it completely depends on your game, doesn't it? A game like *Tetris* might care about a few simple events such as "Brick Created," "Brick Moved," "Brick Rotated," and "Brick Collision." A game like *Thief: Deadly Shadows* had dozens and dozens of different game events. Here's an example of the kind of game events you might send in just about any game:

Game Events	Description
ActorMove	A game object has moved.
ActorCollision	A collision has occurred.
AICharacterState	Character has changed states.
PlayerState	Player has changed states.
PlayerDeath	Player is dead.
GameOver	Player death animation is over.

`ActorCreated`	A new game object is created.
`ActorDestroy`	A game object is destroyed.

Map/Mission Events

`PreLoadLevel`	A new level is about to be loaded.
`LoadedLevel`	A new level is finished loading.
`EnterTriggerVolume`	A character entered a trigger volume.
`ExitTriggerVolume`	A character exited a trigger volume.
`PlayerTeleported`	The player has been teleported.

Game Startup Events.

`GraphicsStarted`	The graphics system is ready.
`PhysicsStarted`	The physics system is ready.
`EventSystemStarted`	The event system is ready.
`SoundSystemStarted`	The sound system is ready.
`ResourceCacheStarted`	The resource system is ready.
`NetworkStarted`	The network system is ready.
`HumanViewAttached`	A human view has been attached.
`GameLogicStarted`	The game logic system is ready.
`GamePaused`	The game is paused.
`GameResumedResumed`	The game is resumed.
`PreSave`	The game is about to be saved.
`PostSave`	The game has been saved.

Animation and Sound Events

`AnimationStarted`	An animation has begun.
`AnimationLooped`	An animation has looped.
`AnimationNotetrack`	An animation dependent command event—used to time sound effects, such as footsteps, exactly with an animation.
`AnimationEnded`	An animation has ended.
`SoundEffectStarted`	A new sound effect has started.
`SoundEffectLooped`	A sound effect has looped back to the beginning.
`SoundEffectEnded`	A sound effect has completed.
`VideoStarted`	A cinematic has started.
`VideoEnded`	A cinematic has ended.

DISTINGUISHING EVENTS FROM PROCESSES

If you recall the CProcess class from Chapter 6, you might be wondering if there is a significant difference between a game event and a process. The difference is easy—a *game event* is something that has happened in the most recent frame, such as an actor has been destroyed or moved. A *process* is something that takes more than one frame to process, such as an animation or monitoring a sound effect.

These two systems are quite powerful by themselves, and can easily create a game of significant complexity with surprisingly little code in your game logic or view classes.

FURTHER READING

Algorithms in C++, Robert Sedgewick

Beyond the C++ Standard Library, Björn Karlsson

Effective STL, Scott Meyers

Introduction to Algorithms, Thomas Cormen

SCRIPTING WITH LUA

by James Clarendon

In This Chapter

- What Is Scripting?
- Common Scripting Paradigms
- Introducing Lua
- Getting Started with a Lua Wrapper—LuaPlus
- Mind the Gap!
- Wanna Buy a Bridge?
- I'm Totally Wired
- Do You Hear What I Hear?
- Let's Get OOP-Able!
- Debugging Script
- Introducing Decoda
- Famous Last Words: "An Exercise for the Reader"
- References

This chapter is authored by James Clarendon, a lead programmer at Red Fly Studio. James and I have collaborated on several projects in the past, most recently Mushroom Men: The Spore Wars *and* Ghostbusters: The Video Game. *He lives in Brooklyn, New York, with entirely too many classic video game systems.*

Picture it: Sicily, 1922. Wait, scratch that—a drizzly October morning, 1983, Sparks Elementary. My fellow first graders and I were led into the bowels of the school and seated before a row of glowing monitors. I was lucky enough to nab a chair in front of one of the color monitors, attached to a TI-99/4A running a cartridge called LOGO. On the lurid blue screen, a small orange truck raced from left to right, wrapping around forever. With a little instruction from Ms. Davis, our teacher, we discovered we could make all sorts of shapes and set them in motion. Soon planes, houses, and a menagerie of others were whizzing to and fro all over the screen.

And then I did it.

I must have hit the function key, because the screen cleared and instead of zooming sprites, I was instead faced with a blinking cursor. What had I done?!?

Ms. Davis came over and explained that I was controlling the turtle. "Oh…" I said, not quite comprehending. Then she pointed me toward a reference card and started giving me some instruction. I started experimenting.

```
FD 10
```

I hit the function key to return to the display. To my amazement, a small black line was in the center of the screen, with a tiny triangle at the end, pointed right. I looked back to the reference card and started typing more.

```
RT 90
```

The triangle had rotated, and was now pointed straight up. That was my "turtle."

```
FD 50
```

Now I had a right angle drawn on my screen. I didn't realize it then, but I had just discovered scripting using the LOGO language.

What Is Scripting?

At its heart, scripting is a way for a user to tell a program how to behave. If you think that sounds a lot like programming, you're partly correct. A script controls the behavior of a program, but it exists as a separate entity that is loaded or entered in and acted upon by the program. Scripts are normally in a human-readable format, and ideally they can be edited by nonprogrammers.

One of the most important things to learn as a modern-day game developer is that it is the *content providers*—not the programmers—who will make the game fun. Sure, you have to fix the bugs and make sure everything runs just right, but the more effort you can invest into making tools that are easy to use for creative types, the more power will be available to them to express their vision.

To that end, you need to shift your programming philosophy from a process-driven one to one where the external data determines the flow and behavior of the game, and where you can expose functionality and open up the game's features to these creative types. This is a data-driven philosophy, which you should adopt as soon as possible.

With a properly engineered design, scripters can bring a game world to life. From a very high-level perspective, scripting can be used to dictate the actions of actors the way a stage director would in a play. By giving these actors a sense of autonomy and interactivity, you can truly leverage the strength of the medium.

Data-Driven Software Design

Writing a good data-driven engine is a difficult task. It requires the software to be architected to accept external data, verify its contents at runtime, handle any problems, and kick off complicated tasks from this data. This sounds simple, but you'll find yourself having to re-think much of an engine's architecture to support this properly. Many explicit calls must be changed to requests that are verified first.

One school of thought holds the ideal engine to be one that could essentially create any type of game, all without changing a single line of code. Content drives this. While this engine still remains a Platonic ideal (or Quixotic folly), realize that the scripters will be the ones building the game, and you will be there to support them.

Data Definition Versus Runtime Game Control

Content can drive a program in one of two ways: straight up data definition, and through runtime control. While you can certainly make a game with just data definition, more powerful engines allow scripters to truly take advantage of exposed functionality. In practice, and in the course of this chapter, I'll be showing you both facets.

Data definition is basically a way to parameterize a program's behavior. INI and XML files are good examples of this; they hold static data that a program reads in at runtime and works around. Most game editors will save out this data for a level, and later read it in to determine the number and types of actors, as well as each of their properties. In a game where all you need is to specify hit points and static behavior values, this is all that is necessary to get moving.

On the other hand, you can have runtime game control from script. This opens up a level of process control to the scripters, and it's one that inspires a lot of fear in programmers. Giving up control?!? Of *my* program?!? Get a hold of yourself now; granting scripters their own functions and access to the game engine's state and behavior will expand the possibilities and interactivity of the final product. And it'll probably save you time, too.

Pros and Cons of Using a Scripting Language

Much like the classic dilemma a certain arachnid-loving superhero was faced with, the power offered by a scripting language brings with it some additional responsibilities and trade-offs that you'll need to be aware of for an optimal implementation. Next, I'll look at what I consider to be the most important considerations.

Resource Efficiency

One concern for a scripting language is its efficiency in controlling resources, particularly memory. Many scripting languages, especially those that dynamically allocate data, use a reference count or garbage collection scheme to maintain memory usage. Still, an interpreted language won't ever be as smart as a good compiler in its use of resources. By and large, this should not be a huge issue, but be aware that it can cause headaches down the road.

Speed

I made this concern purposely vague to illustrate a trade-off: runtime execution speed and workflow speed. A good scripting language may not run as fast as straight C++, but you'll probably wind up saving time in the long run by easily being able to prototype portions of your game. One of the most important aspects of a scripting language is that you don't need to recompile the executable to change the game. Most importantly, nonprogrammers can work on developing the game and don't need to have a copy of Visual Studio, nor do they need a degree in Computer Science.

Besides, with all that time you saved, you'll have plenty of time to profile and find script functions that will run faster when shifted into native C++.

Verifying Data

Since your data will be coming in at runtime, there's no compiler and linker to verify everything *a priori*. This is going to change the way you program, because everything that could handle external data will need to be fault tolerant. Whether you use exceptions or some other scheme, your code must be robust enough to interrupt itself, raise a red flag, and get itself back on track, all the while informing the scripter of his latest bone-headed mistake. Even if it's a completely fatal error, let the user know what data caused it and why it can't continue.

No, you can't just crash to the desktop. Well, you can. Just don't be surprised when they come to your office with torches and pitchforks.

Ease of Use

Isn't this guaranteed to be a "pro"? Isn't it great that we give all this power and freedom to nonprogrammers? What could the "con" be?

The con is that a poorly architected system can hoist an unsuspecting scripter by his or her own petard. A system so complicated and convoluted that it is just impossible to salvage. This can be avoided with some vigilance and some technically minded scripters.

HOISTED BY THEIR WHAT?

I recently learned that a petard was a small explosive used to blow open walls and doors during the Renaissance. Its name comes from the archaic French word *peter*—to fart.

COMMON SCRIPTING PARADIGMS

Below are listed several paradigms used by many engines. Some engines offer one or more of them.

Data Definition Only

While your first instinct may be to sneer, there are some games for which defining static data is perfectly adequate. Simple arcade games and linear action and racing titles can do just fine with this. There's no real "scripting" going on here, but there may not need to be. This method is good for games with minimal or simple dynamic actors.

Graphical

A more modern approach is the graphical scripting system. In such a system (e.g., Unreal's Kismet), the user manipulates various graphical primitives representing concepts to accomplish the runtime scripting. Want the lights to turn on when a player opens the refrigerator door? In a graphical scripting system, you might drag a link object from the door object to the light bulb. This system is very powerful and very user friendly. However, it doesn't offer the kind of freeform and lower-level control that some games may demand.

Interpreted Script Languages

Interpreted script languages are what we'll be focusing on primarily in this chapter. With this paradigm, a scripter works in a high-level language friendlier than C++, but with a lot of power at his disposal. Ideally, it should let the scripter go beyond the bounds of explicit game behavior and allow him to define his own actor types and actions. This kind of scripting paradigm enables scripters to implement (and prototype!) new and deeper systems.

Languages such as BASIC, Python, Lua, and even LOGO may vary in terms of syntax and implementation, but all are interpreted at runtime. Optimizations exist to get around this, such as precompilation, but this interpretation is actually a strength of the language. As we'll see later, a good interpreted language can make explicit calls through a console to help debugging and testing.

THE FUTURE OF SCRIPTING

I've lived for 30 years on this planet (three…elsewhere), and the creativity of the games industry will never cease to amaze me. At the 2007 Game Developers Conference, Sony introduced *Little Big Planet*, a game where the "scripting" is done interactively within the game world, while playing the game. Watching a little sack-person run around, pop open a menu, pull out a wheel from thin air and start it spinning, then jump on it and use it as a platform to hoist himself up to the top of a cliff, left me—as the British would say—"gobsmacked." Could this be the future of scripting?

INTRODUCING LUA

Ah, lovely Lua. Lua is a scripting language developed in the early nineties (back when Mr. Mike was using a 286 to make EGA cave drawings) by a group at the Pontifical University of Rio de Janeiro. The name, as the Brazilian origin would indicate, is the Portuguese word for "moon." Originally intended as a lightweight language usable by nonprogrammers, it borrowed many concepts from contemporary languages. Following an article on Lua in *Dr. Dobbs Journal*, it began to gain traction in the games community.

Looking at a Lua script is intuitive and simple: the structure is fluid, the syntax is lax, and the built-in operations are limited. There's even a runtime interpreter; just go to the *bin* directory of the Lua source and run the executable. It will let you type things in, such as the example code in this chapter, and see

---

SOMEONE'S BEEN MESSING WITH THE MILKMAN'S ANTI-PARANOIA MEDICINE AGAIN

To the best of my knowledge, the first games to use Lua were LucasArts' adventure titles. If you've played *Grim Fandango* or *Psychonauts*—and shame on you if you haven't—you've played a title written primarily in Lua.

---

values spit out. I won't be going into an exhaustive treatise on how to use Lua; better resources will be listed at the end of the chapter for that. For now, you should find the code very C-like and understandable.

So what's so great about Lua?

Lack of Strong Typing

Variables in Lua aren't typed at all. Similar to the boost::any class, you can assign anything to any variable you want. Take, for example, this Lua script snippet:

```
--Let's start 'a' off as a number.
a = 55
print( a )

b = 63.7 + a
print( b )

--Now let's toy with 'a' a little more.
a = "Hello!"
print( a )

--The '..' operator is for concatenation.
print( a .. "  B = " .. b )
```

This produces the result:

```
55
118.7
Hello!
Hello!  B = 118.7
```

Great, so all we did was assign a string to a variable that was once an integer, and then we converted them. Let's look at another, more powerful script:

```
--Calculates the square of the value.
function mySquare( value )
   return ( value * value )
end

--Doubles the input value.
function myDouble( value )
   return ( value * 2 )
end
```

```
f = "I'm about to be a function!"
x = 11
print( f )

f = mySquare
print( f(x) )
f = myDouble
print( f(x) )
```

...which produces:

```
I'm about to be a function!
121
22
```

So even functions can be assigned to variables. You know how many aster-isks, parentheses, incantations, and curses are required to do a function pointer in C++? And it's *still* going to be strongly typed? In Lua, functions can take an arbi-trary number of parameters (if you don't specify them all, Lua will assign them "nil" for you...you can treat it almost like an explicit NULL). But wait there's more! We're not to my favorite part yet.

Tables

The only native data type built in to Lua is the table. A table can be used for almost anything; it's an associative container mapping keys (of any type) to values (of any type). Let's look at an example:

```
function LandRover()
   print( "LAND ROVER" )
end
function GTI()
   print( "GTi" )
end
--Start with empty tables.
tblOne = {}
tblTwo = {}

--We can add elements using two types of syntax,
--the '.' or the '[]' methods, shown below.
tblOne.Name = "Mr. Mike"
tblOne[ "Car" ] = LandRover

tblTwo[ "Name" ] = "James"
tblTwo.Car = GTI
```

Note that the brackets with quote-delimited string produce the same result as the dot method. Let's see what we can do with this now:

```
function displayPerson( personTable )
   --Display the name member.
   print( personTable[ "Name" ] .. " drives a:" )

   --Call the function related to this table.
   --We'll put it into a local variable first.
   local func = personTable.Car
   func()
end


--Display Mike's table.
displayPerson( tblOne )
--Now James' table.
displayPerson( tblTwo )
```

As you can guess, the result of running this is:

```
Mr. Mike drives a:
LAND ROVER
James drives a:
GTi
```

This data structure is so powerful, you can use it to manage an array, a dictionary, lists, and queues. You can easily iterate over a table as well:

```
--Create a table, with last name as key,
--and value as first name.
people =
{
   McShaffry = "Mike",
   Lake = "Jeff",
   Clarendon = "James",
}
--Let's iterate over the table.
--NOTE:  As it's an associative map,
--it may not be in order!
for lastName, firstName in pairs( people ) do
   print( firstName .. " " .. lastName )
end
```

On my machine, this produced the following results:

```
Jeff Lake
Mike McShaffry
James Clarendon
```

Because strings are stored as hashed values, the mapping within a table does not always correspond to the order that they were input. Lua handles strings this way primarily for efficiency.

You can also create an indexed array by assigning entries in *order of index*, or just not specifying any keys:

```
--Create a table to act as an array.
myArray = { 10, 20, 30, 40, 50 }

--NOTE:  We're using ipairs here to iterate over indexed pairs!
for index, value in ipairs( myArray ) do
   print( "Index: " .. index .. " Value: " .. value )
end
```

Something to note here is that the first index is 1, not 0, as you and I would expect.

LUA, LIKE MOST OF HUMANITY, STARTS COUNTING AT ONE

Be careful when treating tables as arrays in C++. All too often, you'll find yourself starting to count at zero, and you'll spend two hours tearing your hair out trying to find the problem.

Tables are a flexible method of dragging around a big quantity of arbitrary data. They're perfect for nonprogrammers to assemble a collection of data without having to jump through lots of hoops. As we'll see later, this flexibility will pay off.

Metatables

Good use of metatables in Lua is an advanced topic, so I won't go too much into detail here. Suffice it to say that a metatable enables you to (among other things) group things into a class of sorts. Not only is this obviously useful for creating an object-oriented style hierarchy, but it can also be used to bring a sort of virtual function table to objects as well.

Throughout the scripts in this book, you'll see things like:

```
EventManager:RegisterEventType( "xyzzy" );
```

This is very similar to calling a member function; here we're calling the `RegisterEventType` method within the `EventManager`.

When we start opening C++ functions up to script, we'll go through metatables to keep them nice and organized.

Garbage Collection

Memory management and tracking down leaky objects vexes programmers. Lua takes care of destroying its own objects. Any object that no longer has any reference to itself will be marked for deletion and taken care of by the system.

Virtual Machines

Lua supports multiple independent instances running as virtual machines (`LuaStates`). This means that you can have a `LuaState` for holding one type of data while another holds different data, and both are completely independent of each other. You could, for example, run a separate `LuaState` for each actor in your world. Or you could put runtime options in one, separate from the game variables, without fear of a name clash.

GETTING STARTED WITH A LUA WRAPPER—LUAPLUS

Lua is written in pure ANSI C. Numerous people have written their own C++ wrappers, with varying success. The best one I have encountered is Joshua Jensen's LuaPlus. Not simply a wrapper, it actually adds new functionality. It is also by far (in my opinion) the most friendly from a programmer's perspective. LuaPlus has been used in several shipped titles, and it is incredibly easy to get up and running scripts quickly.

Where to Get LuaPlus

You can download LuaPlus from http://luaplus.org. Note that the version for direct download isn't always the latest version; you can get that by connecting via a Subversion client.

Once you've gotten it installed, you may elect to link it in your project as a static library or run it as a DLL.

Are We Actually Going to Write Some Code Now?

Now that I've dragged you through the philosophical mud, let's get back into implementer mode. Our core class will be the `LuaStateManager`, and let's take a look at the interface:

```
class LuaStateManager
{
public:
   LuaStateManager(void);

   ~LuaStateManager();

   // I hate two-stage initialization, but due to dependencies,
   // we have to have an Init called after the Event Manager gets built.
   // This function runs the init script.
   bool Init( char const * const pInitFileName );

   // Returns the main state used by the entire game.
   // Other implementations may use multiple LuaStates, but for our purposes
   // a single state will do just fine.
   LuaStateOwner & GetGlobalState(void)  { return m_GlobalState; }

   // Executes a Lua script file.
   bool DoFile(char const * const pFileName);
   static bool ExecuteFile(LuaStateOwner & luaState
                      , char const * const pFileName);

   // Executes an arbitrary Lua command.
   int ExecuteString( char const * const pStringToExecute );

   // Debug function for determining an object's type.
   static void IdentifyLuaObjectType( LuaObject & objToTest );

   // The table where all actor context and data is stored
   // for script accessibility.
   LuaObject GetGlobalActorTable( void );

private:
   // Debug print string function (callable from script).
   void PrintDebugMessage( LuaObject debugObject );

   // Our global LuaState.
   LuaStateOwner m_GlobalState;
```

```
// Our portal to the outside world.
LuaObject m_MetaTable;
};
```

The manager, like any good manager, encapsulates access to its minions. Note the two member variables: m_GlobalState is our LuaState/virtual machine owned by the manager, and the m_MetaTable member will be the interface allowing script to call functions. Let's take a look inside the constructor:

```
LuaStateManager::LuaStateManager( void )
: m_GlobalState( true )    // 'true' Indicates to init the standard Lua library
                           // for dofile, etc.
{
    //Create our metatable...
    m_MetaTable =
      m_GlobalState->
        GetGlobals().CreateTable( "LuaStateManagerMetaTable" );
    m_MetaTable.SetObject( "__index", m_MetaTable );

    // Here we register two functions to make them accessible to script.
    m_MetaTable.RegisterObjectDirect(
        "DoFile", (LuaStateManager *)0, &LuaStateManager::DoFile );
    m_MetaTable.RegisterObjectDirect(
        "PrintDebugMessage", (LuaStateManager *)0,
        &LuaStateManager::PrintDebugMessage );

    LuaObject luaStateManObj = m_GlobalState->BoxPointer( this );
    luaStateManObj.SetMetaTable( m_MetaTable );

    // And here we expose the metatable as a named entity.
    m_GlobalState->GetGlobals().SetObject( "LuaStateManager", luaStateManObj );
}
```

Here you can see that the LuaStateOwner gets initialized with true to indicate that you want LuaPlus to load in the standard Lua libraries for some of the core functionality. Next, you start opening the gate to script via a metatable. These will be callable with script calls like so:

```
LuaStateManager:PrintDebugMessage( "Hello, world!" )
```

Normally, I hate two-stage initialization. I want an object to be fully functional the moment it is created. In this case, however, we have a dependency between the EventManager and the LuaStateManager, which we'll get to in a bit. If you'll recall from Chapter 5, "Game Initialization and Shutdown," we create the

LuaStateManager, followed by the EventManager, and then we call the LuaStateManager::Init(), passing in an initialization script file to execute. Let's look at that function now:

```
bool LuaStateManager::Init( char const * const pInitFileName )
{
    // Create our global actor table.
    // This table will hold context for all actors created in the game world.
    LuaObject globals = m_GlobalState->GetGlobals();
    LuaObject actorTable = globals.CreateTable( "ActorList" );

    return DoFile( pInitFileName );
}
```

This function creates the global table ActorList in script. When we get around to creating actors, they will store any data pertinent to them in that table. Your scripters will then be able to modify and access actors from within script.

The last thing this function does is to execute the initialization Lua script provided. As you'll see later, this is an important detail, because it will set some parameters and context before the game itself gets up and running. This script can also hold any game-specific values you may want to use—think of it as your initial data definition, in lieu of an old school INI file.

MIND THE GAP!

Before we go much further, let's talk about organization of script and code. In this respect, think of them as two separate worlds, and we'll be laying the groundwork of crossing that gap.

What Lives in Code, and What Lives in Script?

Anything engine-specific or processor intensive should go into code. Anything outside the realm of what the basic engine provides, however, should go into script. Script should only refer to entities from the engine via handles/IDs, or through the dedicated objects (like the ActorList above).

Something important to remember is that script can be altered without a recompile. One huge benefit of this is the ability, with a well-architected engine, to do large swaths of prototyping in script. When clean recompiles start to reach dangerously high times (anything in excess of 10 minutes), this flexibility will keep your developers in the zone and moving forward.

ALWAYS USE HANDLES TO REFERENCE CODE-SIDE OBJECTS

Any object created by the code-side of things should be referenced via handle or ID by script. This includes actors, sprites, and just about everything else that needs to allocate or manage resources. While at first it may seem cumbersome to have to look these up to get at your data, it will ultimately serve you well in the end. When you get to the networking chapter, you'll see why synchronizing object IDs across multiple clients is important. Secondly, passing an ID across the script/code gap is more efficient than laboriously copying tables. If your game's biggest bottleneck is looking up objects, there's something wrong.

YOU HIRED SCRIPTERS FOR A REASON

Do as much work as you can in script. Even if it's slow, make it work first. *Slow things can be moved into code easily later on, but iteration speed is important.*

From Code to Script and Back Again

Figuring out how code and script communicate is important. Here we'll look at some of the methods you can use to get data across using explicit functions.

Calling Code Functions from Script

As you saw above in the `LuaStateManager` constructor, we created a metatable that will be the access point for script accessing the manager. The `RegisterObjectDirect` function directly ties a C++ object to a Lua one. Besides mirroring our architecture philosophy for the rest of the engine, this metatable approach offers us several advantages:

- Encapsulates functionality within managers to make a cleaner architecture.
- Reduces namespace collisions in the global state.
- Script-called functions can actually be made private from C++ classes; in the `LuaStateManager` header, note that `PrintDebugMessage` is actually declared in the private section.

Calling Script Functions from Code

LuaPlus also offers a wonderful templated object called the `LuaFunction`. This makes calling arbitrary script functions, with arbitrary return values, nice and simple. For example, let's assume that you have the following script function:

```
function IsGreaterThan5( number )
  return ( number > 5 )
end
```

You can call this function from C++ like so:

```
// This Lua function returns a bool, indicated in the template brackets.
LuaFunction< bool > myLuaFunction( "IsGreaterThan5" );
const bool bIsIt = myLuaFunction( 50 );
```

Executing this will call the appropriate Lua function.

PASS TABLES IN LIEU OF MULTIPLE PARAMETERS

LuaFunction supports passing up to seven parameters. If you're going to pass more than one or two parameters (or if you're passing a variable number of parameters), pass a table with all of the parameters inside it instead. This will also come in handy later when the parameters are necessary for a function change; you won't find yourself changing every single call.

Pros and Cons of Explicit Calls

Explicit calls are nice because they are efficient and fast. When the parameters are known, you can count on exactly what is expected. On the other hand, they're error-prone when a scripter makes a mistake. And what happens if the parameters to a function change?

In the next section, we'll look at a different method of crossing the code/script gap.

WANNA BUY A BRIDGE?

In Chapter 10, "Game Event Management," you were introduced to the event system. What if you could tie the scripting system into this? In this section, we will go from this realm of computer science fiction to computer science *fact*. We'll be building a generic bridge for script and code to communicate with each other. This system will have several advantages:

- Single interface
- Data-driven event system
- Flexibility with optional and variable numbered parameters

Instead of having lots and lots of explicit functions, you'll be communicating through a central point of contact within the EventManager. Besides saving a lot of clutter, this also helps debugging by having all bridge traffic go through central interfaces. Script functions will be written one and only one way, and from the code's perspective, they're simply handling an event. Additionally, you'll be able to create your own event types within script. These event types are identical to the existing event types.

Another important aspect of this method will be a common interface (Lua tables) for transporting event data. This lets you continue to run if function parameters change, as well as supply a variable number of parameters. Lastly, scripters can specify *just the parameters* they want, with defaults being handled by the code.

I'M TOTALLY WIRED

We're going to start by adding some script-callable functions in the `EventManager`'s header file:

```
// Registers a script-based event.
void RegisterScriptEventType( char const * const pEventName );

// Add/remove a script listener.  Note that we pass a Lua *function* as the
// second parameter of each of these, and tie that function to a specific
// event name.  We'll call the Lua function when the event type comes in.
bool AddScriptListener( char const * const pEventName,
                        LuaObject callbackFunction );
bool RemoveScriptListener( char const * const pEventName,
                           LuaObject callbackFunction );

// Triggers an event from script.  The event data will be serialized for any
// code listeners.  Script listeners will receive the data table passed in.
bool TriggerEventFromScript( char const * const pEventName,
                             LuaObject luaEventData );
```

As with the Lua State Manager, you'll be opening these functions up to script via a metatable:

```
LuaObject m_MetaTable;
```

In the `EventManager`'s constructor:

```
//Create our metatable...
m_MetaTable = g_pApp->m_pLuaStateManager->GetGlobalState()->GetGlobals().
              CreateTable("EventManager");
m_MetaTable.SetObject("__index", m_MetaTable);

m_MetaTable.RegisterObjectDirect( "RegisterEventType", (EventManager *)0,
                                  &EventManager::RegisterScriptEventType );
m_MetaTable.RegisterObjectDirect( "TriggerEvent", (EventManager *)0,
                                  &EventManager::TriggerEventFromScript );
m_MetaTable.RegisterObjectDirect( "AddScriptListener", (EventManager *)0,
                                  &EventManager::AddScriptListener );
```

```
m_MetaTable.RegisterObjectDirect( "RemoveScriptListener", (EventManager *)0,
                         &EventManager::RemoveScriptListener );

LuaObject luaStateManObj = g_pApp->m_pLuaStateManager->
                         GetGlobalState()->BoxPointer(this);
luaStateManObj.SetMetaTable(m_MetaTable);
g_pApp->m_pLuaStateManager->GetGlobalState()->GetGlobals().
                         SetObject("EventManager", luaStateManObj);
```

These four functions will be your sole points of entry for the script and code bridge. In the next sections, we'll go into each of these functions, as well as other code required to get them up and running. Before we go into that, let's do a top-down view of what we want to get out of this system.

For a scripter to trigger an event, they will pass in the event name and a Lua table specifying the data for the event, like so:

```
eventData =
{
   Text = "Hello, World!",
   Position =
   {
      --Draw at upper left of screen; X/Y coordinates specified.
      30, 50,
   },
}
EventManager:TriggerEvent( "drawText", eventData )
```

The above Lua snippet creates a table with the parameters for a mythical "draw text" event and then triggers it.

We also want script to be able to listen for events. Here is a sample snippet of script that illustrates that:

```
--Define the listener function.
function DrawTextListener( eventData )
   print( "Attempting to draw the text: " .. eventData.Text )
   print( "At location: (" .. eventData.Position[1] .. ", " ..
         eventData.Position[2] .. ")" )
end

--Add a listener for the function.
EventManager:AddScriptListener( "drawText", DrawTextListener )
```

This snippet defines a listener function and then creates a script listener for the "draw text" event. Whenever a "draw text" event is triggered, the function `DrawTextListener` will be called.

Additions to the Event Data Class

To support what you want, you're going to need some method of transforming Lua event data into the native format of the event. To that end, you're going to be adding some functionality to the `BaseEventData` class:

```
public:
    // Called when sending the event data over to the script-side listener.
    virtual LuaObject VGetLuaEventData( void ) const = 0;

    // Serializes the event data into the LuaObject.
    virtual void VBuildLuaEventData( void ) = 0;

    // Called when testing whether or not the event
    // has been serialized for script
    // (this allows us to only serialize ONCE per event trigger).
    virtual bool VHasLuaEventData( void ) const
    {
        return m_bHasLuaEventData;
    }

protected:
    // We will build Lua data *only if necessary*
    // (i.e., there is a script-side listener).
    bool m_bHasLuaEventData;
```

These additional members will allow you to transform an event's normal data into a Lua table for script listeners. Note that we've implemented an optimization; we only do this transformation (VBuildLuaEventData) when there *is* a script listener. If there is at least one script listener, the `EventManager` only calls `VBuildLuaEventData` once, then the transformed data is sent to each script listener.

Registering Events

Another change you're going to make is to require event types to be *registered* with the `EventManager` before they can be used. This will allow you to define the usage of the events and define the way in which they are created and tracked. It also prevents you from accidentally creating two event types with the same name (as I accidentally did in the process of writing the code for this chapter). This will all make more sense in a moment, I swear. Here's your interface for registration:

```
// This class holds meta data for each event type, and allows
// (or disallows!) creation of code-defined events from script.
class IRegisteredEvent
{
public:
    //Meta data about the type and usage of this event.
    enum eRegisteredEventMetaData
    {
        // Event is defined in script.
        kREMD_ScriptDefined,

        //Event is defined by code, and is *NOT* callable from script.
        kREMD_CodeEventOnly,

        //Event is defined by code, but is callable from script.
        kREMD_CodeEventScriptCallable,
    };

    IRegisteredEvent( const eRegisteredEventMetaData metaData )
        : m_MetaData( metaData )
    {
    }

    virtual ~IRegisteredEvent()
    {
    }

    virtual bool VTriggerEventFromScript( LuaObject & srcData ) const = 0;
    eRegisteredEventMetaData GetEventMetaData( void ) const
    {
        return m_MetaData;
    }
private:
    const eRegisteredEventMetaData m_MetaData;
};
```

As indicated by the enumeration, there are three types of registered events:

- Those defined by script.
- Those defined by code (and creatable by script).
- Those defined by code (but *not* creatable by script!).

This list is reminiscent of a scene from the short "A Fistful of Yen" in *The Kentucky Fried Movie*:

Loo: And who are they?
Dr. Klahn: Refuse, found in waterfront bars.

Loo: Shanghaied?

Dr. Klahn: Just lost drunken men who don't know where they are and no longer care.

Prisoner #1: Where are we?

Prisoner #2: I don't care!

Loo: And these?

Dr. Klahn: These are lost drunken men who don't know where they are, but do care! And these are men who know where they are and care, but don't drink.

Why should you care if a code-defined event is created from script? It allows you to restrict access. It's the only thing you have left between you and the scripters. There are some events that need to be solely in the domain of creation by the coders, such as low-level signals and so on. Script can still *listen* for these events, but it can't *create* them.

The interface also defines two virtual functions called when an event is triggered or queued from script. The LuaObject reference parameter is a table that will hold all of the data for the specific event.

Before we go any further in defining each derivation of IRegisteredEvent, let's look at how they're going to be handled. Here are some additional members of the EventManager's header file:

```
typedef boost::shared_ptr< IRegisteredEvent > IRegisteredEventPtr;


//Verifies that such an event does not already exist, then registers it.
void AddRegisteredEventType( const EventType & eventType,
                             IRegisteredEventPtr metaData );


// one global instance
typedef std::map< EventType, IRegisteredEventPtr >    EventTypeSet;
EventTypeSet    m_typeList;            // list of registered event types
```

So we create a mapping of EventType to IRegisteredEvents, which we can look up when an event comes in:

```
void EventManager::AddRegisteredEventType( const EventType & eventType,
                                           IRegisteredEventPtr metaData )
{
   const EventTypeSet::const_iterator iter = m_typeList.find( eventType );
   if ( iter != m_typeList.end() )
   {
      assert( 0 && "This event type has already been registered!" );
   }
```

```
      else
      {
        // We're good...
        m_typeList.insert( std::make_pair( eventType, metaData ) );
      }
    }
```

When the scripter calls `EventManager:TriggerEvent`, it will then go through the following process:

```
bool EventManager::TriggerEventFromScript( char const * const pEventName,
                                           LuaObject luaEventData )
{
    const EventType eventType( pEventName );

    // Look this event type up.
    const EventTypeSet::const_iterator iter = m_typeList.find( eventType );
    if ( iter == m_typeList.end() )
    {
        assert( 0 && "Attempted to trigger an event type that doesn't exist!" );
        return false;
    }

    // This level of indirection lets us create code-side events
    // or script-side events.
    IRegisteredEventPtr regEvent = iter->second;
    const bool bResult = regEvent->VTriggerEventFromScript( luaEventData );

    return bResult;
}
```

The function looks up the event to find the corresponding `IRegisteredEvent` object and then calls the virtual function necessary to transform the event data from a Lua table into a usable format. This is a lot to process, so take a moment to go over this and ensure you understand it before we move on to the derivations of `IRegisteredEvent`.

REGISTER EVENTS BEFORE YOU USE THEM

Don't forget to register every event type before you use it! Otherwise, the engine will throw a fit when it sees an event it hasn't been told about.

Registering Code-Only Events

The simplest events are those that can only be created by code:

```
// Code defined, but script is NOT allowed to create this event type.
class CodeOnlyDefinedEvent : public IRegisteredEvent
{
public:
   explicit CodeOnlyDefinedEvent( void )
      : IRegisteredEvent( IRegisteredEvent::kREMD_CodeEventOnly )
   {
   }

   virtual bool VTriggerEventFromScript( LuaObject & srcData ) const
   {
      assert( 0 && "Attempted to trigger a code-ONLY triggerable event!" );
      return false;
   }
};
```

Sweet and to the point. Here's how to register a code-only event:

```
void EventManager::RegisterCodeOnlyEvent( const EventType & eventType )
{
   IRegisteredEventPtr metaData( GCC_NEW CodeOnlyDefinedEvent() );
   AddRegisteredEventType( eventType, metaData );
}
```

This just rezzes up a code-only defined registration and adds it to the map. If scripters try to create one of these events, they will be met with only frustration and futile cursing.

Registering Script-Defined Events

Next up on the difficulty scale are the script-defined events. Why would you want script-defined events? For instances where an event would be appropriate for game-specific things, such as PlayerGotAllTheRings or DrawbridgeOpened. A scripter may want several listeners for these events, and may only register these events for specific levels.

Here's your interface:

```
//Script defined event type.
class ScriptDefinedEvent : public IRegisteredEvent
{
```

```
public:
   ScriptDefinedEvent( const EventType & eventType )
      : IRegisteredEvent( IRegisteredEvent::kREMD_ScriptDefined )
      , m_EventType( eventType )
   {
   }

   virtual bool VTriggerEventFromScript( LuaObject & srcData ) const;

private:
   //We need to hold onto the event type for when it gets triggered.
   const EventType m_EventType;
};
```

Before you go delving into the implementation, you need to pause to introduce a new event type:

```
//This type of event data is created by script-defined events.
struct EvtData_ScriptEvtData : public BaseEventData
{
public:
   virtual const EventType & VGetEventType( void ) const
   {
      return m_EventType;
   }

   EvtData_ScriptEvtData( const EventType & eventType, LuaObject & srcData )
      : m_EventType( eventType )
      , m_LuaEventData( srcData )
   {
      m_bHasLuaEventData = true;    //Our Lua event data got passed into us!
   }

   virtual LuaObject VGetLuaEventData(void) const
   {
      return m_LuaEventData;
   }

   virtual void VBuildLuaEventData(void)
   {
      assert( ( false == m_bHasLuaEventData ) &&
              "Already built lua event data!" );
      return;   //Already "built" when the event got created.
   }
```

```
private:
   const EventType   m_EventType;   //Type of this event.
   LuaObject   m_LuaEventData;
};
```

This event is basically a pass-through; when script triggers a script-defined event, you package the data table passed in and send it out to all the listeners. Now let's see how the `ScriptDefinedEvent` works:

```
bool EventManager::ScriptDefinedEvent::VTriggerEventFromScript(
     LuaObject & srcData ) const
{
   const EvtData_ScriptEvtData scriptEvent( m_EventType, srcData );
   return safeTriggerEvent( scriptEvent );
}
```

The above function essentially packages the Lua-generated data table into a `EvtData_ScriptEvtData` event object and sends it out. Now let's look at what the registration actually does; this should be pretty straightforward:

```
void EventManager::RegisterScriptEvent( const EventType & eventType )
{
   IRegisteredEventPtr metaData(
     GCC_NEW EventManager::ScriptDefinedEvent( eventType ) );
   AddRegisteredEventType( eventType, metaData );
}
```

It's all very similar to the `RegisterCodeOnlyEvent` call from before. Since script is defining its own event types, let's look at how it goes about doing that:

```
void EventManager::RegisterScriptEventType( char const * const pEventName )
{
   //Create a new script-defined event object.
   const EventType eventType( pEventName );
   RegisterScriptEvent( eventType );
}
```

So a scripter, if he wanted to make his own event type "xyzzy," would add the following to the script:

```
EventManager:RegisterEventType( "xyzzy" )
```

Registering Code AND Script-Creatable Events

Here's where it starts to get ugly. These are events that code *or* script can trigger, and it's going to require some fancy template work. Let's take a look at the IRegisteredEvent-derived definition:

```
//Code defined, but also creatable from script.
template < class T >
class ScriptCallableCodeEvent : public IRegisteredEvent
{
public:
   explicit ScriptCallableCodeEvent( void )
      : IRegisteredEvent( IRegisteredEvent::kREMD_CodeEventScriptCallable )
   {
   }

   virtual bool VTriggerEventFromScript( LuaObject & srcData ) const
   {
      const T eventData( srcData );   //Construct directly.
      return safeTriggerEvent( eventData );
   }
};
```

The interesting bit here is in the VTriggerEventFromScript; it explicitly creates the event using the event data table as a parameter. This means that the event type *must* have a constructor that accepts just a LuaObject as the sole parameter. If you attempt to register an event that doesn't have such a constructor, the compiler will flip out, but at least it's caught at compile time. Now let's look at the registration function:

```
//Our templated registration function.
template<class T> void EventManager::RegisterEvent( const EventType &
                                                      eventType )
{
   IRegisteredEventPtr metaData( GCC_NEW ScriptCallableCodeEvent< T >() );
   AddRegisteredEventType( eventType, metaData );
}
```

Why would you want an event that is trigger-able from script *or* code? Remember that the ideal engine should be game-agnostic; while there are engine-specific elements that may require these events, you want to define the game largely in script. A good example would be an "abort network game" event: the engine might detect that a networked client has dropped out and send the event. But the scripter might also elect to send that event when a player clicks the quit button.

Serializing Events for Code and Script

Now that we've got a method for telling the engine how each event should work through registration, let's look at how you're actually going to transform event data for script and vice-versa. You'll be working with our hypothetical "draw text" event, which is comprised of a screen position and the text to draw. Here's what the definition of said event looks like:

```
struct EvtData_DrawText : public BaseEventData
{
    // Define our event type and name.
    static const EventType sk_EventType;
    virtual const EventType & VGetEventType( void ) const
    {
        return sk_EventType;
    }

    // Code constructor.
    explicit EvtData_DrawText( const std::string & text, const float xPos,
                               const float yPos )
        : m_Text( text )
        , m_XPos( xPos )
        , m_YPos( yPos )
    {
    }

    // Script constructor.
    Explicit EvtData_DrawText( LuaObject srcData );

    // Converts code data to script.
    virtual void VBuildLuaEventData( void );

    // Provides access to the Lua data when converted from code.
    virtual LuaObject VGetLuaEventData(void) const;

    // OMITTED:  Other members that we'll discuss later.

    // The members of this event.
    std::string m_Text;
    float m_XPos;
    float m_YPos;
```

```
private:
   // Holds all data for a script listener.
   LuaObject m_LuaEventData;
};

// In the implementation file:
const EventType EvtData::sk_EventType( "DrawText" );
```

From Script to Code

The first part you'll handle is converting a Lua table into code-accessible values. Essentially what you'll be doing is reading values from the table and assigning them to the members. You'll do this through the explicit script constructor, which will be invoked by a ScriptCallableCodeEvent register:

```
EvtData_DrawText::EvtData_DrawText( LuaObject srcData )
//Init defaults.
: m_Text( "" )
, m_XPos( 0.0f )
, m_YPos( 0.0f )
{
   //Ensure that what we got was a table.
   assert( srcData.IsTable() && "Wasn't given a table for event!" );
   //See if we have a text member.
   LuaObject textObj = srcData[ "Text" ];
   if ( textObj.IsString() )
   {
      m_Text = textObj.GetString();
   }
   LuaObject posTableObj = srcData[ "Position" ];
   if ( posTableObj.IsTable() )
   {
      //Get each position out.
      m_XPos = posTableObj[ 1 ].GetFloat();
      m_YPos = posTableObj[ 2 ].GetFloat();
   }
}
```

This constructor initializes default values (as the event allows the scripter to specify only the parameters that he wants). This is important, because it allows the scripter to only worry about the elements he wants to change.

The constructor then assesses that the data coming in is of the correct format (a table), and proceeds to attempt to get the members out of it. When this event is triggered, it will make a fully formed one that other listeners can rely upon.

From Code to Script

Now let's go the other way round—taking an event and making it usable by a script listener. When an event is going to be sent to a script listener, the engine asks the event if it already has Lua data via the VHasLuaEventData method. If it *doesn't*, it has to build the event data and send it on. For your sample event, it does it like so:

```
void EvdData_DrawText::VBuildLuaEventData( void )
{
    //Safety check; we shouldn't be building this data twice!
    assert( ( false == VHasLuaEventData() ) &&
            "Attempted to build Lua event data when event already has it!" );

    //Now build the data.
    //Get the global state.
    LuaState * pState = g_pApp->m_pLuaStateManager->GetGlobalState().Get();
    m_LuaEventData.AssignNewTable( pState );

    //Serialize the data necessary.
    m_LuaEventData.SetString( "Text", m_Text.c_str() );
    //Create a position table with exactly two entries.
    LuaObject posTable = m_LuaEventData.CreateTable( "Position", 2 );
    posTable[ 1 ].SetNumber( 1, m_XPos );
    posTable[ 2 ].SetNumber( 2, m_YPos );

    //Indicate that we do, indeed, have Lua data here.
    m_bHasLuaEventData = true;
}
```

Any event that script needs to listen for will need one of these. Note that you don't have to give them *everything* in the event; if an event passes a pointer to a texture, for example, you can omit that from what the script listener will receive.

DO YOU HEAR WHAT I HEAR?

Now that you've wired in your paths to get event data to and from script, let's analyze how it will actually get across the bridge. You'll be modifying Mike's listener class, as well as showing how script can trigger an event.

Script-Side Listeners

You're going to have to create a listener type for scripters. These will tie a Lua function to a specified event type. Here's the definition of that class:

```
//--
// The ScriptEventListener holds a script callback function that responds
// to a particular event.
class ScriptEventListener : public IEventListener
{
public:
    ScriptEventListener( LuaObject explicitHandlerFunction );

    virtual ~ScriptEventListener()
    {
    }

    virtual char const * GetName( void )
    {
        return "Script Listener";
    }

    virtual bool HandleEvent( IEventData const & event );

    const LuaObject & GetHandlerFunction( void ) const
    {
        return m_HandlerFunction;
    }

protected:
    // This function is virtual as sub-classes may pass additional
    // parameters.
    virtual bool VCallLuaFunction( LuaObject & eventData );

    //The callback function itself.
    LuaObject m_HandlerFunction;
};
```

As you can see, the ScriptEventListener derives from the generic IEventListener and extends it. The constructor takes a Lua function as a parameter, and when it is triggered, calls that function:

```
ScriptEventListener::ScriptEventListener( LuaObject explicitHandlerFunction )
: m_HandlerFunction( explicitHandlerFunction )
{
    assert( explicitHandlerFunction.IsFunction() &&
            "Script listener *MUST* be a valid function!" );
}
```

The constructor merely verifies that what it was passed is, indeed, a function. Now let's look at what the listener does when it is provided with an event:

```
bool ScriptEventListener::HandleEvent( IEventData const & event )
{
    // If we don't already have Lua event data built, do so now.
    if ( false == event.VHasLuaEventData() )
    {
        // This goes against everything you are taught in C++ class.
        // We're going to make this const IEventData non-const because
        // we need to serialize the event for Lua to understand it.
        // We're doing this for three reasons:
        //   a) So we only build Lua data ONCE for any triggered event,
        //      and ONLY when the event needs to be sent to a Lua function
        //      (we don't want to ALWAYS build Lua data).
        //   b) We're not technically changing any of the "real" event
        //      *data*...
        //   c) If we make other listener's HandleEvent() calls take
        //      a non-const event, they could alter it.
        // Don't make a habit of doing this.

        // Pray the const away.
        IEventData & NCEventData = const_cast< IEventData & >( event );

        // Build it and never mention this again.
        NCEventData.VBuildLuaEventData();
    }

    LuaObject & eventDataObj = event.VGetLuaEventData();

    //Call the handler function.
    const bool bResult = VCallLuaFunction( eventDataObj );

    return bResult;
}
```

```
bool ScriptEventListener::VCallLuaFunction( LuaObject & eventData )
{
   LuaFunction<bool> function( m_HandlerFunction );
   return function( eventData );
}
```

The listener takes the event in, checks to see if it already has Lua event data, and if it doesn't, builds it. It then passes the event data on to the caller. You'll see later why the VCallLuaFunction event is virtual.

Creating a `ScriptEventListener`

The EventManager will need a method to track all of the ScriptEventListener objects. So you'll track that like so in the EventManager class definition:

```
// Holds all allocated script listeners.
// It maps an event ID to a set of listeners.
typedef boost::shared_ptr< ScriptEventListener > ScriptEventListenerPtr;
typedef std::multimap< unsigned int, ScriptEventListenerPtr >
                      ScriptEventListenerMap;
ScriptEventListenerMap m_ScriptEventListenerMap;
```

So what you have here is an STL multimap, mapping event IDs to one or more script listeners. Why do you use a multimap instead of a map? Because you may have multiple script listeners listening for the same event.

USING MULTIMAPS

I discovered the need for a multimap over a map after banging my head on the keyboard trying to figure out why only one of my listeners was getting called back. It was because the first listener got bumped off when a second one got added for that event!

A script event listener is created whenever a script calls the EventManager:AddScriptListener function:

```
//--
// EventManager::AddScriptListener
// Creates a script-side event listener, given an appropriate Lua function.
bool EventManager::AddScriptListener(
   char const * const pEventName, LuaObject callbackFunction )
```

```
{
    //Ensure this event type exists.
    const EventType testEventType( pEventName );
    const EventTypeSet::const_iterator typeIter =
            m_typeList.find( testEventType );
    if ( m_typeList.end() == typeIter )
    {
        assert( 0 &&
                "Attempted to listen to an event type that wasn't registered!" );
        return false;
    }

    const unsigned int eventID = testEventType.getHashValue();

    //OK, valid event type.  Make sure this isn't a duplicate.
    ScriptEventListenerMap::const_iterator mapIter =
                            m_ScriptEventListenerMap.find( eventID );
    while ( m_ScriptEventListenerMap.end() != mapIter )
    {
        //Iterate through and ensure no duplicates.
        const ScriptEventListenerPtr evtListener = mapIter->second;
        const LuaObject & evtObj = evtListener->GetHandlerFunction();
        if ( evtObj == callbackFunction )
        {
            assert( 0 && "Attempted to listen to the same event handler twice!" );
            return false;
        }
        ++mapIter;
    }

    //Now let's rez up a new script listener.
    ScriptEventListenerPtr listener(
                        GCC_NEW ScriptEventListener( callbackFunction ) );

    m_ScriptEventListenerMap.insert( std::make_pair( eventID, listener ) );

    const bool bSuccess = VAddListener( listener, testEventType );
    return bSuccess;
}
```

The function first verifies that the event type has been registered. It then double-checks that the same listener hasn't already been added; this could cause strange problems if a single event makes multiple calls to the same function.

Finally, it creates the new listener, adds it to the tracking multimap, and puts the listener in the Event Manager's listener list.

Triggering an Event from Script

We've been through a lot, and now the final puzzle piece is coming into place. I admit, it may seem a little bit of a letdown, but by breaking down all the other code elsewhere, we've made it substantially easier to follow.

Ladies and gentlemen, I bring you what will execute when a scripter calls `EventManager:TriggerEvent`...

```
bool EventManager::TriggerEventFromScript( char const * const pEventName,
                                           LuaObject luaEventData )
{
    const EventType eventType( pEventName );

    //Look this event type up.
    const EventTypeSet::const_iterator iter = m_typeList.find( eventType );
    if ( iter == m_typeList.end() )
    {
        assert( 0 && "Attempted to trigger an event type that doesn't exist!" );
        return false;
    }

    //This level of indirection lets us create code-side events
    //or script-side events.
    IRegisteredEventPtr regEvent = iter->second;
    const bool bResult = regEvent->VTriggerEventFromScript( luaEventData );

    return bResult;
}
```

You verify that the event was registered, and then call the register's handler for the event. And away it goes!

LET'S GET OOP-ABLE!

The system you've built works just fine for calling global script functions. But is there a way to encapsulate objects in script, like you do in C++? Of course there is; otherwise, I wouldn't be writing this.

We could use metatables for this kind of encapsulation, but if you'll recall from the `LuaStateManager::Init` function, we created a global script table called `ActorList`, which holds the data specific to an actor and maps Actor IDs (integers) to their specific data. What you'd like to be able to do is have an actor listen for an event, and when the event gets triggered, to pass the equivalent of the actor's this pointer along with it. Here's an example script to depict what you want to be able to do:

```
--These are the functions related to this actor.
function MyActorOnCreate( actorID, actorDataTable )
   print( "MY ACTOR CREATED!" )

   -- Set this actor's data.
   actorDataTable.MyTimer = 0.0

   --Begin letting *this actor* listen for the update tick.
   EventManager:AddScriptActorListener( "update_tick",
                                        MyActorUpdate, actorID )
end

function MyActorOnDestroy( actorID, actorDataTable )
   print( "MY ACTOR DESTROYED!" )

   --Stop listening!
   EventManager:RemoveScriptActorListener( "update_tick", MyActorUpdate,
                                           actorID )
end

function MyActorUpdate( eventData, actorData )
   local dt = eventData[ "Seconds" ]
   actorData.MyTimer = actorData.MyTimer + dt
end

--Now create the actor.
local MyActorParams =
{
   --Constructor and Destructor functions.
   OnCreateFunc = "MyActorOnCreate",
   OnDestroyFunc = "MyActorOnDestroy",
}

--Now that everything is in place, let's create the actor.
EventManager:TriggerEvent( "request_new_actor", MyActorParams )
```

This script creates an actor that listens for the "update_tick" event. The actor, on creation, indicates a constructor and destructor (`OnCreateFunc` and `OnDestroyFunc` keys in the `MyActorParams` table).

The constructor, when called, is passed the actor's ID, as well as its personal data table, `actorDataTable`, from the `ActorList`. It then sets a data member for the actor, called `MyTimer`.

You could look at this actor like a C++ class:

```
class MyActor
{
public:
   MyActor( const int actorID )
   : m_MyTimer( 0.0f )
   {
      OutputDebugString( "MY ACTOR CREATED!" );
   }
   ~MyActor( void )
   {
      OutputDebugString( "MY ACTOR DESTROYED!" );
   }

   void Update( const float dt )
   {
      m_MyTimer += dt;
   }
private:
   float m_MyTimer;
};
```

What you'll need to do is to allow a specific actor to listen for an event, and to get its this pointer passed along with the callback.

Script Actor Listeners

You'll start by adding two functions to the Event Manager:

```
// Actor-specific event listener controls. These will pass in the actor context
// upon calling.
bool AddScriptActorListener( char const * const pEventName,
                        LuaObject callbackFunction, const int actorID );
bool RemoveScriptActorListener( char const * const pEventName,
                        LuaObject callbackFunction, const int actorID );
```

After these functions are exposed in the Event Manager's metatable, they'll be callable from script. Note that they are identical to the `AddScriptListener` and `RemoveScriptListener` functions, except they take an actor ID as a third parameter.

In fact, the code is almost identical:

```
// Creates a script-side *ACTOR* event listener,
// given an appropriate Lua function.
bool EventManager::AddScriptActorListener( char const * const pEventName,
                              LuaObject callbackFunction, const int actorID )
{
   //Ensure this event type exists.
   const EventType testEventType( pEventName );
   const EventTypeSet::const_iterator typeIter =
        m_typeList.find( testEventType );
   if ( m_typeList.end() == typeIter )
   {
      assert( 0 &&
            "Attempted to listen to an event type that wasn't registered!" );
      return false;
   }

   const unsigned int eventID = testEventType.getHashValue();

   //OK, valid event type.  Make sure this isn't a duplicate.
   ScriptActorEventListenerMap::const_iterator mapIter =
                      m_ScriptActorEventListenerMap.find( eventID );
   while ( m_ScriptActorEventListenerMap.end() != mapIter )
   {
      //Iterate through and ensure no duplicates.
      const ScriptActorEventListenerPtr evtListener = mapIter->second;
      const LuaObject & evtObj = evtListener->GetHandlerFunction();
      if ( ( evtObj == callbackFunction ) &&
          ( actorID == evtListener->GetActorID() ) )
      {
         assert( 0 &&  "Attempted to listen to the same event for actor!" );
         return false;
      }
      ++mapIter;
   }

   //Now let's rez up a new script listener.
   ScriptActorEventListenerPtr listener(
        GCC_NEW ScriptActorEventListener( callbackFunction, actorID ) );

   m_ScriptActorEventListenerMap.insert( std::make_pair( eventID, listener ) );

   const bool bSuccess = VAddListener( listener, testEventType );
   return bSuccess;
}
```

The only difference between this and the `AddScriptListener` function is that you check the multimap for identical callback function *and* actor ID, you create a `ScriptActorEventListener` instead of a `ScriptEventListener`, and your multimap now deals with the new listener type.

Let's see what's so unique about the actor-specific listener:

```
//--
// The ScriptActorEventListener holds a script callback function tied
// to a specific actor, and when called, passes in the actor's script
// data.
class ScriptActorEventListener : public ScriptEventListener
{
public:
    ScriptActorEventListener( LuaObject explicitHandlerFunction,
                              const ActorId actorID );

    virtual ~ScriptActorEventListener()
    {
    }

    virtual char const * GetName( void )
    {
        return "Script Actor Listener";
    }

    ActorId GetActorID( void ) const
    {
        return m_SrcActorID;
    }

private:

    // This will pass the event data object as well as
    // look up our actor's specific script data to pass.
    virtual bool VCallLuaFunction( LuaObject & eventData );

    // Our source actor.
    const ActorId m_SrcActorID;
};
```

Not much different from the base class. You keep the actor ID around, and you've overridden the `VCallLuaFunction` member. Let's take a peek in there to see what's up:

```
bool ScriptActorEventListener::VCallLuaFunction( LuaObject & eventData )
{
    // Find our actor to pass in the actor script data context.

    // This is more sanity checking than anything, to ensure that the actor
    // still exists.
    shared_ptr< IActor > gameActor = g_pApp->m_pGame->VGetActor( m_SrcActorID );
    if ( !gameActor )
    {
        assert( 0 && "Attempted to call a script listener for an actor that
                      couldn't be found!  Did you delete the actor without
                      removing all listeners?" );
        return false;
    }

    // Get ahold of the actor's script data.
    LuaState * pState = g_pApp->m_pLuaStateManager->GetGlobalState().Get();
    LuaObject globalActorTable =
        g_pApp->m_pLuaStateManager->GetGlobalActorTable();
    assert( globalActorTable.IsTable()
        && "Global actor table is NOT a table!" );

    LuaObject actorData = globalActorTable[ m_SrcActorID ];

    // We pass in the event data IN ADDITION TO the actor's script data.
    LuaFunction<bool> function( m_HandlerFunction );
    return function( eventData, actorData );
}
```

Voila! This function looks up the actor's script data tied to its ID and then calls the Lua script function with that data as the second parameter.

The only thing remaining is for the engine to take a script constructor and destructor and call them when the actor is created or destroyed, but we'll worry about that in a later chapter.

DEBUGGING SCRIPT

One of the most frustrating things about scripting is that there often isn't an easy method to debug it. Scripters should have tools at their disposal to see their data and to debug it. I'll discuss some of these methods below.

Caveman Debugging

As with C++, sometimes it helps to have a debug print routine. Lua's `print` routine does the job, but you'll probably want to re-route it to another system. An easy method to do this is in your Init.lua file:

```
--Override the print function.
function print( printStuff )
   LuaStateManager:PrintDebugMessage( printStuff )
end
```

The `LuaStateManager::PrintDebugMessage` can then spit it out using `Output-DebugString`, or send it off to another system to sort out debug spew.

Console

A great addition to any game in development is that of an in-game console. id Software's *Quake* was my first introduction to this powerful tool: by pressing the tilde key, a little window would drop down with a blinking cursor. It enabled you to enter commands (and cheats!) and to display information about the game.

Lua gives you the capability to execute arbitrary script commands via the `DoString` method. You can use this to look at the state of variables, change values, or do anything you'd normally do in script. Building a console into your game is an excellent way for scripters to experiment. Figure 11.1 shows an example from the console built in this book.

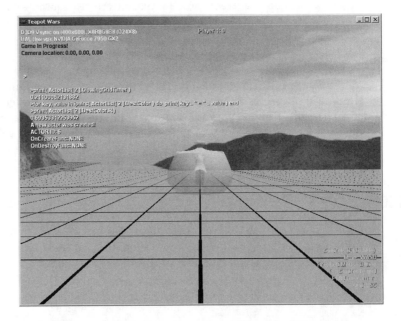

FIGURE 11.1 Use Lua to create a command console for your game.

Symbolic Debuggers

An even more powerful type of debugging comes in the form of a true symbolic debugger for script. These give to script what any proper debugger does for code: freedom to halt the program via breakpoints, look at (and alter) data members, view the call stack, and step through functions. They come in two flavors: integrated and stand-alone IDEs.

Integrated Debuggers

Some debuggers come in the form of plug-ins for an existing IDE, such as Trango Interactive's VSLua, and work directly out of your programming shell. They use the same (or similar) displays as Visual Studio, in theory making it a snap to debug problem scripts. In this sense, the programmer doesn't have to leave the IDE to find out what is happening.

The catch? Well, they're two-fold. First, these debuggers tend to be very finicky and difficult to get working. In my experience, they've been difficult to set up, and don't tend to work very well.

TALES
FROM
THE
PIXEL
MINES

BREAKPOINTS, YES—DEBUGGING, NOT SO MUCH

While writing this chapter, I attempted to get one such debugger working. This took several hours, and when I finally *did* get it working, I could only set a breakpoint and view the data. There was no way to resume the program or to alter data.

More importantly, these debuggers require every scripter to have a copy of the IDE to use them. I don't know about you, but at my company, we don't have the kind of money to provide every scripter with a copy of Visual Studio and training on how to use it.

External Debuggers

Another solution is to package the debugger in with an external program, be it the game editor or a stand-alone IDE. An external program alleviates, requiring scripters to have a copy of the programming IDE, and it can also serve as a text editor with formatting options, and so on. This is the ideal solution for any serious project involving scripting.

Introducing Decoda

The best solution I've found is Unknown Worlds' editor/debugger/IDE hybrid called Decoda. Max McGuire of Unknown Worlds has put together this stellar package, and I was lucky enough to get some sneak peeks at it during development and provide feedback. In Figure 11.2, you can see me running Decoda side-by-side with the running game, with a breakpoint hit and several watch variables active.

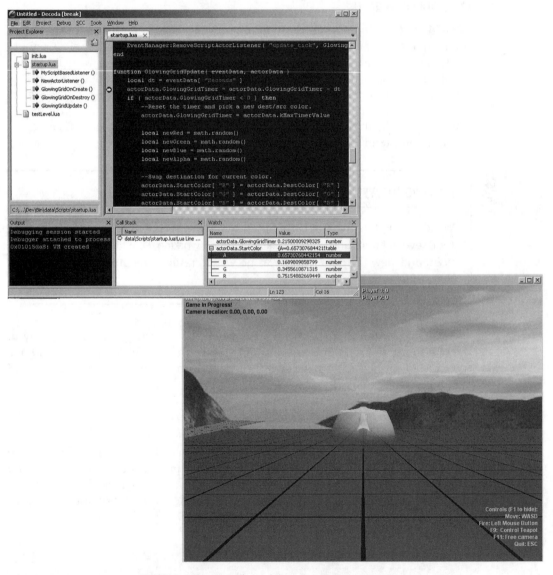

FIGURE 11.2 Use Decoda to debug Lua scripts at runtime.

This wonderful tool will let you do everything you need (and probably more):

- Edit text with color coding.
- Set breakpoints, halting execution of the main program.
- Edit and view data on the fly (even tables!).
- Manage files within a project.
- Integrate with source control.
- Walk the call stack.
- Step into, out of, and over functions.
- Debug multiple virtual machines.
- Support dynamically linked or statically linked Lua libraries.
- You can even attach a (code) debugger to the process during runtime.

…all within a single self-contained editor. It really is a god-send for scripters and programmers alike.

I've included the trial version of Decoda along with the code for this book in the *Tools* directory. You can also find it at www.unknownworlds.com/decoda/. While the product does cost money, it's definitely affordable, and the amount of productivity and iteration will more than make up for the small cost. It's infinitely better than poking around trying to figure out why a certain script won't run, or worse, being pulled out of the programming zone to help a scripter.

Famous Last Words: "An Exercise for the Reader"

I've covered the basic system for bridging the gap between code and script, but there's a lot more out there on the subject of successfully integrating a scripting language into a game engine. Here, I'll discuss some of these topics, as well as a little personal advice.

Pitfalls

In the second edition of this book, Mike wrote the following:

You might believe that programming a game script is easier than C++, and junior programmers or even newbie level builders will be able to increase their productivity using game scripts. This is a trap. What tends to happen is the game scripting system becomes more powerful and complicated as new features are added during development. By the end of the project, their complexity approaches or even exceeds that of C++. The development tools for the game script will fall far short of the compilers and debuggers for common languages. This makes the game scripting job really challenging. If your game depends on complicated game scripts, make sure the development tools are up to the task.

I both agree and disagree with Mike here, and largely my dissent is due to advances in scripting in the years since he originally wrote this. On one hand, a poorly architected scripted system—especially with lots of low-level code functionality exposed—can and will cause tremendous problems. Think twice about exposing a function that, while adding convenience in the short term, may be problematic or abused in the future. There are times for exposing an explicit function, but do your best to prevent your scripters from becoming entangled or causing side effects that they shouldn't. In many cases, you can use the event system to overcome any problems.

Scripting languages such as Lua and Python have come to the point where, while admittedly slower than straight code, are efficient enough to run in real time and do *actual work* instead of being used solely for straight-up data definition. Prototype as much as you can in script; you can always move it into code later if it proves to be too slow.

It's also imperative that someone reviews the scripters' output. Whether this is a programmer or a technically minded scripter is unimportant; the key is that scripts are checked for efficiency, and are using systems correctly. Script listeners should be laser-focused on a single task, and should avoid cobbling together lots of work when multiple listeners would do a better job. Keep listener callbacks succinct, small, and to the point. Regular reviews should be performed to ensure that the scripters' work is up to snuff and written (and commented!) appropriately.

Lastly, as a programmer, you must be ever vigilant to write code that is fault-tolerant. Check data types religiously. Ensure they are within bounds. And only crash the whole shebang when it is absolutely necessary. Your job as a programmer is to support the designers, and your life will be a lot easier when there's much less griping.

Further Study

With the core elements necessary to empower scripters under your belt, you should explore the other features offered by Lua in order to make a more robust and powerful engine. I'll dive into a few, but by no means should this list be considered comprehensive.

Multiple LuaStates

Running multiple virtual machines of Lua can be advantageous. Not only does it prevent clutter, but it also protects your data from inadvertent (or intentionally abusive!) overwrites. It may be wise to put all of your actors' data within a single LuaState, or as some recent MMOs have done, with *each actor* having its own LuaState. The downside to this is it makes the bridges between code and script more complex. Additionally, it can have a performance impact. In a recent postmortem in *Game Developer*, Twisted Pixel Games explained a serious performance hit in their XBLA title, *The Maw*, involving multiple LuaStates and the seemingly arbitrary Lua garbage collection. Ultimately, they altered the code and script to get around this, but keep this in mind before you start creating `LuaStates` willy-nilly.

Metatables

Easily one of the most fascinating and powerful constructs within Lua is the metatable. While there wasn't enough space to go into a full-blown investigation, a metatable provides some very interesting OOP-like functionality. The `__index` property of a metatable can be used in a manner similar to a virtual function table and beyond. I encourage you to look into them further when writing your own tech.

Coroutines

Another construct within Lua is the coroutine. These act like co-operative multitasking threads, yielding control when they feel like it, and are re-entrant. If this sends shivers down your spine with memories of Windows 3.x programming, you're not alone. However, in the right hands, coroutines can be used to properly do "stage direction" for an actor by giving high-level instructions along the lines of the following:

```
WalkToDresser()
OpenDrawer()
PullOutHandgun()
Say( "I always loved you best..." )
SingleTear()
PullTrigger()
```

These high-level instructions may take many frames to execute, as the actor must pathfind to locations, actually perform the locomotion, animate into position, and kick off dialogue. Something worth investigating is how to properly integrate coroutines to pull off this kind of high-level scripting.

Runtime Assertions

While the code presented here relies on `assert` for verification, this was done for space considerations, as well as clarity. In a real life, honest-to-gosh production engine, you'll need to create a runtime assertion routine that lets a content provider know when he has made a mistake. This routine should bring up a dialog box with an informative text description letting him know why and where the mistake was made, specific data values if possible, and ideally, be fault-tolerant enough to not crash back to the desktop. This routine needs to execute even in a Release build, which is what your scripters should be using.

It is important to remember to use this tool on *any single piece of code that gets data from script*. Scripters will break everything you do in new and astounding ways, and getting as much data as possible is important. The more data you can provide in this error message, the more self-sufficient they will become, and the less they will hate you. They will already hate you, but it won't turn into loathing or a conspiracy to assassinate you.

A VERY CLEAR ROUTINE NAME

In an engine I worked with recently, the runtime assertion routine was called `GTFO()`. I'll leave it up to you to decrypt that acronym.

Special Thanks

First and foremost, I'd like to thank Mr. Mike for giving me the opportunity to share what I've been working on for the past few years. I hope some of you take this to heart: Scripters are what make or break a game these days, and we, the programmers, need to support them with the best tools to attain a vision.

I'd also like to thank Joshua Jensen for all his work on LuaPlus. Without it, this chapter would be much longer, harder to follow, and all-around less readable.

Last-but-not-least, a big thanks goes out to Max McGuire for making an excellent scripting tool with Decoda. He worked with me as I struggled with early beta versions, and the final product has saved me immense amounts of time.

REFERENCES

Online

- **www.lua.org**: Your jumping-off point for learning the language. Plenty of excellent tutorials and history here. *Get on the mailing list!* You'll learn plenty, and a searchable index means someone has probably already answered your question.
- **www.luaplus.org**: Homepage for Joshua Jensen's excellent extension of Lua into C++. Newer versions are downloadable via SVN.
- **www.unknownworlds.com/decoda**: The source for Decoda. If you're running into problems, the forums are full of knowledgeable folks who will get you fixed up in no time.

Books

- *Programming in Lua, Second Edition*, Roberto Ierusalimschy—This book is a must-have for learning the language. You'll find yourself picking this up and paging through it during late nights for easy-to-read sample script. Written by one of the language's creators, you'll also get some good insight on how it was developed.
- *Lua 5.1 Reference Manual* by Roberto Ierusalimschy, Luiz Henrique de Figueiredo, and Waldemar Celes—Almost a companion book to the one above, another invaluable reference.
- *Lua Programming Gems* edited by Luiz Henrique de Figueiredo, Waldemar Celes, and Roberto Ierusalimschy—More good tips and script "gems" here; you'll also find some tips on how to integrate Lua into your toolchain and some alternate approaches for tying it into a game engine.
- *Beginning Lua Programming (Programmer to Programmer)*, Kurt Jung and Aaron Brown—Of all the books in the list, this massive tome is probably the one with the most depth to it. Highly recommended.
- *The Art of Interactive Design: A Euphonious and Illuminating Guide to Building Successful Software*, Chris Crawford—With a title as long-winded as its author, this one may be a bit of a struggle. Never have I read anyone I disagree with more—and as a result, felt compelled to out-do—than Chris Crawford. Not that this is a bad book by any means, but it will challenge you and make you think hard about how end users—including your scripters!—will use your software.

GAME AUDIO

In This Chapter

- How Sound Works
- Game Sound System Architecture
- Other Technical Hurdles
- Some Random Notes
- The Last Dance

If you have any doubt about how important sound is in games, try a little experiment. First, find a home theater system that can turn off all the sound except for the center channel. The center channel is almost always used for dialog, and everything else is for music and sound effects. Pop a movie in and feel for yourself how flat the experience is without music and sound.

The same is true for games. Done well, sound and music convey critical information to the player as well as incite powerful emotional reactions. One of my favorite examples of powerful music in any game is the original *Halo* from Bungie. When the music segues into a driving combat tune, you can tell what is coming up—lots of carnage, hopefully on the Covenant side of things!

I'm biased, of course, but an excellent example of sound design and technology comes from *Thief: Deadly Shadows* by Ion Storm. This game integrated the physics, portal, and AI subsystems with the sound system. AI characters would receive propagated sound effect events that happened anywhere near them and react accordingly. If you got clumsy and stumbled Garrett, the main character in *Thief*, into a rack of swords, AI characters around the corner and down the hall would hear it, and they'd come looking for you.

Another great example is from *Mushroom Men: The Spore Wars* for the Wii by Red Fly Studio. In this game, the sound system was actually integrated into the graphics and particles system, creating a subtle but effective effect that had each sparkle of a particle effect perfectly timed with the music.

In this chapter, I'll take you as far as I can into the world of sound. We'll explore both sound effects and music. With a little work and imagination, you should be able to take what you learn here and create your own sound magic.

How Sound Works

Imagine someone on your street working with a hammer. Every time the hammer strikes a nail, or perhaps the poor schmuck's finger, a significant amount of energy is released causing heat, deformation of the hammer, deformation of whatever was hit, and vibrations in all the objects concerned as they return to an equilibrium state. A more complete description of the situation would also include high-amplitude vibration of Mr. Schmuck's vocal cords. Either way, those vibrations are propagated through the air as sound waves.

When these sound waves strike an object, sometimes they make the object vibrate at the same frequency. This only happens if the object is resonant with the frequency of the sound waves. Try this: Go find two guitars and make sure they are properly tuned. Then hold them close together and pluck the biggest, fattest string of one of them. You should notice that the corresponding string on the second guitar will vibrate, too, and you never touched it directly.

The experiment with the guitars is similar to how the mechanical parts of your ear work. Your ears have tiny hairs, each having a slightly different length and resonant frequency. When sound waves get to them and make different sets of them vibrate, they trigger chemical messages in your brain, and your conscious mind interprets the signals as different sounds. Some of them sound like a hammer striking a nail, and others sound more like words you'd rather not say in front of little kids.

The tone of a sound depends on the sound frequency or how fast the vibrations hit your ear. Vibrations are measured in cycles per second, or hertz (abbreviated Hz). The lowest tone a normal human ear can hear is 20Hz, which is so low you almost feel it more than you hear it! As the frequency rises, the tone of the sounds gets higher until you can't hear it anymore. The highest frequency most people can hear is about 20,000Hz, or 20 kilohertz (KHz).

The intensity of a sound is related to the number of air molecules pushed around by the original vibration. You can look at this as the "pressure" applied to anything by a sound wave. A common measurement of sound intensity is the decibel, or dB. This measurement is on a logarithmic scale, which means that a small increase in the dB level can be a dramatic increase in the intensity of the sound. Table 12.1 shows the dB levels for various common sounds.

The reason the scale is a logarithmic one has to do with the sensitivity of our ears. Normal human hearing can detect sounds over an amazing range of intensity, with the lowest being near silence and the highest being something that falls just shy of blowing your eardrums out of your head. The power difference between the two is over one million times. Since the range is so great, it is convenient to use a non-linear, logarithmic scale to measure the intensity of sound.

Did you ever wonder why the volume knob on expensive audio gear is marked with negative dB? This is because volume is actually attenuation, or the level of change of the base level of a sound. Decibels measure relative sound intensity, not absolute intensity, which means that negative decibels measure the amount of sound reduction. Turning the volume to 3dB lower than the current setting reduces the power to your speakers by half. Given that, and I can put this

Table 12.1 Decibel Levels for Different Sounds

dB Level	Description
0	The softest sound a person can hear with normal hearing
10	Normal breathing
20	Whispering at five feet
30	Soft whisper
50	Rainfall
60	Normal conversation
110	Shouting in ear
120	Thunder
150	Mr. Mike screaming when he beats his nephew Chris at *Guitar Hero*

in writing, all the stereo heads out there will be happy to know that if you set your volume level to 0dB, you'll be hearing the sound at the level intended by the audio engineer. This is, of course, usually loud enough to get complaints from your neighbors.

Digital Recording and Reproduction

If you happen to have some speakers with the cones exposed, like my nice Boston Acoustics™ setup, you can watch these cones move in and out in a blur when you crank the music. It turns out that the speakers are moving in correlation to the plot of the sound wave recorded in the studio.

You've probably seen a graphic rendering of a sound wave; it looks like some random up-and-down wiggling at various frequencies and amplitudes (see Figure 12.1).

FIGURE 12.1 A typical sound wave.

This scratching is actually a series of values that map to an energy value of the sound at a particular moment in time. This energy value is the power level sent into a speaker magnet to get the speaker cone to move, either in or out. The frequency, or tone, of the sound is directly related to the number of up/down wiggles you see in the graphic representation of the waveform. The speaker is reproducing, to the best of its ability, the identical waveform of the sound that was recorded in the studio.

If you zoom into the waveform, you'll see these energy values plotted as points above and below the X-axis (see Figures 12.2).

FIGURE 12.2 A closer view of a sound wave.

If all the points were in a straight line at value 0.0f, there would be complete silence. The odd thing is, if all the points were in a straight line at 1.0, you would get a little "pop" at the very beginning and silence thereafter. The reason is the speaker cone would sit at the maximum position of its movement, making no vibrations at all.

The amplitude, or height, of the waveform is a measure of the sound's intensity. Quiet sounds only wiggle close to the 0.0 line, whereas loud noises wiggle all the way from 1.0f to -1.0f. You can also imagine a really loud noise, like an explosion, has an energy level that my Boston Acoustics can't reproduce, and can't be accurately recorded anyway because of the energies involved. Figure 12.3 shows what happens to a sound wave that fails to record the amplitude of a high-energy sound.

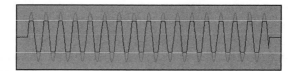

FIGURE 12.3 A clipped sound wave.

Instead of a nice waveform, the tops and bottoms are squared off. This creates a nasty buzzing noise because the speaker cones can't follow a nice smooth waveform. Audio engineers say that a recording like this had the "levels too hot," and they have to rerecord it with the input levels turned down a bit. If you ever see those recording meters on a mixing board, you'd notice the input levels jump into the red when the sound is too hot, creating the clipped waveforms. The same thing can happen when you record sounds straight to your PC from a microphone, so keep an eye on those input levels.

TALES FROM THE PIXEL MINES

CRUSTY GEEZERS SAY THE WILDEST THINGS

On the *Microsoft Casino* project, the actors were encouraged to come up with extemporaneous barks for their characters. Not surprisingly, some of them had to be cut from the game. One was cut by Microsoft legal because they thought it sounded too much like the signature line, "I'll be back," from Arnold Schwarzenegger. Another was cut because it made disparaging remarks toward the waitresses at the Mirage Resorts. My favorite one of all time, though, was a bit of speech from a crusty old geezer, "You know what I REALLY love about Vegas??? The Hookers!!!"

Sound Files

Sound files have many different formats, the most popular being WAV, MP3, OGG, and MIDI. The WAV format stores raw sound data, the aural equivalent of a BMP or TGA file, and is therefore the largest. MP3 and OGG files are compressed sound file formats and can achieve about a 10:1 compression ratio over WAV, with only a barely perceptible loss in sound quality. MIDI files are almost like little sound programs, and are extremely tiny, but the sound quality is completely different—it sounds like those video games from the 1980s. So why would you choose one over the other?

MIDI is popular for downloadable games and games on handheld platforms because they are so small and efficient. Memory can be in incredibly short supply, as well as processing power. The WAV format takes a lot of memory, but it is incredibly easy on your CPU budget. MP3s and OGGs will save your memory budget, but will hit your CPU pretty hard for each stream you decompress into a hearable sound.

If you're short on media space, you can store everything in MP3 or OGG, and decompress the data in memory at load time. This is a pretty good idea for short sound effects that you hear often, like weapons fire and footsteps. Music and background ambiance can be many minutes long, and are almost always played in their compressed form.

ALWAYS KEEP YOUR ORIGINAL HIGH-FIDELITY AUDIO RECORDINGS

Make sure that all of your original sound is recorded in high-resolution WAV format, and plan to keep it around until the end of the project. If you convert all your audio to a compressed format such as MP3, you'll lose sound quality, and you won't be able to reconvert the audio stream to a higher bit-rate if the quality isn't good enough. This is exactly the same thing as storing all your artwork in high-resolution TGAs or TIFFs. You'll always have the original work stored in the highest possible resolution in case you need to mess with it later.

A Quick Word About Threads and Synchronization

Sound systems run in a multithreaded architecture. I'm talking about real multithreading here and not the cooperative multitasking. What's the difference? You should already be familiar with the CProcess and CProcessManager classes from Chapter 6. These classes are cooperative, which means it is up to them to decide when to return control to the calling routine. For those of you who remember coding in the old DOS or Windows 3.x days, this is all we had without some serious assembly level coding. In a way, it was a lot safer, for reasons you'll see in a minute, but it was a heck of a lot harder to get the computer to accomplish many tasks at once.

A classic task in games is to play some neat music in the background while you are playing the game. Like I said at the start of this chapter, sound creates emotion in your game. But what is really going on in the background to make sound come out of your speakers?

Sound data is pushed into the sound card, and the sound card's driver software converts this data into electric signals that are sent to your speakers. The task of reading new data into the sound card and converting it into a usable format takes some CPU time away from your computer. While modern sound cards have CPUs of their own, getting the data from the digital media into the sound card still takes your main CPU.

Since sound data is played at a linear time scale, it's critical to push data into the sound card at the right time. If it is pushed too early, you'll overwrite music that is about to be played. If it is pushed too late, the sound card will play some music you've already heard, only to skip ahead when the right data gets in place.

This is the classic reader/writer problem where you have a fixed memory area with a writer that needs to stay ahead of the reader. If the reader ever overtakes the writer or vice versa, the reader reads data that is either too old or too new. When I heard about this in college, the example presented was always some horribly boring data being read and written, such as employee records or student class enrollment records. I would have paid a lot more attention to this class if they had told me the same solutions could be applied to computer game sound systems.

What makes this problem complicated is there must be a way to synchronize the reader and writer to make sure the writer process only writes when it knows it is safely out of the reader's way. Luckily, the really nasty parts of this problem are handled at a low level in DirectSound, but you should always be aware of it so you don't pull the rug out from the sound system's feet, so to speak. Let me give you an example.

In your game, let's assume there's a portable stereo sitting on a desk, and it is playing music. You take your gun and fire an explosive round into the radio and destroy the radio. Hopefully, the music the radio is playing stops when the radio is destroyed and the memory used by the music is returned to the system. You should be able to see how order-dependent all this is. If you stop the music too early, it looks like the radio was somehow self-aware and freaked out just before it was sent to radio nirvana. If you release all the radio's resources before you notify the sound system, the sound system might try to play some sound data from a bogus area of memory.

Worse still, because the sound system runs in a different thread, you can't count on a synchronous response when you tell the sound system to stop playing a sound. Granted, the sound system will respond to the request in a few milliseconds, far shorter than any human can perceive, but far longer than you could count on using the memory currently allocated to the sound system for something that is still active.

All these complications require a little architecture to keep things simple for programmers who are attaching sounds to objects or music to a game.

GAME SOUND SYSTEM ARCHITECTURE

Just like a graphics subsystem, audio subsystems can have a few different implementations. DirectSound and Miles Audio are two examples. It's a good idea to create an implementation-agnostic wrapper for your sound system so that you are free to choose the implementation right for your game. The audio system presented in this chapter can use DirectSound or Miles, and the only change you have to make for your high-level game code is one line of code. Figure 12.4 shows the class hierarchy for our sound system.

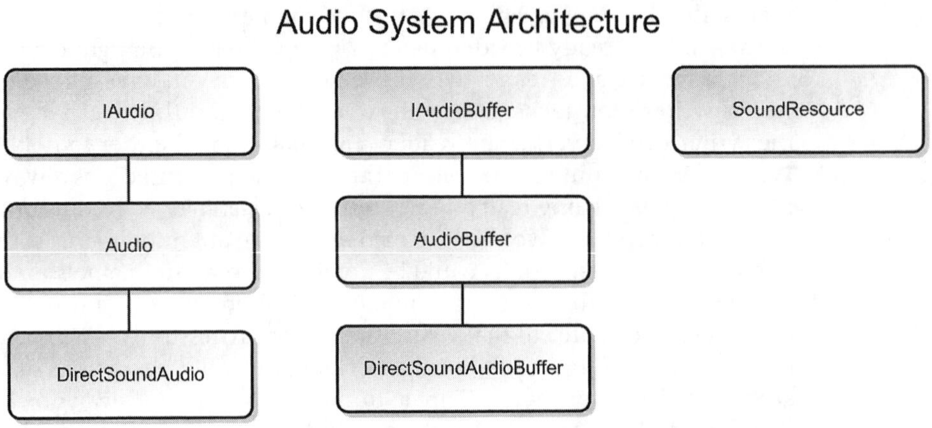

Audio System Architecture

FIGURE 12.4 Sound system class hierarchy.

The sound system inherits from IAudio. This object is responsible for the list of sounds currently active. As you might predict, you only need one of these for your game. The Audio base class implements some implementation-generic routines, and the DirectSoundAudio class completes the implementation with Direct-Sound specific calls.

The sound system needs access to the bits that make up the raw sound. The IAudioBuffer interface defines the methods for an implementation-generic sound buffer. AudioBuffer is a base class that implements some of the IAudioBuffer interface, and the DirectSoundAudioBuffer completes the implementation of the interface class using DirectSound calls. Each instance of a sound effect will use one of these buffer objects.

A CSoundResource encapsulates sound data, presumably loaded from a file or your resource cache. If you had five explosions going off simultaneously, you'd have one CSoundResource object and five DirectSoundAudioBuffer objects.

Sound Resources and Handles

If you want to play a sound in your game, the first thing you do is load it. Sound resources are loaded exactly the same as other game resources; they will likely exist in a resource file. Sound effects can be tiny or quite long. Your game may have thousands of these things, or tens of thousands as many modern games have. Just as you saw in Chapter 7, you shouldn't store each effect in its own file; rather, you should pull it from a resource cache.

A resource cache is convenient if you have many simultaneous sounds that use the same sound data, such as weapons fire. You should load this resource once, taking up only one block of memory, and have the sound driver create many "players" that will use the same resource.

The concept of streaming sound, compressed or otherwise, is beyond the scope of this chapter. The sound system described here uses the resource cache to load the sound data from a resource file, decompresses it if necessary, and manages DirectSound audio buffers if you happen to have the same sound being played multiple times. As usual, I'm exchanging clarity for performance, specifically memory usage, so take this into account when looking at this system. A real sound system would do much more to manage with a lot less memory!

With that caveat in mind, the first thing to do is define a new SoundResource class and SoundResHandle class:

```
class SoundResource : public Resource
{
public:
    SoundResource(std::string name) : Resource(name) { }
    virtual ResHandle *VCreateHandle(
        const char *buffer, unsigned int size, ResCache *pResCache);
};

ResHandle *SoundResource::VCreateHandle(
    const char *buffer, unsigned int size, ResCache *pResCache)
{
    return new SoundResHandle(
        *this, (unsigned char *)buffer, size, pResCache);
}

class SoundResHandle : public ResHandle
{
public:
    SoundResHandle(
        Resource &r,
        unsigned char *buffer,
        unsigned int size,
        ResCache *pResCache);
    virtual ~SoundResHandle();

    char const *GetPCMBuffer() const { return m_PCMBuffer; }
    int GetPCMBufferSize() const { return m_PCMBufferSize; }
    enum SoundType GetSoundType() { return m_SoundType; }
    WAVEFORMATEX const *GetFormat() { return &m_WavFormatEx; }
    int GetLengthMilli() const { return m_LengthMilli; }

    virtual bool VInitialize();
```

```
private:
    enum SoundType m_SoundType;    // is this an Ogg, WAV, etc.?
    bool m_bInitialized;           // has the sound been initialized
    bool m_bFromFile;              // are we reading from a file or a buffer?
    char *m_PCMBuffer;             // the destination PCM buffer of playable sound
    int m_PCMBufferSize;           // the length of the PCM buffer
    WAVEFORMATEX m_WavFormatEx;    // description of the PCM format
    int m_LengthMilli;             // how long the sound is in milliseconds

    const std::string m_SoundFile; // the name of the file or resource

    bool ParseWave(FILE *fd);
    bool ParseOgg(FILE *fd);

    bool ParseOgg(unsigned char *oggStream, size_t length);
    bool ParseWave(unsigned char *wavStream, size_t length);
};
```

Take a look at the private members first. The m_SoundType members store an enumeration that defines the different sound types you support: WAV, OGG, and so on. The next Boolean stores whether the sound has been initialized, which is to say that the sound is ready to play. The m_bFromFile can be set to true if you want to load this sound directly from a file rather than the resource cache, which can be useful for testing sounds outside of the resource cache.

The next two members store the sound in a format that is directly usable by DirectSound, which is a PCM buffer. PCM stands for Pulse Code Modulation, and is a standard data format used in everything from digital telephones to audio CDs and computer audio systems. Because this format is completely uncompressed, it takes up quite a bit of memory space, which is the main reason I consider this class more of a "learning" class instead of something you'd use in a real game.

A real game would keep compressed sounds in memory and send bits and pieces of them into the audio hardware as they were needed, saving precious memory space. For longer pieces such as music, the system might even stream bits of the compressed music from digital media, and then uncompress those bits as they were consumed by the audio card. As you can see, that system could use its own book to describe it thoroughly.

Next up is the SoundResHandle class, which is responsible for sounds that have been loaded by the resource cache:

```
SoundResHandle::SoundResHandle(
Resource &r, unsigned char *buffer,
unsigned int size, ResCache *pResCache)
:   ResHandle(r, (char *)buffer, size, pResCache),
    m_PCMBuffer(NULL),
```

```
        m_PCMBufferSize(0),
        m_SoundType(SOUND_TYPE_UNKNOWN),
        m_SoundFile(r.m_name),
        m_bInitialized(false),
        m_LengthMilli(0),
        m_RawBuffer(buffer),
        m_BufferLength(size)
{
    // don't do anything yet
    // timing sound Initialization is important!
    m_bFromFile = (buffer==NULL);
}


SoundResHandle::~SoundResHandle()
{
// Note - since SoundResources have a lifetime controlled by shared_ptr,
// it's safe for us to nuke the memory without checking the sound system first.
// Once the buffer is deleted, anything trying to read from it will result
// in an Access Violation, like if the sound is still being played in another
// thread. So... that means don't try to play this sound anymore
// after you SAFE_DELETE this buffer

    SAFE_DELETE_ARRAY(m_PCMBuffer);
}
```

You might think for a moment that the destructor might not have "permission" from the audio system to just nuke the PCM buffer. What if the sound is still playing? It turns out that this is fine for multiple reasons. First, just like the ResHandle class you saw in Chapter 7, SoundResHandle objects are always managed through a shared_ptr. If the sound is still in the resource cache or is being actively played by the audio system, the descructor can never be called because of the living reference to the object. Only when the last reference to the SoundResHandle object is released will the descructor get called and the memory released.

Let's take a look at the methods to initialize the sound:

```
bool SoundResHandle::VInitialize()
{
    if (!m_bInitialized)
    {
        m_SoundType = Audio::FindSoundTypeFromFile(m_SoundFile.c_str());
        if (m_bFromFile)
        {
            FILE *file = NULL;
            file = fopen(m_SoundFile.c_str(), "rb");
```

```
        if (file ==  NULL )
          return false;

      switch (m_SoundType)
      {
         case SOUND_TYPE_WAVE:
            ParseWave(file);
            break;

         case SOUND_TYPE_OGG:
            ParseOgg(file);
            break;

         default:
            assert(0 && _T("Sound Type Not Supported"));
      }
      fclose(file);
   }
   else
   {
      // initializing from a memory buffer
      switch (m_SoundType)
      {
         case SOUND_TYPE_WAVE:
            ParseWave(m_RawBuffer, m_BufferLength);
            break;

         case SOUND_TYPE_OGG:
            ParseOgg(m_RawBuffer, m_BufferLength);
            break;

         default:
            assert(0 && _T("Sound Type Not Supported"));
      }
   }
   m_bInitialized = true;
  }
  return true;
}
```

VInitialize() is called separately from construction. This is a good idea for
two reasons. First, sound files can get corrupted, and there's a chance that the
load will fail. If it does fail, you'll want to do something other than throw an
exception in a constructor. Second, you might want to have more control over
when your sound resources actually load. Perhaps you'll want to load them all at

once in one set and in a particular order. Sound tends to be the bulkiest data in your game, and keeping load times down can be tricky.

The `VInitialize()` method only does a few things: it figures out what kind of data to parse, calls the correct parse routine, and calculates the length of the sound in milliseconds. The sound data can come directly from a file, or it can come from a memory buffer.

The meaty methods of the `SoundResHandle` class convert sounds from their native format to PCM format. The class supports both WAV and OGG files. Both `ParseWave()` and `ParseOgg()` can accept a `FILE *` for input or a memory buffer.

BEST PRACTICE

STREAM YOUR MUSIC

A better solution for music files, which tend to be huge in an uncompressed form, is to stream them into memory as the sound data is played. Streaming sound is a complicated subject, so for now we'll simply play uncompressed sound data. Notice that even though a multi-megabyte OGG file is loaded into a decompressed buffer, taking up perhaps 10 times as much memory, it loads many times faster. As you might expect, the Vorbis decompression algorithm is much faster than your hard drive.

After the file is loaded, the `WAVFORMATEX` structure will reflect the nature of the decompressed sound data. Platform-dependent sound systems like DirectSound will need this data to interpret the uncompressed PCM data stream properly.

Loading the WAV Format

WAV files are what old-school game developers call a *chunky* file structure. Each chunk is preceded by a unique identifier, which you'll use to parse the data in each chunk. The chunks can also be hierarchical, that is, a chunk can exist within another chunk. Take a quick look at the code below, and you'll see what I'm talking about. The first identifier, "RIFF," is a clue that the file has an IFF, or Indexed File Format, basically the same thing as saying a chunky format. If the next identifier in the file is "WAVE," you can be sure the file is a WAV audio file.

You'll notice the identifier is always four bytes, and is immediately followed by a 4-byte integer that stores the length of the chunk. Chunky file formats allow parsing code to ignore chunks they don't understand, which is a great way to create extensible file formats. As you'll see next, we're only looking for two chunks from our WAV file, but that doesn't mean that other chunks aren't there:

```
bool SoundResHandle::ParseWave(char *wavStream, size_t bufferLength)
{
    DWORD        file = 0;
    DWORD        fileEnd = 0;
    DWORD        length = 0;
```

```
DWORD      type = 0;
DWORD      pos = 0;

// mmioFOURCC -- converts four chars into a 4 byte integer code.
// The first 4 bytes of a valid .wav file is 'R','I','F','F'

type = *((DWORD *)(wavStream+pos));        pos+=sizeof(DWORD);
if(type != mmioFOURCC('R', 'I', 'F', 'F'))
   return false;

length = *((DWORD *)(wavStream+pos));     pos+=sizeof(DWORD);
type = *((DWORD *)(wavStream+pos));       pos+=sizeof(DWORD);

// 'W','A','V','E' for a legal .wav file
if(type != mmioFOURCC('W', 'A', 'V', 'E'))
   return false;        //not a WAV

// Find the end of the file
fileEnd = length - 4;

memset(&m_WavFormatEx, 0, sizeof(WAVEFORMATEX));

// Load the .wav format and the .wav data
// Note that these blocks can be in either order.
while(file < fileEnd)
{
   type = *((DWORD *)(wavStream+pos));    pos+=sizeof(DWORD);
   file += sizeof(DWORD);

   length = *((DWORD *)(wavStream+pos));   pos+=sizeof(DWORD);
   file += sizeof(DWORD);

   switch(type)
   {
      case mmioFOURCC('f', 'a', 'c', 't'):
      {
         assert(false && "This wav file is compressed.  We don't handle
                          compressed wav at this time");
         break;
      }

      case mmioFOURCC('f', 'm', 't', ' '):
      {
         memcpy(&m_WavFormatEx, wavStream+pos, length);
```

```
            pos+=length;
            m_WavFormatEx.cbSize = length;
            break;
        }

        case mmioFOURCC('d', 'a', 't', 'a'):
        {
            m_PCMBuffer = GCC_NEW char[length];
            m_PCMBufferSize = length;
            memcpy(m_PCMBuffer, wavStream+pos, length);
            pos+=length;
            break;
        }
    }

    file += length;

    // If both blocks have been seen, we can return true.
    if( (m_PCMBuffer != 0 ) && (m_PCMBufferSize != 0) )
    {
        m_LengthMilli = ( GetPCMBufferSize() * 1000 ) /
GetFormat()->nAvgBytesPerSec;
        return true;
    }

    // Increment the pointer past the block we just read,
    // and make sure the pointer is word aligned.
    if (length & 1)
    {
        ++pos;
        ++file;
    }
}

// If we get to here, the .wav file didn't contain all the right pieces.
return false;
}
```

The `ParseWave()` method has two parts. The first part initializes local and output variables and makes sure the WAV file has the right beginning tag: "RIFF," signifying that the file is the IFF type, and the identifier immediately following is "WAVE." If either of these two checks fails, the method returns false.

The code flows into a `while` loop that is looking for two blocks: "fmt" and "data." They can arrive in any order, and there may be other chunks interspersed.

That's fine, because we'll just ignore them and continue looking for the two we care about. Once they are found, we return with success. If for some reason we get to the end of the file and we didn't find the two chunks we were looking for, we return false, indicating a failure.

Loading the OGG Format

The `ParseOgg()` method decompresses an OGG stream already in memory. The `OggVorbis_File` object can load from a normal file or a memory buffer. Loading from a memory buffer is a little trickier since you have to "fake" the operations of an ANSI `FILE *` object with your own code.

This first task is to create a structure that will keep track of the memory buffer, the size of this buffer, and where the "read" position is:

```
struct OggMemoryFile
{
  unsigned char*  dataPtr;// Pointer to the data in memory
  size_t    dataSize;     // Size of the data
  size_t    dataRead;     // Bytes read so far
};
```

The next task is to write functions to mimic `fread`, `fseek`, `fclose`, and `ftell`:

```
size_t VorbisRead(void* data_ptr, size_t byteSize, size_t sizeToRead, void*
            data_src)
{
   OggMemoryFile *pVorbisData = static_cast<OggMemoryFile *>(data_src);
   if (NULL == pVorbisData)
   {
      return -1;
   }

   size_t actualSizeToRead, spaceToEOF =
      pVorbisData->dataSize - pVorbisData->dataRead;
   if ((sizeToRead*byteSize) < spaceToEOF)
   {
      actualSizeToRead = (sizeToRead*byteSize);
   }
   else
   {
      actualSizeToRead = spaceToEOF;
   }
```

```
  if (actualSizeToRead)
  {
    memcpy(data_ptr,
      (char*)pVorbisData->dataPtr + pVorbisData->dataRead, actualSizeToRead);
    pVorbisData->dataRead += actualSizeToRead;
  }

  return actualSizeToRead;
}


int VorbisSeek(void* data_src, ogg_int64_t offset, int origin)
{
  OggMemoryFile *pVorbisData = static_cast<OggMemoryFile *>(data_src);
  if (NULL == pVorbisData)
  {
    return -1;
  }

  switch (origin)
  {
    case SEEK_SET:
    {
      ogg_int64_t actualOffset;
      actualOffset = (pVorbisData->dataSize >= offset) ?
        offset : pVorbisData->dataSize;
      pVorbisData->dataRead = static_cast<size_t>(actualOffset);
      break;
    }

    case SEEK_CUR:
    {
      size_t spaceToEOF =
        pVorbisData->dataSize - pVorbisData->dataRead;

      ogg_int64_t actualOffset;
      actualOffset = (offset < spaceToEOF) ? offset : spaceToEOF;

      pVorbisData->dataRead += static_cast<LONG>(actualOffset);
      break;
    }

  case SEEK_END:
    pVorbisData->dataRead = pVorbisData->dataSize+1;
    break;
```

```
    default:
      assert(false && "Bad parameter for 'origin', requires same as fseek.");
      break;
  };

  return 0;
}


int VorbisClose(void *src)
{
    // Do nothing - we assume someone else is managing the raw buffer
    return 0;
}


long VorbisTell(void *data_src)
{
   OggMemoryFile *pVorbisData = static_cast<OggMemoryFile *>(data_src);
   if (NULL == pVorbisData)
   {
      return -1L;
   }

   return static_cast<long>(pVorbisData->dataRead);
}
```

You might notice that the method that fakes the `fclose()` doesn't do anything. Ordinarily, you might free the memory in the buffer, but since the raw sound data is managed by the resource cache, nothing needs to be done. Here's what the `ParseOgg()` method looks like:

```
bool SoundResHandle::ParseOgg(char *oggStream, size_t length)
{
    OggVorbis_File vf;                        // for the vorbisfile interface
ov_callbacks oggCallbacks;

    OggMemoryFile *vorbisMemoryFile = new OggMemoryFile;
    vorbisMemoryFile->dataRead = 0;
    vorbisMemoryFile->dataSize = length;
    vorbisMemoryFile->dataPtr = (unsigned char *)oggStream;

    oggCallbacks.read_func = VorbisRead;
    oggCallbacks.close_func = VorbisClose;
    oggCallbacks.seek_func = VorbisSeek;
    oggCallbacks.tell_func = VorbisTell;
```

```
int ov_ret =
    ov_open_callbacks(vorbisMemoryFile, &vf, NULL, 0, oggCallbacks);
assert(ov_ret>=0);

// ok now the tricky part
// the vorbis_info struct keeps the most of the interesting format info
vorbis_info *vi = ov_info(&vf,-1);

memset(&m_WavFormatEx, 0, sizeof(m_WavFormatEx));

m_WavFormatEx.cbSize          = sizeof(m_WavFormatEx);
m_WavFormatEx.nChannels       = vi->channels;
// ogg vorbis is always 16 bit
m_WavFormatEx.wBitsPerSample  = 16;
m_WavFormatEx.nSamplesPerSec  = vi->rate;
m_WavFormatEx.nAvgBytesPerSec =
m_WavFormatEx.nSamplesPerSec*m_WavFormatEx.nChannels*2;
m_WavFormatEx.nBlockAlign     = 2*m_WavFormatEx.nChannels;
m_WavFormatEx.wFormatTag      = 1;

DWORD   size = 4096 * 16;
DWORD   pos = 0;
int     sec = 0;
int     ret = 1;

// get the total number of PCM samples
DWORD bytes = (DWORD)ov_pcm_total(&vf, -1);
bytes *= 2 * vi->channels;
m_PCMBuffer = GCC_NEW char[bytes];
m_PCMBufferSize = bytes;

// now read in the bits
while(ret && pos<bytes)
{
    ret = ov_read(&vf, m_PCMBuffer+pos, size, 0, 2, 1, &sec);
    pos += ret;
    if (bytes - pos < size)
    {
        size = bytes - pos;
    }
}

m_LengthMilli = 1000.f * ov_time_total(&vf, -1);
ov_clear(&vf);
delete vorbisMemoryFile;
return true;
}
```

This method shows you how to decompress an OGG memory buffer using the Vorbis API. First, you grab some sound stream information and use it to calculate the size of the uncompressed sound buffer. Next, you allocate the memory for the sound data and enter a loop to decompress the stream.

ALWAYS SHOW SOMETHING MOVING

Any time you have a while loop that might take some time, such as decompressing a large OGG file, it's a good idea to create a callback function that your game can use to monitor the progress of the routine. This might be important for creating a progress bar or some other animation that will give your players something to look at other than a completely stalled screen. Console games are usually required to have on-screen animations during loads, but this is a good idea for PC games too.

If you are just lifting this OGG code into your game and ignoring the rest of this chapter, don't forget to link the Vorbis libraries into your project. Since there's no encoding going on here, you can just link the following libraries: vorbisfile_static.lib, vorbis_static.lib, and ogg_static.lib.

To learn more about the OGG format, go to www.xiph.org/ogg/vorbis. The technology is open source, the sound is every bit as good as MP3, and you don't have to worry about paying annoying license fees. In other words, unless you have money to burn, use OGG for sound data compression. Lots of audio tools support OGG, too. You can go to the Xiph Web site to find out which ones.

Loading WAV or OGG files is extremely similar and actually easier. You can look at those implementations in the *Game Coding Complete* source code.

`IAudioBuffer` Interface and `AudioBuffer` Class

`IAudioBuffer` exposes methods such as volume control, pausing, and monitoring individual sound effects while they are in memory. `IAudioBuffer`, and a partial implementation `AudioBuffer`, are meant to be platform agnostic. Here's the interface class:

```
class IAudioBuffer
{
public:
    virtual ~IAudioBuffer() { }

    virtual void *VGet()=0;
    virtual shared_ptr<SoundResHandle> const VGetResource()=0;
    virtual bool VRestore()=0;
```

```
virtual bool VPlay(int volume, bool looping)=0;
virtual bool VStop()=0;
virtual bool VResume()=0;

virtual bool VTogglePause()=0;
virtual bool VIsPlaying()=0;
virtual bool VIsLooping() const=0;
virtual void VSetVolume(int volume)=0;
virtual int VGetVolume() const=0;
virtual float VGetProgress() const=0;
};
```

The first method is a virtual destructor, which will be overloaded by classes that implement the interface. If this destructor weren't virtual, it would be impossible to release audio resources grabbed for this sound effect.

The next method, VGet(), is used to grab an implementation-specific handle to the allocated sound. When I say implementation specific, I'm talking about the piece of data used by the audio system implementation to track sounds internally. In the case of a DirectSound implementation, this would be a LPDIRECTSOUNDBUFFER. This is for internal use only, for whatever class implements the IAudio interface to call. Your high-level game code will never call this method unless it knows what the implementation is and wants to do something really specific.

The next method, VRestore(), is primarily for Windows games since it is possible for them to lose control of their sound buffers. You might recall a long discussion about losing drawing surfaces in the graphics section, requiring the game to track down every lost surface and call a method to restore it. Sound buffers under Windows operate exactly the same way. The audio system will double-check to see if an audio buffer has been lost before it sends commands to the sound driver to play the sound. If it has been lost, it will call the VRestore() method and everything will be back to normal. Hopefully, anyway.

The next four methods can control the play status on an individual sound effect. VPlay() gets a volume from 0–100 and a Boolean looping, which you set to true if you want the sound to loop. VStop(), VResume(), and VTogglePause() let you control the progress of a sound.

The volume methods do exactly what you'd think they do: set and retrieve the current volume of the sound. The method that sets the volume will do so instantly, or nearly so. If you want a gradual fade, on the other hand, you'll have to use something a little higher level. Luckily, we'll do exactly that later on in this chapter.

The last method returns a floating-point number between 0.0f and 1.0f, and is meant to track the progress of a sound as it is being played. If the sound effect is one-fourth of the way through playing, this method will return 0.25f.

ALL THINGS GO FROM 0.0 TO 1.0

Measuring things like sound effects in terms of a coefficient instead of a number of milliseconds is a nice trick. This abstraction gives you some flexibility if the actual length of the sound effect changes, especially if it is timed with animations.

With the interface defined, we can write a little platform-agnostic code and create the `AudioBuffer` class. The real meat of this class is the management of the smart pointer to a `SoundResource`. This guarantees that the memory for your sound effect can't go out of scope while the sound effect is being played:

```
class AudioBuffer : public IAudioBuffer
{
public:
    virtual shared_ptr<SoundResHandle> VGetResource() { return m_Resource; }
    virtual bool VIsLooping() const { return m_isLooping; }
    virtual int VGetVolume() const { return m_Volume; }
protected:
    AudioBuffer(shared_ptr<SoundResHandle >resource)
    {
        m_Resource = resource;
        m_isPaused = false;
        m_isLooping = false;
        m_Volume = 0;
    }   // disable public construction

    shared_ptr<SoundResHandle> m_Resource;

    // Is the sound paused
    bool m_isPaused;

    // Is the sound looping
    bool m_isLooping;

    //the volume
    int m_Volume;
};
```

This class holds the precious smart pointer to your sound data and implements the `IAudioBuffer` interface. `VIsLooping()` and `VGetVolume()` tell you if your sound is a looping sound and the current volume setting. `VGetResource()` returns a smart pointer to the sound resource, which manages the sound data.

We're nearly to the point where we have to dig into DirectSound. Before that happens, take a look at the classes that encapsulate the system that manages the list of active sounds: IAudio and Audio.

IAudio Interface and Audio Class

IAudio has three main purposes: create, manage, and release audio buffers:

```
class IAudio
{
public:
   virtual bool VActive()=0;

   virtual IAudioBuffer *VInitAudioBuffer(shared_ptr<SoundResHandle>
                                     soundResource)=0;
   virtual void VReleaseAudioBuffer(IAudioBuffer* audioBuffer)=0;

   virtual void VStopAllSounds()=0;
   virtual void VPauseAllSounds()=0;
   virtual void VResumeAllSounds()=0;

   virtual bool VInitialize()=0;
   virtual void VShutdown()=0;
};
```

VActive() is something you can call to determine if the sound system is active. As rare as it may be, a sound card might be disabled or not installed. It is also likely that during initialization or game shutdown, you'll want to know if the sound system has a heartbeat.

The next two methods, VInitAudioBuffer() and VReleaseAudioBuffer(), are called when you want to launch a new sound or tell the audio system you are done with it and it can release audio resources back to the system. This is important, so read it twice. You'll call these for each instance of a sound, even if it is exactly the same effect. You might want to play the same sound effect at two different volumes, such as when two players are firing the same type of weapon at each other, or you have multiple explosions going off at the same time in different places.

You'll notice that the only parameter to the initialize method is a shared pointer to a SoundResHandle object. This object contains the single copy of the actual decompressed PCM sound data. The result of the call, assuming it succeeds, is a pointer to an object that implements the IAudioBuffer interface. What this means is that the audio system is ready to play the sound.

The next three methods are system-wide sound controls, mostly for doing things like pausing and resuming sounds when the player Alt-Tabs away from your game. It's extremely annoying to have game sound effects continue in the background if you are trying to check email or convince your boss you aren't playing a game.

The last two methods, VInitialize() and VShutdown(), are used to create and tear down the sound system. Let's take a look at a platform-agnostic partial implementation of the IAudio interface:

```
extern TCHAR *gSoundExtentions[];
typedef std::list<IAudioBuffer *> AudioBufferList;


class Audio : public IAudio
{
public:
    Audio();
    virtual void VStopAllSounds();
    virtual void VPauseAllSounds();
    virtual void VResumeAllSounds();

    virtual void VShutdown();

    static TCHAR const * const FindExtFromSoundType(SoundType type)
        { return gSoundExtentions[type]; }
    static SoundType FindSoundTypeFromFile(TCHAR const * const ext);
    static bool HasSoundCard(void);

protected:

    AudioBufferList m_AllSamples;    // List of all currently allocated
    bool m_AllPaused;                // Has the sound system been paused?
    bool m_Initialized;              // Has the sound system been initialized?
};
```

We'll use STL to organize the active sounds in a linked list called m_AllSamples. This is probably good for almost any game because you'll most likely have only a handful of sounds active at one time. Linked lists are great containers for a small number of objects. You'd use a more complicated structure for anything with a good population, such as your game objects.

Since the sounds are all stored in the linked list, and each sound object implements the IAudioBuffer interface, we can define routines that perform an action on every sound in the system:

```
void Audio::VShutdown()
{
   IAudioBuffer *audioBuffer = NULL;
   AudioBufferList::iterator i=m_AllSamples.begin();

   while (i!=m_AllSamples.end())
   {
      audioBuffer = (*i);
      audioBuffer->VStop();
      m_AllSamples.pop_front();
   }
}


//Stop all active sounds, including music
void Audio::VPauseAllSounds()
{
   IAudioBuffer *audioBuffer = NULL;

   AudioBufferList::iterator i;
   AudioBufferList::iterator end;
   for(i=m_AllSamples.begin(), end=m_AllSamples.end(); i!=end; ++i)
   {
      audioBuffer = (*i);
      audioBuffer->VPause();
   }

   m_AllPaused=true;
}

void Audio::VResumeAllSounds()
{
   IAudioBuffer *audioBuffer = NULL;
   AudioBufferList::iterator i;
   AudioBufferList::iterator end;
   for(i=m_AllSamples.begin(), end=m_AllSamples.end(); i!=end; ++i)
   {
      audioBuffer = (*i);
      audioBuffer->VResume();
   }

   m_AllPaused=false;
}
```

```
void Audio::VStopAllSounds()
{
   IAudioBuffer *audioBuffer = NULL;

   AudioBufferList::iterator i;
   AudioBufferList::iterator end;
   for(i=m_AllSamples.begin(), end=m_AllSamples.end(); i!=end; ++i)
   {
      audioBuffer = (*i);
      audioBuffer->VStop();
   }

   m_AllPaused=false;
}
```

The code for each of these routines iterates the list of currently playing sounds and calls the appropriate stop, resume, or pause method of the IAudioBuffer object.

DirectSound Implementations

The Audio and AudioBuffer classes are useless on their own; we must still create the platform-specific code. Since DirectSound is completely free to use by anyone, we'll create our platform-specific code around that technology.

You'll need to extend this code if you want to play MP3 or MIDI. Still, Direct-Sound can make a good foundation for a game's audio system. Let's take a look at the implementation for DirectSoundAudio first, which extends the Audio class we just discussed:

```
class DirectSoundAudio : public Audio
{
public:
   DirectSoundAudio()     { m_pDS = NULL; }
   virtual bool VActive() { return m_pDS != NULL; }
   virtual IAudioBuffer *VInitAudioBuffer(
      shared_ptr<SoundResHandle> soundResource);
   virtual void VReleaseAudioBuffer(IAudioBuffer* audioBuffer);
   virtual void VShutdown();
   virtual bool VInitialize(HWND hWnd);

protected:
   IDirectSound8* m_pDS;
   HRESULT SetPrimaryBufferFormat(
```

```
    DWORD dwPrimaryChannels,
    DWORD dwPrimaryFreq,
    DWORD dwPrimaryBitRate );
};
```

The only piece of data in this class is a pointer to an `IDirectSound8` object, which is DirectSound's gatekeeper, so to speak. Initialization, shutdown, and creating audio buffers are all done through this object. One way to look at this is that `DirectSoundAudio` is a C++ wrapper around `IDirectSound8`. Let's look at initialization and shutdown first:

```
bool DirectSoundAudio::VInitialize()
{
    if ( m_Initialized )
        return true;
    m_Initialized=false;
    SAFE_RELEASE( m_pDS );

    HWND hWnd = g_App.m_hWnd;
    HRESULT hr;

    // Create IDirectSound using the primary sound device
    if( FAILED( hr = DirectSoundCreate8( NULL, &m_pDS, NULL ) ) )
        return false;

    // Set DirectSound coop level
    if( FAILED( hr = m_pDS->SetCooperativeLevel( hWnd, DSSCL_PRIORITY) ) )
        return false;

    if( FAILED( hr = SetPrimaryBufferFormat( 8, 44100, 16 ) ) )
        return false;

    m_Initialized = true;
    m_AllSamples.clear();
    return true;
}
```

This code is essentially lifted straight from the DirectX sound samples, so it should look pretty familiar. When you set the cooperative level on the DirectSound object, you're telling the sound driver you want more control over the sound system, specifically how the primary sound buffer is structured and how other applications run at the same time. The `DSSCL_PRIORITY` level is better than `DSSCL_NORMAL` because you can change the format of the output buffer. This is a good setting for games that still want to allow background applications like Microsoft Messenger or Outlook to be able to send something to the speakers.

Why bother, you might ask? If you don't do this, and set the priority level to DSSCL_NORMAL, you're basically informing the sound driver that you're happy with whatever primary sound buffer format is in place, which might not be the same sound format you need for your game audio. The problem is one of conversion. Games use tons of audio, and the last thing you need is for every sound to go through some conversion process so it can be mixed in the primary buffer. If you have 100,000 audio files and they are all stored in 44KHz, the last thing you want is to have each one be converted to 22KHz because it's a waste of time. Take control and use DSSCL_PRIORITY.

The call to SetPrimaryBufferFormat() sets your primary buffer format to a flavor you want; most likely, it will be 44KHz, 16-bit, and some number of channels that you feel is a good trade-off between memory use and the number of simultaneous sound effects you'll have in your game. For the purposes of this class, I'm choosing eight channels, but in a commercial game you could have 32 channels or even more. The memory you'll spend with more channels is dependent on your sound hardware, so be cautious about grabbing a high number of channels—you might find some audio cards won't support it.

```
HRESULT DirectSoundAudio::SetPrimaryBufferFormat(
DWORD dwPrimaryChannels,
DWORD dwPrimaryFreq,
DWORD dwPrimaryBitRate )
{
    // !WARNING! - Setting the primary buffer format and then using this
    // for DirectMusic messes up DirectMusic!
    //
    // If you want your primary buffer format to be 22kHz stereo, 16-bit
    // call with these parameters:   SetPrimaryBufferFormat(2, 22050, 16);

    HRESULT              hr;
    LPDIRECTSOUNDBUFFER pDSBPrimary = NULL;

    if( m_pDS == NULL )
        return CO_E_NOTINITIALIZED;

    // Get the primary buffer
    DSBUFFERDESC dsbd;
    ZeroMemory( &dsbd, sizeof(DSBUFFERDESC) );
    dsbd.dwSize        = sizeof(DSBUFFERDESC);
    dsbd.dwFlags       = DSBCAPS_PRIMARYBUFFER;
    dsbd.dwBufferBytes = 0;
    dsbd.lpwfxFormat   = NULL;

    if( FAILED( hr = m_pDS->CreateSoundBuffer( &dsbd, &pDSBPrimary, NULL ) ) )
        return DXUT_ERR( L"CreateSoundBuffer", hr );
```

```
WAVEFORMATEX wfx;
ZeroMemory( &wfx, sizeof(WAVEFORMATEX) );
wfx.wFormatTag       = (WORD) WAVE_FORMAT_PCM;
wfx.nChannels        = (WORD) dwPrimaryChannels;
wfx.nSamplesPerSec   = (DWORD) dwPrimaryFreq;
wfx.wBitsPerSample   = (WORD) dwPrimaryBitRate;
wfx.nBlockAlign      = (WORD) (wfx.wBitsPerSample / 8 * wfx.nChannels);
wfx.nAvgBytesPerSec  = (DWORD) (wfx.nSamplesPerSec * wfx.nBlockAlign);

if( FAILED( hr = pDSBPrimary->SetFormat(&wfx) ) )
    return DXUT_ERR( L"SetFormat", hr );

SAFE_RELEASE( pDSBPrimary );

return S_OK;
}
```

You have to love DirectSound. This method essentially makes two method calls, and the rest of the code simply fills in parameters. The first call is to `Create-SoundBuffer()`, which actually returns a pointer to the primary sound buffer where all your sound effects are mixed into a single sound stream that is rendered by the sound card. The second call to `SetFormat()` tells the sound driver to change the primary buffer's format to one that you specify.

The shutdown method, by contrast, is extremely simple:

```
void DirectSoundAudio::VShutdown()
{
   if(m_Initialized)
   {
      Audio::VShutdown();
      SAFE_RELEASE(m_pDS);
      m_Initialized = false;
   }
}
```

The base class's `VShutdown()` is called to stop and release all the sounds still active. The `SAFE_RELEASE` on `m_pDS` will release the `IDirectSound8` object and shut down the sound system completely.

The last two methods of the `DirectSoundAudio` class allocate and release audio buffers. An audio buffer is the C++ representation of an active sound effect. In our platform-agnostic design, an audio buffer is created from a sound resource, presumably something loaded from a file or more likely a resource file:

```
IAudioBuffer *DirectSoundAudio::VInitAudioBuffer(shared_ptr<CSoundResource>
                                                 soundResource)
{
   const char* fileExtension =
         Audio::FindExtFromSoundType(soundResource->GetSoundType());

if( m_pDS == NULL )
         return NULL;

   switch(soundResource->GetSoundType())
   {
      case SOUND_TYPE_OGG:
      case SOUND_TYPE_WAVE:
         // We support WAVs and OGGs
         break;

      case SOUND_TYPE_MP3:
      case SOUND_TYPE_MIDI:
         // If it's a midi file, then do nothing at this time...
         // maybe we will support this in the future
         assert(false && "MP3s and MIDI are not supported");
         return NULL;
         break;

      default:
         assert(false && "Unknown sound type");
         return NULL;
   }

   LPDIRECTSOUNDBUFFER sampleHandle;
   // Create the direct sound buffer, and only request the flags needed
   // since each requires some overhead and limits if the buffer can
   // be hardware accelerated
   DSBUFFERDESC dsbd;
   ZeroMemory( &dsbd, sizeof(DSBUFFERDESC) );
   dsbd.dwSize          = sizeof(DSBUFFERDESC);
   dsbd.dwFlags         = DSBCAPS_CTRLVOLUME;
   dsbd.dwBufferBytes   = soundResource->GetPCMBufferSize();
   dsbd.guid3DAlgorithm = GUID_NULL;
   dsbd.lpwfxFormat     = const_cast<WAVEFORMATEX *>(soundResource-
                                                    >GetFormat());

   HRESULT hr;
   if( FAILED( hr = m_pDS->CreateSoundBuffer( &dsbd, &sampleHandle, NULL ) ) )
```

```
    {
        return NULL;
    }

    // Add handle to the list
    IAudioBuffer *audioBuffer =
        (IAudioBuffer *)(new DirectSoundAudioBuffer(sampleHandle,
                                                    soundResource));

    m_AllSamples.insert( m_AllSamples.begin(), audioBuffer);

    return audioBuffer;
}
```

Notice the switch statement at the beginning of this code? It branches on the sound type, which signifies what kind of sound resource is about to play: WAV, MP3, OGG, or MIDI. In our simple example, we're only looking at WAV data, so if you want to extend this system to play other kinds of sound formats, you'll hook that new code in right there. For now, those other formats are short circuited, and will force a failure.

The call to `IDirectSound8::CreateSoundBuffer()` is preceded by setting various values of a `DSBUFFERDESC` structure that informs DirectSound what kind of sound is being created. Take special note of the flags, since that member can have all manner of things set that and control what can happen to the sound. An example here is the `DSBCAPS_CTRLVOLUME` flag, which tells DirectSound that we want to be able to control the volume of this sound effect. Other examples include `DSBCAPS_CTRL3D`, which enables 3D sound, or `DSBCAPS_CTRLPAN`, which enables panning control. Take a look at the DirectSound docs to learn more about this important structure.

After we're sure we're talking about WAV data, there are three things to do. First, we parse the WAV data with the `ParseWave()` method we saw a little earlier in this chapter. The results of that call are passed to DirectSound's `CreateSoundBuffer()` method, which creates an `IDirectSoundBuffer8` object. In the last step, the DirectSound sound buffer is handed to our C++ wrapper class, `DirectSoundAudioBuffer`, and inserted into the master list of sound effects managed by `Audio`.

Releasing an audio buffer is pretty trivial:

```
void DirectSoundAudio::VReleaseAudioBuffer(IAudioBuffer *sampleHandle)
{
    sampleHandle->VStop();
    m_AllSamples.remove(sampleHandle);
}
```

The call to `IAudioBuffer::VStop()` stops the sound effect, and it is then removed from the list of active sounds.

The second piece of this platform-dependent puzzle is the implementation of the `DirectSoundAudioBuffer`, which picks up and defines the remaining unimplemented virtual functions from the `IAudioBuffer` interface:

```
class DirectSoundAudioBuffer : public AudioBuffer
{
protected:
   LPDIRECTSOUNDBUFFER m_Sample;
public:
   DirectSoundAudioBuffer(
      LPDIRECTSOUNDBUFFER sample,
      shared_ptr<SoundResHandle> resource);

   virtual void *VGet();
   virtual bool VRestore();

   virtual bool VPlay(int volume, bool looping);
   virtual bool VStop();
   virtual bool VResume();

   virtual bool VTogglePause();
   virtual bool VIsPlaying();
   virtual void VSetVolume(int volume);

private:
   HRESULT FillBufferWithSound( );
   HRESULT RestoreBuffer( BOOL* pbWasRestored );
};
```

The methods in this class are pretty easy C++ wrappers around `IDirectSound-Buffer8`. The exceptions are `FillBufferWithSound()` and `RestoreBuffer()`:

```
DirectSoundAudioBuffer::DirectSoundAudioBuffer(
   LPDIRECTSOUNDBUFFER sample,
   shared_ptr<CSoundResource> resource)
 : AudioBuffer(resource)
{
   m_Sample = sample;
   FillBufferWithSound();
}
```

```
void *DirectSoundAudioBuffer::VGet()
{
    if (!VRestore())
      return NULL;
    return m_Sample;
}

bool DirectSoundAudioBuffer::VPlay(int volume, bool looping)
{
   VStop();
   m_Volume = volume;
   m_isLooping = looping;

   LPDIRECTSOUNDBUFFER pDSB = (LPDIRECTSOUNDBUFFER)VGet();
   if (!pDSB)
      return false;

   float coeff = (float)volume / 100.0f;
   float range = (DSBVOLUME_MAX - DSBVOLUME_MIN);
   float fvolume = ( range * coeff  ) + DSBVOLUME_MIN;

pDSB->SetVolume( volume );

DWORD dwFlags = looping ? DSBPLAY_LOOPING : OL;

return (S_OK==pDSB->Play( 0, 0, dwFlags ) );
}

bool DirectSoundAudioBuffer::VStop()
{
   LPDIRECTSOUNDBUFFER pDSB = (LPDIRECTSOUNDBUFFER)VGet();

   if(!g_Audio->VActive())
      return false;

if( pDSB == NULL )
      return false;

   m_isPaused=true;
pDSB->Stop();
   return true;
}
```

```
bool DirectSoundAudioBuffer::VResume()
{
   m_isPaused=false;
   return VPlay(VGetVolume(), VIsLooping());
}

bool DirectSoundAudioBuffer::VTogglePause()
{
   if(!g_Audio->VActive())
      return false;

   if(m_isPaused)
   {
      VResume();
   }
   else
   {
      VStop();
   }

   return true;
}

bool DirectSoundAudioBuffer::VIsPlaying()
{
   if(!g_Audio->VActive())
      return false;

   DWORD dwStatus = 0;
   LPDIRECTSOUNDBUFFER pDSB = (LPDIRECTSOUNDBUFFER)VGet();
   pDSB->GetStatus( &dwStatus );
    bool bIsPlaying = ( ( dwStatus & DSBSTATUS_PLAYING ) != 0 );

   return bIsPlaying;
}

void DirectSoundAudioBuffer::VSetVolume(int volume)
{
   if(!g_Audio->VActive())
      return;

   LPDIRECTSOUNDBUFFER pDSB = (LPDIRECTSOUNDBUFFER)VGet();
   assert(volume>=0 && volume<=100 && "Volume must be between 0 and 100");
```

```
// convert volume from 0-100 into range for DirectX
// Don't forget to use a logarithmic scale!

    float coeff = (float)volume / 100.0f;
    float logarithmicProportion = coeff >0.1f  ? 1+log10(coeff)  : 0;
    float range = (DSBVOLUME_MAX - GCC_DSBVOLUME_MIN);
    float fvolume = ( range * logarithmicProportion ) + GCC_DSBVOLUME_MIN;

    pDSB->SetVolume( LONG(fvolume) );

}
```

Most of the previous code has a similar structure and is a lightweight wrapper around IDirectSoundBuffer8. The first few lines check to see if the audio system is running, the audio buffer has been initialized, and parameters have reasonable values. Take one note of the VSetVolume method; it has to renormalize the volume value from 0–100 to a range compatible with DirectSound, and it does so with a logarithmic scale, since sound intensity is logarithmic in nature.

The last three methods in this class are a little trickier, so I'll give you a little more detail on them. The first, VRestore(), looks a little like something you'll recognize from the graphics chapters, and for good reason: sound buffers under DirectSound can be lost just like drawing surfaces or textures under Direct3D. Since Windows is inherently a multitasking system where you can have two games running at the same time, only one of those games will have control of the speakers. If you hit the Alt-Tab key to bring the inactive game to the front, it will have to run some code to restore lost sound and graphics buffers.

If the sound buffer is ever lost, you have to restore it with some DirectSound calls and then fill it with sound data again—it doesn't get restored with its data intact. The VRestore() method calls RestoreBuffer() to restore the sound buffer, and if that is successful, it calls FillBufferWithSound() to put the sound data back where it belongs:

```
bool DirectSoundAudioBuffer::VRestore()
{
    HRESULT hr;
    BOOL    bRestored;

    // Restore the buffer if it was lost
    if( FAILED( hr = RestoreBuffer( &bRestored ) ) )
        return NULL;

    if( bRestored )
    {
        // The buffer was restored, so we need to fill it with new data
```

```
        if( FAILED( hr = FillBufferWithSound( ) ) )
            return NULL;
    }

    return true;
}
```

This implementation of `RestoreBuffer()` is pretty much lifted from the Direct-Sound samples. Hey, at least I admit to it! If you're paying attention, you'll notice an unfortunate bug in the code—see if you can find it:

```
HRESULT DirectSoundAudioBuffer::RestoreBuffer( BOOL* pbWasRestored )
{
    HRESULT hr;

    if( m_Sample == NULL )
        return CO_E_NOTINITIALIZED;
    if( pbWasRestored )
        *pbWasRestored = FALSE;

    DWORD dwStatus;
    if( FAILED( hr = m_Sample->GetStatus( &dwStatus ) ) )
        return DXUT_ERR( L"GetStatus", hr );

    if( dwStatus & DSBSTATUS_BUFFERLOST )
    {
        // Since the app could have just been activated, then
        // DirectSound may not be giving us control yet, so
        // the restoring the buffer may fail.
        // If it does, sleep until DirectSound gives us control.
        do
        {
            hr = m_Sample->Restore();
            if( hr == DSERR_BUFFERLOST )
                Sleep( 10 );
        }
        while( ( hr = m_Sample->Restore() ) == DSERR_BUFFERLOST );

        if( pbWasRestored != NULL )
            *pbWasRestored = TRUE;

        return S_OK;
    }
```

```
    else
    {
        return S_FALSE;
    }
}
```

The bug in the method is the termination condition of the do/while loop; it could try forever, assuming DirectSound was in some wacky state. This could hang your game and cause your players to curse your name and post all kinds of nasty things on the Internet. Making the code better depends on what you want to do when this kind of failure happens. You likely would throw up a dialog box and exit the game. It's totally up to you. The lesson here is that just because you grab something directly from a DirectX sample doesn't mean you should install it into your game unmodified!

The next method is FillBufferWithSound(). Its job is to copy the sound data from a sound resource into a prepared and locked sound buffer. There's also a bit of code to handle the special case where the sound resource has no data—in that case, the sound buffer gets filled with silence. Notice that "silence" isn't necessarily a buffer with all zeros.

```
HRESULT DirectSoundAudioBuffer::FillBufferWithSound( void )
{
    HRESULT hr;
    VOID    *pDSLockedBuffer = NULL;     // DirectSound buffer pointer
    DWORD   dwDSLockedBufferSize = 0;    // Size of DirectSound buffer
    DWORD   dwWavDataRead        = 0;    // Data to read from the wav file

    if( m_Sample == NULL )
        return CO_E_NOTINITIALIZED;

    // Make sure we have focus, and we didn't just switch in from
    // an app which had a DirectSound device
    if( FAILED( hr = RestoreBuffer( NULL ) ) )
        return DXUT_ERR( L"RestoreBuffer", hr );

    int pcmBufferSize = m_Resource->GetPCMBufferSize();
    // Lock the buffer down
    if( FAILED( hr = m_Sample->Lock( 0, pcmBufferSize,
                        &pDSLockedBuffer, &dwDSLockedBufferSize,
                        NULL, NULL, 0L ) ) )
        return DXUT_ERR( L"Lock", hr );
```

```
    if( pcmBufferSize == 0 )
    {
        // Wav is blank, so just fill with silence
        FillMemory( (BYTE*) pDSLockedBuffer,
            dwDSLockedBufferSize,
            (BYTE)(m_Resource->GetFormat()->wBitsPerSample == 8 ? 128 : 0 ) );
    }
    else
    {
        CopyMemory(pDSLockedBuffer,
                m_Resource->GetPCMBuffer(), pcmBufferSize);
        if( pcmBufferSize < (int)dwDSLockedBufferSize )
        {
            // If the buffer sizes are different fill in the rest with silence
            FillMemory( (BYTE*) pDSLockedBuffer + pcmBufferSize,
                dwDSLockedBufferSize - pcmBufferSize,
                (BYTE)(m_Resource->GetFormat()->wBitsPerSample == 8 ? 128 : 0 ) );
        }
    }

    // Unlock the buffer, we don't need it anymore.
    m_Sample->Unlock( pDSLockedBuffer, dwDSLockedBufferSize, NULL, 0 );

    return S_OK;
}
```

There's also some special case code that handles the case where the Direct-Sound buffer is longer than the sound data—any space left over is filled with silence.

There's one last method to implement in the IAudioBuffer interface, the VGet-Progress() method:

```
float DirectSoundAudioBuffer::VGetProgress()
{
    LPDIRECTSOUNDBUFFER pDSB = (LPDIRECTSOUNDBUFFER)VGet();
    DWORD progress = 0;

    pDSB->GetCurrentPosition(&progress, NULL);
    float length = (float)m_Resource->GetPCMBufferSize();
    return (float)progress / length;
}
```

This useful little routine calculates the current progress of a sound buffer as it is being played. Sound plays at a constant rate, so things like music and speech will sound exactly as they were recorded. It's up to you, the skilled programmer, to get your game to display everything exactly in sync with the sound. You do this by polling the sound effect's progress when your game is about to start or change an animation.

Perhaps you have an animation of a window cracking and then shattering. You'd launch the sound effect and animation simultaneously, call VGetProgress() on your sound effect every frame, and set your animation progress accordingly. This is especially important because players can detect even tiny miscues between sound effects and animation.

Sound Processes

All of the classes you've seen so far, CSoundResource, DirectSoundAudio, and Direct-SoundAudioBuffer form the bare bones of an audio system for a computer game. What's missing is some way to launch and monitor a sound effect as it is playing, perhaps to coordinate it with an animation. If you paid some attention in Chapter 6, "Controlling the Main Loop," you'll remember the CProcess class. It turns out to be perfect for this job:

```
class SoundProcess : public CProcess
{
public:
    SoundProcess(
        shared_ptr<SoundResHandle> soundResource,
        int typeOfSound=PROC_SOUNDFX,
        int volume=100,
        bool looping=false);

    virtual ~SoundProcess();

    virtual void    OnUpdate(const int deltaMilliseconds);
    virtual void    OnInitialize();
    virtual void    Kill();

    virtual void    TogglePause();

    void            Play(const int volume, const bool looping);
    void            Stop();

    void            SetVolume(int volume);
    int             GetVolume();
    int             GetLengthMilli();
    bool            IsSoundValid() { return m_SoundResource!=NULL; }
```

```
bool        IsPlaying();
bool        IsLooping() { return m_AudioBuffer->VIsLooping(); }
float       GetProgress();

protected:
    SoundProcess();   //Disable Default Construction

    shared_ptr<SoundResHandle> m_SoundResource;
    shared_ptr<IAudioBuffer> m_AudioBuffer;

    int         m_Volume;
    bool        m_isLooping;
};
```

This class provides a single object that manages individual sounds. Many of the methods are re-implementations of some `IAudioBuffer` methods, and while this isn't the best C++ design, it can make things a little easier in your code.

As you might expect, the parameters are a `CSoundResource` and initial sound settings. One parameter needs a little explanation, `typeOfSound`. Every process has a type, and sound processes use this to distinguish themselves into sound categories such as sound effects, music, ambient background effects, or speech. This creates an easy way for a game to turn off or change the volume level of a particular type of sound, which most gamers will expect. If players want to turn down the music level so they can hear speech better, it's a good idea to let them:

```
SoundProcess::SoundProcess(
    shared_ptr<SoundResHandle> soundResource,
    int typeOfSound, int volume, bool looping)
    : CProcess(typeOfSound, 0),
      m_SoundResource(soundResource),
      m_Volume(volume),
      m_isLooping(looping)
{
}

SoundProcess::~SoundProcess()
{
    if (m_AudioBuffer)
    {
        g_Audio->VReleaseAudioBuffer(m_AudioBuffer.get());
    }
}
```

The meat of the code in `SoundProcess` is in the next few methods. One important concept to understand about sounds is the code might create a sound process long before the sound should be played or even loaded. Since sound effects tend to require a lot of data, it's a good idea to be careful about when you instantiate sound effects. After all, you don't want your game to stutter or suffer wacky pauses. The code shown next assumes the simplest case, where you want the sound to begin playing immediately, but it's good to know that you don't have to do it this way:

```
void SoundProcess::OnInitialize()
{
   if ( ! m_SoundResource )
      return;

   m_SoundResource->Initialize();

   //This sound will manage its own handle in the other thread
   IAudioBuffer *buffer = g_Audio->VInitAudioBuffer(m_SoundResource);

   if (!buffer)
   {
      Kill();
      return;
   }

   m_AudioBuffer.reset(buffer);

   Play(m_Volume, m_isLooping);
}
```

The `VOnUpdate` method monitors the sound effect as it's being played. Once it is finished, it kills the process and releases the audio buffer. If the sound is looping, it will play until some external call kills the process. Again, you don't have to do it this way in your game. Perhaps you'd rather have the process hang out until you kill it explicitly:

```
void SoundProcess::VOnUpdate(const int deltaMilliseconds)
{
   // Call base
   CProcess::OnUpdate(deltaMilliseconds);

   if ( ! m_bInitialUpdate && ! IsPlaying() )
   {
      VKill();
   }
```

```
    if ( IsDead() && IsLooping() )
    {
        Replay();
    }
}
```

This class overloads the VKill() method to coordinate with the audio system. If the process is going to die, so should the sound effect:

```
void SoundProcess::VKill()
{
    if ( IsPlaying() )
        Stop();
    CProcess::VKill();
}
```

Notice that the base class's VKill() is called at the end of the method, rather than the beginning. You can look at VKill() similar to a destructor, which means this calling order is a safer way to organize the code.

As advertised, the remaining methods do nothing more than pass calls into the IAudioBuffer object:

```
bool SoundProcess::IsPlaying()
{
    if ( ! m_SoundResource || ! m_AudioBuffer )
        return false;

    return m_AudioBuffer->VIsPlaying();
}

int SoundProcess::GetLengthMilli()
{
    if ( m_SoundResource )
        return m_AudioBuffer->VGetLengthMilli();
    else
        return 0;
}

void SoundProcess::SetVolume(int volume)
{
    if(m_AudioBuffer==NULL)
        return;
```

```
    assert(volume>=0 &&
          volume<=100 &&
          "Volume must be a number between 0 and 100");

    m_Volume = volume;
    m_AudioBuffer->VSetVolume(volume);
}

int SoundProcess::GetVolume()
{
    if(m_AudioBuffer==NULL)
        return 0;

    m_Volume = m_AudioBuffer->VGetVolume();
    return m_Volume;
}

void SoundProcess::TogglePause()
{
    if(m_AudioBuffer)
        m_AudioBuffer->VTogglePause();
}

void SoundProcess::Play(const int volume, const bool looping)
{
    assert(volume>=0 &&
          volume<=100 &&
          "Volume must be a number between 0 and 100");

    if(!m_AudioBuffer)
        return;

    m_AudioBuffer->VPlay(volume, looping);
}

void SoundProcess::Stop()
{
    if(m_AudioBuffer)
        m_AudioBuffer->VStop();
}
```

```
float SoundProcess::GetProgress()
{
   if (m_AudioBuffer)
      return m_AudioBuffer->VGetProgress();

   return 0.0f;
}
```

Launching Sound Effects

The only thing you need to see now is how to tie all this together to launch and monitor a sound effect in your game. It may seem a little anticlimactic, but here it is:

```
SoundResource resource("SpaceGod7-Level2.ogg");
shared_ptr<ResHandle> rh = g_pApp->m_ResCache->GetHandle(&resource);
shared_ptr<SoundResHandle> srh =
   boost::static_pointer_cast<SoundResHandle>(rh);
shared_ptr<SoundProcess> sfx(new SoundProcess(srh, PROC_MUSIC, 100, true));
m_pProcessManager->Attach(sfx);
```

There's clearly an awful lot of work going on in the background, all of which you now know how to do. Launching a sound effect ties together much of the code you've seen in this book: a cooperative multitasker, a resource system, and a bit of DirectX, which launches an extra thread to manage the problem of getting data to the sound card at exactly the right speed. Still, it's nice to know that all that functionality can be accessed with 6 lines of code.

If you want to launch three sound effects based on the same data, one playing as soon as the other is complete, here's how you'd do it. Each one plays at a lower volume level than the one before it:

```
SoundResource resource("blip.wav");
shared_ptr<SoundResHandle> srh =
boost::static_pointer_cast<SoundResHandle>(g_pApp->m_ResCache-
                                        >GetHandle(&resource));
shared_ptr<SoundProcess> sfx1(new SoundProcess(srh, PROC_SOUNDFX, 100, false));
shared_ptr<SoundProcess> sfx2(new SoundProcess(srh, PROC_SOUNDFX, 60, false));
shared_ptr<SoundProcess> sfx3(new SoundProcess(srh, PROC_SOUNDFX, 40, false));
m_pView->m_pProcessManager->Attach(sfx1);
sfx1->SetNext(sfx2);
sfx2->SetNext(sfx3);
```

OTHER TECHNICAL HURDLES

There are a few more wires to connect, in code and in your brain, before you're ready to install a working sound system in your game. Most sounds are tied directly to game objects or events. Even music is tied to the intensity of the game, or even better, the impending intensity of the game! Tying sounds to game objects and synchronization are critical problems in any game sound system. If you have multiple effects at one time, you'll also have to worry about mixing issues.

Sounds and Game Objects

Imagine the following game situation: A wacky machine in a lab is active, and makes some kind of "wub-wub-wub" sound tied to an animation. Your hero, armed with his favorite plasma grenade, tosses one over to the machine and stands back to watch the fun. The grenade explodes, taking the wacky machine and the "wub-wub-wub" noise with it. What's really going on in the background?

Your game has some grand data structure of game objects, one of which is the doomed machine. When the grenade goes off, there's likely a bit of code or script that searches the local area for objects that can be damaged. Each object in the blast radius will get some damage, and the code that applies damage will notice the machine is a gonner.

What happens next is a core technical problem in computer games: When the machine is destroyed, related game objects or systems should be notified. This can include things like sound effects or animation processes. Most games solve this with the trigger/event system, and this is no exception.

For purposes of clarity, the audio system code presented in this chapter has no such hook, but there's a great chapter in this very book that will show you how to install one! Check out Chapter 10, "Game Event Management," and you'll see how the sound system gets notified when objects are destroyed.

Timing and Synchronization

Imagine the following problem: You have a great explosion graphics effect that has a secondary and tertiary explosion after the initial blast. How could you synchronize the graphics to each explosion? The pacing of the sound is pretty much constant, so the graphics effect should monitor the progress of the sound and react accordingly. We can use the CProcess class to make this work:

```
class ExplosionProcess : public CProcess
{
public:
    ExplosionProcess() : Process(PROC_GAMESPECIFIC) { m_Stage=0; }
```

```
protected:
    int m_Stage;
    shared_ptr<SoundProcess> m_Sound;

    virtual void    VOnUpdate(const int deltaMilliseconds);
    virtual void    VOnInitialize();
};

void ExplosionProcess::VOnInitialize()
{
    CProcess::VOnInitialize();
    SoundResource resource("explosion.wav");
    shared_ptr<SoundResHandle> srh = boost::static_pointer_cast<SoundResHandle>
                                (g_pApp->m_ResCache->GetHandle(&resource));
    m_Sound.reset(GCC_NEW SoundProcess(srh));
    // Imagine cool explosion graphics setup code here!!!!
    //
    //
    //
}

void ExplosionProcess::OnUpdate(const int deltaMilliseconds)
{
    // Since the sound is the real pacing mechanism - we ignore
    // deltaMilliseconds
    float progress = m_Sound->GetProgress();

    switch (m_Stage)
    {
        case 0:
            if (progress>0.55f)
            {
                ++m_Stage;
                // Imagine secondary explosion effect launch right here!
            }
            break;

        case 1:
            if (progress>0.75f)
            {
                ++m_Stage;
                // Imagine tertiary explosion effect launch right here!
            }
            break;
```

```
        default:
            break;
    }
}
```

The `ExplosionProcess` owns a sound effect and drives the imaginary animation code. The sound effect is initialized during the `VOnInitialize()` call, and the `VOnUpdate()` handles the rest as you've seen before. There's a trivial state machine that switches state as the sound progresses past some constant points 55 percent and 75 percent of the way through.

Do you notice the hidden problem with this code? This is a common gotcha in computer game design. What happens if the audio designer decides to change the sound effect and bring the secondary explosion closer to the beginning of the sound? It's equally likely an artist will change the timing of an animated texture, which could have exactly the same effect. Either way, the explosion effect looks wrong, and it's anyone's guess who will get the bug: programmer, artist, or audio engineer.

THE BUTTERFLY EFFECT

Code, animations, and sound data are tightly coupled and mutually dependent entities. You can't easily change one without changing the others, and you can make your life hell by relating all three with hard-coded constants. There's no silver bullet for this problem, but there are preventative measures. It might seem like more work, but you could consider factoring the `ExplosionClass` into three distinct entities, each with its own animation and sound data. Either way, make sure that you have some asset tracking so you can tell when someone changes anything in your game: code, sounds, or animations. When something breaks unexpectedly, the first thing you check is changes to the files.

Mixing Issues

Sound in your game will include sound effects, music, and speech. Depending on what's going on, you might have to change the volume of one or more of these elements to accentuate it. A good example of this is speech, and I'm not talking about the random barks of a drunken guard. Games will introduce clues and objectives with AI dialogue, and it's important that the player be able to hear it. If you played *Thief: Deadly Shadows*, there's a good example of this in the Seaside Mansion mission about halfway through the game. The thunder and lightning outside was so loud it was difficult to hear the AI dialogue.

That's one of the reasons there is this notion of SoundType in our audio system. It gives you a bit of data to hang on to if you want to globally change the volume of certain sounds. In the case of *Thief,* it would have been a good idea to cut the volume of the storm effects so the game clues in the AI dialogue would be crystal clear.

BEST PRACTICE

DON'T DEPEND ON DIALOGUE

Dialogue is great to immerse players in game fiction, but you can't depend on it 100 percent. If you give critical clues and objectives via dialogue, make sure that you have some secondary way to record and represent the objectives, such as a special screen where the player can read a synopsis. It's too easy for a player to miss something.

While we're talking about mixing, you've got to take some care when changing the levels of sound effects. Any discrete jump in volume is jarring. Solve this problem with a simple fade mechanism:

```
CFadeProcess::CFadeProcess(
    shared_ptr<SoundProcess> sound,
    int fadeTime,
    int endVolume)
: CProcess(PROC_INTERPOLATOR)
{
    m_Sound = sound;
    m_TotalFadeTime = fadeTime;
    m_StartVolume = sound->GetVolume();
    m_EndVolume = endVolume;
    m_ElapsedTime = 0;

    OnUpdate(0);
}

void CFadeProcess::OnUpdate(const int deltaMilliseconds)
{
    if (!m_bInitialUpdate)
        m_ElapsedTime += deltaMilliseconds;

    CProcess::OnUpdate(deltaMilliseconds);

    if (m_Sound->IsDead())
        Kill();

    float cooef = (float)m_ElapsedTime / m_TotalFadeTime;
```

```
if (cooef>1.0f)
   cooef = 1.0f;
if (cooef<0.0f)
   cooef = 0.0f;

int newVolume = m_StartVolume + ( float(m_EndVolume - m_StartVolume) *
                                 cooef);

if (m_ElapsedTime >= m_TotalFadeTime)
{
   newVolume = m_EndVolume;
   Kill();
}

m_Sound->SetVolume(newVolume);
}
```

This class can change the volume of a sound effect over time, either up or down. It assumes the initial volume of the sound effect has already been set properly and all the times are given in milliseconds.

Here's how you would create some background music and fade it in over 10 seconds:

```
SoundResource resource("SpaceGod7-Level2.ogg");
shared_ptr<ResHandle> rh = g_pApp->m_ResCache->GetHandle(&resource);
shared_ptr<SoundResHandle> srh = boost::static_pointer_cast
                                 <SoundResHandle>(rh);
shared_ptr<SoundProcess> music(GCC_NEW SoundProcess(srh, PROC_MUSIC, 0, true));
m_pProcessManager->Attach(music);

shared_ptr<CFadeProcess> fadeProc(new CFadeProcess(music, 10000, 100));
m_pProcessManager->Attach(fadeProc);
```

The fade process grabs a smart pointer reference to the sound it is modifying, and once the volume has been interpolated to the final value, the process kills itself. Note that the original sound is created with a zero volume, and the fade process brings it up to 100.

SOME RANDOM NOTES

In the last 50 pages or so, you've read about sound resources, audio buffers, audio systems, and sound processes. This is where most books would stop. Neither my editor nor my readers will find any surprise in me continuing on a bit about sound. Why? I haven't told you a thing about how to actually use sound in your game.

Data-Driven Sound Settings

Sometimes I think this book is equally good at showing you how not to code game technology as it is at showing you how to code correctly. The observant programmer would notice that all my sound examples in the previous pages all had hard-coded constants for things like volume, fade in times, or animation points.

From day one, most programmers learn that hard-coded constants are a bad thing, but they can become a complete nightmare in computer game programming. The reason that I use so many of them in this book is because they make the code easier to read and understand. Real computer games would load all of this data at runtime from a data file. If the data changes, you don't have to recompile. If the game can reload the data at runtime with a cheat key, you can test and tweak this kind of data and get instant feedback.

With this kind of data-driven solution, programmers don't even have to be in the building. This leaves programmers doing what they do best, programming game technology! A bit of volume data can also be tweaked more easily than the original sound file can be re-leveled, so your audio engineer doesn't have to be in the building either.

So who's left to set the level on new sound effects on a Saturday? It's so easy that even a producer could do it. For those of you outside the game industry, I could as well have said, "It's so easy, your boss could do it!"

BEST PRACTICE

RECORD ALL AUDIO AT FULL VOLUME

Every sound effect should be recorded at full volume, even if it is way too loud for the game. This gives the sound the highest degree of waveform accuracy before it is attenuated and mixed with the other sounds in the primary sound buffer.

Background Ambient Sounds and Music

Most games have a music track and an ambient noise track along with the incident sounds you hear throughout the game. These additional tracks are usually long because they'll most likely loop back to their beginning until there's some environmental reason to change them.

An example of an ambient noise track could be the sounds of a factory, crowd noises, traffic, or some other noise. Sounds like these have the effect of placing the player in the environment and give them the impression that there's a lot more going on than what they see. This technique was used brilliantly in *Thief: Deadly Shadows* in the city sections. You could clearly hear city dwellers, small animals, carts, and other such noise, and it made you feel you were in the middle of a medieval city. But, be warned—if the background ambient has recognizable elements, such as someone saying, "Good morning," players will recognize the loop quickly and get annoyed. Keep any ambient background close to "noise" instead of easily discernible sounds.

Music adds to this environment by communicating gut-level intensity. It helps inform the player and add a final polish to the entire experience. Perhaps my favorite example of music used in a game is the original *Halo*. Instead of only reacting to the current events in the game, the music segues just before a huge battle, telling the player he'd better reload his shotgun and wipe the sweat off his controller.

TALES FROM THE PIXEL MINES

LIVE MUSIC ROCKS—FROM PROFESSIONAL MUSICIANS

On the *Microsoft Casino* project, I thought it would be a great idea to record live music. It would be classy and add a unique feel to the game. I'd never produced live music for a game, so I was a little nervous about it. The music was composed by an Austin composer, Paul Baker, who also conducted the band. I got to play the part of the big-time producer guy behind the glass in the recording studio. I thought it was really cool until I heard the band run through the music the first time. It was horrible! I thought I'd be fired and wondered quickly how I could salvage this disaster. My problem was that I'd never seen how professional musicians work. They arrived that day having never seen the music before, and the first time they played it they were all sight-reading. After a break, they played it one more time, and it was nearly flawless. I thought I'd just heard a miracle, but that's just my own naiveté. There was one errant horn note, blurted a little off time, and they cleared everyone out of the room except for the one horn player. He said, "gimme two measures," and they ran the tape back. At exactly the right moment, he played the single note he screwed up, and it was mixed flawlessly into the recording. I was so impressed by the live performance that I'll never be afraid of doing it in other games.

The CPU budget for all this sound decompression is definitely a factor. The longish music and ambient noise tracks will certainly be streamed from a compressed source rather than loaded into memory in uncompressed PCM format. At the time of this writing, decompressing a single MP3 track chews about 25MHz from a single core Intel Pentium. So, it's not horrible, but you should keep track of this. Decompression performance will change much faster than these pages can report, so do some benchmarks on your own and set your budgets accordingly.

Speech

In-game character speech is a great design technique to immerse the player and add dimension to the AI characters. Games use character speech to communicate story, provide clues, and show alert levels in patrolling guards. Players expect a great script, smooth integration of the speech effects with the graphics, and most importantly, the ability to ignore it if they want to.

Random Barks

A *bark* is another way of saying "filler speech." It usually describes any bit of speech that is not part of a scripted sequence. Good examples of this are AI characters talking to themselves or reactions to game events like throwing a grenade around a corner.

Some of my favorite random barks came from the drunk guard in *Thief: Deadly Shadows*. It was perfect comic relief in what is normally a dark game with long stretches of tension. If you hid in a nearby shadow, you'd hear this inebriated and somewhat mentally challenged guard talk to himself for a really long time.

In the background, a piece of code selects a random speech file at random intervals. The code must keep track of the barks so it doesn't play the same thing three times in a row, and it should also make sure that the random barks don't overlap any scripted speech the AI character might have either.

Something that works well is a queue for each AI character regarding speech. Here a high-priority scripted bark will wipe out any random barks in the queue, and you can keep already barked elements in the queue to record which ones have played in recent history.

TALES FROM THE PIXEL MINES

TOO MUCH OF A GOOD THING IS TRUE

Back on *Microsoft Casino*, there was this "blue-haired old lady" character that was our first AI character installed in the game. She only had one random bark: "Have you even been to Hoover Dam?" she would say, waiting for her cards. We sent the build to Microsoft QA, and we waited patiently for the phone call, which came way too quickly for it to be news of acceptance. The lead QA on the phone told us that after just one hour of testing, no one in QA was "ever likely to ever visit the @%$#& Hoover Dam" and could we please remove the bark technology until more barks were recorded. The bark was so reviled, we had to remove it entirely from the game.

Game Fiction

Characters talking amongst themselves or straight to the player are an excellent way to give objectives or clues. If you do this, you must beware of a few gotchas. First, you shouldn't force the player to listen to the speech again if he's heard it before. Second, you should record a summary of the clue or objective in a form that can be referenced later—it's too easy to miss something in a speech-only clue. The third gotcha involves localization.

One game that comes to mind that solved the first gotcha in an interesting way was *Munch's Odyssey*, an Xbox launch title. Throughout the game, this funny mystic character appears and tells you exactly what you need to do to beat the level. If you've heard the spiel before, you can hit a button on the controller and your character, Abe or Munch, will interrupt and say something like, "I've heard all this before," and the mystic guy will bark, "Whatever..." and disappear. Very effective.

The second gotcha is usually solved with some kind of in-game notebook or objectives page. It's too easy to miss something in scripted speech, especially when it tends to be more colorful and therefore a little easier to miss the point entirely. Almost every mission-based game has this design conceit—it keeps the players on track and keeps them from getting lost.

The last gotcha has to do with language translation. What if you record your speech in English and want to sell your game in Japan? Clearly, the solution involves some kind of subtitle to go along with the scripted speech. Re-recording the audio can be prohibitively expensive if you don't have a AAA budget and massive worldwide distribution.

Lip Synching

Synching the speech files to in-game character animations is challenging, both from a technology and tools standpoint. This is one of those topics that could use an entire book, so let me at least convince you that the problem is a big one, and not one to be taken lightly or without experience.

It turns out that human speech has a relatively small number of unique sounds and sound combinations, perhaps only a few dozen. Since each sound is made with a particular position of the mouth and tongue, it follows that an artist can create these positions in a character ahead of time. While the speech is being played, a data stream is fed into the animation system that tells which phoneme to show on the character at each point in time. The animation system interpolates

CHEAP HACKS FOR LIP SYNCHING

There are ways of doing lip synching on the cheap, depending on your game. *Interstate 76* solved the lip synching problem by removing all the lips; none of their characters had mouths at all! Another clever solution is to have the characters animate to a particular phrase like "peas and carrots, peas and carrots." *Wing Commander II*, a game published by Origin Systems in the mid-1990s, had all its characters lip-synched to a single phrase: "Play more games like *Wing Commander II.*"

smoothly between each sound extreme, and you get the illusion that the character is actually talking.

Recording Speech

Most games will use at most a few hundred sound effects. This relatively small number of sound files is trivial to manage compared to speech files in some games. *Thief: Deadly Shadows* had somewhere around 10,000 lines of speech. You can't just throw these files into a single directory. You've got to be organized.

The first thing you need is a script—one for each character. As part of the script, the character should be described in detail, even to the point of including a rendering of the character's face. Voice actors use the character description to get "into character" and create a great performance.

The recording session will most likely have the voice actor read the entire script from top to bottom, perhaps repeating a line or phrase a few times to get it right. It's critical to keep accurate records about which one of the lines you intend to keep and which you'll throw away. A few days later, you could find it difficult to remember.

You'll record to DAT tape or some other high-fidelity media, and later split the session into individual, uncompressed files. Here's where your organization will come into key importance: you should have a database that links each file with exactly what is said. This will help foreign language translators record localized speech or create localized subtitles.

THE LAST DANCE

The one thing I hope you get from this chapter besides a bit of technology advice is that sound is a critically important part of your game. Most programmers and designers tend to wait until the very end of the production cycle before bringing in the sound engineers and composers. By that time, it's usually too late to create a cohesive sound design in your game, and the whole thing will be horribly rushed.

Get organized from the very beginning, and ask yourself whether each task in your game schedule needs an audio component. You'll be surprised how many objects need sound effects, how many levels need their own background ambient tracks, and how much speech you need to record.

Sound technology will also stress more of your core game components than any other system, including resource cache, streaming, memory, main loop, and more. Once your sound system is working flawlessly, you can feel confident about your lower-level systems. That's another good reason to get sound in your game as early as possible.

3D BASICS

In This Chapter

I want to tell you up front that this chapter won't teach you everything you need to know about 3D graphics—actually, far from it. Walk the aisle of any decent computer bookstore, and you'll see racks of books, devoted entirely to 3D graphics. I'm only including two 3D chapters in this book, so I can't compete with the classics on 3D graphics. What's lacking in volume, I'll try to make up in focus and content. My job in the next two chapters is to open the door to 3D graphics, especially in the way game programmers utilize 3D techniques within the Game Code Complete architecture. Once inside, I'll hand you a map of the place and send you on your way.

In this chapter, I'll focus on the essentials, which is a nice way of saying that I'm going to load you down with some math you'll need to know. This will set the foundation so that we can start manipulating objects and perform some of the fun stuff I have planned for later in this chapter and Chapter 14, "3D Scenes."

3D Graphics Pipeline

The word *pipeline* describes the process of getting a 3D scene up on a screen. It's a great word because it implies a beginning that accepts raw materials, a process that occurs along the way, and a conclusion from which pours the refined result. This is analogous to what happens inside 3D game engines. The raw materials at the beginning include collections of the following components:

- **Geometry:** Everything you see on the screen starts with descriptions of their shape. Each shape is broken down into triangles, which is a basic drawable element in 3D engines. Some renderers support points, lines, and even curved surfaces, but the triangle is by far the most common. Meshes are collections of different types of geometry.
- **Materials:** These elements describe appearance. You can imagine materials as paint or wallpaper that you apply to the geometry. Each material can describe colors, translucency, and how the material reflects light.
- **Textures:** These are images that can be applied to objects, just as you might have applied decals to plastic models.
- **Lights:** You must have light to see anything. Light can affect an entire scene or have a local effect that mimics a spotlight.
- **Camera:** Records the scene onto a render target, such as the display. It even describes what kind of lens is used, such as a wide or narrow angle lens. You can have multiple cameras to split the screen for a multiplayer game or render a different view to create a rearview mirror.
- **World:** A data structure that organizes the raw materials so that a minimum set of the above collections can be presented to the rendering hardware. These data structures also relate objects hierarchically to create complicated shapes, such as human figures.

Some of the processes applied to the raw materials include the following:

- **Transformations:** The same object can appear in the world in different orientations and locations. Objects are manipulated in 3D space via matrix multiplications.
- **Culling:** Visible objects are inserted into a draw list.
- **Lighting:** Each object in range of a light source is illuminated by calculating additional colors applied to each vertex.
- **Rasterization:** Polygons are drawn, sometimes in many passes, to handle additional effects such as lighting and shadows.

Graphics pipelines also come in two flavors: fixed function and programmable. The fixed-function pipeline sets rendering states and then uses those states to draw elements with those exact states. A programmable pipeline is much more flexible—it allows programmers detailed control over every pixel on the screen. Many systems, like the Nintendo Wii, still use a fixed-function pipeline. Modern graphics cards and consoles like the Xbox360 and the PS3 use a programmable pipeline. Knowing how to play with both is a good idea. Under DirectX, you can actually use both.

We'll start to see how all of these components and processes act together shortly. I'm going to take a quick shortcut through two math classes you probably slept though in high school or college. I know that because I slept through the same classes—trigonometry and linear algebra.

3D MATH 101

I'll try my best to make this topic interesting. I'll know I've succeeded if I get through writing it without losing consciousness. This stuff can make your eyes glaze over. Remember one thing: You must understand the math or you'll be hopelessly confused if you attempt any 3D programming. Sure, you'll be able to compile a DirectX sample program, tweak some parameters, and make some pretty pictures. Once you leave "Sampleland" and start making changes to your 3D code, however, you won't have a freaking clue why your screen is black and none of the pretty pictures show up. You'll attempt to fix the problem with random tweaks of various numbers in your code, mostly by adding and removing minus signs, and you'll end up with the same black screen and a mountain of frustration.

My advice is to start small. Make sure that you understand each component fully and then move to the next. Have patience, and you'll never tweak a negative sign in anger again.

3D CODE CAN LOOK CORRECT AND STILL BE WRONG

3D programming is easier to get wrong than right, and the difficult part is that a completely miscoded system can look and feel correct. There will be a point where things will begin to break down, but by that time you might have hundreds or thousands of lines of bogus code. If something is wrong, and you randomly apply a negative sign to something to fix it and don't understand why it fixed it, you should back up and review the math.

Coordinates and Coordinate Systems

In a 2D graphics system, you express pixel coordinates with two numbers: (x,y). These are screen coordinates to indicate that each integer number x and y corresponds to a row and column of pixels, respectively. Taken together as a pair, they describe the screen location of exactly one pixel. If you want to describe a 2D coordinate system fully, you need a little more data, such as where (0,0) is on the screen, whether the x coordinate describes rows or columns, and in which direction the coordinates grow—to the left or right. Those choices are made somewhat arbitrarily. There's nothing that says you couldn't create a 2D graphics engine that uses the lower right-hand corner of the screen as your (0,0) point—your origin. There's nothing that would keep you from describing the X-axis as vertical and Y as horizontal, and both coordinates grow positive toward the upper left-hand side of the screen.

Nothing would keep you from doing this, except perhaps the risk of industry-wide embarrassment. I said that these choices of coordinate system are somewhat arbitrary, but they do have a basis in tradition or programming convenience. Here's an example. Since the display memory is organized in row order, it makes sense to locate the origin at the top left-hand side of the screen. Traditional Cartesian mathematics sets the horizontal as the X-axis and the vertical as the Y-axis, which means that programmers can relate to the graphics coordinates with ease. It doesn't hurt that the original designers of text-display systems read text from left to right, top to bottom. If these were reversed, programmers would be constantly slapping their foreheads and saying, "Oh yeah, those idiots made the X-axis vertical!"

A 3D world requires a 3D coordinate system. Each coordinate is expressed as a triplet: (x,y,z). This describes a position in a three-dimensional universe. As you might expect, a location on any of the three axes is described with a floating-point number. The range that can be expressed in a 32-bit floating-point number in IEEE format is shown in Table 13.1.

Table 13.1 Precision of Floating-Point Numbers

Single Precision, 32 bit	Double Precision, 64 bit
$\pm\ 2^{-126}$ to $(2-2^{-23})\times 2^{127}$	$\pm\ 2^{-1022}$ to $(2-2^{-52})\times 2^{1023}$

The diameter of the known universe is on the order of 10^{26} meters. The smallest theoretical structures of the universe, *superstrings*, have an estimated length of 10^{-35} meters. You might believe that a 32-bit floating-point number is more than sufficient to create a 3D simulation of everything in our universe, but you'd be wrong. Even though the range is up to the task, the precision is not. Oddly enough, we may one day find out that the universe is best expressed in terms of 256-bit integers, which would give enough range and precision to represent a number from 0 to $\sim 10^{76}$, plenty to represent the known universe and ignoring irrational or transcendental numbers like p.

So where does that leave you and your 32-bit IEEE floating-point number with its decent range and lacking precision? The IEEE format stores an effective 24 bits of resolution in the mantissa. This gives you a range of 1.67×10^7. How much is that? As Table 13.2 indicates, you should set your smallest unit based on your game design. Most games can safely use the 100 micrometer (μm) basis since your sandbox can be as big as downtown San Francisco. The human eye can barely detect objects 100 μm across, but can't discern any detail.

Table 13.2 Units of Measurement

Smallest Unit	Physical Description of Smallest Representable Object (as a Textured Polygon)	Upper Range In Meters	Physical Description of Area in the Upper Range
100m	A group of redwood trees	1.67×10^9	Earth / Moon System
1m	A human being	1.67×10^7	North and South America
1cm	A coin	1.67×10^6	California
1mm	A flea	1.67×10^5	San Francisco Bay Area
100 μm	A grain of pollen	1.67×10^4	Downtown San Francisco

This is why most games set their basic unit of measurement as the meter, constrain the precision to 1mm, and set their maximum range to 100 kilometers. Most art packages like 3ds Max allow artists to set their basic unit of measurement. If you use such a package, you need to make sure they set it to the right value for your game.

Now that we've nailed the range and precision of the 3D coordinates, let's take a few moments to consider those arbitrary decisions about origin and axes directions. You've probably heard of 3D coordinate systems described as either left- or right-handed, and if you're like me, you tend to forget which is which, and the explanation with your fingers and thumbs was always just a little confusing because I couldn't remember how to hold my hands! Here's another way to visualize it. Imagine that you are standing at the origin of a classic 3D Cartesian coordinate system, and you are looking along the positive X-axis. The positive Y-axis points straight up. If the coordinate system is right-handed, the Z-axis will point to your right. A left-handed coordinate system will have a positive Z-axis pointed to the left.

Why is *handedness* important? For one thing, when you move objects around your world, you'll want to know where your positive Z-axis is and how it relates to the other two, or you might have things zig instead of zag. The tougher answer is that it affects the formulas for calculating important 3D equations, such as a cross product. I'm extremely glad I don't have to explain a 4D coordinate system. I don't think I have it in me.

CONVERTING HANDEDNESS

Since some art packages have different handedness than 3D rendering engines, you have to know how to convert the handedness of objects from one coordinate system to another. Here is how you do it:

1. Reverse the order of the vertices on each triangle. If a triangle started with vertices v0, v1, and v2, they need to be flipped to v2, v1, and v0.

2. Multiply each Z coordinate in the model by -1.

Here's an example:

Original:

V0 = (2.3, 5.6, 1.2)   V1 = (1.0, 2.0, 3.0)   V2 = (30.0, 20.0, 10.0)

Becomes:

V0 = (30.0, 20.0, -10.0)   V1 = (1.0, 2.0, -3.0)   V2 = (2.3, 5.6, -1.2)

Vector Mathematics

Vector and matrix math was always the sleepiest part of linear algebra for me. Rather than just show you the guts of the dot product or cross product for the umpteenth time, I'll also tell you what they do. That's more important anyway. I'll also show you some safety rules regarding matrix mathematics because they don't act like regular numbers.

Before we go any further, you need to know what a unit vector is because it is something you'll use all the time in 3D graphics programming. A unit vector is any vector that has a length of 1.0. If you have a vector of arbitrary length, you can create a unit vector that points in the same direction by dividing the vector by its length. This is also known as *normalizing* a vector:

```
Vec3 v(3, 4, 0);
float length = sqrt ( v.x * v.x + v.y * v.y + v.z * v.z);
Vec3 unit = v / length;
cout "Length=" << length << newline;
cout "Unit vector: X=" << v.x << " Y=" << v.y << " Z=" << v.z << newline;
```

The output generated would be:

```
Length=5.0
Unit vector: X=0.6 Y=0.8 Z=0.0
```

When we talk about dot-and-cross products, their inputs are almost always unit vectors (also called *normalized vectors*). The formulas certainly work on any arbitrary vector, but the results are relatively meaningless unless at least one of them is a unit vector. Take the same formulas and apply unit vectors to them, and you'll find some interesting results that you can use to calculate critical angles and directions in your 3D world.

A dot product of two vectors is a number, sometimes called a *scalar*. The cross product of two vectors is another vector. Remember these two important facts, and you'll never get one confused with the other again. Another way to say this is dot products calculate angles, and cross products calculate direction. The dot product is calculated with the following formula:

```
float dotProduct = ( v1.x * v2.x ) + ( v1.y * v2.y ) + (v1.z * v2.z);
```

Unit vectors never have any coordinate with an absolute value greater than 1.0. Given that, you'll notice that the results of plugging various numbers into the dot product formula have interesting effects. Assuming V1 and V2 are unit vectors:

- **V1 equals V2:** If you calculate the dot product of a vector with itself, the value of the dot product is always 1.0.

- **V1 is orthogonal to V2:** If the two vectors form a right angle to each other and they are the same length, the result of the dot product is always zero.
- **V1 points in the opposite direction to V2:** Two vectors of the same length pointing exactly away from each other have a dot product of -1.0.

If this relationship between vectors, right angles, and the range [-1.0, 1.0] is stirring some deep dark memory, you're correct. The dark memory is trigonometry, and the function you are remembering is the cosine. It turns out that you can use the dot product of two unit vectors to calculate the angle between two vectors. For two unit vectors a and b, the formula for calculating the angle between them is

$$\theta = \cos^{-1}\left(\frac{a \cdot b}{|a||b|}\right)$$

That is a complicated way of saying that if you divide the dot product of two vectors by their lengths multiplied together, you get the cosine of their angle. Take the arccosine of that number, and you have the angle! This is extremely useful in computer games, since you are always trying to figure out the angle between vectors.

Another way to visualize the dot product graphically is that *the dot product projects one vector onto the other, and calculates the length of that vector*. This dot product relationship is shown in Figure 13.1, where the dot product equals the length of the projection of vector A onto B. As it turns out, this length is exactly the same as the projection of vector B onto vector A. Weird, huh?

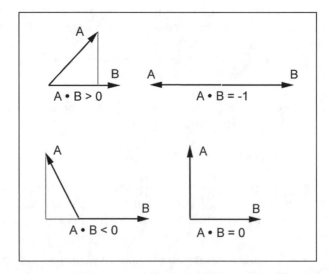

FIGURE 13.1 The dot product projects one vector onto another.

The dot product can be useful by itself, since it can determine whether the angle between two vectors is acute, a right angle, or obtuse. The classic application of the dot product in 3D graphics is determining whether a polygon is facing toward or away from the camera (see Figure 13.2).

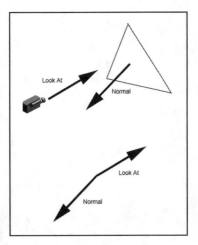

FIGURE 13.2 Dot products are used to see if a polygon is facing the camera—the dot product will be negative.

In Figure 13.2, the camera has a unit vector called the "look at" vector, and it points in the same direction as the camera. Each polygon has a normal vector that is orthogonal to the plane of the polygon. If the dot product between these two vectors is less than zero, the polygon is facing the camera and should be added to the draw list. In the case of Figure 13.2, the dot product for these two vectors is close to -1.0, so the polygon will be drawn.

If you want the actual angle represented by the dot product, you must perform an arccosine operation. If you remember those hazy trig classes at all, you'll know that the arccosine isn't defined everywhere, only between values [-1.0, 1.0]. That's lucky, because dot products from unit vectors have exactly the same range. So where's the problem? The arccosine will always return positive numbers.

The dot product is directionless, giving you the same result no matter which vector you send in first: A dot B is the same as B dot A. Still not convinced this is a problem? Let's assume that you are using the dot product to determine the angle between your current direction and the direction vector that points to something you are targeting.

In Figure 13.3, the white arrow is the current direction, and the gray arrows are oriented 45 degrees away about the Y-axis. Notice that one of the gray arrows is pointing straight to our teapot target, but the other one is pointing in a completely wrong direction. Yet, the dot products between the white direction vector and both gray vectors are the same because the angles are the same!

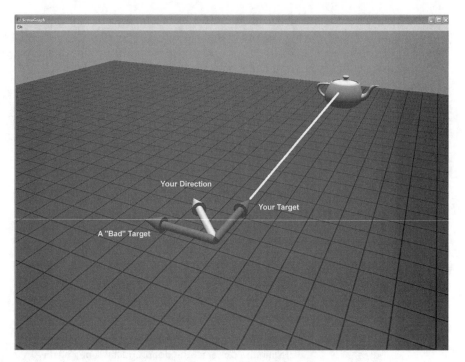

FIGURE 13.3 Dot products can't find targets.

Remember that the dot product measures angles and not direction. As you can see from the diagram, the dot product won't tell you which way to turn, only how much to turn. You need a *cross product*.

Graphically, the cross product returns a vector that is orthogonal to the plane formed by the two input vectors. The cross product vector should be normalized before you use it. Planes have two sides, and the resulting normal vector can only point in one direction. How does it know which way to point? It turns out that cross products are sensitive to the order of their input vectors. In other words, A cross B is not equal to B cross A. As you might expect, it is exactly negative. This is where the handedness of the coordinate system comes back into play. The cross product is always calculated with this formula:

```
cross.x = (A.y * B.z) - (B.y * A.z)
cross.y = (A.z * B.x) - (B.z * A.x)
cross.z = (A.x * B.y) - (B.x * A.y)
```

I'm going to borrow your right hand for a moment. Hold your right hand out in front of you, fingers together and totally flat. Make sure you are looking at your palm. Extend your thumb out, keeping your hand flat. Your thumb is vector

A and your forefinger is vector B. The result of the cross product, A cross B, is a vector pointing up out of your palm. If you did it backward, B cross A, the vector would be pointing away from you. This is the fundamental difference between left- and right-handed coordinate systems—determining which vectors get sent into the cross product in which order. It matters!

The classic use of the cross product is figuring out the normal vector of a polygon (see Figure 13.4). The normal vector is fundamental to calculating which polygons are facing the camera, and therefore, which polygons are drawn and which can be ignored. It is also good for calculating how much light reflects from the polygon back to the camera. By the way, if you take the cross product of two parallel vectors, the result will be a null vector—x, y, and z will all equal zero.

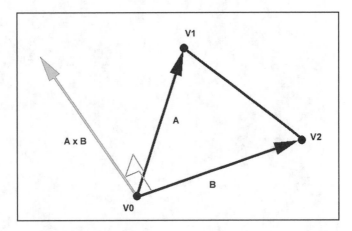

FIGURE 13.4 A cross product.

For any polygon that has three vertices, V0, V1, and V2, the normal vector is calculated using a cross product:

```
Vector A = V1 - V0;
Vector B = V2 - V0;
Vector Cross = CrossProduct(A, B);
```

In a right-handed coordinate system, the vertices are arranged in a counter-clockwise order because they are seen when looking at the drawn side of the polygon.

Another use is figuring the direction. Returning to our chase problem, we have a dot product that tells us that we need to steer either left or right, but we can't figure out which. It turns out that the cross product between the direction vectors contains information about which way to steer.

The cross product between the target vector and your direction vector points up, indicating you should steer right (see Figure 13.5). If the cross product pointed down, the target would have been off to your left. The target example is somewhat contrived because you don't actually need the cross product at all. It makes a good example because it's a useful experiment to visualize the usefulness of the cross product.

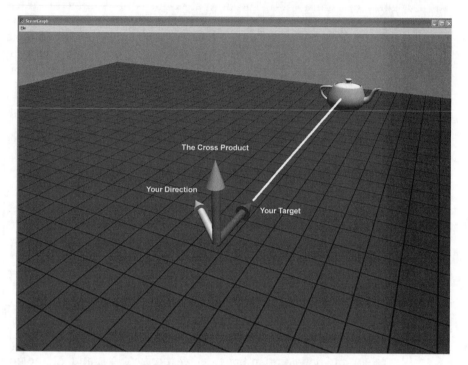

FIGURE 13.5 A cross product and a dot product together can find a target.

FIND TARGETS WITH JUST A DOT PRODUCT

Through a little trickery, you can do it solely with the dot product, as long as you choose the correct vectors. If you use a vector that points to your right instead of straight ahead, your dot product will yield a positive number if you need to steer right, a negative number if you need to steer left, and something close to zero if your target is right in front of you. Even better, if your steering parameters range from -1.0 to steer hard left and 1.0 to lock it all the way to the right, you can send this dot product straight into your steering code. Cool, huh?

C++ MATH CLASSES

Before we get into the guts of a scene graph and how it works, we'll need some simple math classes for handling 3D and 4D vectors, matrices, and quaternions. Most programmers will create a math library with ultra-efficient implementations of these and other useful tidbits. For this book, I'm using DirectX math functions and structures as a base. Here are the two reasons why I'm using this approach:

- The DirectX math functions are fairly well optimized for PC development, and are a fair place to start for console development.
- By creating some platform-agnostic math classes for use in the scene graph code, you can replace them with any C++ implementation you like. Personally I think the C++ versions are much easier to read, too. These classes are bare bones, really not much more than the very basics.

The classes you will use throughout the 3D code in this book include the following:

- `Vec3` & `Vec4`: Three- and four-dimensional vectors.
- `Quaternion`: A quaternion that describes orientation in 3D space.
- `Mat4x4`: A matrix that holds both orientation and translation.
- `Plane`: A flat surface that stretches to infinity; it has an "inside" and an "outside."
- `Frustum`: A shape like a pyramid with the point clipped off, usually used to describe the viewable area of a camera.

Vector Classes

You should already be very familiar with the vector structures used by DirectX—`D3DXVECTOR3` and `D3DXVECTOR4`. Here's a very simple C++ wrapper for both of those structures:

```
class Vec3 : public D3DXVECTOR3
{
public:
   inline float Length()
      { return D3DXVec3Length(this); }
   inline Vec3 *Normalize()
      { return static_cast<Vec3 *>(D3DXVec3Normalize(this, this)); }
   inline float Dot(const Vec3 &b)
      { return D3DXVec3Dot(this, &b); }
   inline Vec3 Cross(const Vec3 &b) const
   {
      Vec3 out;
      D3DXVec3Cross(&out, this, &b);
```

```
        return out;
    }
    Vec3(D3DXVECTOR3 &v3)
        { x = v3.x; y = v3.y; z = v3.z; }
    Vec3() : D3DXVECTOR3() { }
    Vec3(const float _x, const float _y, const float _z)
        { x=_x; y=_y; z=_z; }
    inline Vec3(const class Vec4 &v4)
        { x = v4.x; y = v4.y; z = v4.z; }
};

class Vec4 : public D3DXVECTOR4
{
public:
    inline float Length()
        { return D3DXVec4Length(this); }
    inline Vec4 *Normalize()
        { return static_cast<Vec4 *>(D3DXVec4Normalize(this, this)); }
    inline float Dot(const Vec4 &b)
        { return D3DXVec4Dot(this, &b); }
    // If you want the cross product, use Vec3::Cross

    Vec4(D3DXVECTOR4 &v4)
        { x = v4.x; y = v4.y; z = v4.z; w = v4.w; }
    Vec4() : D3DXVECTOR4() { }
    Vec4(const float _x, const float _y, const float _z, const float _w)
        { x=_x; y=_y; z=_z; w=_w; }
    Vec4(const Vec3 &v3)
        { x = v3.x; y = v3.y; z = v3.z; w = 1.0f; }
};

typedef std::list<Vec3> Vec3List;
typedef std::list<Vec4> Vec4List;
```

The Vec3 and Vec4 classes wrap the DirectX D3DXVECTOR3 and D3DXVECTOR4 structures. The usefulness of the Vec3 class is pretty obvious. As for Vec4, you need a four-dimensional vector to send in to a 4×4-transform matrix. If you remember your high school math, you can't multiply a 4×4 matrix and a three-dimensional vector. Only a four-dimensional vector will do.

The methods that are provided as a part of this class are

- Length: Finds the length of the vector.
- Normalize: Changes the vector to have the same direction, but a length of 1.0f.

- Dot: Computes the dot product of the vector.
- Cross: Computes the cross product of the vector (only Vec3 does this!).

Matrix Mathematics

A 3D world is filled with objects that move around. It would seem like an impossible task to set each vertex and surface normal of every polygon each time an object moves. There's a shortcut, it turns out, and it concerns matrices. Vertices and surface normals for objects in your 3D world are stored in object space. As the object moves and rotates, the only thing that changes is the object's transform matrix. The original vertices and normals remain exactly the same. The object's transform matrix holds information about its position in the world and its rotation about the X-, Y-, and Z-axis.

Multiple instances of an object need not duplicate the geometry data. Each object instance only needs a different transform matrix and a reference to the original geometry. As each object moves, the only things that change are the values of each transform matrix. A transform matrix for a 3D engine is represented by a 4×4 array of floating-point numbers. This is enough information to store both the rotation and position of an object. If you only want to store the rotation and not the position, a 3×3 array is just fine. This is one of the reasons you see both matrices represented in DirectX and other renderers. I'll use the 4×4 D3DXMA-TRIX in this chapter for all of the examples because I want to use one data structure for rotation and translation. The matrix elements are set in specific ways to perform translations and different rotations. For each kind of matrix, I'll show you how to set the elements yourself or how to call a DirectX function to initialize it.

A translation matrix moves vectors linearly. Assuming that you have a displacement vector T, which describes the translation along each axis, you'll initialize the translation matrix with the values shown below.

$$\begin{bmatrix} 1 & 0 & 0 & 0 \\ 0 & 1 & 0 & 0 \\ 0 & 0 & 1 & 0 \\ T.x & T.y & T.z & 1 \end{bmatrix}$$

Here's how to do the same thing in DirectX:

```
// Create a DirectX matrix that will translate vectors
// +3 units along X and -2 units along Z
D3DXVECTOR3 t(3,0,-2);
D3DXMATRIX transMatrix;
D3DXMatrixTranslation(&transMatrix, t.x,t.y,t.z);
```

Let's look at a quick example.

```
D3DXVECTOR4 original(1, 1, 1, 1);
D3DXVECTOR4 result;
D3DXVec4Transform(&result, &original, &transMatrix);
```

The transform creates a new vector with values (4, 1, -1, 1). The DirectX function `D3DXVec4Transform` multiplies the input vector with the transform matrix. The result is a transformed vector.

MAKE SURE YOU MATCH 4 × 4 MATRICES WITH A 4D VECTOR

Did you notice my underhanded use of the D3DXVECTOR4 structure without giving you a clue about its use? Matrix mathematics is very picky about the dimensions of vectors and matrices that you multiply. It turns out that you can only multiply matrices where the number of rows matches the number of columns. This is why a 4 × 4 matrix must be multiplied with a four-dimensional vector. Also, the last value of that 4D vector, w, should be set at 1.0, or you'll get odd results.

There are three kinds of rotation matrices, one for rotation about each axis. The most critical thing you must get through your math-addled brain is this: rotations always happen around the origin. "What in the hell does that mean," you ask? You'll understand it better after you see an example. First, you need to get your bearings. Figure 13.6 shows an image of a teapot sitting at the origin. The squares are one unit across. We are looking at the origin from (x=6, y=6, z=6). The Y-axis points up. The X-axis points off to the lower left, and the Z-axis points to the lower right.

If you look along the axis of rotation, an object will appear to rotate counter-clockwise if you rotate it in a positive angle. One way to remember this is by going back to the unit circle in trig, as shown in Figure 13.7.

A special note to my high school geometry teacher, Mrs. Connally: You were right all along—I did have use for the unit circle after all....

That means if you want to rotate the teapot so that the spout is pointing straight at us, you'll need to rotate it about the Y-axis. The Y-axis points up, so any rotation about that axis will make the teapot appear as if it is sitting on a potter's wheel. How do you calculate the angle? Go back to your unit circle to figure it out. The angle you want is 45 degrees, or p/4. We also know that the angle should be negative. Here's why: If we are looking along the Y-axis, you'd be underneath the teapot looking straight up. The teapot's spout needs to twist clockwise to achieve the desired result, so the angle is negative.

FIGURE 13.6 Displaying a teapot in 3D.

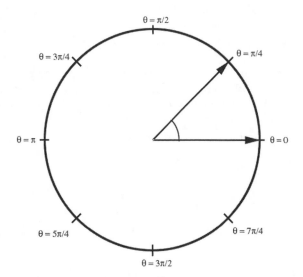

FIGURE 13.7 The ubiquitous unit circle.

A rotation matrix for the Y-axis looks like this:

$$\begin{bmatrix} \cos(\theta) & 0 & \sin(\theta) & 0 \\ 0 & 1 & 0 & 0 \\ -\sin(\theta) & 0 & \cos(\theta) & 0 \\ 0 & 0 & 0 & 1 \end{bmatrix}$$

Here's the code to create this matrix in DirectX:

```
float angle = -D3DX_PI / 4.0f;
D3DXMATRIX rotateY;
D3DXMatrixRotationY(&rotateY, angle);
```

Let's transform a vector with this matrix and see what happens. Since the teapot's spout is pointing down the X-axis, let's transform (x=1, y=0, z=0):

```
D3DXVECTOR4 original(1, 0, 0, 1);
D3DXVECTOR4 result(0,0,0,0);
D3DXVec4Transform(&result, &original, &rotateY);
```

Here's the result:

```
result    {...}           D3DXVECTOR4
    x     0.70710677      float
    y     0.00000000      float
    z     0.70710677      float
    w     1.0000000       float
```

Excellent, that's exactly what we want. The new vector is sitting on the X-Z plane and both coordinates are in the positive. If we take that same transform and apply it to every vertex of the teapot and then redraw it, we'll get the picture shown in Figure 13.8.

This matrix will create a rotation about the X-axis:

$$\begin{bmatrix} 1 & 0 & 0 & 0 \\ 0 & \cos(\theta) & -\sin(\theta) & 0 \\ 0 & \sin(\theta) & \cos(\theta) & 0 \\ 0 & 0 & 0 & 1 \end{bmatrix}$$

FIGURE 13.8 The teapotahedron, rotated -p/4 radians around the Y-axis.

This matrix will create a rotation about the Z-axis:

$$\begin{bmatrix} \cos(\theta) & -\sin(\theta) & 0 & 0 \\ \sin(\theta) & \cos(\theta) & 0 & 0 \\ 0 & 0 & 1 & 0 \\ 0 & 0 & 0 & 1 \end{bmatrix}$$

The DirectX code to create those two rotations is exactly what you'd expect:

```
float angle = -D3DX_PI / 4.0f;
D3DXMATRIX rotateX, rotateZ;
D3DXMatrixRotationX( rotateX, angle);
D3DXMatrixRotationZ( rotateZ, angle);
```

With simple translation and rotation transforms firmly in your brain, you need to learn how to put multiple transforms into action. It turns out that you can multiply, or concatenate, matrices. The result encodes every operation into a single matrix. I know, it seems like magic. There's one important part of this wizardry: The concatenated matrix is sensitive to the order in which you did the original multiplication. Let's look at two examples, starting with two matrices you should be able to visualize:

```
D3DXMATRIX trans, rotateY;
D3DXMatrixTranslation(&trans, 3,0,0);
D3DXMatrixRotationY(&rotateY, -D3DX_PI / 4.0f);
```

The translation matrix will push your teapot down the X-axis, or to the lower left in your current view. The negative angle rotation about the Y-axis you've already seen.

In DirectX, you can multiply two matrices with a function call. I'm not going to bother showing you the actual formula for two reasons. First, you can find it for yourself on the Internet, and second, no one codes this from scratch. There's always an optimized version of a matrix multiply in any 3D engine you find, including DirectX:

```
D3DXMATRIX result;
D3DXMatrixMultiply(&result, &trans, &rotateY);
```

Note the order. This should create a transform matrix that will push the teapot down the X-axis and rotate it about the Y-axis, in that order. Figure 13.9 shows the results.

FIGURE 13.9 Translate down X-axis first and then rotate about the origin.

If you expected the teapot to be sitting on the X-axis, you must remember that any rotation happens about the origin, not the center of the object! This is a common mistake, and I've spent much of my 3D debugging time getting my matrices in the right order.

TRANSLATIONS ALWAYS COME LAST

Always translate last. If you want to place an object in a 3D world, you always perform your rotations first and translations afterward.

Let's follow my own best practice and see if we get a better result. First, we reverse the order of the parameters into the matrix multiplication API:

```
D3DXMATRIX result;
D3DXMatrixMultiply(&result, &rotateY, &trans );
```

Figure 13.10 shows the result.

FIGURE 13.10 Rotate about the origin first and then translate down the X-axis.

I'll show you one more, just to make sure you get it. The goal of this transformation is two rotations and one translation. I want the teapot to sit four units down the Z-axis, on its side with the top toward us, and the spout straight up in the air. Here's the code:

```
D3DXMATRIX rotateX, rotateZ, trans;
D3DXMatrixRotationZ(&rotateZ, -D3DX_PI / 2.0f);
D3DXMatrixRotationX(&rotateX, -D3DX_PI );
D3DXMatrixTranslation(&trans, 0,0,4);
D3DXMATRIX temp, result;
D3DXMatrixMultiply(&temp, &rotateZ, &rotateX);
D3DXMatrixMultiply(&result, &temp, &trans);
```

The first rotation about the Z-axis points our teapot's spout down the negative Y-axis, and the second rotation twists the whole thing around the X-axis to get the spout pointing straight up. The final translation moves it to its resting spot on the Z-axis (see Figure 13.11).

FIGURE 13.11 Rotate the teapot about the Z-axis, then the X-axis, and then translate down the Z-axis.

The Mat4x4 Transform Matrix Class

It can be convenient to wrap DirectX's D3DXMATRIX structure into a C++ class:

```cpp
class Mat4x4 : public D3DXMATRIX
{
public:
    // Modifiers
    inline void SetPosition(Vec3 const &pos)
    {
        m[3][0] = pos.x;
        m[3][1] = pos.y;
        m[3][2] = pos.z;
        m[3][3] = 1.0f;
    }

    inline void SetPosition(Vec4 const &pos)
    {
        m[3][0] = pos.x;
        m[3][1] = pos.y;
        m[3][2] = pos.z;
        m[3][3] = pos.w;
    }

    // Accessors and Calculation Methods
    inline Vec3 GetPosition() const
    {
        return Vec3(m[3][0], m[3][1], m[3][2]);
    }

    inline Vec4 Xform(Vec4 &v) const
    {
        Vec4 temp;
        D3DXVec4Transform(&temp, &v, this);
        return temp;
    }

    inline Vec3 Xform(Vec3 &v) const
    {
        Vec4 temp(v), out;
        D3DXVec4Transform(&out, &temp, this);
        return Vec3(out.x, out.y, out.z);
    }

    inline Mat4x4 Inverse() const
    {
```

```
         Mat4x4 out;
         D3DXMatrixInverse(&out, NULL, this);
         return out;
    }

    // Initialization methods
    inline void BuildTranslation(const Vec3 &pos)
    {
        *this = Mat4x4::g_Identity;
        m[3][0] = pos.x;      m[3][1] = pos.y;      m[3][2] = pos.z;
    }
    inline void BuildTranslation(const float x, const float y, const float z )
    {
        *this = Mat4x4::g_Identity;
        m[3][0] = x; m[3][1] = y;      m[3][2] = z;
    }
    inline void BuildRotationX(const float radians)
        { D3DXMatrixRotationX(this, radians); }
    inline void BuildRotationY(const float radians)
        { D3DXMatrixRotationY(this, radians); }
    inline void BuildRotationZ(const float radians)
        { D3DXMatrixRotationZ(this, radians); }
    inline void BuildYawPitchRoll(
        const float yawRadians, const float pitchRadians,
        const float rollRadians)
        { D3DXMatrixRotationYawPitchRoll(
            this, yawRadians, pitchRadians, rollRadians); }
    inline void BuildRotationQuat(const Quaternion &q)
        { D3DXMatrixRotationQuaternion(this, &q); }

    Mat4x4(D3DXMATRIX &mat) {  memcpy(&m, &mat.m, sizeof(mat.m)); };
    Mat4x4() : D3DXMATRIX() { }

    static Mat4x4 g_Identity;
};

Mat4x4 Mat4x4::g_Identity(D3DXMATRIX(1,0,0,0,0,1,0,0,0,0,1,0,0,0,0,1));

inline Mat4x4 operator * (const Mat4x4 &a, const Mat4x4 &b)
{
    Mat4x4 out;
    D3DXMatrixMultiply(&out, &a, &b);
    return out;
}
```

There are three sections: the modifiers, the accessors and transforms, and finally the initializers. The modifiers simply set position; if you want to set rotations, there's another way I'll show you in a moment. The accessor `GetPosition()` returns the position component of the 4×4 matrix. The `Xform()` methods transform a `Vec3` or `Vec4` object into the space and position of the matrix. Don't worry yet because I'll show you an example of how to use this in a moment.

The initializer methods, those starting with "Build," take various parameters you might have on hand to build a rotation or transform matrix. If you want one that encodes both rotation and transformation, just build two of them and multiply them. Multiplying matrices is the same thing as *concatenating* them.

Here's a quick example in C++ that does the following things:

- Builds two matrices, one for rotation and one for translation.
- Concatenates these matrices in one `Mat4x4` to encode both movements. Remember that rotation always comes first and then translation.
- Determines which direction in the 3D world is considered "forward" by the new orientation and position. This direction is sometimes referred to as a *frame* or *reference*.

```
Mat4x4 rot;
rot.BuildYawPitchRoll(D3DX_PI / 2.0f, -D3DX_PI / 4.0f, 0);

Mat4x4 trans;
trans.BuildTranslation(1.0f, 2.0f, 3.0f);

// don't mess up the order! Multiplying Mat4x4s isn't like ordinary numbers.
Mat4x4 result = rotOnly * trans;
Vec4 fwd(0.0f, 0.0f, 1.0f);    // forward is defined as positive Z
Vec4 fwdWorld = toWorld.Xform(fwd);
```

There you have it. The `fwdWorld` vector points in the "forward" direction of the transform matrix. This is important because of two reasons. First, all of the code in this chapter will continue using these math classes, and this is exactly how you'd tell a missile what direction to move if you fired it from an object that was using the concatenated matrix.

I hope you've followed these bits about rotating things around an axis because it's a critical concept you need to understand before we talk about *quaternions*. If you think you might be hazy on the whole rotation thing, play with a Direct3D sample for a while, and you'll get it.

Quaternion Mathematics

Orientation can be expressed as three angles: yaw, pitch, and roll. In our teapot example, yaw would be around the Y-axis, pitch would be around the Z-axis, and roll would be around the X-axis. By the way, this happens to be called the Euler representation, or Euler angles (you pronounce Euler like "oiler"). This method has a critical weakness. Imagine that you want to interpolate smoothly between two orientations. This would make sense if you had an object like an automated cannon that slowly tracked moving objects. It would know its current orientation and the target orientation, but getting from one to the other might be problematic with Euler angles.

There is a special mathematical construct known as a *quaternion*, and almost every 3D engine supports its use. A quaternion is a fourth-dimensional vector, and it can be visualized as a rotation about an arbitrary axis. Let's look at an example:

```
D3DXQUATERNION q;
D3DXQuaternionIdentity(&q);
D3DXVECTOR3 axis(0,1,0);
float angle = -D3DX_PI / 4.0;
D3DXQuaternionRotationAxis(&q, &axis, angle);
D3DXMATRIX result;
D3DXMatrixRotationQuaternion(&result, &q);
```

This code has exactly the same effect on our teapot as the first rotation example. The teapot rotates around the Y-axis -p/4 degrees. Notice that I'm not setting the values of the quaternion directly, I'm using a DirectX API. I do this because the actual values of the quaternion are not intuitive at all. Take a look at the resulting values from our simple twist around the Y-axis:

```
q     {...}      D3DXQUATERNION
    x     0.00000000    float
    y    -0.38268343    float
    z     0.00000000    float
    w     0.92387950    float
```

Not exactly the easiest thing to read, is it?

The quaternion is sent into another DirectX function to create a transformation matrix. This is done because vectors can't be transformed directly with quaternions—you still have to use a transform matrix.

If you think this seems like a whole lot of work with little gain, let's look at the interpolation problem. Let's assume that I want the teapot to turn so that the spout is pointing down the Z-axis, which would mean a rotation about the Y-axis with an angle of -p/2 degrees. Let's also assume that I want to know what the transformation matrix is at two-thirds of the way through the turn, as shown in Figure 13.12.

FIGURE 13.12 Our teapot two-thirds of the way through a rotation—using quaternions.

Here's the code:

```
D3DXQUATERNION start, middle, end;
D3DXQuaternionIdentity(&start);
D3DXQuaternionIdentity(&middle);
D3DXQuaternionIdentity(&end);

D3DXVECTOR3 axis(0,1,0);
float angle = -D3DX_PI / 2.0;
D3DXQuaternionRotationAxis(&start, &axis, 0);
D3DXQuaternionRotationAxis(&end, &axis, angle);

D3DXQuaternionSlerp(&middle, &end, &start, 0.66f);

D3DXMATRIX result;
D3DXMatrixRotationQuaternion(&result, &middle);
```

The two boundary quaternions, start and end, are initialized in the same way as you saw earlier. The target orientation quaternion, middle, is calculated with the DirectX method D3DXQuaternionSlerp. This creates a quaternion 66 percent of the way between our start and end quaternions.

I might not quite have convinced you yet, but only because I used a trivial rotation that was easy to display. Anyone can interpolate a rotation around a single axis. Since quaternions can represent a rotation about a completely arbitrary axis, like (x=3.5, y=-2.1, z=0.04), and they can be much more useful than Euler angles.

TALES FROM THE PIXEL MINES

COMPRESSING QUATERNIONS? DON'T BOTHER!

When I was on *Thief: Deadly Shadows*, I was sharing an office with a friend of mine who was tasked with the job of compressing streams of quaternions. He was trying to save a few precious megabytes on our animations for the main character. His first few attempts were close, but some of the animations were completely wacko. The character's legs would lift up past his ears in a manner only suitable for a circus performer. The problem was a loss in precision in the quaternion stream, and when we thought about it, and truly understood what a normalized quaternion was, it made perfect sense. A normalized quaternion is a fourth-dimensional vector whose origin sits at (0,0,0,0) and whose endpoint always sits on the surface of a fourth-dimensional hypersphere. Since a well-formed unit quaternion has a length of 1.0f, any loss of accuracy because of compression will trash the unit length and ruin the precision of the quaternion. So what did we do? We used Euler angles. They can lose precision like crazy and still work just fine. Sometimes, the old school solution is what you need.

We've just exposed the first step in getting objects to your screen. All of the matrix concatenation, quaternions, and translations you just learned were used to place a single object in a 3D world with an orientation you wanted and the exact position you desired. This step is called *transforming object space into world space*. Object space is totally untransformed. The vertices exist in exactly the same spots the artist or the programmer placed them. The transform that placed the teapot exactly where you wanted it placed transformed the object space to world space, and is generally called a *world transform*.

In DirectX, you set the current world transform with this line of code:

```
pD3DDevice->SetTransform( D3DTS_WORLD,  &result );
```

Any untransformed polygons sent into the renderer will use this transform. Your teapot will be exactly where you want it. I say untransformed polygons because it is possible to transform polygons yourself and have the renderer do its magic with polygons in screen space. We'll learn more about that in a moment.

The Quaternion Class

The D3DXQUATERNION structure can be wrapped in a useful C++ wrapper class:

```
class Quaternion : public D3DXQUATERNION
{
public:
   // Modifiers
   void Normalize() { D3DXQuaternionNormalize(this, this); };
   void Slerp(const Quaternion &begin, const Quaternion &end, float cooef)
   {
    // performs spherical linear interpolation between begin & end
    // NOTE: set cooef between 0.0f-1.0f
    D3DXQuaternionSlerp(this, &begin, &end, cooef);
   }

   // Accessors
   void GetAxisAngle(Vec3 &axis, float &angle) const
   {
      D3DXQuaternionToAxisAngle(this, &axis, &angle);
   }

   // Initializers
   void BuildRotYawPitchRoll(
             const float yawRadians,
             const float pitchRadians,
             const float rollRadians)
   {
      D3DXQuaternionRotationYawPitchRoll(
         this, yawRadians, pitchRadians, rollRadians);
   }

   void BuildAxisAngle(const Vec3 &axis, const float radians)
   {
      D3DXQuaternionRotationAxis(this, &axis, radians);
   }

   void Build(const class Mat4x4 &mat)
   {
      D3DXQuaternionRotationMatrix(this, &mat);
   }
```

```
    Quaternion(D3DXQUATERNION &q) : D3DXQUATERNION(q) { }
    Quaternion() : D3DXQUATERNION() { }

    static Quaternion g_Identity;
};

inline Quaternion operator * (const Quaternion &a, const Quaternion &b)
{
    // for rotations, this is exactly like concatenating
    // matrices - the new quat represents rot A followed by rot B.
    Quaternion out;
    D3DXQuaternionMultiply(&out, &a, &b);
    return out;
}

Quaternion Quaternion::g_Identity(D3DXQUATERNION(0,0,0,1));
```

The quaternion is useful for orienting objects in a three-dimensional space. The `Quaternion` class just presented gives you the three most used methods for initializing it: from yaw-pitch-roll angles, an axis and rotation around that axis, and a 4×4 matrix. The class also has an operator * to multiply two quaternions, which performs a similar mathematical operation as concatenating matrices. The modifiers let you normalize a quaternion and perform a spherical linear interpolation on them. You saw the interpolation in the previous section when I showed you how to orient the teapot in between two different rotations. `Slerp()` does the same thing.

The identity quaternion is also provided as a global static so you can get to it quickly, especially for initializing a quaternion. This is something I like to do instead of forcing a default initialization all the time. You can use it if you want, and start with the identity, or you can use one of the builder methods.

View Transformation

If you are going to render the scene, you need to have a camera. That camera must have an orientation and a position just like any other object in the world. Similar to any other object, the camera needs a transform matrix that converts world space vertices to camera space.

Calculating the transform matrix for a camera can be tricky. In many cases, you want the camera to look at something, like a teapot. If you have a desired camera position and a target to look at, you don't quite have enough information to place the camera. The missing data is a definition of the *up* direction for your world. This last bit of data gives the camera a hint about how to orient itself. The view matrix for our previous teapot experiment used a DirectX function, `D3DXMatrixLookAtLH`:

```
D3DXMATRIX matView;
D3DXVECTOR3 vFromPt   = D3DXVECTOR3( 6.0f, 6.0f, 6.0f );
D3DXVECTOR3 vLookatPt = D3DXVECTOR3( 0.0f, 0.0f, 0.0f );
D3DXVECTOR3 vUpVec    = D3DXVECTOR3( 0.0f, 1.0f, 0.0f );
D3DXMatrixLookAtLH( &matView, &vFromPt, &vLookatPt, &vUpVec );
m_pd3dDevice->SetTransform( D3DTS_VIEW, &matView );
```

By the way, the LH at the end of the DirectX function's name is a hint that this function assumes a left-handed coordinate system. There is a right-handed version of this, and most other matrix functions, as well.

The vFromPt is out along the positive values of X, Y, and Z, and the vLookatPt point is right back at the origin. The last parameter defines the up direction. If you think about a camera as having an orientation constraint similar to a camera boom like you see on ESPN, it can move anywhere, pan around to see its surroundings, and pitch up or down. It doesn't tilt, at least not normally. This is important, because if tilting were allowed in constructing a valid view transform, there could be many different orientations that would satisfy your input data.

STRAIGHT UP AND STRAIGHT DOWN AREN'T SUPPORTED!

This system isn't completely perfect because there are two degenerate orientations. Given the definition of up as (x=0, y=1, z=0) in world space, the two places you can't easily look are straight up and straight down. You can construct the view transform yourself quite easily, but don't expect the look-at function to do it for you.

Remember that the camera's view transform is a matrix, just like any other. You don't have to use the look-at function to calculate it, but it tends to be the most effective camera positioning function there is.

Projection Transformation

So far, we've taken vertices from object space and transformed them into world space, and taken vertices from world space and transformed them into camera space. Now we need to take all those 3D vertices sitting in camera space and figure out where they belong on your computer screen and which objects sit in front of other objects.

Imagine sitting in front of a computer screen and seeing four lines coming from your eyeball and intersecting with the corners of the screen. For the sake of simplicity, I'll assume you have only one eyeball in the center of your head. These lines continue into the 3D world of your favorite game. You have a pyramid shape with the point at your eyeball and its base somewhere out in infinity somewhere. Clip the pointy end of the pyramid with the plane of your computer screen and form a base of your pyramid at some arbitrary place in the distance. This odd clipped pyramid shape is called the viewing *frustum*. The shape is actually a cuboid, since it is topologically equivalent to a cube, although pushed out of shape.

Every object inside this shape, the viewing frustum, will be drawn on your screen. The projection transformation takes the camera space (x,y,z) of every vertex and transforms it into a new vector that holds the screen pixel (x,y) location and a measure of the vertices' distance into the scene.

Here's the code to create the viewing frustum of the teapot experiments:

```
D3DXMATRIX matProj;
FLOAT fAspect = ((FLOAT)m_d3dsdBackBuffer.Width) / m_d3dsdBackBuffer.Height;
D3DXMatrixPerspectiveFovLH( &matProj, D3DX_PI/4, fAspect, 1.0f, 100.0f );
m_pd3dDevice->SetTransform( D3DTS_PROJECTION, &matProj );
```

The DirectX function that helps you calculate a projection matrix—something you don't want to do by yourself—accepts four parameters after the address of the matrix:

- **Field of view:** Expressed in radians, this is the width of the view angle. p/4 is a pretty standard angle. Wider angles such as 3p/4 make for some weird results. Try it and see what happens.
- **Aspect ratio:** This is the aspect ratio of your screen. If this ratio were 1.0, the projection transform would assume you had a square screen. A 640 × 480 screen has a 1.333 aspect ratio.
- **Near clipping plane:** This is the distance between your eye and the near view plane. Any object closer will get clipped. The units are usually meters, but feel free to set them to whatever standard makes sense for your game.
- **Far clipping plane:** The distance between your eye and the far clipping plane. Anything farther away will be clipped.

SET FAR CLIPPING PLANE DISTANCE TO SOMETHING FAR, BUT NOT TOO FAR

Don't set your far clipping plane to some arbitrarily large number in the hopes that nothing in your huge 3D world will get clipped. The trade-off is that the huge distance between your near and far clipping plane will create sorting problems in objects very close or very far from the camera—depending on your renderer. These weird sorting problems manifest themselves as if two polygons were run through a paper shredder, since the individual pixels on two coincident polygons will sort incorrectly. This problem is caused by numerical inaccuracy, and the polygons will sort into exactly the depth in 3D space. If you see this problem, first check the art to make sure the artists actually placed the polygons correctly and then check your far clipping plane distance. This problem is sometimes called "Z fighting."

Also, don't set your near clipping plane to zero, with the hope that you'll be able to see things very close to the camera. There's a relationship between the near clipping plane and the field of view. If you arbitrarily move the near clipping plane closer to the camera without changing the field of view, weird things begin to happen. My suggestion is to write a little code and see for yourself.

ENOUGH MATH—PLEASE STOP

I'm done torturing you with linear algebra, but I'm not quite done with geometry. Hang in there because you'll soon find out some interesting things about triangles.

Triangles

Did you know that everything from teapots to cars to volleyball-playing beach bunnies can be made out of triangles? We all know that a geometric triangle is made up of three points. In a 3D world, a triangle is composed of three vertices. A vertex holds all of the information the renderer will use to draw the triangle, and as you might expect, there can be a lot more than its location in a 3D space.

Different renderers will support different kinds of triangles, and therefore different kinds of vertices that create those triangles. Once you get your feet wet with one rendering technology, such as DirectX 9, you'll quickly find analogs in any other rendering technology, such as OpenGL. Since I've already sold my soul to Bill Gates, I'll show you how you create vertices in DirectX 9. A DirectX 9 vertex is a structure you define yourself. When you send your vertex data to the renderer, you send in a set of flags that informs it about the contents of the vertex data.

DIRECTX VERTEX STRUCTURES HAVE SPECIFIC ORDER

You may define the structure yourself, but DirectX 9 expects the data in the structure to exist in a particular order. For example, the vertex position always comes before the normal, which always comes before texture coordinates. Search for "Vertex Formats" in the DirectX SDK to see this order. All hell will break loose if you don't.

First, you should understand the concepts of a *transformed vertex* versus an *untransformed vertex*. A transformed vertex is defined directly in screen space. It doesn't need the transformations we discussed in the last section—object to world, world to camera, and camera to screen. You would use this kind of vertex to build triangles that create user interface components, since they don't need to exist in anything else but screen space.

SCREEN SPACE CAN BE MADDENING

Don't think that you can easily get away with defining triangles in screen space that "look" like they exist in world space. On the first *Microsoft Casino* project, we defined our card animations in screen space. Every corner of every card was painstakingly recorded and entered into the card animation code. These coordinates looked fairly good, but the second we needed to tweak the camera angle, all the coordinates had to be recomputed, rerecorded, and entered into the code by hand. It seemed like a good idea at the time, but we finally ditched this approach in favor of real cards animating through world space.

An untransformed vertex exists in object space, like the triangles that make up our teapot. Before the triangles are drawn, they'll be multiplied with the concatenated matrix that represents the transformations that will change a location in object space to projected screen space. Here's how you define a DirectX 9 vertex structure for a transformed vertex and an untransformed vertex:

```
struct TRANSFORMED_VERTEX
{
    D3DXVECTOR3 position;   // The screen x, y, z - x,y are pixel coordinates
    float rhw;              // always 1.0, the reciprocal of homogeneous w
};
#define D3DFVF_TRANSFORMED_VERTEX (D3DFVF_XYZRHW)

struct UNTRANSFORMED_VERTEX
{
    D3DXVECTOR3 position;   // The position in 3D space
};
#define D3DFVF_UNTRANSFORMED_VERTEX (D3DFVF_XYZ)
```

The #defines below the vertex definitions are the flags that you send into renderer calls that inform the renderer how to treat the vertex data. A renderer needs to know more than the location of a vertex in 3D space or screen space. It needs to know what it looks like. There are a few categories of this appearance information, but the first one on your list is lighting and color.

Lighting, Normals, and Color

In DirectX 9 and many other rendering technologies, you can assign colors to vertices yourself, or you can instruct the renderer to calculate those colors by looking at vertex data and the lights that illuminate the vertex. You can even do both. Everyone has seen games that show subtle light pools shining on walls and floors—a nice and efficient effect but completely static and unmoving. Other illumination is calculated in real time, such as when your character shines a flashlight around a scene. Multiple lights can affect individual vertices, each light adding a color component to the vertex color calculation.

Two flavors of dynamic lighting effects are *diffuse* and *specular* lighting. The DirectX fixed function pipeline can calculate these values for you if you want to send unlit vertices to the renderer, but you can also set the diffuse and specular colors directly. Almost all 3D cards have hardware acceleration for lighting calculations. DirectX makes use of this hardware automatically. To do this, you need to know about *normal* vectors, which are added to the vertex definition to enable lighting calculations.

When light hits an object, the color of light becomes a component of the object's appearance. Perform a little experiment to see this in action. Take a playing card, like the ace of spades, and place it flat on a table lit by a ceiling lamp. The card takes on a color component that reflects the color of that lamp. If your lamp is a fluorescent light, the card will appear white with a slight greenish tint. If your lamp is incandescent, the card will take on a slightly yellowish color.

If you take the card in your hand and slowly turn it over, the brightness and color of the card changes. As the card approaches an edge-on orientation to the lamp, the effects of the lighting diminish to their minimum. The light has its maximum effect when the card is flat on the table, and its minimum effect when the card is edged-on to the light. This happens because when light hits a surface at a low angle it spreads out and has to cover a larger area with the same number of photons. This gives you a dimming effect.

Diffuse lighting attempts to simulate this effect. With the card sitting flat on the table again, take a pencil and put the eraser end in the middle of the card and point the tip of the pencil straight up in the air toward your ceiling lamp. You've just created a normal vector. Turn the card as before, but hold the pencil and turn it as well, as if it were glued to the card. Notice that the light has a maximum effect when the angle between the pencil and the light is 180 degrees and minimum effect when the angle between the light and the pencil is 90 degrees, and no effect when the card faces away from the light.

Each vertex gets its own normal vector. This might seem like a waste of memory, but consider this: If each vertex has its own normal, you can change the direction of the normal vectors to "fool" the lighting system. You can make the 3D object take on a smoother shading effect. This is a common technique to blend the edges of coincident triangles. The illusion you create allows artists to create 3D models with fewer polygons.

The normals on the teapot model are calculated to create the illusion of a smooth shape, as shown in Figure 13.13.

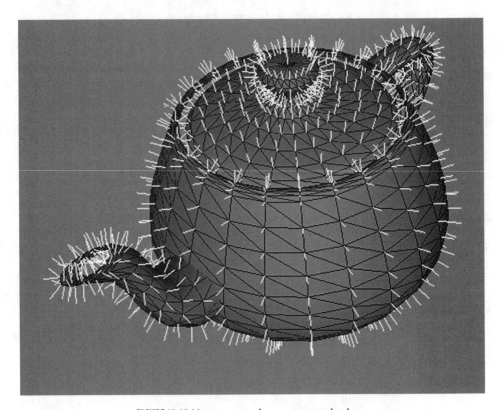

FIGURE 13.13 Vertex normals on a teapotahedron.

Now that you know what a normal vector is, you need to know how to calculate one. If you want to find the normal vector for a triangle, you'll need to use a cross product as shown here:

```
Vec3 triangle[3];
triangle[0] = Vec3(0,0,0);
triangle[1] = Vec3(5,0,0);
triangle[2] = Vec3(5,5,0);

Vec3 edge1 = triangle[1]-triangle[0];
Vec3 edge2 = triangle[2]-triangle[0];

Vec3 normal = edge1.Cross(edge2);
normal.Normalize();
```

Our polygon is defined with three positions in 3D space. These positions are used to construct two edge vectors, both pointing away from the same vertex. The two edges are sent into the cross product function, which returns a vector that is pointing in the right direction, but the wrong size. All normal vectors must be exactly one unit in length to be useful in other calculations, such as the dot product. The D3DXVec3Normalize function calculates the unit vector by dividing the temp vector by its length. The result is a normal vector you can apply to a vertex.

If you take a closer look at the teapot figure, you'll notice that the normal vectors are really the normals of multiple triangles, not just a single triangle. You calculate this by averaging the normals of each triangle that shares your vertex. Calculate the average of multiple vectors by adding them together and dividing by the number of vectors, exactly as you would calculate the average of any other number.

CALCULATE YOUR NORMALS AHEAD OF TIME

Calculating a normal is a somewhat expensive operation. Each triangle will require two subtractions, a cross product, a square root, and three divisions. If you create 3D meshes at runtime, try to calculate your normals once, store them in object space, and use transforms to reorient them.

Specular lighting is calculated slightly differently. It adds shininess to an object by simulating the reflection of the light on the object. The light calculation takes the angle of the camera into account along with the normal vector of the polygon and the light direction.

You might be wondering why I didn't mention ambient lighting—a color value that is universally applied to every vertex in the scene. This has the effect of making an object glow like a light bulb, and it isn't very realistic. Ambient lighting values are a necessary evil in today's 3D games because they simulate low-light levels on the back or underside of objects due to light reflecting all about the scene. In the next few years, I expect this light hack to be discarded completely in favor of the latest work with pixel shaders and environment-based lighting effects. I can't wait!

Here are the DirectX 9 vertex definitions for lit and unlit vertices:

```
struct UNTRANSFORMED_LIT_VERTEX
{
   D3DXVECTOR3 position;   // The position in 3D space
   D3DCOLOR    diffuse;    // The diffuse color
   D3DCOLOR    specular;   // The specular color
};
```

```
#define D3DFVF_UNTRANS_LIT_VERTEX (D3DFVF_XYZ | D3DFVF_DIFFUSE |
                                  D3DFVF_SPECULAR)

struct UNTRANSFORMED_UNLIT_VERTEX
{
    D3DXVECTOR3 position;   // The position in 3D space
    D3DXVECTOR3 normal;     // The normal vector (must be 1.0 units in length)
    D3DCOLOR    diffuse;    // The diffuse color
    D3DCOLOR    specular;   // The specular color
};
#define FVF_UNTRANS_UNLIT_VERT    \
    (D3DFVF_XYZ | D3DFVF_NORMAL | D3DFVF_DIFFUSE | D3DFVF_SPECULAR)
```

Notice that both vertex definitions were of the untransformed variety, but there's nothing keeping you from making the transformed versions of these things. It's entirely up to you and what you need for your game. Remember that the transformed versions will bypass the transformation and lighting pipeline entirely. The transformation and lighting pipeline are inseparable.

Note also that the unlit vertex still had definitions for diffuse and specular color information. This is kind of like having the best of both worlds. You can set specific diffuse and specular lighting on each vertex for static lights and the renderer will add any dynamic lights if they affect the vertex.

Textured Vertices

A texture is a piece of two-dimensional art that is applied to a model. Each vertex gets a texture coordinate. Texture coordinates are conventionally defined as (U,V) coordinates, where U is the horizontal component and V is the vertical component. Classically, these coordinates are described as floating-point numbers where (0.0f,0.0f) signifies the top left of the texture and grows to the left and down. The coordinate (0.5f, 0.5f) would signify the exact center of the texture. Each vertex gets a texture coordinate for every texture. DirectX 9 supports up to eight textures on a single vertex.

Here's an example of a vertex with a texture coordinate:

```
// A structure for our custom vertex type. We added texture coordinates
struct COLORED_TEXTURED_VERTEX
{
    D3DXVECTOR3 position;   // The position
    D3DCOLOR  color;        // The color
    FLOAT  tu, tv;          // The texture coordinates
};
```

```
// Our custom FVF, which describes our custom vertex structure
#define D3DFVF_COLORED_TEXTURED_VERTEX \
   (D3DFVF_XYZ | D3DFVF_DIFFUSE | D3DFVF_TEX1)
```

This vertex happens to include a diffuse color component as well, and you should also be able to tell by the flags that this vertex is untransformed, which means it exists in 3D world space, as opposed to screen space. This kind of vertex is not affected by any dynamic lighting in a scene, but it can be prelit by an artist, creating nicely lit environments. This vertex is also extremely efficient, since it isn't sent into the lighting equations.

Numbers greater than 1.0 can tile the texture, mirror it, or clamp it, depending on the addressing mode of the renderer. If you wanted a texture to tile three times in the horizontal direction and four times in the vertical direction on the surface of a single polygon, the texture (U,V) coordinate that would accomplish that task would be (3.0f, 4.0f). Numbers less than 0.0f are also supported. They have the effect of mirroring the texture.

Other Vertex Data

If you happen to have the DirectX SDK documentation open and you are following along, you'll notice that I skipped over a few additional vertex data components, such as blending weight and vertex point size, and also tons of texturing minutia. All I can say is that these topics are beyond the scope of this simple 3D primer. I hope you'll forgive me and perhaps write a note to my publisher begging for me to write a more comprehensive book on the subject. That is, of course, if my wife ever lets me write another book. You have no idea how much housework I've been able to get out of by writing.

Triangle Meshes

We've been talking so far about individual vertices. Its time to take that knowledge and create some triangle meshes. There are three common approaches to defining sets of triangles:

- **Triangle list:** A group of vertices defines individual triangles, each set of three vertices defines a single triangle.
- **Triangle strip:** A set of vertices that define a strip of connected triangles; this is more efficient than a triangle list because fewer vertices are duplicated. This is probably the most popular primitive because it is efficient and can create a wide variety of shapes.
- **Triangle fan:** Similar to a triangle strip, but all the triangles share one central vertex; also very efficient.

When you define sets of vertices in DirectX 9, you put them in a *vertex buffer*. The vertex buffer is sent to the renderer in one atomic piece, which implies that every triangle defined in the buffer is rendered with the current state of the renderer. Every triangle will have the same texture, be affected by the same lights, and so on.

This turns out to be a staggeringly good optimization. The teapot you saw earlier in this chapter required 2,256 triangles and 1,178 vertices, but it could be drawn with around 50 triangle strips. It turns out that DirectX meshes are always triangle lists. Lists or strips are much faster than sending each triangle to the card and rendering it individually, which is what happened in the dark ages—circa 1996.

In DirectX 9, you create a vertex buffer, fill it with your triangle data, and then use it for rendering at a time of your choosing. Before you read this code, please know that no rational programmer would create an entire vertex buffer for a single triangle, this is just a simple example:

```
class Triangle
{
   LPDIRECT3DVERTEXBUFFER9 m_pVerts;
   DWORD m_numVerts;

public:
   Triangle()  { m_pVerts = NULL;  m_numVerts = 3; }
   ~Triangle() { SAFE_RELEASE(m_pVerts); }

   HRESULT Create(LPDIRECT3DDEVICE9 pDevice);
   HRESULT Render(LPDIRECT3DDEVICE9 pDevice);
};

HRESULT Triangle::Create(LPDIRECT3DDEVICE9 pDevice)
{
   // Create the vertex buffer.
   m_numVerts = 3;
   if( FAILED( pDevice->CreateVertexBuffer(
                  m_numVerts*sizeof(TRANSFORMED_VERTEX),
                  D3DUSAGE_WRITEONLY, D3DFVF_TRANSFORMED_VERTEX,
                  D3DPOOL_MANAGED, &m_pVerts, NULL ) ) )
   {
      return E_FAIL;
   }

   // Fill the vertex buffer. We are setting the tu and tv texture
   // coordinates, which range from 0.0 to 1.0
   TRANSFORMED_VERTEX* pVertices;
```

```
if( FAILED( m_pVerts->Lock( 0, 0, (void**)&pVertices, 0 ) ) )
   return E_FAIL;

pVertices[0].position = D3DXVECTOR3(0,0,0);
pVertices[0].rhw = 1.0;
pVertices[1].position = D3DXVECTOR3(0,50,0);
pVertices[1].rhw = 1.0;
pVertices[2].position = D3DXVECTOR3(50,50,0);
pVertices[2].rhw = 1.0;

m_pVerts->Unlock();

return S_OK;
}
```

This is a simple example of creating a vertex buffer with a single triangle, and a transformed one at that. The call to CreateVertexBuffer is somewhat scary looking, but all it does is set up a piece of memory the right size, the kind of vertex that will inhabit the buffer, and how the memory will be managed.

After the buffer is created, you have to lock it before writing data values. This should remind you somewhat of locking a 2D surface. The single triangle has three vertices—no surprise there. Take a quick look at the position values, and you'll see that I've defined a triangle that will sit in the upper left-hand corner of the screen with a base and height of 50 pixels. This triangle is defined in screen space, since the vector is defined as a transformed vertex.

When I'm ready to render this vertex buffer, I call this code:

```
HRESULT Triangle::VRender(LPDIRECT3DDEVICE9 pDevice)
{
    pDevice->SetStreamSource( 0, m_pVerts, 0, sizeof(TRANSFORMED_VERTEX) );
    pDevice->SetFVF( D3DFVF_TRANSFORMED_VERTEX );
    pDevice->DrawPrimitive( D3DPT_TRIANGLELIST , 0, 1 );
    return S_OK;
}
```

The first call sets the stream source, or vertex buffer, to our triangle. The second call tells D3D what kind of vertices to expect in the stream buffer using the flags that you or'ed together when you defined the vertex structure. The last call to DrawPrimitive() actually renders the triangle. This is an example of the fixed-function pipeline. You tell Direct3D what vertex data to expect and send the vertex data in with a call to DrawPrimitive(). Direct3D then uses all of the current rendering settings to render the vertices.

THIS ISN'T THE WHOLE STORY

You can't call any drawing functions in Direct3D without first calling `IDirect3D9Device::BeginScene()`, and you must call `IDirect3DDevice::EndScene()` when you are done drawing! The previous example encapsulates the rendering of a single triangle and would be called only from within the context of the beginning and ending of a scene.

Indexed Triangle Meshes

There's one more wrinkle to defining triangle meshes. Instead of sending vertex data to the renderer alone, you can send an index along with it. This index is an array of 16- or 32-bit numbers that define the vertex order, allowing you to avoid serious vertex duplication and therefore save memory. Let's take a look at a slightly more complicated mesh example. Here's the code that created the grid mesh in the teapot example:

```
class Grid
{
protected:
    LPDIRECT3DTEXTURE9      m_pTexture;    // the grid texture
    LPDIRECT3DVERTEXBUFFER9 m_pVerts;      // the grid verts
    LPDIRECT3DINDEXBUFFER9  m_pIndices;    // the grid index
    DWORD                   m_numVerts;
    DWORD                   m_numPolys;

public:
    Grid();
    ~Grid();
    HRESULT Create (
        LPDIRECT3DDEVICE9 pDevice, const DWORD gridSize, const DWORD color);
    HRESULT Render(LPDIRECT3DDEVICE9 pDevice);
};

Grid::Grid()
{
    m_pTexture = NULL;
    m_pVerts = NULL;
    m_pIndices = NULL;
    m_numVerts = m_numPolys = 0;
}
```

```
Grid::~Grid()
{
   SAFE_RELEASE(m_pTexture);
   SAFE_RELEASE(m_pVerts);
   SAFE_RELEASE(m_pIndices);
}

HRESULT Grid::Create(
   LPDIRECT3DDEVICE9 pDevice,
   const DWORD gridSize,
   const DWORD color)
{
   if( FAILED( D3DUtil_CreateTexture(
      pDevice, "Textures\\Grid.dds", &m_pTexture ) ) )
   {
      return E_FAIL;
   }

   // Create the vertex buffer - we'll need enough verts
   // to populate the grid. If we want a 2x2 grid, we'll
   // need 3x3 set of verts.
   m_numVerts = (gridSize+1)*(gridSize+1);

   if( FAILED( pDevice->CreateVertexBuffer(
                  m_numVerts*sizeof(COLORED_TEXTURED_VERTEX),
                  D3DUSAGE_WRITEONLY, D3DFVF_COLORED_TEXTURED_VERTEX,
                  D3DPOOL_MANAGED, &m_pVerts, NULL ) ) )
   {
      return E_FAIL;
   }

   // Fill the vertex buffer. We are setting the tu and tv texture
   // coordinates, which range from 0.0 to 1.0
   COLORED_TEXTURED_VERTEX* pVertices;
   if( FAILED( m_pVerts->Lock( 0, 0, (void**)&pVertices, 0 ) ) )
      return E_FAIL;

   for( DWORD j=0; j<(gridSize+1); j++ )
   {
      for (DWORD i=0; i<(gridSize+1); i++)
      {
         // Which vertex are we setting?
         int index = i + (j * (gridSize+1) );
         COLORED_TEXTURED_VERTEX *vert = &pVertices[index];
```

```
            // Default position of the grid is at the origin, flat on
            // the XZ plane.
            float x = (float)i;
            float y = (float)j;
            vert->position =
                ( x * D3DXVECTOR3(1,0,0) ) + ( y * D3DXVECTOR3(0,0,1) );
            vert->color    = color;

            // The texture coordinates are set to x,y to make the
            // texture tile along with units - 1.0, 2.0, 3.0, etc.
            vert->tu       = x;
            vert->tv       = y;
        }
    }
    m_pVerts->Unlock();

    // The number of indicies equals the number of polygons times 3
    // since there are 3 indicies per polygon. Each grid square contains
    // two polygons. The indicies are 16 bit, since our grids won't
    // be that big!
    m_numPolys = gridSize*gridSize*2;
    if( FAILED( pDevice->CreateIndexBuffer(
                sizeof(WORD) * m_numPolys * 3,
                D3DUSAGE_WRITEONLY, D3DFMT_INDEX16,
                D3DPOOL_MANAGED, &m_pIndices, NULL ) ) )
    {
        return E_FAIL;
    }

    WORD *pIndices;
    if( FAILED( m_pIndices->Lock( 0, 0, (void**)&pIndices, 0 ) ) )
        return E_FAIL;

    // Loop through the grid squares and calc the values
    // of each index. Each grid square has two triangles:
    //
    //    A - B
    //    | / |
    //    C - D

    for( DWORD j=0; j<gridSize; j++ )
    {
        for (DWORD i=0; i<gridSize; i++)
        {
```

```
        // Triangle #1  ACB
        *(pIndices) = WORD(i + (j*(gridSize+1)));
        *(pIndices+1) = WORD(i + ((j+1)*(gridSize+1)));
        *(pIndices+2) = WORD((i+1) + (j*(gridSize+1)));

        // Triangle #2  BCD
        *(pIndices+3) = WORD((i+1) + (j*(gridSize+1)));
        *(pIndices+4) = WORD(i + ((j+1)*(gridSize+1)));
        *(pIndices+5) = WORD((i+1) + ((j+1)*(gridSize+1)));
        pIndices+=6;
    }
}

m_pIndices->Unlock();
return S_OK;
}
```

I've commented the code pretty heavily to help you understand what's going on. An index buffer is created and filled in much the same way as vertex buffers. Take a few minutes to stare at the code that assigns the index numbers—it's the last nested for loop. If you have trouble figuring it out, trace the code with a 2 × 2 grid, and you'll get it.

This code creates an indexed triangle list. If you wanted to be truly efficient, you'd rewrite the code to create an indexed triangle strip. All you have to do is change the index buffer. I'll leave that to you. If you can get that working, you'll know you have no trouble understanding index buffers. The code that renders the grid looks very similar to the triangle example:

```
HRESULT Grid::Render(LPDIRECT3DDEVICE9 pDevice)
{
  // Setup our texture. Using textures introduces the texture stage states,
  // which govern how textures get blended together (in the case of multiple
  // textures) and lighting information. In this case, we are modulating
  // (blending) our texture with the diffuse color of the vertices.
  pDevice->SetTexture( 0, m_pTexture );
  pDevice->SetTextureStageState( 0, D3DTSS_COLOROP,   D3DTOP_MODULATE );
  pDevice->SetTextureStageState( 0, D3DTSS_COLORARG1, D3DTA_TEXTURE );
  pDevice->SetTextureStageState( 0, D3DTSS_COLORARG2, D3DTA_DIFFUSE );

  pDevice->SetStreamSource( 0, m_pVerts, 0, sizeof(COLORED_TEXTURED_VERTEX) );
  pDevice->SetIndices(m_pIndices);
  pDevice->SetFVF( D3DFVF_COLORED_TEXTURED_VERTEX );
  pDevice->DrawIndexedPrimitive(
    D3DPT_TRIANGLELIST , 0, 0, m_numVerts, 0, m_numPolys );
  return S_OK;
}
```

You'll note the few extra calls to let the renderer know that the triangles in the mesh are textured, and that the texture is affected by the diffuse color of the vertex. This means that a black-and-white texture will take on a colored hue based on the diffuse color setting of the vertex. It's a little like choosing different colored wallpaper with the same pattern.

Materials

There's a lot more to texturing than the few calls you've seen so far. One thing you'll need to check out in DirectX 9 is materials. When you look at the structure of D3DMATEIRAL9, you'll see things that remind you of those color settings in vertex data:

```
typedef struct _D3DMATERIAL9 {
    D3DCOLORVALUE Diffuse;
    D3DCOLORVALUE Ambient;
    D3DCOLORVALUE Specular;
    D3DCOLORVALUE Emissive;
    float Power;
} D3DMATERIAL9;
```

If the DirectX 9 renderer doesn't have any specific color data for vertices, it will use the current material to set the color of each vertex, composing all the material color information with the active lights illuminating the scene.

BLACK OBJECTS EVERYWHERE? SET YOUR DEFAULT MATERIAL!

One common mistake with using the fixed-function pipeline in DirectX 9 is not setting a default material. If your vertex data doesn't include diffuse or specular color information, your polygons will appear completely black. If your game has a black background, objects in your scene will completely disappear!

Other than the critical information about needing a default material and texture, the DirectX SDK documentation does a pretty fair job of showing you what happens when you play with the specular and power settings. They can turn a plastic ping-pong ball into a ball bearing, highlights and everything.

The material defines how light reflects off the polygons. In Direct3D, this includes different colors for ambient, diffuse, specular, and emissive light. It is convenient to wrap the D3DMATERIAL9 structure in a class, which will be used in the next chapter to control how objects look, or even if they are transparent. Here is the source code for the class:

```
#define fOPAQUE (1.0f)
#define fTRANSPARENT (0.0f)

typedef D3DXCOLOR Color;

Color g_White( 1.0f, 1.0f, 1.0f, fOPAQUE );
Color g_Black( 0.0f, 0.0f, 0.0f, fOPAQUE );
Color g_Cyan( 0.0f, 1.0f, 1.0f, fOPAQUE );
Color g_Red( 1.0f, 0.0f, 0.0f, fOPAQUE );
Color g_Green( 0.0f, 1.0f, 0.0f, fOPAQUE );
Color g_Blue( 0.0f, 0.0f, 1.0f, fOPAQUE );
Color g_Yellow( 1.0f, 1.0f, 0.0f, fOPAQUE );
Color g_Gray40( 0.4f, 0.4f, 0.4f, fOPAQUE );
Color g_Gray25( 0.25f, 0.25f, 0.25f, fOPAQUE );
Color g_Gray65( 0.65f, 0.65f, 0.65f, fOPAQUE );
Color g_Transparent (1.0f, 0.0f, 1.0f, fTRANSPARENT );

class Material
{
   D3DMATERIAL9 m_D3DMaterial;
public:
   Material();
   void SetAmbient(const Color &color);
   void SetDiffuse(const Color &color);
   void SetSpecular(const Color &color, const float power);
   void SetEmissive(const Color &color);
   void Set(const Color &color);
   void SetAlpha(const float alpha);
   bool HasAlpha() const { return GetAlpha() != fOPAQUE; }
   float GetAlpha() const { return m_D3DMaterial.Diffuse.a; }
   void Use();
};

Material::Material()
{
   ZeroMemory( &m_D3DMaterial, sizeof( D3DMATERIAL9 ) );
   Set(g_White);
}

void Material::SetAmbient(const Color &color)
{
   m_D3DMaterial.Ambient = color;
}
```

```
void Material::SetDiffuse(const Color &color)
{
   m_D3DMaterial.Diffuse = color;
}

void Material::SetSpecular(const Color &color, const float power)
{
   m_D3DMaterial.Specular = color;
   m_D3DMaterial.Power = power;
}

void Material::SetEmissive(const Color &color)
{
   m_D3DMaterial.Emissive = color;
}

void Material::Set(const Color &color)
{
   m_D3DMaterial.Diffuse = color;
   m_D3DMaterial.Ambient = color;
   m_D3DMaterial.Specular = g_White;
   m_D3DMaterial.Emissive = g_Black;
}

void Material::SetAlpha(float alpha)
{
   m_D3DMaterial.Diffuse.a =
      m_D3DMaterial.Ambient.a =
      m_D3DMaterial.Specular.a = alpha;
}

void Material::Use()
{
   DXUTGetD3DDevice()->SetMaterial( &m_D3DMaterial );
}
```

The material has four different color components. Generally, you'll set the ambient and diffuse color to the same thing, but you might get a black object by mistake. If you set an object's diffuse and ambient material to 100% blue, and you put that object in an environment with 100% red light, it will appear black. That's because a 100% blue object doesn't reflect any red light. Fix this by putting a little red in either the diffuse or ambient colors. The specular color is usually set to white or gray, and defines the color of the shininess the object takes on. Lastly, the emissive component allows an object to light itself. This is a good idea for things like explosions or light bulbs—anything that emits light.

The last property is used to classify how the scene node is drawn, opaque or transparent. There are four different ways transparency can work, the first of which is completely opaque, or not transparent.

```
enum AlphaType
{
   AlphaOpaque,
   AlphaTexture,
   AlphaMaterial,
   AlphaVertex
};
```

One way is by using a texture with an alpha channel, such as you might do to create a nice-looking set of leaves on a tree or pickets in a fence. You might think the alpha channel makes a bigger texture, but if your texture is 24-bit RGB, your video card will create a 32-bit ARGB space for it. You can finely control which pixels look transparent and how transparent they are. This is the method used for `AlphaTexture`.

The second way is to use the material. You can make the entire object transparent by setting the alpha component of the material. This is the method used for `AlphaMaterial`.

The last method is by vertex color. If you have the kind of vertices that have a color component, you can set the alpha value of the vertex in any way you want. The simple 3D engine in this book doesn't support that method, but perhaps you'll have a free weekend to implement it. Don't forget to check the Web site, www.mcshaffry.com/GameCode/portal.php, and if you're lucky, it might be up there right now. Or check out www.courseptr.com/downloads.

Texturing

Back in `Grid::Create()`, I quietly included some texture calls into the code. Let's start with what I did to actually create the texture in the first place and go through the calls that apply the texture to a set of vertices. The first thing you'll do to create a texture is pop into Photoshop, Paint, or any bitmap editing tool. That leaves out tools like Macromedia Flash or Illustrator because they are vector tools and are no good for bitmaps.

Go into one of these tools and create an image 128 × 128 pixels in size. Figure 13.14 shows my version.

FIGURE 13.14 A sample texture.

Save the texture as a TIF, TGA, or BMP. If you are working in Photoshop, you'll want to save the PSD file for future editing, but our next step can't read PSDs. While you can use the DirectX Texture Tool to save your texture in DirectX's DDS format, DirectX can load BMP, DIB, HDR, JPG, PFM, PNG, PPM, and TGA files, too.

```
HRESULT hr;
LPDIRECT3DTEXTURE9 pTexture;
hr = D3DXCreateTextureFromFile (
    DXUTGetD3D9Device(), "texture.dds", &pTexture ) ) )
return hr;
```

Sometimes you might also want to create a texture from memory, such as when you have a resource cache load your texture files:

```
Resource resource("texture.dds");
shared_ptr<ResHandle> texture =
   g_pApp->m_ResCache->GetHandle(&resource);

hr = D3DXCreateTextureFromFileInMemory(
   DXUTGetD3D9Device(), texture->Buffer(), texture->Size(),
   &pTexture ) ) )
return hr;
```

There is much more to creating and loading textures than you see here, because I'm only scratching the surface. Take a look at DirectX 9's documentation on texture creation functions D3DXCreateTextureFromFileEx(), D3DXCreateTexture-FromResourceEx(), and D3DXCreateTextureFromFileInMemoryEx().

There is one important concept, *mip-mapping*, that needs special attention. If you've ever seen old 3D games, or perhaps just really bad 3D games, you'll probably recall an odd effect that happens to textured objects as you back away from them. This effect, called *scintillation*, is especially noticeable on textures with a regular pattern, such as a black-and-white checkerboard pattern. As the textured objects recede in the distance, you begin to notice that the texture seems to jump around in weird patterns. This is due to an effect called *subsampling*.

Subsampling

Assume for the moment that a texture appears on a polygon very close to its original size. If the texture is 128 × 128 pixels, the polygon on the screen will look almost exactly like the texture. If this polygon were reduced to half of this size, 64 × 64 pixels, the renderer must choose which pixels from the original texture must be applied to the polygon. So what happens if the original texture looks like the one shown in Figure 13.15?

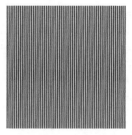

FIGURE 13.15 A texture particularly sensitive to subsampling.

This texture is 128×128 pixels, with alternating vertical lines exactly one pixel in width. If you reduced this texture in a simple paint program, you might get nothing but a 64×64 texture that is completely black. What's going on here?

When the texture is reduced to half its size, the naive approach would select every other pixel in the grid, which in this case happens to be every black pixel on the texture. The original texture has a certain amount of information, or frequency, in its data stream. The frequency of the above texture is the number of alternating lines. Each pair of black-and-white lines is considered one wave in a waveform that makes up the entire texture. The frequency of this texture is 64, since it takes 64 waves of black-and-white lines to make up the texture.

Subsampling is what occurs if any waveform is sampled at less than twice its frequency. In the above case, any sample taken at less than 128 samples or less will drop critical information from the original data stream.

It might seem weird to think of textures having a frequency, but they do. A high frequency implies a high degree of information content. In the case of a texture, it has to do with the number of undulations in the waveform that make up the data stream. If the texture were nothing more than a black square, it has a minimal frequency, and therefore carries only the smallest amount of information. A texture that is a solid black square, no matter how large, can be sampled at any rate whatsoever. No information is lost because there wasn't that much information to begin with.

In case you were wondering whether or not this subject of subsampling can apply to audio waveforms, it can. Let's assume that you have a high-frequency sound, say a tone at 11KHz. If you attempt to sample this tone in a WAV file at 11KHz, exactly the frequency of the tone, you won't be happy with the results. You'll get a subsampled version of the original sound. Just as the texture turned completely black, your subsampled sound would be a completely flat line, erasing the sound altogether.

It turns out there is a solution for this problem, and it involves processing and filtering the original data stream to preserve as much of the original waveform as possible. For sounds and textures, the new sample isn't just grabbed from an original piece of data in the waveform. The data closest to the sample is used to figure out what is happening to the waveform, instead of one value of the waveform at a discrete point in time.

In the case of our lined texture used previously, the waveform is alternating from black to white as you sample horizontally across the texture, so naturally if the texture diminishes in size the eye should begin to perceive a 50 percent gray surface. It's no surprise that if you combine black and white in equal amounts you get 50 percent gray.

For textures, each sample involves the surrounding neighborhood of pixels—a process known as *bilinear filtering*. The process is a linear combination of the pixel values on all sides sampled pixel—nine values in all. These nine values are weighted and combined to create the new sample. The same approach can be used with sounds as well, as you might have expected.

This processing and filtering is pretty expensive so you don't want to do it in real time for textures or sounds. Instead, you'll want to create a set of reduced images for each texture in your game. This master texture is known as a *mip-map*.

Mip-Mapping

Mip-mapping is a set of textures that has been preprocessed to contain one or more levels of size reduction. In practice, the size reduction is in halves, all the way down to one pixel that represents the dominant color of the entire texture. You might think that this is a waste of memory but it's actually more efficient than you'd think. A mip-map uses only one-third more memory than the original texture, and considering the vast improvement in the quality of the rendered result, you should provide mip-maps for any texture that has a relatively high frequency of information. It is especially useful for textures with regular patterns, such as our black-and-white line texture.

REALLY LONG POLYGONS CAN BE TROUBLE

One last thing about mip-maps: As you might expect, the renderer will choose which mip-map to display based on the screen size of the polygon. This means that it's not a good idea to create huge polygons on your geometry that can recede into the distance. The renderer might not be able to make a good choice that will satisfy the look of the polygon edge, both closest to the camera and the one farthest away. Some older video cards might select one mip-map for the entire polygon, and it would therefore look strange. You can't always count on every player to have modern hardware. If you have to support these older cards, you should consider breaking up longer polygons into ones that are more square.

Also, while we're on the subject, many other things can go wrong with huge polygons in world space, such as lighting and collision. It's always a good idea to tessellate, or break up, larger surfaces into smaller polygons that will provide the renderer with a good balance between polygon size and vertex count.

The DirectX Texture Tool can generate mip-maps for you. To do this, you just load your texture and select Format, Generate Mip Maps. You can then see the resulting reduced textures by pressing PageUp and PageDn.

You might have heard of something called *trilinear filtering*. If the renderer switches between one mip-map level on the same polygon, it's likely that you'll notice the switch. Most renderers can sample the texels from more than one mip-map and blend their color in real time. This creates a smooth transition from one mip-map level to another, a much more realistic effect. As you approach something like a newspaper, the mip-maps are sampled in such a way that eventually the blurry image of the headline can resolve into something you can read and react to.

3D Graphics—It's Just the Beginning

You've seen enough to be dangerous in DirectX 9, and perhaps even be dangerous in any other renderer you choose, such as OpenGL. The concepts I presented are the same. The only thing different are the function calls, the coordinate systems, the texturing support, how they expect your geometry, and so on. This chapter's goal was really not much more than a vocabulary lesson, and a beginning one at that. We'll get to more 3D material in the next chapter, so don't worry.

I suggest that you go play around a bit in DirectX 9's sample projects and get your bearings. Don't feel frustrated when you get lost either. Even while writing this book, you could see me holding my hands in front of myself twisted like some madman, attempting to visualize rotations and cross products. With any luck, you've got just enough knowledge in your head to perform some of your own twisting and cursing.

3D SCENES

In This Chapter

In the previous chapter, you learned something about how to draw 3D geometry, but there's much more to a 3D game than drawing a few triangles. Even a relatively boring 3D game has characters, interesting environments, dynamic objects, and a few special effects here and there. Your first attempt at a 3D engine might be to just draw everything. You might think that your blazing fast ATI video card can handle anything you throw at it, but you'd be wrong. It turns out to be pretty tricky to get 3D scenes to look right and draw quickly.

In only one chapter, there's not enough time to talk about every aspect of 3D engines because there is way too much material to cover. You will, however, develop the knowledge of how a prototype for a 3D game engine gets its start. With any luck, you'll end this chapter with a healthy respect for the programmers who build 3D engines.

First, a little more geometry.

THE PLANE CLASS

The plane is an extremely useful mathematical device for 3D games. Here's a simple wrapper around the DirectX plane structure, D3DXPLANE:

```
class Plane : public D3DXPLANE
{
public:
    inline void Normalize();

    // normal faces away from you if you send in verts
    // in counter clockwise order....
    inline void Init(const Vec3 &p0, const Vec3 &p1, const Vec3 &p2);
    bool Inside(const Vec3 &point, const float radius) const;
    bool Inside(const Vec3 &point) const;
};

inline void Plane::Normalize()
{
    float mag;
    mag = sqrt(a * a + b * b + c * c);
    a = a / mag;
    b = b / mag;
    c = c / mag;
    d = d / mag;
}
```

```
inline void Plane::Init(const Vec3 &p0, const Vec3 &p1, const Vec3 &p2)
{
   D3DXPlaneFromPoints(this, &p0, &p1, &p2);
   Normalize();
}


bool Plane::Inside(const Vec3 &point) const
{
   // Inside the plane is defined as the direction the normal is facing
   float result = D3DXPlaneDotCoord(this, &point);
   return (result >= 0.0f);
}


bool Plane::Inside(const Vec3 &point, const float radius) const
{
   float fDistance;    // calculate our distances to each of the planes

   // find the distance to this plane
   fDistance = D3DXPlaneDotCoord(this, &point);

   // if this distance is < -radius, we are outside
   return (fDistance >= -radius);
}
```

Basically, if you know three points on the surface of the plane, you'll have enough information to create it mathematically. You can also create planes in other ways, and you're perfectly free to extend this bare-bones class to create more constructors, but this simple version goes a surprisingly long way.

Once the plane is initialized, you can ask whether a point or a circle (defined by a point and a radius) is on the inside or outside of the plane. Inside is defined by being on the same side as the plane normal. The plane normal is defined by the coefficients a, b, and c inside the D3DXPLANE structure, and it is calculated for you when the plane class is constructed.

The plane is rarely used by itself. It is usually used to create things like BSP trees, portals, and a camera view frustum, which you'll see how to create next.

THE FRUSTUM CLASS

A *frustum* is defined as the portion of a solid, usually a cone or a pyramid, which lies between two parallel planes that cut the solid (see Figure 14.1). View frustums are of the pyramid variety. If you have a U.S. dollar bill in your pocket, you can see one in the form of the unfinished pyramid that is the reverse side of the Great Seal of the United States.

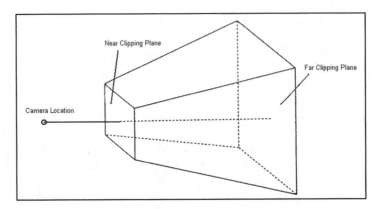

FIGURE 14.1 The view frustum with near and far clipping planes.

The camera is at the tip of the pyramid, looking at the frustum through the near clipping plane. Any object that is totally outside the six planes that describe the frustum are outside the viewing area, which means they can be skipped during the rendering passes. The six planes include the near and far clipping planes and the four other planes that make up the top, left, right, and bottom of the frustum. It turns out to be really efficient to test a point or a sphere against a frustum, and that is exactly how this frustum will be used to cull objects in the scene graph.

A frustum is defined with four parameters: the field of view, the aspect ratio, the distance to the near clipping plane, and the distance to the far clipping plane. The field of view, or FOV, is the full angle made by the tip of the pyramid at the camera location (see Figure 14.2). The aspect ratio is the width of the near clipping plane divided by the height of the near clipping plane. For a 640 × 480 pixel screen, the aspect ratio would be 640.f/480.f or 1.33333334. The distance to the near and far clipping planes should be given in whatever units your game uses to measure distance—feet, meters, cubits, whatever. With these parameters safely in hand, the six plane objects can be built.

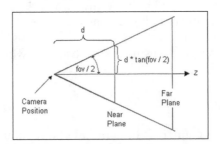

FIGURE 14.2 Calculating the points of the view frustum.

Here's the code for defining the Frustum class:

```
class Frustum
{
public:
    enum Side { Near, Far, Top, Right, Bottom, Left, NumPlanes };

    Plane m_Planes[NumPlanes];    // planes of the frustum in camera space
    Vec3 m_NearClip[4];           // verts of the near clip plane in camera space
    Vec3 m_FarClip[4];            // verts of the far clip plane in camera space

    float m_Fov;                  // field of view in radians
    float m_Aspect;               // aspect ratio - width divided by height
    float m_Near;                 // near clipping distance
    float m_Far;                  // far clipping distance

public:
    Frustum();

    bool Inside(const Vec3 &point) const;
    bool Inside(const Vec3 &point, const float radius) const;
    const Plane &Get(Side side) { return m_Planes[side]; }
    void SetFOV(float fov) { m_Fov=fov; Init(m_Fov, m_Aspect, m_Near, m_Far); }
    void SetAspect(float aspect)
       { m_Aspect=aspect; Init(m_Fov, m_Aspect, m_Near, m_Far); }
    void SetNear(float nearClip)
       { m_Near=nearClip; Init(m_Fov, m_Aspect, m_Near, m_Far); }
    void SetFar(float farClip)
       { m_Far=farClip; Init(m_Fov, m_Aspect, m_Near, m_Far); }
    void Init(const float fov, const float aspect,
       const float near, const float far);

    void Render();
};

Frustum::Frustum()
{
    m_Fov = D3DX_PI/4.0f;   // default field of view is 90 degrees
    m_Aspect = 1.0f;        // default aspect ratio is 1:1
    m_Near = 1.0f;          // default near plane is 1m away from the camera
    m_Far = 1000.0f;        // default near plane is 1000m away from the camera
}
```

```
bool Frustum::Inside(const Vec3 &point) const
{
   //for (int i=0; i<NumPlanes; ++i)
   for (int i=0; i<=Far; ++i)
   {
      if (!m_Planes[i].Inside(point))
         return false;
   }

   return true;
}

bool Frustum::Inside(const Vec3 &point, const float radius) const
{
   for(int i = 0; i < NumPlanes; ++i)
   {
      if (!m_Planes[i].Inside(point, radius))
         return false;
   }

   // otherwise we are fully in view
   return(true);
}
```

The next method, Init(), is a little heavy on the math. The algorithm is used to find the eight points in space made by corners of the view frustum and use those points to define the six planes. If you remember your high school geometry, you'll remember that the tangent of an angle is equal to the length of the opposite side divided by the adjacent side. Since we know the length D from the camera to the near clipping plane, we can find the length between the center point of the near clipping plane to the right edge and also the top using the aspect ratio. The same operation is repeated for the far clipping plane, and that gives us the 3D location of the corner points:

```
void Frustum::Init(const float fov, const float aspect, const float nearClip,
                   const float farClip)
{
   m_Fov = fov;
   m_Aspect = aspect;
   m_Near = nearClip;
   m_Far = farClip;

   double tanFovOver2 = tan(m_Fov/2.0f);
   Vec3 nearRight = (m_Near * tanFovOver2) * m_Aspect * g_Right;
   Vec3 farRight = (m_Far * tanFovOver2) * m_Aspect * g_Right;
```

```
Vec3 nearUp = (m_Near * tanFovOver2 ) * g_Up;
Vec3 farUp = (m_Far * tanFovOver2)  * g_Up;

// points start in the upper right and go around clockwise
m_NearClip[0] = (m_Near * g_Forward) - nearRight + nearUp;
m_NearClip[1] = (m_Near * g_Forward) + nearRight + nearUp;
m_NearClip[2] = (m_Near * g_Forward) + nearRight - nearUp;
m_NearClip[3] = (m_Near * g_Forward) - nearRight - nearUp;

m_FarClip[0] = (m_Far * g_Forward) - farRight + farUp;
m_FarClip[1] = (m_Far * g_Forward) + farRight + farUp;
m_FarClip[2] = (m_Far * g_Forward) + farRight - farUp;
m_FarClip[3] = (m_Far * g_Forward) - farRight - farUp;

// now we have all eight points. Time to construct six planes.
// the normals point away from you if you use counter clockwise verts.

Vec3 origin(0.0f, 0.0f, 0.0f);
m_Planes[Near].Init(m_NearClip[2], m_NearClip[1], m_NearClip[0]);
m_Planes[Far].Init(m_FarClip[0], m_FarClip[1], m_FarClip[2]);
m_Planes[Right].Init(m_FarClip[2], m_FarClip[1], origin);
m_Planes[Top].Init(m_FarClip[1], m_FarClip[0], origin);
m_Planes[Left].Init(m_FarClip[0], m_FarClip[3], origin);
m_Planes[Bottom].Init(m_FarClip[3], m_FarClip[2], origin);
}
```

With the location of the corner points correctly nabbed, the planes of the view frustum can be created with three known points for each one. Don't forget that the order in which the points are sent into the plane equation is important. The order determines the direction of the plane's normal, and therefore which side of the plane is the inside versus the outside.

There's one more useful method of the Frustum class—one to render to the screen in its familiar clipped pyramid shape:

```
void Frustum::Render()
{
   COLORED_VERTEX verts[24];
   for (int i=0; i<8; ++i)
      verts[i].color = g_White;

   for (int i=0; i<8; ++i)
      verts[i+8].color = g_Red;

   for (int i=0; i<8; ++i)
      verts[i+16].color = g_Blue;
```

```
// Draw the near clip plane
verts[0].position = m_NearClip[0];    verts[1].position = m_NearClip[1];
verts[2].position = m_NearClip[1];    verts[3].position = m_NearClip[2];
verts[4].position = m_NearClip[2];    verts[5].position = m_NearClip[3];
verts[6].position = m_NearClip[3];    verts[7].position = m_NearClip[0];

// Draw the far clip plane
verts[8].position = m_FarClip[0];     verts[9].position = m_FarClip[1];
verts[10].position = m_FarClip[1];    verts[11].position = m_FarClip[2];
verts[12].position = m_FarClip[2];    verts[13].position = m_FarClip[3];
verts[14].position = m_FarClip[3];    verts[15].position = m_FarClip[0];

// Draw the edges between the near and far clip plane
verts[16].position = m_NearClip[0];   verts[17].position = m_FarClip[0];
verts[18].position = m_NearClip[1];   verts[19].position = m_FarClip[1];
verts[20].position = m_NearClip[2];   verts[21].position = m_FarClip[2];
verts[22].position = m_NearClip[3];   verts[23].position = m_FarClip[3];

DXUTGetD3DDevice()->SetRenderState( D3DRS_LIGHTING, FALSE );
DXUTGetD3DDevice()->SetFVF( COLORED_VERTEX::FVF );
DXUTGetD3DDevice()->DrawPrimitiveUP(
    D3DPT_LINELIST, 12, verts, sizeof(COLORED_VERTEX) );
}
```

Scene Graph Basics

A *scene graph* is a dynamic data structure, similar to a multiway tree. Each node represents an object in a 3D world or perhaps an instruction to the renderer. Every node can have zero or more children nodes. The scene graph is traversed every frame to draw the visible world. Many commercial renderers use a scene graph as their basic data structure, one of which is Gamebryo from Emergent Game Technologies. Before you get too excited, what you are about to see is a basic introduction to the concepts and code behind a scene graph—not something you can simply install into a commercial product. Think of this as a scene graph with training wheels.

ISceneNode Interface Class

The base class for all nodes in the scene graph is the interface class ISceneNode. Everything else inherits from that class and extends the class to create every part of your 3D world, including the simple geometry, meshes, a camera, and so on. Here's the ISceneNode class:

```
class ISceneNode
{
protected:

public:
    virtual const SceneNodeProperties * const VGet() const=0;

    virtual void VSetTransform(const Mat4x4 *toWorld, const Mat4x4
                              *fromWorld=NULL)=0;

    virtual HRESULT VOnUpdate(Scene *, DWORD const elapsedMs)=0;
    virtual HRESULT VOnRestore(Scene *pScene)=0;

    virtual HRESULT VPreRender(Scene *pScene)=0;
    virtual bool VIsVisible(Scene *pScene) const=0;
    virtual HRESULT VRender(Scene *pScene)=0;
    virtual HRESULT VRenderChildren(Scene *pScene)=0;
    virtual HRESULT VPostRender(Scene *pScene)=0;

    virtual bool VAddChild(shared_ptr<ISceneNode> kid)=0;

    virtual ~ISceneNode() { };
};
```

Each node has certain properties that affect how the node will draw, such as its material, its geometric extents, what game actor it represents, and so on. We'll cover the details of the SceneNodeProperties structure in the next section.

As you learned in the previous chapter, every object in a 3D universe needs a transform matrix. The matrix encodes the orientation and position of the object in the environment. In a scene graph, this idea is extended to a hierarchy of objects. This is easy to understand with an example. Imagine a boat with people on it, and those people have guns in their hands. When the boat moves, all the people on the boat move with it. Their position and orientation stay the same relative to the boat. When the people aim their weapons, the bones of their arms move and the guns move with them.

This effect is done by concatenating matrices. Every node in the hierarchy has a matrix that describes position and orientation relative to its parent node. As the scene graph is traversed, the matrices are multiplied to form a single matrix that perfectly describes the position and orientation of the node in the 3D world—even if it is a gun attached to a hand attached to a forearm attached to a shoulder attached to a guy standing on a boat.

Take notice that the VSetTransform() method takes two Mat4x4 objects, not just one. It turns out to be really convenient to store two matrices for each scene node—the one we just discussed about transforming object space to the space of its parent (usually world space if there's no complicated hierarchy involved). This is the `toWorld` parameter in the `SetTransform()` and `GetTransform()` APIs. The second one does the opposite; it transforms 3D world back into object space. This is great if you want to know where a bullet strikes an object. The bullet's trajectory is usually in world space, and the `fromWorld` transform matrix will tell you where that trajectory is in object space.

This can be a little confusing, so if your brain is swimming a bit don't worry. Mine did too when I first read it. You can imagine this by thinking about your hand as a self-contained hierarchical object. The root would be your palm, and attached to it are five children—the first segment of each of your five fingers. Each of those finger segments has one child, the segment without a fingernail. Finally, the segment with the fingernail attaches, making the palm its great-grandfather. If the transform matrix for one of those finger segments is rotated around the right axis, the finger should bend, carrying all the child segments with it. If I change the translation or rotation of the palm (the root object), everything moves. That is the basic notion of a hierarchical animation system.

TALES FROM THE PIXEL MINES

THAT'S GOTTA HURT!

It's common for artists to create human figures with the hips, or should I say, groin, as the root node. It's convenient because it is close to the center of the human body, and has three children: the torso and the two legs. One fine day the *Ultima VIII* team went to the park for lunch and played a little Ultimate Frisbee. As happens frequently in that game, two players went to catch the Frisbee at the same time and collided, injuring one of the players. He was curled up on the ground writhing in pain, and when I asked what happened I was told that he took a blow to the root of his hierarchy.

The call to `VSetTransform()` will calculate the inverse transform matrix for you if you don't send it in. Yes, it's somewhat expensive. If you've ever seen the formula for calculating the determinant of a 4 × 4 matrix, you know what I'm talking about. If you've never seen it, just imagine an entire case of alphabet soup laid out on a recursive grid. It's gross.

The two methods, `VOnRestore()` and `VOnUpdate()`, simply traverse their children nodes and recursively call the same methods. When you inherit from `SceneNode` and create a new object, don't forget to call the base class's `VOnRestore()` or `VOnUpdate()` if you happen to overload them. If you fail to do this, your children nodes won't get these calls. The `VOnRestore()` method is meant to re-create any programmatically created data after it has been lost. This is a similar concept to the section on lost 2D DirectDraw surfaces.

The VOnUpdate() method is meant to handle animations or anything else that is meant to be decoupled from the rendering traversal. That's why it is called with the elapsed time, measured in milliseconds. You can use the elapsed time to make sure animations or other movements happen at a consistent speed, regardless of computer processing power. A faster CPU should always create a smoother animation, not necessarily a faster one!

The VPreRender() method is meant to perform any task that must occur before the render, such as setting render states. The VIsVisible() method performs a visibility test. The VRender() method does exactly what it advertises: it renders the object. A recursive call to VRenderChildren() is made to traverse the scene graph, performing all these actions for every node. The VPostRender() method is meant to perform a post-rendering action, such as restoring a render state to its original value.

The VAddChild() method adds a child node. You'll see different implementations of this interface class add children in different ways. No, you shouldn't attach a node to itself; you'll run out of stack space in your infinitely recursive scene graph before you know what happened.

SceneNodeProperties and RenderPass

When I first designed the ISceneNode class and the implementation class you'll see in a few pages, SceneNode, the first attempt loaded the class full of virtual accessor methods: VGetThis(), VGetThat(), and VGetTheOtherDamnThing(). What I really wanted was a structure of these properties and a single virtual accessor that would give me read-only access to the data in that structure. The structure, SceneNode-Properties, is defined as follows:

```
typedef unsigned int ActorId;

class SceneNodeProperties
{
    friend class SceneNode;

protected:
    optional<ActorId>    m_ActorId;
    std::string          m_Name;
    Mat4x4               m_ToWorld, m_FromWorld;
    float                m_Radius;
    RenderPass           m_RenderPass;
    Material             m_Material;
    AlphaType            m_AlphaType;

    void SetAlpha(const float alpha)
        { m_AlphaType=AlphaMaterial; m_Material.SetAlpha(alpha); }
```

```
public:
    optional<ActorId> const &ActorId() const { return m_ActorId; }
    Mat4x4 const &ToWorld() const { return m_ToWorld; }
    Mat4x4 const &FromWorld() const { return m_FromWorld; }
    void Transform(Mat4x4 *toWorld, Mat4x4 *fromWorld) const;

    const char * Name() const { return m_Name.c_str(); }

    bool HasAlpha() const { return m_Material.HasAlpha(); }
    virtual float Alpha() const { return m_Material.GetAlpha(); }

    RenderPass RenderPass() const { return m_RenderPass; }
    float Radius() const { return m_Radius; }

    Material const &Material() const { return m_Material; }
};

void SceneNodeProperties::Transform(Mat4x4 *toWorld, Mat4x4 *fromWorld) const
{
    if (toWorld)
        *toWorld = m_ToWorld;

    if (fromWorld)
        *fromWorld = m_FromWorld;
}
```

All of the accessors to this class are const, which gives the read-only access I wanted. The implementation of SceneNode will perform all of the modifying, which is important since modifying some of these values can have repercussions throughout the scene graph.

The first two data members, m_ActorId and m_Name, help to relate the scene node to an object in your game logic and identify the scene node or the scene node type. Game engines typically assign unique identifiers to objects in the game. An ActorId that is basically an unsigned integer is easy for game engines to handle, but string-based names are easy for programmers to read.

The Mat4x4 data members, m_ToWorld and m_FromWorld, define the transform matrices. Transform() copies the member variables into memory you pass in. Generally, you don't want to just allow direct access to the transform matrices because changing them directly might break something. Various inherited classes of SceneNode or ISceneNode might filter or otherwise set the transforms themselves.

The next data member, m_Radius, defines the radius of a sphere that includes the visible geometry of a scene node. Spheres are really efficient for various tests, such as visibility tests or ray-intersection tests. The only problem with spheres is that they don't closely match most geometry, so you can't use them alone. Some commercial games actually do this, though, and you can tell when you play. An easy way to tell is if gunshots seem to hit, even though you aimed too far to the left or right. Better games will use the sphere as a first pass test, since it is so fast, and go to other more expensive tests if needed.

When a scene graph is traversed, like most tree-like data structures, it is traversed in a particular order. This order, when combined with various render state settings, creates different effects or enables an efficient rendering of the entire scene. Every node of your scene graph belongs to one of a few different possible render passes—one for static objects, one for dynamic objects, one for the sky, and perhaps others.

The reason you want to do this is mainly for efficiency. The goal is to minimize re-drawing pixels on the screen each frame. It makes sense to draw your scenery, objects, and sky in whatever order approaches this goal, hoping to draw things mostly from front to back to get all your closest objects drawn first. With any luck, by the time you get to your sky, you won't have to render hardly any pixels from it at all. After everything, you run through your transparent objects from back to front to make sure they look right. The m_RenderPass data member keeps track of which render pass your scene node belongs to, and should hold one value from the following enumeration:

```
enum RenderPass
{
    RenderPass_0,                       // A constant to define the starting pass
    RenderPass_Static = RenderPass_0,   // environments and level geometry
    RenderPass_Actor,                   // objects and things that can move
    RenderPass_Sky,                     // the background 'behind' everything
    RenderPass_Last                     // not used - a counter for for loops
};
```

SceneNode—It All Starts Here

That's it for the basics. You've now seen the design for the ISceneNode interface and what each scene node is supposed to implement. You've also seen SceneNode-Properties and how it stores read-only data that affect how the scene node draws.

Here's the base implementation of SceneNode that inherits from the ISceneNode interface class:

```
typedef std::vector<shared_ptr<ISceneNode> > SceneNodeList;

class SceneNode : public ISceneNode
{
    friend class Scene;
```

```
protected:
    SceneNodeList           m_Children;
    SceneNode               *m_pParent;
    SceneNodeProperties     m_Props;

public:
    SceneNode(optional<ActorId> actorId,
              std::string name,
              RenderPass renderPass,
              const Mat4x4 *to,
              const Mat4x4 *from=NULL)
    {
        m_pParent= NULL;
        m_Props.m_ActorId = actorId;
        m_Props.m_Name = name;
        m_Props.m_RenderPass = renderPass;
        m_Props.m_AlphaType = AlphaOpaque;
        VSetTransform(to, from);
        SetRadius(0);
    }

    virtual ~SceneNode();
    virtual const SceneNodeProperties * const VGet() const { return &m_Props; }
    virtual void VSetTransform(
        const Mat4x4 *toWorld, const Mat4x4 *fromWorld=NULL);

    virtual HRESULT VOnRestore(Scene *pScene);
    virtual HRESULT VOnUpdate(Scene *, DWORD const elapsedMs);
    virtual HRESULT VPreRender(Scene *pScene);
    virtual bool VIsVisible(Scene *pScene) const;
    virtual HRESULT VRender(Scene *pScene);
    virtual HRESULT VRenderChildren(Scene *pScene);
    virtual HRESULT VPostRender(Scene *pScene);

    virtual bool VAddChild(shared_ptr<ISceneNode> kid);

    void SetAlpha(float alpha) { return m_Props.SetAlpha(alpha); }

    Vec3 GetPosition() const { return m_Props.m_ToWorld.GetPosition(); }
    void SetPosition(const Vec3 &pos) { m_Props.m_ToWorld.SetPosition(pos); }

    void SetRadius(const float radius) { m_Props.m_Radius = radius; }
    void SetMaterial(const Material &mat) { m_Props.m_Material = mat; }
};
```

Every scene node has an STL `<vector>` of scene nodes attached to it. These child nodes, and child nodes of child nodes and so on, create the scene graph hierarchy. Most of the scene graph will be pretty flat, but some objects, such as articulated vehicles and characters, have a deep hierarchy of connected parts.

You might wonder why I chose an STL `<vector>` instead of a `<list>`. It's an easy choice since all scene nodes tend to keep a similar number of children. Even if the number of children changes, say when a car loses a wheel in a crash, it's easy enough to make the node invisible. Lists are much better for structures that need fast insertion and deletion, and vectors are fastest for iteration and random access, which makes them a better candidate to store child nodes. There's nothing stopping you, of course, in creating a special scene node that uses STL `<list>` to store its children.

Here's how the `SceneNode` class implements the `VSetTransform` method:

```
void SceneNode::VSetTransform(const Mat4x4 *toWorld, const Mat4x4 *fromWorld)
{
   m_Props.m_ToWorld = *toWorld;
   if (!fromWorld)
      m_Props.m_FromWorld = m_Props.m_ToWorld.Inverse();
   else
      m_Props.m_FromWorld = *fromWorld;
}
```

If the calling routine already has the `fromWorld` transform, it doesn't have to be calculated with a call to the expensive `D3DXMatrixInverse` function. The `fromWorld` transformation is extremely useful for things like *picking*, or finding the exact intersection of a ray with a polygon on a scene node. You certainly shouldn't do this for every object in your scene, but in this "training wheels" scene graph, it is convenient for every node to have it.

This kind of picking is similar to the ray cast provided by most physics systems, but this one is for visible geometry, not physical geometry. Most games actually consolidate the calls to both, giving the caller the opportunity to grab the right target based on what it looks like or how it is physically represented in the game world. These are usually very different, since the visible geometry is usually finely detailed, and the physical geometry is a simplified version of that.

The `VOnRestore()` and `VOnUpdate()` implementations iterate through `m_Children` and call the same method; child classes will usually do something useful, such as create geometry, load textures, or handle animations and call these methods of `SceneNode` to make sure the entire scene graph is handled:

```
HRESULT SceneNode::VOnRestore(Scene *pScene)
{
   SceneNodeList::iterator i = m_Children.begin();
   SceneNodeList::iterator end = m_Children.end();
```

```
      while (i != end)
      {
         (*i)->VOnRestore(pScene);
         i++;
      }
      return S_OK;
}

HRESULT SceneNode::VOnUpdate(Scene *pScene, DWORD const elapsedMs)
{
   SceneNodeList::iterator i = m_Children.begin();
   SceneNodeList::iterator end = m_Children.end();
   while (i != end)
   {
      (*i)->VOnUpdate(pScene, elapsedMs);
      i++;
   }
   return S_OK;
}
```

The next two methods, VPreRender() and VPostRender(), call some of the scene graph's matrix management methods. They deal with setting the world transform matrix before the render and then restoring it to its original value afterwards. You'll see how this is done in detail when I talk about the Scene class, in the next section.

```
HRESULT SceneNode::VPreRender(Scene *pScene)
{
   pScene->PushAndSetMatrix(m_Props.m_ToWorld);
   return S_OK;
}

HRESULT SceneNode::VPostRender(Scene *pScene)
{
   pScene->PopMatrix();
   return S_OK;
}
```

VIsVisible() is responsible for visibility culling. In real commercial games, this is usually a very complicated and involved process, much more than you'll see here. You have to start somewhere, though, and you can find a staggering amount of material on the Internet that will teach you how to test for object visibility in a 3D rendered scene. What's really important is that you know that you can't ignore it, no matter how simple your engine is. Here is VIsVisible():

```
bool SceneNode::VIsVisible(Scene *pScene) const
{
    // transform the location of this node into the camera space
    // of the camera attached to the scene

    Mat4x4 toWorld, fromWorld;
    pScene->GetCamera()->VGet()->Transform(&toWorld, &fromWorld);
    Vec3 pos = VGet()->ToWorld().GetPosition();

    pos = fromWorld.Xform(pos);

    Frustum const &frustum = pScene->GetCamera()->GetFrustum();
    return frustum.Inside(pos, VGet()->Radius());
}
```

If you recall from the first section in this chapter that discussed the Frustum object, you'll realize that this object was in camera space, with the camera at the origin and looking down the positive Z-axis. This means we can't just send the object location into the Frustum::Inside() routine; we have to transform it into camera space first. The first lines of code in VIsVisible() do exactly that. The location of the scene node is transformed into camera space and sent into the frustum for testing. If the object passes the visibility test, it can be rendered.

The code in VRender() handles two things. First, it sets the current material. Second, it sets the proper render states in case the node has a transparent texture or material:

```
HRESULT SceneNode::VRender(Scene *pScene)
{
    m_Props.m_Material.Use();

    switch (m_Props.m_AlphaType)
    {
        case AlphaTexture:
            // Nothing to do here....
            break;

        case AlphaMaterial:
            DXUTGetD3DDevice()->SetRenderState( D3DRS_COLORVERTEX, true);
            DXUTGetD3DDevice()->SetRenderState(
                D3DRS_DIFFUSEMATERIALSOURCE, D3DMCS_MATERIAL );
            break;
```

```
      case AlphaVertex:
        assert(0 && _T("Not implemented!"));
        break;
    }


    return S_OK;
}
```

Any class that inherits from `SceneNode` will overload `VRender()` and do something more interesting. I'll get to that when I talk about different child classes of `SceneNode`, such as `CameraNode` or `SkyNode`.

The real meat and potatoes of a scene graph happens inside `VRenderChildren()`. This method is responsible for iterating the other scene nodes stored in `m_Children` and calling the main rendering methods:

```
HRESULT SceneNode::VRenderChildren(Scene *pScene)
{
    // Iterate through the children....
    SceneNodeList::iterator i = m_Children.begin();
    SceneNodeList::iterator end = m_Children.end();
    while (i != end)
    {
        if ((*i)->VPreRender(pScene)==S_OK)
        {
            // You could short-circuit rendering
            // if an object returns E_FAIL from
            // VPreRender()

            // Don't render this node if you can't see it
            if ((*i)->VIsVisible(pScene))
            {
                float alpha = (*i)->VGet()->m_Material.GetAlpha();
                if (alpha==fOPAQUE)
                {
                    (*i)->VRender(pScene);
                }
                else if (alpha!=fTRANSPARENT)
                {
                    // The object isn't totally transparent...
                    AlphaSceneNode *asn = GCC_NEW AlphaSceneNode;
                    assert(asn);
                    asn->m_pNode = *i;
                    asn->m_Concat = *pScene->GetTopMatrix();
```

```
                Vec4 worldPos(asn->m_Concat.GetPosition());
                Mat4x4 fromWorld = pScene->GetCamera()->VGet()->FromWorld();
                Vec4 screenPos = fromWorld.Xform(worldPos);
                asn->m_ScreenZ = screenPos.z;

                pScene->AddAlphaSceneNode(asn);
            }
        }

        (*i)->VRenderChildren(pScene);
    }
    (*i)->VPostRender(pScene);
    i++;
    }


    return S_OK;
}
```

Every child scene node in the `m_Children` vector gets the same processing. First, `VPreRender()` is called, which at a minimum pushes the local transform matrix onto the matrix stack. A visibility check is made with `VIsVisible()`, and if this method returns false, the scene node isn't visible and doesn't need to be drawn. If it is visible, the scene node is checked if it is in any way transparent, because the renderer draws them after everything else. If the scene node is 100 percent opaque, `VRender()`, `VRenderChildren()`, and `VPostRender()` are called to draw the scene node and its children.

As I mentioned above, transparent objects need to draw after everything else in a special render pass. If they drew in the regular order, they wouldn't look right, since some of the background objects might actually draw after the transparent objects. What needs to happen is this: All transparent objects get stuck in a special list, and after the scene graph has been completely traversed, the scene nodes in the alpha list get drawn.

But wait, there's more. You can't just stick a pointer to the scene node in a list. You have to remember a few more things like the value of the top of the matrix stack. When the list gets traversed, it won't have the benefit of the entire scene graph and all the calls to `VPreRender()` and `VPostRender()` to keep track of it. To make things easy, there's a little structure that can help remember this data:

```
struct AlphaSceneNode
{
    shared_ptr<ISceneNode> m_pNode;
    Mat4x4 m_Concat;
    float m_ScreenZ;
```

```
// For the STL sort...
bool const operator < (AlphaSceneNode const &other)
    { return m_ScreenZ < other.m_ScreenZ; }
};

typedef std::list<AlphaSceneNode *> AlphaSceneNodes;
```

The m_ScreenZ member stores the depth of the object in the scene. Larger values are farther away from the camera, and are therefore farther away. When you draw transparent objects together, such as a forest of trees with transparent textures on them, you have to draw them from back to front, or they won't look right. The list of alpha objects is stored in the Scene class, which you'll see in the next section.

There's only VAddChild left, and besides adding a new scene node to the m_Children member, it also sets a new radius for the parent. If the child node extends geometry beyond the parent's radius, the parent's radius should be extended to include the children:

```
bool SceneNode::VAddChild(shared_ptr<ISceneNode> kid)
{
    m_Children.push_back(kid);

    // The radius of the sphere should be fixed right here
    Vec3 kidPos = kid->VGet()->ToWorld().GetPosition();
    Vec3 dir = kidPos - m_Props.ToWorld().GetPosition();
    float newRadius = dir.Length() + kid->VGet()->Radius();
    if (newRadius > m_Props.m_Radius)
        m_Props.m_Radius = newRadius;
    return true;
}
```

Don't forget that SceneNode is just a base class. You'll need to inherit from it to get anything useful to draw on the screen. I'll show you the Scene class first—the thing that manages the entire scene graph, and then move on to some interesting types of scene nodes.

The Scene Graph Manager Class

The top-level management of the entire scene node hierarchy rests in the capable hands of the Scene class. It serves as the top level entry point for updating, rendering, and adding new SceneNode objects to the scene hierarchy. It also keeps track of which scene nodes are visible components of dynamic actors in your game.

Here's the definition of the Scene, a container for SceneNode objects of all shapes and sizes:

```
typedef std::map<ActorId, shared_ptr<ISceneNode> > SceneActorMap;

class CameraNode;
class SkyNode;

class Scene
{
protected:
    shared_ptr<SceneNode>      m_Root;
    shared_ptr<CameraNode>     m_Camera;
    ID3DXMatrixStack           *m_MatrixStack;
    AlphaSceneNodes            m_AlphaSceneNodes;
    SceneActorMap              m_ActorMap;
    EffectManager              m_Effects;

    void RenderAlphaPass();

public:

    Scene();
    virtual ~Scene();

    HRESULT OnRender();
    HRESULT OnRestore();
    HRESULT OnUpdate(const int deltaMilliseconds);

    shared_ptr<ISceneNode> FindActor(ActorId id);
    bool AddChild(optional<ActorId> id, shared_ptr<ISceneNode> kid)
    {
        if (id.valid())
        {
            // This allows us to search for this later based on actor id
            m_ActorMap[*id] = kid;
        }
        return m_Root->VAddChild(kid);
    }

    bool RemoveChild(ActorId id)
    {
        m_ActorMap.erase(id);
        return m_Root->VRemoveChild(id);
    }
```

```
// Camera accessor / modifier
void SetCamera(shared_ptr<CameraNode> camera) { m_Camera = camera; }
const shared_ptr<CameraNode> GetCamera() const { return m_Camera; }

void PushAndSetMatrix(const Mat4x4 &toWorld);
void PopMatrix()
const Mat4x4 *GetTopMatrix() ;

ID3DXEffect *GetEffect(std::wstring name)
    { return m_Effects.Get(name); }

void AddAlphaSceneNode(AlphaSceneNode *asn)
    { m_AlphaSceneNodes.push_back(asn); }
};
```

The Scene class has seven data members:

- m_Root: The root scene node of the entire visible world. It has no parents and everything that is drawn is attached either as a child or to a descendant scene node.
- m_Camera: The active camera. In this simple scene graph, there is only one camera, but there's nothing that says you can't have a list of these objects.
- m_MatrixStack: A nifty DirectX object that manages a stack of transform matrices, this data structure holds the current world transform matrix as the scene graph is traversed and drawn.
- m_AlphaSceneNodes: A list of structures that holds the information necessary to draw transparent scene nodes in a final render pass.
- m_ActorMap: An STL map that lets the scene graph find a scene node matched to a particular ActorId.
- m_Effects: An STL map that lets the scene graph find a ID3DXEffect matched to a particular effect name. This is used by the DirectX programmable pipeline, and lets you apply vertex and pixel shaders to scene nodes in your scene graph.
- m_Light: A D3DLIGHT9 structure. This is used by the DirectX fixed-function pipeline, and lets you define a light source for the scene.

The root node is the top-level scene node in the entire scene graph. There is some special code associated with the root node, which I'll show you shortly. For now, you can consider the root node as the same kind of object that all tree-like data structures have.

The camera node is a little special. It could be attached anywhere in the scene graph, especially if it is a first- or third-person camera that targets a particular object. All the same, the scene graph needs quick access to the camera node, because just before rendering the scene, the scene graph uses the camera location and orientation to set the rendering device's view transform. I'll show you how that is done when I talk about the `CameraNode` class.

The interesting bit that you might not have seen before is a Direct3D matrix stack. In the previous chapter, we did plenty of work with matrix concatenation. Any number of matrices could be multiplied, or concatenated, to create any bizarre and twisted set of rotation and translation operations. In the case of a hierarchical model like a human figure, these matrix concatenations can get tedious unless you can push them onto and pop them from a stack. Hang tight—examples are coming soon.

The next data member is the actor map. This is an STL map that relates unique ActorId's (really just a plain old unsigned integer) with a particular scene node. This is needed when the scene graph needs to change a scene node based on an ActorId. A good example of this is when the physics system bounces something around. Since the physics system doesn't know or care anything about a pointer to a scene node, it will inform game subsystems of the bouncing via an event with an ActorId. When the scene graph hears about it, it uses the ActorId to find the right scene node to manipulate.

The next data member is the effects list. Each time an effect is requested for a scene node, it is loaded and managed by an effects list manager. The manager is ultra simple and assumes that effects will stay loaded once they've been used. This allows easy sharing of effects by multiple scene nodes that happen to need the same effect.

The final data member is the light source that illuminates the scene. This scene graph supports only the single light source, but it wouldn't be difficult for you to create a `LightNode` and use it to create dynamic lights in your scene.

Here's the implementation of the `Scene` class:

```
Scene::Scene()
{
   m_Root.reset(GCC_NEW RootNode());
   D3DXCreateMatrixStack(0, &m_MatrixStack);
}

Scene::~Scene()
{
   SAFE_RELEASE(m_MatrixStack);
}
```

The constructor and destructor are simple enough. They simply manage the creation and release of the root node and the DirectX matrix stack object. The other data structures have default constructors and are managed by smart pointers, so there is a little more happening here behind the scene. Yes, that was a terrible pun, but I'm not sorry.

Let's now look at OnRender, OnRestore, and OnUpdate:

```
HRESULT Scene::OnRender()
{
   DXUTGetD3D9Device()->SetLight( 1, &m_Light );
   DXUTGetD3D9Device()->LightEnable( 1, TRUE );
   DXUTGetD3D9Device()->SetRenderState( D3DRS_LIGHTING, TRUE );

   if (m_Root && m_Camera)
   {
      // The scene root could be anything, but it
      // is usually a SceneNode with the identity
      // matrix

      m_Camera->SetViewTransform(this);

      if (m_Root->VPreRender(this)==S_OK)
      {
         m_Root->VRender(this);
         m_Root->VRenderChildren(this);
         m_Root->VPostRender(this);
      }
   }

   RenderAlphaPass();

   return S_OK;
}

HRESULT Scene::OnRestore()
{
   if (!m_Root)
      return S_OK;

   D3DXVECTOR3 vecLightDirUnnormalized(1.0f, -6.0f, 1.0f);
   ZeroMemory( &m_Light, sizeof(D3DLIGHT9) );
   m_Light.Type        = D3DLIGHT_POINT;
   m_Light.Diffuse = g_White / 5.0f;
   m_Light.Specular = g_Black;
   m_Light.Ambient = g_White / 50.0f;

   D3DXVec3Normalize( (D3DXVECTOR3*)&m_Light.Direction,
      &vecLightDirUnnormalized );

   // Hard coded constants are dumb, I know.
   m_Light.Position.x      = 5.0f;
```

```
    m_Light.Position.y     = 5.0f;
    m_Light.Position.z     = -2.0f;
    m_Light.Range          = 100.0f;
    m_Light.Falloff        = 1.0f;
    m_Light.Attenuation0   = 0.1f;
    m_Light.Attenuation1   = 0.0f;
    m_Light.Attenuation2   = 0.0f;
    m_Light.Theta          = 0.0f;
    m_Light.Phi            = 0.0f;

    return m_Root->VOnRestore(this);
}


HRESULT Scene::OnUpdate(const int deltaMilliseconds)
{
    static DWORD lastTime = 0;
    DWORD elapsedTime = 0;
    DWORD now = timeGetTime();

    if (!m_Root)
        return S_OK;

    if (lastTime == 0)
    {
        lastTime = now;
    }

    elapsedTime = now - lastTime;
    lastTime = now;

    return m_Root->VOnUpdate(this, elapsedTime);
}
```

These methods clearly use the root node for all the heavy lifting. (I'll bet you thought there was going to be a little more meat to these methods!)

You'll notice that OnRender() must first check for the existence of a root node and a camera. Without either of these, there's not much more that can be done. If everything checks out fine, the camera's SetView() method is called to send the camera position and orientation into the rendering device. Then the rendering methods of the root node are called, which in turn propagate throughout the entire scene graph. Finally, the scene graph calls the RenderAlphaPass() method to handle any scene nodes that were found to have some translucency during this render.

The OnRestore() method is so trivial I think I can trust you to figure it out. There is one trick, though. The camera node must clearly be attached to the scene graph as a child of a scene node, in addition to having it as a member of the scene graph. If it isn't, it would never have its critical virtual functions called properly.

Lastly, OnUpdate() is what separates rendering from updating. Updating is generally called as fast as possible, where the render pass might be delayed to keep a particular frame rate. Rendering is usually much more expensive than updating, too. You'll also notice that the update pass is called with a delta time in milliseconds, where the render is called with no parameters. That in itself is telling since there shouldn't be any time variant code running inside the render pass, such as animations. Keep that stuff inside the update pass, and you'll find your entire graphics system will be flexible enough to run on pokey hardware and still have the chops to blaze on the fast machines.

```
void Scene::PushAndSetMatrix(const Mat4x4 &toWorld)
{
   m_MatrixStack->Push();
   m_MatrixStack->MultMatrixLocal(&toWorld);
   DXUTGetD3DDevice()->SetTransform(D3DTS_WORLD, m_MatrixStack->GetTop());
}

void Scene::PopMatrix()
{
   m_MatrixStack->Pop();
   DXUTGetD3DDevice()->SetTransform(D3DTS_WORLD, m_MatrixStack->GetTop());
}

const Mat4x4 *Scene::GetTopMatrix()
{
   return static_cast<const Mat4x4 *>(m_MatrixStack->GetTop());
}
```

Remember matrix concatenation? I don't think I've gone two paragraphs without mentioning it. There's a useful thing in DirectX called a *matrix stack*, and it is used to keep track of matrices in a hierarchy. The call to VPreRender() pushes a new matrix on the matrix stack and then concatenates it with what was already there, creating a new matrix. Once that is done, the new matrix is used to draw anything sent into the render pipeline.

This is a little confusing, and I won't ask you to visualize it because when I tried I got a pounding headache—but here's the gist of it. The matrix that exists at the top of the stack is either the identity matrix or the result of all the concatenated matrices from the hierarchy in your scene nodes in the scene graph. As you traverse to child nodes deeper in the scene graph during rendering, these methods manage the transform matrix on the stack and cause it to be concatenated with every transform up the chain, but by only doing one matrix multiplication. As you can see, this is quite efficient, and extremely flexible for implementing hier-archical objects. The push/pop methods are called by the `SceneNode::VPreRender()` and `SceneNode::VPostRender()`. The `GetTopMatrix()` method gives you read-only access to the top matrix, which is useful for storing off the world matrix of a scene node during the render pass.

Here's how the `Scene` class implements `FindActor()`:

```
shared_ptr<ISceneNode> Scene::FindActor(ActorId id)
{
   SceneActorMap::iterator i = m_ActorMap.find(id);
   if (i==m_ActorMap.end())
   {
      shared_ptr<ISceneNode> null;
      return null;
   }

   return (*i).second;
}
```

This is pretty standard STL `<map>` usage, and since we have defined the `ActorId` to be unique, we don't have to worry about finding multiple actors for a particular scene node.

The last method of the `Scene` class is `RenderAlphaPass`. This method is called after the normal rendering is done, so all the transparent scene nodes will draw on top of everything else. Here's basically what happens in this method:

- The current world transform is saved off.
- Z-sorting is disabled.
- Alpha blending is turned on.
- The alpha nodes in the alpha list are sorted.
- Each node in the alpha list is rendered and then removed from the list.
- The old render states are restored to their old values.

```
void Scene::RenderAlphaPass()
{
   Mat4x4 oldWorld;
   DXUTGetD3DDevice()->GetTransform(D3DTS_WORLD, &oldWorld);

   DWORD oldZWriteEnable;
   DXUTGetD3DDevice()->GetRenderState(D3DRS_ZWRITEENABLE, &oldZWriteEnable);
   DXUTGetD3DDevice()->SetRenderState(D3DRS_ZWRITEENABLE, false);

   DXUTGetD3DDevice()->SetRenderState(D3DRS_ALPHABLENDENABLE, true);
   DXUTGetD3DDevice()->SetRenderState(D3DRS_SRCBLEND, D3DBLEND_SRCCOLOR);
   DXUTGetD3DDevice()->SetRenderState(D3DRS_DESTBLEND, D3DBLEND_INVSRCCOLOR);
```

```
m_AlphaSceneNodes.sort();
while (!m_AlphaSceneNodes.empty())
{
    AlphaSceneNodes::reverse_iterator i = m_AlphaSceneNodes.rbegin();
    DXUTGetD3DDevice()->SetTransform(D3DTS_WORLD, &((*i)->m_Concat));
    (*i)->m_pNode->VRender(this);
    delete (*i);
    m_AlphaSceneNodes.pop_back();
}

DXUTGetD3DDevice()->SetRenderState(D3DRS_COLORVERTEX, false);
DXUTGetD3DDevice()->SetRenderState(D3DRS_ALPHABLENDENABLE, false);
DXUTGetD3DDevice()->SetRenderState(D3DRS_ZWRITEENABLE, oldZWriteEnable);
DXUTGetD3DDevice()->SetTransform(D3DTS_WORLD, &oldWorld);
}
```

The SceneNode::VRender() or any virtual overload is responsible for doing anything else to handle special transparency render states, such as if you wanted to use texture-based alpha blending.

SPECIAL SCENE GRAPH NODES

The naked SceneNode class doesn't draw anything at all. It just performs a lot of DirectX and 3D homework. We need some classes that inherit from SceneNode to construct an interesting scene. Here are the ones I'll show you:

- class RootNode: Manages children as separate render passes for different kinds of scene nodes.
- class CameraNode: Manages the camera and view frustum culling.
- class TestObject: Creates a textured grid.
- class SkyNode: Creates a sky that appears to be infinitely far away.
- class MeshNode: Wraps a DirectX mesh object.
- class ShaderMeshNode: Wraps a DirectX mesh object and draws the mesh with a vertex and pixel shader.

Implementing Separate Render Passes

Different render passes help optimize the rendering. Drawing things in the right order can do wonders for performance. Many rendering engines are fill-rate bound, which means that it's relatively expensive for them to draw pixels once everything has been set up. Every pixel you don't draw saves time, which sounds pretty obvious. How you do that gets pretty complicated, but one obvious way to do this is don't draw any pixels that are completely behind other pixels because it's a waste of time.

This means that it makes sense to draw big foreground stuff first and small background stuff later. Draw the sky absolutely as the last thing before your transparent objects, since it could cover the entire screen. One way to do this is by creating a special scene node that manages all this, and that scene node happens to be the root node of the entire scene graph:

```
class RootNode : public SceneNode
{
public:
   RootNode();
   virtual bool VAddChild(shared_ptr<ISceneNode> kid);
   virtual HRESULT VRenderChildren(Scene *pScene);
   virtual bool VIsVisible(Scene *pScene) const { return true; }
};


RootNode::RootNode()
: SceneNode(optional_empty(), "Root", RenderPass_0, &Mat4x4::g_Identity)
{
   m_Children.reserve(RenderPass_Last);

   shared_ptr<SceneNode> staticGroup(
      new SceneNode(optional_empty(),
         "StaticGroup", RenderPass_Static, &Mat4x4::g_Identity));
   m_Children.push_back(staticGroup);    // RenderPass_Static = 0

   shared_ptr<SceneNode> actorGroup(
      new SceneNode(optional_empty(),
         "ActorGroup", RenderPass_Actor, &Mat4x4::g_Identity));
   m_Children.push_back(actorGroup);    // RenderPass_Actor = 1

   shared_ptr<SceneNode> skyGroup(
      new SceneNode(optional_empty(),
         "SkyGroup", RenderPass_Sky, &Mat4x4::g_Identity));
   m_Children.push_back(skyGroup);    // RenderPass_Sky = 2
}
```

The root node has child nodes that are added directly as a part of the constructor—one child for each render pass you define. In the previous case, there are three render passes: one for static actors, one for dynamic actors, and one for the sky. When other scene nodes are added to the scene graph, the root node actually adds them to one of these children based on the new scene node's m_RenderPass member variable:

```
bool RootNode::VAddChild(shared_ptr<ISceneNode> kid)
{
   // Children that divide the scene graph into render passes.
   // Scene nodes will get added to these children based on the value of the
   // render pass member variable.

   if (!m_Children[kid->VGet()->RenderPass()])
   {
      assert(0 && _T("There is no such render pass"));
      return false;
   }

   return m_Children[kid->VGet()->RenderPass()]->VAddChild(kid);
}
```

This lets the root node have a very fine control over when each pass gets rendered and even what special render states get set for each one:

```
HRESULT RootNode::VRenderChildren(Scene *pScene)
{
   // This code creates fine control of the render passes.

   for (int pass = RenderPass_0; pass < RenderPass_Last; ++pass)
   {
      switch(pass)
      {
         case RenderPass_Static:
         case RenderPass_Actor:
            m_Children[pass]->VRenderChildren(pScene);
            break;

         case RenderPass_Sky:
         {
            DWORD oldZWriteEnable;
            DXUTGetD3DDevice()->GetRenderState(
               D3DRS_ZWRITEENABLE, &oldZWriteEnable);
            DXUTGetD3DDevice()->SetRenderState( D3DRS_ZWRITEENABLE, false);

            DWORD oldLightMode;
            DXUTGetD3DDevice()->GetRenderState( D3DRS_LIGHTING, &oldLightMode);
            DXUTGetD3DDevice()->SetRenderState( D3DRS_LIGHTING, FALSE );

            DWORD oldCullMode;
            DXUTGetD3DDevice()->GetRenderState( D3DRS_CULLMODE, &oldCullMode );
            DXUTGetD3DDevice()->SetRenderState( D3DRS_CULLMODE, D3DCULL_NONE );
```

```
        m_Children[pass]->VRenderChildren(pScene);

        // Notice that the render states are returned to
        // their original settings.....
        // Could there be a better way???

        DXUTGetD3DDevice()->SetRenderState( D3DRS_LIGHTING, oldLightMode );
        DXUTGetD3DDevice()->SetRenderState( D3DRS_CULLMODE, oldCullMode );

        DXUTGetD3DDevice()->SetRenderState(
            D3DRS_ZWRITEENABLE, oldZWriteEnable);
        break;
      }
    }
  }

  return S_OK;
}
```

For static and dynamic actors, the root node doesn't do anything special other than draw them. The sky node needs a little extra attention though—with three render states changed for its benefit. First, the Z-write is turned off since you know that the sky node and anything that draws after it, like transparent objects, doesn't care about Z and therefore the drawing will go faster. Lighting is also turned off because you expect the textured sky will essentially have the color and lighting baked into the texture. Lastly, culling is turned off since you will clearly draw the sky polygons. They all face the camera, no matter where it is looking.

You could easily define other render passes, perhaps one for shadows or other special effects like light bloom. It's totally up to you and what you want your game to look like.

A Simple Camera

You'll need a camera if you want to take pictures, right? The camera in a 3D scene inherits from SceneNode just like everything else and adds some data members to keep track of its viewable area, the projection matrix, and perhaps a target scene node that it will follow around:

```
class CameraNode : public SceneNode
{
protected:

    Frustum        m_Frustum;
    Mat4x4         m_Projection;
    bool           m_bActive;
```

```
        bool             m_DebugCamera;
        optional< shared_ptr<SceneNode> > m_pTarget;

    public:
        CameraNode(Mat4x4 const *t, Frustum const &frustum)
         : SceneNode(optional_empty(), "Camera", RenderPass_0, t),
           m_Frustum(frustum),
           m_bActive(true),
           m_DebugCamera(false)
        {
        }

        virtual HRESULT VRender(Scene *pScene);
        virtual HRESULT VOnRestore(Scene *pScene);
        virtual bool VIsVisible(Scene *pScene) const { return m_bActive; }

        virtual HRESULT SetView(Scene *pScene);

        const Frustum &GetFrustum() { return m_Frustum; }
        void SetTarget(shared_ptr<SceneNode> pTarget)
        {
            m_pTarget = pTarget;
        }
    };
```

The VRender() method calls the Frustum::Render() method to draw the camera's viewable area:

```
HRESULT CameraNode::VRender(Scene *pScene)
{
    if (m_DebugCamera)
    {
        m_Frustum.Render();
    }

    return S_OK;
}
```

The VOnRestore() chain can be called when the player resizes the game screen to a different resolution. If this happens, the camera view frustum shape will probably change, and so will the projection matrix, which is really a Mat4x4 structure that describes the shape of the view frustum in a transform matrix. Notice the D3DXMatrixPerspectiveFovLH call—the LH stands for "left-handed." You'll see tons of DirectX methods dealing with transform matrices that are either left-handed or

CREATE A SPECIAL CAMERA FOR DEBUGGING

When I was working on Thief: Deadly Shadows, *it was really useful to have a special "debug" camera that moved about the scene without affecting the code that was being checked against the "real" camera. The process worked like this: I would key in a special debug command, and the debug camera would be enabled. I could free-fly it around the scene, and the "normal" camera was visible because the view frustum of the normal camera would draw, and I could visually debug problems like third-person movement issues, scene culling issues, and so on. It was kind of like having a backstage pass to the internals of the game!*

right-handed, and using one over the other is simply a matter of choice. Sometimes, you have better compatibility with importing meshes from modeling tools in one versus the other, but besides that they are mathematically identical.

```
virtual HRESULT CameraNode::VOnRestore(Scene *pScene)
{
   m_Frustum.SetAspect(
      DXUTGetBackBufferSurfaceDesc()->Width /
        (FLOAT)DXUTGetBackBufferSurfaceDesc()->Height);
   D3DXMatrixPerspectiveFovLH( &m_Projection,
      m_Frustum.m_Fov, m_Frustum.m_Aspect, m_Frustum.m_Near, m_Frustum.m_Far );
   DXUTGetD3DDevice()->SetTransform( D3DTS_PROJECTION, &m_Projection );
      return S_OK;
}
```

The camera's `SetView()` method is called just before rendering the scene. It reads the "from world" transform stored in the scene node and sends that into the rendering device:

```
HRESULT CameraNode::SetView(Scene *pScene)
{
   //If there is a target, make sure the camera is
   //rigidly attached right behind the target
   if(m_pTarget.valid())
   {
      Mat4x4 mat = (*m_pTarget)->VGet()->ToWorld();
      Vec4 at = g_Forward4 * -10.0f;
      Vec4 atWorld = mat.Xform(at);
      Vec3 pos = mat.GetPosition() + Vec3(atWorld);
      mat.SetPosition(pos);
      VSetTransform(&mat);
   }
```

```
DXUTGetD3DDevice()->SetTransform( D3DTS_VIEW, &VGet()->FromWorld() );
    return S_OK;
}
```

The simple example above also implements a bare-bones third-person follow camera—the camera's position and orientation is sucked from the target scene node and moved 10 meters back. Of course, a real third-person camera would detect environment geometry and have all kinds of interpolators to make sure the camera movement was smooth and pleasing to the player. Sadly, that technology is beyond the scope of this chapter.

Building and Rendering Simple Geometry

We still haven't seen anything that will actually draw a shape on the screen yet. Here's a class that will create a perfect cube or an asymmetric cuboid, useful for testing your renderer and physics system:

```
class TestObject : public SceneNode
{
protected:
    LPDIRECT3DVERTEXBUFFER9 m_pVerts;
    DWORD                   m_numVerts;
    DWORD                   m_numPolys;
    DWORD                   m_color;
    bool                    m_squashed;

public:
    TestObject(ActorId id, DWORD color, bool squashed, std::string name);
    virtual ~TestObject();
    HRESULT VOnRestore(Scene *pScene);
    HRESULT VRender(Scene *pScene);

    static WORD g_TestObjectIndices[][3];
    static Vec3 g_CubeVerts[];
    static Vec3 g_SquashedCubeVerts[];
};

TestObject::TestObject(
    ActorId id, DWORD color, bool squashed, std::string name)
    : SceneNode(id, name, RenderPass_0, &p.m_Mat)
{
    m_color = color;
    m_pVerts = NULL;
    m_numVerts = m_numPolys = 0;
```

```
   Material mat;
   mat.Set(g_Green);
   SetMaterial(mat);
}


TestObject::~TestObject()
{
   SAFE_RELEASE(m_pVerts);
}

Vec3 TestObject::g_CubeVerts[] =
{
   Vec3( 0.5,0.5,-0.5),        // Vertex 0.
   Vec3(-0.5,0.5,-0.5),        // Vertex 1.
   Vec3(-0.5,0.5,0.5),         // And so on.
   Vec3(0.5,0.5,0.5),
   Vec3(0.5,-0.5,-0.5),
   Vec3(-0.5,-0.5,-0.5),
   Vec3(-0.5,-0.5,0.5),
   Vec3(0.5,-0.5,0.5)
};

Vec3 TestObject::g_SquashedCubeVerts[] =
{
   Vec3( 0.5,0.5,-0.25),       // Vertex 0.
   Vec3(-0.5,0.5,-0.25),       // Vertex 1.
   Vec3(-0.5,0.5,0.5),         // And so on.
   Vec3(0.75,0.5,0.5),
   Vec3(0.75,-0.5,-0.5),
   Vec3(-0.5,-0.5,-0.5),
   Vec3(-0.5,-0.3f,0.5),
   Vec3(0.5,-0.3f,0.5)
};

WORD TestObject::g_TestObjectIndices[][3] =
{
   { 0,1,2 },                  // Face 0 has three vertices.
   { 0,2,3 },                  // And so on.
   { 0,4,5 },
   { 0,5,1 },
   { 1,5,6 },
   { 1,6,2 },
   { 2,6,7 },
```

```
        { 2,7,3 },
        { 3,7,4 },
        { 3,4,0 },
        { 4,7,6 },
        { 4,6,5 }
};

HRESULT TestObject::VOnRestore(Scene *pScene)
{
    // Call the base class's restore
    SceneNode::VOnRestore(pScene);

    Vec3 center;
    Vec3 *verts = m_squashed ? g_SquashedCubeVerts : g_CubeVerts;
    float radius;
    HRESULT hr = D3DXComputeBoundingSphere(
        static_cast<D3DXVECTOR3*>(verts), 8,
          D3DXGetFVFVertexSize(D3DFVF_XYZ),
        &center, &radius );

    SetRadius(radius);

    // Create the vertex buffer - this object is essentially
    // a squashed cube, but since we want each face to be flat shaded
    // each face needs its own set of verts - because each vert has a normal
    // and thus can't have any vert shared by adjacent faces.
    m_numPolys = 12;
    m_numVerts = m_numPolys * 3;

     if( FAILED( DXUTGetD3D9Device()->CreateVertexBuffer(
       m_numVerts*sizeof(UNTRANSFORMED_UNLIT_VERTEX),
       D3DUSAGE_WRITEONLY, UNTRANSFORMED_UNLIT_VERTEX::FVF,
         D3DPOOL_MANAGED, &m_pVerts, NULL ) ) )
     {
         return E_FAIL;
     }

    // Fill the vertex buffer. We are setting the tu and tv texture
    // coordinates, which range from 0.0 to 1.0
    UNTRANSFORMED_UNLIT_VERTEX* pVertices;
    if( FAILED( m_pVerts->Lock( 0, 0, (void**)&pVertices, 0 ) ) )
        return E_FAIL;

    static Color colors[6] =
      { g_White, g_Gray65, g_Cyan, g_Red, g_Green, g_Blue };
```

```
    for (DWORD face=0; face<m_numPolys; ++face )
    {
       UNTRANSFORMED_UNLIT_VERTEX* v = &pVertices[face * 3];
       v->position = verts[g_TestObjectIndices[face][0]];
       v->diffuse = colors[face/2];
       v->specular   = colors[face/2];
       (v+1)->position = verts[g_TestObjectIndices[face][1]];
       (v+1)->diffuse = colors[face/2];
       (v+1)->specular   = colors[face/2];
       (v+2)->position = verts[g_TestObjectIndices[face][2]];
       (v+2)->diffuse = colors[face/2];
       (v+2)->specular   = colors[face/2];

       Vec3 a = v->position - (v+1)->position;
       Vec3 b = (v+2)->position - (v+1)->position;

       Vec3 cross = a.Cross(b);
       cross /= cross.Length();
       v->normal = cross;
       (v+1)->normal = cross;
       (v+2)->normal = cross;
    }

    m_pVerts->Unlock();
    return S_OK;
}


HRESULT TestObject::VRender(Scene *pScene)
{
    if (S_OK != SceneNode::VRender(pScene) )
       return E_FAIL;

    DXUTGetD3D9Device()->SetRenderState( D3DRS_LIGHTING, TRUE );

    DXUTGetD3D9Device()->SetRenderState( D3DRS_CULLMODE, D3DCULL_CCW );
    DXUTGetD3D9Device()->SetTexture (0, NULL);

    // If you want colored verts, still affected by the D3DLIGHT9 in
    // the fixed function pipeline you need to call these two
    // render states:
    DXUTGetD3D9Device()->SetRenderState( D3DRS_COLORVERTEX , TRUE );
    DXUTGetD3D9Device()->SetRenderState(
       D3DRS_DIFFUSEMATERIALSOURCE, D3DMCS_COLOR1);
```

```
DXUTGetD3D9Device()->SetStreamSource(
    0, m_pVerts, 0, sizeof(UNTRANSFORMED_UNLIT_VERTEX) );
DXUTGetD3D9Device()->SetFVF( UNTRANSFORMED_UNLIT_VERTEX::FVF );
DXUTGetD3D9Device()->DrawPrimitive( D3DPT_TRIANGLELIST , 0, 12);

return S_OK;
}
```

One thing is important to note about the scene graph architecture: you can't be sure what the render state is at the beginning of a call to VRender(). You have two choices here. First, you can just always set the states you need at the beginning of each call to VRender(). That is the method I tend to choose. Another choice is to grab the current render states with GetRenderState() and restore them before you return from VRender().

If you think this will result in calling SetRenderState() way too many times, or perhaps mistakenly leave the renderer with a weird state setting, you are absolutely right. This is one of the limitations of a scene-graph architecture, whether you use a fixed-function or programmable pipeline.

First, it's way too easy to forget to set the render state to something "neutral" after rendering a node that uses special render states. Second, being very cautious about saving and restoring render states as the scene graph is traversed results in too many calls to SetRenderState(). So what is a programmer to do?

One thing you might consider is to decouple the scene graph traversal with the actual rendering. As the scene graph is traversed, you send the geometry, render states, and transform matrices into a lower-level system that is smart enough to sort the geometry by texture and material, keep large monolithic vertex and index buffers around to hold this geometry, and above all minimize render state changes. A by-product of this system is that it tends to send bits to the video card in larger batches, which tends to keep the video card's GPU and the computers CPU busy in parallel.

Rendering the Sky

The sky in computer games is usually a very simple object, such as a cube or faceted dome. The trick to making the sky look like it is infinitely far away is to keep its position coordinated with the camera. The following class implements a cube-shaped sky. The textures that are placed on the cube are created to give the players the illusion they are looking at a dome-shaped object.

```
class SkyNode : public SceneNode
{
protected:
    LPDIRECT3DTEXTURE9        m_pTexture[5]; // the sky textures
    LPDIRECT3DVERTEXBUFFER9   m_pVerts;      // the sky verts
```

```
DWORD                          m_numVerts;
DWORD                          m_sides;
const char *                   m_textureBaseName;
shared_ptr<CameraNode>         m_camera;
bool                           m_bActive;
public:
    SkyNode(const char *textureFile, shared_ptr<CameraNode> camera);
    virtual ~SkyNode();
    HRESULT VOnRestore(Scene *pScene);
    HRESULT VRender(Scene *pScene);
    HRESULT VPreRender(Scene *pScene);
    bool VIsVisible(Scene *pScene) const { return m_bActive; }
};
```

This class is extremely similar in construction to the TestObject class, with the small exception of how the geometry is built and the addition of some textures. Everything else is pretty similar:

```
SkyNode::SkyNode(const char *pTextureBaseName, shared_ptr<CameraNode> camera)
: SceneNode(optional_empty(), "Sky", RenderPass_Sky, &Mat4x4::g_Identity)
, m_camera(camera)
, m_bActive(true)
{
    m_textureBaseName = pTextureBaseName;
    for (int i=0; i<5; ++i)
    {
        m_pTexture[i] = NULL;
    }
}

SkyNode::~SkyNode()
{
    for (int i=0; i<5; ++i)
    {
        SAFE_RELEASE(m_pTexture[i]);
    }
    SAFE_RELEASE(m_pVerts);
}
```

There are five textures mapped on the sky, one each for north, east, south, west, and top sides of the cube. The texture base name sent into the constructor lets a programmer set a base name, like "Daytime" or "Nighttime," and the textures that are actually read append side name suffixes to the actual texture filename:

```
HRESULT SkyNode::VOnRestore(Scene *pScene)
{
    // Call the base class's restore
    SceneNode::VOnRestore(pScene);

    const char *suffix[] =
        { "_n.jpg", "_e.jpg",  "_s.jpg",  "_w.jpg",  "_u.jpg" };
    for (int i=0; i<5; ++i)
    {
        char name[256];
        strcpy(name, m_textureBaseName);
        strcat(name, suffix[i]);

        Resource resource(name);
        shared_ptr<ResHandle> texture = g_pApp->m_ResCache->GetHandle(&resource);
        if ( FAILED ( D3DXCreateTextureFromFileInMemory( DXUTGetD3D9Device(),
                    texture->Buffer(), texture->Size(), &m_pTexture[i] ) ) )
            return E_FAIL;
    }

    m_numVerts = 20;

    if( FAILED( DXUTGetD3DDevice()->CreateVertexBuffer(
        m_numVerts*sizeof(COLORED_TEXTURED_VERTEX),
        D3DUSAGE_WRITEONLY, COLORED_TEXTURED_VERTEX::FVF,
        D3DPOOL_MANAGED, &m_pVerts, NULL ) ) )
    {
        return E_FAIL;
    }

    // Fill the vertex buffer. We are setting the tu and tv texture
    // coordinates, which range from 0.0 to 1.0
    COLORED_TEXTURED_VERTEX* pVertices;
    if( FAILED( m_pVerts->Lock( 0, 0, (void**)&pVertices, 0 ) ) )
        return E_FAIL;

    // Loop through the grid squares and calc the values
    // of each index. Each grid square has two triangles:
    //
    //      A - B
    //      | / |
    //      C - D
```

```
COLORED_TEXTURED_VERTEX skyVerts[4];
D3DCOLOR skyVertColor = 0xffffffff;
float dim = 50.0f;

skyVerts[0].position = Vec3( dim, dim, dim );
skyVerts[0].color=skyVertColor; skyVerts[0].tu=1; skyVerts[0].tv=0;
skyVerts[1].position = Vec3(-dim, dim, dim );
skyVerts[1].color=skyVertColor; skyVerts[1].tu=0; skyVerts[1].tv=0;
skyVerts[2].position = Vec3( dim,-dim, dim );
skyVerts[2].color=skyVertColor; skyVerts[2].tu=1; skyVerts[2].tv=1;
skyVerts[3].position = Vec3(-dim,-dim, dim );
skyVerts[3].color=skyVertColor; skyVerts[3].tu=0; skyVerts[3].tv=1;

Mat4x4 rotY;
rotY.BuildRotationY(D3DX_PI/2.0f);
Mat4x4 rotX;
rotX.BuildRotationX(-D3DX_PI/2.0f);

m_sides = 5;

for (DWORD side = 0; side < m_sides; side++)
{
   for (DWORD v = 0; v < 4; v++)
   {
      Vec4 temp;
      if (side < m_sides-1)
      {
         temp = rotY.Xform(Vec3(skyVerts[v].position));
      }
      else
      {
         skyVerts[0].tu=1; skyVerts[0].tv=1;
         skyVerts[1].tu=1; skyVerts[1].tv=0;
         skyVerts[2].tu=0; skyVerts[2].tv=1;
         skyVerts[3].tu=0; skyVerts[3].tv=0;

         temp = rotX.Xform(Vec3(skyVerts[v].position));
      }
      skyVerts[v].position = Vec3(temp.x, temp.y, temp.z);
   }
   memcpy(&pVertices[side*4], skyVerts, sizeof(skyVerts));
}

m_pVerts->Unlock();
return S_OK;
}
```

You might even notice a cameo from the resource caching chapter; just before the texture is created, you see a call to create a resource and g_pApp->m_ResCache->GetHandle(resource) to load the resource from the resource cache. You could just as easily load the texture straight from the file using the D3DXCreateTextureFromFile() API, if you decide the resource cache isn't for you.

The real trick to making the sky node special is the code inside VPreRender().

```
HRESULT SkyNode::VPreRender(Scene *pScene)
{
   Vec3 cameraPos = m_camera->VGet()->ToWorld().GetPosition();
   Mat4x4 mat = m_Props.ToWorld();
   mat.SetPosition(cameraPos);
   VSetTransform(&mat);

   return SceneNode::VPreRender(pScene);
}
```

This code grabs the camera position and moves the sky node into place. This gives a completely convincing illusion that the objects like sun, moon, mountains, and other backgrounds rendered into the sky textures are extremely far away, since they don't appear to move as the player moves.

The VRender() method is pretty similar to what you've already seen, with the exception that the sky has five textures, and these textures need to be set for each face as it is rendered:

```
HRESULT SkyNode::VRender(Scene *pScene)
{
   DXUTGetD3DDevice()->SetTextureStageState(
      0, D3DTSS_COLOROP,   D3DTOP_MODULATE );
   DXUTGetD3DDevice()->SetTextureStageState(
      0, D3DTSS_COLORARG1, D3DTA_TEXTURE );
   DXUTGetD3DDevice()->SetTextureStageState(
      0, D3DTSS_COLORARG2, D3DTA_DIFFUSE );

   DXUTGetD3DDevice()->SetStreamSource(
      0, m_pVerts, 0, sizeof(COLORED_TEXTURED_VERTEX) );
   DXUTGetD3DDevice()->SetFVF( COLORED_TEXTURED_VERTEX::FVF );

   for (DWORD side = 0; side < m_sides; side++)
   {
      // TODO: A good optimization would be to transform the camera's
      // world look vector into local space and do a dot product. If the
```

```
    // result is positive, we shouldn't draw the side since it has to be
    // behind the camera!

    // Sky boxes aren't culled by the normal mechanism
    DXUTGetD3DDevice()->SetTexture( 0, m_pTexture[side] );
    DXUTGetD3DDevice()->DrawPrimitive( D3DPT_TRIANGLESTRIP , 4 * side, 2);
}

DXUTGetD3DDevice()->SetTexture (0, NULL);
return S_OK;
}
```

If you read this and say to yourself, "What a fool—McShaffry is setting a different texture for each face of the sky and that's too expensive!" you'd be absolutely right. I think it is just as informative watching programmers, in this case me, make mistakes as it is watching them be brilliant. Believe me, I'm much better at the former than the latter.

So how would you optimize this code? I'd do two things. First, I'd bake all five sky textures into one monolithic texture, taking some care I didn't ruin a texture size limitation somewhere. I'd have to tweak the (u,v) coordinates when the geometry was built, but that's pretty easy. Another thing I'd do would be to check to see which parts of the sky the camera was actually looking at, so I didn't set a texture for something that never drew. Clearly, you never have to draw the east sky and the west sky if your camera view frustum is narrow enough.

Using Meshes in Your Scene

A 3D game would be pretty boring with nothing but grids drawing at various positions and rotations. If you want interesting shapes, you'll need to create them in a modeling tool like 3D Studio Max. Modeling tools are precise tools for creating shapes for your game levels or dynamic objects. DirectX can't read a MAX or 3DS file directly; you'll need to convert it to a X file with DirectX's conv3ds.exe utility. You can find help for this program in MSDN and elsewhere on the Web.

Once you have a X file, you can create a mesh object that DirectX can read natively, and all you need is a way to plug this object into the scene graph.

The node you are looking for is MeshNode, which encapsulates ID3DXMesh, a D3D object that represents an object mesh and applied materials in a 3D scene. You can create simple meshes with the DirectX Mesh Viewer Utility, such as boxes, spheres, and all the teapots you could ever want.

This class has two constructors. The first is used for sending in a prebuilt mesh, such as a sphere, which can be built by DirectX. The other constructor takes a filename of a valid X file:

```
class MeshNode : public SceneNode
{
protected:
    ID3DXMesh *m_pMesh;
    std::wstring m_XFileName;

public:
    MeshNode(const optional<ActorId> actorId,
        std::string name,
        ID3DXMesh *mesh,
        RenderPass renderPass,
        const Mat4x4 *t,
        const Color &color);

    MeshNode(const optional<ActorId> actorId,
        std::string name,
        std::wstring xFileName,
        RenderPass renderPass,
        const Mat4x4 *t,
        const Color &color);

    virtual ~MeshNode() { SAFE_RELEASE(m_pMesh); }
    HRESULT VRender(Scene *pScene);
    virtual HRESULT VOnRestore(Scene *pScene);

    float CalcBoundingSphere();
};
```

There are two data members of this class. The first, m_pMesh, stores a pointer to the constructed mesh, which by the way is a COM object like many DirectX objects. This means you'll see the expected call to SAFE_RELEASE in the methods that destruct or restore the MeshNode class. There's also an STL string that stores the name of the X file if the mesh was loaded from one. It is assumed that if the string is empty, the mesh was prebuilt instead of being loaded from a file:

```
MeshNode::MeshNode(const optional<ActorId> actorId,
    std::string name,
    ID3DXMesh *mesh,
    RenderPass renderPass,
    const Mat4x4 *t,
    const Color &color)
  : SceneNode(actorId, name, renderPass, t)
```

```
{
   m_pMesh = mesh;
   m_pMesh->AddRef();

   Material mat;
   mat.Set(color);
   SetMaterial(mat);
}

MeshNode::MeshNode(const optional<ActorId> actorId,
   std::string name,
   std::wstring xFileName,
   RenderPass renderPass,
   const Mat4x4 *t,
   const Color &color)
 : SceneNode(actorId, name, renderPass, t)
{
   m_pMesh = NULL;
   m_XFileName = xFileName;

   Material mat;
   mat.Set(color);
   SetMaterial(mat);
}
```

The VRender() method is pretty trivial, since all it does is call the parent class's VRender() method and then the DrawSubset() API of the DirectX mesh:

```
HRESULT MeshNode::VRender(Scene *pScene)
{
   if (S_OK != SceneNode::VRender(pScene) )
      return E_FAIL;

   return m_pMesh->DrawSubset(0);
}
```

The parameter sent into DrawSubset() identifies a subset of the mesh to draw. Every subset of a mesh uses a different material, which could be a different texture or alpha blend mode. The DirectX X file format stores all of these subsets so a single mesh can be a very complicated object—even one that can animate. For this simple scene graph, you can assume that a mesh will have one subset.

Modeling tools allow definition of multiple subsets per mesh to separate different parts of the mesh that have different attributes like texture or material.

The VOnRestore() method is responsible for loading the mesh, as shown here:

```
HRESULT MeshNode::VOnRestore(Scene *pScene)
{
   if (m_XFileName.empty())
   {
      SetRadius(CalcBoundingSphere());
      return S_OK;
   }

   SAFE_RELEASE(m_pMesh);

   WCHAR str[MAX_PATH];
   HRESULT hr;

   // Load the mesh with D3DX and get back a ID3DXMesh*.  For this
   // sample we'll ignore the X file's embedded materials since we know
   // exactly the model we're loading.  See the mesh samples such as
   // "OptimizedMesh" for a more generic mesh loading example.
   V_RETURN( DXUTFindDXSDKMediaFileCch( str, MAX_PATH, m_XFileName.c_str() ) );

   V_RETURN( D3DXLoadMeshFromX(str, D3DXMESH_MANAGED,
      DXUTGetD3DDevice(), NULL, NULL, NULL, NULL, &m_pMesh) );

   DWORD *rgdwAdjacency = NULL;

   // Make sure there are normals which are required for lighting
   if( !(m_pMesh->GetFVF() & D3DFVF_NORMAL) )
   {
      ID3DXMesh* pTempMesh;
      V( m_pMesh->CloneMeshFVF( m_pMesh->GetOptions(),
                                m_pMesh->GetFVF() | D3DFVF_NORMAL,
                                DXUTGetD3DDevice(), &pTempMesh ) );
      V( D3DXComputeNormals( pTempMesh, NULL ) );

      SAFE_RELEASE( m_pMesh );
      m_pMesh = pTempMesh;
   }

   // Optimize the mesh for this graphics card's vertex cache
   // so when rendering the mesh's triangle list the vertices will
   // cache hit more often so it won't have to re-execute the vertex shader
   // on those vertices so it will improve perf.

   rgdwAdjacency = GCC_NEW DWORD[m_pMesh->GetNumFaces() * 3];
   if( rgdwAdjacency == NULL )
      return E_OUTOFMEMORY;
```

```
V( m_pMesh->ConvertPointRepsToAdjacency(NULL, rgdwAdjacency) );
V( m_pMesh->OptimizeInplace(D3DXMESHOPT_VERTEXCACHE,
    rgdwAdjacency, NULL, NULL, NULL) );

SAFE_DELETE_ARRAY(rgdwAdjacency);
SetRadius(CalcBoundingSphere());
 return S_OK;
}
```

This method is lifted almost verbatim from the DirectX sample code. It is responsible for opening and loading the mesh file, calculating normals, and optimizing the mesh for the current hardware. This optimization does slow down load times, if you are loading hundreds of mesh files. Assuming your players can sit through that, they'll be rewarded with a faster frame rate.

BEST PRACTICE

WATCH THOSE LONG LOAD TIMES

Balancing load times and runtime frame rate is one of the trickiest problems in game development. Load times tend to be slow because the files are intentionally stripped down to the bare bones and compressed to pack as many game assets on the digital media as possible. Frame rate suffers if the game assets have to be tweaked every frame or if they simply aren't formatted for the fastest rendering on the player's hardware. Here's a good rule of thumb: Don't make the player wait more than 60 seconds for a load for every 30 minutes of gameplay. And whatever you do, make sure you have a nice screen animation during the load so players don't confuse your long load times with a game crash!

There's a useful DirectX method to calculate the bounding sphere of a group of vertices. Since the scene node class requires the right value in m_Props.m_Radius to be properly checked against the view frustum, the D3DXComputeBoundingSphere method comes in quite handy:

```
float MeshNode::CalcBoundingSphere()
{
   HRESULT hr;

   // Find the mesh's center, then generate a centering matrix.
   IDirect3DVertexBuffer9* pVB = NULL;
   V_RETURN( m_pMesh->GetVertexBuffer( &pVB ) );

   void* pVertices = NULL;
   hr = pVB->Lock( 0, 0, &pVertices, 0 );
```

```
      if( FAILED(hr) )
      {
        SAFE_RELEASE( pVB );
        return hr;
      }

      Vec3 center;
      float radius;
      hr = D3DXComputeBoundingSphere(
            (D3DXVECTOR3*)pVertices, m_pMesh->GetNumVertices(),
            D3DXGetFVFVertexSize(m_pMesh->GetFVF()), &center, &radius );
      pVB->Unlock();
      SAFE_RELEASE( pVB );
      return radius;
    }
```

The array of vertices are hidden safely away in the mesh's vertex buffer, and to get to them, the vertex buffer has to be locked. Assuming the lock is successful, the vertices are sent into the D3DXComputeBoundingSphere routine, and that gives us the right value to store in the scene node properties.

WHAT ABOUT SHADERS?

When I first started the third edition of this book, one of my most important goals was an ultra simple introduction to vertex and pixel shaders. Much of my own learning about them was pretty frustrating, actually. It seemed there was no middle ground between drawing a very lame triangle and drawing fur. I hope the following introduction will help you see a path to getting started with shaders.

A shader is a program that can affect the position of a vertex, or the color of a pixel, or both. Shaders can create interesting effects by manipulating geometry, as is frequently done for water surfaces, or changing the appearance of something as mundane as a teapotahedron (see Figure 14.3).

Shaders can be written in assembly or high-level languages. Microsoft developed HLSL, which stands for High Level Shader Language, for use within DirectX. There is also a standard for OpenGL. There is also Nivida's Cg, or C for Graphics, which is very similar to HLSL. All look and feel a lot like C, but don't be fooled. They aren't C.

Just like any high-level language, shaders compile to assembler language. The shader compiler lives in your graphics drivers, and depending on your graphics card, the compiler can do some pretty interesting things with the resulting assembly. One example is loops, which are generally unrolled instead of actually looping in the way you are used to. Different shader versions have drastically different support for numbers of texture coordinates or even the size of the shader.

FIGURE 14.3 Different effects created by pixel and vertex shaders.

You can compile shaders ahead of time for all the different shader versions and test them against your video cards, and this is definitely recommended for a commercial environment. Compiling at runtime is the way most programmers develop shaders. In the example you are about to see, the shader will be loaded and compiled at runtime just as you would do when developing them.

The .FX File

Let's have a look at the code stored in the GameCode3.fx file. This particular shader is a simple one, because all it does is light vertices and apply a texture. The shader starts, like all programs, by declaring variables:

```
//--------------------------------------------------------------
// Global variables
//--------------------------------------------------------------
float4 g_MaterialAmbientColor;      // Material's ambient color
float4 g_MaterialDiffuseColor;      // Material's diffuse color
int g_nNumLights;
```

```
float3 g_LightDir[3];        // Light's direction in world space
float4 g_LightDiffuse[3];    // Light's diffuse color
float4 g_LightAmbient;       // Light's ambient color
float g_fAlpha;          // Alpha value (0.0 totally transparent, 1.0 opaque)

texture g_MeshTexture;               // Color texture for mesh

float    g_fTime;                    // App's time in seconds
float4x4 g_mWorld;                   // World matrix for object
float4x4 g_mWorldViewProjection;     // World * View * Projection matrix

//-----------------------------------------------------------------
// Texture samplers
//-----------------------------------------------------------------
sampler MeshTextureSampler =
sampler_state
{
    Texture = <g_MeshTexture>;
    MipFilter = LINEAR;
    MinFilter = LINEAR;
    MagFilter = LINEAR;
};
```

You'll recognize the names from the set value calls in ShaderMeshNode::VRender(). The MeshTextureSampler is a declaration that allows the pixel shader to draw texels from g_MeshTexture.

The next bit in the shader file is the declaration of the output of the vertex shader:

```
//-----------------------------------------------------------------
// Vertex shader output structure
//-----------------------------------------------------------------
struct VS_OUTPUT
{
    // vertex position
    float4 Position   : POSITION;

    // vertex diffuse color (note that COLOR0 is clamped from 0..1)
    float4 Diffuse    : COLOR0;

    // vertex texture coords
    float2 TextureUV  : TEXCOORD0;
};
```

This might jog your memory from the fixed-function pipeline. Video hardware is still video hardware, and you'll notice that you still have to get data to it so it can render triangles.

Next, a function is declared that calculates each vertex:

```
//--------------------------------------------------------------
// This shader computes standard transform and lighting
//--------------------------------------------------------------
VS_OUTPUT RenderSceneVS( float4 vPos : POSITION,
                         float3 vNormal : NORMAL,
                         float2 vTexCoord0 : TEXCOORD0,
                         uniform int nNumLights,
                         uniform bool bTexture,
                         uniform bool bAnimate )
{
    VS_OUTPUT Output;
    float3 vNormalWorldSpace;

    // Transform the position from object space
    // to homogeneous projection space
    Output.Position = mul(vPos, g_mWorldViewProjection);

    // Transform the normal from object space to world space
    vNormalWorldSpace = normalize(mul(vNormal, (float3x3)g_mWorld));
    // Compute simple directional lighting equation
    float3 vTotalLightDiffuse = float3(0,0,0);
    for(int i=0; i<nNumLights; i++ )
        vTotalLightDiffuse += g_LightDiffuse[i] *
            max(0,dot(vNormalWorldSpace, g_LightDir[i]));

    Output.Diffuse.rgb = g_MaterialDiffuseColor * vTotalLightDiffuse +
                         g_MaterialAmbientColor * g_LightAmbient;

    Output.Diffuse.a = 1.0f;

    // Just copy the texture coordinate through
    if( bTexture )
        Output.TextureUV = vTexCoord0;
    else
        Output.TextureUV = 0;

    return Output;
}
```

The input parameters to the vertex shader come from the mesh subset: position, normal, and texture coordinate. The parameters with the uniform keyword are set by the shader technique, which you'll see in a moment.

Looking at this code, you should quickly realize that all the neat stuff in the DirectX fixed function pipeline is clearly not at work anymore. All of the world, view, and projection calculations, lighting calculations, and anything else you might have desired is not working—at least not here. You'll see shortly that this is intentional, and you can enable certain render states, such as alpha blending, in another part of the shader. This one is bare bones, even to the point of calculating lighting just like I did back in the *Ultima IX* days.

Of course, the real power of a vertex shader is that you can also physically move the vertex around, which is how many programmers implement cool surfaces like water or even cloth.

The output of the vertex shader is fed into the pixel shader, whose format is defined next. This particular pixel shader is so trivial there's no reason we should have used it at all, because a fixed-function method would have worked just fine. But this will give you a place to start experimenting:

```
//---------------------------------------------------------------
// Pixel shader output structure
//---------------------------------------------------------------
struct PS_OUTPUT
{
    float4 RGBColor : COLOR0;   // Pixel color
};


//---------------------------------------------------------------
// This shader outputs the pixel's color by modulating the texture's
//        color with diffuse material color
//---------------------------------------------------------------
PS_OUTPUT RenderScenePS( VS_OUTPUT In, bool bTexture )
{
    PS_OUTPUT Output;

    // Lookup mesh texture and modulate it with diffuse
    if( bTexture )
      Output.RGBColor =
          tex2D(MeshTextureSampler, In.TextureUV) * In.Diffuse;
    else
      Output.RGBColor = In.Diffuse;
    return Output;
}
```

Notice that the RenderScenePS takes as its input a VS_OUTPUT parameter, which is the output of the vertex shader. This pixel shader grabs the right texel from the texture and modulates it with the diffuse color calculated in the vertex shader's lighting calculation.

The only thing that remains is the definition of the shader techniques, which allow you to define shaders for different shader versions and set the parameters defined by the uniform keyword. The example below will show six different techniques:

```
//--------------------------------------------------------------
// Renders scene to render target
//--------------------------------------------------------------

technique RenderSceneWith1Light
{
   pass P0
   {
      VertexShader = compile vs_2_0 RenderSceneVS( 1, false, true );
      PixelShader  = compile ps_2_0 RenderScenePS( false );
   }
}


technique RenderSceneWith1LightAlpha
{
   pass P0
   {
      AlphaBlendEnable = true;
      SrcBlend         = SrcAlpha;
      DestBlend        = InvSrcAlpha;
      VertexShader = compile vs_2_0 RenderSceneVS( 1, false, true );
      PixelShader  = compile ps_2_0 RenderScenePS( false );
   }
}


technique RenderSceneWithTexture1Light
{
   pass P0
   {
      VertexShader = compile vs_2_0 RenderSceneVS( 1, true, true );
      PixelShader  = compile ps_2_0 RenderScenePS( true );
    }
}
```

```
technique RenderSceneWithTexture2Light
{
    pass P0
    {
        VertexShader = compile vs_2_0 RenderSceneVS( 2, true, true );
        PixelShader  = compile ps_2_0 RenderScenePS( true );
    }
}

technique RenderSceneWithTexture3Light
{
    pass P0
    {
        VertexShader = compile vs_2_0 RenderSceneVS( 3, true, true );
        PixelShader  = compile ps_2_0 RenderScenePS( true );
    }
}

technique RenderSceneNoTexture
{
    pass P0
    {
        VertexShader = compile vs_2_0 RenderSceneVS( 1, false, false );
        PixelShader  = compile ps_2_0 RenderScenePS( false );
    }
}
```

There are a number of techniques listed here, some with single or multiple lights, a texture, or an alpha component. If you wanted to support earlier pixel shader standards, such as 1.0, you would do so as follows:

```
VertexShader = compile vs_1_0 RenderSceneVS( 1, false, false );
PixelShader  = compile ps_1_0 RenderScenePS( false );
```

If you attempted that with the above shader, you would be sad to discover that it has too many instructions to work on a 1.0 video card, and the effect wouldn't even load.

The EffectManager Class

Shaders, like textures, need a class to load and manage them. Here's a simple class to manage shaders:

```
typedef std::map<std::wstring, ID3DXEffect *> EffectNameMap;
class EffectManager
{
protected:
   EffectNameMap    m_EffectMap;
public:
   ~EffectManager() { OnLostDevice(); }
   ID3DXEffect *Get(std::wstring);
   void OnLostDevice();
};

ID3DXEffect *EffectManager::Get(std::wstring name)
{
   ID3DXEffect *pEffect = m_EffectMap[name];
   if (pEffect == NULL)
   {
      // Load the effect file
      DWORD dwShaderFlags =
         D3DXFX_NOT_CLONEABLE | D3DXSHADER_DEBUG | D3DXSHADER_NO_PRESHADER;
      WCHAR effectFile[MAX_PATH];
      DXUTFindDXSDKMediaFileCch( effectFile, MAX_PATH, name.c_str() );
      D3DXCreateEffectFromFile(
         DXUTGetD3D9Device(), effectFile, NULL, NULL,
         dwShaderFlags, NULL, &pEffect, NULL );
      m_EffectMap[name] = pEffect;
   }

   return pEffect;
}



void EffectManager::OnLostDevice()
{
   while (! m_EffectMap.empty() )
   {
      EffectNameMap::iterator i = m_EffectMap.begin();
      ID3DXEffect *effect = (*i).second;
      SAFE_RELEASE(effect);
      m_EffectMap.erase ( i );
   }
}
```

This simple manager class loads effects directly from their .FX files if they haven't already been loaded. If the Direct3D device is ever lost, all of the effects will be released and they will be reloaded the next time they are accessed.

The effect manager is a member of the Scene class, so loading an effect is easy:

```
m_pScene->GetEffect(L"GameCode3.fx")
```

There is some discussion on forums about the relative efficiency of shader effects managed though the ID3DXEffect interface, which is not just an interface to a shader, but also a high-level framework to control how rendering is done. As always, the code in this book is meant to give you a start, but needs significant work to be deployed in a commercial game.

The ShaderMeshNode Class

In order to demonstrate a simple shader, I've created a child class of the MeshNode class you saw earlier. In addition to all the MeshNode members, ShaderMeshNode can use a vertex and pixel shader to render itself. From a high-level perspective, you access a shader almost like you would set a material, but in reality, it is a very different beast that can do some amazing things.

Let's drill down into ShaderMeshNode:

```
class ShaderMeshNode : public MeshNode
{
protected:
    ID3DXEffect *m_pEffect;
    std::wstring m_fxFileName;

public:
    ShaderMeshNode(const optional<ActorId> actorId,
        std::string name,
        ID3DXMesh *mesh,
        ID3DXEffect *effect,
        RenderPass renderPass,
        const Mat4x4 *t,
        const Color &color);

    ShaderMeshNode(const optional<ActorId> actorId,
        std::string name,
        std::wstring xFileName,
        std::wstring fxFileName,
        RenderPass renderPass,
        const Mat4x4 *t,
        const Color &color);
```

```
virtual ~ShaderMeshNode() { SAFE_RELEASE(m_pEffect); }
HRESULT VRender(Scene *pScene);
virtual HRESULT VOnRestore(Scene *pScene);

};


ShaderMeshNode::ShaderMeshNode(const optional<ActorId> actorId,
    std::string name,
    ID3DXMesh *mesh,
    ID3DXEffect *effect,
    RenderPass renderPass,
    const Mat4x4 *t,
    const Color &color)
 : MeshNode(actorId, name, mesh, renderPass, t, color)
{
    m_pEffect = effect;
    m_pEffect->AddRef();
}

ShaderMeshNode::ShaderMeshNode(const optional<ActorId> actorId,
    std::string name,
    std::wstring xFileName,
    std::wstring fxFileName,
    RenderPass renderPass,
    const Mat4x4 *t,
    const Color &color)
 : MeshNode(actorId, name, xFileName, renderPass, t, color)
{
    m_fxFileName = fxFileName;
}
```

The only addition to the class and constructor is a `ID3DXEffect` object, which is the interface class that gains you access to DirectX shader utility functions. The class can even use `MeshNode::VOnRestore()` since the effects themselves are managed from the `Scene` class.

As you might expect, `ShaderMeshNode::VRender()` is a completely new animal:

```
HRESULT ShaderMeshNode::VRender(Scene *pScene)
{
    if (S_OK != SceneNode::VRender(pScene) )
        return E_FAIL;

    HRESULT hr;
```

```
// Update the effect's variables.  Instead of using strings, it would
// be more efficient to cache a handle to the parameter by calling
// ID3DXEffect::GetParameterByName

Mat4x4 worldViewProj = pScene->GetCamera()->GetWorldViewProjection(pScene);

D3DXCOLOR ambient =  m_Props.GetMaterial().GetAmbient();
V_RETURN( m_pEffect->SetValue(
    "g_MaterialAmbientColor", &ambient, sizeof( D3DXCOLOR ) ) );
D3DXCOLOR diffuse =  m_Props.GetMaterial().GetDiffuse();
V_RETURN( m_pEffect->SetValue(
    "g_MaterialDiffuseColor", &diffuse, sizeof( D3DXCOLOR ) ) );


V( m_pEffect->SetMatrix( "g_mWorldViewProjection", &worldViewProj ) );
V( m_pEffect->SetMatrix( "g_mWorld", pScene->GetTopMatrix() ) );
V( m_pEffect->SetFloat( "g_fTime", ( float )1.0f ) );

D3DXVECTOR3 vLightDir[3];
D3DXCOLOR vLightDiffuse[3];

D3DXCOLOR vLightAmbient(0.35f, 0.35f, 0.35f, 1.0f);
D3DXVECTOR3 vecLightDirUnnormalized(1.0f, 6.0f, 1.0f);
D3DXVECTOR3 vecLightDirNormalized;

D3DXVec3Normalize( &vecLightDirNormalized, &vecLightDirUnnormalized );

// Render the light arrow so the user can visually see the light dir
for( int i = 0; i < 3; i++ )
{
    vLightDir[i] = vecLightDirNormalized;
    vLightDiffuse[i] = D3DXCOLOR( 1, 1, 1, 1 );
}

V( m_pEffect->SetValue(
    "g_LightDir", vLightDir, sizeof( D3DXVECTOR3 ) * 3 ) );
V( m_pEffect->SetValue(
    "g_LightDiffuse", vLightDiffuse, sizeof( D3DXVECTOR4 ) * 3 ) );
V( m_pEffect->SetInt( "g_nNumLights", 1 ) );
V( m_pEffect->SetValue(
    "g_LightAmbient", &vLightAmbient, sizeof( D3DXVECTOR4 ) * 1 ) );
V( m_pEffect->SetFloat( "g_fAlpha",  m_Props.GetMaterial().GetAlpha() ) );

V( m_pEffect->SetTechnique( "RenderSceneWith1Light" ) );
```

```
    // Apply the technique contained in the effect
    UINT iPass, cPasses;
    V( m_pEffect->Begin( &cPasses, 0 ) );

    for( iPass = 0; iPass < cPasses; iPass++ )
    {
        V( m_pEffect->BeginPass( iPass ) );

        // The effect interface queues up the changes and performs them
        // with the CommitChanges call. You do not need to call CommitChanges if
        // you are not setting any parameters between the BeginPass and EndPass.
        // V( g_pEffect->CommitChanges() );

        // Render the mesh with the applied technique
        V( m_pMesh->DrawSubset( 0 ) );

        V( m_pEffect->EndPass() );
    }
    V( m_pEffect->End() );

    return S_OK;
}
```

You'll notice calls to various methods of the ID3DXEffect interface, which are summarized below:

- SetValue: Sets a shader parameter; the parameter can be of any size or type. You can think of this as a memcpy().
- SetMatrix: Sets a matrix parameter of the shader.
- SetInt: Sets an integrer parameter of the shader.
- SetTechnique: FX files can have multiple "techniques," and you can think of them as templatized versions of the shader.

You'll see each of these variables referenced in the shader, which you saw earlier. Notice also that the ID3DXEffect::Begin() and ID3DXEffect::End() calls surround a loop that calls ID3DXMesh::DrawSubset() for each pass of the shader. Shaders can have multiple passes, and this is how they are activated.

WHAT'S MISSING?

That is all you need to create a simple scene graph. It may seem like an extremely simplistic architecture, but it's more flexible than you'd think. Each node you design can add functionality and special effects to all its children nodes. Here are some examples.

- **Full support for mesh subsets:** See the `CDXUTXFileMesh` class in the DirectX Framework to see how to fully support mesh subsets.
- **Billboard node:** Sets the transform matrix of all the child nodes so that they always face the camera. Use this for trees or light glare.
- **Level of detail node:** A node that chooses one node in its child list for rendering based on the node's distance from the camera.
- **BSP node:** A node that sets its visibility based on which side of the BSP plane the camera is and where it is facing.
- **Material node:** Sets the default material for all children nodes.
- **World sector node:** Defines a 3D volume that completely contains all of its children nodes. You use it to determine if any children need to be drawn based on camera direction or interposed opaque world sectors.
- **Mirror node:** Defines a portal through which the scene is rerendered from a different point of view and stenciled onto a texture.
- **Lots more shader effects!**

I'm sure you can come up with other cool stuff.

The scene graph in this chapter is a fun toy. It's not nearly ready to install into a real game engine. You'll want tons of new nodes, articulated figures, and other visible objects. There are also a few other things you'll need to add to this system. The first and foremost is a better way of creating and editing your world. I'm pretty sure I mentioned somewhere in this book that any good game engine is a data-driven creature, and then I showed you a completely hard-coded scene graph! No, I'm not a slacker. I opted for the cheap and easy route because it's also easy to understand. Lucky for you that you can use what you learned about Lua in Chapter 11, "Scripting with Lua," to create scripts to put all those hard-coded constants into a Lua file.

Still Hungry?

When this chapter was first outlined, I knew that I was going to leave plenty of questions completely unanswered. The chapter was going to end too soon, and I would leave the readers with just enough vocabulary and ideas to play around in 3D without enough knowledge to make *Quake*. There's a lot to know, for one thing.

Way back in 2003 at the Computer Game Developer's Conference, I watched a simulation of fluid dynamics programmed completely with pixel shaders. Instead of manipulating texture values and red, green, and blue components of a texture, the values were things like pressure and velocity. The graphics card was performing partial differential equations entirely in the GPU.

I don't know about you, but I haven't seen anything that cool since the first hardware-accelerated 3D graphics card.

I hope you're hungry for more—I certainly am.

FURTHER READING

- *3D Game Engine Design*, David H. Heberly
- *3D Game Engine Architecture*, David H. Heberly
- *Programming Vertex and Pixel Shaders*, Wolfgang Engel

COLLISION AND SIMPLE PHYSICS

by Jeff Lake

In This Chapter

- Mathematics for Physics Refresher
- Choosing a Physics SDK
- Object Properties
- Collision Hulls
- Using a Collision System
- Integrating a Physics SDK
- But Wait, There's So Much More

Jeff Lake is an inveterate gameplay programmer. He started in the game industry at Edge of Reality in Austin working on a PS2/Xbox title. He then moved to Wolfpack Studios and Stray Bullet Games and between the two, he worked on more unreleased MMO prototypes than you could shake a stick at. He's spent the last few years at Red Fly Studio wrestling with the Nintendo Wii. His most recent released title was Mushroom Men: The Spore Wars. *Jeff helped Mike with the code in this chapter and wrote details on how you integrate a game engine with Bullet Physics.*

Even the simplest 2D game needs collision. After all, if the objects in a game can't interact, how fun could the game possibly be? *Breakout* is a great example of a simple game. A ball bounces off walls, bricks, and the paddle. If you look at it this way, the core of the game experience is created by the 2D collision algorithm. It's almost impossible to design a game without at least some rudimentary collision. Perhaps a text adventure like *Zork* is one example, but, hey, it hasn't exactly been flying off the shelves lately. If you are familiar with *Zork*, that's great because you know your game history. If you've actually played *Zork*, well, then you are probably as "mature" as I am.

Collision is a purely mathematical calculation to determine the spatial relationship between objects such as points, lines, planes, or polygonal models. I'll show you a few in this chapter to get you going, but mostly I'll point you to some great resources outside of this book that provide good solutions. I'm not going to pretend I can offer something better.

Physics, on the other hand, is a much more complicated beast altogether. A physics simulation in your game will make it possible to stack objects on top of each other, fall down slopes and stairs accurately, and interact with other dynamic objects in a visually realistic fashion. It can also create motion under force such as you'd see with motors and springs. It can constrain the movements of objects similar to a door on hinges or a pendulum swinging in a grandfather clock.

In the spring of 2004, I worked on *Thief: Deadly Shadows*. This game used the Havok physics engine on every movable object, including rag dolls for characters. *Thief* might not use physics as the core game experience, but it certainly creates a convincing illusion of a complete world in which the player can interact with objects in a meaningful way and affect the events of the game. Here's an example: You could knock a barrel down a flight of stairs, and each impact reported by the collision system would trigger a sound effect that you heard through the speakers. The actions would also trigger sound events into the AI subsystem. This would bring curious guards around to investigate the noise.

You might think for a moment that you could have a similar game experience without a complicated physics simulation, and you are right. The aforementioned barrel could have simply shattered into bits when you knocked into it, and the same guard could have investigated it. The fundamental difference is one of realism and how far the player has to go to imagine what happens versus seeing it in front of his eyes.

Many games don't have super accurate physics simulations, something you've probably suspected, but perhaps wondered why the designers and programmers stopped short. A truly accurate physics simulation for every game object is an expensive proposition, CPU wise. Every game will make reasonable optimizations to make things faster. For example, most physics simulations assume that buildings and other architecture are essentially infinite weight and impossible to break. Load *Project Gotham 4* and try running into a barricade with a Ferrari at over 200 mph and tell me that a real barricade would survive that impact without being horribly mangled. It won't, and therefore that simulation isn't completely accurate.

But it is quite a bit of fun to rebound off barricades in games like *Project Gotham* at high speed to get around corners faster, isn't it? The point I'm trying to make is that you have to understand your game before you decide that a physics simulation will actually add to the fun. A game like *Thief* benefited from accurate physics, but *Project Gotham* would have been remiss to create something perfectly accurate in every way, even if it could have afforded the CPU budget.

Think about this for a moment: Is it better to have the pendulum in a grandfather clock act under a completely realistic physics simulation or a simple scripted animation? The answer is completely dependent on your game, and by the end of this chapter, hopefully, you'll be able to answer that question for yourself.

Since I only have one chapter to talk about collision and physics, I only have time to show you how to use an existing system (specifically the open source library, Bullet) in your game. We'll cover the basics and get right into how you can best use these complicated pieces of technology.

MATHEMATICS FOR PHYSICS REFRESHER

I don't know about you, but every time I read anything that has anything to do with math, I somehow feel all the intelligence leak out of my skull. I think it has something to do with the presentation. I hope to do better here because if you can't get past understanding these concepts, you'll be pretty lost when you get around to debugging physics and collision code.

Meters, Feet, Cubits, or Kellicams?

What you are about to read is true (even though you might not believe it), so read it over and over until you have no doubt:

Units of measure don't matter in any physics calculation. All the formulas will work, as long as you are consistent.

I'm sure you remember the unfortunate story about the Mars Lander that crashed because two different units of measurement were used? One team used meters, and the other team used feet. This error is frighteningly simple to make, so don't laugh too hard. It's not just the programmers who need to agree on the units of measure for a game project. Artists use units of measurement, too, and they can cause all kinds of trouble by choosing the wrong ones.

A unitless measure of distance can therefore be anything you like: meters, feet, inches, and so on. There are two other properties that can also be unitless: mass and time. You'll generally use kilograms or pounds for mass, and I'll go out on a limb here and suggest you use seconds for time. Whatever you use, just be consistent. All other measurements, such as velocity and force, are derived from various combinations of distance, mass, and time.

By the way, if you are wondering how I knew how to spell Kellicams (the unit of measure used by the Klingon Empire), I did what any author would do: I searched Google and chose the spelling that gave me the most returns.

Distance, Velocity, and Acceleration

When you need to work with objects moving through space, you'll be interested in their position, velocity, and acceleration. Each one of these is represented by a 3D vector:

```
Vec3 m_Pos;
Vec3 m_Vel;
Vec3 m_Accel;
```

Velocity is the change in position over time, and likewise acceleration is the change in velocity over time. You calculate them like this:

```
Vec3 CalcVel(const Vec3 &pos0, const Vec3 &pos1, const float time)
{
    return (pos1 - pos0) / time;
}

Vec3 CalcAccel(const Vec3 &vel0, const Vec3 &vel1, const float time)
{
    return (vel1 - vel0) / time;
}
```

This is fairly pedantic stuff, and you should remember this from the math you learned in high school. In computer games, you frequently need to go backward. You'll have the acceleration as a vector, but you'll want to know what happens to the position of an object during your main loop. Here's how to do that:

```
inline Vec3 HandleAccel(Vec3 &pos, Vec3 &vel, const Vec3 &accel, float time)
{
    vel += accel * time;
    pos += vel * time;
    return pos;
}
```

Notice that when the acceleration is handled, both the velocity and the position change. Both are sent into `HandleAccel()` as references that will hold the new values.

Now that you've seen the code, take a quick look Table 15.1, which contains mathematical formulas for calculating positions and velocities. Hopefully, you won't pass out.

You probably recognize these formulas. When you first learned these formulas, you were using scalar numbers representing simple one-dimensional measurements like distance in feet or meters. In a 3D world, we're going to use the same formulas, but the inputs are going to be 3D vectors to represent position,

Table 15.1 Formulas for Calculating Positions and Velocities

Formula	Description
$p = p_0 + v_t$	Find a new position (p) from your current position (p_0), velocity (v), and time (t)
$v = v_0 + a_t$	Find a new velocity (v) from your current velocity (v_0), acceleration (a), and time (t)
$p = p_0 + v_0 t + (at_2)/2$	Find a new position (p) from your current position (p_0), velocity (v_0), acceleration (a), and time (t)

speed, and acceleration in 3D space. Luckily, these vectors work exactly the same as scalar numbers in these equations, because they are only added together or multiplied by time, a scalar number itself.

Mass, Acceleration, and Force

Whenever I have a particularly nasty crash when mountain biking, some joker in my mountain biking group quips, "F=ma, dood. You okay?" This formula is Newton's 2nd Law of Motion, and says that force is calculated by multiplying the mass of the object in question with its acceleration. In the case of an unfortunate mountain biker taking an unexpected exit from the bike, the acceleration is the change in the biker's velocity over time, or deceleration actually, multiplied by the biker's weight. Crashing at the same speed, the heavier biker gets hurt more. If the same biker crashes twice in one day, the slightly faster speed does quite a bit more damage because acceleration has a time squared component, and is therefore much more serious than a change in mass.

If you use metric units, force is measured in Newtons. One Newton, symbolized by the letter N, is defined as one kilogram accelerated over one meter in exactly one second, or said another way:

$$N = \frac{kg}{ms^2}$$

Try not to confuse acceleration and force. Gravity is a force, and when it is applied to an object, it causes acceleration. Galileo discovered an interesting property about this acceleration by dropping things from the Leaning Tower of Pisa: it doesn't matter how much something weighs because they all fall at the same rate. This turns out to be false, as the acceleration due to gravity has to do with the masses of both objects, since they both exert a gravitational field. In Galileo's time, the tiny gravitational field of a handheld object was way too small for it to make any difference in his experiment.

WHO WINS, A TISSUE OR THE PLANET?

While it might not feel this way to you, gravitation is an incredibly weak force compared to something like electricity. You can prove it to yourself by placing an object, like your cell phone, on a piece of tissue paper. Grab both sides of the tissue paper and lift it, suspending your cell phone over the ground. The force that keeps the cell phone from tearing through the tissue paper is the electrical force binding the material of the tissue paper together. So the electrical bonds present in that tiny piece of tissue paper are sufficient to withstand the gravitational force exerted on the cell phone *by the entire planet Earth.*

Heavier things exert a larger force in a gravitational field, such as when you place a weight on your chest. At sea level, Earth's gravity causes an acceleration of exactly 9.80665 meters/s² on every object. Thus, a one kilogram object exerts a force of 9.80665N. To get an idea of how big that force is, set this book on your chest. It turns out to be about a kilogram, give or take Chapter 5. So, one Newton is not all that big, really, if you are the size of a human being and the force is somewhat distributed over a book-sized area. Balance this book on a fork, tines downward, and you'll see how that distribution will change your perception of one Newton. Area, as it seems, makes a huge difference.

Let's look at the code that would apply a constant acceleration, like gravity, to an object. We'll also look at code that applies an instantaneous force. Forces are vectors, and are therefore additive, so multiple forces (f_0, f_1, f_2, ...) on one object are added together to get an overall force (f):

$f_0 + f_1 + f_2 + ...$

or in shorthand, we write

$$F = \sum_{x=0}^{n} f_x$$

Just so you know, the C++ version of that math formula is a simple `for` loop:

```
Vec3 AddVectors(const Vec3 *f, int n)
{
    Vec3 F = Vec3(0,0,0);
    for (int x = 0; x < n; x++)
        F += f[x];

    return F;
}
```

A constant force over time equates to some acceleration over time, depending on the object's mass. An impulse is instantaneous, so it only changes the acceleration once. Think of it like the difference between the force of a rocket motor and the force of hitting something with a golf club: one happens over time, the other is instantaneous. Take a look at a simple game object class:

```
typedef std::list<Vec3> Vec3List;

class GameObject
{
    Vec3 m_Pos;
    Vec3 m_Vel;
    Vec3 m_Accel;
    Vec3List m_Forces;
    Vec3List m_Impulses;
    float m_Mass;

    void AddForce(const Vec3 &force) { m_Forces.push_back(force); }
    void AddImpulse(const Vec3 &impulse) { m_Impulses.push_back(impulse); }
    void OnUpdate(const float time);
};
```

This class contains 3D vectors for position, velocity, and acceleration. It also has two lists: one for constant forces and the other for impulses, each of which is modified by accessor methods that push the force or impulse onto the appropriate list. The real action happens in the OnUpdate call:

```
void GameObject::OnUpdate(const float time)
{
    if (m_Mass == 0.0f)
        return;

    // Add constant forces...
    Vec3 F(0,0,0);
    for (Vec3List::iterator it=m_Forces.begin(); it!=m_Forces.end(); it++)
    {
        F += *it;
    }

    // Also add all the impulses, and remove them from the list
    while (!m_Impulses.empty())
    {
        Vec3List::iterator impulse=m_Impulses.begin();
        F += *impulse;
        m_Impulses.pop_front();
    }
```

```
// calculate new acceleration
m_Accel = F / m_Mass;
m_Vel += m_Accel * time;
m_Pos += m_Vel * time;
}
```

The two loops add all the forces being applied to the game object. The first loop just iterates through and accumulates a result. The second loop is different, because as it accumulates the result, the list is emptied. This is because the forces are impulses, and thus they only happen once. The resulting acceleration is calculated by dividing the accumulated force (F) by the object's mass. Once that is done, you can update the object's velocity and position.

PHYSICS ENGINES ARE VERY TIME SENSITIVE

You must be extremely careful with the value of time. If you send in a value either too big or too small, you'll get some unpredictable results. Very small values of time can accentuate numerical imprecision in floating-point math, and since time is essentially squared in the position calculation, you can run into precision problems there, too. To be safe, keep time in the (0.005f - 0.1f) seconds for best results in any force or physics calculation.

Rotational Inertia, Angular Velocity, and Torque

When an object moves through space, its location always references the center of mass. Intuitively, you know what the center of mass is, but it is interesting to note some special properties about it. For one thing, when the object rotates freely, it always rotates about the center of mass. If the object is sitting on the ground, you can tip it, and it will only fall when the center of mass is pushed past the base of the object. That's why it's easier to knock over a cardboard tube standing on its end than a pyramid sitting on its base.

Different objects rotate very differently, depending on their shape and how weight is distributed around the volume of the shape. A Frisbee spins easily when I throw it, but doesn't spin as well end-over-end, like when my youngest nephew throws it! Mathematically, this property of physical objects is called the *inertia tensor*. It has a very cool name, and you can impress your friends by working it into conversations.

The inertia tensor is something that is calculated ahead of time and stored in the physical properties of the object. It's pretty expensive to create at runtime. It is a 3 × 3 matrix describing how difficult it is to rotate an object on any possible axis. An object's shape, density, and mass are all used to compute the inertia tensor. It is usually done when you create an object; it's much more preferable to precompute the inertia tensor and store it. This calculation isn't trivial. As you might expect, the inertia tensor is to orientation as mass is to position; it is a property of the object that will completely change how the object rotates.

Angular velocity is a property of physics objects that describes the axis of spin and the speed at the same time in one 3D vector. The magnitude of the vector is the spin in whatever units per second, and the direction of the vector shows the rotational axis.

Angular force is called *torque,* and is measured by a force applied about a spin radius. Think of a wrench. As you push on it to get a bolt loose, you apply a certain force to the end of a wrench of some length. A particularly stubborn bolt might come loose if you put a long pipe over the end of your wrench, but the wise mechanic knows that you have a pretty good chance to break the end right off that nice wrench. This is a good reason to buy Craftsman.

Torque is measured by force, specified in Newton-meters for metric system or foot-pounds for the medieval system. As you might expect, 5 Newton-meters is a 5 Newton force applied about a 1 meter length.

Distance Calculations and Intersections

The best resource I've found for calculating distances is a Web site, and it would be crazy of me to simply regurgitate the content they have. Just visit www.real-timerendering.com/intersections.html. This resource is so great because it has collected the best of the best in finding these collisions and intersections, and listed them all in a big matrix. This took a lot of research, and I'd be completely remiss if I didn't point you to it.

As of this printing, this Web site is a great resource for finding collisions/intersections between any of the following objects:

- Ray
- Plane
- Sphere
- Cylinder
- Cone
- Triangle
- Axis-Aligned Bounding Box (AABB)
- Oriented Bounding Box (OBB)
- Viewing Frustum
- Convex Polyhedron

If you want to perform collision detection on arbitrary static and dynamic meshes, such as a teapot against a stairway, you'll need more firepower. For that, I'd suggest going straight to a real physics SDK like Bullet Physics—an open source SDK with source code. You can also choose a commercial physics SDK, like Novodex or Havok.

CHOOSING A PHYSICS SDK

There are a lot of options these days for programmers who don't want to write their own collision system or a system to handle dynamics. Some of these systems have really interesting components for handling nonrigid bodies like bowls of Jell-o or vehicles.

Whether you choose to grab one off-the-shelf or write your own, it should have the following minimum set of features:

- Allow user data to relate physics objects with your game objects.
- Optimize collisions for static actors or geometry.
- Trap and report collision events.
- Provide a fast raycaster.
- Draw debug information visually.
- Output errors in a rational way.
- Override memory allocation.
- Add and remove objects, or regions of objects, from the physics simulation for optimal CPU usage.
- Save and load its own state.

As the physics system simulates the movements of physical objects in a game, it will need some way to associate objects in its data structures to actual objects in your game. This is especially true since the physics object will usually have a simpler geometry than the visible object—a good reason to keep them separate. When physics objects are created, look for a way to provide a reference, or special user data, to these objects so you can figure out which physics and game object pairs match.

Most physics systems allow static actors by setting their mass to zero. These objects would be the geometry that makes the walls, floors, terrain, and the rest of the environment, as well as any really heavy object that will never be moved, like a tree. Most physics systems treat any object with zero mass as unmovable, and they usually take advantage of that fact to speed dynamics calculations.

Besides moving objects around, you'll want to know if and when they collide. You'll also want to know all kinds of things about the collision, such as the force of the collision, the collision normal, and the two objects that collided. All these things are great for playing back sounds, spawning particle effects, or imparting damage and destruction to the objects concerned.

Any game is going to need a good raycaster. A raycaster is something that returns one or more objects that intersect with a probe ray. It is an extremely useful routine for finding out whether objects are in the line of sight of an AI process, where to put bullet holes, and probing the surrounding geometry for moving cameras, objects, or characters. This routine is called so often that it should be either really snappy, or you should be extra careful to call the routine only when you really need it. If possible, you should also be able to do something called a *shape cast*, which takes an entire object, like a sphere, and casts it instead of a simple ray. This kind of thing is invaluable for creating good third-person cameras.

Most physics SDKs can send lots of debug information into your rendering pipeline so that things like collision shapes, acceleration vectors, and contact points are drawn so you can actually see their magnitudes and directions. Watching physics data structures visually is the only way to debug physics. You simply can't just look at the data structures and easily diagnose problems. Consider this example: Two objects seem to react in unexpected ways when they collide. When you look at the collision mesh data, you find that they look correct in the debugger's watch window. When you turn the physics debug renderer on, you might notice that one of the collision hulls is simply the wrong shape and needs to be fixed. You'd never figure this out looking at a long list of points in 3D space.

Most physics errors come from bad data or misuse of the API. For this reason, any decent physics SDK should have a good way to report errors back to you in the debug build. DirectX does this by sending error or informational messages to the debugger's output window. A good physics system should do the same thing. If your artists have created a collision mesh the physics system can't handle, it's nice to know right away rather than after you've spent all night debugging the problem.

Memory allocation is always a concern in computer games. They simply don't use memory in the manner that best suits the standard C-runtime memory allocator, and for that reason, most games write their own memory allocation scheme. A physics system can be just as hard on memory as a graphics subsystem, and thus it needs to use the same optimized memory system as the rest of your game. Look for hooks in the SDK that let you circumvent the default memory allocator with your own.

Physics is expensive enough that you only want to simulate areas of the game the player can actually see or be affected by. For this reason, most good physics systems have easy ways for groups of objects to be enabled or disabled as a group, which allows you to turn on and off areas to make the very best use of your CPU budget.

A physics system should be able to stream so that you can save and load its state. Even if your game doesn't have a load/save feature, it is likely that your game editor has a save feature; otherwise, it wouldn't be much of a game editor. In many game editors, physics objects are placed in the level and simulated until they find a stable position. Usually, you'd do this for candles sitting on tables and other props, but you could do it for something as complicated as a stone bridge. It might be fun to blow something like that up in your game! Either way, you can't count on designers to place the objects with such accuracy, so it's best to let the physics system simulate it until it stabilizes and then save the state.

Now that you've got a physics SDK with everything on your checklist, let's talk a little about how to actually use it.

Object Properties

Physical objects have properties that affect their movement and interactions with other objects. We've already talked about mass, position, velocity, force, the inertia tensor, angular velocity, and torque. These properties describe object motion under force in free space. When objects bump into each other, or into infinitely heavy objects, their reactions are dependent on three more properties: restitution, static friction, and dynamic friction.

Restitution is the amount of bounce that an object has when it hits something, and is usually expressed in a positive floating-point number. A good way to think of this is how high a ball will bounce when you drop it. If the restitution is 0.0f, you've got a piece of playdough, and when it hits it will simply stick to the ground. If you've got something like 0.99f, you've got a nice superball that will bounce around for a long time. It's a bad idea to assign restitutions of greater than 1.0f, since the object will simply continue to gain energy forever.

Static friction and *dynamic friction* describe how much energy is lost when two materials touch each other. Oddly enough, friction changes drastically when things are simply touching but immobile, and when they are sliding over one another. This is why it's so hard to regain control of a car once it's in a skid—the dynamic friction is lower than the static friction. You experience this same issue when moving heavy objects; it's easier to keep them moving than it is to get them moving initially.

The coefficient of friction, usually represented by μ, is a number that is calculated by the ratio of the force (F) required to move an object over the normal force (N), which on a flat surface is simply the mass of the object multiplied by the acceleration due to gravity:

$$F = \mu N$$
$$\mu = F / N$$

So, if it took a 700N force to move an object that weighed 100Kg (thus exerting a 980N force on whatever surface it was sitting on), the coefficient of static friction would be about 0.714f. Once the object was moving, if all you had to apply was 490N to keep it moving at a steady speed, the coefficient of dynamic friction (or sliding friction) would be 0.5f.

Intuitively, the static or dynamic friction for two objects has everything to do with what those objects are made of. Many physics systems let you specify this coefficient on a material-by-material basis, which isn't exactly accurate. If you look on the Web, you'll find that these numbers are presented in tables that match two materials together, such as steel on steel or brass on oak or steel on ice. In other words, you'll likely need to tweak values for your objects until they seem right. A good safety tip is to make this a data file somewhere that you can tweak at runtime. Trust me, you will need to do this. Here are some of the examples of this used in the *Game Coding Complete* source code base:

```
MaterialData g_PhysicsMaterials[] =
{
    // restitution      friction
    {    0.05f,      0.9f  },   // playdough
    {    0.25f,      0.5f  },   // a 'normal' material
    {    0.95f,      0.5f  },   // a 'bouncy' material
    {    0.25f,      0.0f  },   // a 'slippery' material
};
```

One final note on the properties of restitution and friction: You'd better have a physics SDK that can assign these materials to specific triangles of a mesh. While this isn't that critical for dynamic objects, it is surely needed for your environment mesh, or you might have to decide to make your entire world out of plastic!

COLLISION HULLS

Your physics objects will require representations in the physical world, and these might be very different from their visible geometry. For example, a perfect sphere is a mathematical construct in a physical world and has only a location and a radius, whereas a visible representation might need quite a few polygons to look good. You should use mathematical representations in the physical world where and when you can, and you'll save memory and CPU time.

The trade-off is whether things will act like they appear. In the case of the sphere object representing a bowling ball in your game, you'll be quite happy. If the same sphere were representing a box or a crate, I think you'd be a lot less happy. That example is pretty trivial to make a point, but there are tougher problems. Before we cover some of those, let's talk about how collision geometry is built. You'll need to know this if you want to use a mesh editor such as 3ds Max.

Requirements of Good Collision Geometry

A collision mesh has to have a few properties to make the math in the physics SDK efficient, or even possible. First, the mesh has to be convex. Good examples of convex meshes are those that represent any regular solid such as a sphere, cube, or even dodecahedron. Concave meshes, on the other hand, have valleys and holes.

The classic teapot is a good example of a concave mesh (see Figure 15.1). If I had the actual teapot in front of me, and I had a piece of string, it would be trivial for me to place the string on two parts of the object and observe the string cross

FIGURE 15.1 The Classic teapot is concave.

empty space. On a concave mesh, this can't be done anywhere on the object's surface. An easier way to remember is by using the name *concave* because, simply put, it has caves.

Another requirement of a collision hull is that it be *manifold*, a mathematical term that describes how the triangles fit together and form edges. A manifold edge has exactly two triangles on either side. A manifold mesh has no holes or dangling polygons. It represents a completely solid object. It also has no T-joints on any triangle edge. This usually isn't a problem for artists because they know it screws up the object's lighting anyway.

This might be hard to visualize, so I've dusted off my Photoshop skills and made a drawing for you (see Figure 15.2). The left-hand triangles are clearly nonmanifold because of the T-joint. The triangles on the right satisfy the requirement that each edge must border exactly two triangles. The remaining requirement is that the mesh be completely closed and have no holes in it.

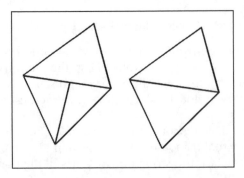

FIGURE 15.2 The left-hand triangles are nonmanifold—the right-hand triangles are okay.

If you're worried that it might be tough to make meshes that always satisfy the requirements of your physics system, you're right. It's sometimes easy for artists to forget what the requirements are, especially when the heat is on and they're trying to get a ton of work done. The best thing is to make sure that your artists double-check their work, hopefully, by actually importing their work into the game and seeing for themselves if anything is awry.

Visible Geometry Versus Collision Geometry

It's a good thing to note that while the position and orientation of a physics object is related to the visual position and orientation, they aren't necessarily the same. They are probably the same for symmetrical objects like a sphere or a cube, but not much else. The position of an object in the physical world is always the center of mass, and that might not be the anchor point of the visible geometry. When you set the location for a 3D object, it is the anchor point on that object that will be positioned precisely at the new location. Likewise, the default orientation of an object in the physics simulation is usually an inertia tensor, such that it aligns with the X-, Y-, and Z-axes. Maybe you can visualize this, but I certainly can't, and it won't necessarily match a reasonable orientation for the object for programmers and artists, such as orienting a gun with the barrel pointed straight down one of the X-, Y-, or Z-axes. Therefore, you'll probably need to apply a transformation to get from the orientation and position of your physics object to find the correct position and orientation for your visible geometry.

BEST PRACTICE

ASYMMETRIC OBJECTS ARE GREAT FOR TESTING

One test object you should definitely create is a completely asymmetric object. A good example is a cube with three corner vertices pulled or pushed around, as long as the shape is still convex. This will help you if you think your physical and visible coordinate systems are out of whack. If they are, the wireframe for the physical geometry won't match the visible geometry. If you integrate a new physics SDK with your game engine, and you use only balls or cubes as test objects, there's almost no way to tell if your transforms are correct. Use a crazy, convex object, and you'll notice problems right away.

If the collision and visible geometry are different, and they usually are, there are a couple of things you'll want to keep in mind:

- If you can simplify the physical geometry, without sacrificing too much in the way of geometrical accuracy, go for it.
- Lean on the side of making physical geometry a little smaller than the visible geometry for objects and static environment meshes. This will create some graphical errors, but the objects that move won't get stuck so much, or appear to hit something that isn't there.

Collision Hulls for Human Characters

You might think that you'd want to represent a human character by a rag doll. If the character is unconscious or dead and is therefore under complete control of the physics system, that is probably okay. However, while the character is under kinematic control, in other words under control of the animation system, you'll probably want something a lot simpler. The same thing goes for the player character as human AIs. Take a look at Figure 15.3. Here, the collision hull has four parts. I'll describe them from top to bottom.

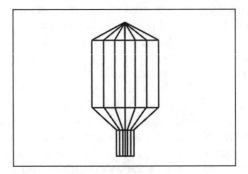

FIGURE 15.3 A collision hull for a human character.

The pointed cap at the top of the hull sits over the character's head. This keeps anything from landing on the character and simply sitting there. Everything, including other characters, will slide off to the ground.

The cylinder shape surrounds the character from shoulder height to about knee height, and keeps the character far enough away from walls and other objects so that most animations will look good. I say most because some animations, like wild staff swinging, will surely leave the collision hull, which will enable the staff and likely part of the arm to intersect walls and whatnot. This is usually normal and expected because the trade-off of making the collision hull too big around is you can't slide in between closely placed columns or trees or other tight geometry. There's also a problem if you make the radius of this cylinder too small; it won't be able to slip easily around square objects like beams set in walls. If you've ever ridden a bicycle, you know that bigger wheels can go up bigger ledges and other obstacles. The analogy works for your character hull; make it just big enough to get around your most common environment geometry.

The sloped shape from the knees to the bottom of the character's feet allows the character to slide up or step up objects, such as stairs or small boxes. If the character has a special animation to climb that's great—I'm talking about normal walking or running. If an object intersects with the area below the knees, you'll know you don't have to halt the character's movement, but slide up. If the object is big enough to stop the character or trigger a different animation state, it will hit

CROWDED GAMES REQUIRE SMALLER COLLISION HULLS

If you've played Valve's Left 4 Dead, *you probably recognize that the collision hulls for the player characters and the zombies don't interact with each other that much, or at least not so that you can tell. That's because there are so many human characters running around that large collision hull circumferences would cause you to get stuck behind your fellow AIs and cause all manner of frustration. Also, if you notice the game environments, there's not a lot of vertical objects like pipes or beams to get stuck on. Make sure you take your game design into careful consideration when designing the collision hulls, and that will influence the design of your game environment.*

above the knees and intersect with the main body of the character hull. Notice that the shape of the bottom of the knee-feet area is still a flat circle; this lets the character proxy sit stable on a small flat area.

The area below the character feet will usually be below the ground, except when the character walks off a ledge. This area is useful for detecting when there is some geometry below the character to cause it to go into a normal step-down animation or an actual fall.

The exact shape of this character hull is totally tunable and is completely dependent on your game. Experiment with different widths, heights, and angles until you've got the kind of behavior you are looking for. Of course, there's still quite a bit of code to write in the background to detect collisions with all these shapes and impart the right impulses to dynamic objects or move the character in the right direction, but the general shape of it should get you started.

Just in case I wasn't clear, the character hull isn't under physics control. It is a shape that you move around yourself and check the physics system for collisions only when you move it. How you move the hull is completely dependent on your game. You could choose to allow the animation data to help you and minimize foot sliding. Or you could find some flexibility by having a totally analog movement system tied right to the controller, and have the animation system queue off the distance you actually moved. You'll still get some feet sliding, but you'll also have some freedom to move exactly how you want. The choice is yours.

THE MOVEMENT GYM

As part of this tuning process, you should create a special map level in your game that looks like an obstacle course. Create every kind of environment and object your character can navigate: stairs, ladders, slopes, ledges, doorways, and windows of every width, a forest of trees or columns, crawlspaces, and anything else you can think of. Every time you make a change to any code or data, including the shape of the character hull, run through the obstacle course and make sure that everything still works. You'll be surprised how easy it is to tweak something and completely break your entire character movement system.

I could probably write a whole chapter just on character movement. It's a big subject, and one not tackled lightly. One bit of advice, if you are just starting out: Don't worry about sliding feet, and certainly don't worry about hovering feet above stairs and ramps, at least at first. Some games solve this problem, but they also tend to have huge budgets. The important bit is to make your game fun first. You can spend any amount of money on cool ankle blending on your main character, but no one will give a damn if your game isn't fun to start with.

Special Objects: Stairs, Doorways, and Trees

Some objects need special collision hulls because they interact with characters or objects in ways that don't necessarily have a direct correlation to their visible shape. Good examples of these objects are stairs, doorways, and trees.

Stairs are tough because you really want two completely different collision shapes, depending on the dynamic object interacting with them. Most objects like crates and barrels would use a pretty similar, although simplified, version of the visible geometry. When they fall or roll down stairs, they'll react to the edges and corners and bounce around exactly as you'd expect. Characters, on the other hand, are usually a different story.

When you watch someone ascend or descend a staircase, their head doesn't follow a sharp square wave. Instead, it bobs smoothly with each step, but not too much. This bobbing is even less when the character is moving quickly, such as running. If you put a naive solution in your character/physics model, your character would probably follow the exact shape of the stairway, causing a very unnatural and jerky movement. The easiest solution to this problem is to make two collision hulls for stairs—one for characters and one for every other kind of object. The collision hull for characters should be a simple ramp, which will create a nice movement when characters move up and down stairs. The second collision hull for the stairway will look like stairs, although perhaps a very low polygon version of them for efficiency. Using this second collision hull, normal objects will roll and bounce, instead of sliding. Using two hulls for stairways is a good economical trick to make your game look good for characters and objects.

GET CHARACTER MOVEMENT DONE EARLY

Your character movement really is at the heart of your game, if you think about it. You should therefore make sure that your character movement system is scheduled extremely early in development, before the level geometry is built. Then designers will be able to test everything against a completely final character movement system. Wait too long, and the designers will have to guess how high your character can jump or what slopes it can climb. Believe me, you don't want them to guess on stuff like that.

I like running through doorways in games, which is probably why I get fragged a lot. Your artists probably don't know this, but it's easy to create a door that's hard to walk through by making it too small or by having odd door jamb geometry. Doors should be a little bigger than you experience every day. This helps the player have some leeway on either side when walking through. If the character is running all the time, you'll want even more slop in the door size, or the collision hull will get caught on the sides too easily. Rebounding is a possible solution, but if the door is too small, you'll just hit the other side and come to a complete halt.

Vegetation, especially trees, should have collision geometry for the big woody parts like the trunk, but be sure to leave it completely off of the foliage. These objects are usually part of the physics simulation as static (mass=0) objects, and as such, they won't move even if they are hit by a huge force. This includes landing a 1969 Buick in the canopy of something as wispy as an ornamental pear tree. Basically, any object stuck in a tree in your game will likely look a little stupid or be annoying.

USING A COLLISION SYSTEM

Any collision system worth its salt should be able to do a few basic things: report collision events, raycast, shapecast, and handle phantom objects. Collision events have more than just a location and two objects, and this extra information will help you spawn some important game logic changes or game view changes. Raycasting and shapecasting are important for a number of reasons, some of which will become apparent shortly. Phantom volumes that can detect entry and exit events, sometimes called *triggers*, are usually simple enough to be handled with your own code, unless they aren't simple shapes. Finally, a good collision system should support collision groups, because not every object needs to be able to collide with every other object.

A collision event should give you at a very minimum the following data: the two objects that collided (or separated), the sum normal of the collision, and the force of the collision. While it might not have occurred to you yet, objects separating are equally as important in computer games as objects colliding. If two objects collide, the game might impart damage to them or cause a sound effect to play. The force of the collision might alter these events. You might want to run some kind of particle-effect animation for forceful collisions, for example.

Some collision systems will give you more data, such as a list of contact points and the collision normal for each of those points. This might be useful for spreading out the particle effect, or determining whether one object had sufficient force at one point to penetrate the other object or cause some kind of special damage. I admit, that last example is a bit of a reach. I can't think of any game that really goes that far just yet, but someone might figure out a good use for this data.

Raycasting is both a savior and a curse. It stabs a ray from a start location in your game world to any other point and gives you the collision information for anything it intersects along the way. This is really useful for detecting line of sight from an AI creature to your player's character, or perhaps it can be used to probe the surrounding geometry to figure out where to place a third-person camera. The problem with raycasting is that it's only accurate to a point.

I know that was a horrible pun, but I'm actually serious. The ray is infinitely thin, and can therefore slip through the smallest cracks in your geometry. If you want to know something about the general shape of the local geometry, such as if your character is standing next to an open window, you can make a few stabs with these rays, but they might miss something important, such as bars over the windows. Your raycasts could instruct your character animation system to allow your player to climb right through those bars. I'll give you one more example. Let's say you want to make a single raycast to determine if an AI creature can see your player. You could easily hide behind the thinnest pole, if you were lucky enough to stand in exactly the right place. The ray could intersect the pole, causing it to believe there was a solid object in the way. A simple hack uses more raycasts from the center of the creature's forehead to various parts of the players body, like an arm or a foot. Then it's very difficult to hide, but those raycasts are more performance intensive. Everything is a trade-off.

This can get expensive fast, though. Raycasts can be pretty expensive, especially if you want a list of objects sorted by distance, rather than a simple yes or no answer to the "did my ray hit anything" question. Back to the line-of-sight question—a good trick is to cache the results of multiple raycasts over many game loops. If you cast one ray per loop from an AI character, and your game is running at 30Hz, that's 30 rays per second you can cast! Since human beings can only perceive delays lasting longer than about 100ms or 1/10th of a second—a good general rule—you can even spread these raycasts out farther to once every other frame or perhaps more. This is a game tuning thing, and you'll just have to play with it.

Another option is the shapecast. Think of this as pushing a geometrical shape from a start location in your game world along a straight line to somewhere else. This is more expensive than a single raycast, but can be much more accurate if you are moving an object in your game and want it to follow geometry closely. A good example of this is a wall-following scheme, where your character closely follows the geometry of a wall, including beams and wall sconces. Once you've validated the move direction, move the character away from the wall a bit and shape cast it back into the wall. If something like a beam or sconce is in the way, the new position of your character will accommodate the annoying geometry. This is exactly how the wall-flattening algorithm worked in *Thief: Deadly Shadows*.

Phantom objects, or triggers, are usually pretty simple to code without a physics or collision system. They are usually simple proximity alarms that fire when some dynamic object gets within range or leaves the active area. You use these things to open automatic doors, or perhaps fire poison darts, or something like that. If you have a physics system, however, you can make these areas into any arbitrary shape, as long as it is convex. This can be really useful for tuning triggers into tight areas in your level. If all your trigger shapes have to be spheres or cubes, you'd have to make enough room for them to stay out of other rooms or hallways nearby.

The idea behind a collision group is simple: it optimizes the entire collision system. As you might expect, a collision system's algorithmic complexity grows with the complexity of the geometry in question. Remove some of this geometry, and you speed up your simulation. This is done by sorting objects into collision groups, essentially lists of objects that can collide with one another and those that can't. For example, objects like a bunch of crates on the first floor can't collide with another group of crates on the second floor if they are physically separated by something like an elevator. Set those objects into different collision groups, and your physics system will thank you for it by running a few milliseconds faster.

Integrating a Physics SDK

Most programmers aren't going to write their own physics system. They'll most likely grab a physics SDK off-the-shelf and integrate it into their game. Since I'm likely describing most of the readers of this book, let's discuss this important integration task.

Note that the code presented in this section is only a tiny part of integrating a physics SDK into a complete game. The functionality here won't get you much past bouncing balls on a ground plane, so don't expect more than that. The goal is to show you how a third-party physics system fits into the game architecture presented in this book. It's up to you to extend this class for additional functionality or use a different SDK than the one I chose.

It helps to discuss an interface class for a simple physics system. The interface shown here creates a few objects and manages their movements. If you want to abstract an entire physics system, you'd extend this class quite a lot. Actually, you'd extend this interface and probably create a few new ones. We'll keep it simple for now, just to get you started. After the interface discussion, we'll implement it using the Bullet Physics SDK available from www.bulletphysics.com, which is available for free under the Zlib license.

```
class IGamePhysics
{
public:
  virtual void VOnUpdate(int deltaMilliseconds) = 0;
  virtual void VSyncVisibleScene() = 0;
  virtual void VRenderDiagnostics() = 0;

  virtual void VCreateSphere(float radius, ISceneNode *sceneNode)=0;
```

```
// ... you can create methods here, for other shapes or meshes

virtual void VCreateTrigger(Vec3 const &pos, float dim, int triggerID)=0;

virtual ~IGamePhysics() { };
};
```

The first method, VOnUpdate(), starts the physics simulation, which recalculates new positions and orientations for moving objects and queues physics event callbacks like collision or trigger events. The second method, VSyncVisibleScene(), is responsible for iterating through all of the physics objects and updating the visible geometry with new locations and orientations. The VRenderDiagnostics() method is a special routine that draws physics debug data to the renderer. It is a critical tool for you to debug physics problems. The remaining interface methods create different physics objects and attach them to the simulation, such as a sphere. It is through methods like VCreateSphere() that you add physical presence to your game objects so they can move just like they would in the real world.

Here's the implementation of that interface using the Bullet Physics SDK:

```
class BulletPhysics : public IGamePhysics, boost::noncopyable
{
    // use auto pointers to automatically call delete on these objects
    //    during ~BulletPhysics

    // these are all of the objects that Bullet uses to do its work.
    //    see BulletPhysics::VInitialize() for some more info.
    std::auto_ptr<btDynamicsWorld>                m_dynamicsWorld;
    std::auto_ptr<btBroadphaseInterface>          m_broadphase;
    std::auto_ptr<btCollisionDispatcher>          m_dispatcher;
    std::auto_ptr<btConstraintSolver>             m_solver;
    std::auto_ptr<btDefaultCollisionConfiguration> m_collisionConfiguration;
    std::auto_ptr<BulletDebugDrawer>              m_debugDrawer;

    // keep track of the existing rigid bodies:  To check them for updates
    //    to the actors' positions and to remove them when their lives are
    //    over.
    typedef std::map<ActorId, BulletActor*> ActorIDToBulletActorMap;
    ActorIDToBulletActorMap m_actorBodies;

    // also keep a map to get the actor ID from the btRigidBody*
    typedef std::map<btRigidBody const *, ActorId> RigidBodyToActorIDMap;
    RigidBodyToActorIDMap m_rigidBodyToActorId;

    // data used to store which collision pair (bodies that are touching)
    //    need collision events sent.  When a new pair of touching bodies are
```

```
//    detected, they are added to m_previousTickCollisionPairs and an
//    event is sent.  When the pair is no longer detected, they are
//    removed and another event is sent.
typedef std::pair< btRigidBody const *, btRigidBody const * >
    CollisionPair;
typedef std::set< CollisionPair > CollisionPairs;
CollisionPairs m_previousTickCollisionPairs;

// helpers for sending events relating to collision pairs
void SendCollisionPairAddEvent( btPersistentManifold const * manifold,
                                btRigidBody const * body0,
                                btRigidBody const * body1 );
void SendCollisionPairRemoveEvent( btRigidBody const * body0,
                                   btRigidBody const * body1 );

// common functionality used by VAddSphere, VAddBox, etc
void AddShape( IActor * actor,
               btCollisionShape * shape,
               btScalar mass,
               enum PhysicsMaterial mat );

// helper for cleaning up objects
void RemoveCollisionObject( btCollisionObject * removeMe );

// find the rigid body associated with the given actor ID
btRigidBody * FindActorBody( ActorId id ) const;

// find the BulletActor object with the given actor ID
BulletActor* FindBulletActor(ActorId id) const;

// find the actor ID associated with the given body
optional<ActorId> FindActorID( btRigidBody const * ) const;

// callback from bullet for each physics time step.  set in VInitialize
static void BulletInternalTickCallback( btDynamicsWorld * const world,
                                        btScalar const timeStep );

public:
    BulletPhysics();
    virtual ~BulletPhysics();

    // Initialiazation and Maintenance of the Physics World
    virtual bool VInitialize();
    virtual void VSyncVisibleScene();
    virtual void VOnUpdate( float deltaSeconds );
```

```
// Initialization of Physics Objects
virtual void VAddSphere(float radius,
                        IActor *actor,
                        float specificGravity,
                        enum PhysicsMaterial mat);
virtual void VAddBox(const Vec3& dimensions,
                     IActor *gameActor,
                     float specificGravity,
                     enum PhysicsMaterial mat);
virtual void VAddPointCloud(Vec3 *verts,
                            int numPoints,
                            IActor *gameActor,
                            float specificGravity,
                            enum PhysicsMaterial mat);
virtual void VRemoveActor(ActorId id);

// Debugging
virtual void VRenderDiagnostics();

// Physics world modifiers
virtual void VCreateTrigger(const Vec3 &pos,
                            const float dim,
                            int triggerID);
virtual void VApplyForce(const Vec3 &dir, float newtons, ActorId aid);
virtual void VApplyTorque(const Vec3 &dir, float newtons, ActorId aid);
virtual bool VKinematicMove(const Mat4x4 &mat, ActorId aid);

virtual void VRotateY(ActorId actorId, float angleRadians, float time);
};
```

You'll notice our new class wraps the Bullet data structures for the SDK and a set of components, including a world, a collision dispatcher, a constraint solver, and other components of the Bullet physics system. They are created separately so the user (that's you!) can easily customize the various behaviors of Bullet.

For our example, we'll use the most common default components that Bullet provides: btBroadphaseInterface, btCollisionDispatcher, btConstraintSolver, and btDefaultCollisionConfiguration. I'll describe these components in more detail in a second.

You'll also notice when you look at the code that our physics system uses a physics system-specific vector class, btVector3. It is quite common for a physics system to have its own data structures or classes for common fundamental mathematics: vectors, matrices, and so on. To be honest, this is one thing that annoys me, since you'll be forced to make conversion functions between your physics

> ### THE DIFFERENCES BETWEEN `std::auto_ptr` AND `boost::shared_ptr`
>
> `BulletPhysics` uses `std::auto_ptrs` to store its components. These are handy little components out of the C++ standard whose sole purpose is to call delete on their stored pointers when they are destructed. So, you don't have to remember to call delete on them during `~BulletPhysics`!
>
> `std::auto_ptrs` are a class of "smart pointers," like the `boost::shared_ptrs` used elsewhere. The difference is that `std::auto_ptrs` have slightly less overhead, but the downside is they can't be safely copied like a `boost::shared_ptr` can. I use them here because we never copy these pointers, but if you need full "copyability" (or you're just not sure), use `boost::shared_ptr`!

system's 3D vector and your game system's 3D vector, and quite possibly your renderer's 3D vector. Yuck. I hate it too. You almost wish you could recompile the whole thing with your own data types! Ah well....

Components of the Bullet SDK

The most important component managed by Bullet is the `btDynamicsWorld` object. This is the parent object that manages the other components and provides the main interface point to Bullet's internal physics system. When `btDynamicsWorld's` constructor is called, we pass in pointers to the other components in order to specify our desired behavior.

One of those components is a subclass of the `btBroadphaseInterface`. This class manages the "broad phase" of collision detection, which is the first test. This phase is fast but inaccurate, and once a possible collision has passed this test, it is sent to the "narrow phase," which is managed by `btCollisionDispatcher`. We use Bullet's `btDbvtBroadphase`, which has good default behavior.

The `btCollisionDispatcher` handles very precise collision detection between objects in the system. Detecting collisions this way can be very slow, however, so it only tests collisions that have passed the broad phase. Once collisions are detected, this object also dispatches the collision pairs to the world to be handled, hence the name.

Next, let's look at the subclass of `btConstraintSolver`. In Bullet, a "constraint" is a spring, hinge, or motor—basically anything that restricts an object's freedom of motion. You can have hinge constraints on a door, or slider constraints like a piston, or basically anything you can think of. The `btSequentialImpulseConstraint-Solver` manages these. Unfortunately, the scope of our physics system is too narrow to really demonstrate constraints, but trust me, they're cool.

The final initialization component is `btDefaultCollisionConfiguration`. This object manages some aspects of memory usage for the physics system. We're using the default configuration because we don't want to do anything fancy with memory allocation.

The last object created here is `BulletDebugDrawer`, which actually handles debugging tasks for your game engine. After all, a physics system can't draw a line with a renderer it knows nothing about, so you get to help it along. The same goes with error reporting. Your game should be able to define how it wants to handle physics system errors or informational messages.

For more information about any of these classes, consult the Bullet documentation, or better yet, read the Bullet source code and examples. Open source is great that way!

Initialization

Let's take a look at the implementation of the `IGamePhysics` interface, `Bullet-Physics`. The init function for this implementation class runs through the following tasks:

- Initializes the `btDynamicsWorld` and components' members.
- Creates the internal tick callback, which is used to send collision events.
- Sets debug rendering parameters.

```
bool BulletPhysics::VInitialize()
{
    // VInitialize creates the components that Bullet uses

    // this controls how Bullet does internal memory management during the
    // collision pass
    m_collisionConfiguration.reset( new btDefaultCollisionConfiguration() );

    // this manages how Bullet detects precise collisions between pairs of
    // objects
    m_dispatcher.reset(
        new btCollisionDispatcher( m_collisionConfiguration.get() ) );

    // Bullet uses this to quickly (imprecisely) detect collisions between
    // objects.  Once a possible collision passes the broad phase, it will be
    // passed to the slower but more precise narrow-phase collision detection
    // (btCollisionDispatcher).
    m_broadphase.reset( new btDbvtBroadphase() );

    // Manages constraints which apply forces to the physics simulation.
    //  Used for e.g. springs, motors.  We don't use any constraints right now.
    m_solver.reset( new btSequentialImpulseConstraintSolver );
```

```
// This is the main Bullet interface point.  Pass in all these components
//   to customize its behavior.
m_dynamicsWorld.reset(
    new btDiscreteDynamicsWorld( m_dispatcher.get(),
                                 m_broadphase.get(),
                                 m_solver.get(),
                                 m_collisionConfiguration.get() ) );

// also set up the functionality for debug drawing
m_debugDrawer.reset( new BulletDebugDrawer );
m_dynamicsWorld->setDebugDrawer( m_debugDrawer.get() );

// and set the internal tick callback to our own method
//   "BulletInternalTickCallback"
m_dynamicsWorld->setInternalTickCallback( BulletInternalTickCallback );
m_dynamicsWorld->setWorldUserInfo( this );

return true;
}
```

This is nice and straightforward. This function creates the components of the physics system and then passes them into the constructor of the physics world.

One important piece of code in the initialize function turns on a few rendering diagnostics by setting up the `BulletDebugDrawer`, which has the capability of visibly rendering collision shapes, contact points, and contact normals. Depending on what your problem is, you might want other things, but this is a good basic set. If you were really smart, you'd create a little command line debug console in your game, and be able to turn on/off different physics debug information at a whim. That's exactly what we had for *Thief: Deadly Shadows*, and it saved our butts on more than one occasion. You don't want to draw them all because there's too much information. In fact, you might even want to filter the information for particular objects, which is something you can do in the debug renderer class you write yourself.

Shutdown

Shutting down the physics system is pretty easy. Clean up all of the `btRigidBody` objects that you've allocated and added to the physics system and then delete the physics system components. In the sample code, those components are stored with `auto_ptrs`, which will handily invoke delete on them for us, so all you need to do is clean up the active bodies in the system.

```
BulletPhysics::~BulletPhysics()
{
   // delete any physics objects which are still in the world

   // iterate backwards because removing the last object doesn't affect the
   //  other objects stored in a vector-type array
   for ( int i=m_dynamicsWorld->getNumCollisionObjects()-1; i>=0; --i )
   {
      btCollisionObject * const obj
         = m_dynamicsWorld->getCollisionObjectArray()[i];

      RemoveCollisionObject( obj );
   }

   // destroy all the BulletActor objects
   for (ActorIDToBulletActorMap::iterator it = m_actorBodies.begin();
        it != m_actorBodies.end();
        ++it)
   {
      BulletActor* pBulletActor = it->second;
      delete pBulletActor;
   }
   m_actorBodies.clear();

   // auto_ptrs will handle deletion of m_dynamicsWorld et. al.
}
```

Updating the Physics System

Somewhere in the main loop of your game, you'll call two methods of this physics class to update the physics simulation and then pass those updates along to the visible geometry. It will probably look something like this:

```
if (m_pBaseGamePhysics)
{
   m_pBaseGamePhysics->VOnUpdate(deltaMilliseconds);
   m_pBaseGamePhysics->VSyncVisibleScene();
}
```

Let's look at the guts of these methods:

```
void BulletPhysics::VOnUpdate( float const deltaSeconds )
{
    // Bullet uses an internal fixed timestep (default 1/60th of a second)
    //   We pass in 4 as a max number of sub steps.  Bullet will run the
    //   simulation in increments of the fixed timestep until "deltaSeconds"
    //   amount of time has passed, but will only run a maximum of 4 steps
    //   this way.
    m_dynamicsWorld->stepSimulation( deltaSeconds, 4 );
}
```

Simple, eh? The important thing to know here is that Bullet's stepSimulation() function makes sure that even if your game is running slower than 60Hz, the physics system is always ticked at a maximum time delay of 1/60th of a second. This is important because a large time delay can create instability in the simulation. Physics systems generally don't deal well with deep interpenetrations of objects, which happens a lot when objects move a large distance in between simulation steps.

TALES FROM THE PIXEL MINES

THE INCREDIBLE BOUNCING CAMERA

Physics systems are horribly sensitive to frame rate. When I was working on *Thief: Deadly Shadows*, I had to program a simple spring attached to the camera system, which created a smooth movement of the camera under lots of game situations, for example, when the main character jumped off a wall. On my first attempt, I noticed that the camera could easily bounce out of control, as if the spring were getting more and more energy until the camera system crashed. After a little debugging, I noticed the system crashed more easily in areas with a low frame rate. The problem was that my spring system wasn't being ticked at a high enough frame rate, say 60Hz, and the spring calculation would accumulate energy. The solution was pretty easy. I just called the spring calculation in a tight loop, with a delay of no more than 1/60th of a second, and everything was fine.

The trade-off is that ticking your physics simulation multiple times in one game loop is expensive, so try your best to keep enough CPU budget around for everything: rendering, AI, sound decompression, resource streaming, and physics.

Another important note is that Bullet automatically calls an "internal callback" once every internal time step. This callback is specified by the user. For our purposes, let's set it as BulletInternalTickCallback. This function handles dispatching collision events.

After the physics system has updated itself, you can grab the results and send it to your game's data structures. Any decent physics system lets you set a user data member of its internal physics objects. Doing this step is critical to getting the new position and orientation data to your game. Take a look at this in action:

```
void BulletPhysics::VSyncVisibleScene()
{
    // Keep physics & graphics in sync

    // check all the existing actor's bodies for changes.
    //  If there is a change, send the appropriate event for the game system.
    for ( ActorIDToBulletActorMap::const_iterator it = m_actorBodies.begin();
         it != m_actorBodies.end();
         ++it )
    {
        ActorId const id = it->first;

        // get the MotionState.  This object is updated by Bullet.
        // It's safe to cast the btMotionState to ActorMotionState,
        //   because all the bodies in m_actorBodies were created through
        //   AddShape()
        ActorMotionState const * const actorMotionState =
            static_cast<ActorMotionState*>
            (it->second->m_pRigidBody->getMotionState());
        assert( actorMotionState );

        shared_ptr<IActor> gameActor = g_pApp->m_pGame->VGetActor( id );
            if ( gameActor )
            {
               if ( gameActor->VGetMat()
                   != actorMotionState->m_worldToPositionTransform )
            {
               // bullet has moved the actor's physics object.
               //   update the actor.
               safeQueEvent( IEventDataPtr(
                   GCC_NEW EvtData_Move_Actor( id,
                   actorMotionState->m_worldToPositionTransform ) ) );
            }
        }
    }
}
```

In Bullet, each physics actor has a `MotionState` that manages how the physics system communicates with the game engine. As Bullet processes the physics world, it updates the position and orientation stored in each `MotionState` for each actor. There are many ways you could implement a `MotionState` to handle these position changes, but our system simply stores the new data so that it can be processed in `VSyncVisibleScene()`.

So once you get to `VSyncVisibleScene`, you loop through all the motion states. For each motion state that has different data from the `IActor`'s position, an event is sent so the actor can update itself based on the physics data.

Creating A Simple Physics Object

Bullet represents all nondynamic physical bodies with the `btRigidBody` class. Let's take a look at how you'd create a sphere object, given a radius and a related game actor:

```
void BulletPhysics::VAddSphere( float const radius,
                                IActor * const actor,
                                float const specificGravity,
                                enum PhysicsMaterial const mat)
{
    assert( actor );

    // create the collision body, which specifies the shape of the object
    btSphereShape * const collisionShape = new btSphereShape( radius );

    // calculate absolute mass from specificGravity
    float const volume = (4.f / 3.f) * M_PI * radius * radius * radius;
    btScalar const mass = volume * specificGravity;

    AddShape( actor, collisionShape, mass, mat );
}

void BulletPhysics::AddShape( IActor * const actor,
                              btCollisionShape * const shape,
                              btScalar const mass,
                              enum PhysicsMaterial const mat )
{
    // actors get one body apiece
    optional<ActorId> const maybeID = actor->VGetID();
    assert( maybeID.valid() && "Actor with invalid ID?" );
```

```
ActorId const actorID = *maybeID;
assert( m_actorBodies.find( actorID ) == m_actorBodies.end()
                    && "Actor with more than one physics body?" );

// localInertia defines how the object's mass is distributed
btVector3 localInertia( 0.f, 0.f, 0.f );
if ( mass > 0.f )
   shape->calculateLocalInertia( mass, localInertia );

// set the initial position of the body from the actor
ActorMotionState * const myMotionState
 = GCC_NEW ActorMotionState( actor->VGetMat() );

btRigidBody::btRigidBodyConstructionInfo rbInfo( mass,
        myMotionState, shape, localInertia );

// set up the materal properties
rbInfo.m_restitution = g_PhysicsMaterials[mat].m_restitution;
rbInfo.m_friction    = g_PhysicsMaterials[mat].m_friction;

btRigidBody * const body = new btRigidBody(rbInfo);

m_dynamicsWorld->addRigidBody( body );

// create the BulletActor
BulletActor* pBulletActor = GCC_NEW BulletActor(body);

// add it to the collection to be checked for changes in
//     VSyncVisibleScene
m_actorBodies[actorID] = pBulletActor;
m_rigidBodyToActorId[body] = actorID;
}
```

Most physics systems have easy ways to create basic shapes like spheres, boxes, and capsules. In Bullet, spheres are represented by the btSphereShape class. Creating an object in the physics system is as simple as creating the object's shape and then passing that shape to a new btRigidBody.

You'll notice that we've separated out the creation of the shape in VAddSphere() and the creation of the body in AddShape(). This is good practice because you can then reuse the code in AddShape() when you create other types of objects.

Although we don't do it in this example, physics actors can be described with multiple base shapes, which is a great feature. You could describe a hammer quite accurately with two bodies, each with different sizes, shapes, and properties. In this case, we only have the one sphere shape. The mass is calculated based on the volume and density of the material, so the user can customize whether he wants an object that is dense like iron or light like styrofoam.

Next comes the position, which is sucked right out of the actor's transform matrix. You pass this in to a new `MotionState`. As discussed earlier, the `MotionState` is the interface object that the physics system uses to notify your game of changes to the physics object's position and orientation (from gravity, collisions, and so on). You pass this motion state along with other configuration info into the constructor for the new `btRigidBody` and add the `btRigidBody` object to the physics system.

The last part of the `AddShape()` method creates a `BulletActor`, which you can use as a handle to the created physics object. Let's use it to check for updates to the `MotionState` and also for removing the physics objects on shutdown.

Creating a Convex Mesh

Spheres are nice, but they aren't all that interesting. You'll probably want to create an object that has a more interesting shape, and one way to do that is to use a *convex mesh*. This is an object that has an arbitrary shape, with one restriction: it can't have any holes or empty space in between parts of the same object. So, a potato is a convex mesh but a donut is not.

Creating them in Bullet is pretty easy:

```
void BulletPhysics::VAddPointCloud(Vec3 *verts,
                                   int numPoints,
                                   IActor *actor,
                                   float specificGravity,
                                   enum PhysicsMaterial mat)
{
   assert( actor );

   btConvexHullShape * const shape = new btConvexHullShape();

   // add the points to the shape one at a time
   for ( int ii=0; ii<numPoints; ++ii )
      shape->addPoint( Vec3_to_btVector3( verts[ii] ) );

   // approximate absolute mass using bounding box
   btVector3 aabbMin(0,0,0), aabbMax(0,0,0);
   shape->getAabb( btTransform::getIdentity(), aabbMin, aabbMax );

   btVector3 const aabbExtents = aabbMax - aabbMin;
```

```
float const volume = aabbExtents.x() * aabbExtents.y() * aabbExtents.z();
btScalar const mass = volume * specificGravity;

AddShape( actor, shape, mass, mat );
}
```

Notice we're using our friend `AddShape()` to avoid duplicating work.

What this does is add the vertices of the convex mesh one by one, and Bullet will create a shrink-wrap of polygons that represents the minimum volume object that contains all the points. It will even reorder the polygons from your rendering representation, so it might turn out more efficient for the collision system's algorithms. That's cool!

Creating a Trigger

Another useful object is the trigger. A trigger is something that gives you a callback if objects enter or leave it, which can be very useful for many things. For example, you can spawn some AIs when the player moves through a certain doorway.

Bullet triggers are the same as other objects, except they have no mass and they don't collide with anything. Not colliding means that objects will move straight through them as if they're not even there. The only thing they need to do is generate an event for the game system when something touches them.

```
void BulletPhysics::VCreateTrigger(
    const Vec3 &pos, const float dim, int triggerID )
{
    // create the collision body, which specifies the shape of the object
    btBoxShape * const boxShape
        = new btBoxShape( Vec3_to_btVector3( Vec3(dim,dim,dim) ) );

    // triggers are immoveable.  0 mass signals this to Bullet.
    btScalar const mass = 0;

    // set the initial position of the body from the actor
    Mat4x4 triggerTrans = Mat4x4::g_Identity;
    triggerTrans.SetPosition( pos );
    ActorMotionState * const myMotionState
        = GCC_NEW ActorMotionState( triggerTrans );

    btRigidBody::btRigidBodyConstructionInfo
        rbInfo( mass, myMotionState, boxShape, btVector3(0,0,0) );
    btRigidBody * const body = new btRigidBody(rbInfo);
```

```
m_dynamicsWorld->addRigidBody( body );

// a trigger is just a box that doesn't collide with anything.  That's
//    what "CF_NO_CONTACT_RESPONSE" indicates.
body->setCollisionFlags(
    body->getCollisionFlags() | btRigidBody::CF_NO_CONTACT_RESPONSE );
body->setUserPointer( GCC_NEW int(triggerID) );
}
```

Of course, as long as the mesh components are convex, you could create a complicated trigger zone on virtually any shape at all. Zones like that can be quite useful if you want something to fire the trigger when it is in exactly the right place, and yet not intruding on other spaces, perhaps behind walls.

The Physics Debug Renderer

One other important method of the IPhysics interface is VRenderDiagnostics:

```
void BulletPhysics::VRenderDiagnostics()
{
   m_dynamicsWorld->debugDrawWorld();
}
```

This method obviously doesn't do any of the rendering. Part of the BaseGame-Physics class is a member that does the heavy lifting. Bullet lets you inherit from one of their base classes and implement your own draw routines.

A physics system can't know or care how you render your visible geometry. It could be a text display, and it wouldn't know any different except for all the extra CPU time it would get! You simply can't debug physics problems looking at raw data, so the easiest debugging technique for physics problems is to draw physics data as visible geometry. Collision hulls show up as wireframes around your objects. Contact points and normals are drawn as lines, and forces can be drawn as lines of different lengths in the direction of the force. Bullet provides an easy way for you to do this. You simply inherit from the btIDebugDraw class, overload a few methods, and you'll see everything you need to debug physics:

```
class BulletDebugDrawer : public btIDebugDraw
{
public:
   // btIDebugDraw interface
   virtual void    drawLine(const btVector3& from,
                            const btVector3& to,
                            const btVector3& color);
```

```
virtual void    drawContactPoint(const btVector3& PointOnB,
                                 const btVector3& normalOnB,
                                 btScalar distance,
                                 int lifeTime,
                                 const btVector3& color);
virtual void    reportErrorWarning(const char* warningString);
virtual void    draw3dText(const btVector3& location,
                           const char* textString);
virtual void    setDebugMode(int debugMode);
virtual int     getDebugMode() const;
};
```

Pretty simple. You just overload the provided methods to render on-screen and there's your debug info! There's an incredible amount of useful stuff you can do with this data, including histories, averages, and statistics of all sorts, but for this example, you just draw on-screen in the simplest manner possible.

The most important method that we've overridden is drawLine():

```
void BulletDebugDrawer::drawLine(const btVector3& from,
                                 const btVector3& to,
                                 const btVector3& lineColor)
{
    if ( IDirect3DDevice9 * d3ddevice = DXUTGetD3D9Device() )
    {
        DWORD oldLightingState;
        d3ddevice->GetRenderState( D3DRS_LIGHTING, &oldLightingState );

        // disable lighting for the lines
        d3ddevice->SetRenderState( D3DRS_LIGHTING, FALSE );

        COLORED_VERTEX verts[2];

        verts[0].position.x = from.x();
        verts[0].position.y = from.y();
        verts[0].position.z = from.z();
        verts[0].color = D3DCOLOR_XRGB( BYTE(255*lineColor.x()),
                                        BYTE(255*lineColor.y()),
                                        BYTE(255*lineColor.z()) );
        verts[1].position.x = to.x();
        verts[1].position.y = to.y();
        verts[1].position.z = to.z();
        verts[1].color = verts[0].color;
```

```
d3ddevice->SetFVF( COLORED_VERTEX::FVF );
d3ddevice->DrawPrimitiveUP(
    D3DPT_LINELIST, 1, verts, sizeof(COLORED_VERTEX) );

// restore original lighting state
d3ddevice->SetRenderState( D3DRS_LIGHTING, oldLightingState );
    }
}
```

Most of this information should be pretty familiar from the rendering chapter. One point of interest is that lighting is turned off, so the debug lines will always be seen, even in pitch darkness. The color of the lines is set by the physics system so you can tell the different points, lines, and triangles apart from each other and what they mean. Keeping the vertex buffer around from call to call is a good optimization at the cost of video memory, but your development machines will likely have video cards with a little more headroom anyway.

DON'T COUNT MEMORY USED ONLY FOR DEBUGGING

This tip might be a little off the subject, but the last paragraph reminded me of it so here goes. Whenever you have memory allocated for diagnostic or debugging purposes, make sure that you don't count it in your game's memory budget! You can send the testers into a panic if they see the memory budget skyrocket, and the only reason it did so was that you allocated a couple of megabytes for some debugging routine.

Another simple yet interesting method is reportErrorWarning:

```
void BulletDebugDrawer::reportErrorWarning(const char* warningString)
{
    OutputDebugString( warningString );
}
```

The reason you want to do send errors and warnings to the debug window is pretty simple; there is a wealth of information that can help you diagnose problems sitting in the error stream. You must trap it yourself and send it somewhere useful, such as the output window in the debugger, a log file, or preferably both. While writing this chapter, I used this very code to figure out that I was sending in incorrect data while trying to create a collision hull for a test object. If that's not good advertising, I don't know what is.

This version merely forwards the error message to the debug output stream. It's a good start, but there's a whole world of things you can do with this information, including popping up a dialog box, recording the data in a database, emailing a message to your physics programmer, and so on.

Receiving Collision Events

Moving objects around realistically provides a great visual look to your game, but when objects collide and interact, your game gets really interesting. A collision event can be defined as when two objects change their contacts either by colliding or separating. In Bullet, generating these events is a little tricky, but you can do it by using the internal tick callback. This callback is set up in VInitialize(), and Bullet calls it once every internal time step. It's a great place to put any work that needs to happen continuously within the physics system.

```
void BulletPhysics::BulletInternalTickCallback( btDynamicsWorld * const world,
                                                btScalar const timeStep )
{
   assert( world );

   assert( world->getWorldUserInfo() );
   BulletPhysics * const bulletPhysics
      = static_cast<BulletPhysics*>( world->getWorldUserInfo() );

   CollisionPairs currentTickCollisionPairs;

   // look at all existing contacts
   btDispatcher * const dispatcher = world->getDispatcher();
   for ( int manifoldIdx=0;
         manifoldIdx<dispatcher->getNumManifolds();
         ++manifoldIdx )
   {
      // get the "manifold", which is the set of data corresponding to a
      //   contact point between two physics objects
      btPersistentManifold const * const manifold
         = dispatcher->getManifoldByIndexInternal( manifoldIdx );
      assert( manifold );

      // get the two bodies used in the manifold.  Bullet stores them as
      //   void*, so we must cast them back to btRigidBody*s.
      //   Manipulating void* pointers is usually a bad idea, but we
      //   have to work with the environment that we're given.  We know
      //   this is safe because we only ever add btRigidBodys to the
      //   simulation
      btRigidBody const * const body0
         = static_cast<btRigidBody const *>(manifold->getBody0());
      btRigidBody const * const body1
         = static_cast<btRigidBody const *>(manifold->getBody1());
```

```
    // always create the pair in a predictable order
    bool const swapped = body0 > body1;

    btRigidBody const * const sortedBodyA = swapped ? body1 : body0;
    btRigidBody const * const sortedBodyB = swapped ? body0 : body1;

    CollisionPair const thisPair
       = std::make_pair( sortedBodyA, sortedBodyB );
    currentTickCollisionPairs.insert( thisPair );

    if ( bulletPhysics->m_previousTickCollisionPairs.find( thisPair )
       == bulletPhysics->m_previousTickCollisionPairs.end() )
    {
        // this is a new contact, which wasn't in our list before.
        //   send an event to the game.
        bulletPhysics->SendCollisionPairAddEvent(
           manifold, body0, body1 );
    }
}


CollisionPairs removedCollisionPairs;

// use the STL set difference function to find collision pairs that
//   existed during the previous tick but not any more
std::set_difference( bulletPhysics->m_previousTickCollisionPairs.begin(),
                     bulletPhysics->m_previousTickCollisionPairs.end(),
                     currentTickCollisionPairs.begin(),
                     currentTickCollisionPairs.end(),
                     std::inserter( removedCollisionPairs,
                        removedCollisionPairs.begin() ) );

for ( CollisionPairs::const_iterator it = removedCollisionPairs.begin(),
      end = removedCollisionPairs.end(); it != end; ++it )
{
    btRigidBody const * const body0 = it->first;
    btRigidBody const * const body1 = it->second;

    bulletPhysics->SendCollisionPairRemoveEvent( body0, body1 );
}

// the current tick becomes the previous tick.  this is the way of all
//   things.
bulletPhysics->m_previousTickCollisionPairs = currentTickCollisionPairs;
}
```

This code does three things: First it collects all of the collision pairs from the physics system. A *collision pair* is any two objects whose physics shapes overlap in the physics world. So a box sitting on the floor is a collision pair, just like an arrow passing through a tent is a collision pair. Our code finds all the pairs of objects that are touching each other this tick.

Next, once all the collision pairs are collected, it compares them with the previous tick's collision pairs. If there are any new ones, then an event is sent indicating that the two objects came into contact with one another. If there are any pairs that existed in the previous tick but no longer exist, an event is sent to tell the game system that the objects separated from each other. Both of these events are quite useful in a game.

The great thing about using an event system for handling collision and separation is that the physics system doesn't have to interpret the event and figure out what to do with it. That should be up to the subsystems themselves. The sound system, for example, will listen for collisions and play sounds based on the force and type of object. You might have a damage manager that controls things like hit point reduction or spawning a destruction event. Either way, the physics system doesn't have to know or care about all these other things in your game.

Also note that usually we send a generic collision event for each collision, but we handle triggers differently. Although they are handled the same by Bullet, triggers and collision objects are logically different, and the game expects them to work differently. So the game gets different events when the objects colliding include a trigger, and the game engine doesn't know anything about what goes on under the hood. This way, you can change the implementation if you want and the game engine doesn't have to know anything about it. That's the beauty of this polymorphic interface.

The final thing that this internal tick callback does is store the list of collision pairs. This saves them for you so you can compare them during the *next* tick.

A Final Word on Integrating Physics SDKs

Throughout this chapter, I've described physics in general and one SDK in particular from Bullet (www.bulletphysics.com). There are certainly others:

- **Havok (www.havok.com):** An extremely fully-featured commercially licensable physics engine, but expensive and likely out of reach for small game companies or individuals.
- **PhysX (www.nvidia.com/object/nvidia_physx.html):** A commercial grade physics engine owned by NVidia and optimized for use with GPU based physics. A software driver is also available.
- **Newton Game Dynamics (http://physicsengine.com):** A commercially licensable game engine within reach of budget games.

- **Open Dynamics Engine (www.ode.org):** An open source engine that anyone can use for free.
- **Tokamak Physics Engine (www.tokamakphysics.com):** Older versions are free, newer versions are commercially licensable and within reach of budget games.

The SDKs are developed so rapidly that an exhaustive review of each of them in this book would quickly become stale. I suggest you go to their Web sites, check out the developer forums and licensing terms, and do a little surfing for others. New ones come out all the time.

Whatever you do, don't think for a minute that you can plug in one of these physics systems in a day or two and completely change the feel of your game. Integrating this technology is much more than making it link and getting collision events sent around. You have to write a lot of code to have your game react to what the physics system does to your dynamic objects and the events it detects. That, my young Feynman, is an amazing amount of work, and you shouldn't underestimate it.

SUPER BOUNCY BARRELS

I think I mentioned before that *Thief: Deadly Shadows* used the Havok Physics SDK. The version of Unreal didn't really have a good dynamics simulation, and Havok seemed to be pretty cool. For the longest time the correct impulses created by kinematic animation, such as characters bumping into things, were drastically exaggerated. These huge impulses would send huge barrels and crates spinning across the map just by touching them, and while it was funny at first, after a few weeks everyone just wanted things to work. The problem was that the two physics programmers were so busy wiring everything else that they didn't get around to fixing this problem until after it had been seen by many a head honcho, none of whom understood the real problem. There was just too much work and too few people doing it.

BUT WAIT, THERE'S SO MUCH MORE

I have to admit to you right now that I changed my major in college from Computer Science, Science Option to the Business Option because I failed a physics test. Granted, I had totally forgotten that the test was going to happen, and had I studied for it, I probably would have stuck with it.

I suggest you have a little more patience than I do. This stuff is devilishly difficult, and is probably one of the most challenging areas of game programming. It tricks you by making a 20-minute task to get a sphere bouncing around on a checkerboard floor seem easy, and then forces you into six months of solid hell getting elevators to lift objects properly.

Physics is already being hardware accelerated in our game machines, especially those equipped with NVidia graphics cards. When I wrote the second edition of this book, I predicted it would take until the fourth edition for this to happen, and I guess I was wrong. It happened faster than that. I did predict that it would be integrated into video cards, though! Read the second edition if you don't believe me.

Either way, collision, physics, and dynamics are in our games to stay. The challenge is making a great physics simulation in your game translate directly to the fun factor. That's not as easy as you think, but I have faith, and I can't wait to see where this goes.

NETWORK PROGRAMMING PRIMER

In This Chapter

- How the Internet Works
- Sockets API
- Making a Multiplayer Game with Sockets
- Core Client-Side Classes
- Core Server-Side Classes
- Wiring Sockets into the Event System
- Gosh, if It's That Easy

I remember the very moment the Internet became relevant to my job, and it completely changed the way I worked. A colleague of mine walked into my office and showed me a Web site for the very first time. He'd made it himself, and although it was very simple, I knew right away that the Internet was going to change the world. Well, maybe it wasn't quite that clear. I missed out on the Netscape IPO, but it was certainly clear after that.

At the time, computer games could be played via modem or over a LAN, but they were quite the bear to program. Once gamers populated the Net, game companies started using the Internet, and the communications protocols it uses, for hooking up fragfests. Now, whether you're playing with a buddy in the next office or a friend from overseas, pretty much all the network games use Internet protocols to communicate.

As it turns out, getting two computers to talk to each other is pretty dang easy. The trouble happens when you try to make some sense of the bits coming in from the other side: keeping track of them and their memory buffers, changing the raw data stream into useful game data, and trying to create a plug-in architecture that doesn't care if you are playing locally or from afar.

This chapter covers moving bits across the network, how you come up with the bits to send, and how you transform that raw data back into something your game can use just as if there were no network at all. First, we'll start with a little primer on the Internet and its two most common Internet protocols: the *transport control protocol* (TCP) and *user datagram protocol* (UDP).

How the Internet Works

You probably have some familiarity with TCP and UDP. You might have heard that UDP is what all good network games use and TCP is for chat windows. The truth, as usual, is a little more complicated than that. TCP is a guaranteed, full-duplex protocol. It looks and feels just as if there were no remote connection at all. You can write code that simply pulls bits out just as they were sent in, in the right order, with nothing missing and no duplications. It is easier to program because you don't have to worry so much about wacky Internet problems that can happen during packet transmission: packet loss, packet splitting, or even corruption. The best analogy is a pipe—what goes in will come out the other side, or you'll receive an error telling you something bad happened to the connection. The possibility of problems exists, and you should watch out for socket exceptions. Unlike files or UNIX-style pipes, you won't get an "end of file" marker.

UDP is a little more like sending messages by using those crazy bicycle messengers you see in downtown areas. You don't know when or even if your package will get to its destination. You also won't be informed if the package (your data) was split into multiple pieces during the transmission. I guarantee you that if you required a bicycle messenger to carry a 10,000-page document, that person would get friends to help, and it would be up to the receiver to make some sense of it when it all arrived.

By design, UDP is fairly lightweight, but the messages aren't guaranteed to arrive at their destination in any order, to arrive in one piece, or to arrive at all. TCP, the guaranteed delivery service, doesn't give its guarantees of a pipe-like connection lightly. It does its work by having the receiver acknowledge the reception of a complete, uncorrupted packet of data by sending a message back, essentially saying, "OK, I got packet #34, and it checks out, thanks." If the sender doesn't receive an acknowledgement, or an *ACK*, it will resend the missing or otherwise corrupted packet.

Of course, you don't have to wait to receive the ACK before sending another message; you can set your TCP connection to allow you to stuff data in as fast as you want. It will send the data as quickly as possible and worry about keeping track of the ACKs internally. This kind of socket is called a *nonblocking* socket because it operates asynchronously. A blocking socket can be useful if you want to enforce a rigid exchange between two computers, something like talking over a two-way radio. One computer sends data, and it blocks until the data is received by the other side. When I say "blocks," I mean exactly that—the socket function that sends data will not return until the data actually gets to the other side. You can see that this kind of thing would be bad for servers or clients; you generally want to send and receive data without waiting for the other side to get it and answer. This is the same, regardless of whether you use TCP or UDP.

Winsock or Berkeley?

You may have heard about Berkeley sockets, or the Berkeley implementation of the sockets API. It's called that because it was developed for the Berkeley UNIX operating system, and it is a commonly used implementation of the TCP/UDP protocols. Of course, Microsoft developed an implementation of TCP/UDP as well, called *WinSock*. You might wonder which one is better and debate endlessly about it, but I'll leave it to the experts and Internet forums. I like to use Berkeley sockets for multiplayer games, even under Windows. There's a caveat to that, and I'll clue you in on it later.

Here is why I like to use Berkeley. When there's a more standard API out there that works, I'll tend to gravitate toward it. It's really a little like why Sony VHS won over Betamax; it had more to do with the fact that more people were using VHS and nothing at all to do with the fact that Betamax was a superior format. Actually, the people that were using VHS represented the porn industry, and some say that's why it succeeded so quickly! But I digress....

You are free to use Berkley style sockets on a Windows machine, as I have done throughout this chapter. Since space is such a premium—God knows this book is heavy enough to give you cramps if you hold it too long—I'll show you how to use TCP to get your game running as a multiplayer game. You can investigate UDP once you've mastered TCP. First, you have to know something about the Internet. After all, you can't send data to another computer on the Internet until you connect to the computer, and you can't connect to it until you can identify it uniquely from every other computer on the Net.

You are also free to use WinSock or Berkeley and as long as you use the same protocols, which you'll see in a moment, you can set up network communications with any other computer on the Internet. You can use your program to connect to Web servers, FTP sites, whatever you want. You just have to know what IP address to connect to, how to format the bytes you send, and how to parse the bytes you receive.

Internet Addresses

Every computer that has TCP/IP installed has an IP address to identify the computer on the network. I say "the network" and not "the Internet" very specifically because not every network is visible to the Internet. Some, like the one in my house and the network where I work, are hidden from the Internet at large. They act like their very own mini-Internets. The computers on these mini-Internets only need a unique IP address for their network. Other computers, like the one that hosts my Web site, are attached directly. These computers need a unique IP address for the Internet at large.

The IP address is a 4-byte number, something you can store in an unsigned int. Here's the address for the computer that hosts my Web site, for example: 3486000987, or expressed in hexadecimal: 0xCFC8275B. People usually write Internet addresses in dotted decimal format to make them easier to remember. The above address would be expressed like this: 207.200.39.91. This may be easier to remember than 3486000987, but it's still no cakewalk.

This address has two parts: the network ID number and the host ID number. The host ID is the individual computer. Different networks have different sizes, and the designers of the Internet were wise to realize this. If they had simply chosen to use two bytes to represent the network ID and the host ID, the Internet would be limited to 65,536 networks and 65,536 computers on each network. While that might have seemed fine back in 1969 when the first four computers inaugurated ARPANET, as it was called, it would hardly seem sufficient now. The solution was to separate the network into address classes, as shown in Table 16.1.

Table 16.1 provides a summary of the IP address classes that are used to create IP addresses. The total size of the Internet, if you have a calculator handy, is about 3.7 billion computers on 2.1 million networks of various sizes, most of them

Table 16.1 IP Address Classes

Class	Network ID Bytes	Hosts on Network	Networks on Internet
A	1	16,777,216	127
B	2	65,536	16,384
C	3	254	2,097,152

very small. Here's a quick example of some of the holders of Class A address blocks on the Internet:

- BBN Planet, MA (NET-SATNET)
- IBM Corporation, NY (NET-IBM)
- DoD Intel Information Systems, Defense Intelligence Agency, Washington DC (NET-DODIIS)
- AT&T (NET-ATT)
- Xerox Palo Alto Research Center, CA (NET-XEROX-NET)
- Hewlett-Packard Company, CA (NET-HP-INTERNET)
- Apple Computer Inc., CA (NET-APPLE-WWNET)
- Massachusetts Institute of Technology, MA (NET-MIT-TEMP)
- Ford Motor Company, MI (NET-FINET)
- Computer Sciences Corporation, VA (NET-CSC)
- U.S. Defense Information Systems Agency (DDN-RVN), VA (NET-DDN-RVN)
- Defense Information Systems Agency, Washington DC (NET-DISNET)
- U.S. Cable Networks
- Royal Signals and Radar Establishment, UK (NET-RSRE-EXP)
- Defense Information Systems Agency, VA (NET-MILNET)
- ARPA DSI JPO, VA (NET-DSI-NORTH)
- IBM Global Services, NH (NETBLK-IBMGLOBALSERV)
- Halliburton Company, TX (NET-HALLIBURTON)
- Stanford University, CA (NET-SU-NET-TEMP)
- Japan Inet, Japan (NET-JAPAN-A)
- Bell-Northern Research, Canada (NET-BNR)
- Joint Tactical Command, Control, and Communications Agency, AZ (NET-JITCNET1)
- Joint Tactical Command, Control, and Communications Agency, AZ (NET-JITCNET2)
- Department of Social Security of UK, England (NET-ITSANET)
- Merck and Co., Inc., NJ (NET-MERCK2)
- Army National Guard Bureau, VA (NET-RCAS2)
- U.S. Postal Service, NC (NET-USPS1)
- Asia Pacific Network Information Center (NETBLK-APNIC2)
- European Regional Internet Registry/RIPE NCC (NETBLK-RIPE-C3)
- InterNIC Registration (NETBLK-INTERNIC-2)

Interesting list of organizations, isn't it? It's a virtual who's who of the military industrial complex.

As you might have guessed, there's a central authority for handing out unique network ID numbers to those who want to get on the Net. This authority is called the Internet Corporation for Assigned Names and Numbers (ICANN). Once the network ID is assigned, it's up to the local network administrator to hand out unique host IDs. In the case of the network in my house, the unique host IDs are handed out by a device I have hooked up to my network. Whenever one of my computers boots, it is assigned a host ID automatically. The device that hands out the addresses is called a Dynamic Host Configuration Protocol (DHCP) server, and is exactly what you find on most wireless routers. If I didn't have one of these devices, I'd have to assign each of my computers a unique IP address. What a hassle.

There are some special IP addresses you should know about, as well as some special network IDs (see Table 16.2).

Table 16.2 Special IP Addresses and Network IDs

Address	Description
127.0.0.1	Called the loopback address, and always refers to your computer. It is also called the localhost.
127.x.x.x	Loopback subnet; this network ID is used for diagnostics.
255.255.255.255	This IP address refers to all hosts on the local network.
10.x.x.x 172.(16-31).x.x 192.168.x.x	Private networks; any address with these network IDs is considered on the local network, and not on the Internet at large. Use these addresses for your home or local company network if they don't need to be visible on the Internet.

The Domain Name System

When you browse the Web, your Web browser program attaches to another computer on the Internet, downloads a Web page and anything attached to it, and renders the Web page so you can see it. But when you browse the Web, you don't go to http://207.46.19.254, do you? If you put this specific address in your browser, you'll be rewarded with Microsoft's Web page.

Luckily for us, there's an easier way to find computers on the Internet. Clearly, www.microsoft.com is easier to read and remember than 207.46.245.42. The designers of the Internet designed a distributed database called the Domain Name System, or DNS.

This system is structured like a hierarchical tree. The first level of the tree consists of the top-level domains (TLD), as listed in Table 16.3.

TLDs are also available for foreign countries to use, although they are generally used in as free and open a manner as the rest of the Internet. For example, .uk is used for the United Kingdom and .cn is used for mainland China. Funny, the Pacific island of Tuvalu that sits midway between Hawaii and Australia got lucky and pulled .tv as its TLD. The television industry has made excellent use of these addresses.

Table 16.3 Top-Level Domains

TLD	Description
.edu	Educational institutions, mainly in the U.S. (reserved)
.gov	United States government (reserved)
.int	International Organizations (reserved)
.mil	United States military (reserved)
.com	Commercial (open for general use)
.net	Networks (open for general use)
.org	Organizations (open for general use)
.coop	Cooperatives (sponsored)
.aero	Air-Transport Industry (sponsored)
.museum	Museums (sponsored)
.biz	Business (open for general use)
.info	Information (open for general use)
.name	Individuals, by name (open for general use)
.pro	Profession (open for general use)

As you can tell from Table 16.3, some of these TLDs are restricted and either managed by ICANN or somehow sponsored by an authority agreed upon to manage assigning unique names within their domain. The open, general use TLDs like .com, .net, and .org are managed by ICANN.

Domain names within these top-level domains are issued by ICANN or another sponsoring authority. When you register for a domain name, you have to provide all kinds of information, but the really important piece of information is the primary name server. The primary name server is the IP address of the computer that retains the authoritative version of your domain name. It propagates this information to other name servers all over the Internet. Name servers generally update themselves every few hours. Any new or changed domain name takes a few days to register with enough name servers to be resolved quickly by anyone on the Internet.

I'll show you how to use the sockets API to find Internet addresses in just a bit.

Useful Programs and Files

There are a couple of useful programs you'll find installed on virtually any computer, UNIX or Windows. You'll use them for checking Internet connectivity and other useful things. They are listed in Table 16.4.

Table 16.4 Useful Programs and Files for Internet Work

Name	Description
ping	This little program attempts to send information to another computer, and tells you the time in milliseconds it took for the packets to arrive.
netstat	This program can show you the state of current sockets on your computer. It can tell you if they are listening for connections, connected, or about to be closed.
tracert	This program tells you what Internet hops your packets have to make before they are received by the host computer.
telnet	This program attaches to a host computer and sends/receives text messages. It can be great for debugging network code if your debug code can send/receive in text mode.
hosts	This is a file that holds locally overridden DNS information. If you want to force a DNS name, like goober.mcfly.com to be any legal IP address, you can do it in this file. On Windows machines, look for it in the system32\drivers\etc directory. Windows machines also have a file "lmhosts," which stands for LanManHosts, which is used by the Windows peer networking protocol, or SMB protocol. UNIX machines running the free Samba server may also have an "lmhosts" file.

SOCKETS API

Well, I've now given you enough knowledge to be dangerous. All you need is some source code. The sockets API is divided into a few different useful areas of code:

- Utility functions
- Domain Name Service (DNS) functions
- Initialization and shutdown
- Creating sockets and setting socket options
- Connecting client sockets to a server
- Server functions
- Reading and writing from sockets

Sockets Utility Functions

There are some useful conversion functions that help you deal with Internet addresses and data that has been sent by another computer. The first two functions, inet_addr() and inet_ntoa(), perform conversions from a text string dotted decimal IP address and the four-byte unsigned integer. You'll notice the input parameter for inet_ntoa() is a structure called in_addr:

`unsigned long inet_addr(`
`    const char* cp`
`);`
	Takes a string value like "127.0.0.1" and converts it to an unsigned integer you can use as an IP address.

`char* FAR inet_ntoa(`
`    struct in_addr in`
`);`
	Takes an in_addr structure and converts it to a string. Note: Copy the string from the return pointer; don't assume it will be there for long. It points to a static char buffer and may be overwritten the next time a socket's function is called.

The in_addr structure is something that helps you break up IP addresses into their component parts. It's not just a normal unsigned integer, because the values of the bytes are in a specific order. This might seem confusing until you recall that different machines store integers in Big-endian or Little-endian order. In a Big-endian system, the most significant value in the sequence is stored at the lowest storage address (for example, "big end first"). In a Little-endian system, the least significant value in the sequence is stored first. Take a look at how the two systems store the 4-byte integer 0x80402010:

```
Big-endian     80 40 20 10
Little-endian  10 20 40 80
```

It's exactly backward from each other. Intel processors use Little-endian, and Motorola processors use Big-endian. The Internet standard is Big-endian. This means that you have to be really careful with the data you get from strange computers because it might be in the wrong order. For certain sockets data structures, you are also expected to put things in network order. Luckily, there are some helper functions for that.

BEST
PRACTICE

THE RULES ARE THERE FOR A REASON

It's a good idea to always use the converter functions, even if you know you'll never have an Internet application that has to talk to something with a different endian-ness. After all, there were a lot of programmers in the 1960s that never thought they'd need more than two digits to store the year, right?

The helper functions convert 4-byte and 2-byte values to and from network order:

```u_long htonl(u_long hostlong);```	Converts a 4-byte value from the host-byte order to network-byte order.
```u_long ntohl(u_long hostlong);```	Converts a 4-byte value from the network-byte order to host-byte order.
```u_short htons(u_short hostshort);```	Converts a 2-byte value from the host-byte order to network-byte order.
```u_short ntohs(u_short hostshort);```	Converts a 2-byte value from the network-byte order to host-byte order.

Here's a short bit of code that uses the utility/conversion functions:

```
unsigned long ipAddress = inet_addr("128.64.16.2");

struct in_addr addr;
addr.S_un.S_addr = htonl(0x88482818);

char ipAddressString[16];
strcpy(ipAddressString, inet_ntoa(addr));

printf("0x%08x 0x%08x %s\n:", ipAddress, addr.S_un.S_addr, ipAddressString);
```

The output, on my decidedly Little-endian Dell Inspiron, is this:

```
0x02104080 0x18284888 136.72.40.24
```

The first value, 0x02104080, is the unsigned long that is the converted IP address for 128.64.16.2. This is already in network order, so you can use it in sockets functions without converting it. The next value, 0x18288488, shows you what happens when you send 0x88482818 through the htonl() function on my Dell. Your mileage may vary if you happen to use a Mac! The last string on the output line is 136.72.40.24, which is the dotted decimal format for the IP address given by htonl(0x88482818).

This can be devilishly confusing, so choose a nice calm day to start playing with network programming.

Domain Name Service (DNS) Functions

The next set of functions helps you make use of DNS:

```struct hostent* FAR gethostbyname(const char* name);```	Retrieves host information, such as IP address, from a dotted-decimal format string. If the host doesn't exist, you'll get back NULL.
```struct hostent* FAR gethostbyaddr(const char* addr, int len, int type);```	Retrieves host information given a network address in network byte order, the network address length, and network type, such as AF_INET.

Both of these functions look up host information based on an address, either a text string in dotted-decimal notation or an IP address in network order. Don't let the const char * fool you in gethostbyaddr() because it doesn't want a text string. Here's a quick example of using both of these:

```
const char *host = "ftp.microsoft.com";
struct hostent *pHostEnt = gethostbyname(host);

if (pHostEnt == NULL)
{
   fprintf(stderr, "No such host");
}
else
{
   struct sockaddr_in addr;
   memcpy(&addr.sin_addr,pHostEnt->h_addr,pHostEnt->h_length);

   printf("Address of %s is 0x%08x\n", host, ntohl(addr.sin_addr.s_addr));
}
```

Both functions return a pointer to a data structure, hostent. The data structure stores information about the host, such as its name, IP address, and more. It is allocated and managed by the sockets system, so don't do anything other than read it. Notice the liberal sprinkling of network-to-host conversion functions.

The output of the code is this line:

```
Address of ftp.microsoft.com is 0xcf2e858c
```

Instead of using the `gethostbyname()` function, I could have used these lines and used `gethostbyaddr()`:

```
unsigned int netip = inet_addr("207.46.133.140");
pHostEnt = gethostbyaddr((const char *)&netip, 4, PF_INET);
```

The DNS lookup functions make it easy for you to specify IP addresses in a human readable form, which is important for setting up a server IP address in an options file or in a dialog box without getting out the calculator.

> ## DNS FUNCTIONS FAILING?
>
> You can call the conversion functions anytime you want, but the DNS lookup functions will fail if you try to call them before you've initialized the sockets API.

Sockets Initialization and Shutdown

Even if you are programming Berkeley style sockets on a Windows machine, you'll call the Windows Sockets API to initialize the sockets system and shut it down:

```
int WSAStartup(
    WORD wVersionRequested,
    LPWSADATA lpWSAData
);
```
Initializes the sockets API; you must call it before calling any other sockets function.

```
int WSACleanup(void);
```
Call this to deregister the application from using sockets, usually in your application cleanup code.

In the first function, `WSAStartup()`, you send in the version number of the sockets implementation you want. At this writing, the most recent version of sockets is version 2.2, and it has been that way for years. Notice that you want to send in the minor version number in the high order byte, and the major version in the low order byte. If for some reason you wanted to initialize Windows Sockets version 2.0, you'd send in 0x0002 into the `WSAStartup()` function. As you can see below, you can also use the `MAKEWORD` macro to set the version number properly:

```
WORD wVersionRequested = MAKEWORD( 0, 2 );    // set to 2.0
WSADATA wsaData;
int err WSAStartup( wVersionRequested, &wsaData );
```

WSAStartup() also takes a pointer to the WSADATA structure. This structure is filled with data that describes the socket implementation and its current status, but that's about it.

WSACleanup() is called when you are ready to shut down your application.

Creating Sockets and Setting Socket Options

The embodiment of a socket is the socket handle. You should already be familiar with using handles for everything from files to resources in a resource cache. The difference comes in the multistep manner in which you create a connected socket. The easiest connection style is a client-side connection. Doing this requires three steps. First, you ask the sockets API to create a socket handle of a particular type. You have the option of changing socket options, which tells the sockets API more information about how you want the socket to act. After that, you can connect the socket with another computer. It is a little more involved than opening a file, but sockets are a little more complicated.

socket()

The following is the API to create a socket, interestingly enough:

```
SOCKET socket (
   int address_family,
   int socket_type,
   int protocol );
```

Parameters:

- **Address family:** Will always be PF_INET for communicating over the Internet. Other address families include PF_IPX, PF_DECnet, PF_APPLETALK, PF_ATM, and PF_INET6.
- **Socket type:** Use SOCK_STREAM for connected byte streams. SOCK_DGRAM is for connectionless network communication and SOCK_RAW is for raw sockets, which lets you write socket programs at a lower level than TCP or UDP.
- **Protocol:** Use IPPROTO_TCP for TCP and IPPROTO_UDP for UDP sockets.

Return Value:

The socket() function returns a valid handle for a socket if one was created or INVALID_SOCKET if there was some kind of error.

Here's an example of how to create a TCP socket handle:

```
SOCKET sock  = socket(PF_INET, SOCK_STREAM, IPPROTO_TCP);
if ((sock == INVALID_SOCKET)
{
   // handle error!
}
```

setsockopt()

Now that you have a socket handle, you can decide how you'd like the socket to act when it is open. You do this by setting the socket options through a function called setsockopt(). There are a wide variety of options, and I'm happy to show you some common ones, specifically the ones used in the client/server code in this chapter. Make sure you look at the complete sockets documentation for socket options. I'm only scratching the surface here:

```
int setsockopt (
    SOCKET socket,
    int level,
    int optionName,
    const char* optionValue,
    int optLen );
```

Parameters:

- **Socket:** A valid socket handle.
- **Level:** Either SOL_SOCKET or IPPROTO_TCP, depending on the option chosen.
- **Option Name:** The identifier of the socket option you want to set.
- **Option Value:** The address of the new value for the option. For Boolean values, you should send in a 4-byte integer set to either 1 or 0.
- **Option Length:** The length in bytes of the option value.

Return Value:
Returns zero if the option was set or SOCKET_ERROR if there was an error.
Here are some examples of setting socket options:

```
int x = 1;
setsockopt(sock, IPPROTO_TCP, TCP_NODELAY, (char *)&x, sizeof(x));
setsockopt(sock, SOL_SOCKET, SO_DONTLINGER, (char *)&x, sizeof(x));
setsockopt(sock, SOL_SOCKET, SO_KEEPALIVE, (char *)&x, sizeof(x));
```

The first option, TCP_NODELAY, disables an internal buffering mechanism in an attempt to sacrifice some network bandwidth for a speedier sending of packets. It is especially important when you want to send a high number of small packets, as is common in many multiplayer computer games.

The next option, SO_DONTLINGER, ensures a speedy return from a call to close the socket. The socket will be closed gracefully, but the call will essentially happen in the background. This is a clear win for any application that has to support a high number of connections, but is still good for a computer game, no matter how many connections you have.

The last one of interest is SO_KEEPALIVE. It sends a packet of data at regular intervals if no other data has been sent. The default interval is two hours, but on some systems it can be configurable. This is probably only useful for a server system that supports a high number of connections. In a multiperson shooter, it will be pretty obvious if someone's remote connection goes dark.

ioctlsocket()

Another useful socket control function is `ioctlsocket()`, which has a few uses but the most important one to you, the fledgling multiplayer game programmer, is to set whether a socket is a blocking socket or a nonblocking socket:

```
int ioctlsocket( SOCKET s,  long command,  u_long* argumentPointer );
```

Parameters:

- **Socket:** A valid socket handle.
- **Command:** `FIONBIO` controls blocking. `FIONREAD` will return the number of bytes ready in the socket's input buffer, and `SIOCATMARK` will tell you if there is any out-of-band (OOB) data to be read. OOB data is only available for sockets that have the `SO_OOBINLINE` socket options set.
- **Argument Pointer:** A pointer to a `u_long` that holds the argument to the command or stores the result of the command.

Return Value:
Returns zero if the option was set or `SOCKET_ERROR` if there was an error.

A blocking socket is one that will wait to send or receive data. A nonblocking socket performs these tasks asynchronously. When you call the socket's function to receive data on a blocking socket, it won't return until there is actually data to receive. Blocking sockets are easier to program, but aren't nearly as useful in game programming. Imagine using a blocking socket on a multiplayer game. Each client would be completely stopped, frozen in place, until some data was received. A nonblocking socket is the only way a game can continue processing anything in the same thread, which is why it is used overwhelmingly over the blocking sort.

Here's how you call the `ioctlsocket()` function to set your socket to nonblocking:

```
const unsigned long BLOCKING = 0;
const unsigned long NONBLOCKING = 1;
unsigned long val = NONBLOCKING;
ioctlsocket(m_sock, FIONBIO, &val);
```

There's one thing you should watch out for, however. You can only call this function on a "live" socket, meaning that it is a client socket that has been connected to a server or a server socket that is listening for clients.

Connecting Sockets to a Server and Understanding Ports

Once you have a socket handle and set the options with `ioctlsocket()`, the socket will be ready to connect to another computer. For a socket to connect, the computer accepting the connection must be listening for it. This differentiates server-side sockets from client-side sockets, even though they all use the same `SOCKET` handle structure and they all use the same functions to send and receive data.

For now, imagine you are simply creating a socket to attach to something like an FTP server, such as ftp.microsoft.com. Here you are, over a dozen pages into a networking chapter, and I haven't even mentioned ports yet. Well, I can't put it off any longer.

The designers of the Internet realized that computers on the Internet might have multiple connections to other computers simultaneously. They facilitated this by adding ports to the IP protocol. In addition to specifying an IP address of a computer, you must specify a port as well. Ports can be numbered from 1 to 65535, 0 is reserved. Various client/server applications like FTP and Telnet use well-known port assignments, which is simply an agreement that certain server applications will use certain ports. Most popular server applications like Telnet and FTP use ports in the 0..1024 range, but new server applications, like those for common chat programs and multiplayer games, use higher port numbers. This keeps popular client/server applications from using the same port. Table 16.5 provides a short list of commonly used ports you might recognize.

If you are creating a server, it's up to you to choose a good port that isn't already dominated by something else that everyone uses. There are plenty to go around, and some quick searches on the Internet will give you plenty of current information about which applications are using which port.

Table 16.5 Commonly Used Internet Ports

Protocol	Port Number	Protocol	Port Number
Echo	7	HTTP	80
Daytime	13	*Doom*	666
Quote of the Day	17	Kazaa	1214
FTP-data	20	MSN Messenger	1863
FTP	21	Apple iTunes	3689
SSH	22	*Ultima Online*	5001-5010
Telnet	23	Yahoo Messenger	5050
SMTP	25	AOL Instant Messenger	5190
Time	37	*Quake*	26000
Whois	43		

The port and IP address make a unique connection identifier. A server that listens on a particular port, like 5190 for AOL Instant Messenger, can accept many hundreds, if not thousands, of connections. A client can even make multiple connections to the same server on the same port. The IP protocol distinguishes actual connections internally so they don't get confused, although I'd hate to be a programmer trying to debug an application like that!

connect()

Enough already. Here's the API for actually connecting a socket to a server that is listening for connections:

```
int connect( SOCKET s, const struct sockaddr* name, int namelen);
```

Parameters:

- **Socket:** A valid socket handle.
- **Name:** A structure that holds the address family, port, and address of the server.
- **NameLen:** Always sizeof(struct sockaddr).

Return Value:

Returns zero if the function succeeded or SOCKET_ERROR if there was an error. Here's an example of how you connect a socket:

```
struct sockaddr_in sa;
sa.sin_family = AF_INET;
sa.sin_addr.s_addr = htonl(ip);
sa.sin_port = htons(port);

if (connect(m_sock, (struct sockaddr *)&sa, sizeof(sa)))
{
    // HANDLE ERROR HERE
}
```

The address family is set to AF_INET since we're using the Internet. The IP address and port are set, and the structure is sent into the connect() function along with the socket handle. If this didn't work for some reason, there are two things to try to help figure out what the problem is.

- First, try connecting with Telnet, one of the utility programs you can access from the command line. If it doesn't work, there's something wrong with the address, port, or perhaps your network can't see the remote computer.
- If Telnet works, try reversing the byte order of the port or IP address. This is easy to screw up.

Server Functions

You've seen how to create sockets on the client side, so now you're ready to create a server-side socket. You create the socket handle with the same `socket()` function you saw earlier, and you are free to also call the `setsockopt()` function to set the options you want. Instead of calling `connect()`, though, you call two other functions: `bind()` and `listen()`.

bind()

A server has to bind a socket to a particular IP address and port within the system before it can accept connections. After it is bound to an address and a port, you call `listen()` to open the server side for client connections:

```
int bind( SOCKET s, const struct sockaddr* name, int namelen);
```

Parameters:

- **Socket:** A valid socket handle.
- **Name:** A structure that holds the address family, port, and address of the server.
- **NameLen:** always `sizeof(struct sockaddr)`.

Return Value:

Returns zero if the function succeeded or `SOCKET_ERROR` if there was an error.
Here's an example of how you bind a socket to a particular port using the local IP address of the server. The port is specified in the `struct sockaddr` in network byte order. The address family is `AF_INET` for Internet addresses, and since we want the socket to be bound to the local IP address, the address member is set to `ADDR_ANY`:

```
struct sockaddr_in sa;
sa.sin_family = AF_INET;
sa.sin_addr = ADDR_ANY;
sa.sin_port = htons(portnum);

if (bind(m_sock, (struct sockaddr *)&sa, sizeof(sa)))
{
    // HANDLE ERROR HERE
}
```

listen()

After you've bound a socket to a particular port, you can open it up to accept connections with the `listen()` function:

```
int listen(  SOCKET s,  int backlog);
```

Parameters:

- **Socket:** A valid socket handle.
- **Backlog:** The maximum length of the queue of incoming connections. Set it to SOMAXCONN if you want the underlying service provider to use its default value. If a client attempts to connect and the backlog is full, the connection will be refused.

Return Value:

Returns zero if the function succeeded or SOCKET_ERROR if there was an error. Here's an example of using listen() to set the backlog to 256:

```
if (listen(m_sock, 256) == SOCKET_ERROR)
{
    // HANDLE ERROR HERE
}
```

accept()

When a remote client attaches to the listen socket with connect(), the server side will detect input on the listen socket. Exactly how this happens you'll see in a moment with the select() function. Once input is detected on a listen socket, you call accept() to establish the connection:

```
SOCKET accept(  SOCKET listenSock,  const struct sockaddr* name,  int namelen);
```

Parameters:

- **Listen Socket:** A valid socket handle to a listen socket.
- **Name:** A structure that receives the address of the connecting client.
- **NameLen:** Always sizeof(struct sockaddr).

Return Value:

Returns zero if the function succeeded or INVALID_SOCKET if there was an error.

There are a few things to be aware of when using accept(). First and foremost, it will block if there are no client connections ready and the listen socket is set to blocking. If the listen socket is set to nonblocking and there are no client connections ready, it will return an error and could put the listen socket in an unusable state. Basically, don't call accept() until you have input on the listen socket connection and can be sure you have at least one client ready to start talking. You can check for this by calling the select() function, which is up next.

The last server side method is `select()`. This function lets you poll the state of all your open sockets. You create three arrays of socket pointers that will be polled. The first set will be polled for input, the second set for output, and the third set for exceptions. Here's the `fd_set` structure definition and the definition for `select()`.

```
typedef struct fd_set {
  u_int fd_count;
  SOCKET fd_array[FD_SETSIZE];
} fd_set;

int select(
    int nfds,
    fd_set* readfds,
    fd_set* writefds,
    fd_set* exceptfds,
    const struct timeval* timeout );
```

Parameters:

- **nfds:** Ignored in WinSock; only included for compatibility with Berkeley sockets.
- **readfds, writefds, exceptfds:** The arrays of pointers to sockets to be polled for input, output, and exceptions.
- **timeout:** A pointer to a timeout structure. Set it to NULL if you want `select()` to block until something happens on one of the sockets, or set it to a valid timeout structure with all zeros to make a quick poll.

Return Value:

Returns zero if the function timed out, `SOCKET_ERROR` if there was an error, or the number of sockets contained within the structures that are ready to process.

This function is a real boon for the server-side programmer. It helps with servers that have tons of client connections and you don't want to block on any of

MAXIMUM CLIENT CONNECTIONS IS 64 BY DEFAULT

By default, the `fd_set` structure can hold 64 sockets. That size is defined as FD_SET-SIZE in the WINSOCK2.H header file. In C++, you can define your own FD_SETSIZE, as long as it's defined before the WINSOCK2 header file is included. You can set this compiler `#define` in the command line or project properties. If it is defined anywhere after `#include WinSock2.h`, it will break horribly.

them, whether they are set to blocking or nonblocking. This function can tell your program which sockets are ready to read from, write to, or have suffered an exception of some kind. By the way, one of those exceptions is the reception of out-of-band data.

Socket Reading and Writing

The two most common functions used for sending and receiving data are send() and recv(). They each take similar parameter lists, with the exception that they use different flags and one of them will clearly stomp all over the buffer you send in:

```
int send(  SOCKET s,  const char* buffer,  int length,  int flags);
int recv(  SOCKET s,  char* buffer,        int length,  int flags);
```

Parameters:

- **Socket:** A valid socket handle.
- **Buffer:** Either the source data buffer for sending or the destination buffer for receiving.
- **Length:** The size of the buffer in bytes.
- **Flags:**
  - **For Send:** MSG_DONTROUTE informs sockets you don't want the data routed, which can be ignored on WinSock. MSG_OOB tells sockets to send this packet as out-of-band data.
  - **For Recv:** MSG_PEEK peeks at the data, but doesn't remove it from the input buffer, and MSG_OOB processes out-of-band data.

Return Value:

Returns the number of bytes actually sent or received or SOCKET_ERROR if there was an error. The recv() function will return 0 if the socket was gracefully closed.

There's a few points to clarify. If you have a 10-byte receive buffer, and there are 20 bytes ready to read, the remaining 10 bytes will be there when you call recv() a second time. Conversely, if you have a 10-byte buffer, and there are only 5 bytes ready to read, the function will dutifully return 5, and the first 5 bytes of your buffer will have new data.

Also, MSG_PEEK and MSG_OOB seem to be ill supported and even broken, depending on the various implementations of TCP/IP on all the equipment and operating systems between the two connected computers. Trust them at your own risk.

That's certainly a whirlwind tour of the most used sockets functions. There are certainly more of them to learn, but what you just read will give you an excellent start. What you are about to see next is one way to organize these C functions into a usable set of classes designed to make your single-player game a multiplayer game.

Making a Multiplayer Game with Sockets

If you've followed the advice in this book, you've organized your game into three major components: the application layer, the game logic layer, and the game view layer. The game logic and game view can call directly into the application layer for performing tasks like opening files and allocating memory. The game view and game logic talk to each other through an event system, as described in Chapter 11, "Scripting with Lua."

If you guessed that the sockets classes belong in the application layer, you'd be exactly right. They are similar to files, really, in that they provide a stream of data your game can use. Sockets also tend to be slightly different on Windows and UNIX platforms, which is another good reason to stick them in the application layer.

I provided an important diagram in Chapter 2, "What's in a Game?" to describe how the logic/view architecture could easily support a networked game. Figure 16.1 shows this diagram again so that you don't have to go all the way back to Chapter 2.

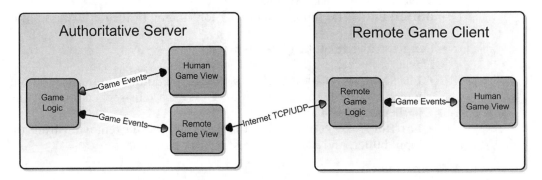

FIGURE 16.1 A remote game client attaching to a server.

Recall that this game architecture supports game logic and multiple views on that logic. These might include a human player view, an AI player view, and a remote player view. The events that are being generated by the authoritative machine acting as the game server can be serialized, sent over the Internet, and reconstructed as the same events on the remote machine. The remote machine can also send events in the form of game commands, like "fire my 105mm cannon at the newbie" back to the server.

While this high-level explanation seems easy, the reality is, as always, a bit more complicated. I'll take you through the whole thing, step-by-step. I'm going to break this job into four pieces so our brains don't explode.

- **Packet Classes:** Create objects to handle packets of data that will be sent and received through socket connections.
- **Core Socket Classes:** Create base objects to handle client connections.

- **Core Server Classes:** Create base objects to handle server connections.
- **Wire Sockets Classes into the Event System:** Create an event forwarder that listens to events locally and sends them on to a remote computer.

One thing you should know right away—all the code samples in this chapter assume a single-threaded environment. There are plenty of network programming examples out there that use one thread per connection and blocking calls to every socket. This may be an easy way to implement network communications, but it isn't the most efficient way.

Packet Classes

Data that is sent or received via sockets has a format, just like any file you would read from beginning to end. The format of the data will usually come in chunks, or packets, of discrete units, each of which is essentially a stand-alone piece of data. The format and interpretation of these packets is totally up to you. Just as you define the structure of your data files, you can define the structure of your packet stream. These packets might carry username and password data, data for events like "change game state missile" or "move actor," or game commands like "set throttle to 100%."

As your program reads data from a socket, it needs to have some way of determining what kind of packet is coming in and how many bytes to expect. When the correct number of bytes is ready, the packet is read from the socket as an atomic unit, encapsulated with a C++ packet object, and then handled by your game.

The exact opposite happens when you want to send a packet. The block of bytes that makes up the packet is assembled, or streamed, into a memory buffer. The size of the buffer is sent along with the packet, as well as some identifier that distinguishes the type of packet. The receiving end will probably handle packets of different types in different ways. A good example of this might be the difference between a text packet and a binary packet. The text packet might require additional processing for carriage returns and line feeds for the host system, whereas the binary packet might simply be a block of data.

The classes you are about to see encapsulate these ideas into C++ classes. The first class is an interface class that defines the API for any kind of packet that you'd care to define:

```
class IPacket
{
public:
    virtual char const * const VGetType() const=0;
    virtual char const * const VGetData() const=0;
    virtual u_long VGetSize() const =0;
    virtual ~IPacket() { }
};
```

This definitely follows the KISS (keep it simple, stupid!) rule. A packet's basic accessors simply gain access to the packet type, which I've defined as a unique text string, the packet data, and the size in bytes.

Most multiplayer games send binary data over network connections. This is because the information in the packets contains things like game events, movement deltas, and game commands that can be encoded very efficiently in a binary format. If this data were sent in clear text, it would be much larger. Think of it as the same thing as storing your data in a database or XML. XML might be easier to read, but it takes more space.

The first packet class is for binary packets. It allocates its own buffer of bytes and stores the size of the buffer in the first four bytes, but note that it stores them in network order. This is generally a good idea, even though I know I might never be using this system on anything other than my Dell:

```cpp
class BinaryPacket : public IPacket
{
protected:
    char *m_Data;

public:
    inline BinaryPacket(char const * const data, u_long size);
    inline BinaryPacket(u_long size);
    virtual ~BinaryPacket() { SAFE_DELETE(m_Data); }
    virtual char const * const VGetType() const { return g_Type; }
    virtual char const * const VGetData() const { return m_Data; }
    virtual u_long VGetSize() const { return ntohl(*(u_long *)m_Data); }
    inline void MemCpy(char const *const data, size_t size, int destOffset);

    static const char *g_Type;
};
```

Here I've defined two different constructors, both of which take the size of the buffer as an expected parameter. The first one takes a pointer to a data buffer that the BinaryPacket object will copy into its own buffer. The second expects the API programmer, that's you, to make repeated calls to MemCpy() to fill the buffer.

Here's the implementation of the constructors and MemCpy().

```cpp
const char *BinaryPacket::g_Type = "BinaryPacket";

inline BinaryPacket::BinaryPacket(char const * const data, u_long size)
{
    m_Data = GCC_NEW char[size + sizeof(u_long)];
    assert(m_Data);
```

```
      *(u_long *)m_Data = htonl(size+sizeof(u_long));
      memcpy(m_Data+sizeof(u_long), data, size);
}


inline BinaryPacket::BinaryPacket(u_long size)
{
   m_Data = GCC_NEW char[size + sizeof(u_long)];
   assert(m_Data);
   *(u_long *)m_Data = htonl(size+sizeof(u_long));
}


inline void BinaryPacket::MemCpy(char const *const data, size_t size, int
                                 destOffset)
{
   assert(size+destOffset <= VGetSize()-sizeof(u_long));
   memcpy(m_Data + destOffset + sizeof(u_long), data, size);
}
```

Another kind of packet that is pretty useful to have around is the `TextPacket`. It is a trivial class that takes a pointer to a character string, determines its own size, and sets the type as a text packet:

```
class TextPacket : public BinaryPacket
{
public:
   TextPacket(char const * const text);
   virtual char const * const VGetType() const { return g_Type; }

   static const char *g_Type;
};


TextPacket::TextPacket(char const * const text)
 : BinaryPacket(static_cast<u_long>(strlen(text) + 2))
{
   MemCpy(text, strlen(text), 0);
   MemCpy("\r\n", 2, 2);
   *(u_long *)m_Data = 0;
}


const char *TextPacket::g_Type = "TextPacket";
```

Core Socket Classes

As you might expect, I've written a class to encapsulate a socket handle. It has four virtual functions that can be overridden by implementers of child classes, or the class can even be used as is.

```
#define MAX_PACKET_SIZE (256)
#define RECV_BUFFER_SIZE (MAX_PACKET_SIZE * 512)

typedef std::list< shared_ptr <IPacket> > PacketList;

class NetSocket
{
public:
    NetSocket();
    NetSocket(SOCKET new_sock, unsigned int hostIP);
    virtual ~NetSocket();

    bool Connect(unsigned int ip, unsigned int port, int fCoalesce = 0);
    void SetBlocking(int block);

    void Send(shared_ptr<IPacket> pkt, bool clearTimeOut=1);

    virtual int  HasOutput() { return !m_OutList.empty(); }
    virtual void HandleOutput();
    virtual void HandleInput();
    virtual void TimeOut() { m_timeOut=0; }

    void HandleException() { m_deleteFlag |= 1; }


    void SetTimeOut(int ms=45*1000) { m_timeOut = timeGetTime() + ms; }

protected:
    SOCKET m_sock;        // the socket handle
    int m_id;             // a unique ID given by the socket manager

    // note: if deleteFlag has bit 2 set, exceptions only close the
    //   socket and set to INVALID_SOCKET, and do not delete the NetSocket
    int m_deleteFlag;

    PacketList m_OutList;              // packets to send
    PacketList m_InList;              // packets just received
```

```
    char m_recvBuf[RECV_BUFFER_SIZE];        // receive buffer
    unsigned int m_recvOfs, m_recvBegin;     // tracking the read head of the
                                             // buffer
    bool m_bBinaryProtocol;            // is the socket in binary or text mode

    int m_sendOfs;                     // tracking the output buffer
    unsigned int m_timeOut;            // when will the socket time out
    unsigned int m_ipaddr;             // the ipaddress of the remote connection

    int m_internal;                    // is the remote IP internal or external?
    int m_timeCreated;                 // when the socket was created
};
```

The class is relatively self-documenting, but there are a couple of things worthy of discussion. First, the delete flag is set to different values by the socket manager class if it wants to delete the class object, or simply close the socket but keep the class object around. This can help handle reconnections if the remote side drops out for a little while. Next, the input and output lists are ordered lists of packets to be sent and received, and they are implemented as STL lists. There is no output buffer, since it can use the already allocated memory of the packets in the output list. There is an input buffer, since you'll use it to compose packets as they stream in from the remote computer.

Also, note the maximum packet size and the size of the receive buffer defined just before the class. These sizes are totally up to you and what you expect to receive in the way of packets from the remote computers. Your mileage may vary with different choices, especially in terms of server memory. If you expect to have a few hundred clients attached, this memory buffer can get pretty big indeed.

Here are the constructors and destructor:

```
NetSocket::NetSocket()
{
    m_sock = INVALID_SOCKET;
    m_deleteFlag = 0;
    m_sendOfs = 0;
    m_timeOut = 0;

    m_recvOfs = m_recvBegin = 0;
    m_internal = 0;
}


NetSocket::NetSocket(SOCKET new_sock, unsigned int hostIP)
{
    // set everything to zero
    m_sock = INVALID_SOCKET;
```

```
        m_deleteFlag = 0;
        m_sendOfs = 0;
        m_timeOut = 0;

        // set the socket to receive binary packets
        m_bBinaryProtocol = 1;

        m_recvOfs = m_recvBegin = 0;
        m_internal = 0;

        // check the time
        m_timeCreated = timeGetTime();

        m_sock = new_sock;
        m_ipaddr = hostIP;

        // ask the socket manager if the socket is on our internal network
        m_internal = g_pSocketManager->IsInternal(m_ipaddr);

        setsockopt (m_sock, SOL_SOCKET, SO_DONTLINGER, NULL, 0);

        // NOTE! Don't do the following if you want high performance on a server!!!!
        if (m_ipaddr)
        {
            TCHAR buffer[128];
            const char *ansiIpaddress = g_pSocketManager->GetHostByAddr(m_ipaddr);
            if (ansiIpaddress)
            {
                TCHAR genIpaddress[64];
                AnsiToGenericCch(
                    genIpaddress,
                    ansiIpaddress,
                    static_cast<int>(strlen(ansiIpaddress)+1));
                _tcssprintf(buffer,
                    _T("User connected: %s %s"),
                    genIpaddress,
                    (m_internal) ? _T("(internal)") : _T(""));
                OutputDebugString(buffer);
            }
        }
    }
```

```
NetSocket::~NetSocket()
{
   if (m_sock != INVALID_SOCKET)
   {
      closesocket(m_sock);
      m_sock = INVALID_SOCKET;
   }
}
```

The only thing to watch out for is the code at the last part of the second constructor, which takes a valid socket handle and the IP address of the remote computer. It calls a method of the socket manager, which you'll see shortly. But as you can probably tell by the name of the method, it wraps one of those DNS utility functions. These functions are not usable for super-fast server applications, as DNS lookups take hundreds of milliseconds, maybe more, if the DNS system can't find the name of the IP address in question. If you have a high-performance server application, you can just eliminate the call to GetHostByAddr(), since it is really only used for a debug message.

Also, notice the conversion function AnsiToGenericCch(). This function is adapted from some early DirectX utility code that converts text strings, by force if necessary, from generic format to ANSI format. The function is actually in the source code that goes along with this book, and you can find it on the book's Web site. The point is, sometimes you have to do these forced conversions when dealing with older APIs, like you find in sockets, that don't have any internal support for wide character strings. It's a pain in the butt, I know, but you've got to do it if you have a UNICODE or MBCS application that uses sockets like this.

The next method is called when you want to connect a new NetSocket to a remote client:

```
bool NetSocket::Connect(unsigned int ip, unsigned int port, int fCoalesce)
{
   struct sockaddr_in sa;
   int x = 1;

   // create the socket handle
   if ((m_sock = socket(AF_INET, SOCK_STREAM, 0)) == INVALID_SOCKET)
      return false;

   // set socket options - in this case turn off Nagle algorithm if desired
   if (!fCoalesce)
   {
      setsockopt(m_sock, IPPROTO_TCP, TCP_NODELAY, (char *)&x, sizeof(x));
   }
```

```
// last step - set the IP adress and port of the server, and call connect()
sa.sin_family = AF_INET;
sa.sin_addr.s_addr = htonl(ip);
sa.sin_port = htons(port);

if (connect(m_sock, (struct sockaddr *)&sa, sizeof(sa)))
{
   closesocket(m_sock);
   m_sock = INVALID_SOCKET;
   return false;
}

return true;
}
```

Just as described in the socket primer earlier in this chapter, the process for connecting a socket to a server has three steps. First, you create the socket handle. Second, you call the socket options. In this case, NetSocket supports disabling the packet-grouping algorithm by default. This increases network traffic, but can improve performance if you send/receive tons of tiny packets like games tend to do. Finally, you connect the socket to the remote server.

Right after the socket is connected, you probably want to set it to nonblocking. Here's a method that does exactly that, and it is exactly like you saw in the primer:

```
void NetSocket::SetBlocking(int block)
{
      unsigned long val = block ? 0 : 1;
      ioctlsocket(m_sock, FIONBIO, &val);
}
```

It's now time to learn how this class sends packets to the remote computer. Whenever you have a packet you want to send, the Send() method simply adds it to the end of the list of packets to send. It doesn't send the packets right away. This is done once per update loop by the HandleOutput() method:

```
void NetSocket::Send(shared_ptr<IPacket> pkt, bool clearTimeOut)
{
   if (clearTimeOut)
      m_timeOut = 0;

   m_OutList.push_back(pkt);
}
```

The HandleOutput() method's job is to iterate the list of packets in the output list and call the sockets send() API until all the data is gone or there is some kind of error:

```
void NetSocket::HandleOutput()
{
   int fSent = 0;
   do
   {
      assert(!m_OutList.empty());
      PacketList::iterator i = m_OutList.begin();

      shared_ptr<IPacket> pkt = *i;
      const char *buf = pkt->VGetData();
      int len = static_cast<int>(pkt->VGetSize());

      int rc = send(m_sock, buf+m_sendOfs, len-m_sendOfs, 0);
      if (rc > 0)
      {
         g_pSocketManager->m_Outbound += rc;
         m_sendOfs += rc;
         fSent = 1;
      }
      else if (WSAGetLastError() != WSAEWOULDBLOCK)
      {
         HandleException();
         fSent = 0;
      }
      else
      {
         fSent = 0;
      }

      if (m_sendOfs == pkt->VGetSize())
      {
         m_OutList.pop_front();
         m_sendOfs = 0;
      }

   } while ( fSent && !m_OutList.empty() );
}
```

The idea behind reading the socket for input is similar, but there's some buffer management to worry about. For efficiency's sake, there's a single monolithic buffer for each NetSocket object. Depending on how the remote sends data, you might get your packet in chunks. TCP is guaranteed to send things in the right order and it won't split them up, but you might attempt to send something large, like a movie file. In any case, you want to collect bytes in the read buffer until you have a valid packet and then copy those bytes into a dynamic data structure like BinaryPacket or TextPacket so your game can process it.

Since you might receive multiple packets in a single read, the read buffer operates in a round-robin fashion. The read/write heads continually advance until they get too close to the end of the buffer and then they copy any partial packets to the beginning of the buffer and start the whole process over:

```
void NetSocket::HandleInput()
{
   bool bPktReceived = false;
   u_long packetSize = 0;
   int rc = recv(m_sock,
                 m_recvBuf+m_recvBegin+m_recvOfs,
                 RECV_BUFFER_SIZE-m_recvOfs, 0);
   if (rc==0)
      return;

   if (rc < 0)
   {
      m_deleteFlag = 1;
      return;
   }

   const int hdrSize = sizeof(u_long);
   unsigned int newData = m_recvOfs + rc;
   int processedData = 0;

   while (newData > hdrSize)
   {
      // There are two types of packets at the lowest level of our design:
      // BinaryPacket - Sends the size as a positive 4 byte integer
      // TextPacket - Sends 0 for the size, the parser will search for a CR

      packetSize = *(reinterpret_cast<u_long*>(m_recvBuf+m_recvBegin));
      packetSize = ntohl(packetSize);
```

```
if (m_bBinaryProtocol)
{
    // we don't have enough new data to grab the next packet
    if (newData < packetSize)
        break;

    if (packetSize > MAX_PACKET_SIZE)
    {
        // prevent nasty buffer overruns!
        HandleException();
        return;
    }

    if (newData >= packetSize)
    {
        // we know how big the packet is...and we have the whole thing
        shared_ptr<BinaryPacket> pkt(
            GCC_NEW BinaryPacket(
                &m_recvBuf[m_recvBegin+hdrSize], packetSize-hdrSize));
        m_InList.push_back(pkt);
        bPktRecieved = true;
        processedData += packetSize;
        newData -= packetSize;
        m_recvBegin += packetSize;
    }
}
else
{
    // the text protocol waits for a carriage return and creates a string
    char *cr = static_cast<char *>(
        memchr(&m_recvBuf[m_recvBegin], 0x0a, rc));
    if (cr)
    {
        *(cr+1) = 0;
        shared_ptr<TextPacket> pkt(
            GCC_NEW TextPacket(&m_recvBuf[m_recvBegin]));

        m_InList.push_back(pkt);
        packetSize = cr - &m_recvBuf[m_recvBegin];
        bPktRecieved = true;

        processedData += packetSize;
        newData -= packetSize;
        m_recvBegin += packetSize;
```

```
            }
        }
    }

    g_pSocketManager->m_Inbound += rc;
    m_recvOfs = newData;

    if (bPktRecieved)
    {
        if (m_recvOfs == 0)
        {
            m_recvOfs = 0;
            m_recvBegin = 0;
        }
        else if (m_recvBegin + m_recvOfs + MAX_PACKET_SIZE > RECV_BUFFER_SIZE)
        {
            // we don't want to overrun the buffer - so we copy the leftover bits
            // to the beginning of the receive buffer and start over
            int leftover = m_recvOfs;
            memcpy(m_recvBuf, &m_recvBuf[m_recvBegin], m_recvOfs);
            m_recvBegin = 0;
        }
    }
}
```

Notice the predicate in the middle that checks for m_bBinaryProtocol? The Net-Socket class by default reads binary packets. It is up to child classes to switch between a binary and text packet protocol. If this annoys you, you could even encode the packet type inside the packet itself at the cost of additional network bytes. It's a better plan, perhaps, to define a special binary packet that signals the socket to switch.

When you are coding a server application, such as *Ultima Online*, believe me every byte counts. It makes tons of sense to save bytes if you can. In the case of this class, one way you could clearly save space is to change the amount of space saved for the packet size. Right now, we are using a u_long, which is clearly way too big for a single packet.

BEST PRACTICE

EASY TO READ OR SUPER EFFICIENT? DO BOTH!

When you define your packet definitions and protocols, make sure you can easily switch between a tight, efficient packet definition and an easy-to-read definition such as clear text. You'll use one for production, but the other is invaluable for debugging.

A Socket Class for Listening

A listen socket is an easy extension of the `NetSocket` class. It adds the capability to listen for client connections and accept them, adding new sockets to the global socket manager:

```
class NetListenSocket: public NetSocket
{
public:
   NetListenSocket() { };
   NetListenSocket(int portnum) { port = 0; Init(portnum); }

   void Init(int portnum);
   SOCKET AcceptConnection(unsigned int *pAddr);

   unsigned short port;
};
```

There are five steps to create a listen socket: You create a socket handle, set the socket options, bind the socket to a listen port, set it to nonblocking, and finally call `listen()`:

```
void NetListenSocket::Init(int portnum)
{
   struct sockaddr_in sa;
   int x = 1;

   // create socket handle
   if ((m_sock = socket(AF_INET, SOCK_STREAM, 0)) == INVALID_SOCKET)
   {
      EXIT_ASSERT
   }

   // set socket options to reuse server socket addresses even if they are
   // busy - this is important if your server restarts and you don't want
   // to wait for your sockets to time out.

   if (setsockopt(
      m_sock, SOL_SOCKET, SO_REUSEADDR, (char *)&x, sizeof(x))== SOCKET_ERROR)
   {
      closesocket(m_sock);
      m_sock = INVALID_SOCKET;
      EXIT_ASSERT
   }
```

```
memset(&sa, 0, sizeof(sa));
sa.sin_family = AF_INET;
sa.sin_port = htons(portnum);

// bind to port
if (bind(m_sock, (struct sockaddr *)&sa, sizeof(sa)) == SOCKET_ERROR)
{
   closesocket(m_sock);
   m_sock = INVALID_SOCKET;
   EXIT_ASSERT
}

// set nonblocking - accept() blocks under some odd circumstances otherwise
SetBlocking(NONBLOCKING);

// start listening
if (listen(m_sock, 256) == SOCKET_ERROR)
{
   closesocket(m_sock);
   m_sock = INVALID_SOCKET;
   EXIT_ASSERT
}

port = portnum;
}
```

If the listen socket gets any input, it means there's a client ready to attach. The method that handles the attachment and creates a new socket handle is AcceptConnection():

```
SOCKET NetListenSocket::AcceptConnection(unsigned int *pAddr)
{
   SOCKET new_sock;
   struct sockaddr_in sock;
   int size;

   size = sizeof(sock);

   if ((new_sock = accept(m_sock, (struct sockaddr *)&sock, &size))==
                                   INVALID_SOCKET)
      return INVALID_SOCKET;
```

```
if (getpeername(new_sock, (struct sockaddr *)&sock, &size) == SOCKET_ERROR)
{
   closesocket(new_sock);
   return INVALID_SOCKET;
}
*pAddr = ntohl(sock.sin_addr.s_addr);
return new_sock;
}
```

This method is a simple wrapper around `accept()`, which does all the heavy lifting. There's a utility function, `getpeername()`, which basically grabs the IP address of the new client and returns it in an output parameter.

You should be asking two questions right now. First, why don't I simply create a `NetSocket()` object right here and return that? Second, who or what ever actually calls this `AcceptConnect()` method? The answer to the first question is: I don't return a `NetSocket` object because I assume you'll want to create your own child class that inherits from `NetSocket`, but overloads the `HandleInput()` and `HandleOutput()` methods. You'll see a class that does exactly that when I show you some more server-side code. Here's the answer to the second question: the server-side code itself! You'll see that in a few pages.

A Socket Manager Class

Sockets need a socket manager, whether they are on a client or on a server. A socket manager organizes multiple sockets into a manageable group, takes care of handling the initialization and shutdown of the sockets system, and provides some useful utility functions. It also provides a useful base class for more specialized socket managers for servers and clients:

```
// defines a socket list
typedef std::list<NetSocket *> SocketList;
// maps an ID number to a socket handle
typedef std::map<int, NetSocket *> SocketIdMap;
class BaseSocketManager
{
   friend class NetSocket;

public:
   BaseSocketManager();
   virtual ~BaseSocketManager() { Shutdown(); }

   bool Init();
   void Shutdown();
```

```
    int AddSocket(NetSocket *socket);
    void RemoveSocket(NetSocket *socket);

    bool Send(int sockId, shared_ptr<IPacket> packet);
    void DoSelect(int pauseMicroSecs, int handleInput = 1);

    void SetSubnet(unsigned int subnet, unsigned int subnetMask)
    {
        m_Subnet = subnet;
        m_SubnetMask = subnetMask;
    }
    bool IsInternal(unsigned int ipaddr);

    unsigned int GetHostByName(std::string hostName);
    const char *GetHostByAddr(unsigned int ip);

protected:
    WSADATA m_WsaData;          // describes sockets system implementation

    SocketList m_SockList;      // a list of sockets
    SocketIdMap m_SockMap;      // a map from integer IDs to socket handles

    int m_NextSocketId;         // a ticker for the next socket ID

    int m_Inbound;              // statistics gathering - inbound data
    int m_Outbound;             // statistics gathering - outbound data
    int m_MaxOpenSockets;       // statistics gathering - max open sockets

    unsigned int m_SubnetMask;  // the subnet mask of the internal network
    unsigned int m_Subnet;      // the subnet of the internal network

    NetSocket *FindSocket(int sockId);
};
```

One of the core features of the socket manager is the notion that each socket has a companion identifier. In this implementation of the manager, a counter is used to guarantee a unique ID for each socket in the system. This is different than a handle because this ID could be something much more significant, such as a player ID number or an account ID number or whatever. On *Ultima Online*, this ID was a unique player ID number that was assigned to it by the account login system when new accounts were created. You can use whatever you want, but it is a good thing to associate an unchanging ID number with each socket, since socket handles can change if the socket is dropped and reconnected.

Another thing that the socket manager tracks is statistics for socket traffic and the maximum number of sockets the manager has managed at one time. This can be useful if you decide to track that sort of thing in production or even after release. As an example, *Ultima Online* tracked all manner of statistics about player activity, network activity, and so on.

If you set the subnet members, the socket manager can tell if a socket is coming from an internal IP address. For example, it can ensure an IP address is on the local network and deny access from an IP address coming from the Internet. This feature proved to be pretty useful to mask off special functions, like the "God" commands in *Ultima Online*, from anyone outside of the development team.

Like other members of the application layer, the socket manager is a singular object that exists once for the application. It can manage both client and listen sockets, although the implementations in this chapter favor a straight client or straight server paradigm:

```
BaseSocketManager *g_pSocketManager = NULL;

BaseSocketManager::BaseSocketManager()
{
    m_Inbound = 0;
    m_Outbound = 0;
    m_MaxOpenSockets = 0;
    m_SubnetMask = 0;
    m_Subnet = 0xffffffff;

    g_pSocketManager = this;
    ZeroMemory(&m_WsaData, sizeof(WSADATA));
}

bool BaseSocketManager::Init()
{
    int errorCode = WSAStartup(0x0202, &m_WsaData);
    testCode();

    if (errorCode==0)
        return true;
    else
    {
        assert(0 && "WSAStartup failure!");
        return false;
    }
}
```

```
void BaseSocketManager::Shutdown()
{
    // Get rid of all those pesky kids...
    while (!m_SockList.empty())
    {
        delete *m_SockList.begin();
        m_SockList.pop_front();
    }

    WSACleanup();
}
```

You've seen before that performing any task that can fail in a constructor is generally a bad idea. Therefore, the socket manager class uses an initialization method that can return a Boolean value. It also uses a Shutdown() method apart from the destructor so you can have more control over the life and death of sockets in your application.

Once a NetSocket object exists, it is added to the socket manager with the AddSocket() method. It adds the socket to the socket list, updates the map of socket IDs to socket handles, and updates the maximum number of sockets opened. The RemoveSocket() method removes the socket from the list and the map, and then it frees the socket:

```
int BaseSocketManager::AddSocket(NetSocket *socket)
{
    socket->m_id = m_NextSocketId;
    m_SockList.push_front(socket);

    int openSockets = static_cast<int>(m_SockList.size());

    if (openSockets > m_MaxOpenSockets)
        ++m_MaxOpenSockets;

    m_SockMap[m_NextSocketId] = socket;
    ++m_NextSocketId;

    return socket->m_id;
}

void BaseSocketManager::RemoveSocket(NetSocket *socket)
{
    m_SockList.remove(socket);
    m_SockMap.erase(socket->m_id);
    SAFE_DELETE(socket);
}
```

Your game needs a high-level function to send a packet to a particular socket ID. High-level game systems certainly won't care to have a direct reference to a socket handle, so they use the socket ID to figure out which socket is going to get the packet. In the case of a server system with hundreds of attached clients, this function makes short work of finding a socket handle that corresponds to a generic socket ID:

```
NetSocket *BaseSocketManager::FindSocket(int sockId)
{
   SocketIdMap::iterator i = m_SockMap.find(sockId);
   if (i==m_SockMap.end())
      return NULL;

   return (*i).second;
}

bool BaseSocketManager::Send(int sockId, shared_ptr<IPacket> packet)
{
   NetSocket *sock = FindSocket(sockId);
   if (!sock)
      return false;
   sock->Send(packet);
   return true;
}
```

The real meat of the socket manager class is `DoSelect()`. There are four stages of this method:

- Set up which sockets are going to be polled for activity.
- Call the `select()` API.
- Handle processing of any socket with input, output, or exceptions.
- Close any sockets that need closing.

```
void BaseSocketManager::DoSelect(int pauseMicroSecs, int handleInput)
{
   timeval tv;
   tv.tv_sec = 0;
   // 100 microseconds is 0.1 milliseconds or .0001 seconds
   tv.tv_usec = pauseMicroSecs;

   fd_set inp_set, out_set, exc_set;
   int maxdesc;
   NetSocket *pSock;
```

```
FD_ZERO(&inp_set);
FD_ZERO(&out_set);
FD_ZERO(&exc_set);

maxdesc = 0;

// set everything up for the select
for (SocketList::iterator i = m_SockList.begin();
    i != m_SockList.end(); ++i)
{
   pSock = *i;
   if ((pSock->m_deleteFlag&1) || pSock->m_sock == INVALID_SOCKET)
      continue;

   if (handleInput)
      FD_SET(pSock->m_sock, &inp_set);

   FD_SET(pSock->m_sock, &exc_set);

   if (pSock->HasOutput())
      FD_SET(pSock->m_sock, &out_set);

   if ((int)pSock->m_sock > maxdesc)
      maxdesc = (int)pSock->m_sock;

 }

int selRet = 0;

// do the select (duration passed in as tv, NULL to block until event)
selRet = select(maxdesc+1, &inp_set, &out_set, &exc_set, &tv) ;
if (selRet == SOCKET_ERROR)
{
   // todo - handle error!
   return;
}

// handle input, output, and exceptions
if (selRet)
{
   for (SocketList::iterator i = m_SockList.begin();
      i != m_SockList.end(); ++i)
```

```
        {
            pSock = *i;

            if ((pSock->m_deleteFlag&1) || pSock->m_sock == INVALID_SOCKET)
                continue;

            if (FD_ISSET(pSock->m_sock, &exc_set))
                pSock->HandleException();

            if (!(pSock->m_deleteFlag&1) && FD_ISSET(pSock->m_sock, &out_set))
                pSock->HandleOutput();

            if (   handleInput
                && !(pSock->m_deleteFlag&1) && FD_ISSET(pSock->m_sock, &inp_set))
            {
                pSock->HandleInput();
            }
        }
    }

    unsigned int timeNow = timeGetTime();

    // handle deleting any sockets
    for (SocketList::iterator i = m_SockList.begin();
        i != m_SockList.end(); ++i)
    {
        pSock = *i;
        if (pSock->m_timeOut)
        {
            if (pSock->m_timeOut < timeNow)
                pSock->TimeOut();
        }

        if (pSock->m_deleteFlag&1)
        {
            switch (pSock->m_deleteFlag)
            {
              case 1:
                  --i;
                  g_pSocketManager->RemoveSocket(pSock);
                  break;
```

```
            case 3:
               pSock->m_deleteFlag = 2;
               if (pSock->m_sock != INVALID_SOCKET)
               {
                    closesocket(pSock->m_sock);
                    pSock->m_sock = INVALID_SOCKET;
               }
               break;
         }
      }
   }
}
```

Notice the liberal use of FD_ZERO, FD_SET, and FD_ISSET. These are accessors to the fd_set structures that are sent into the select() method and store the results. This method's job is to poll all the sockets you send into it for input, output, and exceptions. The socket list is iterated three times in this method, which may seem inefficient. The truth is if you use select(), which polls sockets, the real inefficiency is inside the select statement itself. The other code doesn't really take that much more time. Sockets could also have their delete flags set inside calls to HandleInput() or HandleOutput(), so it makes sense to iterate through them after those methods are finished.

The code at the end of the method has two kinds of socket shutdown. The first, if the delete flag is set to 1, removes the socket entirely from the socket manager. This would occur if the socket were shut down elegantly from both sides, perhaps by trading an "L8R" packet or something. The second case allows the NetSocket object to exist, but the socket handle will be shut down. This allows for a potential reconnection of a socket if a player drops off the game for a moment, but then comes back. If that happened, the unsent packets still in the NetSocket object would still be ready to send to the newly reconnected player.

The DoSelect() method is the only thing you need to call in your main loop to make the entire sockets system work. You'll want to call this method after you tick the Event Manager but before updating the game, assuming you are using the socket system to send events across the network:

```
safeTickEventManager( 20 ); // allow event queue to process for up to 20 ms

if (g_pApp->m_pBaseSocketManager)
   g_pApp->m_pBaseSocketManager->DoSelect(0);   // pause 0 microseconds

g_pApp->m_pGame->VOnUpdate(fTime, fElapsedTime);
```

The last three methods in the socket manager class are some utility methods. The first one uses the subnet and subnet mask members to figure out if a particular IP address is coming from the internal network or from somewhere outside:

```cpp
bool BaseSocketManager::IsInternal(unsigned int ipaddr)
{
    bool internal = false;
    if (m_SubnetMask)
    {
        unsigned int hostSubnet = ipaddr & m_SubnetMask;
        if (hostSubnet == m_Subnet)
        {
            internal = 1;
        }
    }
    return internal;
}
```

The next two methods wrap the DNS functions you already know how to use: gethostbyname() and gethostbyaddr().

```cpp
unsigned int BaseSocketManager::GetHostByName(const std::string &hostName)
{
    struct hostent *pHostEnt;
    struct sockaddr_in tmpSockAddr; //placeholder for the ip address

    //This will retrieve the ip details and put it into pHostEnt structure
    pHostEnt = gethostbyname(hostName.c_str());

    if(pHostEnt == NULL)
    {
        assert(0 && _T("Error occurred"));
        return 0;
    }

    memcpy(&tmpSockAddr.sin_addr,pHostEnt->h_addr,pHostEnt->h_length);
    return ntohl(tmpSockAddr.sin_addr.s_addr);
}

const char *BaseSocketManager::GetHostByAddr(unsigned int ip)
{
    static char host[32];
```

```
int netip = htonl(ip);
LPHOSTENT lpHostEnt = gethostbyaddr((const char *)&netip, 4, PF_INET);

if (lpHostEnt)
{
    strcpy(host, lpHostEnt->h_name);
    return host;
}

return NULL;
}
```

The `BaseSocketManager` class is about 99 percent of what you need to create a client-side socket manager or a server-side socket manager. Classes that inherit from it can make it easy to create connections between clients and servers.

CORE CLIENT-SIDE CLASSES

An easy example of an extension of the `BaseSocketManager` class is a class to manage the client side of a game. Its job is to create a single socket that attaches to a known server:

```
class ClientSocketManager : public BaseSocketManager
{
    std::string m_HostName;
    unsigned int m_Port;

public:
    ClientSocketManager(const std::string &hostName, unsigned int port)
    {
        m_HostName = hostName;
        m_Port = port;
    }

    bool Connect();
};

bool ClientSocketManager::Connect()
{
    if (!BaseSocketManager::Init())
        return false;

    RemoteEventSocket *pSocket = GCC_NEW RemoteEventSocket;
```

```
      if (!pSocket->Connect(GetHostByName(m_HostName), m_Port) )
      {
         SAFE_DELETE(pSocket);
         return false;
      }
      AddSocket(pSocket);
      return true;
}
```

I haven't shown you the `RemoteEventSocket` class yet, so hang tight because you'll see it shortly. All you need to know for now is that `RemoteEventSocket` is an extension of the `NetSocket` class, and it handles all the input and output for the local game client. In practice, you'd define whatever socket you want to handle all your client packets and initialize it in your version of the `ClientSocketManager` class.

Here's an example of how you might use this class to create a client connection to a server at shooter.fragfest.com, listening on port 3709:

```
ClientSocketManager *pClient = GCC_NEW
                    ClientSocketManager(_T("shooter.fragfest.com", 3709));
if (!pClient->Connect())
{
   assert(0 && _T("Couldn't attach to game server."));
}
```

CORE SERVER-SIDE CLASSES

The server side is a little trickier, but not terribly so. The complexity comes from how sockets work on the server side. Let's review what happens on the server side once the sockets system is running and the server has a listen socket open:

- Initialize the server socket manager and attach a listen socket.
- Call `DoSelect()` on the server socket manager.
- If there's input on the listen socket, create a new socket and attach it to the socket manager.
- Handle input/output/exceptions on all other sockets.

What we need is a class that extends `NetListenSocket` by overloading `HandleIn-put()` to create new clients. The clients are encapsulated by the `RemoteEventSocket`, which is the final piece to this puzzle. Its job is to send game events generated on the server to a remote client and fool the client into thinking that the events were actually generated locally:

```
class GameServerListenSocket: public NetListenSocket
{
public:
   GameServerListenSocket(int portnum) { Init(portnum); }
   void HandleInput();
};

void GameServerListenSocket::HandleInput()
{
   SOCKET new_sock;
   unsigned int theipaddr;

   new_sock = AcceptConnection(&theipaddr);

   int x = 1;
   setsockopt(new_sock, SOL_SOCKET, SO_DONTLINGER, (char *)&x, sizeof(x));

   if (new_sock != INVALID_SOCKET)
   {
      RemoteEventSocket * sock =
         GCC_NEW RemoteEventSocket(new_sock, theipaddr);
      int sockId = g_pSocketManager->AddSocket(sock);
      safeQueEvent( EventPtr( GCC_NEW Evt_Remote_Client( sockId ) ) );
   }
}
```

Notice another cameo from Chapter 10, "Game Event Management"? The call to safeQueEvent() with a new event: Evt_Remote_Client. The event takes the socket ID and passes it onto any game subsystem that is listening. This is how the game attaches new players. It relates the socket ID to an object or actor in the game, and a special game view that fools the server into thinking that the client is actually a human player playing on the same system.

You are now ready to see the final piece of this puzzle—how the sockets system ties into the event system and the game views.

WIRING SOCKETS INTO THE EVENT SYSTEM

Let's take inventory. What have you learned so far in this chapter?

- NetSocket() and ClientSocketManager() work together to create the generic client side of the network communications.
- NetListenSocket() and BaseSocketManager() work together to create the generic server side of the network communications.

- `GameServerListenSocket()` is a custom server-side class that creates special sockets that can take network data and translate them into events that game systems can listen to, just like you saw in Chapter 10.

So what's left? A few things, actually. You need a socket that can translate network data into events, and you also need a class that can take events and create network packets to be sent along to remote computers—client or server. Both the client and the server will do this because they both generate and listen for events coming from the other side.

Translating C++ objects of any kind requires streaming. There are tons of useful implementations of streams out there, and in my great practice of doing something rather stupid to make a point, I'm going to show you how to use STL `istrstream` and `ostrstream` templates.

Even though I'm an old-school C hound and still use `printf()` everywhere, I'm sure many of you have seen streams like this:

```
char nameBuffer[1024];
cout << "Hello World! What is your name?";
cin >> name;
```

The `istrstream` and `ostrstream` work very similarly. Think of them as a string-based memory stream that you can read from and write to very easily. At some point in this book, I mentioned how useful it was to use streams to initialize C++ objects and use them to save them out to disk for saved games. Well, here's an example of what this looks like with a simple C++ object:

```
struct ActorParams
{
   int m_Size;
   optional<ActorId> m_Id;
   Vec3 m_Pos;
   ActorType m_Type;

   ActorParams()
      { m_Pos=Vec3(0,0,0); m_Type=AT_Unknown; m_Size=sizeof(ActorParams); }
   virtual bool VInit (std::istrstream &in)
   {
      int hasActorId = 0;

      in >> m_Size;
      in >> hasActorId;
      if (hasActorId)
      {
         in >> hasActorId;
```

```
            m_Id = hasActorId;
        }
        in >> m_Pos.x >> m_Pos.y >> m_Pos.z;
        return true;
    }

    virtual void VSerialize(std::ostrstream &out)
    {
        out << m_Type << " ";
        out << m_Size << " ";
        out << static_cast<int>(m_Id.valid()) << " ";
        if (m_Id.valid())
        {
            out << *m_Id << " ";
        }
        out << m_Pos.x << " " << m_Pos.y << " " << m_Pos.z << " ";
    }
};
```

This object represents the parameters that are common to many actors in a game: it stores the size of the structure, the actor ID, location, and type. Notice two virtual functions for initializing the object and serializing the object with streams? The methods are virtual so that entire class hierarchies can stream themselves to and from files for save games or even network communications. By the way, my choice for the stream class being string-based and not binary makes my network packets completely enormous, but they are easy on my eyes and easy to debug. The best thing is, once the basic system is running, I can even replace these text stream objects with something cool—like something that compresses streams on the fly. Look on the Internet, and you'll find neat stream technology out there.

Back to the task at hand, you've seen a quick introduction into using streams to turn C++ objects into raw bits that can be sent to a disk or across the Internet. Now you're ready to see the RemoteEventSocket class, which converts the network socket data into events that can be sent on to the local event system. There are only two methods in this class, one overloads HandleInput() and the other takes the incoming packets and turns them into events:

```
class RemoteEventSocket: public NetSocket
{
public:
    enum
    {
        NetMsg_Event,
        NetMsg_PlayerLoginOk,
    };
```

```
    // server accepting a client
    RemoteEventSocket(SOCKET new_sock, unsigned int hostIP)
    : NetSocket(new_sock, hostIP)
    {
    }

    // client attach to server
    RemoteEventSocket() { };

    virtual void HandleInput();

protected:
    void CreateEvent(std::istrstream &in);
};

void RemoteEventSocket::HandleInput()
{
    NetSocket::HandleInput();

    // traverse the list of m_InList packets and do something useful with them
    while (!m_InList.empty())
    {
        shared_ptr<IPacket> packet = *m_InList.begin();
        m_InList.pop_front();
        const char *buf = packet->VGetData();
        int size = static_cast<int>(packet->VGetSize());

        std::istrstream in(buf+sizeof(u_long), (size-sizeof(u_long)));

        int type;
        in >> type;
        switch(type)
        {
            case NetMsg_Event:
                CreateEvent(in);
                break;

            case NetMsg_PlayerLoginOk:
            {
                int vid;
                in >> vid;
                g_pApp->m_pGame->SetPlayer(GameView_Human, vid, 0);
                break;
            }
        }
    }
}
```

```
            default:
                assert(0 && _T("Unknown message type."));
        }
    }
}
```

You'll see that I've created a little handshaking; actually, it's completely one-sided, so it's not really handshaking in the sense that I'm reading one byte from the incoming packet and using that byte to determine a message type. There are two types of messages in this simple design. The first is a normal event, in which case, the packet is sent on to CreateEvent(). The second is a special case message from the server that tells the local client what its game view ID is. This is how different clients, all playing the same multiplayer game, tell each other apart: their game views will all have a unique ID set by the server. If they didn't do this, all their game view IDs would be set to zero, and it would be difficult for the local clients to do the right thing with all manner of things, such as displaying a score for each player. After all, if I'm playing poker, I need to know what seat I'm sitting in.

The CreateEvent() method looks in the stream for an event type, which is sent in string format. The event type is used to create a new event object, which then uses the stream to initialize itself:

```
void RemoteEventSocket::CreateEvent(std::istrstream &in)
{
    char eventType[256];
    in >> eventType;

    if (!stricmp(eventType, Evt_New_Game::gkName))
    {
        safeQueEvent(EventPtr(GCC_NEW Evt_New_Game(in)));
    }
    else if (!stricmp(eventType, Evt_Game_State::gkName))
    {
        safeQueEvent(EventPtr(GCC_NEW Evt_Game_State(in)));
    }
    else if (!stricmp(eventType, Evt_New_Actor::gkName))
    {
        safeQueEvent(EventPtr(GCC_NEW Evt_New_Actor(in)));
    }
    else if (!stricmp(eventType, Evt_Move_Actor::gkName))
    {
        safeQueEvent(EventPtr(GCC_NEW Evt_Move_Actor(in)));
    }
```

```
   else if (!stricmp(eventType, Evt_Destroy_Actor::gkName))
   {
      safeQueEvent(EventPtr(GCC_NEW Evt_Destroy_Actor(in)));
   }
   else
   {
      char debugMessage[256];
      sprintf(debugMessage,
         "ERROR Unknown event type from remote: %s\n", eventType);
      OutputDebugStringA(debugMessage);
   }
}
```

This event was generated on a remote machine, sent over the network, re-created from the bit stream, and put back together again just like Dr. McCoy in a transporter beam. The local game systems really have no idea the event was generated from afar.

One last thing—you need to see how local events are sent into the network. If you think I'm going to use streams again, you are right. The class inherits from the IEventListener class you read about in Chapter 10, but it knows about a socket ID:

```
class NetworkEventForwarder : public IEventListener
{
public:
   // IEventListener
   NetworkEventForwarder(int sockId) { m_sockId = sockId; }
   bool HandleEvent( Event const & event );
   char const * GetName(void) { return "NetworkEventForwarder"; }

protected:
   int m_sockId;
};
```

The HandleEvent() implementation creates a stream that has the event message identifier first, followed by the event type (which is really the name of the event), followed finally by the event itself. This stream object now contains the serialized event and enough data to be reconstructed on the remote computer.

```
bool NetworkEventForwarder::HandleEvent( Event const & event )
{
   std::ostrstream out;

   out << static_cast<int>(RemoteEventSocket::NetMsg_Event) << " ";
```

```
out << event.getType().getStr() << " ";
event.serialize(out);
out << "\r\n";

shared_ptr<BinaryPacket> eventMsg(
   GCC_NEW BinaryPacket(out.rdbuf()->str(), out.pcount()));

g_pSocketManager->Send(m_sockId, eventMsg);
return true;
}
```

YOU CAN'T SERIALIZE POINTERS

You have to be really careful when designing any C++ objects that are going to be serialized. For one thing, they can't contain pointers. If a local C++ object had a direct pointer to another game data structure like an actor or a sound, once it got to the remote computer the pointer would surely point to garbage. This is why you see so many handles, ID numbers, and other stuff that refers to objects indirectly through a manager of some sort. An actor ID should be guaranteed to be unique on the server, and thus it will be unique on all the clients, too.

There's one last class you need to know about—the `NetworkGameView`. This is a "fake" view that fools the authoritative game server into thinking someone is sitting right there playing the game, instead of a few hundred milliseconds by photon away. As you can see, it's not much more than a pretty face:

```
class NetworkGameView : public IGameView
{
public:
   // IGameView Implementation - everything is stubbed out.
   virtual HRESULT VOnRestore() { return S_OK; }
   virtual void VOnRender(double fTime, float fElapsedTime) { }
   virtual void VOnLostDevice() { }
   virtual GameViewType VGetType() { return GameView_Remote; }
   virtual GameViewId VGetId() const { return m_ViewId; }
   virtual void VOnAttach(GameViewId vid, optional<ActorId> aid);
   virtual LRESULT CALLBACK VOnMsgProc( AppMsg msg ) { return 0; }
   virtual void VOnUpdate( int deltaMilliseconds ) { };
```

```
   NetworkGameView(int sockId)
   {
      m_SockId = sockId;
   }

protected:
   GameViewId m_ViewId;
   optional<ActorId> m_PlayerActorId;
   int m_SockId;
};
```

There's really only one method, VOnAttach(), which is called by the game logic when new views are added. You should see the other side of that NetMsg_Player-LoginOk message you saw a moment ago. This is where the server sends the unique view ID number down to the client so all the players of a multiplayer game don't get confused:

```
void NetworkGameView::VOnAttach(GameViewId viewId, optional<ActorId> aid)
{
   m_ViewId = viewId;
   m_PlayerActorId = aid;

   // this is the first thing that happens when the
   // network view is attached. The view id is sent,
   // which we'll add to the binary events that get sent.

   std::ostrstream out;

   out << static_cast<int>(RemoteEventSocket::NetMsg_PlayerLoginOk) << " ";
   out << viewId << " ";
   out << "\r\n";

   shared_ptr<BinaryPacket> gvidMsg(
      GCC_NEW BinaryPacket(out.rdbuf()->str(), out.pcount()));
   g_pSocketManager->Send(m_SockId, gvidMsg);
}
```

GOSH, IF IT'S THAT EASY

There is much more to network programming than I've had the pages to teach you here. First, remote games need to be very smart about handling slow Internet connectivity by predicting moves and handling things elegantly when those predictions are wrong. For enterprise games like *Star Wars Galaxies, Everquest,* or *Ultima Online,* you have to take the simple architecture in this book and extend it into a hierarchy of server computers. You also have to create technology that prevents cheating and hacking. These tasks could use a book all by themselves to cover them adequately.

Still, I feel that what you've seen in this chapter is an excellent start. Certainly, if you want to learn network programming without starting from scratch, the code in this chapter and on the book's Web site will give you something you can play with. You can experiment with it, break it, and put it back in good order. That's the best way to learn.

That is, of course, how I started, only I believe the little record player I ruined when I was a kid never did work again. Sorry Mom!

ADVANCED TOPICS AND BRINGING IT ALL TOGETHER

AN INTRODUCTION TO GAME AI

by David "Rez" Graham

In This Chapter

- Intro to AI concepts
- Movement
- Path Finding
- Simple Decision Making
- Advanced Decision Making
- Types of Game AI
- Further Reading

David "Rez" Graham works at Planet Moon Studios as an AI pro-grammer. His credits include: Barbie Diaries: High School Mys-tery, Rat Race, *and* Brain Quest. *He lives in Berkeley, California with two cats and enjoys playing music, performing random pro-gramming experiments, and changing his hair color to various odd shades. I met Rez at the Game Developer's Conference through the Game Coding Complete forums.*

Put simply, artificial intelligence (or simply "AI") is our attempt to make computers think. While we've gotten rather good at mimicking certain behaviors, especially in a medium such as games where the suspension of disbelief is very much present, we have yet to come anywhere close to truly emulating the human brain. I have no doubt that we will one day achieve this feat, and very much hope that I'm alive to see it. I am forced to wonder what will become of these artificial creations of ours and how they will be treated. Think about it—an artificial brain with the capability to think and reason as we do. Will it also be able to feel? Dream? Love? Hate? If so, what does that say about our own consciousness?

Artificial intelligence is a very broad subject that covers a number of real-world applications. Many of them are not at all related to games. A patient may call into a hospital and speak with an automated representative controlled by complex speech recognition software and ask about test results. These tests may have been performed by an expert system written and trained to deal with his particular illness. The fuel he puts into his car on his way to pick up his prescription is a mixture that's refined and processed by complex analysis software. The opponent he curses under his breath in the video game he plays on his handheld in the waiting room is really just a set of simple control states with transitional branches between those states, but it still manages to out-maneuver his troops.

Game AI seems to be in a class all its own. We have a unique set of problems where we have to make the game "fun" while not bringing the CPU to a grinding halt. Whenever I go to the AI round-tables at the Game Developer's Conference, I'm continually intrigued by the dichotomy between experienced video game AI developers and developers coming from academia or other fields of AI. They tend to want to create as intelligent an agent as possible, whereas we just want the player to have fun. Game AI is not about trying to make something smart, it's about making something *look* smart while still being able to be beaten, though not too easily. That's what makes the game fun, and the key to game AI is fun through illusion, not true intelligence. If you have a military shooter game, who cares whether or not the enemies really work together as a team as long as the player believes they do? As AI programmers, we're the ultimate illusionists. And we have to do it all within a tiny fraction of CPU time.

Intro to AI Concepts

AI programming is one part science and two parts art. As I write this chapter, I'm working at Planet Moon Studios on an unannounced title. It took me a week or so to write the core AI system, but I've spent nearly twice that time just making little tweaks and rewriting behaviors for specific enemies. It's hard to strike that perfect balance between too easy and too hard. The best thing you can do for yourself is to expose as much relevant data as possible to the designers, especially all those little things that will constantly change. Should the creature see you at 300 units or 600 units? Should they move at a velocity of 50 or 150?

On the other hand, you have to be careful about exposing too much to the designers. If you do, they'll be too afraid to make changes because they won't understand what ramifications their changes will have, which means you'll end up having to make all the tweaks yourself. Remember, as the AI programmer, your job is to enable designers to do their jobs.

The AI on *Barbie Diaries: High School Mystery* was a goal-based system that was balanced through a series of desires, which were tempered by drives. These were all configured with a gigantic XML file that allowed the designer to define the agent's needs, how much they desired that need, which entities in the world could satisfy the need, and so on. The system was nice and generic and allowed tons of different options. Unfortunately, that agility came with a cost. The XML file was very hard to read because it contained arcane names and values that really didn't mean anything to anyone who didn't know the underlying code (which was me and the original author of the system). There was no way a designer without significant scripting experience was going to touch that file. In retrospect, a better solution would have been to split it into two files. The first would contain those arcane values and configurations, while the second would be simple values a designer might want to mess with, such as an agent's desire to speak versus its desire to sit down and do homework.

MOVEMENT

Before we start looking at decision making and providing the illusion of intelligence, we need to learn the fundamentals of movement. If you're simply trying to move in a straight line toward some destination, the following code is all you need:

```
// get the direction vector from the actor to the target and normalize it
Vec3 diff = m_target - pActor->VGetMat().GetPosition();
diff.Normalize();

// calculate our speed this frame
float speed = AI_TEAPOT_SPEED * ((float)deltaMilliseconds / 1000.0f);

// multiply the direction vector by our speed and translate to our new point
diff *= speed;
pPhysics->VTranslate(m_actorId,diff);
```

As you can see, the position of the agent is subtracted from the target's position, which is then normalized and multiplied by the calculated speed. This calculates the position the agent needs to be at by the end of the frame. The physics system is told to translate the actor to the correct position. Depending on the system you're working on, this function may look very different. You might simply give the physics system a scalar velocity value and tell it to apply a force to your agent, which will send it in the direction it's currently facing. For simpler games, you may end up updating the model-to-world transform matrix directly. There may be some animation syncing that needs to happen as well.

Most of the time, you'll want to have your agent face where it's going before you move it, which involves rotating the agent to face that orientation. Here's a simple snippet of code that does just that:

```
// get our current world orientation
float orientation = pPhysics->VGetOrientationY(m_actorId);

// figure our what direction we need to be facing
Vec3 diff = m_target - pActor->VGetMat().GetPosition();

// calculate the target orientation
Vec3 zUnit(0,0,1); // 0 orientation means staring down the positive Z axis

// calculate the world orientation
float angle = (atan2(diff.z,diff.x*-1) - atan2(zUnit.z,zUnit.x));
m_targetOrientation = WrapPi(angle);   // WrapPi() just wraps the angle so
                                       // it's between -PI and PI

// if we're not facing the right direction, start rotating
if (fabs(m_targetOrientation - orientation) > 0.001f)
   pActor->VRotateY(m_targetOrientation);
```

Of course, you usually don't want to snap to a particular orientation, so this is typically done over time. To see an example of how this works, check out the MoveState::RotateAndMove() function in TeapotStates.cpp of the *Game Coding Complete* source code in Source\TeapotWars\TeapotStates.cpp. The code snippets above were adapted from this function, which we will look at in greater detail later in this chapter.

I haven't started talking about AI states yet, but this should give you an idea of how to rotate and move something over time.

Path Finding

The code in the previous section is fine for simple, short movements in unobstructed terrain, but what happens when you want to move the agent long distances through more complicated terrain? While it's possible to write code that will scan every possibility and find the best route, this really isn't the most efficient way. Trying to have every creature analyze the terrain in real time is typically way too expensive in terms of CPU time to be a viable option. A better solution would be to find a way to represent the world in much simpler terms to cut the cost of trying to find a path. One such technique for doing this is by using a graph where the nodes and arcs connecting them define the movable space. This is the technique we used at Super-Ego Games in *Rat Race* (see Figure 17.1).

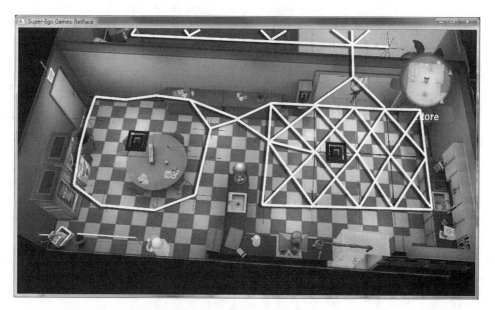

FIGURE 17.1 Pathing graph for *Rat Race*.

So how do we go about creating such a system? Let's start with the nodes. A node describes a point in space that the agent must reach. Nodes are connected by arcs, which are essentially straight lines. For our graph, we're going to guarantee that an agent may freely move between any two nodes directly connected by an arc. Thus, in order to move from one node to its neighboring node, all you need to do is rotate to face the correct direction and move in a straight line as described earlier in this chapter.

There's a slight problem with this method. Since the nodes are all connected by straight lines, it's possible that the agent's motion will look a bit robotic, especially if the graph is laid out like a grid. If the agent wanted to move onto a perpendicular arc, it would walk to the node, make a 90-degree turn, and then walk to the next point. This doesn't look natural at all. There are two things we can do to combat this problem. The first is to ensure that the nodes are not placed in an obvious grid-like fashion. Place a few nodes around a turn to create a curve instead of simply placing the corner node with two perpendicular arcs. I like to make a little Y-shaped triangle of nodes and arcs near such corners.

The second thing we can do is allow each node to have a tolerance that describes how close the agent has to be to the node in order to be considered to have hit it. Using these two techniques together, you can get a much smoother path. If you really want to go for broke, you can do a little prediction and figure out when to start turning and how sharply you need to turn. This will give your agents a very smooth curve, though perhaps it will be too smooth in some instances. For example, when someone is near a wall and turns a corner, there is very little curve. Another alternative would be to add that information into the node classes, but this may be a bit much to ask the designers (who typically create and tweak these graphs) to do. I've found that you can get some pretty decent results with the first two methods.

Now we need to describe the arc that connects these nodes. We could make arcs unidirectional, bidirectional, or both. We could give each arc a weight that gives a rough description of the difficulty for traversing that area. We could even allow multiple arcs to connect the same nodes but have different weights on those arcs for different types of agents. For example, we could have one arc used by ground-based agents and another used by flying agents. That way, you could easily have it so the ground agents tend to stick to the roads while the flying agents wouldn't really care. The weights can even be dynamic. Let's say you're making a real-time strategy game, and you want the flying units to avoid the guard towers the player sets up. One way of solving this problem would be to have the guard towers themselves increase the weight of nearby arcs. The flying units would tend to avoid them. For now, let's just give our arcs a weight.

RUDE NPC BEHAVIOR SHOULD BE CORRECTED

When I was working at Super-Ego Games, I worked on an adventure game for the PlayStation 3 called *Rat Race*, which was set in an office. Being an adventure game, one of the major things you did was talk to the NPCs. Unfortunately, other NPCs would plow right through the middle of these conversations. We ended up creating conversation pathing objects that would spawn in the middle of conversations, which would significantly raise the weight of any arcs within a radius around that point. We also forced NPCs with affected arcs in their path to replan. This caused NPCs to do the polite thing and walk around the conversation.

Okay, let's take a look at our node class. Here's the `PathingNode` class:

```cpp
typedef std::list<PathingNode*> PathingNodeList;
typedef std::list<PathingArc*> PathingArcList;

class PathingNode
{
   float m_tolerance;
   Vec3 m_pos;
   PathingArcList m_arcs;

public:
   explicit PathingNode(
      const Vec3& pos, float tolerance = PATHING_DEFAULT_NODE_TOLERANCE)
      : m_pos(pos)
      { m_tolerance = tolerance; }
   const Vec3& GetPos(void) const { return m_pos; }
   float GetTolerance(void) const { return m_tolerance; }
   void AddArc(PathingArc* pArc);
   void GetNeighbors(PathingNodeList& outNeighbors);
   float GetCostFromNode(PathingNode* pFromNode);
private:
   PathingArc* FindArc(PathingNode* pLinkedNode);
};
```

The `PathingNode` class has three members: `m_tolerance` is the tolerance of the node, `m_pos` is the position of the node, and `m_arcs` is a list of arcs connecting this node to other nodes.

Most of the functions are pretty self-explanatory. `GetPos()` and `GetTolerance()` are just getters. `AddArc()` pushes a new arc onto the list. `GetNeighbors()` fills the `outNeighbors` parameter with a list of all neighboring nodes. `GetCostFromNode()` looks at the arc connecting this node to the other node and returns the cost, which is the distance between the two nodes multiplied by the arc's weight. `FindArc()` is a helper function that finds the arc connecting this node with the `pLinkedNode` parameter. As you can see, this class is very simple.

Here's the `PathingArc` class:

```cpp
class PathingArc
{
   float m_weight;
   PathingNode* m_pNodes[2];   // an arc always connects two nodes
```

```
public:
    explicit PathingArc(float weight = PATHING_DEFAULT_ARC_WEIGHT;)
        { m_weight = weight; }
    float GetWeight(void) const { return m_weight; }
    void LinkNodes(PathingNode* pNodeA, PathingNode* pNodeB);
    PathingNode* GetNeighbor(PathingNode* pMe);
};
```

The `PathingArc` class only has two members. The first is `m_weight`, which is the weight of this arc. It gets multiplied by the distance between the nodes this arc connects (for example, the length of the arc). `m_pNodes` is an array of `PathingNode` objects and has exactly two elements. Each arc is guaranteed to connect exactly two nodes and each arc is bidirectional. This simplifies things considerably.

As for the member functions, `GetWeight()` is a simple getter. `LinkNodes()` links the two passed-in nodes together by calling `AddArc()` on each and adding them to its own internal array. `GetNeighbor()` gets the node this arc is pointing to that's not equal to the node we pass in.

As you can see, these classes are very straightforward with a minimal set of features, yet they are also easily extended. This is how I prefer to design my systems.

START SIMPLE AND TRY TO STAY THAT WAY

It's usually best to write the least amount of code possible to get the job done, while still allowing the system to be flexible enough to be easily expanded. The system I'm designing here could be easily modified to add any of the features I discussed previously without a lot of refactoring.

Now that you have a couple of nice classes that define your pathing primitives, you need to have a way to encapsulate all the objects you're about to create. This brings us to the `PathingGraph` class. The `PathingGraph` class acts as the main interface into the whole pathing system. There is currently only one `PathingGraph` object alive in the system at any given time, but there's no reason you couldn't have more. For example, one possible solution to having both flying enemies and ground enemies in your game would be to have two separate `PathingGraph` objects, one for each type of enemy. Let's take a look at this important class in detail:

```
typedef std::list<PathingArc*> PathingArcList;
typedef std::vector<PathingNode*> PathingNodeVec;

class PathingGraph
{
    PathingNodeVec m_nodes;   // master list of all nodes
    PathingArcList m_arcs;    // master list of all arcs
```

```
public:
    PathingGraph(void) {}
    ~PathingGraph(void) { DestroyGraph(); }
    void DestroyGraph(void);

    PathingNode* FindClosestNode(const Vec3& pos);
    PathingNode* FindFurthestNode(const Vec3& pos);
    PathingNode* FindRandomNode(void);
    PathPlan* FindPath(const Vec3& startPoint, const Vec3& endPoint);
    PathPlan* FindPath(const Vec3& startPoint, PathingNode* pGoalNode);
    PathPlan* FindPath(PathingNode* pStartNode, const Vec3& endPoint);
    PathPlan* FindPath(PathingNode* pStartNode, PathingNode* pGoalNode);

    void BuildTestGraph(void);

private:
    // helpers
    void LinkNodes(PathingNode* pNodeA, PathingNode* pNodeB);
};
```

The `m_nodes` and `m_arcs` members are the master lists of those objects. The `PathingGraph` class owns the creation and destruction of all `PathingNode` and `PathingArc` objects. The `DestroyGraph()` iterates over the two lists and destroys all the objects. This function is public so you can call it to reset the `PathingGraph` object. This is useful when you load a new level.

There are three functions for finding a particular node. `FindClosestNode()` finds the node closest to the position passed in. `FindFurthestNode()` does the opposite. `FindRandomNode()` will return a completely random node, which is nice if you just want the agent to wander somewhere. `FindClosestNode()` is used extensively since most agents will never be right on top of a node.

`BuildTestGraph()` is a simple helper function that generates the pathing graph. There are two major ways to create a pathing graph. The first is to have someone create it by hand. This can be very tedious, especially for large worlds, but it's the best way to get exactly what you want. The second way is to generate it with code, usually as an offline process. Many projects do both. They'll generate the first pass in code and then hand it off to a designer who can then tweak weights and move nodes around to optimize the map.

The four overloaded `FindPath()` functions call your path-finding algorithm to get a `PathPlan` object. The `PathPlan` object represents a single path through the world from a start node to an end node. Here's the class definition:

```
typedef std::list<PathingNode*> PathingNodeList;

class PathPlan
{
    friend class AStar;

    PathingNodeList m_path;
    PathingNodeList::iterator m_index;

public:
    PathPlan(void) { m_index = m_path.end(); }

    void ResetPath(void) { m_index = m_path.begin(); }
    const Vec3& GetCurrentNodePosition(void) const
        { assert(m_index != m_path.end()); return (*m_index)->GetPos(); }
    bool CheckForNextNode(const Vec3& pos);
    bool CheckForEnd(void);

private:
    void AddNode(PathingNode* pNode);
};
```

The m_path member is a list of PathingNode objects sorted in the order in which they are meant to be traversed. The m_index member is the tracking variable used to track the agent's progress.

The ResetPath() and GetCurrentNodePosition() functions are self-explanatory. The CheckForEnd() function simply returns true if the agent has reached the end of the path, and the AddNode() helper function adds a node to the list.

The CheckForNextNode() function does most of the useful housekeeping:

```
bool PathPlan::CheckForNextNode(const Vec3& pos)
{
    if (m_index == m_path.end())
        return false;

    Vec3 diff = pos - (*m_index)->GetPos();

    if (diff.Length() <= (*m_index)->GetTolerance())
    {
        ++m_index;
        return true;
    }
    return false;
}
```

This function checks to see if the agent is close enough to the node based on the node's tolerance. If it is, the `m_index` variable is updated and this function returns true. Otherwise, the function returns false.

A* (A-Star)

Now we have a system for building a graph of nodes connected by arcs and even returning a path through that graph, but how do we use it? How do we efficiently scan this graph to find the best route through it to our destination? There are many different searching algorithms to choose from, but A* (pronounced *A-Star*) happens to be the best choice for our purposes. It will find the path with the smallest cost and do it fairly quickly. There are many different implementations of A*, but they all come from the same basic algorithm. A* was first described in 1968 by Peter Hart, Nils Nilsson, and Bertram Raphael. In their paper, it was called *algorithm A*. Since using this algorithm yields optimal behavior, it has been called A*.

The A* algorithm works by analyzing each node it comes across and assigning three values to each. The first is the total cost to this node by the current path so far. This value is usually referred to as *g*, or *goal*. The second value is an estimated cost from this node to the goal. It's often referred to as *h*, or *heuristic*. The third value is an estimated cost from the start of the path through this node to the goal, which is really just *g + h*. This value is often called *f*, or *fitness*.

The point of these three values is to keep track of your progress so you know how well you're doing. The value of *g* is something you know for sure since it's a calculated value (the sum of the costs of every node in the path so far), but how do you find out how to calculate *h* and by extension, *f*? The only rule for calculating *h* is that it can't be greater than the actual cost between this node and the goal node. Of course, the more accurate the guess, the faster you can find a path. In this case, a simple distance check will suffice:

```
Vec3 diff = m_pPathingNode->GetPos() - s_pGoalNode->GetPos();
m_heuristic = diff.Length();
```

This allows us to easily calculate *f*.

The algorithm also maintains a priority queue called the *open set*. The open set is a list of nodes that are being considered, and the node with the lowest fitness score is at the front of the queue. The process starts with the node nearest the starting location. During each iteration of the algorithm, the front node is popped off the queue. The neighbors of this node are evaluated (potentially updating their magic values) and added to the open set. This process continues until the node removed from the queue is the goal node. Note that it's quite possible to see the goal node from a particular neighbor and ignore it if its *f* score is not low enough. This simply means that you haven't found the best path yet. Once you have processed a node, you mark it as closed. This allows you to ignore neighbors you've already processed. If the open set ever becomes empty before finding the goal node, it means you're done and no path could be found.

YOU CAN'T ALWAYS GET THERE FROM HERE

No matter how solid you think the data is, there are times when you won't be able to find a path. Make sure that you have a graceful recovery plan.

AGENTS CAN BE STUBBORN

While working on *Rat Race* for Super-Ego Games, our solution to failing to find a path was to re-run the higher decision-making logic. Unfortunately, the decision was almost always to try and do the exact same thing. Since AI was only updating once a second, the NPC would take a half step, stop, play a confused-looking idle animation (many of our idle animations were confused looking; it was a comedy game after all), and then repeat the process. The solution was to have them abandon that particular decision, which meant that they couldn't choose it the second time around.

Okay, enough theory! Let's look at an A* implementation. First, we'll need a new node class. This is a special class used only during pathing. We can't use the `PathingNode` class because multiple agents may be building completely different paths through the same node. These two paths will have very different *g*, *h*, and *f* values. The solution is to create a new `PathPlanNode` class that links to the `PathingNode` object it represents. Here's our new class:

```
class PathPlanNode
{
    PathPlanNode* m_pPrev;  // node we just came from
    PathingNode* m_pPathingNode;  // pointer to the pathing node from
                                  // the pathing graph
    PathingNode* m_pGoalNode;  // pointer to the goal node
    bool m_closed;  // the node is closed if it's already been processed
    float m_goal;  // cost of the entire path up to this point (often called g)
    float m_heuristic;  // estimated cost of this node to the goal
                        // (often called h)
    float m_fitness;  // estimated cost from start to the goal through this
                      // node (often called f)
```

```
public:
    explicit PathPlanNode(PathingNode* pNode, PathPlanNode* pPrevNode,
                          PathingNode* pGoalNode);
    PathPlanNode* GetPrev(void) const { return m_pPrev; }
    PathPlanNode* GetNext(void) const { return m_pNext; }
    PathingNode* GetPathingNode(void) const { return m_pPathingNode; }
    bool IsClosed(void) const { return m_closed; }
    float GetGoal(void) const { return m_goal; }
    float GetHeuristic(void) const { return m_heuristic; }
    float GetFitness(void) const { return m_fitness; }

    void UpdatePrevNode(PathPlanNode* pPrev);
    void SetClosed(bool toClose = true) { m_closed = toClose; }

    bool operator<(PathPlanNode* pRight)
        { return (m_fitness < pRight->GetFitness()); }

private:
    void UpdateHeuristics(void);
};
```

The m_pPrev member is a pointer to the previous node. This is used to help calculate the magic values and to rebuild the path when a solution is found. The m_pPathingNode member is a pointer to the PathingNode object this node represents, and the m_pGoalNode is a pointer to the node the agent is trying to reach. If m_closed is true, the node has been processed and is in the "closed set." The m_goal, m_heuristic, and m_fitness members were explained in detail previously.

Most of the functions are simple getters except for the private UpdateHeuristics() function, which calculates the three magic values. Notice the overloaded operator< function. The open set is really a priority queue, so this function is needed to figure out where in the queue to insert the node.

Next, let's take a look at the AStar class:

```
typedef std::map<PathingNode*, PathPlanNode*> PathingNodeToPathPlanNodeMap;
typedef std::list<PathPlanNode*> PathPlanNodeList;

class AStar
{
    PathingNodeToPathPlanNodeMap m_nodes;
    PathingNode* m_pStartNode;
    PathingNode* m_pGoalNode;
    PathPlanNodeList m_openSet;
```

```
public:
   AStar(void);
   ~AStar(void);
   void Destroy(void);

   PathPlan* operator()(PathingNode* pStartNode, PathingNode* pGoalNode);

private:
   PathPlanNode* AddToOpenSet(PathingNode* pNode, PathPlanNode* pPrevNode);
   void AddToClosedSet(PathPlanNode* pNode);
   void InsertNode(PathPlanNode* pNode);
   void ReinsertNode(PathPlanNode* pNode);
   PathPlan* RebuildPath(PathPlanNode* pGoalNode);
};
```

This class is a *functor*, which is simply a class whose objects are meant to be called like functions (see the `PathingGraph::FindPath()` functions to see an example of how they're called).

The m_nodes member is a mapping of `PathingNode` objects to `PathPlanNode` objects. This map keeps track of all the `PathPlanNode` objects that are created so they can be destroyed when this class is destroyed. Whenever a new node is evaluated, the map is searched to see if a `PathPlanNode` object representing this node already exists and what its status is. I chose to use a map here because it has to be searched in every iteration, and searching a map is a lot faster than searching a list or array.

m_pStartNode and m_pGoalNode are the nodes to start at and end at, respectively.

m_openSet is the priority queue of nodes being evaluated. Notice that it's really just an STL list under the covers. A simple insertion sort is used to turn it into a priority queue:

```
void AStar::InsertNode(PathPlanNode* pNode)
{
   assert(pNode);

   // just add the node if the open set is empty
   if (m_openSet.empty())
   {
      m_openSet.push_back(pNode);
      return;
   }

   // otherwise, perform an insertion sort
   PathPlanNodeList::iterator it = m_openSet.begin();
   PathPlanNode* pCompare = *it;
```

```
   while (pCompare < pNode)
   {
      ++it;

      if (it != m_openSet.end())
         pCompare = *it;
      else
         break;
   }
   m_openSet.insert(it,pNode);
}
```

The first thing that happens is a test to see if the open set is empty. If it is, the node is simply pushed to the back. Otherwise, the list is searched until the appropriate insertion spot is found, at which point the node is inserted and the loop is broken.

The bulk of the work in this class is done in the overloaded function call operator:

```
PathPlan* AStar::operator()(PathingNode* pStartNode, PathingNode* pGoalNode)
{
   assert(pStartNode);
   assert(pGoalNode);

   // if the start and end nodes are the same, we're close enough to
   // b-line to the goal
   if (pStartNode == pGoalNode)
      return NULL;

   // set our members
   m_pStartNode = pStartNode;
   m_pGoalNode = pGoalNode;

   // The open set is a priority queue of the nodes to be evaluated.
   // If it's ever empty, it means we couldn't find a path to the goal.
   // The start node is the only node that is initially in the open set.
   AddToOpenSet(m_pStartNode, NULL);

   while (!m_openSet.empty())
   {
      // grab the most likely candidate
      PathPlanNode* pNode = m_openSet.front();
```

```
        // If this node is our goal node, we've successfully found a path.
        if (pNode->GetPathingNode() == m_pGoalNode)
            return RebuildPath(pNode);

        // we're processing this node so remove it from the open set and
        // add it to the closed set
        m_openSet.pop_front();
        AddToClosedSet(pNode);

        // get the neighboring nodes
        PathingNodeList neighbors;
        pNode->GetPathingNode()->GetNeighbors(neighbors);

        // loop though all the neighboring nodes and evaluate each one
        for (PathingNodeList::iterator it = neighbors.begin();
             it != neighbors.end(); ++it)
        {
            PathingNode* pNodeToEvaluate = *it;

            // Try and find a PathPlanNode object for this node.
            PathingNodeToPathPlanNodeMap::iterator findIt =
                m_nodes.find(pNodeToEvaluate);

            // If one exists and it's in the closed list, we've already
            // evaluated the node.  We can safely skip it.
            if (findIt != m_nodes.end() && findIt->second->IsClosed())
                continue;

            // figure out the cost for this route through the node
            float costForThisPath = pNode->GetGoal() +
                pNodeToEvaluate->GetCostFromNode(pNode->GetPathingNode());
            bool isPathBetter = false;

            // Grab the PathPlanNode if there is one.
            PathPlanNode* pPathPlanNodeToEvaluate = NULL;
            if (findIt != m_nodes.end())
                pPathPlanNodeToEvaluate = findIt->second;

            // No PathPlanNode means we've never evaluated this pathing node
            // so we need to add it to the open set, which has the side effect
            // of setting all the heuristic data.  It also means that this is
            // the best path through this node that we've found so the nodes are
            // linked together (which is why we don't bother setting isPathBetter
            // to true; it's done for us in AddToOpenSet()).
```

```
    if (!pPathPlanNodeToEvaluate)
       pPathPlanNodeToEvaluate = AddToOpenSet(pNodeToEvaluate,pNode);

    // If this node is already in the open set, check to see if this
    // route to it is better than the last.
    else if (costForThisPath < pPathPlanNodeToEvaluate->GetGoal())
       isPathBetter = true;

    // If this path is better, relink the nodes appropriately, update
    // the heuristics data, and reinsert the node into the open list
    // priority queue.
    if (isPathBetter)
    {
       pPathPlanNodeToEvaluate->UpdatePrevNode(pNode);
       ReinsertNode(pPathPlanNodeToEvaluate);
    }
  }
}

// If we get here, there's no path to the goal.
return NULL;
}
```

To start everything off, the member variables are set and the starting node is added to the open set. As long as there are nodes left in the open set, there is still a chance to find the path. The first node is removed from the queue and checked to see if it's a goal node. If it is, the path is rebuilt from this spot and the plan is returned. Otherwise, this node is added to the closed set so that it's not double-processed. The node is then asked for a list of all its neighbors. The m_nodes list is searched to see if the first neighbor exists there. If it's found and has been closed, it can safely be ignored and the neighbor is evaluated. Next, the cost to this node for the current path is calculated. If there isn't a PathPlanNode object for this node, it means it has never been looked at it and will need to be added to the open set. If it already has one, the node is evaluated to see if this path through then node is better. If it is, the node is updated with the new path and magic values. This is repeated for every neighbor and then the algorithm starts all over, evaluating the highest priority in the queue.

An interesting side note about A* is that it's not specific to path finding. It's really just a search algorithm suited to find the lowest cost solution to any problem that can be represented by a graph or tree. For example, in the game *Fear* by Monolith Productions, the agents used a decision tree to decide what they wanted to do next, like toss a grenade, shoot, patrol, etc. This decision tree was traversed using an A* algorithm.

Take some time to read through the code—it all lives in the Game Code Complete source files, in Source\AI\Pathing.h and Source\AI\Pathing.cpp. Make sure that you have a good grasp of what's going on and how it all fits together.

The techniques and code presented here are by no means the only way to navigate through the world. Remember, the key to successful navigation is to simplify the agents' view of the world so you can cut down on how much you have to process. A few hundred or even a few thousand pathing nodes are *much* faster to process than trying to deal with world geometry at runtime.

Another very common technique is something called a *navigation mesh,* which is a simple mesh that can be built by the artists or designers and represents the walkable terrain. The concept is really no different than the graph above. The center of each triangle is a node, and the edges that connect to other triangles are the arcs. There will probably have to be a bit more smoothing involved or else the paths may not look good, but if your meshes are dense enough with decent tolerances, it may not be much of an issue. *Game Programming Gems* has an article called "Simplified 3D Movement and Pathfinding Using Navigation Meshes" that serves as a great introduction to using navigation meshes if you find yourself interested in learning more.

Making a Professional Game

This is a nice little path-finding system we've developed together, but is it ready for prime time? Probably not. There are a few issues that would need to be resolved before this would fly in a commercial game. The biggest one is probably optimization. I wrote the code to be easy to understand, not fast. The A* algorithm itself could definitely stand some optimization. I think a big performance gain could be made by simply pooling the `PathPlanNode` objects. We're constantly destroying and re-creating them, which is thrashing memory and fragmenting it all to hell. This will kill you on a console, and you'll probably end up with some mysterious out-of-memory error that will take you weeks to track down. Allocating 100 or so of these `PathPlanNode` objects isn't such a bad idea. It's a bit more wasteful on memory, but it'll be considerably faster. An even better solution would be to write a custom memory pool allocator that already had chunks of memory set aside of the appropriate size for this data structure. This is what we did at Planet Moon for *Brain Quest,* our GameBoy DS title, and it worked very well.

Most of the time, you'll probably want to have multiple agents all navigating through the world at once. What happens if two or more agents are trying to hit the same node at the same time? What about two agents coming toward each other along the same arc? Figure 17.2 shows exactly what could happen.

The simplest solution to both of these issues is to turn off the node or arc in question. As soon as an agent starts traveling down an arc, give it exclusive access to that arc. If another agent happens to reach a point in its path where it has to travel down that same arc in the opposite direction, force it to replan from its current node to its target node, ignoring that particular arc.

FIGURE 17.2 Multiple agents trying to reach a single node.

The above scenario works well for relatively open areas, but what happens when your agents are in a confined space, like an office building? When I worked on *Rat Race* at Super-Ego Games, we had this exact problem. There were over a dozen agents in a small office building all pathing around the world. It was okay most of the time, but there were several choke points where it all just broke down, like the stairwell. The solution to this problem was to implement a dynamic avoidance algorithm. Each agent was given a personal comfort radius around it. If another agent enters that radius and they're both moving, they calculate how much they have to turn to avoid each other's comfort zones. This ended up working really well and solved most of our issues concerning people running into each other.

Having multiple agents all moving around using complex pathing graphs can be very taxing on the system. In larger game worlds, a common practice is to allow the A* algorithm to stop at any time so that a single path can be built across multiple frames. This is easy enough to implement with the system you've built. All you need to do is to store the `AStar` object for each path being built and have an event sent when the path is done. This sounds like a perfect job for a `CProcess` object. In Chapter 18, "Introduction to Multiprogramming," you'll learn an even better solution using threads.

SIMPLE DECISION MAKING

By now, you should have a good grasp of how an agent moves from point A to point B, but how does the agent decide that he wants to be at point B instead of point C? After all, point C might be closer.

There are many different kinds of agents and many different types of decision making. Some agents are proactive, likes the ones in *The Sims* or the opponent AI in *Dawn of War*. Other agents are very reactive, like the NPCs in *Assassin's Creed* or the soldiers in *Thief: Deadly Shadows*. They just run their routine until something interesting happens, like the player killing someone he shouldn't. In either case, the foundation for most AI systems is the state machine.

State Machines

A state machine consists of a set of states, each encapsulating a particular behavior such as moving, attacking, getting a soda from the refrigerator, assaulting the player's town, or even just loitering. State machines usually have an event for entering a state, leaving a state, and an update function called every frame. Hmm, this is starting to sound a lot like the CProcess class you learned about in Chapter 6, "Controlling the Main Loop." In fact, states are a perfect candidate to be children of CProcess. Let's take a look at the base AiState class:

```
class AiState : public CProcess
{
protected:
    int m_timer;
    PathPlan* m_pPlan;
    Vec3 m_target;
    ActorId m_actorId;
    StateMachine* m_pStateMachine;

public:
    AiState(const ActorId& actorId, StateMachine* pStateMachine,
            int processType);
    virtual ~AiState(void);
    virtual void VOnUpdate(const int deltaMilliseconds);
};
```

This is a pretty simple class. All it does is add a bit of extra AI-related data to the functionality that CProcess already had.

BEST PRACTICE

DON'T REINVENT THE WHEEL

If you're working as part of a team, always take the time to look through the code base for something you need. It's often already been written for you. A real-life example of this is the WrapPi() function you may have noticed in the pathing code. I started to write that function myself and did a quick search for something similar. There it was in CMath.cpp, kindly written by someone before me.

The purpose of the `m_timer` member variable is to allow states to delay execution. This is particularly useful for noncritical states that don't need to be updated every frame. In fact, most AI states probably don't need to be updated every single frame. The `m_pPlan` variable is a pointer to the agent's current pathing plan (see the path-finding section previously) or NULL if the agent doesn't have a path. `m_target` is the agent's current target, which is either a specific location or the location of the current path node. You need a way to talk to the actor itself, so you can store the actor ID in the `m_actorId` variable. `m_pStateMachine` is a pointer to the `StateMachine` object that created this state.

All states are managed by a `StateMachine` class, which can be thought of as the agent's brain. The `StateMachine` class is responsible for creating and destroying the appropriate `AiState` objects and is owned by the agent's game view object.

Intelligent agents need to have a view of the game world, similar in many ways to the `HumanView` class you read about in Chapter 9, "User Interface Programming." An AI view would subscribe to various game events that it would use to evaluate the changing state of the world and to make decisions. As you'll see in Chapter 19, "A Game of Teapot Wars," a class called `AITeapotView` will do exactly that, and handle the AI behavior of teapots by using the `StateMachine` class. While AI agents can easily ask about the state of the world, such as where actors are or where the exit for the room is, they can also use the Event Manager to receive information about the changing state of the world. In *Thief: Deadly Shadows*, for example, the agents listened for collision events and if they were energetic enough, they would begin a search to see what made the noise. You can drastically alter AI behavior by changing what game events an AI cares about and how they will change their state.

Let's take a look at the `StateMachine` class and see how it works:

```
class StateMachine
{
protected:
    shared_ptr<PathingGraph> m_pPathingGraph;
    shared_ptr<AiState> m_pCurrState;
    ActorId m_actorId;

public:
    StateMachine(const ActorId& actorId, shared_ptr<PathingGraph>
                pPathingGraph);
    virtual ~StateMachine(void);

    void SetState(const std::string& stateName);

    shared_ptr<PathingGraph> GetPathingGraph(void) { return m_pPathingGraph; }
```

```
protected:
   // This is the factory method for spawning concrete state objects.
   // Since the state classes all live in the game layer, it's up to that
   // layer to inherit from this class and implement this function.
   virtual void CreateState(const std::string& stateName) = 0;
};
```

The m_pPathingGraph variable is a smart pointer to the PathingGraph object, which is passed in upon construction. This allows you to easily have multiple pathing graphs if you want, or to swap out the existing graph. m_pCurrState is the base class pointer to the current AI state and m_actorId is the actor's ID.

The process for setting AI states is a bit tricky. There's a protected pure virtual function hiding at the bottom of this class definition named CreateState(). This is the factory method used for creating states. In order to use this class, you must write a game-specific class that inherits from this one and implement CreateState(). Here's the subclass I created for the *Teapot Wars* demo:

```
class TeapotStateMachine : public StateMachine
{
public:
   TeapotStateMachine(const ActorId& actorId,
                      shared_ptr<PathingGraph> pPathingGraph) :
                      StateMachine(actorId,pPathingGraph) {}
   virtual void CreateState(const std::string& stateName);
};
```

As you can see, this class is pretty trivial. All it does is implement the CreateState() function:

```
void TeapotStateMachine::CreateState(const std::string& stateName)
{
   if (stateName == "attack")
      m_pCurrState.reset(GCC_NEW AttackState(m_actorId,this));
   else if (stateName == "chase")
      m_pCurrState.reset(GCC_NEW ChaseTargetState(m_actorId,this));
   else if (stateName == "wander")
      m_pCurrState.reset(GCC_NEW WanderState(m_actorId,this));
   else if (stateName == "spin")
      m_pCurrState.reset(GCC_NEW SpinState(m_actorId,this));
   else if (stateName == "wait")
      m_pCurrState.reset(GCC_NEW WaitState(m_actorId,this));
   else
      OutputDebugString(_T("Couldn't find state"));
}
```

This function is a simple series of if/then blocks that figures out what state you're asking for and instantiates the correct concrete class. This function is called from the SetState() function in StateMachine:

```
void StateMachine::SetState(const std::string& stateName)
{
   // kill the old state if there is one
   if (m_pCurrState)
   {
      m_pCurrState->VKill();
      m_pCurrState.reset();
   }

   // instantiate the concrete state object
   CreateState(stateName);

   // attach the state process
   if (m_pCurrState)
      g_pApp->m_pGame->AttachProcess(m_pCurrState);
}
```

This function checks to see if the agent already has a state. If it does, it sends the kill message, which will safely remove it from the list. Next, the CreateState() function is called, and if a valid AiState was created, the process is attached to the process manager.

One very common bug in state systems is something known as *state oscillation*, which is caused by one state transitioning to another and that state transitioning right back. For example, say you have a conditional statement that says this:

```
if (playerDistance < 600.0f)
   m_pStateMachine->SetState("chase");
```

And then in the chase state, you have a conditional that says this:

```
if (playerDistance > 300.0f)
   m_pStateMachine->SetState("wander");
```

If the player were 400 units away, the agent would get confused and constantly shift between those two states. These bugs are hard enough in a simple, deterministic system like the one that's been built in this chapter, but they become nightmarish in a really complex, nondeterministic system like some of the ones described next.

Let's take a look at a sample state, ChaseTargetState:

```
class ChaseTargetState : public MoveState
{
   ActorId m_victim;
   int m_pathingTimer;
public:
   ChaseTargetState(const ActorId& actorId, StateMachine* pStateMachine) :
                    MoveState(actorId,pStateMachine,PROC_AISTATE_CHASETARGET)
                    { m_hasStartedRotation = false; m_pathingTimer = 0; }
   virtual void VOnUpdate(const int deltaMilliseconds);
   virtual void VOnInitialize(void);
};
```

This class inherits from the `MoveState` class:

```
class MoveState : public AiState
{
protected:
   bool m_hasStartedRotation;
   float m_targetOrientation;
public:
   MoveState(const ActorId& actorId, StateMachine* pStateMachine,
            int processType) : AiState(actorId,pStateMachine,processType)
            {m_hasStartedRotation = false; m_targetOrientation = FLT_MAX;}
protected:
   void RotateAndMove(const int deltaMilliseconds);
};
```

This class is simply a helper. As I was writing these states, I noticed that I was starting to write some of the same code over again, so I extracted some common functionality and put it in a base class. This way, `RotateAndMove()` can be used by other classes. `m_hasStartedRotation` and `m_targetOrientaton` are used by `RotateAndMove()` to keep track of rotations.

The purpose of the `ChaseTarget` state is to find a target and chase it. Once it gets within firing range, the agent will launch a deadly assault! It has an `m_victim` variable to keep track of its poor target and an `m_pathingTimer` variable to ensure that the expensive A* algorithm isn't run too often.

The `VOnInitialize()` function just calls the base class `VOnInitialize()` and grabs a random actor from the global list of actors as its victim. The juicy part is in the `VOnUpdate()` function:

```
void ChaseTargetState::VOnUpdate(const int deltaMilliseconds)
{
   AiState::VOnUpdate(deltaMilliseconds);
   m_pathingTimer += deltaMilliseconds;
```

```
// grab the necessary interfaces
shared_ptr<IGamePhysics> pPhysics = g_pApp->m_pGame->VGetGamePhysics();
assert(pPhysics);
shared_ptr<IActor> pActor = g_pApp->m_pGame->VGetActor(m_actorId);
assert(pActor);

// Try to grab the victim.  If we can't, he's probably dead already
// so switch to wander.
shared_ptr<IActor> pVictim = g_pApp->m_pGame->VGetActor(m_victim);
if (!pVictim)
{
   m_pStateMachine->SetState("wander");
   return;
}

// grab the actors' positions
Vec3 actorPos(pActor->VGetMat().GetPosition());
Vec3 victimPos(pVictim->VGetMat().GetPosition());
Vec3 diff = victimPos - actorPos;
float dist = diff.Length();

// check to see if we're close enough to start attacking
if (dist >= AI_TEAPOT_ATTACK_MIN && dist <= AI_TEAPOT_ATTACK_MAX)
{
   m_pStateMachine->SetState("attack");
   return;
}

// If we're not within range, path to where we need to be.  We
// need to actually reach our goal because the agent will be
// within weapons range first.
else
{
   // if we have an invalid pathing plan or the plan we do have is
   // stale, replan
   if (!m_pPlan || m_pathingTimer >= AI_TEAPOT_PATHING_TIMER ||
       m_pPlan->CheckForEnd())
   {
      // path to victim
      SAFE_DELETE(m_pPlan);
      if (dist > AI_TEAPOT_ATTACK_MAX)  // too far away, try and path
                                        // to his location
         m_pPlan = m_pStateMachine->GetPathingGraph()->FindPath(actorPos,
                                                         victimPos);
```

```
        else  // too close, try and path to furthest node away from him
        {
            PathingNode* pFurthestNode =
                m_pStateMachine->GetPathingGraph()->
                    FindFurthestNode(victimPos);
            m_pPlan = m_pStateMachine->GetPathingGraph()->
                FindPath(actorPos,pFurthestNode);
        }

        // if we can't find a path to the victim, give up
        if (!m_pPlan)
        {
            m_pStateMachine->SetState("wander");
            return;
        }

        // set our target pos
        m_pPlan->ResetPath();
        m_target = m_pPlan->GetCurrentNodePosition();
        m_pathingTimer = 0;
    }

    // If we get here, we have a valid plan that we're executing.
    // Calculate our target orientation.

    // check to see if we're close enough to the next node
    if (m_pPlan->CheckForNextNode(actorPos))
    {
        m_target = m_pPlan->GetCurrentNodePosition();
        m_hasStartedRotation = false;
        return;
    }

    // still too far so check to see that we facing the right way
    else
        RotateAndMove(deltaMilliseconds);
    }
}
```

First, the base class VOnUpdate() function is called, the timer is updated, and the interfaces that are needed are stored. Then an attempt to get the victim is made. If it fails, the victim is assumed to be dead and the agent's state is set to "wander." Next, a little math is done to get the actor's positions and the difference between them. The next block checks to see if the agent is close enough to the victim to start attacking. Incidentally, these constants are perfect candidates to be moved out of the C++ code and into a Lua file somewhere.

If the agent is not close enough to the victim, it will try to path there. Notice the checks to make sure the plan is stale or invalid before attempting to replan. A* is an algorithm you want to run as seldom as you can, especially when you have many agents pathing around the world. Five might be okay, but 50 certainly wouldn't be!

It's possible that the agent is either too close or too far from the victim since the bullets travel in a pretty big arc. If this is the case, the agent figures out which direction it needs to go and finds a path there. If it can't, its state is set to "wander" (remember, always handle the failure to find a path). The PathingPlan object is reset, and the agent heads off in the appropriate direction.

The next section of the function is executed if the agent is running a valid plan. All it does is check to see if the agent is at the next node. If it is, then m_has-StartedRotation flag is reset so that RotateAndMove() knows that a rotation may be needed. If the agent is not yet at the next node, RotateAndMove() is called to update its position. Let's take a look at that function to see how it works:

```
void MoveState::RotateAndMove(const int deltaMilliseconds)
{
   // grab the necessary interfaces
   shared_ptr<IGamePhysics> pPhysics = g_pApp->m_pGame->VGetGamePhysics();
   assert(pPhysics);
   shared_ptr<IActor> pActor = g_pApp->m_pGame->VGetActor(m_actorId);
   assert(pActor);

   // calculate orientation
   float orientation = pPhysics->VGetOrientationY(m_actorId);
   Vec3 diff = m_target - pActor->VGetMat().GetPosition();
   if (m_targetOrientation == FLT_MAX)
      m_targetOrientation = GetYRotationFromVector(diff);

   // if we're not facing the right direction, start rotating if we
   // haven't already
   if (fabs(m_targetOrientation - orientation) > 0.001f)
   {
      if (!m_hasStartedRotation)
      {
         pActor->VRotateY(m_targetOrientation);
         m_hasStartedRotation = true;
      }
   }
}
```

```
// if we're already facing the right direction, pretend we rotated there
else if (!m_hasStartedRotation)
    m_hasStartedRotation = true;


// if we get here, we're done rotating so start moving
else
{
    m_targetOrientation = FLT_MAX;
    m_hasStartedRotation = false;
    diff.Normalize();
    float speed = AI_TEAPOT_SPEED * ((float)deltaMilliseconds / 1000.0f);
    diff *= speed;
    pPhysics->VTranslate(m_actorId,diff);
}
}
```

The code in this function should look familiar. It's based on the principles discussed in the very beginning of this chapter. The first thing that happens (besides grabbing the appropriate interfaces) is a query to the physics system for the agent's current orientation about the Y axis. The agent's target orientation is then calculated. If it's not facing the right direction and hasn't started rotating, the physics system is told to start the rotation and the m_hasStartedRotation flag is set. The next time through this function, the target orientation is calculated again and, if the agent hasn't reached the target yet, the function returns. This effectively causes the state to wait until the agent has completed its rotation. Once the rotation is complete, the final else block at the bottom of the function gets executed. This signals that the agent is ready to be moved. The agent will move until something tells it to stop, which is exactly what happens when it's close enough to the target. This is checked back in the ChaseTargetState::VOnUpdate() function.

Spend some time studying ChaseTargetState and get to know how it works. It's a nice vertical slice of the AI system and uses everything we've covered.

Making a Professional Game

What needs to change in your StateMachine system before you can use this in a commercial game? The CreateState() factory method isn't exactly ideal. You really don't want to create a series of if/then statements that do a bunch of string compares. Furthermore, the state transitions are all hard coded. This is fine if you're making a relatively simple game, but once you delve into something more complex, you'll want to abstract the transitions themselves. One way to do this would be to create functors (similar to the A* functor described above) that can be instantiated just like states. Each functor represents a conditional that can be mapped to a state. If the condition is true, you transition to that state. You can build a sorted list of these transition-to-state pairs and in the VOnUpdate() function of each state, it simply goes through its list of transitions and checks each one.

Another thing this system sorely lacks is some exposure to Lua. These states should all be exposed and designers should have the ability to force state changes on script events. Right now, it's all controlled by the programmer. The pathing graph is currently generated with a simple grid-building algorithm. The designers need to have some control over this, too. One solution would be to write an offline tool that analyzes the world geometry and builds a simple pathing graph based on that. Then the designers can go into the level editing tool and muck around with values as needed.

ADVANCED DECISION MAKING

State machines are really just the beginning. I want to touch on a few advanced techniques for decision making to give you an idea of what else is out there. I can't do these topics any justice in a single chapter since entire books have been written about each one, but this should be enough to pique your curiosity to start looking into them when you're ready.

Fuzzy Logic

In traditional logical systems, things are very Boolean. Either you are tired, or you are not; there's no in between. At its most basic, fuzzy logic simply turns this into a variable.

For example, let's say you have an agent with a value for "rest" that goes from 0–100 where 0 is passed out and 100 is fully rested. In your state transition code, you have it set that if the agent's "rest" falls to 50, it starts heading for bed. If it falls below 25, it urgently looks for a safe place to sleep. This is pretty standard rigid logic.

A fuzzy approach to this same problem would be to define a fuzzy set called "rested" and another called "tired." The agent would usually belong to both of these sets, but in different degrees. For example, if its rest meter were at 75, it would be 0.75 in the rested set and 0.25 in the tired set. As its membership in the tired set increases, it becomes more and more important for it to find a place to sleep. With this simple example, you could define its percentage chance of wanting to find a place to sleep as the degree of membership in the tired set divided by 0.80. This means it's guaranteed to find a place to sleep once its degree of membership is greater than 0.8. If its meter were at 75 (giving him a 0.25 degree of membership in the tired set), it would have a 31.25% chance to want to rest.

Fuzzy systems get really interesting when you introduce several fuzzy sets to which all agents belong. You can get some really complex emergent behavior with just a few simple fuzzy sets. For example, your agent might be really tired, but if it's starving to death, it shouldn't matter how hungry it is.

One of the really interesting side effects of fuzzy systems is that agents will sometimes behave unpredictably. They'll do the expected thing *most* of the time, but every now and then they'll do something a bit strange. In my experience, I've found that a little tuning of simple fuzzy systems can imbue otherwise static NPCs with personality and life.

Goal-Oriented Agents

Goal-oriented agents just want to be happy. All of their decision making is a prediction of the future, and they always try to choose the option that will maximize their happiness. In AI terms, this happiness is often called *utility*. Each agent has a series of desires and a number of possible actions that may or may not satisfy those desires. The desires can be thought of as little meters or buckets that the agent wants to fill. Sometimes, they go down with time (like hunger), and sometimes it takes an event (like taking damage). In a simple world, all desires are equal, and the agent simply chooses to satisfy the one that has the lowest value. However, in most cases, things are not at all equal, and the agent ends up doing a juggling act. Whenever it has to make a decision about what to do next, it looks at all of its options and chooses the one that it feels will maximize his overall utility score. Goal-oriented agents can be hard to tune, especially if there are a lot of desires. Usually, there's some fuzzy logic going on there as well, so the system becomes very nondeterministic.

The Sims is a perfect example of how goal-oriented agents behave. Each sim has a series of needs, and all of their AI controlled actions are based on satisfying those needs. In their case, nearly every need decays with time, though they are clearly not all weighted equally. If your sim is about to starve to death but also smells really bad, it will typically go get something to eat first.

TALES FROM THE PIXEL MINES

AGENTS CAN COMPLAIN ABOUT WORK JUST LIKE US

Rat Race used a system called *UtilEcon*, which stood for *Utility Economy*. The system was designed to be a goal-oriented system where agents would wander around the world and trade utility with each other through speech. We had a whole speech system tied into this so there were different types of utility for different types of conversations. That way you'd tend to hear the gossipy people in the office say the gossip lines while the workaholics would say the work lines. The system worked really well and added quite a bit to the atmosphere. "Oh look, there's Joy complaining again."

Types of Game AI

Before I wrap up this chapter, I want to talk briefly about a few different genres of games and some of the challenges AI developers face with them.

Simple Action Games and Platformers

Simple action/platformer games rely on reflex and patterns. Some examples include the various *Mega Man* games, *Little Big Planet*, *Paper Mario* for the Wii, and *Braid*. The AI for this genre tends to be very simple. It's often just simple, preprogrammed patterns with a very simple state machine. For some games (like *Mega Man*), the fun is trying to figure out that pattern so you can use it to defeat the enemy. Other games are even simpler.

The techniques presented in this book are more than sufficient to build a game like this. In fact, many platformers (especially side-scrollers like *Mega Man*) don't use path-finding algorithms at all.

Shooters

Shooters are the next generation of action game where the primary goal is typically to destroy the enemy. Examples of these games are *Half Life*, *Quake*, *Doom*, *Fear*, *Gears of War*, and *Left 4 Dead*. The AI in these games is often a bit more complex. The enemies need to move around in a bigger, more complex space. They'll need some shooting control code and perception algorithms (line-of-sight, hearing, and so on). Decision making is often handled with a more complex state machine, and the enemies will probably need a way to communicate with each other so they can work together. It would look pretty dumb if two enemies closed in on the player while a third threw a grenade at him!

The principles you learned in this chapter still hold true. Keep in mind that the average lifetime of a single AI-controlled enemy in a shooter game is pretty short; doing much more than simple tactics is usually overkill. The system in this chapter would need to be expanded, but the core of it would be perfectly suited to this genre of game.

Strategy Games

Strategy games are an order of magnitude more complex than shooters, especially real-time strategy games. Some examples of strategy games include *Civilization*, *Dawn of War*, *Starcraft*, and *Warcraft*. Strategy games typically have two major components to their AI. The first is the individual unit AI, which includes path finding, basic attack states, and so on. A relatively simple state machine is usually enough for these guys. Path finding is another story. The path finding in real-time strategy (RTS) games is usually very complex and often involves a considerable amount of optimization. At the very least, it should be run in a separate thread.

The second component of strategy AI is the opponent. This is a much higher level of AI that determines which units to build and when to attack. A goal-oriented agent would be appropriate here as would adding some simple learning algorithms to help anticipate the player's attacks.

Role-Playing Games

Role-playing games come in many different flavors. Some have very scripted NPCs while others have living, breathing worlds. The former is created easily enough using simple waypoints. The latter is much more of an interesting challenge. Games like *Oblivion*, *Fallout 3*, and the *Ultima* series would simulate entire worlds. People wake up, eat breakfast, wander outside, go to work, hunt, come home, and sleep. *Ultima VII* did this with an internal schedule for each NPC that would dictate what it was doing at any given time.

Games like this usually require complex state machines with some decent culling techniques. As you get farther away from a particular area, the game can give the NPC less CPU time to update. Maybe in the beginning, it just runs a really dumb but really fast path-finding algorithm. As you get farther away, perhaps pathing is turned off completely, and it merrily clips through any geometry in its way (at this point, it probably has no physical presence, just a position). It will eventually get turned off completely. This is the basis behind LOD (level of detail). LOD has been in use in the graphics world for quite some time. You can think of AI LOD as a form of logical mip-mapping. As the player gets farther away, the AI is swapped for more simplified versions. This helps tremendously when there are dozens of very complex agents roaming around the world.

FURTHER READING

Here is a short list of books I've found very helpful in becoming a better AI programmer:

- *Artificial Intelligence for Games*, Ian Millington, published by The Morgan Kaufmann Series in Interactive 3D Technology
- *Artificial Intelligence: A Modern Approach*, Stuart Russell and Peter Norvig, published by Prentice-Hall Inc.
- The *AI Game Programming Wisdom* series, Charles River Media
- The *Game Programming Gems* series, Charles River Media

INTRODUCTION TO MULTIPROGRAMMING

In This Chapter

I'll be honest with you, gentle reader, that the thought of writing this chapter was quite intimidating. I've spent many hours of my programming career attempting to solve bugs that were caused by some multithreaded or multicore madness. Adding this potential source of pain and suffering to the Game Code 3 source was somewhat terrifying. But, as it turned out, I was saved by a few things: a great core architecture, very careful coding with constant testing, and lots of planning ahead of time.

The general term for creating software that can figuratively or actually run in multiple, independent pieces simultaneously is *multiprogramming*.

There are few subjects in programming as tricky as this. It turns out to be amazingly simple to get multiple threads chewing on something interesting, like calculating π to 1,000,000 digits. The difficulty comes in getting each of these jobs to play nice with each other's memory, and getting them to send information to each other so that the results of their work can be put to good use.

The code you will learn in this chapter will work on single or multiprocessor Win32 systems, but it is easy enough to port to others. The concepts you will learn, such as process synchronization, are also portable to any system that has threading built into the operating system.

The first question you should ask is why should we bother with multithreading at all? Isn't one thread on one CPU enough?

What Multiprogramming Does

A CPU is amazingly fast, and many desktop CPUs are now sitting solidly in the 2-3GHz range. If you happen to have a really nice lab and can get your CPU down to near absolute zero, you can squeeze 500GHz out of one, like IBM and Georgia Tech did back in 2006. But what does that really mean?

Gigahertz as it is applied to CPUs, measure the *clock speed* of the CPU. The clock speed is the basic measure of how fast things happen—anything from loading a bit of memory into a register or doing a mathematical operation like addition. Different instructions take different cycles, or ticks, of the clock. With the advent of multicore processors, it is even possible to perform more than one instruction in a single cycle. Many processors are capable of executing instructions in parallel in a single core if they use different parts of the processor.

As fast as CPUs are, they spend most of their time waiting around. Take a look at Figure 18.1, a snapshot of the CPU load running *Teapot Wars*, which you'll see in Chapter 19.

The figure shows a few spikes, but there's still plenty of headroom—so what's going on? Is *Teapot Wars* written so efficiently? Hardly. The CPU, or CPUs in this case, spend most of their time waiting on the video hardware to draw the scene. This is a pretty common thing in computer game software, since preparing the scene and communicating to the video card takes so much time.

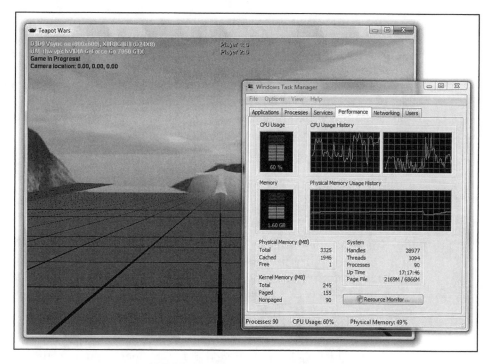

FIGURE 18.1 CPU load running *Teapot Wars*.

It turns out there is a solution for this problem, and it involves *multithreading*. Instead of creating a monolithic program that runs one instruction after another, the programmer splits the program into multiple, independent pieces. Each piece is launched independently, and can run on its own. If one piece, or *thread*, becomes stuck waiting for something, like the CD-ROM to spin up so a file can be read, the processor can switch over to another thread and process whatever instructions it has.

If you think this is similar to what happens when you run 50 different applications on your desktop machine, you are very close to being right. Each application exists independently of other applications and can access devices like your hard drive or your network without any problems at all, at least until you run out of memory or simply bog your system down.

Under Windows and most operating systems, applications run as separate processes, and the operating system has very special rules for switching between processes since they run in their own memory space. This switching is relatively expensive, since a lot of work has to happen so that each application believes it has the complete and full attention of the CPU.

The good news is that under Win32 and other operating systems each process can have multiple threads of its own, and switching between them is relatively inexpensive. Each thread has its own stack space and full access to the same memory as the other threads created by the process. Being able to share memory is extremely useful, but it does have its problems.

The operating system can switch from one thread to another at any time. When a switch happens, the values of the current thread's CPU registers are saved. They are then overwritten by the next thread's CPU registers, and the CPU begins to run the code for the new thread. This leads to some interesting behaviors if multiple threads manipulate the same bit of memory. Take a look at the assembler for incrementing a global integer:

```
++g_ProtectedTotal;
006D2765  mov        eax,dword ptr [g_ProtectedTotal (9B6E48h)]
006D276A  add        eax,1
006D276D  mov        dword ptr [g_ProtectedTotal (9B6E48h)],eax
```

There are three instructions. The first loads the current value of the variable from main memory into eax, one of the general purpose registers. The second increments the register, and the third stores the new value back into memory. Remember that each thread has full access to the memory pointed to by g_ProtectedTotal, but its copy of eax is unique. A thread switch can happen after each assembler level instruction completes.

If a dozen or so threads were running these three instructions simultaneously, it wouldn't be long before a switch would happen right after the add instruction but before the results were stored back to main memory.

In my own experiments, the results were pretty sobering: 20 threads each incrementing the variable 100,000 times created an end result of 1,433,440. This means 566,560 additions were completely missed. I ran this experiment on a Dell M1710 equipped with an Intel Centrino Duo.

Lucky for you and everyone else out there wanting to take full advantage of their CPUs, there are ways to solve this problem. First, you should know how you create the thread in the first place.

CREATING THREADS

Under Win32, you use the CreateThread() API. For you programmers who desire a more portable solution, you can also choose the ANSI C _beginthread() call. They are similar enough that with a little work you can port this code to ANSI C thread calls.

```
DWORD g_maxLoops = 20;              // shouldn't be on a stack!
DWORD g_UnprotectedTotal = 0;       // the variable we want to increment
```

```
DWORD WINAPI ThreadProc( LPVOID lpParam )
{
   DWORD maxLoops = *static_cast<DWORD *>(lpParam);
   DWORD dwCount = 0;
   while( dwCount < maxLoops )
   {
      ++dwCount;
      ++g_UnprotectedTotal;
   }
   return TRUE;
}


void CreateThreads()
{
   for (int i=0; i<20; i++)
   {
      HANDLE m_hThread = CreateThread(
               NULL,        // default security attributes
               0,           // default stack size
               (LPTHREAD_START_ROUTINE) ThreadProc,
               &g_maxLoops,  // thread parameter is how many loops
               0,           // default creation flags
               NULL);       // receive thread identifier
   }
}
```

To create a thread, you call the CreateThread() API with a pointer to a function that will run as the thread procedure. The thread will cease to exist when the thread procedure exits, or something external stops the thread, such as a call to TerminateThread(). The thread procedure, ThreadProc, takes one variable, a void pointer which you may use to send any bit of data your thread procedure needs. In the previous example, a DWORD was set to the number of loops and used as the thread parameter. The thread can be started in a suspended state if you set the default creation flags to CREATE_SUSPENDED, in which case you'll need to call ResumeThread(m_hThread) to get it started.

Take special note of where the parameter to the thread process is stored, because it is a global. Had it been local to the CreateThreads() function, it would have been stored on the stack. The address of this would have been passed to the thread procedures, and goodness knows what it would have in it at any given moment. This is a great example of how something seemingly trivial can have a huge effect on how your threads run.

THE STACK CAN BE A DANGEROUS PLACE

Be careful about where you store data that will be accessed by thread procedures. The stack is right out, since it will be constantly changing. Allocate specific memory for your thread procedures or store them globally.

When you have multiple threads running in your game, you can debug each of them, to a point. In Visual Studio you can show the Threads window by selecting Debug->Window->Threads from the main menu (see Figure 18.2).

ID	Name	Location	Priority	Suspend
3116	std::locale::_Locimp::_Makeushloc	CreateThreads	Normal	0
356	Win32 Thread	77279a94	Normal	0
5540	Win32 Thread	77279a94	Time Critical	0
2344	Win32 Thread	77279a94	Time Critical	0
628	Win32 Thread	77279a94	-3	0
2004	Win32 Thread	ThreadProc	Normal	0
4828	Win32 Thread	ThreadProc	Normal	0

FIGURE 18.2 The Threads window in Visual Studio.

When you hit a breakpoint, all threads stop execution. If you double-click on a row in the Threads window, you will see where execution has stopped in that thread. You can easily set breakpoints in the thread procedure, but if you run multiple threads using the same procedure, you can never tell which thread will hit the breakpoint first! It can become a little confusing.

Creating a thread is pretty trivial, as you have seen. Getting these threads to work together, and not wipe out the results of other threads working on the same memory, is a little harder.

PROCESS SYNCHRONIZATION

There's really no use in having threads without having some way to manage their access to memory. In the early days of computing, programmers tried to solve this with software. When I was in college, one of my favorite instructors, Dr. Rusinkiewicz, had a great story he told to show us how these engineers tried to create a heuristic to handle this problem.

Imagine two railways that share a section of track in the Andes Mountains in South America. One railway runs in Bolivia and the other runs in neighboring Peru. The engineers are both blind and deaf, so they can't hear or see the other. For a few months, nothing bad happened—the trains simply weren't in the pass long enough to be a problem. But, one day the trains crashed. The governments of the two countries agreed that something must be done.

No, they didn't hire train engineers that could see and hear. That would be too easy.

A bowl was placed at the beginning of the shared section of track. When an engineer arrived, he would check the bowl. If it was empty, he would put a rock in it and drive across the pass. He would then walk back, remove the rock, and continue on his trip. This worked for a few days, and then the Peruvians noticed that their train never arrived. Fearing the worst, a search team was sent out to find the train. It was waiting at the junction, and as the search team watched, the Bolivian train roared by, not even stopping. The Bolivian engineer ignored the rules, just put a rock in the bowl, and never intended to take it out. He was fired and another, more honest, blind and deaf Bolivian engineer replaced him.

For years nothing bad happened, but one day neither train arrived. A team was sent to investigate, and they found that the trains had crashed, and two rocks were in the bowl. The two countries decided that the current system wasn't working, and something must be done to fix the problem. Yes, they still hired blind and deaf engineers. Instead, they decided that the bowls were being used the wrong way. The Bolivian engineer would put a rock in the bowl when he was driving across, and the Peruvian engineer would always wait until the bowl was empty before driving across.

This didn't even work for a single day. The Peruvian train had until this time run twice per day, and the Bolivian train once per day. The new system prevented crashes, but now each train could only run once per day since it relied on trading permission to run through the pass. Again, the governments put their best minds at work to solve the problem.

They bought another bowl.

Now, two bowls were used at the pass. Each engineer had his own bowl. When he arrived, he would drop a rock into his bowl, walk to the other engineer's bowl, and check it. If there was a rock there, he would go back to his bowl, remove the rock, and take a siesta. This seemed to work for many years, until both trains were so late a search team was sent out to find out what happened.

Luckily, both trains were there, and both engineers were simultaneously dropping rocks into their bowls, checking the other, finding a rock, and then taking a siesta. Finally, the two governments decided that bowls and rocks were not going to solve this problem.

What they needed was a semaphore.

Test and Set, the Semaphore, and the Mutex

The computer software version of a semaphore relies on a low-level hardware instruction called a test-and-set instruction. It checks the value of a bit, and if it is zero, it sets the bit to one, all in one operation that cannot be interrupted by the CPU switching from one thread to another.

Traditionally, a semaphore is set to an integer value that denotes the number of resources that are free. When a process wishes to gain access to a resource, it decrements the semaphore in an atomic operation using a test-and-set. When it is done with the resource, it increments the semaphore in with the same atomic operation. If a process finds the semaphore equal to zero, it must wait.

A mutex is a binary semaphore, and it is generally used to give access to a resource for a single process. All others must wait.

Win32 has many different ways to handle process synchronization. A mutex can be created with CreateMutex(), and a semaphore can be created with Create-Semaphore(). But since these synchronization objects can be shared between Windows applications, they are fairly heavyweight and shouldn't be used for high performance. Windows programmers should use the *critical section*.

The Win32 Critical Section

The critical section under Windows is a less expensive way to manage synchronization among the threads of a single process. Here's how to put it to use:

```
DWORD g_ProtectedTotal = 0;
DWORD g_maxLoops = 20;
CRITICAL_SECTION g_criticalSection;

DWORD WINAPI ThreadProc( LPVOID lpParam )
{
   DWORD maxLoops = *static_cast<DWORD *>(lpParam);
   DWORD dwCount = 0;
    while( dwCount < maxLoops )
     {
       ++dwCount;

       EnterCriticalSection(&g_criticalSection);
       ++g_ProtectedTotal;
       LeaveCriticalSection(&g_criticalSection);
   }
   return TRUE;
}


void CreateThreads()
{
   DWORD maxLoops = 100000;
   InitializeCriticalSection(&g_criticalSection);
```

```
for (int i=0; i<20; i++)
{
    HANDLE m_hThread = CreateThread(
            NULL,           // default security attributes
            0,              // default stack size
            (LPTHREAD_START_ROUTINE) ThreadProc,
            &g_maxLoops,    // thread parameter is how many loops
            0,              // default creation flags
            NULL);          // receive thread identifier
}
}
```

The call to `InitializeCriticalSection()` does exactly what it advertises—initializes the critical section object, declared globally as `CRITICAL_SECTION g_criticalSection`. You should treat the critical section object as opaque, and do not copy it or attempt to modify it. The thread procedure makes calls to `EnterCriticalSection()` and `LeaveCriticalSection()` around the access to the shared global variable, `g_ProtectedTotal`.

If another thread is already in the critical section, the call to `EnterCriticalSection()` will block and wait until the other thread leaves the critical section. Windows does not guarantee any order in which the threads will get access, but it will be fair to all threads. Notice that the critical section is made as small as possible—not even the increment to the `dwCount` member variable is inside. This is to illustrate an important point about critical sections: in order to achieve the maximum throughput, you should minimize the time spent in critical sections as much as possible.

If you don't want your thread to block when it attempts to enter a critical section, you can call `TryEnterCriticalSection()`, which will return true only if the critical section is validly entered.

INTERESTING THREADING PROBLEMS

There are a number of interesting threading problems you should be aware of: racing, starvation, and deadlock.

Racing is a condition where two or more threads are reading or writing shared data and the final result requires the threads to run in a precise order, which can never be guaranteed. The classic problem is the writer-reader problem, where a writer thread fills a buffer and a reader thread processes the buffer. If the two threads aren't synchronized properly, the reader will overtake the writer and read garbage.

The solution to this problem is easy with a shared count of bytes in the buffer, changed only by the writer thread using a critical section.

Starvation and deadlock is a condition where one or more threads gains access to a shared resource and continually blocks access to the starving thread. The classic illustration of this problem is called the *dining philosophers problem*, first imagined by Tony Hoare, a British computer scientist best known for creating the Quicksort algorithm. It goes like this. Five philosophers sit around a circular table, and they are doing one of two things: eating or thinking. When they are eating, they are not thinking, and when they are thinking, they are not eating. The table has five chopsticks, one sitting between each philosopher. In order to eat, each person must grab two chopsticks, and he must do this without speaking to anyone else.

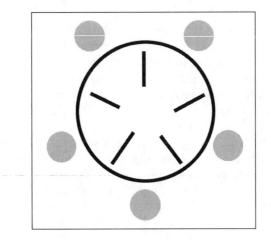

FIGURE 18.3 The dining philosophers.

You can see that if every philosopher grabbed the chopstick on his left and held onto it, none of them could ever grab a second chopstick, and they would all starve. This is analogous to deadlock.

If they were eating and thinking at different times, one philosopher could simply get unlucky and never get the chance to get both chopsticks. He would starve, even though the others could eat. That is similar to *process starvation*.

There are two solutions to the dining philosophers problem: one of them involves something I told you about way back in Chapter 5, "Game Initialization and Shutdown." If you want to avoid deadlock in any shared resource situation, always ask for resources in a particular order and release them in the reverse order. If you find yourself at a table with four other people and only five chopsticks between you, simply agree to pick up the left chopstick first, and the right chopstick second. When you are ready to stop eating and start thinking, put them down in the reverse order. Believe it or not, no deadlock will happen, and no one will starve.

There are a number of these interesting problems, which you should look up and try to solve on your own:

- Cigarette smokers problem
- Sleeping barbers problem
- Dining cryptographers protocol

THREAD SAFETY

As you might imagine, there are often more things you *shouldn't* do in a thread than you should. For one thing, most STL and ANSI C calls are not thread safe. In other words, you can't manipulate the same `std::list` or make calls to `fread()` from multiple threads without something bad happening to your program. If you need to do these things in multiple concurrent threads, you need to manage the calls with critical sections. A good example of this is included in the Game Code 3 source code, which manages any `std::basic_ostream< char_type, traits_type>` and allows you to safely write to it from multiple threads. Look in the Multicore\SafeStream.h file for the template class and an example on how it can be used.

MULTITHREADING CLASSES

You are ready to see how these concepts are put to work in the Game Code 3 architecture. There are two systems that make this easy: the Process Manager and the Event Manager. If you recall from Chapter 6, "Controlling the Main Loop," the Process Manager is a container for cooperative processes that inherit from the `CProcess` class. It is simple to extend the `CProcess` class to create a real-time version of it, and while the operating system manages the thread portion of the class, the data and existence of it is still managed by the `CProcessManager` class. This turns out to be really useful, since initialization and process dependencies are still possible, even between normal and real-time processes.

Communication between real-time processes and the rest of the game happens exactly where you might expect—in the Event Manager. A little bit of code has to be written to manage the problem of events being sent to or from real-time processes, but you'll be surprised how little.

After the basic classes are written, you'll see how you can write a background real-time process to handle decompression of a part of a ZIP file.

The `RealtimeProcess` Class

The goal with the `RealtimeProcess` class is to make it really easy to create real-time processes. Here's the class definition:

```cpp
class RealtimeProcess : public CProcess
{
protected:
    HANDLE m_hThread;
    DWORD m_ThreadID;
    int m_ThreadPriority;
    LPTHREAD_START_ROUTINE m_lpRoutine;
public:
    // Other prioities can be:
    // THREAD_PRIORITY_ABOVE_NORMAL
    // THREAD_PRIORITY_BELOW_NORMAL
    // THREAD_PRIORITY_HIGHEST
    // THREAD_PRIORITY_TIME_CRITICAL
    // THREAD_PRIORITY_LOWEST
    // THREAD_PRIORITY_IDLE
    //
    RealtimeProcess( LPTHREAD_START_ROUTINE lpRoutine,
        int priority = THREAD_PRIORITY_NORMAL );
    virtual void   VKill()
    {
        CloseHandle(m_hThread);
        CProcess::VKill();
    }
    virtual void   VTogglePause()
    {
        assert(0 && "This is not supported.");
    }
    virtual void   VOnInitialize();
};

RealtimeProcess::RealtimeProcess(
    LPTHREAD_START_ROUTINE lpRoutine, int priority )
    : CProcess(PROC_REALTIME)
{
    m_lpRoutine = lpRoutine;
    m_ThreadID = 0;
    m_ThreadPriority = priority;
}
```

The members of this class include a Win32 HANDLE to the thread, the thread ID, and the current thread priority. This is set to THREAD_PRIORITY_NORMAL, but depending on what the process needs to do, you might increase or decrease the priority. Note that if you set it to THREAD_PRIORITY_TIME_CRITICAL, you'll likely notice a serious sluggishness of the user interface, particularly the mouse pointer. It's a good idea to play nice and leave it at the default or even put it at a lower priority.

The thread process is pointed to by LPTHREAD_START_ROUTINE m_lpRoutine. The RealtimeProcess class is meant to be a base class. Child classes will write their own thread process and send a pointer to it in the constructor.

The VKill() method calls CloseHandle() and then CProcess::VKill(). By design, the VKill() method does not call TerminateThread(). Following the same rules as other cooperative processes, VKill() is only called by itself when the process has finished its work.

VOnInitialize() is where the call to CreateThread() happens:

```
void RealtimeProcess::VOnInitialize(void)
{
   CProcess::VOnInitialize();
   m_hThread = CreateThread(
               NULL,        // default security attributes
               0,           // default stack size
               (LPTHREAD_START_ROUTINE) m_lpRoutine,
               this,        // thread parameter is a pointer to the process
               0,           // default creation flags
               &m_ThreadID); // receive thread identifier

   if( m_hThread == NULL )
   {
      assert(0 && "Could not create thread!");
      VKill();
   }

   SetThreadPriority(m_hThread, m_ThreadPriority);
}
```

Note the thread parameter in the call to CreateThread(). It is a pointer to the instance of the calling class, which will make it possible to access a member variable in the thread process. The only new call you haven't seen yet is the call to SetThreadPriority(), where you tell Win32 how much processor time to allocate to this thread.

Here's how you would create a real-time process to increment a global integer, just like you've seen earlier:

```
class ProtectedProcess : public RealtimeProcess
{
public:
    static DWORD WINAPI ThreadProc( LPVOID lpParam );
    static DWORD g_ProtectedTotal;
    static CRITICAL_SECTION g_criticalSection;
    DWORD m_MaxLoops;
    ProtectedProcess(DWORD maxLoops)
        : RealtimeProcess(ThreadProc)
        { m_MaxLoops = maxLoops; }
};

DWORD ProtectedProcess::g_ProtectedTotal = 0;
CRITICAL_SECTION ProtectedProcess::g_criticalSection;

DWORD WINAPI ProtectedProcess::ThreadProc( LPVOID lpParam )
{
    ProtectedProcess *proc = static_cast<ProtectedProcess *>(lpParam);
    DWORD dwCount = 0;

    while( dwCount < proc->m_MaxLoops )
    {
        ++dwCount;

        // Request ownership of critical section.
        EnterCriticalSection(&g_criticalSection);
        ++g_ProtectedTotal;
        LeaveCriticalSection(&g_criticalSection);
    }

    proc->VKill();
    return TRUE;
}
```

The thread process is defined by the static member function, `ThreadProc()`. Two other static members of this class are the variable the process is going to increment and the critical section that will be shared between multiple instances of the real-time process. Just before the thread process returns, `proc->VKill()` is called to tell the Process Manager to clean up the process and launch any dependent processes.

As it turns out, you instantiate a real-time process in exactly the same way you do a cooperative process:

```
for( i=0; i < 20; i++ )
{
   shared_ptr<CProcess> proc(GCC_NEW ProtectedProcess(100000));
   procMgr->Attach(proc);
}
```

The above example instantiates 20 processes that will each increment the global variable 100,000 times. The use of the critical sections ensure that when all the processes are complete, the global variable will be set to exactly 2,000,000.

Sending Events from Real-Time Processes

There's probably no system in the Game Code 3 architecture that uses STL containers more than the `EventManager` class. Given that STL containers aren't thread safe by themselves, there's one of two things that can be done.

We could make all the containers in the Event Manager thread safe. This includes two `std::map` objects, three `std::pair` objects, and two `std::list` objects. This would be a horrible idea, since the vast majority of the event system is accessed only by the main process and doesn't need to be thread safe. A better idea would be to create a single, thread-safe container that could accept events that were sent by real-time processes. When the event system runs its `VTick()` method, it can empty this queue in a thread-safe manner and handle the events sent by real-time processes along the rest.

A thread-safe queue was posted by Anthony Williams on www.justsoftwares-olutions.co.uk. It uses two synchronization mechanisms in the Boost C++ Thread library, `boost::mutex` and `boost::condition_variable`:

```
template<typename Data>
class concurrent_queue
{
private:
   std::queue<Data> the_queue;
   mutable boost::mutex the_mutex;
   boost::condition_variable the_condition_variable;
public:
   void push(Data const& data)
   {
      boost::mutex::scoped_lock lock(the_mutex);
      the_queue.push(data);
      lock.unlock();
      the_condition_variable.notify_one();
   }
```

```
bool empty() const
{
    boost::mutex::scoped_lock lock(the_mutex);
    return the_queue.empty();
}

bool try_pop(Data& popped_value)
{
    boost::mutex::scoped_lock lock(the_mutex);
    if(the_queue.empty())
    {
        return false;
    }

    popped_value=the_queue.front();
    the_queue.pop();
    return true;
}

void wait_and_pop(Data& popped_value)
{
    boost::mutex::scoped_lock lock(the_mutex);
    while(the_queue.empty())
    {
        the_condition_variable.wait(lock);
    }

    popped_value=the_queue.front();
    the_queue.pop();
}
};
```

The boost::mutex is similar to the critical section object you've already seen. It has a useful scoped_lock object that blocks on construction until the shared resource is available, then automatically releases the resource on destruction.

The boost::condition_variable is a mechanism that allows one thread to notify another thread that a particular condition has become true. Without it, a reader thread manipulating the queue would have to lock the mutex, check the queue, find that it was empty, release the lock, and then find a way to wait for a while before checking it all over again. Using the condition variable, a writer thread can notify the reader thread the moment something interesting is in the queue. This increases concurrency immensely.

Here's how the `EventManager` class you saw in Chapter 10 needs to change to be able to receive events from real-time processes:

```
typedef concurrent_queue<IEventDataPtr> ThreadSafeEventQueue;

class EventManager : public IEventManager
{
   // Add a new method and a new member:
public:
   virtual bool VThreadSafeQueueEvent ( IEventDataPtr const & inEvent );

private:
   ThreadSafeEventQueue m_RealtimeEventQueue;

}

bool EventManager::VThreadSafeQueueEvent ( IEventDataPtr const & inEvent )
{
   m_RealtimeEventQueue.push(inEvent);
   return true;
}
```

The concurrent queue template is used to create a thread-safe queue for `IEventDataPtr` objects, which are the mainstay of the event system. The method `VThreadSafeQueueEvent()` can be called by any process in any thread at any time. All that remains is to add the code to `EventManager::VTick()` to read the events out of the queue:

```
bool EventManager::VTick ( unsigned long maxMillis )
{
   unsigned long curMs = GetTickCount();
   unsigned long maxMs =
      maxMillis == IEventManager::kINFINITE
      ? IEventManager::kINFINITE
      : (curMs + maxMillis );

   EventListenerMap::const_iterator itWC = m_registry.find( 0 );

   // This section added to handle events from other threads
   // -------------------------------------------------------
   IEventDataPtr rte;
   while (m_RealtimeEventQueue.try_pop(rte))
   {
      VQueueEvent(rte);
```

```
        curMs = GetTickCount();
        if ( maxMillis != IEventManager::kINFINITE )
        {

            if ( curMs >= maxMs )
            {
                assert(0 && "A realtime process is spamming the event manager!");
            }
        }
    }
    // -------------------------------------------------------

    // swap active queues, make sure new queue is empty after the
    // swap ...

    // THE REST OF VTICK IS UNCHANGED!!!!
```

There is a new section of code at the top of the method to handle events from real-time processes. The call to try_pop grabs an event out of the real-time queue if it exists, but if the queue is empty, it returns immediately. Since real-time processes can run at a higher priority, it is possible they could spam the Event Manager faster than the Event Manager could consume them, so a check is made to compare the current tick count against the maximum amount of time the Event Manager is supposed to run before exiting.

The RealtimeEventListener Class

Real-time processes should also be able to receive events from other game subsystems. This requires the same strategy as before, using a thread-safe queue. The RealtimeEventListener class inherits from IEventListener just like other listeners, but instead of handling the event as it is received, the event is placed in the thread-safe queue:

```
class RealtimeEventListener : public IEventListener
{
   ThreadSafeEventQueue m_RealtimeEventQueue;
public:
   char const* GetName(void) { return "RealtimeEventListener"; }
   virtual bool HandleEvent( IEventData const & event )
   {
      IEventDataPtr pEvent = event.VCopy();
      g_RealtimeEventQueue.push(pEvent);
      return true;
   };
};
```

Then the thread process reads events out of this queue and handles them as a part of its inner loop:

```
DWORD WINAPI MyRealtimeProcess::ThreadProc( LPVOID lpParam )
{
   MyRealtimeProcess *proc =
      static_cast< MyRealtimeProcess *>(lpParam);

   while (1)
   {
      // check the queue for events we should consume
      IEventDataPtr e;
      if (g_RealtimeEventQueue.try_pop(e))
      {
         // there's an event! Something to do....
         if (EvtData_Random_Event::sk_EventType == e->VGetEventType())
         {
            // Handle the event right here!!!
         }
      }

      // other random thread code goes here
   }

   proc->VKill();
   return true;
}
```

With those tools, you have everything you need to write your own real-time processes, including having them send and receive events from other threads and game subsystems.

BACKGROUND DECOMPRESSION OF A ZIP FILE

One classic problem in game software is how to decompress a stream without halting the game. The stream could be anything from a portion of a music file, to a movie, to level data. The following class and code shows how you can set up a background process to receive requests from the game to decompress something in the background and send an event when the decompression is complete.

```
class DecompressionProcess : public RealtimeProcess
{
public:
   EventListenerPtr m_pListener;
   static DWORD WINAPI ThreadProc( LPVOID lpParam );
   static void Callback(int progress, bool &cancel);
   DecompressionProcess();
};

DecompressionProcess::DecompressionProcess()
   : RealtimeProcess(ThreadProc)
{
   m_pListener = EventListenerPtr (GCC_NEW RealtimeEventListener);
   safeAddListener( m_pListener, EvtData_Decompress_Request::sk_EventType );
}
```

The DecompressionProcess class has an EventListenerPtr member that is initialized to a new RealtimeEventListener. It has one event that it listens for, the EvtData_Decompress_Request event, which simply stores the name of the ZIP file and the name of the resource in the ZIP file to decompress. It is declared exactly the same as other events you've seen.

Here's the ThreadProc():

```
DWORD WINAPI DecompressionProcess::ThreadProc( LPVOID lpParam )
{
   DecompressionProcess *proc = static_cast<DecompressionProcess *>(lpParam);

   while (1)
   {
      // check the queue for events we should consume
      IEventDataPtr e;
      if (g_RealtimeEventQueue.try_pop(e))
      {
         // there's an event! Something to do....
         if (EvtData_Decompress_Request::sk_EventType == e->VGetEventType())
         {
            shared_ptr<EvtData_Decompress_Request> decomp =
               boost::static_pointer_cast<EvtData_Decompress_Request>(e);

            ZipFile zipFile;
            bool success = FALSE;
```

```
        if (zipFile.Init(decomp->m_zipFileName.c_str()))
        {
            int size = 0;
            optional<int> resourceNum =
                zipFile.Find(decomp->m_fileName.c_str());
            if (resourceNum.valid())
            {
                size = zipFile.GetFileLen(*resourceNum);
                void *buffer = GCC_NEW char[size];
                zipFile.ReadFile(*resourceNum, buffer);

                // send decompression result event
                threadSafeQueEvent(IEventDataPtr (
                    GCC_NEW EvtData_Decompression_Progress (
                        100, decomp->m_zipFileName,
                        decomp->m_fileName, buffer) ) );
            }
        }
    }
    }
    else
    {
        Sleep(10);
    }
    }
    proc->VKill();
    return TRUE;
}
```

This process is meant to loop forever in the background, ready for new decompression requests to come in from the Event Manager. Once the decompression request comes in, the method initializes a ZipFile class, exactly as you saw in Chapter 7, "Loading and Caching Game Data."

After the resource has been decompressed, an event is constructed that contains the progress (100%), the ZIP file name, the resource name, and the buffer. It is sent to the Event Manager with threadSafeQueueEvent() helper function.

The event is handled in the usual way:

```
if ( EvtData_Decompression_Progress::sk_EventType == event.VGetEventType() )
{
    const EvtData_Decompression_Progress & castEvent =
        static_cast< const EvtData_Decompression_Progress & >( event );
```

```
    if (castEvent.m_buffer != NULL)
    {
        const void *buffer = castEvent.m_buffer;
        // do something with the buffer!!!!
    }
}
```

Note that I'm bending one of my own rules here by allowing a pointer to sit in an event. The only reason that I can sleep at night is that I know that this particular event won't ever be serialized, so the pointer will always be good.

FURTHER WORK

Decompressing a data stream is a good example, but there are plenty of other tasks you could use this system for if you had a spare weekend. These include AI tasks such as path finding, physics, and others.

AI is a great choice to put in a background process. Whether you are programming a chess game or calculating an A* solution in a particularly dense path network, doing this in its own thread might buy you some great results. The magic length of time a human can easily perceive is 1/10th of one second, or 100 milliseconds. A game running at 60 frames per second has exactly 16 milliseconds to do all the work needed to present the next frame, and believe me, rendering and physics are going to take most of that. This leaves AI with a paltry 2–3 milliseconds to work. Usually, this isn't nearly enough time to do anything interesting.

So, running a thread in the background, you can still take those 2–3 milliseconds per frame, spread it across 10 or so frames, and all the player will perceive is just a noticeable delay between the AI changing a tactic or responding to something new. This gives your AI system much more time to work, and the player just notices a better game.

Running physics in a separate thread is a truly interesting problem. On one hand, it seems like a fantastic idea, but the moment you dig into it, you realize there are significant process synchronization issues to solve. Remember that physics is member of the game logic, which runs the rules of your game universe. Physics is tied very closely with the game logic, and having to synchronize the game logic and the physics systems in two separate threads seems like an enormous process synchronization problem, and it is.

Currently, the physics system sends movement events when actors move under physics control. Under a multithreaded system, more concurrent queues would have to buffer these movement events, and since they would happen quite a bit, would drop the system's efficiency greatly.

One solution to this would be to tightly couple the physics system to the game logic and have the game logic send movement messages to other game subsystems, like AI views or human views. Then it might be possible to detach the entire game logic into its own thread, running separately from the HumanView. With a little effort, it may even be possible to efficiently separate each view into its own thread. I'll leave that exercise to a sufficiently motivated reader.

ABOUT THE HARDWARE

Games have had multiple processors since the early 1990s, but the processors were very dedicated things. They were a part of audio hardware first, and then in the mid to late 1990s, the advent of dedicated floating-point (FPU) and video processors revolutionized the speed and look of our games. Both were difficult for programmers to deal with, and in many ways, most game programmers, except for perhaps John Miles, the author of the Miles Sound System, were happily coding in a completely single-threaded environment. They let the compiler handle anything for the FPU, and pawned tough threading tasks off to gurus who were comfortable with the reader/writer problems so common with sound systems.

The demands of the gaming public combined with truly incredible hardware from Intel, IBM, and others has firmly put those days behind us. Mostly, anyway. The Nintendo Wii is the only holdout of the bunch, sporting a single core PowerPC CPU built especially for the Wii by IBM.

TALES
FROM
THE
PIXEL
MINES

NINTENDO WII MIGHT WIN?

While the other consoles have a much more capable architecture, which you'll be introduced to shortly, I have to observe that as I write this in the first months of 2009, the Nintendo Wii is outselling the other consoles, and it will be tough for Sony or Microsoft to beat. I'll let the pundits and industry yahoos debate about why, but perhaps the fact that my Mom, a retired schoolteacher, bought one for herself and now loves bowling is the best example of why this is occurring. Go figure.

The other consoles have a much more interesting and capable hardware. The PS3 has a Cell processor jointly designed by IBM, Sony Computer Entertainment, and Toshiba. The main processor, the Power Processing Element, or PPE, is a general purpose 64-bit processor and handles most of the workload on the PS3. In addition, there are eight other special purpose processors called Synergistic Processing Elements or SPEs. Each has 256KB of local memory that may be used to store instructions and data. Each SPE runs at 3.2GHz, which is quite amazing since there are *eight* of them.

To get the best performance out of the PS3, a programmer would have to create very small threads on each one to handle one step of a complicated task. That last sentence, I assure you, was about 1,000,000 times easier for me to write than it would be to actually accomplish on a game.

The Xbox360 from Microsoft has a high-performance processor, also designed by IBM, based on a slightly modified version of the Cell PPE. It has three cores on one die, runs at 3.2GHz each, and has six possible total hardware threads available to the happy engineer writing the next Xbox360 blockbuster.

While it doesn't take a math genius to see that the PS3 cell processor seems to have the upper hand on the Xbox360 Xenon, from a programming perspective, the Xenon is a much friendlier programming environment, capable of handling general purpose threads that don't need to fit in a tiny 256KB space.

ABOUT THE FUTURE

Looking at the past, it is easy to see a trend. Smaller sizes and higher speeds are getting exponentially more difficult for companies like IBM to achieve on new processor designs. It seems the most cost-effective solution for consumers is to simply give the box more CPUs, albeit extremely capable ones. The truth is that programmers who haven't played in the somewhat frightening but challenging multiprogramming arena are going to be left behind. It takes an order of magnitude of more planning and sincere care and dedication to avoid seriously difficult bugs in this kind of environment.

At some point, we can all hope that compilers will become smart enough, or will develop languages specifically for the purpose of handling tricky multiprogramming problems. There have been attempts, such as Modula and concurrent Pascal, but nothing so far seems to be winning out over us monkeys smashing our femur bones on the monolith of C++.

Perhaps a reader of this book will think about that problem and realize we don't need new techniques, but simply a new language to describe new techniques.

Either way, multiprogramming is in your future whether you like it or not. So go play, carefully, and learn.

A GAME OF *TEAPOT WARS!*

You've seen a lot of source code in this book, including everything from resource management to rendering to network code. In the first edition, I tried to give good source examples, and I found out firsthand how hard that was. It was important to me that the code you saw had come directly from, or had been adapted from, a computer game that actually saw real players and some time in the sun. It turned out that those two goals were quite lofty indeed, and the source code in the first edition was like a family reunion on the Jerry Springer Show—nobody got along, and it was generally pretty ugly all around!

With the second edition, I decided to create a little game using the code you've seen so far in this book. Not being a great artist, I used the DirectX teapot mesh as my main characters in the game, and lo and behold *Teapot Wars* was born! A screen for the game is shown in Figure 19.1.

Teapot Wars is a game where teapots battle each other to the death utilizing their fearsome spout cannon. This game features the use of advanced physics, networked multiplayer, AI, and everything else you've learned. This is a simple game, but in this simplicity is hidden nearly all of the code you've seen in this book. It ties together the architecture I've been pushing; it uses the application layer, the game logic, and game views as a basis for the game and ties them

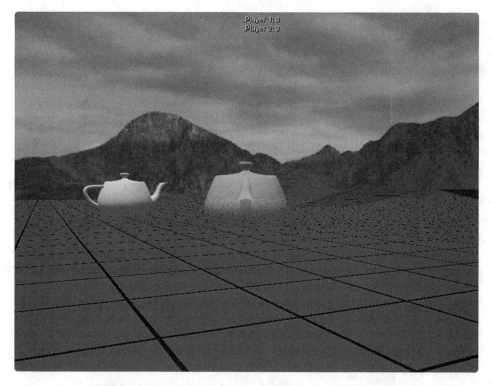

FIGURE 19.1 *Teapot Wars*—the next AAA game on the Xbox 360!

together with the event system. The game even works as a multiplayer game over the Internet, believe it or not. Some of the new things you're going to see are how to create and manage game actors, and how to extend the basic logic and human view classes into game-specific classes.

The teapot has an interesting history. You might wonder why you see it virtually everywhere. DirectX even has a built-in function to create one. I did a little research on the Internet and found this explanation:

> "Aside from that, people have pointed out that it is a useful object to test with. It's instantly recognizable, it has complex topology, it self-shadows, there are hidden surface issues, it has both convex and concave surfaces, as well as 'saddle points.' It doesn't take much storage space—it's rumored that some of the early pioneers of computer graphics could type in the teapot from memory," quoted directly from http://sjbaker.org/teapot.

Some 3D graphics professionals have even given this shape a special name—the "teapotahedron." It turns out that the original teapot that has come to be the official symbol of SIGGRAPH now lies in the Ephemera Collection of the Computer History Museum in Mountain View, California. Someday, I should make a pilgrimage. These lovely teapots, in a way, are the founding shapes of the 3D graphics industry, and therefore the computer game industry.

It's quite fitting that we make them the heroes of our game.

GAME ACTORS

Game actors are objects in your game, and they can be either static or dynamic. Games need ways to define and create actors, and they usually have some common properties like position, type, color, and a unique ID. Different types of actors will inherit from the common data and extend it, perhaps adding things like color or what player is controlling them.

Since actors are common to both the game logic and the game view, you can bet that when the game sends a new actor event, it will contain all the parameters necessary for the game logic, game view, or any other subsystem to handle the "new actor" event in its own way.

Most games have different actor types, and *Teapot Wars* is no exception. Actor types are meant to be broad categories that have identical property types and are managed by the game's logic and view classes in a similar way. In *Teapot Wars*, there are four main types of actors: the ubiquitous teapotahedron for the player, teapots for the AI agents, a sphere that serves as a projectile, and a grid actor that serves as a surface for teapots to roam on or bump against. These are defined in a simple enum of actor types:

```
enum ActorType { AT_Unknown, AT_Sphere, AT_Teapot, AT_Grid };
```

enum ActorType MIGHT BE A DUMB IDEA

By the way, `ActorType` should probably be a string or stringhash, like you saw in the event subsystem. Left as an `enum`, any new actor classes that get created in the future would require the coder to touch this base class and update enumerations, and cause the entire universe to recompile. A simple `enum` was fine for this simple example, but you'll want to do something more robust in your game.

Every actor object in the game inherits from the `IActor` interface:

```
class IActor
{
    friend class IGame;
public:
    virtual ~IActor() { }

    virtual Mat4x4 const &VGetMat()=0;
    virtual void VSetMat(const Mat4x4 &newMat)=0;

    virtual ActorId VGetID()=0;
    virtual void VSetID(ActorId id)=0;

    virtual const int VGetType()=0;
    virtual shared_ptr<ActorParams> VGetParams()=0;

    virtual bool VIsPhysical()=0;
    virtual bool VIsGeometrical()=0;
    virtual void VOnUpdate(int deltaMilliseconds)=0;
    virtual void VRotateY(float angleRadians) = 0;
};
```

This class defines the most basic capabilities of a game actor. A commercial game would likely define a few more operations—it would be completely dependent on what kinds of things your game actors could do. Add to the `IActor` class frugally. Here's my implementation of the `IActor` interface:

```
class BaseActor : public IActor
{
    friend class BaseGameLogic;
```

```
protected:
   ActorId m_id;
   Mat4x4 m_Mat;
   int m_Type;
   shared_ptr<ActorParams> m_Params;

   virtual void VSetID(ActorId id) { m_id = id; }
   virtual void VSetMat(const Mat4x4 &newMat) { m_Mat = newMat; }

public:
   BaseActor(Mat4x4 mat, int type, shared_ptr<ActorParams> params)
      { m_Mat=mat; m_Type=type; m_Params=params; }

   virtual Mat4x4 const &VGetMat()            { return m_Mat; }
   virtual const int VGetType()               { return m_Type; }
   virtual ActorId VGetID()                   { return m_id; }
   virtual shared_ptr<ActorParams> VGetParams() { return m_Params; }
   virtual bool VIsPhysical()                 { return true; }
   virtual bool VIsGeometrical()              { return true; }
   virtual void VOnUpdate(int deltaMilliseconds) { }
};
```

The `BaseActor` class is pretty simple. It contains various get and set methods that the game logic will use to manipulate actors in the game world. The `BaseActor` class is so simple, that you might wonder how it is useful at all. By itself, it isn't that useful. The really useful class is the `ActorParams` class.

The `ActorParams` Class

Since actors can be saved onto disk or streamed across a network, it is a good design to create a general purpose parameter class that all actors can use to manage their parameters. These parameters are the core of how most games manage different kinds of actors in their game world.

```
struct ActorParams
{
   int m_Size;
   optional<ActorId> m_Id;
   Vec3 m_Pos;
   ActorType m_Type;
   Color m_Color;
```

```
// Lua functions to call for actors upon creation or destruction.
static const int sk_MaxFuncName = 64;
char m_OnCreateLuaFunctionName[ sk_MaxFuncName ];
char m_OnDestroyLuaFunctionName[ sk_MaxFuncName ];

ActorParams();

virtual ~ActorParams() { }

virtual bool VInit(std::istrstream &in);
virtual void VSerialize(std::ostrstream &out) const;

typedef std::deque< std::string > TErrorMessageList;
virtual bool VInit(
LuaObject srcData, TErrorMessageList & errorMessages );
static ActorParams *CreateFromStream(std::istrstream &in);
static ActorParams *CreateFromLuaObj( LuaObject srcData );

virtual shared_ptr<IActor> VCreate(BaseGameLogic *logic)
     { shared_ptr<IActor> p; return p; }
virtual shared_ptr<SceneNode> VCreateSceneNode(shared_ptr<Scene> pScene)
     { shared_ptr<SceneNode> p; return p; }
};
```

The ActorParams class is meant to be a base class. New actor types inherit from it and define specialized parameters and virtual methods. The m_Size member holds the size of the structure, and helps with streaming since child classes will add new parameter members and increase the size. Other members include an actor ID, the actor's position in the world, its type, and finally color.

The next two members hold the name of a Lua function to run when actors are created or destroyed, which can be especially useful if you want to push some game-specific actor code out of the engine and into a Lua script.

The next two methods, VInit() and VSerialize(), allow actors to be streamed:

```
bool ActorParams::VInit(std::istrstream &in)
{
   int hasActorId = 0;

   in >> m_Size;
   in >> hasActorId;
   if (hasActorId)
   {
      in >> hasActorId;
      m_Id = hasActorId;
   }
```

```
   in >> m_Pos.x >> m_Pos.y >> m_Pos.z;
   in >> m_Color.r >> m_Color.g >> m_Color.b >> m_Color.a;
   in >> m_OnCreateLuaFunctionName;
   in >> m_OnDestroyLuaFunctionName;
   return true;
}


void ActorParams::VSerialize(std::ostrstream &out) const
{
   out << m_Type << " ";
   out << m_Size << " ";
   out << static_cast<int>(m_Id.valid()) << " ";
   if (m_Id.valid())
   {
      out << *m_Id << " ";
   }
   out << m_Pos.x << " " << m_Pos.y << " " << m_Pos.z << " ";
   out << m_Color.r << " " << m_Color.g << " "
   << m_Color.b << " " << m_Color.a << " ";
   out << m_OnCreateLuaFunctionName << " ";
   out << m_OnDestroyLuaFunctionName << " ";
}
```

Streaming is useful if you want to save the actor parameters, either on disk or send them over a network. In fact, this is exactly how new actors are marshalled from a server to a client, as you learned in Chapter 16, "Network Programming for Multiplayer Games."

The next three methods create an interface between actor parameters and Lua:

```
bool ActorParams::VInit( LuaObject srcData, TErrorMessageList & errorMessages )
{
   LuaObject actorIDObj = srcData[ "ActorID" ];
   if ( actorIDObj.IsInteger() )
   {
      m_Id = actorIDObj.GetInteger();
   }

   LuaObject posObj = srcData[ "Pos" ];
   if ( posObj.IsTable() )
   {
      const int tableCount = posObj.GetTableCount();
      if ( 3 != tableCount )
      {
```

```
          const std::string err(
             "Incorrect number of parameters in the 'Pos' member." );
          errorMessages.push_back( err );
          return false;
       }
       else
       {
          //Get the three values.
          m_Pos.x = posObj[ 1 ].GetFloat();
          m_Pos.y = posObj[ 2 ].GetFloat();
          m_Pos.z = posObj[ 3 ].GetFloat();
       }
    }

    LuaObject colorObj = srcData[ "Color" ];
    if ( colorObj.IsTable() )
    {
       //Get the RGBA off of it.
       LuaObject r = colorObj[ "R" ];
       if ( r.IsNumber() )
       {
          m_Color.r = r.GetFloat();
       }
       LuaObject g = colorObj[ "G" ];
       if ( g.IsNumber() )
       {
          m_Color.g = g.GetFloat();
       }
       LuaObject b = colorObj[ "B" ];
       if ( b.IsNumber() )
       {
          m_Color.b = b.GetFloat();
       }
       LuaObject a = colorObj[ "A" ];
       if ( a.IsNumber() )
       {
          m_Color.a = a.GetFloat();
       }
    }

    //See if we have any on create/destroy handlers.
    LuaObject onCreateObj = srcData[ "OnCreateFunc" ];
    if ( onCreateObj.IsString() )
    {
```

```
        const char * pString = onCreateObj.GetString();
        strcpy_s( m_OnCreateLuaFunctionName,
            sk_MaxFuncName, onCreateObj.GetString() );
    }
    LuaObject onDestroyObj = srcData[ "OnDestroyFunc" ];
    if ( onDestroyObj.IsString() )
    {
        strcpy_s( m_OnDestroyLuaFunctionName,
            sk_MaxFuncName, onDestroyObj.GetString() );
    }

    return true;
}
```

VInit() is used to create an ActorParams object from a Lua object, such as you might define in a Lua script, to create a long list of actors. In this engine, Lua is used not only as a scripting language, but also as a game world definition system. The *Teapot Wars* editor, as you will see in the next chapter, saves your work in a Lua file. When this Lua file is loaded by the game, it re-creates ActorParams objects using VInit().

The two static functions are helpers that encode two different ways: Actor-Params objects can be created from Lua—either a clear text stream formatted with Lua syntax or directly from a LuaObject:

```
ActorParams *ActorParams::CreateFromStream(std::istrstream &in)
{
    int actorType;
    in >> actorType;

    ActorParams *actor = NULL;
    switch (actorType)
    {
        case AT_Sphere:
            actor = GCC_NEW SphereParams;
            break;

        case AT_Teapot:
            actor = GCC_NEW TeapotParams;
            break;

        case AT_Grid:
            actor = GCC_NEW GridParams;
            break;
```

```
        default:
            assert(0 && _T("Unimplemented actor type in stream"));
            return 0;
    }

    if (! actor->VInit(in))
    {
        // something went wrong with the serialization...
        assert(0 && _T("Error in Actor stream initialization"));
        SAFE_DELETE(actor);
    }

    return actor;

}

ActorParams * ActorParams::CreateFromLuaObj( LuaObject srcData )
{
    //Make sure this is legit.
    if ( false == srcData.IsTable() )
    {
        assert( 0 && "No table was passed with actor params!" );
        return NULL;
    }

    //Find out the actor type.
    LuaObject actorTypeObj = srcData[ "ActorType" ];
    if ( false == actorTypeObj.IsString() )
    {
        assert( 0 && "Member 'ActorType' wasn't found!" );
        return NULL;
    }

    // OK, we've got a string.
    // Match it up with the appropriate constructor to build the data.
    const char * pActorType = actorTypeObj.GetString();
    ActorParams * pActorParams = NULL;
    if ( 0 == stricmp( pActorType, "sphere" ) )
    {
        pActorParams = GCC_NEW SphereParams();
    }
    else if ( 0 == stricmp( pActorType, "teapot" ) )
    {
        pActorParams = GCC_NEW TeapotParams();
    }
```

```
else if ( 0 == stricmp( pActorType, "grid" ) )
{
    pActorParams = GCC_NEW GridParams();
}
else
{
    assert( 0 && "Unknown/unsupported member in 'ActorType' encountered!" );
    return NULL;
}

if ( NULL != pActorParams )
{
    TErrorMessageList errorMessages;
    if ( false == pActorParams->VInit( srcData, errorMessages ) )
    {
        assert( 0 && "Error in actor parameter creation from script!" );
        SAFE_DELETE( pActorParams );
    }
}

return pActorParams;
}
```

Both static methods require you to do a little bit of ugly wiring to get the full benefit of linking Lua scripts with your actor system, but it is worth it. If you create totally new actor types, such as a SkeletalActor or a ClothActor, you would add them to these methods only if you wanted a tight integration with Lua scripts. It's totally up to you.

The last two methods of the ActorParams class are used by the game logic and game view to create their representations of the actor. The game logic calls VCreate(), which creates an object that implements the IActor interface, something you will see shortly. The game view calls VCreateSceneNode(), which implements the ISceneNode interface that you learned back in Chapter 14, "3D Scenes." You'll see a concrete example of both with the TeapotParams class.

TALES FROM THE PIXEL MINES

ACTOR PARAMETERS ON *THIEF: DEADLY SHADOWS*

Thief: Deadly Shadows had a pretty amazing and extensible actor parameter system. It was hierarchical in nature, and allowed multiple actors to share the same parameter set or break off and have their own copy. This was all managed at run-time, and while the designers really loved it, it was hard to tell if the complexity of the system really paid off in something players noticed.

TeapotParams and TeapotMeshNode Classes

Now that you've seen the ActorParams class, take a look at the TeapotParams class:

```
struct TeapotParams : public ActorParams
{
   float m_Length;
   GameViewId m_ViewId;
   Mat4x4 m_Mat;

   TeapotParams();

   virtual bool VInit(std::istrstream &in);
   virtual bool VInit(
   LuaObject srcData, TErrorMessageList & errorMessages );
   virtual void VSerialize(std::ostrstream &out) const;
   virtual shared_ptr<IActor> VCreate(BaseGameLogic *logic);
   virtual shared_ptr<SceneNode> VCreateSceneNode(shared_ptr<Scene> pScene);
};
```

This class adds the physical length of the teapot, a view ID, and a transform matrix to the basic ActorParams class. Take a look at the constructor:

```
TeapotParams::TeapotParams()
  : ActorParams()
{
   m_Type=AT_Teapot;
   m_Length=1.0f;
   m_ViewId = VIEWID_NO_VIEW_ATTACHED;
   m_Mat=Mat4x4::g_Identity;
   m_Size=sizeof(TeapotParams);
}
```

The constructor sets the type to AT_Teapot and its game world length to 1.0 units. Since teapots are agents that will be controlled by either a human player or an AI, it also holds a view ID that is currently set to a default value. Finally, the transform matrix is intialized to a reasonable value and the m_Size member is set to the size of the TeapotParams class. If you create your own extension of the Actor-Params class, you'll want to write a similar constructor, taking special care to set the m_Size and m_Type member properly.

The stream based VInit() and VSerialize() methods look exactly as you would expect:

```
bool TeapotParams::VInit(std::istrstream &in)
{
   if (ActorParams::VInit(in))
   {
      m_Type=AT_Teapot;
      in >> m_Length;
      in >> m_ViewId;
      for (int i=0; i<4; ++i)
         for (int j=0; j<4; ++j)
            in >> m_Mat.m[i][j];

      return true;
   }
   return false;
}

void TeapotParams::VSerialize(std::ostrstream &out) const
{
   ActorParams::VSerialize(out);
   out << m_Length << " ";
   out << m_ViewId;
   for (int i=0; i<4; ++i)
      for (int j=0; j<4; ++j)
         out << m_Mat.m[i][j] << " ";
}
```

CLEAR TEXT IS USEFUL, BUT NOT ALWAYS

The previous streaming code uses std::istrstream *and* std::ostrstream *from STL. This is fine for a game engine on training wheels like* Game Coding Complete, *but you'll want to ditch this for a high-powered, efficient binary stream. With luck, this mythical stream class will have an option to switch from binary to clear text, especially if you need to debug a heinous network or load/save problem.*

Next up is the VInit() method that can load our TeapotParams object from Lua:

```
bool TeapotParams::VInit(
   LuaObject srcData, TErrorMessageList & errorMessages )
{
   if ( false == ActorParams::VInit( srcData, errorMessages ) )
   {
      return false;
   }
```

```
m_Type = AT_Teapot;

LuaObject lengthObj = srcData[ "Length" ];
if ( lengthObj.IsNumber() )
{
   m_Length = lengthObj.GetFloat();
}

m_Mat = Mat4x4::g_Identity;

LuaObject matObj = srcData[ "Mat" ];
if ( matObj.IsTable() )
{
   const int tableCount = matObj.GetTableCount();
   if ( 16 != tableCount )
   {
      const std::string err( "Incorrect number of parameters in 'Mat'" );
      errorMessages.push_back( err );
      return false;
   }
   else
   {
      char name[4] = "_00";

      for( int i = 1; i <= 4; ++i )
      {
         name[1] = '0' + i;

         for( int j = 1; j <= 4; ++j )
         {
            name[2] = '0' + j;

            LuaObject entry = matObj[ name ];
            if( entry.IsNumber() )
            {
                m_Mat.m[i - 1][j - 1] = entry.GetFloat();
            }
         }
      }
   }
}

LuaObject viewIDObj = srcData[ "GameViewID" ];
```

```
if ( viewIDObj.IsInteger() )
{
   m_ViewId = viewIDObj.GetInteger();
}


return true;
}
```

This should look a little familiar to you, assuming you didn't skip Chapter 11, "Scripting with Lua." The srcData object passed in is queried for each and every member the TeapotParams class needs to intialize.

Next, let's looks at the all-important method used by the game logic to actually create an instance of an actor given an object based on ActorParams. Here's the method to create an actual teapot actor:

```
shared_ptr<IActor> TeapotParams::VCreate(BaseGameLogic *logic)
{
   Mat4x4 mat;
   mat = m_Mat;
   shared_ptr<IActor> pTeapot(
   GCC_NEW BaseActor(mat, AT_Teapot,
      shared_ptr<TeapotParams>(GCC_NEW TeapotParams(*this))));
   logic->VAddActor(pTeapot, this);
   logic->VGetGamePhysics()->VAddBox(
Vec3(m_Length, m_Length/3, m_Length), &*pTeapot,
   SpecificGravity(PhysDens_Water)*.8f, PhysMat_Normal);
   return pTeapot;
}
```

The teapot actor is really a BaseActor class, created with its own copy of the teapot parameters object. Having a separate copy lets you change the color of one teapot without changing them all at the same time, although that might be a cool feature. Once created, the actor is added to the game logic and the physics system.

Finally, here's how the teapot is created for the view:

```
shared_ptr<SceneNode> TeapotParams::VCreateSceneNode(shared_ptr<Scene> pScene)
{
   shared_ptr<SceneNode> teapot(
   GCC_NEW TeapotMeshNode(m_Id, "Teapot", L"GameCode3.fx",
      RenderPass_Actor, &m_Mat, m_Color));
   return teapot;
}
```

The `TeapotMeshNode` class is a simple extension of the `ShaderMeshNode` class you saw in Chapter 14.

```
class TeapotMeshNode : public ShaderMeshNode
{
public:
    TeapotMeshNode(
        const optional<ActorId> actorId,
        std::string name,
        std::wstring fxFileName,
        RenderPass renderPass,
        const Mat4x4 *t,
        const Color &color);
    virtual HRESULT VOnRestore(Scene *pScene);
};

TeapotMeshNode::TeapotMeshNode(
    const optional<ActorId> actorId,
    std::string name,
    std::wstring fxFileName,
    RenderPass renderPass,
    const Mat4x4 *t,
    const Color &color)
: ShaderMeshNode(actorId, name, NULL, fxFileName, renderPass, t, color)
{
    // do nothing
}
```

The only tricky bit is the `VOnRestore()` method. It calls the `D3DXCreateTeapot()` API, but by default, the teapot's spout is pointing off to the side instead of straight ahead. By default, our game's direction vectors are set to

```
Vec3 g_Right(1.0f, 0.0, 0.0f);
Vec3 g_Up(0.0f, 1.0f, 0.0f);
Vec3 g_Forward(0.0f, 0.0f, 1.0f);
```

As you can see, the forward direction is defined as down the positive Z-axis. The DirectX teapots, by default, have their spouts turned down the positive X-axis. The `VOnRestore()` method fixes this problem by locking the vertex buffer and transforming each one 90 degrees about the up vector, or Y-axis. Doing this once for each teapot is much smarter than performing this transformation every time the teapot renders.

```
HRESULT TeapotMeshNode::VOnRestore(Scene *pScene)
{
    HRESULT hr;

    IDirect3DDevice9 * pDevice = DXUTGetD3D9Device();
    V( D3DXCreateTeapot( pDevice, &m_pMesh, NULL ) );

    // Rotate the teapot 90 degrees from default so that the spout faces forward
    Mat4x4 rotateY90 = m_Props.ToWorld();
    rotateY90.SetPosition(Vec3(0.0f, 0.0f, 0.0f));
    IDirect3DVertexBuffer9* pVB = NULL;
    m_pMesh->GetVertexBuffer(&pVB);
    Vec3* pVertices = NULL;
    pVB->Lock( 0, 0, (void**)&pVertices, 0 );
    for (unsigned int i=0; i<m_pMesh->GetNumVertices(); ++i)
    {
        *pVertices = rotateY90.Xform(*pVertices);
        ++pVertices;
        // The structs depicted in this vertex buffer actually store
        // information for normals in addition to xyz, thereby
        // making the vertices in pVB twice the size of the one described
        // by *pVertices.  So we address that here.
        *pVertices = rotateY90.Xform(*pVertices);    //rotate the normals, too
        ++pVertices;
    }
    pVB->Unlock();
    SAFE_RELEASE( pVB );
    //...end rotation

    // Note - the mesh is needed BEFORE calling the base class VOnRestore.
    V ( ShaderMeshNode::VOnRestore ( pScene ) );

    return S_OK;
}
```

Another gotcha in `VOnRestore()` is that the call to the parent class's `VOnRestore()` method happens at the end of the method, rather than the traditional beginning. `ShaderMeshNode::VOnRestore()` assumes that the mesh already exists, so it is up to us to create the mesh before calling it. Had I called `ShaderMeshNode::VOnRestore()` at the beginning of this method, it would have caused a crash because of a NULL mesh.

WHICH WAY IS UP?

The badly oriented teapot mesh implies something very serious about how your artists create their 3D models. One standard sets "up" as the Y-axis and "forward" as the Z-axis. You'll want to communicate this standard clearly to any artist making models for your game. Otherwise, an artist might create a rocket model in the classic pose, standing straight up, ready for launch. This would be wrong. The artist should create it with its body skewered on the Z-axis. When you move it "forward," along its transformed Z-axis in world space, it will do exactly as you expect and look like it is being pushed by the rocket exhaust.

One more nit about model creation: Try to think about convenient origins for each model. For example, an artist might create a model of a door standing straight up, centered on the origin, which would also be wrong. The door should be able to rotate around its hinge without figuring out wacky interim translations. A better approach would have the artist place the door's hinge directly above the origin. When someone opens the door, all that will be needed in the game is a simple rotation about the up vector. This kind of thing can be unintuitive for artists and programmers, and also isn't encouraged by many modeling tools. Most tools like 3D Studio Max tend to model things centered on the origin, and not every object has a natural rotation about its center of mass—a door being the best example.

How About `GridParams` and `SphereParams`?

The code for creating a `GridParams` object and `SphereParams` object is so similar to `TeapotParams` that I'll assign you, my reader, to not only study it in the *Game Coding Complete* source code, but also to create your own special actor type. Doing this "homework" involves nearly all of the systems you've learned in this book, making it an excellent exercise.

GAME EVENTS

You've already seen most of the events that will be fired during a highly addictive session of *Teapot Wars*. When objects collide, for example, the physics system sends a collision event just like the one you saw in Chapter 15, "Collision and Simple Physics." There are three new events that are specific to *Teapot Wars*: `EvtData_Fire_Weapon`, `EvtData_Thrust`, and `EvtData_Steer`:

```
class EvtData_Fire_Weapon : public BaseEventData
```

```
{
public:
   static const EventType sk_EventType;
   virtual const EventType & VGetEventType() const
      { return sk_EventType; }

   explicit EvtData_Fire_Weapon( ActorId id )
      : m_id( id )    {    }

   explicit EvtData_Fire_Weapon( std::istrstream & in )
      { in >> m_id; }

   virtual IEventDataPtr VCopy() const
   {
      return IEventDataPtr ( GCC_NEW EvtData_Fire_Weapon (m_id) );
   }

   virtual ~EvtData_Fire_Weapon() {}

   virtual LuaObject VGetLuaEventData() const
   {
      assert( ( true == m_bHasLuaEventData ) &&
   "Call BulidLuaEventData() first!" );
      return m_LuaEventData;
   }

   virtual void VBuildLuaEventData()
   {
      assert( ( false == m_bHasLuaEventData ) &&
   "Already built lua event data!" );

      // Get the global state.
      LuaState * pState = g_pApp->m_pLuaStateManager->GetGlobalState().Get();
      m_LuaEventData.AssignNewTable( pState );

      // Serialize the data necessary.
      m_LuaEventData.SetInteger( "ActorId", m_id );

      m_bHasLuaEventData = true;
   }

   virtual void VSerialize( std::ostrstream & out ) const
   {
      out << m_id << " ";
   }

   ActorId m_id;
```

```
private:
   LuaObject    m_LuaEventData;
};
```

The "fire weapon" event is pretty similar to what you've seen in other chapters.

Events for thrusting send game commands to move the teapot forward or backward, and steering sends commands to steer left or right. For these kinds of control events, it is common to send control values in terms of a floating-point number from -1.0 to 1.0. For the thruster, 0.0 means no thrust at all; -1.0 means 100% backward; and 1.0 means 100% forward. For the steering, -1.0 means 100% left and 1.0 corresponds to 100% right. It makes it pretty easy to map keyboard commands to these coefficients:

```
struct EvtData_Thrust : public BaseEventData
{
   static const EventType sk_EventType;
   virtual const EventType & VGetEventType( void ) const
   {
      return sk_EventType;
   }

   explicit EvtData_Thrust( ActorId id, float throttle )
      : m_id(id),
        m_throttle(throttle)
   {}

   explicit EvtData_Thrust( std::istrstream & in )
   {
      in >> m_id;
      in >> m_throttle;
   }

   virtual IEventDataPtr VCopy() const
   {
      return IEventDataPtr ( GCC_NEW EvtData_Thrust (m_id, m_throttle) );
   }

   virtual ~EvtData_Thrust()
   {
   }

   ActorId m_id;
   float m_throttle;
```

```
      virtual LuaObject VGetLuaEventData(void) const
      {
         assert( ( true == m_bHasLuaEventData ) &&
            "Can't get lua event data yet - call BulidLuaEventData() first!" );
         return m_LuaEventData;
      }

      virtual void VBuildLuaEventData(void)
      {
         assert( ( false == m_bHasLuaEventData ) &&
            "Already built lua event data!" );

         // Get the global state.
         LuaState * pState = g_pApp->m_pLuaStateManager->GetGlobalState().Get();
         m_LuaEventData.AssignNewTable( pState );

         // Set the appropriate data.
         m_LuaEventData.SetInteger( "ActorId", m_id );
         m_LuaEventData.SetNumber( "Throttle", m_throttle );

         m_bHasLuaEventData = true;
      }

      virtual void VSerialize( std::ostrstream & out ) const
      {
         out << m_id << " ";
         out << m_throttle << " ";
      }

private:
   LuaObject    m_LuaEventData;
};

//////////////////////////////////////////////////////////////////////////////
struct EvtData_Steer : public BaseEventData
{
   static const EventType sk_EventType;
   virtual const EventType & VGetEventType( void ) const
   {
      return sk_EventType;
   }

   explicit EvtData_Steer( ActorId id, float dir)
      : m_id(id),
        m_dir(dir)
   {}
```

```
explicit EvtData_Steer( std::istrstream & in )
{
   in >> m_id;
   in >> m_dir;
}

virtual IEventDataPtr VCopy() const
{
   return IEventDataPtr ( GCC_NEW EvtData_Steer (m_id, m_dir) );
}

virtual ~EvtData_Steer()
{
}

virtual LuaObject VGetLuaEventData(void) const
{
   assert( ( true == m_bHasLuaEventData ) &&
      "Can't get lua event data yet - call BulidLuaEventData() first!" );
   return m_LuaEventData;
}

virtual void VBuildLuaEventData(void)
{
   assert( ( false == m_bHasLuaEventData ) &&
      "Already built lua event data!" );

   // Get the global state.
   LuaState * pState = g_pApp->m_pLuaStateManager->GetGlobalState().Get();
   m_LuaEventData.AssignNewTable( pState );

   // Set appropriate data.
   m_LuaEventData.SetInteger( "ActorId", m_id );
   m_LuaEventData.SetNumber( "Dir", m_dir );

   m_bHasLuaEventData = true;
}

virtual void VSerialize( std::ostrstream & out ) const
{
   out << m_id << " ";
   out << m_dir << " ";
}
```

```
    ActorId m_id;
    float m_dir;      // -1.0 is all the way left, 0 is straight, 1.0 is right

private:
    LuaObject    m_LuaEventData;
};

char const * const Evt_Fire_Weapon::gkName = "fire_weapon";
char const * const Evt_Thrust::gkName = "thrust";
char const * const Evt_Steer::gkName = "steer";
```

NETWORK GAMES SHOULDN'T TRUST CLIENT DATA

While the event data just presented is easy to learn and use, it isn't a good choice for a networked game. Network game clients shouldn't be allowed to set the thrust value for just any actor in the game, and even though there might not be a way in your game client to actually tweak the actor ID illegally, you can bet that someone will hack into your packet data and figure out how to replace that actor ID with something that will let them cheat. Real networking code has many layers of security built into the packet definitions.

THE APPLICATION LAYER

The application layer is the object that holds all the operating system dependent code like initialization, strings, the resource cache, and so on. *Teapot Wars* extends the GameCodeApp class you saw in Chapter 5, "Game Initialization and Shutdown." It adds three methods. The virtual overload of VCreateGameAndView() is responsible for initializing the game logic and any game views. VLoadGame() loads the game from an initial state. GetGame() is an accessor for getting a pointer to the base game logic class:

```
class TeapotWarsGameApp : public GameCodeApp
{
private:
    void RegisterGameSpecificEvents( void );  // Registers game-specific events
                                              // for later usage.

protected:
    virtual BaseGameLogic *VCreateGameAndView();
    virtual bool VLoadGame();
```

```
public:
    TeapotWarsGameApp() : GameCodeApp() { }
    inline TeapotWarsBaseGame const * const GetGame() const
{
    return dynamic_cast<TeapotWarsBaseGame*>(m_pGame);
}

    virtual TCHAR *VGetGameTitle() { return _T("Teapot Wars"); }
    virtual TCHAR *VGetGameAppDirectory()
        { return _T("Game Coding Complete 3.0\\Teapot Wars\\3.0"); }
    virtual HICON VGetIcon();
};

BaseGameLogic *TeapotWarsGameApp::VCreateGameAndView()
{
    BaseGameLogic *game = NULL;
    assert(m_pOptions && _T("The game options object is uninitialized."));

    // Register any game-specific events here.
    RegisterGameSpecificEvents();

    if (m_pOptions->m_gameHost.empty())
    {
        game = GCC_NEW TeapotWarsGame(*m_pOptions);
    }
    else
    {
        game = GCC_NEW TeapotWarsGameProxy(*m_pOptions);

        EventListenerPtr listener ( GCC_NEW NetworkEventForwarder( 0 ) );
        extern void ListenForTeapotGameCommands(EventListenerPtr listener);
        ListenForTeapotGameCommands(listener);

    }

    shared_ptr<IGameView> gameView(GCC_NEW MainMenuView());
    game->VAddView(gameView);

    return game;
}
```

There are two types of possible game logic that can be created here, based on the value of the m_gameHost member of the GameOptions class. Game options are commonly loaded from an initialization file like you saw in Chapter 5, and this one was no exception. If the game is going to be the authoritative server, the game logic class called for is TeapotWarsGame. If the game is a client attaching to a remote server, the `TeapotWarsGameProxy` class is a stand-in for the real game logic on the server. It basically does nothing but convince the game subsystems that a valid game logic is instantiated. You'll see both of them in the next section on game logic.

The method to load the game could actually do something complicated, like search the local directory tree and send messages to the game view so it can present a menu of load games to choose from, or have the player start a new game. We're not going to be nearly that complicated. We'll simply tell the game logic to build a new game through a special text command:

```
bool TeapotWarsGameApp::VLoadGame()
{
    // Ordinarily you'd read the game options and see what the current game
    // needs to be - or perhaps pop up a dialog box and ask which game
    // needed loading. All of the game graphics are initialized by now, too...
    return m_pGame->VLoadGame("NewGame");
}
```

That's all there is to the *Teapot Wars* application layer. The base class `Game-CodeApp` does almost all the work for you.

THE GAME LOGIC

As you saw before, there are two classes for game logic: a smart one and a side-kick. The smart one is the authoritative game logic for any game of *Teapot Wars*, and the dumb one is a stand-in for clients that are playing remotely. They have things in common, including some game data, and these common elements are stored in a base class.

The game data is nothing more than the scores of the players. But wait, you say, where are all the actors managed? Actors are stored and managed in the `BaseGameLogic` class. You can see the `BaseGameLogic` class in its full glory in the companion source code, but some of the more important methods are included and discussed here.

Let's get back to the *Teapot Wars* common game data and logic class:

```
class TeapotWarsGameData
{
public:
    ActorScoreMap m_actorScores;

    const ActorScoreMap &GetActorScores() const { return m_actorScores; }
    void RemoveActor(ActorId id) { m_actorScores.erase(id); }
};
```

```
class TeapotWarsBaseGame : public BaseGameLogic
{
protected:
  TeapotWarsGameData m_data;

public:
  TeapotWarsBaseGame(GameOptions const &options)
    : BaseGameLogic(options)
  { }

  bool VLoadGame(std::string gameName);
  void VRemoveActor(ActorId id);
  void VAddActor(shared_ptr<IActor> actor, ActorParams *p);
  void VSetProxy() { BaseGameLogic::VSetProxy(); }

  // overloadable
  virtual void VRegisterHit(const ActorId sphere, const ActorId teapot) { }

  const TeapotWarsGameData& GetData() const { return m_data; }
};
```

The common game logic for *Teapot Wars* is pretty simple: it is responsible for loading games, adding some actor management tasks to keep the score data up to date, and creating a virtual stub for VRegisterHit(), which the "real" logic will overload.

Three methods that are defined are VLoadGame(), VAddActor(), and VRemoveActor():

```
bool TeapotWarsBaseGame::VLoadGame(std::string gameName)
{
  if (gameName=="NewGame")
  {
    VBuildInitialScene();
    safeTriggerEvent( EvtData_New_Game() );
  }

  return true;
}
```

You probably thought you were going to see a little game loading/creating code, but really all VLoadGame() does is call VBuildInitialScene() and send an event. VBuildInitialScene() is not defined in this class—it depends on child classes to implement it.

Next is VAddActor(), which adds the actor to the BaseGameLogic class, sets actor scores if the actor happens to be a teapot or AI teapot, and manages the calls to Lua scripts that activate when actors are created:

```
void TeapotWarsBaseGame::VAddActor(shared_ptr<IActor> actor, ActorParams *p)
{
    BaseGameLogic::VAddActor(actor, p);
    if (p->m_Type==AT_Teapot && p->m_Id.valid())
    {
        m_data.m_actorScores[*p->m_Id] = 0;
    }

    // Ensure script knows about this actor, too.
    LuaState * pState = g_pApp->m_pLuaStateManager->GetGlobalState().Get();
    LuaObject globalActorTable =
        g_pApp->m_pLuaStateManager->GetGlobalActorTable();
    assert( globalActorTable.IsTable() &&
        "Global actor table is NOT a table!" );

    // The actor ID is the key.
    LuaObject addedActorData = globalActorTable.CreateTable( *p->m_Id );
    addedActorData.SetInteger( "ActorID", *p->m_Id );

    if ( 0 != p->m_OnCreateLuaFunctionname[0] )
    {
      addedActorData.SetString( "OnCreateFunc", p->m_OnCreateLuaFunctionName );
    }
    if ( 0 != p->m_ OnDestroyLuaFunctionName[0] )
    {
      addedActorData.SetString( "OnDestroyFunc", p->m_OnDestroyLuaFunctionName );
    }

    //If this actor has any script-specific functions to call, do so now.
    if ( 0 != strlen( p->m_OnCreateLuaFunctionName ) )
    {
        //First attempt to FIND the function specified.
        LuaObject foundObj = g_pApp->m_pLuaStateManager->
          GetGlobalState()->GetGlobal( p->m_OnCreateLuaFunctionName );
        if ( foundObj.IsNil() )
        {
            assert( 0 && "Unable to find specified OnCreateFunc function!" );
        }
        else
```

```
      {
         // Make sure it actually *IS* a function.
         if ( false == foundObj.IsFunction() )
         {
            assert( 0 && "Specified OnCreateFunc doesn't exist!" );
         }
         else
         {
            // Attempt to call the function.
            LuaFunction< void > onCreateFunc( foundObj );
            // Pass in the actor ID and this actor's user-owned data table.
            onCreateFunc( *p->m_Id, addedActorData );
         }
      }
   }
}
}
```

Notice the first few lines of Lua interface code? The Lua state manager and the actor table are accessed, which are needed to grab the Lua actor data for this actor instance. If there is an "on create" Lua method defined for this actor, it is called.

Besides being in reverse order from VAddActor(), VRemoveActor() is almost identical, so to save a little paper I'll ask you to find it in the *Game Coding Complete* source code.

The TeapotWarsBaseGame class is meant to serve as a base class for one of two implementations: an authoritative server and a proxy. The proxy is something that would exist on a remote client machine attached to a game server over the Internet.

The `TeapotWarsGame` Class

Now you're ready to see the real *Teapot Wars* game logic class, TeapotWarsGame. This is the authoritative server, and it makes all the decisions regarding changes to the game world. If a teapot dies, this class swings the ax:

```
class TeapotWarsGame : public TeapotWarsBaseGame
{
   friend class TeapotWarsEventListener;

protected:
   float m_Lifetime;    //indicates how long this game has been in session
   Vec3 m_StartPosition;
   int m_HumanPlayersAttached;
   int m_AIPlayersAttached;
   EventListenerPtr m_teapotWarsEventListener;
```

```
public:
    TeapotWarsGame(struct GameOptions const &options);

    ~TeapotWarsGame();

    // TeapotWars Methods

    // Update
    virtual void VOnUpdate(float time, float elapsedTime);
    virtual void VSetProxy();

    // Overloads
    virtual void VRegisterHit(const ActorId sphere, const ActorId teapot);
    virtual void VBuildInitialScene();
    virtual void VChangeState(BaseGameState newState);
    virtual void VAddView(
        shared_ptr<IGameView> pView, optional<ActorId> actor=optional_empty());
    virtual shared_ptr<IGamePhysics> VGetGamePhysics(void)
        { return m_pPhysics; }

    // set/clear render diagnostics
    void ToggleRenderDiagnostics() { m_RenderDiagnostics = !m_RenderDiagnostics; }

private:
    //Allows access for script calls.
    LuaObject m_MetaTable;

    //Script accessible functions.
    void SetCameraOffset( LuaObject gameViewIndex, LuaObject offsetTable );
};
```

This class has members to track the lifetime of the game, what players or AI agents are attached, the next teapot starting position, and a member to listen for events. Here's the constructor for the TeapotWarsGame class:

```
TeapotWarsGame::TeapotWarsGame(GameOptions const &options)
    : TeapotWarsBaseGame(options)
    , m_Lifetime(0)
    , m_StartPosition(6.0f, 1.5f, 3.0f)
    , m_HumanPlayersAttached(0)
    , m_AIPlayersAttached(0)
{
    m_pPhysics.reset(CreateGamePhysics());
```

```
m_teapotWarsEventListener = shared_ptr<TeapotWarsEventListener>
    (GCC_NEW TeapotWarsEventListener ( this ) );
safeAddListener(m_teapotWarsEventListener,
    EvtData_Remote_Client::sk_EventType);
safeAddListener( m_teapotWarsEventListener,
    EvtData_PhysCollision::sk_EventType );
safeAddListener( m_teapotWarsEventListener,
    EvtData_New_Actor::sk_EventType );
safeAddListener( m_teapotWarsEventListener,
    EvtData_Destroy_Actor::sk_EventType );
safeAddListener( m_teapotWarsEventListener,
    EvtData_Move_Actor::sk_EventType );
safeAddListener( m_teapotWarsEventListener,
    EvtData_Request_New_Actor::sk_EventType );
safeAddListener( m_teapotWarsEventListener,
    EvtData_Request_Start_Game::sk_EventType );
safeAddListener( m_teapotWarsEventListener,
    EvtData_Network_Player_Actor_Assignment::sk_EventType );
safeAddListener( m_teapotWarsEventListener,
    EvtData_UpdateActorParams::sk_EventType );

extern void ListenForTeapotGameCommands(EventListenerPtr listener);
ListenForTeapotGameCommands(m_teapotWarsEventListener);

// Open up access to script.
{
    // Create our metatable...
    m_MetaTable = g_pApp->m_pLuaStateManager->
        GetGlobalState()->GetGlobals().CreateTable("TeapotWarsGame");
    m_MetaTable.SetObject("__index", m_MetaTable);

    m_MetaTable.RegisterObjectDirect( "SetCameraOffset",
        (TeapotWarsGame *)0, &TeapotWarsGame::SetCameraOffset);
    LuaObject luaStateManObj = g_pApp->m_pLuaStateManager->
        GetGlobalState()->BoxPointer(this);
    luaStateManObj.SetMetaTable(m_MetaTable);
    g_pApp->m_pLuaStateManager->GetGlobalState()->
        GetGlobals().SetObject("TeapotWarsGame", luaStateManObj);
}
}
```

Besides initializing the member variables and the physics system, the game logic registers to receive game events. The last few lines open access to Lua script, creating the right tables and objects for Lua to be wired into our game logic.

VOnUpdate() is the method that is called once per game loop, and may be called at a different rate than the screen is rendered, depending on the speed of the renderer and the logic:

```
void TeapotWarsGame::VOnUpdate(float time, float elapsedTime)
{
    int deltaMilliseconds = int(elapsedTime * 1000.0f);
    m_Lifetime += elapsedTime;

    BaseGameLogic::VOnUpdate(time, elapsedTime);

    if (m_bProxy)
        return;

    switch(m_State)
    {
    case BGS_LoadingGameEnvironment:
        break;

    case BGS_MainMenu:
        break;

    case BGS_WaitingForPlayers:
        if (m_ExpectedPlayers + m_ExpectedRemotePlayers ==
            m_HumanPlayersAttached )
        {
            VChangeState(BGS_LoadingGameEnvironment);
        }
        break;

    case BGS_SpawnAI:
        // five seconds to wait for a human opponent
        if(g_pApp->m_pOptions->m_numAIs && m_Lifetime>5)
        {
            for (int i=0; i<g_pApp->m_pOptions->m_numAIs; ++i)
            {
                shared_ptr<IGameView> gameView(
                    GCC_NEW AITeapotView(m_pPathingGraph));
                VAddView(gameView);
                m_Lifetime = 0;
            }
            VChangeState(BGS_Running);
        }
        break;
```

```
    case BGS_Running:
        break;

    default:
        assert(0 && _T("Unrecognized state."));
    }

    // look in Chapter 15, page 563 for more on this bit of code
    if(m_pPhysics)
    {
        m_pPhysics->VOnUpdate(elapsedTime);
        m_pPhysics->VSyncVisibleScene();
    }
}
```

VOnUpdate() does a few other jobs besides calling the base class's update method. The first is to detect if the game logic is acting as a proxy—if so, the meaty parts of the logic are short-circuited. The rest of the method works as a simple state machine with the following states:

```
enum BaseGameState
{
    BGS_Initializing,               // resource check and systems initialization
    BGS_LoadingGameEnvironment,     // loading the game environment
    BGS_MainMenu,                   // present the main menu
    BGS_WaitingForPlayers,          // wait for all human players to join
    BGS_SpawnAI,                    // spawn AI
    BGS_Running                     // run the game!
};
```

The states follow one after the other, and are controlled by the game logic class. The game view classes respond to the game states, such as when they need to show a main menu or display messages that the game is starting.

When the game state is set to BGS_SpawnAI, a timer detects when five seconds have passed before creating the AI views. It's a good idea to give the human players a moment to get their bearings. The AI teapots are, as you will shortly see, so smart they can nearly predict the future. I'm joking, of course.

Now that you've been introduced to the game logic's state machine, take a look at the VChangeState() methods for both the BaseGameLogic class and the TeapotWarsGame class:

```
void BaseGameLogic::VChangeState(BaseGameState newState)
{
    if (newState==BGS_WaitingForPlayers)
    {
```

```
      // Note: Split screen support would require this to change!
      m_ExpectedPlayers = 1;
      m_ExpectedRemotePlayers = g_pApp->m_pOptions->m_expectedPlayers - 1;
      m_ExpectedAI = g_pApp->m_pOptions->m_numAIs;

      if (!g_pApp->m_pOptions->m_gameHost.empty())
      {
         // REMOTE CLIENT!
         VSetProxy();
         m_ExpectedAI = 0;                  // the server will create these
         m_ExpectedRemotePlayers = 0;    // the server will create these
         ClientSocketManager *pClient = GCC_NEW ClientSocketManager(
            g_pApp->m_pOptions->m_gameHost,
            g_pApp->m_pOptions->m_listenPort);
         if (!pClient->Connect())
         {
            VChangeState(BGS_MainMenu);
            return;
         }
         g_pApp->m_pBaseSocketManager = pClient;
      }
      else if (m_ExpectedRemotePlayers > 0)
      {
         // WE ARE CREATING A SERVER!
         BaseSocketManager *pServer = GCC_NEW BaseSocketManager();
         if (!pServer->Init())
         {
            // TODO: Throw up a main menu
            VChangeState(BGS_MainMenu);
            return;
         }

         pServer->AddSocket(GCC_NEW
            GameServerListenSocket(g_pApp->m_pOptions->m_listenPort));
         g_pApp->m_pBaseSocketManager = pServer;
      }
   }

   m_State = newState;
   if (!m_bProxy)
   {
      safeQueEvent( IEventDataPtr(GCC_NEW EvtData_Game_State(m_State)) );
   }
}
```

The `BaseGameLogic` state machine handles some core aspects of the `BGS_Waiting-ForPlayers` state, namely the network connection for multiplayer games. Some method, such as a menu interface or simple game options file, will set the game host before the `BGS_WaitingForPlayers` state is entered. If the game is a remote client, the logic is set to a proxy logic by setting the `m_bProxy` member of the `BaseGameLogic` class to true. After that point, most of the game logic is short-circuited, and the game events will simply come in from the remote server. If the game is an authoritative server expecting remote players, a `GameServerListenSocket` is created. This class was covered in Chapter 16. Finally, an event is sent telling other game subsystems that the state has changed.

The grandchild of `BaseGameLogic`, `TeapotWarsGame`, also has a `VChangeState()` method:

```
void TeapotWarsGame::VChangeState(BaseGameState newState)
{
    TeapotWarsBaseGame::VChangeState(newState);

    switch(newState)
    {
    case BGS_WaitingForPlayers:
        if (m_bProxy)
            break;

        for (int i=0; i<m_ExpectedPlayers; i++)
        {
            shared_ptr<IGameView> playersView(GCC_NEW TeapotWarsGameView());
            VAddView(playersView);

            TeapotParams tp;
            tp.m_Mat = Mat4x4::g_Identity;
            tp.m_Mat.BuildRotationY(-D3DX_PI / 2.0f);
            tp.m_Mat.SetPosition(m_StartPosition);
            tp.m_Length = 2.5;
            tp.m_ViewId = playersView->VGetId();
            tp.m_Color = g_Green;
            const EvtData_Request_New_Actor requestActor( &tp );
            safeTriggerEvent( requestActor );
            m_StartPosition += Vec3(8, 0, 8);
        }

        for (int i=0; i<m_ExpectedRemotePlayers; i++)
        {
            TeapotParams tp;
            tp.m_Mat = Mat4x4::g_Identity;
            tp.m_Mat.BuildRotationY(-D3DX_PI / 2.0f);
```

```
        tp.m_Mat.SetPosition(m_StartPosition);
        tp.m_Length = 2.5;
        tp.m_ViewId = VIEWID_NO_VIEW_ATTACHED;
        tp.m_Color = g_Red;
        const EvtData_Request_New_Actor requestActor( &tp );
        safeTriggerEvent( requestActor );
        m_StartPosition += Vec3(8, 0, 8);
    }

    for (int i=0; i<m_ExpectedAI; i++)
    {
        shared_ptr<IGameView> aiView(GCC_NEW AITeapotView(m_pPathingGraph));
        VAddView(aiView);

        TeapotParams tp;
        tp.m_Mat = Mat4x4::g_Identity;
        tp.m_Mat.BuildRotationY(-D3DX_PI / 2.0f);
        tp.m_Mat.SetPosition(m_StartPosition);
        tp.m_Length = 2.5;
        tp.m_ViewId = aiView->VGetId();
        tp.m_Color = g_Yellow;
        const EvtData_Request_New_Actor requestActor( &tp );
        safeTriggerEvent( requestActor );
        m_StartPosition += Vec3(8, 0, 8);
    }

    break;
    }
}
```

VChangeState() will wait for the game state to be set to BGS_WaitingForPlayers, then look at the members for m_ExpectedPlayers, m_ExpectedRemotePlayers, and m_ExpectedAI and create the correct views for each. The code will send "request new actor" events, and each teapot will get matched with a view. A normal human player gets a green teapot. The network player gets a red one, and the AI gets a yellow one. Each time the starting position gets moved so the teapots aren't sitting on top of one another.

There are two more methods for the TeapotWarsGame class. The first adds new views of various flavors to logic:

```
void TeapotWarsGame::VAddView(
    shared_ptr<IGameView> pView, optional<ActorId> actor)
{
    TeapotWarsBaseGame::VAddView(pView, actor);
```

```
if (boost::dynamic_pointer_cast<NetworkGameView>(pView))
{
   m_HumanPlayersAttached++;
}
else if (boost::dynamic_pointer_cast<TeapotWarsGameView>(pView))
{
   m_HumanPlayersAttached++;
}
else if (boost::dynamic_pointer_cast<AITeapotView>(pView))
{
   m_AIPlayersAttached++;
}
}
```

Besides calling the base class method, all this does is track the counters for the different number of views attached. Notice that this is one of the methods that isn't short-circuited by the m_bProxy member, since views are always added by authoritative methods and are therefore legal to do whether the logic is in proxy mode or not.

The last method of the game logic for *Teapot Wars* is VRegisterHit(), which is called when an accurate teapot lands a blue sphere of doom on one of its brethren:

```
void TeapotWarsGame::VRegisterHit(const ActorId sphere, const ActorId teapot)
{
   if (m_bProxy)
      return;

   //Make the teapot dizzy if it hits

   const float hitForce = 80.f;

   m_pPhysics->VApplyTorque(Vec3(0,1,0), hitForce, teapot);

   //everyone else gets a point, hahaha
   for( ActorScoreMap::iterator i=m_data.m_actorScores.begin()
      ;i!=GetData().GetActorScores().end(); ++i )
   {
      if( i->first!=teapot )
      {
         ++(i->second);
      }
   }

   VRemoveActor(sphere);
}
```

The game logic does two things when a teapot gets hit with a sphere. First, it tells the physics system to spin the thing about the Y-axis like there's no tomorrow. A dizzying effect, if you happen to be the one that gets hit. Second, the scoreboard is updated. In *Teapot Wars*, everyone but the damaged teapot gets a point. If you wanted to be a little greedier, it would require a little more data on the sphere actor. If extra data were stored with the sphere that contained the actor ID of the teapot that shot it, it would be trivial to give the shooting teapot the points it so gallantly earned.

The `TeapotWarsEventListener` Class

The real meat of the *Teapot Wars* game is in the event listener class. There's still a lot more logic code to run through, and that code belongs to the `TeapotWarsEventListener`. Since the `HandleEvent()` method is so long, I'll show how each event is handled one at a time rather than list the entire method in one chunk:

The first event is the "request start game" event:

```
if ( EvtData_Request_Start_Game::sk_EventType == event.VGetEventType() )
{
    m_TeapotWars->VChangeState(BGS_WaitingForPlayers);
}
```

The response to this event is simply to change state to `BGS_WaitingForPlayers`. You might do other things in extensions to the game, such as check a player's account balance or something that would gate the beginning of a game.

Here's how the game logic reponds to the "remote client" event, which is sent when a remote player attaches to the game logic:

```
else if ( EvtData_Remote_Client::sk_EventType == event.VGetEventType() )
{
    // This event is always sent from clients to the game server.
    const EvtData_Remote_Client & castEvent =
        static_cast< const EvtData_Remote_Client & >( event );
    const int sockID = castEvent.m_socketId;
    const int ipAddress = castEvent.m_ipAddress;

    // The teapot has already been created - we need to go find it.
    ActorMap::iterator i = m_TeapotWars->m_ActorList.begin();
    ActorMap::iterator end = m_TeapotWars->m_ActorList.end();
    shared_ptr<IActor> actor = shared_ptr<BaseActor>();
    while (i != end)
    {
        actor = (*i).second;
```

```
        if (actor->VGetType() == AT_Teapot)
        {
            shared_ptr<ActorParams> params = actor->VGetParams();
            shared_ptr<TeapotParams> teapotParams =
                boost::static_pointer_cast<TeapotParams>(params);
            if (teapotParams->m_ViewId == VIEWID_NO_VIEW_ATTACHED)
            {
                break;
            }
        }
        ++i;
    }

    if (actor != shared_ptr<BaseActor>())
    {
        NetworkGameView *netGameView = GCC_NEW NetworkGameView( sockID );

        shared_ptr<IGameView> gameView(netGameView);
        m_TeapotWars->VAddView(gameView, actor->VGetID());

        extern void ListenForTeapotViewEvents(EventListenerPtr listener);

        EventListenerPtr listener ( GCC_NEW NetworkEventForwarder( sockID ) );
        ListenForTeapotViewEvents( listener );
    }
}
```

The code searches the actor lists for an `AT_Teapot` that doesn't have a view attached to it. Once found, a `NetworkGameView` is created and wired to listen for events sent to teapot view classes.

The other side of this equation is when a remote player gets an actor ID assignment. This message is sent by the `NetworkGameView::VOnAttach()` method, which is marshalled from the server across the network to the client:

```
else if ( EvtData_Network_Player_Actor_Assignment::sk_EventType ==
    event.VGetEventType() )
{
    // we're a remote client getting an actor assignment.
    // the server assigned us a playerId when we first attached
    // (the server's socketId, actually)
    const EvtData_Network_Player_Actor_Assignment & castEvent =
        static_cast<const EvtData_Network_Player_Actor_Assignment &>( event );
```

```
        shared_ptr<IGameView> playersView(GCC_NEW TeapotWarsGameView());
        m_TeapotWars->VAddView(playersView, castEvent.m_actorId);
    }
```

This code instructs the remote client to create a `TeapotWarsGameView()` object and associate it with the actor ID sent by the server.

Next up is the "physics collision" event, which is sent by the physics system whenever a moving object collides with something:

```
else if ( EvtData_PhysCollision::sk_EventType == event.VGetEventType() )
{
    const EvtData_PhysCollision & castEvent =
        static_cast< const EvtData_PhysCollision & >( event );
    shared_ptr<IActor> pGameActorA =
        m_TeapotWars->VGetActor(castEvent.m_ActorA);
    shared_ptr<IActor> pGameActorB =
        m_TeapotWars->VGetActor(castEvent.m_ActorB);
    if (!pGameActorA || !pGameActorB)
        return false;

    int typeA = pGameActorA->VGetType();
    int typeB = pGameActorB->VGetType();

    if (AT_Sphere==typeA && AT_Teapot==typeB)
    {
        m_TeapotWars->VRegisterHit(pGameActorA->VGetID(),
            pGameActorB->VGetID());
        m_TeapotWars->VRemoveActor(pGameActorA->VGetID
    }
    if (AT_Teapot==typeA && AT_Sphere==typeB)
    {
        m_TeapotWars->VRegisterHit(pGameActorB->VGetID(),
            pGameActorA->VGetID());
        m_TeapotWars->VRemoveActor(pGameActorB->VGetID
    }
}
```

This one is pretty simple. The code detects if one actor was a teapot and the other actor was a sphere, and if so, registers a hit on the teapot and destroys the sphere.

Let's look at the "thrust" event, which is sent by the game view class in response to a player pressing the right button on the mouse or keyboard:

```
else if ( EvtData_Thrust::sk_EventType == event.VGetEventType() )
{
   const EvtData_Thrust & castEvent =
      static_cast<const EvtData_Thrust &>( event );
   shared_ptr<IActor> pActor = m_TeapotWars->VGetActor(castEvent.m_id);
   if( pActor )
   {
      static const float newtonForce = 1.f;
      float thrustForce = castEvent.m_throttle * newtonForce;

      Mat4x4 rotation = pActor->VGetMat();
      rotation.SetPosition(Vec3(0,0,0));
      Vec3 dir = rotation.Xform(g_Forward);
      dir.Normalize();
      m_TeapotWars->m_pPhysics->
         VApplyForce(dir, thrustForce, castEvent.m_id);
   }
}
```

Even though the "thrust" event just applies the thrust via the `VApplyForce()` method of the physics class, you could have just as well checked the teapot's fuel supply and done nothing. This is a great example of how the view and logic work together.

The next two events, "steer" and "fire," are similar to the "thrust" event:

```
else if ( EvtData_Steer::sk_EventType == event.VGetEventType() )
{
   static const float newtonForce = -.25 * 1.8f;

   const EvtData_Steer & castEvent =
      static_cast< const EvtData_Steer & >( event );
   float steerForce = -castEvent.m_dir * newtonForce;
   m_TeapotWars->m_pPhysics->VApplyTorque(
      Vec3(0,1,0), steerForce, castEvent.m_id);
}
else if ( EvtData_Fire_Weapon::sk_EventType == event.VGetEventType() )
{
   const EvtData_Fire_Weapon & castEvent =
      static_cast< const EvtData_Fire_Weapon & >( event );
   ActorId gunnerId = castEvent.m_id;

   shared_ptr<IActor> pGunner = m_TeapotWars->VGetActor(gunnerId);
   if (pGunner)
   {
      // TODO: You should check his stores of ammo right here!!!
```

```
    // Calculate depth offset from the controller
    Vec4 at = g_Forward4 * 2.0f;
    Vec4 atWorld = pGunner->VGetMat().Xform(at);

    // Calculate up offset from the controller
    Vec4 up = g_Up4 * 2.f;
    Vec4 upWorld = pGunner->VGetMat().Xform(up);

    Vec4 direction = atWorld + upWorld;
    Vec3 normalDir(direction);
    normalDir.Normalize();

    SphereParams sp;
    sp.m_Pos = pGunner->VGetMat().GetPosition() + Vec3(direction);
    sp.m_Radius = 0.25;
    sp.m_Segments = 16;
    sp.m_Color = g_Cyan;
    sp.m_NormalDir = normalDir;
    sp.m_Force = g_WeaponForce;

    //Request creation of this actor.
    const EvtData_Request_New_Actor cannonBallEvt( &sp );
    safeTriggerEvent( cannonBallEvt );
    }
 }
```

Both simply do what is asked, but if you wanted the teapots to have limited ammunition, you could check the ammo supply before firing. Notice the 3D math in the "fire" event code. If you are a little shaky on that, here's what's going on. The g_Forward4 vector is transformed into at, which now is the world space vector of the gunner teapot's spout. The same happens with the g_Up4 vector, and when you add these together, you get a 45-degree angle pointing along the direction of the gunner's spout. Because the global direction vectors are only 1.0 units long, each is doubled in length before they are added, which places the initial spot of the sphere far enough away from the teapot that it won't collide with it. After all that, the sphere actor is requested.

That event, as it turns out, is the next one on our list: "request new actor."

```
else if ( EvtData_Request_New_Actor::sk_EventType == event.VGetEventType() )
{
   const EvtData_Request_New_Actor & castEvent =
      static_cast< const EvtData_Request_New_Actor & >( event );

   ActorParams * pActorParams = NULL;
   const bool bCreateEventData = castEvent.VHasLuaEventData();
```

```
        if ( false == bCreateEventData )
        {
            // Actor params were created FOR us, so we won't need to allocate it.
            pActorParams = castEvent.m_pActorParams;
        }
        else
        {
            // Create actor params from the Lua object.
            LuaObject actorDef = castEvent.VGetLuaEventData();
            pActorParams = ActorParams::CreateFromLuaObj( actorDef );
        }

        // Did we get valid actor params?
        if ( NULL == pActorParams )
        {
            assert( 0 && "Invalid parameters specified for actor!" );
            return false;
        }

        // Valid params.
        const ActorId actorID = m_TeapotWars->GetNewActorID();
        pActorParams->m_Id = actorID;
        // Package as a new actor event.
        const EvtData_New_Actor actorEvent( actorID, pActorParams );
        const bool bSuccess = safeTriggerEvent( actorEvent );
        if ( bCreateEventData )
        {
            SAFE_DELETE( pActorParams );
        }
        return bSuccess;
    }
```

Since new actors can be requested from virtually anywhere, their parameters
should be checked, which is exactly what the "request new actor" event does. If
the parameters check out, a new event, "new actor," is sent:

```
else if ( EvtData_New_Actor::sk_EventType == event.VGetEventType() )
{
    const EvtData_New_Actor & castEvent =
        static_cast< const EvtData_New_Actor & >( event );
    ActorParams * pActorParams = castEvent.m_pActorParams;

    if ( NULL == pActorParams )
    {
```

```
        assert( 0 && "NULL actor parameters!" );
        return false;
    }

    // ActorParams::VCreate actually creates the actor for the logic
    pActorParams->VCreate(m_TeapotWars);

    if ( false == castEvent.m_id )
    {
        assert( 0 && "Unable to construct desired actor type!" );
        return false;
    }
    else
    {
        return true;
    }
}
```

After all the preliminary checking, the actor is created with the `ActorParams::VCreate()` method, which you learned about earlier in this chapter. Each actor type get its own `ActorParams` child class and overloads the `VCreate()` method.

The next event is received if anything in the `ActorParams` class changes via a Lua script, such as if a Lua script changed the color of an actor:

```
else if ( EvtData_UpdateActorParams::sk_EventType == event.VGetEventType() )
{
    //Update the parameters for the specified actor.
    const EvtData_UpdateActorParams & castEvent =
        static_cast< const EvtData_UpdateActorParams & >( event );
    shared_ptr< IActor > destActor =
        g_pApp->m_pGame->VGetActor( castEvent.m_ActorID );

    //Re-jigger the actor params.
    BaseActor * pBaseActor = static_cast< BaseActor * >( destActor.get() );
    shared_ptr<ActorParams> params = pBaseActor->VGetParams();

    ActorParams::TErrorMessageList errorMessages;
    params->VInit( castEvent.VGetLuaEventData(), errorMessages );
}

return false;
}
```

Earlier in this chapter, you learned about the `ActorParams::VInit()` method that took a `LuaObject` as its first parameter—this is where this method actually gets called.

Last, but most certainly not least, is the "move actor" event, which is sent if an authoritative source needs to move an actor:

```
else if ( EvtData_Move_Actor::sk_EventType == event.VGetEventType() )
{
    const EvtData_Move_Actor & castEvent = static_cast< const
                                    EvtData_Move_Actor & >( event );
    m_TeapotWars->VMoveActor(castEvent.m_Id, castEvent.m_Mat);
}
```

That wraps up the `TeapotWarsGame` class, which controls the "rules" of *Teapot Wars*. Next is the view class for a human player, so you can see what's going on and interact with the game.

THE GAME VIEW FOR A HUMAN PLAYER

The game view's job is to present the game, accept input, and translate that input into commands for the game logic. There are three kinds of views that can attach to *Teapot Wars*: a view for a local human player, a view for an AI player, and a view that represents a player on a remote machine. The last one, `NetworkGameView`, was presented at the end of Chapter 16.

The view for the human player is responsible for the 3D graphics, audio, and user interface of the game. There are four classes that make this system work:

- `ScreenElementScene`: Inherits from the `Scene` class presented in Chapter 14 to draw a 3D view of the game world and also from the `ISceneElement` interface class in Chapter 9, "User Interface Programming," to hook into the base game view's layered user interface system.
- `TeapotWarsGameView`: Inherits from the `HumanView` class presented in Chapter 9, which has hooks into the Windows application layer message pump for user interface processing and organizes user interface objects, like buttons and text strings on top of a 3D scene background.
- `TeapotWarsGameViewListener`: Listens to and handles events coming from the game logic, such as object movement events.
- `TeapotController`: Reads input from the keyboard and mouse and translates input into commands that are sent to the game logic.

The `ScreenElementScene` Class

Chapter 9 used a layered approach to drawing objects on a window. All of the objects attached to the draw list in the `HumanView` class were required to implement the `IScreenElement` interface. In the case of *Teapot Wars*, the background layer is actually a 3D scene. Interface classes are safe to use in a multiple inheritance situation, which is exactly how a 3D scene can become a screen element of a `HumanView`:

```
class ScreenElementScene : public IScreenElement, public Scene
{
public:
    ScreenElementScene() : Scene() { }

    // IScreenElement Implementation
    virtual void VOnUpdate(int deltaMS) { OnUpdate(deltaMS); };
    virtual HRESULT VOnRestore()
        { OnRestore(); return S_OK; }
    virtual HRESULT VOnRender(double fTime, float fElapsedTime)
        { OnRender(); return S_OK; }
    virtual int VGetZOrder() const { return 1; }
    virtual void VSetZOrder(int const zOrder) { }

    // Don't handle any messages
    virtual LRESULT CALLBACK VOnMsgProc( AppMsg msg ) { return 0; }

    virtual bool VIsVisible() const { return true; }
    virtual void VSetVisible(bool visible) { }
    virtual bool VAddChild(optional<ActorId> id, shared_ptr<ISceneNode> kid)
        { return Scene::AddChild(id, kid); }
};
```

Since the 3D scene doesn't accept any messages from the application layer, such as a keyboard or mouse event, it is always visible, and it is always in the background. This class is trivial to define. Most of the methods needed to implement the `IScreenElement` interface are one-liners. If you ever wondered whether interface classes were worth the trouble, this example should seal the deal.

The `TeapotWarsGameView` Class

The code for the `TeapotWarsGameView` is quite a bit longer. It has a lot of work to do, keeping track of the 3D scene, audio, graphical object creation, and presenting the user interface.

```cpp
class TeapotWarsGameView : public HumanView
{
   friend class TeapotWarsGameViewListener;

protected:
   bool  m_bShowUI;                    // If true, it renders the UI control text
   BaseGameState m_BaseGameState;      // what is the current game state

   shared_ptr<ScreenElementScene> m_pScene;
   shared_ptr<SoundProcess> m_music;
   shared_ptr<TeapotController> m_pTeapotController;
   shared_ptr<MovementController> m_pFreeCameraController;
   shared_ptr<CameraNode> m_pCamera;
   shared_ptr<SceneNode> m_pTeapot;
   shared_ptr<StandardHUD> m_StandardHUD;

   void BuildInitialScene();
   void MoveActor(ActorId id, Mat4x4 const &mat);
   void HandleGameState(BaseGameState newState);
public:

   TeapotWarsGameView();

   virtual LRESULT CALLBACK VOnMsgProc( AppMsg msg );
   virtual void VRenderText(CDXUTTextHelper &txtHelper);
   virtual void VOnUpdate(int deltaMilliseconds);
   virtual void VOnAttach(GameViewId vid, optional<ActorId> aid);

   virtual void VSetCameraOffset(const Vec4 & camOffset );
};

TeapotWarsGameView::TeapotWarsGameView()
{
   m_BaseGameState = BGS_Initializing;
   m_bShowUI = true;

   m_pScene.reset(GCC_NEW TeapotWarsScene());

   Frustum frustum;
   frustum.Init(D3DX_PI/4.0f, 1.0f, 1.0f, 100.0f);
   m_pCamera.reset(GCC_NEW CameraNode(&Mat4x4::g_Identity, frustum));
   assert(m_pScene && m_pCamera && _T("Out of memory"));

   m_pScene->VAddChild(optional_empty(), m_pCamera);
   m_pScene->SetCamera(m_pCamera);
```

```
   EventListenerPtr listener ( GCC_NEW TeapotWarsGameViewListener( this ) );
   ListenForTeapotViewEvents(listener);
}

void ListenForTeapotViewEvents(EventListenerPtr listener)
{
   // hook in the physics event listener
   safeAddListener( listener, EvtData_PhysCollision::sk_EventType );
   safeAddListener( listener, EvtData_Destroy_Actor::sk_EventType );
   safeAddListener( listener, EvtData_Fire_Weapon::sk_EventType );
   safeAddListener( listener, EvtData_New_Game::sk_EventType );
   safeAddListener( listener, EvtData_New_Actor::sk_EventType );
   safeAddListener( listener, EvtData_Move_Actor::sk_EventType );
   safeAddListener( listener, EvtData_Game_State::sk_EventType );
   safeAddListener( listener, EvtData_Request_New_Actor::sk_EventType );
   safeAddListener( listener, EvtData_Debug_String::sk_EventType );
   safeAddListener( listener, EvtData_UpdateActorParams::sk_EventType );
   safeAddListener( listener, EvtData_Decompression_Progress::sk_EventType );

}
```

The constructor creates the `ScreenElementScene` object and a camera, and it registers to listen for events coming from the game logic. There is a C function that takes a listener as a parameter and registers a group of events for any human views of *Teapot Wars*, local or remote. It's in a C function because it is convenient to group these calls into a function that any view class can call.

Here's how the game view builds the initial scene. This is done as soon as the game logic signals the view that a new game needs to be loaded:

```
void TeapotWarsGameView::BuildInitialScene()
{
   SoundResource resource("SpaceGod7-Level2.ogg");
   shared_ptr<ResHandle> rh = g_pApp->m_ResCache->GetHandle(&resource);
   shared_ptr<SoundResHandle> srh =
      boost::static_pointer_cast<SoundResHandle>(rh);
   shared_ptr<SoundProcess> music(
      GCC_NEW SoundProcess(srh, PROC_MUSIC, 0, true));
   m_pProcessManager->Attach(music);

   shared_ptr<CFadeProcess> fadeProc(new CFadeProcess(music, 10000, 100));
   m_pProcessManager->Attach(fadeProc);

   // Here's our sky node
   shared_ptr<SkyNode> sky(GCC_NEW SkyNode("Sky2", m_pCamera));
   m_pScene->VAddChild(optional_empty(), sky);
```

```
   m_StandardHUD.reset(GCC_NEW StandardHUD);

   VPushElement(m_pScene);
   VPushElement(m_StandardHUD);

   // A movement controller is going to control the camera,
   // but it could be constructed with any of the objects you see in this
   // function. You can have your very own remote controlled sphere.
   m_pFreeCameraController.reset(
      GCC_NEW MovementController(m_pCamera, 0, 0, false));

   VOnRestore();
}
```

The initial scene is pretty simple. A piece of music is loaded using the audio classes you read about in Chapter 12, "Game Audio." There's also a nice fade process that fades the music in over time so it doesn't hit you all at once. This is a pretty common thing to do in games when you have discrete pieces of music you want to play, but don't have custom transitions to seamlessly go from one piece to another. You might also recognize the process manager code from Chapter 6, "Controlling the Main Loop." The process manager keeps track of the sound as it plays, but it could also handle animations or other objects that move outside of the control of the physics system.

Finally, the sky is added to the scene. VOnRestore() is called immediately, since most of the constructors for these objects don't really do much of anything. Rather, each object is wired into the VOnRestore() call, which recurses all of the objects attached to the game that need to be restored. Restoring must happen when the objects are first created, as you see here, but it can also happen if the objects are somehow lost to DirectX. If the D3D device loses scope to another 3D game all objects need to be restored. Switching to other 3D games happens mostly in the test department at Microsoft, but you should make sure your game also handles this kind of thing elegantly.

BEST
PRACTICE

SHAME ON MR. MIKE—HARD-CODED SCENE ELEMENTS?

I actually left this remnant of code in from the second edition of the book and the 2.x version of the source code to make a point, and to give you an assignment. The second edition didn't have a Lua scripting system, and the entire scene, grid actors, teapots, the works, was all hard coded. Try your hand at extending the Lua scripting system, and the C# editor you will see in the next chapter, to completely retire BuildInitialScene().

It's now time to see a little bit of user interface code. First, we'll look at the method that grabs some messages sent by the application layer:

```
LRESULT CALLBACK TeapotWarsGameView::VOnMsgProc( AppMsg msg )
{
    if (HumanView::VOnMsgProc(msg))
        return 1;

    if (msg.m_uMsg==WM_KEYDOWN)
    {
        if (msg.m_wParam==VK_F1)
        {
            m_bShowUI = !m_bShowUI;
            m_StandardHUD->VSetVisible(m_bShowUI);
            return 1;
        }
        else if (msg.m_wParam=='Q')
        {
            if (GameCodeApp::Ask(QUESTION_QUIT_GAME)==IDYES)
            {
                g_pApp->SetQuitting(true);
            }
            return 1;
        }
    }

    return 0;
}
```

In this case, the only message handled is a keyboard event. If the player hits the F1 key, the `m_bShowUI` member variable is toggled, which controls some extra text on the screen, such as a frame counter or help text. The other key, Q, allows the player to quit the game.

The next method is `VRenderText()`, which is called after all the other screen elements of the human view have been drawn:

```
void TeapotWarsGameView::VRenderText(CDXUTTextHelper &txtHelper)
{
    HumanView::VRenderText(txtHelper);

    const D3DSURFACE_DESC* pd3dsdBackBuffer =
        DXUTGetD3D9BackBufferSurfaceDesc();
    txtHelper.Begin();
```

```
// Scoreboard (with shadow)...
const ActorScoreMap& actorScores =
    g_TeapotWarsApp.GetGame()->GetData().GetActorScores();
std::wstring scoreStr;
TCHAR tempBuffer[256];
int player = 1;
for( ActorScoreMap::const_iterator i=actorScores.begin();
    i!=actorScores.end(); ++i )
{
    // It's good practice to use the string table
    wsprintf( tempBuffer, _T("%s %d: %d\n"),
        g_pApp->GetString(IDS_PLAYER).c_str(), player, i->second );
    ++player;
    scoreStr.append( tempBuffer );
}
txtHelper.SetInsertionPos( pd3dsdBackBuffer->Width/2, 5 );
txtHelper.SetForegroundColor( D3DXCOLOR( 0.0f, 0.0f, 0.0f, 1.0f ) );
txtHelper.DrawTextLine(scoreStr.c_str());
txtHelper.SetInsertionPos( pd3dsdBackBuffer->Width/2-1, 5-1 );
txtHelper.SetForegroundColor( D3DXCOLOR( 0.25f, 1.0f, 0.25f, 1.0f ) );
txtHelper.DrawTextLine(scoreStr.c_str());

//...Scoreboard
if( m_bShowUI )
{
    // Output statistics...
    txtHelper.SetInsertionPos( 5, 5 );
    txtHelper.SetForegroundColor( D3DXCOLOR( 1.0f, 1.0f, 0.0f, 1.0f ) );
    txtHelper.DrawTextLine( DXUTGetFrameStats() );
    txtHelper.DrawTextLine( DXUTGetDeviceStats() );
    txtHelper.SetForegroundColor( D3DXCOLOR( 0.0f, 0.0f, 0.0f, 0.5f ) );

    //Game State...
    switch (m_BaseGameState)
    {
        case BGS_Initializing:
            txtHelper.DrawTextLine(
                g_pApp->GetString(IDS_INITIALIZING).c_str());
            break;

        case BGS_MainMenu:
            txtHelper.DrawTextLine(L"Main Menu");
            break;
```

```
    case BGS_SpawnAI:
        txtHelper.DrawTextLine(L"Spawn AI");
        break;

    case BGS_WaitingForPlayers:
        txtHelper.DrawTextLine(g_pApp->GetString(IDS_WAITING).c_str());
        break;

    case BGS_LoadingGameEnvironment:
        txtHelper.DrawTextLine(g_pApp->GetString(IDS_LOADING).c_str());
        break;

    case BGS_Running:
        txtHelper.DrawTextLine(g_pApp->GetString(IDS_RUNNING).c_str());
        break;
}
//...Game State

//Camera...
TCHAR buffer[256];
const TCHAR *s = NULL;
Mat4x4 toWorld;
Mat4x4 fromWorld;
if (m_pCamera)
{
    m_pCamera->VGet()->Transform(&toWorld, &fromWorld);
}
swprintf(buffer, g_pApp->GetString(IDS_CAMERA_LOCATION).c_str(),
    toWorld.m[3][0], toWorld.m[3][1], toWorld.m[3][2]);
txtHelper.DrawTextLine( buffer );
//...Camera

//Help text.  Right justified, lower right of screen.
RECT helpRect;
helpRect.left = 0;
helpRect.right = pd3dsdBackBuffer->Width - 10;
helpRect.top = pd3dsdBackBuffer->Height-15*8;
helpRect.bottom = pd3dsdBackBuffer->Height;
txtHelper.SetInsertionPos( helpRect.right, helpRect.top );
txtHelper.SetForegroundColor( D3DXCOLOR( 1.0f, 0.75f, 0.0f, 1.0f ) );
txtHelper.DrawTextLine( helpRect, DT_RIGHT,
    g_pApp->GetString(IDS_CONTROLS_HEADER).c_str() );
helpRect.top = pd3dsdBackBuffer->Height-15*7;
txtHelper.DrawTextLine( helpRect, DT_RIGHT,
```

```
        g_pApp->GetString(IDS_CONTROLS).c_str() );
    //...Help
}//end if (m_bShowUI)

txtHelper.End();
}
```

The text renderer draws text for the player scores and some optional text for things like frame rate and game state. Notice that there are no hard-coded strings here. This code loads strings using the game's application layer. The application layer loads them from a string table, which makes your game much easier to localize into foreign languages. What's more, your game could easily load these string tables on game initialization, which means you could ship your game in multiple languages with the same executable. Not to brag, but this is very similar to what we did back at Origin to ship *Ultima VIII: Pagan*. We didn't have string tables, per se, but the U8.EXE could run in English, French, or German just by swapping a command line parameter.

Next is VOnUpdate():

```
void TeapotWarsGameView::VOnUpdate( int deltaMilliseconds )
{
    HumanView::VOnUpdate( deltaMilliseconds );

    if (m_pFreeCameraController)
    {
        m_pFreeCameraController->OnUpdate(deltaMilliseconds);
    }

    if (m_pTeapotController)
    {
        m_pTeapotController->OnUpdate(deltaMilliseconds);
    }

    //Send out a tick to script listeners.
    const EvtData_Update_Tick tickEvent( deltaMilliseconds );
    safeTriggerEvent( tickEvent );
}
```

VOnUpdate() calls the base class version and also updates the controller, whichever one happens to be active. I found it useful to be able to have multiple controllers in a game, one of which was always a free camera that could fly any-where and look at anything. It made things really easy to debug. It also sends a "tick" event, which could be listened to by any subsystem but is really meant for Lua script listeners.

`VOnAttach()` is pretty straightforward:

```
void TeapotWarsGameView::VOnAttach(GameViewId vid, optional<ActorId> aid)
{
   HumanView::VOnAttach(vid, aid);
   BuildInitialScene();
}
```

It simply calls the base class and `BuildInitialScene()`. Once you follow my assignment and get rid of `BuildInitialScene()` and replace it with a Lua file, you will be able to get rid of this overload as well.

`MoveActor()` is what is called if the view is informed that an actor in the game logic has changed position:

```
void TeapotWarsGameView::MoveActor(ActorId id, Mat4x4 const &mat)
{
    shared_ptr<ISceneNode> node = m_pScene->FindActor(id);
    if (node)
    {
       node->VSetTransform(&mat);
    }
}
```

Again, very simple—all it does is find the actor using the ID and set the transform to the requested value.

Finally, let's look at `HandleGameState()`:

```
void TeapotWarsGameView::HandleGameState(BaseGameState newState)
{
   m_BaseGameState = newState;
}
```

This method might do more if certain actions were needed when the game state changed, but for now all *Teapot Wars* needs to do is record the new value in a member variable.

The `TeapotWarsGameViewListener` Class

Just as you saw with the `TeapotWarsGame` class, the view class has a companion event listener. This event listener responds to all the events sent to the view from any subsystem in the game, including the game logic. Just as I did before, I'll show you how each event is handled one at a time, as it appears in the listener's `HandleEvent()` method:

First on the list is the "collide" event, which is sent when the physics system detects a collision:

```
if ( EvtData_PhysCollision::sk_EventType == event.VGetEventType() )
{
    EvtData_PhysCollision const & ed =
        static_cast< const EvtData_PhysCollision & >( event );
    shared_ptr<IActor> pGameActorA = g_pApp->m_pGame->VGetActor(ed.m_ActorA);
    shared_ptr<IActor> pGameActorB = g_pApp->m_pGame->VGetActor(ed.m_ActorB);
    if (!pGameActorA || !pGameActorB)
        return false;

    int typeA = pGameActorA->VGetType();
    int typeB = pGameActorB->VGetType();

    if(    (AT_Teapot==typeA && AT_Sphere==typeB)
        || (AT_Sphere==typeA && AT_Teapot==typeB) )
    {
        // play the sound a bullet makes when it hits a teapot
        SoundResource resource("computerbeep3.wav");
        shared_ptr<SoundResHandle> srh =
            boost::static_pointer_cast<SoundResHandle>(
                g_pApp->m_ResCache->GetHandle(&resource));
        shared_ptr<SoundProcess> sfx(
            GCC_NEW SoundProcess(srh, PROC_SOUNDFX, 100, false));
        m_pView->m_pProcessManager->Attach(sfx);
    }
}
```

The view responds by detecting if the collision was between any kind of teapot and a sphere, and if so, a sound effect is played. Notice that the human view interprets this event and does things that only matter to the human player and are inconsequential to any other system. You might also spawn a particle effect here, since that doesn't affect anything in the game logic.

Now, let's look at the "destroy actor," which simply finds the actor requested and removes it from the scene:

```
else if ( EvtData_Destroy_Actor::sk_EventType == event.VGetEventType() )
{
    const EvtData_Destroy_Actor & castEvent = static_cast< const
                                    EvtData_Destroy_Actor & >( event );
    ActorId aid = castEvent.m_id;
    m_pView->m_pScene->RemoveChild(aid);
}
```

The "fire weapon" event is interesting. It is sent when the game logic deter-mines a valid request to fire results in an actual sphere arcing away from the gun-ner teapot:

```
else if ( EvtData_Fire_Weapon::sk_EventType == event.VGetEventType() )
{
    // play a weapon fire sound
    SoundResource resource("blip.wav");
    shared_ptr<SoundResHandle> srh =
        boost::static_pointer_cast<SoundResHandle>(
            g_pApp->m_ResCache->GetHandle(&resource));
    shared_ptr<SoundProcess> sfx1(
        GCC_NEW SoundProcess(srh, PROC_SOUNDFX, 100, false));
    shared_ptr<SoundProcess> sfx2(
        GCC_NEW SoundProcess(srh, PROC_SOUNDFX, 60, false));
    shared_ptr<SoundProcess> sfx3(
        GCC_NEW SoundProcess(srh, PROC_SOUNDFX, 40, false));
    m_pView->m_pProcessManager->Attach(sfx1);
    sfx1->SetNext(sfx2);
    sfx2->SetNext(sfx3);
}
```

You can set up a chain of processes to run one after another in sequence. In this example, three `SoundProcess` objects are created and chained so that you hear three "blip" sounds, one after another, with decreasing volume. As you recall from Chapter 6, the `SetNext()` set the process chain in action.

The next two events are fairly simple housekeeping things, "move actor" and "game state":

```
else if ( EvtData_Move_Actor::sk_EventType == event.VGetEventType() )
{
    const EvtData_Move_Actor & ed =
        static_cast< const EvtData_Move_Actor & >( event );
    m_pView->MoveActor(ed.m_Id, ed.m_Mat);
}
else if ( EvtData_Game_State::sk_EventType == event.VGetEventType() )
{
    const EvtData_Game_State & ed =
        static_cast< const EvtData_Game_State & >( event );
    BaseGameState gameState = ed.m_gameState;
    m_pView->HandleGameState(gameState);
}
```

Both events simply call the right view methods to respond to the event.

Next is the "new actor" event, which is sent by the game logic when a new actor should be created:

```
else if ( EvtData_New_Actor::sk_EventType == event.VGetEventType() )
{
    const EvtData_New_Actor & ed =
        static_cast< const EvtData_New_Actor & >( event );

    // These next lines actually create the actor through ActorParams...
    shared_ptr<SceneNode> node =
        ed.m_pActorParams->VCreateSceneNode(m_pView->m_pScene);
    m_pView->m_pScene->VAddChild(ed.m_pActorParams->m_Id, node);
    node->VOnRestore(&(*(m_pView->m_pScene)));

    if (ed.m_pActorParams->m_Type == AT_Teapot)
    {
        TeapotParams *p = static_cast<TeapotParams *>(ed.m_pActorParams);
        if (p->m_ViewId == m_pView->m_ViewId)
        {
            m_pView->m_pTeapot = node;
            m_pView->m_pTeapotController.reset(
                GCC_NEW TeapotController(m_pView->m_pTeapot, 0, 0));
            m_pView->m_KeyboardHandler = m_pView->m_pTeapotController;
            m_pView->m_MouseHandler = m_pView->m_pTeapotController;
            m_pView->m_pCamera->SetTarget(m_pView->m_pTeapot);
            m_pView->m_pTeapot->SetAlpha(0.8f);
        }
    }
}
return false;
}
```

Just as the game logic called a virtual member of the ActorParams class to create the game actor, the view class calls ActorParams::VCreateSceneNode() to create the visual representation of an actor. It is added to the scene and ISceneNode::VOnRestore() is called to create the actual geometry or load mesh files.

If the actor happens to be a teapot, and the ID of the view class is the same as the view ID sent with the teapot actor parameters, then this particular teapot is the one controlled by the human player. In that case a TeapotController is created.

The Teapot Controller

A game view that presents the game to a human needs a way for that very human to affect the game. It's a common practice to factor control systems that have a particular interface, like the keyboard WASD controls, into a class that can be attached and detached as necessary. This controller class isn't exactly WASD, since the A and D keys control steering rather than strafing, but I'm sure you'll forgive the departure:

```
class TeapotController : public IMouseHandler, public IKeyboardHandler
{
protected:
    BYTE              m_bKey[256];              // Which keys are up and down
    shared_ptr<SceneNode>    m_object;

public:
    TeapotController(shared_ptr<SceneNode> object,
        float initialYaw, float initialPitch);
    void OnUpdate(DWORD const elapsedMs);

public:
    bool VOnMouseMove(const CPoint &mousePos) { return true; }
    bool VOnLButtonDown(const CPoint &mousePos);
    bool VOnLButtonUp(const CPoint &mousePos) { return true; }
    bool VOnRButtonDown(const CPoint &) { return false; }
    bool VOnRButtonUp(const CPoint &) { return false; }

    bool VOnKeyDown(const BYTE c) { m_bKey[c] = true; return true; }
    bool VOnKeyUp(const BYTE c) { m_bKey[c] = false; return true; }
};

TeapotController::TeapotController(shared_ptr<SceneNode> object,
    float initialYaw, float initialPitch)
: m_object(object)
{
    memset(m_bKey, 0x00, sizeof(m_bKey));
}
```

As you can see from the class definition, really the only methods that have any meat to them are the response to the left mouse button and OnUpdate(). Keyboard events are recorded as they happen, which are used in OnUpdate().

Here's what happens when the player clicks the left mouse button:

```
bool TeapotController::VOnLButtonDown(const CPoint &mousePos)
{
    optional<ActorId> aid = m_object->VGet()->ActorId();
    assert(aid.valid() && _T("Invalid actor!"));
    safeQueEvent( IEventDataPtr( GCC_NEW EvtData_Fire_Weapon( *aid ) ) );
    return true;
}
```

The code queues a "fire weapon" event. Note that in a commercial game, this wouldn't be hard coded to the left mouse button necessarily. Instead, there would be an intermediate layer that translates specific user interface events into mappable game events, which enables users to set up their keyboard and mouse the way they like it.

Here's the OnUpdate() method of the controller:

```
void TeapotController::OnUpdate(DWORD const deltaMilliseconds)
{
    if (m_bKey['W'] || m_bKey['S'])
    {
        const ActorId actorID = *m_object->VGet()->ActorId();
        safeQueEvent( IEventDataPtr(
            GCC_NEW EvtData_Thrust( actorID, m_bKey['W']? 1.0f : -1.0 ) ) );
    }
    if (m_bKey['A'] || m_bKey['D'])
    {
        const ActorId actorID = *m_object->VGet()->ActorId();
        safeQueEvent( IEventDataPtr(
            GCC_NEW EvtData_Steer( actorID, m_bKey['A']? -1.0 : 1.0 ) ) );
    }
}
```

The controller keeps a record of what keys are down on the keyboard, and it responds to the mouse-down event as well. Since the controller implements the IMouseHandler and IKeyboardHandler interfaces, it wires in nicely to the base Human-View class. The interface events are translated into the two game command events you've already seen: "thrust" and "steer."

THE AI VIEW AND LISTENER

What you learned in Chapter 17, "An Introduction to Game AI," will be put to good use in this section. In the second edition of this book, the teapot AI was nothing more than a random series of pauses, thrusts, fires, and whatnot. Not anymore!

What's important here is how the AI plugs into the system as another type of view of the game. Between what you learned in Chapter 17 and the many excellent books available on AI, you will soon have an excellent framework to plug them into *Teapot Wars*. There are two classes that interface to AI systems such as path finding and state machines. The first is the AITeapotView class, which implements the IGameView interface:

```cpp
class AITeapotView : public IGameView
{
   friend class AITeapotViewListener;

private:
   shared_ptr<PathingGraph> m_pPathingGraph;
   StateMachine* m_pStateMachine;

protected:
   GameViewId   m_ViewId;
   optional<ActorId> m_PlayerActorId;

public:
   AITeapotView(shared_ptr<PathingGraph> pPathingGraph);
   virtual ~AITeapotView();

   virtual HRESULT VOnRestore() { return S_OK; }
   virtual void VOnRender(double fTime, float fElapsedTime) {}
   virtual void VOnLostDevice() {}
   virtual GameViewType VGetType() { return GameView_AI; }
   virtual GameViewId VGetId() const { return m_ViewId; }
   virtual void VOnAttach(GameViewId vid, optional<ActorId> aid)
      { m_ViewId = vid; m_PlayerActorId = aid; }
   virtual LRESULT CALLBACK VOnMsgProc( AppMsg msg ) {    return 0; }
   virtual void VOnUpdate( int deltaMilliseconds ) {}

   shared_ptr<PathingGraph> GetPathingGraph(void) const
      { return m_pPathingGraph; }
   void RotateActorY(float angleRadians);
};

AITeapotView::AITeapotView(shared_ptr<PathingGraph> pPathingGraph)
   : IGameView(), m_pPathingGraph(pPathingGraph)
{
   m_pStateMachine = NULL;
   EventListenerPtr listener ( GCC_NEW AITeapotViewListener( this ) );
   safeAddListener( listener, EvtData_New_Actor::sk_EventType );
}

AITeapotView::~AITeapotView(void)
{
   SAFE_DELETE(m_pStateMachine);
   OutputDebugString(_T("Destroying AITeapotView\n"));
}
```

This class contains the pathing graph and state machine through a view class that can be wired into the game logic, and therefore an actor in the game world. It is really not much more than a simple container to encapsulate these objects.

The AI has a companion listener class, `AITeapotViewListener`.

```cpp
class AITeapotViewListener : public IEventListener
{
   AITeapotView *const m_pView;
public:
   explicit AITeapotViewListener(AITeapotView *pView)
      : IEventListener(), m_pView(pView) {}
   virtual char const* GetName(void) { return "AITeapotViewListener"; }
   virtual bool HandleEvent(IEventData const& event);
};


bool AITeapotViewListener::HandleEvent( IEventData const & event )
{
    if ( EvtData_New_Actor::sk_EventType == event.VGetEventType() )
    {
        const EvtData_New_Actor & ed =
            static_cast< const EvtData_New_Actor & >( event );
        switch(ed.m_pActorParams->m_Type)
        {
            case AT_Sphere:
            {
                // somebody took a shot!
                break;
            }
            case AT_Teapot:
            {
                TeapotParams *p =
                    static_cast<TeapotParams *>(ed.m_pActorParams);
                if (p->m_ViewId == m_pView->m_ViewId)
                {
                    // we need a valid ID
                    assert(p->m_Id.valid());
                    m_pView->m_PlayerActorId = p->m_Id;

                    // create the state machine, set the initial state
                    m_pView->m_pStateMachine = GCC_NEW
                        TeapotStateMachine(*(p->m_Id),
                            m_pView->m_pPathingGraph);
```

```
                    m_pView->m_pStateMachine->SetState("wander");
            }
            break;
        }

        default:
            OutputDebugString(
                _T("AI Listener - Unsupported Actor Type\n"));
        }
    }

    return false;
}
```

The only event that the listener responds to is the "new actor" event. Just as you saw with the human view class, the code looks through the game actors to find an actor that has the same view ID stored in the actor parameters as the `AITeapotView` ID. Once found, a new `TeapotStateMachine` object is created and set to "wander."

Once that is done, the AI system described in Chapter 17 takes over, giving AI teapots the power to attack, chase, wander, spin, or wait around.

MORE *TEAPOT WARS*, IF YOU ARE WILLING

As I'm sure you are aware, *Game Coding Complete* is really an architecture book that paints broad strokes through a vast array of tools and technologies that make up professional computer gaming. One of the observations about the first edition of this book, and I'm sure of this one, is that the book doesn't cover each subject in rigorous detail, completely exposing every last bit. That was by design, not fiat.

Sometimes the hardest part of writing code is knowing where to begin. Once you get started and build a suitable framework around a new system, your fingers fly across the keyboard until numbness takes them, and still you don't stop. My goal with this book and all the code therein was to give you some interesting tidbits, save you from nasty pitfalls, tell a few funny stories, and cover as much territory of game programming as I possibly could.

I have also given you, my valued reader and colleague, a place to start.

A SIMPLE GAME EDITOR IN C#

by Quoc Tran

In This Chapter

Quoc Tran is a programmer/designer for Gendai Games. Quoc and Mr. Mike also work on the side creating MrMike's Addins, *tasked with the noble goal of making Microsoft Project usable for the majority of project managers in the game industry. In a prolonged fit of wanderlust, Quoc has worked as a producer, designer, and programmer and hopes to become the game industry equivalent of Dick Van Dyke from* Mary Poppins.

Back in Chapter 11, "Scripting with Lua," we talked about how the content providers make the game fun, and since modern games require so much content, it stands to reason that you'll want to make it as easy as possible for content providers to generate content for your games. That's why you need a variety of tools to help support your content providers: so they spend less time trying to figure out how to add art assets or generate levels, and spend more time tweaking the content to make the game better. Game engines provide a variety of tools, but the most common tool is the level editor.

What Should a Level Editor Do?

One of the most popular level editors, the Unreal Editor, allows its users control over things like lighting, scripted camera control, and shader creation, as well as basic geometry placement. Let's not forget about saving and loading the levels as well, which is also pretty important. Some editors allow you to view animations on characters, while other engines break things like that into separate tools. For our purposes, we want to make sure that our editor handles the most essential task for a level editor—adding objects to our level, adjusting its properties, and saving the level to file.

You'll see things you've learned over the previous chapters, while adding a new wrinkle. The application layer, view, and logic will be written in C++, but the editor application itself will be written in C#.

Why C#?

Why would anyone want to write an editor in C#? C# isn't very fast, and for performance-intensive applications, you'll still want to use C++. Try Googling "C# performance," and you should find multiple C++ to C# performance benchmarks. However, C# enables you to develop Windows applications quickly with a minimum of fuss, and if your application doesn't need to run at 60fps, you should be in good shape. C# has great GUI integration, and for you C++ programmers out there, C# should look much more familiar than VB.net. The lack of semicolons in VB.net consistently throws me for a loop, although fortunately not an infinite one. In my opinion, C# code also looks much cleaner than writing Windows Forms using C++. All in all, you can throw a decent application together pretty quickly in C#.

How the Editor Is Put Together

A level editor is an application with a complicated user interface, which makes it a good candidate for C#. The core game technologies that you've seen throughout this book are written in C++. You can't just force them into the same application—some gentle persuasion is required. What you are going to see is how a C# application can load and interface with a DLL created from C++.

There are three steps to this. First, the editor architecture is created in C++, including the application layer, the logic layer, and the view layer. Next, a C++ DLL is created that wraps key editor classes and methods with C free functions that create an easy interface into the DLL. Finally, a C# application is created that can load the DLL and use these free functions to access the editor DLL and create game worlds.

THE EDITOR ARCHITECTURE

Just like you've seen in the game architecture, you need to create the application layer, logic, and view for the editor. They'll be written in C++, since these objects are performance critical. Since the engine code is in C++, creating derived classes will have to be done in C++ as well. There's some trickiness involved in getting C# to talk to C++, but we'll handle that further down the line.

BEST
PRACTICE

THE EDITOR IS AN EXTENSION OF THE GAME

As you review the code for the application layer, logic, and view, you'll notice that their classes look very similar to their Teapot Wars *counterparts. When writing a real editor, you'll want your level editor to use the same engine that runs your game. In our case, the classes look like simplified versions of their* Teapot Wars *counterparts to make it easier to explain how the level editor works.*

The Application Layer

The level editor's application layer does not differ significantly from the application layer for *Teapot Wars*. We'll look at the differences below. For the rest of the code, be sure to look at *Source\Editor\Editor.cpp*:

```
BaseGameLogic* Editor::VCreateGameAndView()
{
    BaseGameLogic *game = NULL;
    assert(m_pOptions && _T("The game options object is uninitialized."));

    // Register any game-specific events here.
    RegisterGameSpecificEvents();

    game = GCC_NEW EditorGame(*m_pOptions);
```

```
    shared_ptr<IGameView> gameView(GCC_NEW EditorGameView());
    game->VAddView(gameView);

    return game;
}

inline EditorGame const * const  Editor::GetGame() const
{
    return dynamic_cast<EditorGame*>(m_pGame);
}
```

This should be pretty familiar, because you looked at code like this in Chapter 5, "Game Initialization and Shutdown." This code creates an instance of the game logic class `EditorGame`, which will inherit from `BaseGameLogic`. It also creates a view class, `EditorGameView`:

```
void Editor::RegisterGameSpecificEvents( void )
{
    // We only care about two events - when the game is starting, and when
    // a new actor is being requested. All other relevant events are registered
    // by GameCode.
    m_pEventManager->RegisterCodeOnlyEvent( EvtData_New_Game::sk_EventType );
    m_pEventManager->RegisterEvent< EvtData_Request_New_Actor >(
        EvtData_Request_New_Actor::sk_EventType );
}
```

Events the editor cares about are registered with the Event Manager. In this case, the editor wants to know when new actors are requested and when a new game has started. The editor is not actually running a game, but this event will let it know when it can start doing things like adding basic geometry and setting up input controllers.

The Editor's Logic Class

The editor logic is pretty simple. Since this is a basic level editor, it doesn't need physics. In a level editor for a commercial game, a running physics system will ensure legal placement of objects and make sure they settle properly. In the example below, there is a physics system, but it is completely empty of code—a NULL physics system. I'll leave implementing a real physics system in the editor to you as an exercise. Throughout this chapter, you'll see calls to the physics system, but just remember that right now it doesn't do anything.

The `EditorGame` class will look familiar to you if you've looked over the `Teapot-WarsBaseGame` class in the previous chapter:

```
class EditorGame : public BaseGameLogic
{
    friend class EditorEventListener;

protected:
    float m_Lifetime;    //indicates how long this game has been in session
    EventListenerPtr m_editorEventListener;

public:
    EditorGame(GameOptions const &options);
    ~EditorGame();

    bool VLoadGame(string gameName);
    virtual void VOnUpdate(float time, float elapsedTime);

    // We need to expose this information so that the C# app can
    // know how big of an array to allocate to hold the list of
    // actors
    int GetNumActors() { return (int)m_ActorList.size(); }

    // Exposes the actor map so that the global functions
    // can retrieve actor information
    ActorMap::iterator GetActorMapBegin() { return m_ActorList.begin(); }
    ActorMap::iterator GetActorMapEnd() { return m_ActorList.end(); }

    bool IsRunning() { return (BGS_Running == m_State); }
    shared_ptr<IGameView> GetView();

    void OpenLevelFile( char* fileName );
};
```

As you can see, most of the EditorGame class is defined right in the constructor. EditorGame is a thin wrapper around BaseGameLogic, since all it has to do is provide some accessor methods to the actor lists and manage a view. Here's the constructor:

```
EditorGame::EditorGame(GameOptions const &options)
: BaseGameLogic(options)
, m_Lifetime(0)
{
    m_pPhysics.reset(CreateNullPhysics());
    m_editorEventListener = shared_ptr<EditorEventListener> (GCC_NEW
        EditorEventListener ( this ) );
    safeAddListener( m_editorEventListener, EvtData_New_Actor::sk_EventType );
```

```
safeAddListener( m_editorEventListener,
   EvtData_Destroy_Actor::sk_EventType );
safeAddListener( m_editorEventListener, EvtData_Move_Actor::sk_EventType );
safeAddListener( m_editorEventListener,
   EvtData_Request_New_Actor::sk_EventType );
}
```

The constructor initializes the physics system with a NULL physics stub and adds listeners for the "new actor" and "move actor" events. Next up is the update loop:

```
void EditorGame::VOnUpdate(float time, float elapsedTime)
{
   int deltaMilliseconds = int(elapsedTime * 1000.0f);
   m_Lifetime += elapsedTime;

   BaseGameLogic::VOnUpdate(time, elapsedTime);

   switch(m_State)
   {
   case BGS_MainMenu:
      // If we are at the main menu, go ahead and
      // start loading the game environment since the
      // editor doesn't have a main menu.
      VChangeState(BGS_LoadingGameEnvironment );
      break;
   case BGS_LoadingGameEnvironment:
      break;
   case BGS_WaitingForPlayers:
      break;
   case BGS_Running:
      break;
   case BGS_SpawnAI:
      break;
   default:
      assert(0 && _T("Unrecognized state."));
   }

   if(m_pPhysics)
   {
      m_pPhysics->VOnUpdate(elapsedTime);
      m_pPhysics->VSyncVisibleScene();
   }
}
```

The game logic for `EditorGame` doesn't have to worry about waiting for players or spawning AI. As `BaseGameLogic` initializes, it sets its state to `BGS_MainMenu`. Since you also don't have a main menu (you'll be handling UI within C#), you can set your state directly to `BGS_LoadingGameEnvironment`.

We have a few more functions to look at, and then we'll be finished with the editor's logic class:

```
void EditorGame::OpenLevelFile( char* fileName )
{
    while (m_ActorList.size() > 0)
    {
        ActorId id = m_ActorList.begin()->first;
        const EvtData_Destroy_Actor destroyActor( id );
        safeTriggerEvent( destroyActor );
    }
    const bool bStartupScriptSuccess =
        g_pApp->m_pLuaStateManager->DoFile(fileName );
    if ( false == bStartupScriptSuccess )
    {
        assert( 0 && "Unable to execute level file!" );
    }
}


shared_ptr<IGameView> EditorGame::GetView()
{
    shared_ptr<IGameView> pGameView = *m_gameViews.begin();
    return pGameView;
}
```

`OpenLevelFile()` executes a Lua script. Level files will be stored as Lua files, which will contain parameters on the actors in our level and a Lua command for each actor that will trigger a "request new actor" event.

The last function returns a function pointer to the game view. Again, since we don't have any AIs or extra players, we'll only have one view for the editor, which simplifies things greatly.

Just like the game, the editor has a `VLoadGame()` method:

```
bool EditorGame::VLoadGame(string gameName)
{
    if (gameName=="NewGame")
    {
        VBuildInitialScene();
        // After we build the initial scene, change the game
        // to New Game. The Editor Game View will do what it
```

```
        // needs to do, and then GameCode will transition
        // the game state into Running.
        safeTriggerEvent( EvtData_New_Game() );
    }

    return true;
}
```

This code should look familiar because it is implemented identically to what you saw in the `TeapotWarsBaseGame` class. In a real game, you might change this method to automatically load whatever level was worked on last.

FEWER CLICKS MAKE HAPPIER GAME DEVELOPERS

In any software development, from Web sites to tool development, it makes sense to do every-thing you can to minimize the number of mouse clicks it takes to do anything. This is espe-cially true with the most commonly used features. Put buttons for them right on the main menu and provide hot keys!

Before we move on to the editor view, a quick mention about the `EditorEventListener`. This listener listens for events and runs code to handle each one. It is very similar to the `TeapotWarsEventListener` you saw in Chapter 19, "A Game of Teapot Wars!" but handles only the events related to creating, moving, and destroying actors. For more information, take a look at *Source\Editor\Editor.cpp* in the *Game Coding Complete* source code.

The Editor View

The classes for the editor view are very similar to their *Teapot Wars* counterparts.

In a normal game, the human view is responsible for the sound manager, drawing the world, and grabbing user input. The editor view is a little simpler in one way, not needing a sound system, but more complicated since it receives input from the C# side of things. The following code is in *Source\Editor\ EditorGameView.cpp*:

```
void ListenForEditorEvents(EventListenerPtr listener)
{
    // Note that the only events we really care about are related
    // to when the app is starting up, and events related to
    // creating, destroying, or moving actors in the scene
    safeAddListener( listener, EvtData_Destroy_Actor::sk_EventType );
    safeAddListener( listener, EvtData_New_Game::sk_EventType );
```

```
    safeAddListener( listener, EvtData_New_Actor::sk_EventType );
    safeAddListener( listener, EvtData_Move_Actor::sk_EventType );
}


EditorGameView::EditorGameView()
{
    // The EditorGameView differs from its counterpart in TeapotWars primarily
    // in the fact that we don't have any UI classes. Any level information
    // should be displayed in the C# app.

    m_pScene.reset(GCC_NEW EditorScene());

    Frustum frustum;
    frustum.Init(D3DX_PI/4.0f, 1.0f, 1.0f, 100.0f);
    m_pCamera.reset(GCC_NEW CameraNode(&Mat4x4::g_Identity, frustum));
    assert(m_pScene && m_pCamera && _T("Out of memory"));

    m_pScene->VAddChild(optional_empty(), m_pCamera);
    m_pScene->SetCamera(m_pCamera);

    EventListenerPtr listener ( GCC_NEW EditorGameViewListener( this ) );
    ListenForEditorEvents(listener);
}
```

The same conceit you saw earlier with the game logic works here, too; there is a C function that takes a listener as a parameter and registers a group of events for any human views of the editor. We only register events that create, modify, or remove actors.

Here's what the view does when a new game is started:

```
void EditorGameView::BuildInitialScene()
{
    // EditorGameView::BuildInitialScene differs from the TeapotWarsView
    // version of this function in that we don't have a sound manager
    // or HUD.

    // Here's our sky node
    // This would be good to put into a file loaded into the editor,
    // rather than hardcoded. Another homework assignment!
    shared_ptr<SkyNode> sky(GCC_NEW SkyNode("Sky2", m_pCamera));
    m_pScene->VAddChild(optional_empty(), sky);

    VPushElement(m_pScene);
```

```
// We also make sure that the MovementController is hooked up
// to the keyboard and mouse handlers, since this is our primary method
// for moving the camera around.
m_pFreeCameraController.reset(GCC_NEW MovementController(m_pCamera, 90, 0));
m_KeyboardHandler = m_pFreeCameraController;
m_MouseHandler = m_pFreeCameraController;
m_pCamera->ClearTarget();

VOnRestore();
}
```

This is a simplified version of `TeapotWarsView::BuildInitialScene()`, since we don't have to worry about stuff like music. Just as in *Teapot Wars*, the sky node should really be in a Lua file, and the entire `BuildInitialScene()` method should be retired. Take a weekend and see if you can do it.

The `EditorEventListener` listens for registered events and calls code within the view class. This looks like the corresponding listener within `TeapotWarsView`, except the `EditorEventListener` doesn't need any code for teapots firing weapons and other game-specific events.

```
bool EditorGameViewListener::HandleEvent( IEventData const & event )
{
    // As mentioned earlier, the only events we really care about here
    // are events related to changes in the actors in the scene

    if ( EvtData_Destroy_Actor::sk_EventType == event.VGetEventType() )
    {
        const EvtData_Destroy_Actor & castEvent =
            static_cast< const EvtData_Destroy_Actor & >( event );
        ActorId aid = castEvent.m_id;
        m_pView->m_pScene->RemoveChild(aid);
    }
    else if ( EvtData_New_Game::sk_EventType == event.VGetEventType() )
    {
        m_pView->BuildInitialScene();
    }
    else if ( EvtData_Move_Actor::sk_EventType == event.VGetEventType() )
    {
        const EvtData_Move_Actor & ed =
            static_cast< const EvtData_Move_Actor & >( event );
        m_pView->MoveActor(ed.m_Id, ed.m_Mat);
    }
```

```
        else if ( EvtData_New_Actor::sk_EventType == event.VGetEventType() )
        {
            const EvtData_New_Actor & ed =
                static_cast< const EvtData_New_Actor & >( event );
            shared_ptr<SceneNode> node =
                ed.m_pActorParams->VCreateSceneNode(m_pView->m_pScene);
            m_pView->m_pScene->VAddChild(ed.m_pActorParams->m_Id, node);
            node->VOnRestore(&(*(m_pView->m_pScene)));
        }
        return false;
}
```

The `EditorGameViewListener` handles four events, and "move actor" and "destroy actor" are handled exactly the same way the game view does. The other two events are different. The `Editor::VLoadGame()` method you saw earlier sends the "new game" event, and the view responds by building its initial scene. The "new actor" event is handled similarly, but has no need to marry a teapot with a controller as the game does.

Wrapping Up the Editor Architecture

The editor is a stripped-down version of a game engine. It can add actors to a scene, render them, and receive events on how to modify the actors, either by moving them around or deleting them. It doesn't handle a lot of the higher functions of a game, which this simple editor doesn't really need. Next, we need to wire the editor game engine into our C# application.

BEST

PRACTICE

FAST ITERATION MAKES GAMES MORE FUN

In a commercial game editor, rather than using a stripped-down version of the game, many editors completely surround and extend the game. This enables content developers like level designers and artists to run the game inside the editor so they can test their work. Editors that don't work this way force content developers to change something in the editor, save the level, load the game, find the spot they changed, see the change in the game, and decide whether they like what they did. If they don't like it, and I guarantee they won't, they exit the game, load the editor, find the spot they changed again, and start the whole process over.

Before you can start adding features essential to the level editor, you need to add new things to the Editor C++ library to get the editor game engine and the C# editor app communicating. This part gets a little tricky, and for context, we need to go over differences between managed and unmanaged code.

Differences Between Managed-Code Land and Unmanaged-Code Land

With .Net, managed code is not actually compiled into machine code, but is instead written into an intermediary format. The .Net common language runtime (CLR) compiles the intermediary code into machine code at the time of execution and caches this machine code for when the application is run again. Unmanaged code is compiled directly into machine code. Some of the benefits from managed code are that it is portable to any machine that has the .Net CLR installed, but this comes at the cost of performance. In addition, C# uses a garbage collector, meaning that programs are not strictly responsible for cleaning up memory after themselves, although there are exceptions.

In addition, C# cannot load static libraries, but only dynamically linked libraries. Any unmanaged code that you call from C# will have to live inside a DLL.

Functions to Access the Editor Game Engine

Before you begin, a quick note on how you'll be passing data and calling functions in C++ from C#. While it is possible to instantiate objects in C++ and pass their pointers to C#, doing so requires a lot of preparation work, and it makes this sample editor a lot more complicated. Instead of creating an instance of the editor application layer and passing that pointer to the C# editor app, I'll use C-style functions that will access the global instance of the application layer. This will greatly simplify the explanation on how to wire the C# application with the editor game engine.

One of the functions that definitely needs to be exposed is our old friend WinMain(), which you read about back in Chapter 5. It is very similar to the original, but there it had a different beginning and end:

```
// This function is similar to the Main in GameCode3, but with a few
// key differences. We don't want to use GameCode's main loop since
// that would lock out the C# app.
int EditorMain(int *instancePtrAddress,
    int *hPrevInstancePtrAddress,
    int *hWndPtrAddress,
    int nCmdShow,
    int screenWidth, int screenHeight)
{
    // C# gets unhappy passing pointers to unmanaged dlls, so instead we pass
    // the actual address of the pointer itself as an int. Then we convert
    // the ints into pointer values.

    // In general, we do this for any pointers that we pass
    // from C# to the unmanaged dll.
```

```
HINSTANCE hInstance = (HINSTANCE)instancePtrAddress;
HINSTANCE hPrevInstance = (HINSTANCE) hPrevInstancePtrAddress;
HWND hWnd = (HWND)hWndPtrAddress;
WCHAR *lpCmdLine = L"";

// Set up checks for memory leaks.
//
int tmpDbgFlag = _CrtSetDbgFlag(_CRTDBG_REPORT_FLAG);

// set this flag to keep memory blocks around
tmpDbgFlag |= _CRTDBG_DELAY_FREE_MEM_DF;
   // this flag will cause intermittent pauses in your game!

// perform memory check for each alloc/dealloc
//tmpDbgFlag |= _CRTDBG_CHECK_ALWAYS_DF;
   // remember this is VERY VERY SLOW!

// always perform a leak check just before app exits.
tmpDbgFlag |= _CRTDBG_LEAK_CHECK_DF;

_CrtSetDbgFlag(tmpDbgFlag);

 // Set the callback functions. These functions allow the sample framework
 // to notify the application about device changes, user input, and windows
 // messages.  The callbacks are optional so you need only set callbacks for
 // events you're interested in. However, if you don't handle the device
 // reset/lost callbacks,  the sample framework won't be able to reset
 // your device since the application must first release all device
 // resources before resetting.  Likewise, if you don't handle the
 // device created/destroyed callbacks,  the sample framework won't be
 // able to recreate your device resources.

DXUTSetCallbackD3D9DeviceCreated( GameCodeApp::OnCreateDevice );
DXUTSetCallbackD3D9DeviceDestroyed( GameCodeApp::OnDestroyDevice );
DXUTSetCallbackMsgProc( GameCodeApp::MsgProc );
DXUTSetCallbackD3D9DeviceReset( GameCodeApp::OnResetDevice );
DXUTSetCallbackD3D9DeviceLost( GameCodeApp::OnLostDevice );
DXUTSetCallbackD3D9FrameRender( GameCodeApp::OnRender );
DXUTSetCallbackFrameMove( GameCodeApp::OnUpdateGame );

// Show the cursor and clip it when in full screen
DXUTSetCursorSettings( true, true );
```

```
// Perform application initialization
if (!g_pApp->InitInstance (hInstance, lpCmdLine, hWnd, screenWidth,
    screenHeight))
{
    return FALSE;
}

// Instead of calling Main Loop, we set up everything for the main loop
DXUTSetUpMainLoop();
return true;
}
```

EditorMain() looks very similar to GameCode3() except for the very beginning and the very end. The first few lines of EditorMain() cast some integer pointers into Windows handles for the application instance and window. C# pointers are very different beasts since the CLR uses managed memory. But, all we need for C# to do is hold these pointers and pass them into the C free functions that access the editor code. Because of this, it's safe to hold these pointers as integers in C# and cast them to real C++ pointers inside the free functions. One more note—any C# methods that do this should be declared with the unsafe keyword.

The very end of the function is different from its game engine counterpart. Instead of starting the main loop with DXUTMainLoop(), you call DXUTSetUpMainLoop(). If you look inside DXUTMainLoop(), you'll see that you call DXUTSetUpMainLoop() just before entering the message loop. You avoid entering the main loop here because you want the C# app to handle messages from its own loop. Otherwise, if you called the main loop here, control wouldn't return to the C# application until the main loop quit.

If the C# editor application's main loop is going to be responsible for handling messages, the editor needs to expose a few other functions as C free functions:

```
void RenderFrame()
{
    // In TeapotWars, this would be called by GameCode's main loop
    // Since the C# app has its own main loop, we expose this
    // function so that C# app can call from its main loop
    DXUTRender3DEnvironment();
}

void WndProc(int *hWndPtrAddress, int msg, int wParam, int lParam)
{
    HWND hWnd = (HWND)hWndPtrAddress;
    DXUTStaticWndProc( hWnd, msg, WPARAM(wParam), LPARAM(lParam) );
}
```

```
int DXShutdown()
{
   // Normally this is called after the GameCode main loop ends. We
   // expose this here so that the C# app can shut down after it finishes
   // its main loop
   DXUTShutdown();
   _CrtDumpMemoryLeaks();                 // Reports leaks to stderr

   return g_pApp->GetExitCode();
}
```

RenderFrame() exposes the rendering call, DXUTRender3DEnvironment(), to the C# app, so it can render a frame if the editor isn't handling any other messages. WndProc() exposes the editor's message handling function so that the editor can forward any appropriate messages to be handled by the editor game engine, such as user input to move the camera position around. Finally, DXShutdown() shuts down the DirectX device and exits the editor.

These C-style functions are in *Source\Editor\EditorGlobalFunctions.cpp*, which is part of the Editor project in Visual Studio, which compiles to the Editor.Dll loaded by the C# editor.

CREATING THE DLL

When you create a DLL, you usually want to expose functions to any consumer of that DLL. This is done with the _declspec keyword in a C++ header file. Here's what this looks like:

```
#define DllExport _declspec(DLLexport)

#include "..\Editor\EditorGlobalFunctions.h"

//====================================================================
//
// This file exposes the functions in the EditorGlobalFunctions file
// for use by the C# app.
//
//====================================================================

extern "C" DllExport int EditorMain(
   int *instancePtrAddress,
   int *hPrevInstancePtrAddress,
   int *hWndPtrAddress,
   int nCmdShow, int screenWidth, int screenHeight);
```

```
extern "C" DllExport void RenderFrame();
extern "C" DllExport void DXShutdown();
extern "C" DllExport void WndProc(int *hWndPtrAddress, int msg,
    int wParam, int lParam);
```

Let's start by looking at this line:

```
#define DllExport _declspec(DLLexport)
```

Each exported function must have `extern "C" _declspec(DLLexport)` before the declaration. The macro at the top of the last code segment helps keep the code looking cleaner.

THE C# EDITOR APPLICATION

Get ready to switch gears from C++ to C#. It feels like we haven't touched this in a while, huh? When the editor is complete, it should look like what you see in Figure 20.1.

The window on the left is what you created at the beginning of this chapter, a panel that forms the surface for DirectX to render the game world. The C# form

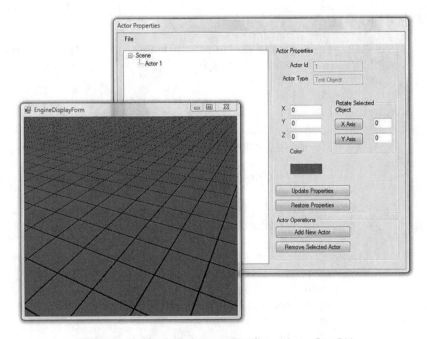

FIGURE 20.1 The final product—a C# editor using a C++ DLL.

on the right is the Actor Properties form, which is used to create new actors in the game world and manipulate their properties. During the rest of this chapter, you'll hear references to the `EngineDisplayForm` and `ActorProperties` classes, all of which belong to the `EditorApp` C# namespace.

ONE WINDOW ISN'T ENOUGH

Most commercial game editors have multiple windows rendering simultaneously. One of these windows looks like the `EngineDisplayForm` in Figure 20.2, which renders the game world from any angle and looks pretty much as you would expect the game to look. Other windows show the world in wireframe, usually directly along the X-, Y-, and Z-axes. This can really help content creators see exactly where an object is placed in the world. In many of these editors, each window is completely configurable, too, allowing the user to set up his display panels in exactly the right way to help him work quickly and correctly.

C# Basic Editor App

For starters, you'll want to create a simple application using C#. Rather than going over the minutiae of how to create a C# project, I recommend using MSDN. MSDN is at times infuriating, especially when you need information on how to use a function call and the only information MSDN has is basically the parameters. But in this case, you should be able to find a lot of information on how to set up C# projects using Visual Studio.

First, create a new form and add a `Systems.Windows.Form.Panel` to the form. Check out `Source\EditorApp\EngineDisplayForm.cs` in the *Game Coding Complete* source for an example.

You should have an empty form that looks like the one shown in Figure 20.2.

FIGURE 20.2 `EngineDisplayForm`.

If you run the app, you should see an empty Windows form appear on your screen. This isn't too exciting, but it will eventually be used by the application layer to render your level.

C# NativeMethods Class

You are now ready to see how C# loads the editor DLL. The NativeMethods class declares hooks into the C++ DLL so that they can be called from C#:

```
namespace EditorApp
{
   // We also need to import some functions that will allow us to load
   // the dll, and free it when we're done.
   static class NativeMethods
   {
#if DEBUG
      const string editorDllName = "Editord.dll";
#else
      const string editorDllName = "Editor.dll";
#endif
      [DllImport(editorDllName)]
      public unsafe static extern int EditorMain(
         IntPtr instancePtrAddress,
         IntPtr hPrevInstancePtrAddress,
         IntPtr hWndPtrAddress,
         int nCmdShow,
         int screenWidth, int screenHeight);
      [DllImport(editorDllName)]
      public static extern void RenderFrame();
      [DllImport(editorDllName)]
      public static extern void DXShutdown();
      [DllImport(editorDllName)]
      public unsafe static extern void WndProc(
         IntPtr hWndPtrAddress, int msg, int wParam, int lParam);
   }
}
```

This code lives in Source\EditorApp\NativeMethods.cs and shows you how to import functions from an unmanaged DLL. Anytime you export a C free function with the DLLExport macro, you'll also need to change the NativeMethods class so C# can see it.

The EngineDisplayForm Class

The EngineDisplayForm class is the primary interface into the game world, not only visually but programmatically as well. It loads the C++ DLL and makes calls through the NativeMethods class to access the C++ data structures and objects. The C++ DLL is loaded with the constructor of the EngineDisplayForm class:

```
public partial class EngineDisplayForm : Form
{
   const int INVALID_ID = -1;
   private MessageHandler m_messageFilter;

   public unsafe EngineDisplayForm()
   {
      InitializeComponent();
      try
      {
         // This is how we get the instance handle for our C# app.
         System.IntPtr hInstance =
System.Runtime.InteropServices.Marshal.GetHINSTANCE(this.GetType().Module);

         // This is how we get the window handle for
         // the panel we'll be rendering into.
         IntPtr hwnd = this.DisplayPanel.Handle;

         // Call into our Dll main function, which will set up an
         // instance of the EditorApp project.
         // Remember that we can't pass the pointer itself,
         // so we'll pass the pointer value.
         // The int will be converted into a pointer value later.
         NativeMethods.EditorMain(
            hInstance, IntPtr.Zero, hwnd, 1,
            this.DisplayPanel.Width, this.DisplayPanel.Height);

         m_messageFilter = new MessageHandler(
            this.Handle, this.DisplayPanel.Handle, this);
          m_actorPropertiesForm = new ActorPropertiesForm(this);
         m_actorPropertiesForm.Show();
      }
      catch() { }
   }
}
```

First, you specify the name of the DLL itself. You should make sure the DLL is in the same directory as the C# editor application executable. This example takes into account the fact that the DLL has a different name for debug and release builds.

The call to GetHINSTANCE() grabs the instance handle for this application, and the next line gets the window handle for the panel that will become the main rendering area on the C# form. These handles are converted into integer values and then passed into the EditorMain function in the unmanaged C++ DLL.

The next methods manage initialization of the ActorPropertiesForm:

```
public void SetEditorReadyForUse()
{
    m_actorPropertiesForm.InitScene();
}
public EditorActorParams GetActorInformation(uint actorId)
{
    EditorActorParams actorParams;

    try
    {
        // We're getting a position array from the unmanaged DLL, so
        // allocate space in memory that can hold 3 floats.
        IntPtr tempArray = Marshal.AllocCoTaskMem(3 * sizeof(float));

        NativeMethods.GetActorPos(tempArray, actorId);

        // Copy the memory into a float array and dispose of our memory.
        float[] actorPos = new float[3];
        Marshal.Copy(tempArray, actorPos, 0, 3);
        Marshal.FreeCoTaskMem(tempArray);

        int actorType = NativeMethods. GetActorType(actorId);
        UInt32 actorColor = NativeMethods. GetActorColor(actorId);
        actorParams = new EditorActorParams(actorId, (ActorType)actorType,
          actorPos, Color.FromArgb((int)actorColor), 0.0f, 0.0f);

        return actorParams;
    }
    catch
    {
        return actorParams =
            new EditorActorParams(EditorActorParams.INVALID_ID);
    }
}
```

```
public unsafe int[] GetActorList()
{
    // We need to know how many actors there are,
    // in order to find out how much memory to allocate
    int numActors = NativeMethods.GetNumActors();

    IntPtr tempArray = Marshal.AllocCoTaskMem(numActors * sizeof(int));
    NativeMethods.GetActorList(tempArray.ToInt32(), numActors);

    // Copy the memory into an array of ints, and dispose of our memory
    int[] actorList = new int[numActors];
    Marshal.Copy(tempArray, actorList, 0, numActors);
    Marshal.FreeCoTaskMem(tempArray);

    return actorList;
}

public unsafe void SelectActor()
{
    IntPtr hWnd = this.DisplayPanel.Handle.
    int actorId = NativeMethods.PickActor(hWnd);
    if (actorId != INVALID_ID)
    {
        m_actorPropertiesForm.SelectTreeNode(actorId);
    }
}
```

SetEditorReadyForUse() is called when the application layer, game logic, and views have finished with their initialization tasks. You can see that SetEditorReady-ForUse() calls InitScene(), which populates the tree view with actor IDs from this level.

GetActorInformation(), if you recall, is called by the ActorPropertiesForm whenever the user clicks on a TreeNode or directly on an actor in the level. You allocated space in memory that can hold three floating-point values. Pass the pointer address and actor ID into DllWrapperGetActorPos(), and that memory should be filled with the three floating-point values for the actor's X, Y, and Z coordinates. You can copy this into a floating-point array and then make sure to free this memory. Then you grab the actor type and color, and then return a new Editor-ActorParams object containing the actor information.

GetActorList is called whenever you are populating the TreeView. GetActorList first finds out how many actors are in this level. It allocates memory to hold the specified number of integers and passes the pointer address into DllWrapperGet-ActorList, which will copy the actor IDs into that memory location. You copy these values into an integer array and then free the memory.

SelectActor is called whenever you click directly on an actor in the level. Remember that the PickActor function in your accessor functions directly grabs the cursor position, so you don't need to pass the cursor address. You just need to pass the window handle for the Panel in the EngineDisplayForm. Once you get the actor ID back from the unmanaged DLL, you call SelectTreeNode.

The C# MessageHandler Class

Next, you set up your message filter with both the window handle for this form and the window handle for the Panel. So here's something slightly annoying about C#—there are tons of event handlers you can use, ranging from key presses on forms to button presses or mouse actions, but the event handlers require work to convert the data into traditional Win32 message data. However, the IMessage-Filter class actually does give you the Win32 message data, and you need a helper class to manage this, NativeMessageHandler:

```
using System;
using System.Collections.Generic;
using System.Text;
using System.Windows.Forms;

namespace EditorApp
{
    //==========================================================================
    //
    // We need to hook up our own message handler, since it's difficult
    // getting the proper C wndProc params from using the standard C#
    // event handlers.
    //
    //==========================================================================
    public class MessageHandler : IMessageFilter
    {
        const int WM_LBUTTONDOWN = 0x0201;
        const int WM_LBUTTONUP = 0x0202;
        const int WM_LBUTTONDBLCLK = 0x0203;
        const int WM_RBUTTONDOWN = 0x0204;
        const int WM_RBUTTONUP = 0x0205;
        const int WM_RBUTTONDBLCLK = 0x0206;
        const int WM_MBUTTONDOWN = 0x0207;
        const int WM_MBUTTONUP = 0x0208;
        const int WM_MBUTTONDBLCLK = 0x0209;

        const int WM_KEYDOWN = 0x0100;
        const int WM_KEYUP = 0x0101;
```

```
const int WM_SYSKEYDOWN = 0x0104;
const int WM_SYSKEYUP = 0x0105;
const int WM_CLOSE = 0x0010;

IntPtr m_formHandle;
IntPtr m_displayPanelHandle;
EngineDisplayForm m_parent;
bool m_gameIsRunning;

// We take both the EngineDisplayForm's handle and its
// displayPanel handle, since messages will sometimes be for the
// form, or the display panel.

public MessageHandler( IntPtr formHandle,
   IntPtr displayPanelHandle, EngineDisplayForm parent )
{
   m_formHandle = formHandle;
   m_displayPanelHandle = displayPanelHandle;
   m_parent = parent;
   m_gameIsRunning = false;
}

public bool PreFilterMessage(ref Message m)
{
   // Intercept messages only if they occur for the EngineDisplayForm
   // or its display panel.
   if (m.HWnd == m_displayPanelHandle || m.HWnd == m_formHandle)
   {
      switch (m.Msg)
      {
         case WM_LBUTTONDOWN:
         case WM_LBUTTONUP:
         case WM_LBUTTONDBLCLK:
         case WM_RBUTTONDOWN:
         case WM_RBUTTONUP:
         case WM_RBUTTONDBLCLK:
         case WM_MBUTTONDOWN:
         case WM_MBUTTONUP:
         case WM_MBUTTONDBLCLK:
         case WM_KEYDOWN:
         case WM_KEYUP:
         case WM_SYSKEYDOWN:
         case WM_SYSKEYUP:
         case WM_CLOSE:
```

```
        {
            NativeMethods.WndProc(m_displayPanelHandle,
                m.Msg, m.WParam.ToInt32(), m.LParam.ToInt32());
            // If the left mouse button is up, try doing a
            // ray cast to see if it intersects with an actor
            if (m.Msg == WM_LBUTTONUP)
            {
                m_parent.SelectActor();

            }
            return true;
        }
    }
}
return false;
}
```

The `PreMessageFilter` class lives in the `Source\Editor\MessageHandler.cs` file. This class determines if the window handle for these messages matches either the `EngineDisplayForm` or the `Panel`. This would happen if the `EngineDisplayForm` had focus and the user moves his mouse around or presses keys on the keyboard. In this instance, it would be appropriate for the editor game engine to handle these messages, so you call the unmanaged DLL's function `WndProc()`. If this were a message that occurred for some other form, `PreMessageFilter` would simply ignore the message. You would run into this occurrence if the user clicked on a form that wasn't the `EngineDisplayForm`, such as a form that displayed properties for the objects in the level. You'll see that in a little bit.

One message that the C# editor application needs to trap is `WM_LBUTTONUP`. This will call `EngineDisplayForm::SelectActor()` so that you can click directly on the actor you are interested in and have its properties show up in the `ActorProperties-Form`.

Similar to the main loop in C++, when the editor application isn't processing messages, it is idle, and can do other jobs like render the 3D world:

```
public void Application_Idle(object sender, EventArgs e)
{
    try
    {
        // Render the scene if we are idle
        NativeMethods.RenderFrame();
        if (!m_gameIsRunning)
        {
            // In addition, test to see if the editor is
            // fully initialized and running.
```

```
            bool isRunning = false;
            isRunning = NativeMethods.IsGameRunning();
            if (isRunning)
            {
                // If the editor is running, then we should
                // populate the editor form with information
                // about the scene.
                // We just need to do this once.
                m_actorPropertiesForm.InitScene();
                m_gameIsRunning = true;
            }
        }
    }
    catch (Exception ex)
    {
        MessageBox.Show(ex.Message);
    }
    m_parent.Invalidate();
    }
}
```

`Application_Idle()` calls into `NativeMethods.RenderFrame()`. Obviously, this function is called during any idle time, at which point you render the level. Remember in the constructor for `EngineDisplayForm` that you passed the window handle for the `EngineDisplayForm`'s `Panel` into the unmanaged DLL? The editor game engine will use the `Panel` as a surface to render onto.

The check `m_gameIsRunning` handles the time when the unmanaged DLL is still initializing. When the game logic is running, then you can start querying the game logic for information about actors in the level.

At the end of the `Application_Idle()`, you call `m_parent.Invalidate()` so that `Application_Idle()` will continue to be called as long as there aren't any other messages.

The C# Program Class

The C# `Program` class is the main entry point to the C# editor application. It constructs a new `EngineDsplayForm` and hooks up the `MessageHandler` so it can handle Windows messages and rendering.

```
using System;
using System.Collections.Generic;
using System.Windows.Forms;
```

```
namespace EditorApp
{
    static class Program
    {
        /// <summary>
        /// The main entry point for the application.
        /// </summary>
        [STAThread]
        static void Main()
        {
            Application.EnableVisualStyles();
            Application.SetCompatibleTextRenderingDefault(false);
            EngineDisplayForm form = new EngineDisplayForm();

            // Hook up our message handler
            MessageHandler messageHandler = form.GetMessageHandler();
            Application.AddMessageFilter(messageHandler);
            Application.Idle += new EventHandler(messageHandler.Application_Idle);
            Application.Run(form);
        }
    }
}
```

We're looking at the entry point to the C# editor app in `Source\Editor\Program.cs`. This code tells the application to use the message handler described in the last section. C# applications can process a special event handler just before they go idle, defined by `Application.Idle`. This is when the `NativeMessageHandler::Application_Idle()` will get called, which will render the view of the game world on the `EngineDisplayForm` window.

Now you can build everything and fire up a basic version of the editor. `WM_KEYDOWN` and `WM_MOUSEMOVE` messages are forwarded from `EngineDisplayForm` into the C++ Editor.Dll, letting you define how they change the world state or camera position by changing the `EditorGameView` class.

This is definitely important for a level editor. You need to be able to move around and survey your level. There's still no way for you to add actors or change their properties. That's what you'll see next.

GETTING INFORMATION ABOUT ACTORS IN THE LEVEL

What information do you need about actors in the level? At a minimum, you want to know about their location. You may also want to know the unique identifier for each actor in the level. In this case, it will be the actor ID for each actor. You may also want to know if there are any AI scripts attached to your actor, and some level editors allow you to attach special tags to your actors so that the actors respond to events in the world. In this case, let's just grab the basic information in the ActorParams—the actor ID, actor type, position, and color.

Adding Accessor Functions to the Editor Game Engine

In order to provide actor information to the C# editor application, a few more C style functions are added to the Source\Editor\EditorGlobalFunctions.h file:

```
int GetNumActors()
{
   EditorGame* pGame = (EditorGame*)g_pApp->m_pGame;
   if ( pGame )
   {
      return pGame->GetNumActors();
   }
   else
   {
      return 0;
   }
}


void GetActorList( int *ptr, int numActors )
{
   // To keep things simple, we pass the actor ids to the C# app
   // the C# app iterates through the actor ids, and calls back into
   // the unmanaged DLL to get the appropriate information about each
   // actor
   EditorGame* pGame = (EditorGame*)g_pApp->m_pGame;
   if ( pGame )
   {
      ActorMap::iterator itr;
      int actorArrayIndex;
      for ( itr = pGame->GetActorMapBegin(), actorArrayIndex = 0;
         itr != pGame->GetActorMapEnd() && actorArrayIndex < numActors; itr++,
         actorArrayIndex++ )
      {
         ActorId actorId = itr->first;
         ptr[actorArrayIndex] = actorId;
      }
   }
}
```

GetNumActors() is pretty simple. It uses the global application layer pointer to get to the game logic. Once it has a pointer to the game logic, it gets the number of actors in the level and returns that. The reason why you need the number of actors is that the C# editor application will be allocating space for an array of integers. The editor will use the number of actors to determine how large of an array to allocate. GetActorList() fills that array with the actors in this level by iterating through the actor data structure stored in the editor logic.

The next three functions get information about actors:

```
void GetActorPos( int *actorPosPtrAddress, ActorId actorId )
{
    float* ptr = (float*)actorPosPtrAddress;

    shared_ptr<IActor> pActor = g_pApp->m_pGame->VGetActor( actorId   );
    if ( !pActor )
    {
        return;
    }

    // Just to keep things simple, the C# app allocates memory,
    // and we populate that memory with position information.
    // This way, the C# app can free this memory when it's
    // finished.
    Vec3 position = pActor->VGetMat().GetPosition();
    ptr[0]=position.x;
    ptr[1]=position.y;
    ptr[2]=position.z;
}

int GetActorType( ActorId actorId )
{
    shared_ptr<IActor> pActor = g_pApp->m_pGame->VGetActor( actorId );
    if ( !pActor )
    {
        return 0;
    }

    return pActor->VGetType();
}

DWORD GetActorColor( ActorId actorId )
{
    shared_ptr<IActor> pActor = g_pApp->m_pGame->VGetActor(
        actorId );
```

```
    if (!pActor)
    {
        return 0;
    }

    shared_ptr<ActorParams> pActorParams = pActor->VGetParams();
    if (!pActorParams)
    {
        return 0;
    }


    return pActorParams->m_Color;
}
```

These functions provide information on the actor's position and the actor type. `GetActorPos()` receives a pointer to an array of floating-point values and copies the position information into that array. `GetActorType()` returns the type of actor, and `GetActorColor()` returns a `DWORD` containing the RGBA values of the actor, given a valid actor ID.

Every game editor needs a method to select an actor from the visual display. To do this requires a special bit of technology called a *raycaster*, which mathematically calculates which objects in the game world are intersected by a ray given two endpoints. `PickActor()` is a function that does exactly this:

```
int PickActor(int hWndPtrAddress)
{
    HWND hWnd = (HWND)hWndPtrAddress;

    CPoint ptCursor;
    GetCursorPos( &ptCursor );

    // Convert the screen coordinates of the mouse cursor into
    // coordinates relative to the client window
    ScreenToClient( hWnd, &ptCursor );
    RayCast rayCast(ptCursor);
    EditorGame* pGame = (EditorGame*)g_pApp->m_pGame;

    if (!pGame)
    {
        return INVALID_ID;
    }

    shared_ptr<IGameView> pView = pGame->GetView();
    if (!pView)
```

```
    {
        return INVALID_ID;
    }

    shared_ptr<EditorGameView> gameView =
        boost::static_pointer_cast<EditorGameView>( pView );

    // Cast a ray through the scene. The RayCast object contains an array of
    // Intersection objects.
    gameView->GetScene()->Pick(&rayCast);
    rayCast.Sort();

    // If there are any intersections, get information from the first
    // intersection.
    if (rayCast.m_NumIntersections)
    {
        Intersection firstIntersection = rayCast.m_IntersectionArray[0];
        optional<ActorId> maybeID = firstIntersection.m_actorId;
        if (maybeID.valid())
        {
            ActorId id = *maybeID;
            return id;
        }
    }
    return INVALID_ID;
}
```

PickActor() will take the current cursor position and convert the position into coordinates relative to the editor window. If you remember the Frustum class from Chapter 14, "3D Scenes," the ray will go from the camera location through the near clipping plane at exactly the mouse position.

The RayCast class is designed with this purpose in mind, and is a part of the *Game Coding Complete* source code. RayCast::Pick() will fill member variables, indicating the number of intersections and the actor information of all actors intersected by the ray sorted by their distance from the camera. The code grabs the first actor ID in the list of intersection and returns the actor ID. This will allow users to click on objects in the world and then find out information about them.

One last function will return whether the editor logic has been initialized and is running:

```
bool IsRunning()
{
    EditorGame* game = (EditorGame*)g_pApp->m_pGame;
    if (game)
```

```
   {
      bool isRunning = game->IsRunning();
      return isRunning;
   }
   return false;
}
```

By this point, you could have probably written that function yourself! It simply grabs a pointer to the EditorGame object and queries the IsRunning() method, indicating whether the game logic has finished initializing and building the initial scene. If this returns true, then you are ready to start querying the game logic for actors and eventually add and modify actors.

Adding Functions to the Editor DLL

Now that you have functions that can access actor information in the level, you need to expose them so that the C# editor app can query the editor game engine for information. The C free functions need to be exported, and declared in Source\Editor\EditorGlobalFunctions.h:

```
extern "C" DllExport bool IsGameRunning();
extern "C" DllExport int GetActorType( ActorId actorId );
extern "C" DllExport int GetNumActors();
extern "C" DllExport void GetActorList( int *actorIdArrayPtrAddress,
   int size );
extern "C" DllExport DWORD GetActorColor( ActorId actorId );
extern "C" DllExport void GetActorPos( int *actorPosPtrAddress,
   ActorId actorId );
extern "C" DllExport int PickActor(int *hWndPtrAddress);
```

To plug in the other end of your DLL wire, the NativeMethods class in the C# code needs to have this code:

```
public static extern bool IsGameRunning();
[return: MarshalAs(UnmanagedType.I1)]
[DllImport(editorDllName)]
public static extern int GetActorType(uint actorId);
[DllImport(editorDllName)]
public static extern int GetNumActors();
[DllImport(editorDllName)]
public unsafe static extern void GetActorList(IntPtr actorIdArrayPtrAddress,
                                              int size);
[DllImport(editorDllName)]
```

```
public static extern UInt32 GetActorColor(uint actorId);
[DllImport(editorDllName)]
public unsafe static extern void GetActorPos(IntPtr actorPosPtrAddress, uint
                                    actorId);
[DllImport(editorDllName)]
public unsafe static extern int PickActor(IntPtr hWndPtrAddress);
```

One minor thing to note is the return value for IsGameRunning. An ANSI C-style bool is a single byte value, while most Win 32 APIs return a bool as a 4-byte value. You need to marshal the return type so that you get the proper value.

Displaying Actor Properties in the Editor

On the C# side, you need to call these functions and display the information using C# user interface controls on the ActorPropertiesForm. An example of this is using a Treeview to show a list of all the actors in the world. Textboxes can be used to enter and display actor properties, such as its position in the world. Look at Source\Editor\ActorPropertiesForm.cs to see how it's put together.

The ActorPropertiesForm is shown in Figure 20.3.

For the C# editor to view and modify actor parameters, it needs a parallel structure to the ActorParams in C++. This is declared in Source\Editor\ EngineDisplayForm.cs:

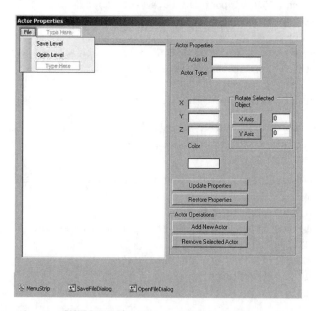

FIGURE 20.3 The ActorPropertiesForm.

```csharp
public enum ActorType
{
    AT_Unknown,
    AT_Sphere,
    AT_Teapot,
    AT_Grid,
    AT_GenericMeshObject
};

public struct EditorActorParams
{
    public const uint INVALID_ID = 0;

    public uint m_actorId;
    public ActorType m_actorType;
    public float[] m_pos;
    public Color m_color;
    public float m_length;
    public float m_radius;
    public string m_effectFile;
    public string m_meshFile;

    public EditorActorParams( uint actorId )
    {
        m_actorId = actorId;
        m_actorType = ActorType.AT_Unknown;
        m_pos = new float[0];
        m_color = Color.White;
        m_length = 0;
        m_radius = 0;
        m_effectFile = String.Empty;
        m_meshFile = String.Empty;
    }

    public EditorActorParams(uint actorId, ActorType actorType, float[] pos,
        Color color, float length, float radius)
    {
        m_actorId = actorId;
        m_actorType = actorType;
        m_pos = pos;
        m_color = color;
        m_length = length;
        m_radius = radius;
```

```
        m_effectFile = String.Empty;
        m_meshFile = String.Empty;
    }
}
```

The unmanaged C++ DLL won't actually be passing any `ActorParams` pointers. Instead, `EngineDisplayForm` will query for various pieces of information on the different actors, using that information to create an `EngineActorParams` object, and then passing that object to the `ActorPropertiesForm` to populate the form with information on each actor. Since you haven't exposed the `ActorTypes` in the DLL, you'll need to create your own `ActorTypes` enumeration here as well.

KEEP THE GAME AND EDITOR IN SYNC

Note that we create two structures that have to remain in sync. As previously stated, we don't export the C++ version of `ActorTypes` to keep the C++/C# interoperability simple, so whenever you change one, you have to remember to change the other.

This kind of thing happens in commercial game editors all the time. When a particular bit of the editor changes to manipulate something new in the game, both the editor and the game code have to change simultaneously. Making this even trickier is the whole development team must usually update their code and tools in a coordinated fashion, lest the editor or game not match the latest data on the development server. If you think this causes headaches in game development, believe me you have no idea.

Now let's go back to the `ActorPropertiesForm` and see how it is structured to get and set actor properties viewed in the 3D scene in the `EngineDisplayForm`. You'll see the entire class from top to bottom, with some explanations in between snippets of code:

```
using System;
using System.Collections.Generic;
using System.ComponentModel;
using System.Data;
using System.Drawing;
using System.Text;
using System.Collections;
using System.Windows.Forms;
using System.IO;
```

```csharp
namespace EditorApp
{
    public partial class ActorPropertiesForm : Form
    {
        EngineDisplayForm m_parent;
        ArrayList m_types;
        TreeNode m_mainNode;
        ActorCreationForm m_createForm;

        public ActorPropertiesForm( EngineDisplayForm parent )
        {
            InitializeComponent();
            m_parent = parent;
            m_types = new ArrayList();
            m_types.Add("Unknown");
            m_types.Add("Sphere");
            m_types.Add("Teapot");
            m_types.Add("AiTeapot");
            m_types.Add("Test Object");
            m_types.Add("Grid");
            m_types.Add("Generic Mesh Object");

            m_createForm = new ActorCreationForm();

            m_mainNode = new TreeNode();
            m_mainNode.Name = "mainNode";
            m_mainNode.Text = "Scene";
            this.m_treeView.Nodes.Add(m_mainNode);

            // Make sure nothing that can change the scene
            // is active until the Editor itself has been
            // initialized
            m_fileToolStripMenuItem.Enabled = false;
            m_addActorBtn.Enabled = false;
            m_removeActorBtn.Enabled = false;
            m_updateActorPosBtn.Enabled = false;
            m_restoreActorPosBtn.Enabled = false;
            m_rotateActorYAxisBtn.Enabled = false;
            m_rotateActorXAxisBtn.Enabled = false;
        }

        public void InitScene()
        {
            // This gets called when we are ready to make
            // adjustments to the scene.
```

```
        m_fileToolStripMenuItem.Enabled = true;
        m_addActorBtn.Enabled = true;
        m_removeActorBtn.Enabled = true;
        m_updateActorPosBtn.Enabled = true;
        m_restoreActorPosBtn.Enabled = true;
        m_rotateActorXAxisBtn.Enabled = true;
        m_rotateActorYAxisBtn.Enabled = true;

        m_mainNode.Nodes.Clear();
        int[] actorList = m_parent.GetActorList();
        // Get a list of actors in the scene, and add
        // the appropriate information to our treeview
        PopulateTreeView(actorList);
    }
```

InitScene() is called to enable the forms buttons and initialize the TreeView with the actors in the level. It is also called when you add or remove an actor to the level. The real work to initialize the TreeView is done in PopulateTreeView():

```
    private void PopulateTreeView(int[] actorList)
    {
        // Add each actor as its own node in the treeview.
        for (int i = 0; i < actorList.GetLength(0); i++)
        {
            TreeNode node = new TreeNode();
            node.Name = actorList[i].ToString();
            node.Text = "Actor " + actorList[i];
            m_mainNode.Nodes.Add(node);
        }
    }
```

PopulateTreeView takes an array of actor IDs as integers and creates new TreeNodes. Each TreeNode is identified by an actor ID.

When you click on a node in the TreeView, the ActorPropertiesForm should display information about the tree node's corresponding actor. That happens in Tree-View_NodeMouseClick():

```
    private void TreeView_NodeMouseClick(object sender,
        TreeNodeMouseClickEventArgs e)
    {
        TreeNode node = e.Node;
        if (node != m_mainNode)
        {
            // If we click on an actor node, have the EngineDisplayForm
            // get information on that actor from the unmanaged DLL.
```

```
        EditorActorParams actorParams =
            m_parent.GetActorInformation(UInt32.Parse(node.Name));
        PopulateActorInformation(actorParams);
    }
}
```

`TreeView_NodeMouseClick` checks to make sure the node isn't the main or root node and then accesses the actor ID associated with the node. Then it asks the `EngineDisplayForm` to grab information about this actor. The information is returned as an `EditorActorParams` object.

```
private void PopulateActorInformation(EditorActorParams actorParams)
{
    m_actorIdTextbox.Text = actorParams.m_actorId.ToString();
    m_actorTypeTextbox.Text = (String)m_types[(int)actorParams.m_actorType];
    m_actorXTextbox.Text = actorParams.m_pos[0].ToString();
    m_actorYTextbox.Text = actorParams.m_pos[1].ToString();
    m_actorZTextbox.Text = actorParams.m_pos[2].ToString();
    m_colorPreviewPanel.BackColor = actorParams.m_color;
}
```

The `ActorPropertiesForm` uses `PopulateActorInformation` to display information about the currently selected actor in the `TreeView`. Use the `ActorType` to index into the `m_types` `ArrayList` to find the appropriate string to display, describing this actor's type.

A similar thing needs to happen if you click on the graphics version of the actor in the `EngineDisplayForm`. If an actor is returned from `PickActor()`, the corresponding actor in the `TreeView` is found, selected, and its properties are displayed in the `ActorPropertiesForm`:

```
public void SelectTreeNode(int actorId)
{
    // There are two methods of populating actor information. We can
    // select a node in the treeview, or we can click on the actor
    // in the world view. If we click on the actor in the world view,
    // we use this function to update the actor information.
    TreeNode[] node = m_mainNode.Nodes.Find(actorId.ToString(), true);
    if (node.GetLength(0) > 0)
    {
        m_treeView.SelectedNode = node[0];
        EditorActorParams actorParams =
            m_parent.GetActorInformation((uint)actorId);
        PopulateActorInformation(actorParams);
    }
}
```

An actor ID is used to find the corresponding `TreeNode` in the `TreeView`. Then `EngineDisplayForm::GetActorInformation()` is called to get the `ActorParams` from this actor, and that in turn is passed into `PopulateActorInformation`.

CREATING, CHANGING, AND REMOVING ACTORS

The very first thing you'll do to a new level is add its first actor. You also want to remove actors and change their properties. Just as you saw with displaying actor properties, new accessor functions need to be added to the C++ DLL in `Source\Editor\EditorGlobalFunctions.cpp`. The first are `CreateActor()` and `RemoveActor()`:

```
void CreateActor( ActorType type, DWORD color, float length, float radius,
                  char* effectFileName, char* meshFileName )
{
    Vec3 startPosition(0.0f, 1.5f, 0.0f);
    switch (type)
    {
    case AT_Teapot:
        {
            TeapotParams tp;
            tp.m_Mat.SetPosition(startPosition);
            tp.m_Length = 2.5;
            tp.m_Color = color;
            const EvtData_Request_New_Actor requestActor( &tp );
            safeTriggerEvent( requestActor );
        }
        break;
    case AT_Grid:
        {
            GridParams grid;
            grid.m_Color = color;
            strcpy_s( grid.m_Texture, GridParams::sk_MaxTextureNameLen,
                "grid.dds" );
            grid.m_Mat = Mat4x4::g_Identity;
            grid.m_Squares = length;
            grid.m_Mat.SetPosition(startPosition);
            const EvtData_Request_New_Actor gridEvt( &grid );
            safeTriggerEvent( gridEvt );
        }
        break;
    case AT_Sphere:
```

```
        {
            SphereParams sp;
            sp.m_Pos = startPosition;
            sp.m_Radius = radius;
            sp.m_Segments = 16;
            sp.m_Color = color;
            const EvtData_Request_New_Actor requestActor( &sp );
            safeTriggerEvent( requestActor );
        }
        break;
    case AT_GenericMeshObject:
        {
            GenericMeshObjectParams gmp;
            gmp.m_Color = color;
            strcpy_s( gmp.m_FXFileName,
                GenericMeshObjectParams::sk_MaxFileNameLen, effectFileName );
            strcpy_s( gmp.m_XFileName, GenericMeshObjectParams::sk_MaxFileNameLen,
                meshFileName );
            gmp.m_Mat = Mat4x4::g_Identity;
            gmp.m_Mat.SetPosition(startPosition);
            const EvtData_Request_New_Actor gmpEvt( &gmp );
            safeTriggerEvent( gmpEvt );
        }
        break;
    default:
        break;
    }
}


void RemoveActor( ActorId actorId )
{
    EditorGame* pGame = (EditorGame*)g_pApp->m_pGame;
    if (pGame)
    {
        const EvtData_Destroy_Actor destroyActor( actorId );
        safeTriggerEvent( destroyActor );
    }
}
```

CreateActor() takes several parameters and triggers a "request new actor" event for an actor with the requested properties. Not all actors share the same properties. Teapots don't have a segment or radius property, for example. As a result, you create the specific subclass of ActorParams that corresponds to the type of actor being created. `RemoveActor()` simply takes the actor ID for the actor to be removed and triggers a "destroy actor" event.

The next functions can change the actor's position or its orientation in the world:

```
void SetActorPos( ActorId actorId,
   const float x, const float y, const float z )
{
   shared_ptr<IActor> pActor = g_pApp->m_pGame->VGetActor( actorId );
   if ( !pActor )
   {
      return;
   }
   Mat4x4 position = pActor->VGetMat();
   position.SetPosition( Vec3(x, y, z) );
   safeQueEvent( IEventDataPtr( GCC_NEW
      EvtData_Move_Actor( actorId, position) ) );
}

void RotateActorXAxis( ActorId actorId, float radians )
{
   shared_ptr<IActor> pActor = g_pApp->m_pGame->VGetActor( actorId );
   if ( !pActor )
   {
      return;
   }

   Mat4x4 initialRotationMatrix = pActor->VGetMat();
   Vec3 position = initialRotationMatrix.GetPosition();
   initialRotationMatrix.SetPosition( Vec3(0.0f, 0.0f, 0.0f) );

   Mat4x4 rotation = Mat4x4::g_Identity;;
   rotation.BuildRotationX( radians );

   initialRotationMatrix *= rotation;
   initialRotationMatrix.SetPosition( position );
   safeQueEvent( IEventDataPtr( GCC_NEW
      EvtData_Move_Actor( actorId, initialRotationMatrix) ) );
}
```

`SetActorPos()` takes an actor ID and the three coordinates for the actor's position. It takes the transformation matrix, updates the position, and then queues a move event for the actor.

`RotateActorXAxis()` operates in the same manner. It takes an actor ID and the rotation amount in radians. It grabs the transformation matrix and caches away the position, before setting the transformation matrix's position to the zero vector. You always want to handle rotation before translation. The code does this by calculating the rotation in `initialRotationMatrix` and then calling `SetPosition()` to translate.

These functions need to be exported, so these lines are added to EditorGlobal-Functions.h:

```
extern "C" DllExport void CreateActor( ActorType actorType,
    DWORD color, float length, float radius, LPCTSTR lEffectFileName,
    LPCTSTR lMeshFileName );
extern "C" DllExport void RemoveActor( ActorId actorId );
extern "C" DllExport void SetActorPos(ActorId actorId, const float x,
    const float y, const float z);
extern "C" DllExport void RotateActorXAxis( ActorId actorId,
    float radians );
```

The C# editor application needs parallel definitions in `Source\EditorApp\NativeMethods.cs`:

```
[DllImport(editorDllName)]
public static extern void CreateActor(int type, UInt32 color,
    float length, float radius, string lEffectFileName, string lMeshFileName);
[DllImport(editorDllName)]
public static extern void RemoveActor(uint actorId);
[DllImport(editorDllName)]
public static extern void SetActorPos(uint actorId, float x, float y, float z);
[DllImport(editorDllName)]
public static extern void RotateActorXAxis(uint actorId, float radians);
```

C# does not have a `DWORD` data type, so you use a `UInt32` for the color value in `CreateActor()`.

The `ActorCreationForm` Class

If you are going to create new actors, you need a dialog to enter parameters for the new actor. Take a look at it in Figure 20.4.

The `ActorCreationForm` has controls that let you enter initial values for any of the actor parameters. In this architecture, the parameter types of different actors are hard coded to the form. In a real editor, the parameter types would be data defined, and the form would be created on the fly. Since my editor is already wincing at the length of this chapter, I'll go for the simple and easy-to-explain

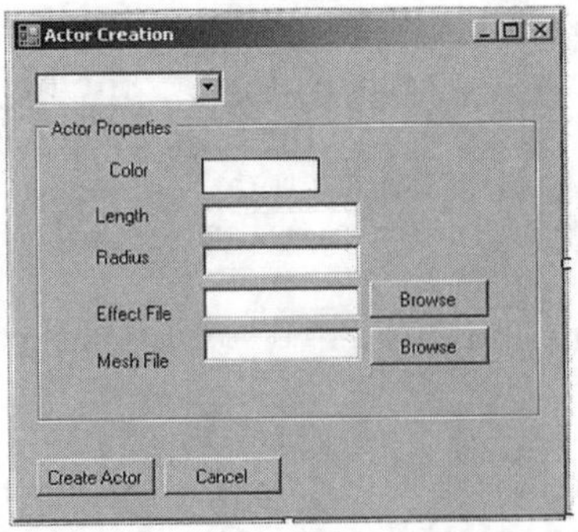

FIGURE 20.4 The ActorCreationForm.

route. You can try your hand at extending this system to allow for completely data-defined actor parameters. Now, on to the code for the ActorCreationForm:

```
namespace EditorApp
{
    //=========================================================================
    //
    // This form is used to gather information about new actors that will be
    // added to the scene.
    //
    //=========================================================================

    public partial class ActorCreationForm : Form
    {
        EditorActorParams m_actorParams;

        public ActorCreationForm()
        {
            InitializeComponent();

            m_actorParams.m_color = Color.White;
            m_actorParams.m_length = 0;
            m_actorParams.m_radius = 0;
            m_actorParams.m_actorType = ActorType.AT_Unknown;

            m_actorTypeComboBox.Items.Add("Sphere");
            m_actorTypeComboBox.Items.Add("Grid");
            m_actorTypeComboBox.Items.Add("Teapot");
            m_actorTypeComboBox.Items.Add("Test Object");
            m_actorTypeComboBox.Items.Add("Generic Mesh Object");
```

```
            // Display the controls for modifying actor properties
            // only after the user has selected what type of actor
            // to create
            m_createActorBtn.Visible = false;
            m_cancelBtn.Visible = false;
            m_colorDisplayPanel.Visible = false;
            m_colorLabel.Visible = false;
            m_LengthTextbox.Visible = false;
            m_lengthLabel.Visible = false;
            m_RadiusTextbox.Visible = false;
            m_radiusLabel.Visible = false;
            m_effectFileLabel.Visible = false;
            m_meshFileLabel.Visible = false;
            m_effectFileTextbox.Visible = false;
            m_meshFileTextbox.Visible = false;
            m_browseEffectFileBtn.Visible = false;
            m_browseMeshFileBtn.Visible = false;
        }

        public EditorActorParams GetParams()
        {
            return m_actorParams;
        }
```

The constructor makes most of the controls invisible. Since controls will be selectively displayed depending on the type of the actor selected in the combo box, the form starts with them all invisible.

`ActorTypeComboBox_SelectedIndexChanged()` is called whenever the user selects a new value in the combo box. This function selectively displays controls on the form. If the user wants a teapot, it doesn't make much sense to display the controls for radius.

```
// Display the appropriate controls for each actor type
switch (m_actorTypeComboBox.Text)
{
    case "Sphere":
        m_createActorBtn.Visible = true;
        m_cancelBtn.Visible = true;
        m_colorDisplayPanel.Visible = true;
        m_colorLabel.Visible = true;
        m_RadiusTextbox.Visible = true;
        m_radiusLabel.Visible = true;
        break;
```

```
case "Teapot":
case "Test Object":
    m_createActorBtn.Visible = true;
    m_cancelBtn.Visible = true;
    m_colorDisplayPanel.Visible = true;
    m_colorLabel.Visible = true;
    break;

// more actor types will follow...
```

When the parameters for the selected actor are filled in and the "Create Actor" button is pressed, the CreateActorBtn_Click() method is called. It copies the control values into the m_actorParams member variable and closes the dialog.

```
*private void CreateActorBtn_Click(object sender, EventArgs e)
{
        switch (m_actorTypeComboBox.Text)
        {
            case "Sphere":
                m_actorParams.m_actorType = ActorType.AT_Sphere;
                m_actorParams.m_radius = float.Parse(m_RadiusTextbox.Text);
                m_actorParams.m_color = m_colorDisplayPanel.BackColor;
                this.DialogResult = DialogResult.OK;
                this.Close();
                break;
            case "Teapot":
                m_actorParams.m_actorType = ActorType.AT_Teapot;
                m_actorParams.m_color = m_colorDisplayPanel.BackColor;
                this.DialogResult = DialogResult.OK;
                this.Close();
                break;
            case "Grid":
                m_actorParams.m_actorType = ActorType.AT_Grid;
                m_actorParams.m_color = m_colorDisplayPanel.BackColor;
                m_actorParams.m_length = float.Parse(m_LengthTextbox.Text);
                this.DialogResult = DialogResult.OK;
                this.Close();
                break;
            case "Generic Mesh Object":
                m_actorParams.m_actorType = ActorType.AT_GenericMeshObject;
                m_actorParams.m_color = m_colorDisplayPanel.BackColor;
                m_actorParams.m_effectFile = m_effectFileTextbox.Text;
                m_actorParams.m_meshFile = m_meshFileTextbox.Text;
```

```
                    this.DialogResult = DialogResult.OK;
                    this.Close();
                    break;
               default:
                    MessageBox.Show("You must select an actor type!");
                    break;
        }
    }
}
```

There are a few more methods that are wired into the controls on the Actor-PropertiesForm:

```
private void ColorDisplayPanel_MouseDown(object sender, MouseEventArgs e)
{
   m_colorDialog.ShowDialog();
   m_colorDisplayPanel.BackColor = m_colorDialog.Color;
   }

   private void BrowseEffectFileBtn_Click(object sender, EventArgs e)
   {
      DialogResult res = m_openFileDialog.ShowDialog();
      if (res != DialogResult.OK)
      {
         return;
      }
      m_effectFileTextbox.Text = m_openFileDialog.FileName;
   }

   private void BrowseMeshFileBtn_Click(object sender, EventArgs e)
   {
      DialogResult res = m_openFileDialog.ShowDialog();
      if (res != DialogResult.OK)
      {
         return;
      }
   m_meshFileTextbox.Text = m_openFileDialog.FileName;
}
```

These methods use other C# dialogs, such as the ColorDialog and the Open-FileDialog, to make it easy for users of the ActorPropertiesForm to fill in actor para-meters. Now that that little sidetrack is completed, I can get back to explaining how the actor update methods are wired into the ActorPropertiesForm.

Adding Actor Update Methods to `ActorPropertiesForm`

There are just a few methods to add, since the editor is so basic. These will update the actor position, revert to an old position, rotate the actor, and remove the actor:

```
private void UpdateActorPosBtn_Click(object sender, EventArgs e)
{
    m_parent.SetActorInformation(UInt32.Parse(this.m_actorIdTextbox.Text),
        float.Parse(this.m_actorXTextbox.Text),
        float.Parse(this.m_actorYTextbox.Text),
        float.Parse(this.m_actorZTextbox.Text));
}


private void RestoreActorPosBtn_Click(object sender, EventArgs e)
{
    // The position has been changed in the EditorForm, but the user wants to
    // get the old position information on this actor before updating the
    // position. The EngineDisplayForm should retrieve information on this
    // actor, which the EditorForm will use to repopulate actor information.
    EditorActorParams actorParams =
        m_parent.GetActorInformation(UInt32.Parse(this.m_actorIdTextbox.Text));
    PopulateActorInformation(actorParams);
}


private void RotateActorXAxisBtn_Click(object sender, EventArgs e)
{
    if (m_treeView.SelectedNode != m_mainNode)
    {
        float degrees = float.Parse(m_rotateActorXAxisDegreesTextbox.Text);
        m_parent.RotateObjectX(UInt32.Parse(m_treeView.SelectedNode.Name),
            (float)(Math.PI * degrees / 180.0));
    }
}


private void RemoveActorBtn_Click(object sender, EventArgs e)
{
    if (m_treeView.SelectedNode != m_mainNode)
    {
        UInt32 id = UInt32.Parse(m_treeView.SelectedNode.Name);
        m_mainNode.Nodes.Remove(m_treeView.SelectedNode);
        m_parent.RemoveActor(id);
    }
}
```

The first function, `UpdateActorPosBtn_Click`, grabs the values from the textboxes containing coordinate information and sends the actor ID and coordinate information to the `EngineDisplayForm`. If the user makes any changes to the position, this information gets passed onward.

`RestoreActorPosBtn_Click` simply restores the position, in case you entered any new position information into the form but decided you would rather revert to the existing values. The rotate function converts the value of the rotate textboxes from degrees into radians and then passes that information on to the `EngineDisplayForm`.

`RemoveActorBtn_Click` checks to be sure a legitimate actor is selected and then tells `EngineDisplayForm` to remove the actor.

BEST PRACTICE

EDITORS NEED ROBUST ERROR CHECKING

One thing that is missing is checks on the data types. This occurred because the author was focusing most of his time on getting C# and C++ to play nice and trying to stamp out linker errors! However, you should make sure that data being passed to the editor game engine is all legitimate. You don't want to send any data that isn't appropriate to the unmanaged DLL. At best, nothing happens. At worst, the entire application crashes, taking with it several hours of work! There is nothing more dangerous to a programmer's well being than a person whose finest work has been lost by an editor bug.

Now the editor can add objects to the level, move them around, rotate them, and remove them if they displease you. The editor also needs to save its fabulous creations out to a file and reload them.

SAVING AND LOADING LEVELS

The game's save game format is a Lua table. Loading it is relatively trivial since you can just call `LuaStateManager::DoFile()` with the level filename. Saving out the files isn't tricky, but it is a little tedious.

Switch gears again to the C++ Editor DLL since it needs C-style accessor functions added to `Source\Editor\EditorGlobalFunctions.cpp`:

```
*void OpenLevel( char* fileName )
{
    EditorGame* pGame = (EditorGame*)g_pApp->m_pGame;
    if (pGame)
    {
        pGame->OpenLevelFile(fileName);
    }
}
```

`OpenLevel()` checks to make sure the pointer to the game logic is valid and then calls the `EditorGame::OpenLevelFile()` method with the name of your level file. Believe it or not you saw that back at the beginning of the chapter in the section on "The Editor's Logic Class."

For a file to be opened, it must first be saved. Take a look at what the save file will ultimately look like:

```
*local gridParams2=
{
   ActorType = "grid",
   Color =
   {
      R = 0.400000,  G = 0.400000,  B = 0.400000,  A = 1.000000,
   },
   Mat =
   {
      _11 = 1.000000, _12 = 0.000000, _13 = 0.000000, _14 = 0.000000,
      _21 = 0.000000, _22 = 1.000000, _23 = 0.000000, _24 = 0.000000,
      _31 = 0.000000, _32 = 0.000000, _33 = 1.000000, _34 = 0.000000,
      _41 = 0.000000, _42 = 0.000000, _43 = 0.000000, _44 = 1.000000,
   },
   Texture = "grid.dds",
   Squares = 100,
}
EventManager:TriggerEvent( "request_new_actor", gridParams2 )
local genericMeshObjectParams3=
{
   ActorType = "genericMeshObject",
   Color =
   {
      R = 1.000000,  G = 0.501961,  B = 0.000000,  A = 1.000000,
   },
   Mat =
   {
      _11 = -0.866025,  _12 = 0.000000,  _13 = 0.500000,   _14 = 0.000000,
      _21 = 0.000000,   _22 = 1.000000,  _23 = 0.000000,   _24 = 0.000000,
      _31 = -0.500000,  _32 = 0.000000,  _33 = -0.866025,  _34 = 0.000000,
      _41 = 5.000000,   _42 = 1.500000,  _43 = 0.000000,   _44 = 1.000000,
   },
   XFile = "C:\\GCC root\\GameCode3\\Dev\\test\\airplane 2.x",
   FXFile = "C:\\GCC root\\GameCode3\\Dev\\test\\GameCode3.fx",
}
EventManager:TriggerEvent( "request_new_actor", genericMeshObjectParams3 )
local sphereParams5=
```

```
{
    ActorType = "sphere",
    Pos =
    {
        0.000000,    5.000000,    0.000000,
    },
    Radius = 1.000000,
    Segments = 16,
    Color =
    {
        R = 0.000000,    G = 0.501961,    B = 1.000000,    A = 1.000000,
    },
}
EventManager:TriggerEvent( "request_new_actor", sphereParams5 )
local teapotParams6=
{
    ActorType = "teapot",
    Color =
    {
        R = 0.501961,    G = 0.000000,    B = 0.501961,    A = 1.000000,
    },
    Mat =
    {
        _11 = 1.000000,    _12 = 0.000000,    _13 = 0.000000,    _14 = 0.000000,
        _21 = 0.000000,    _22 = 1.000000,    _23 = 0.000000,    _24 = 0.000000,
        _31 = 0.000000,    _32 = 0.000000,    _33 = 1.000000,    _34 = 0.000000,
        _41 = 0.000000,    _42 = 1.500000,    _43 = 0.000000,    _44 = 1.000000,
    },
}
EventManager:TriggerEvent( "request_new_actor", teapotParams6 )
```

Each actor's parameters are stored in a Lua table. The name of the table is the type of ActorParams you are saving and the actor ID. This ensures that every table has a unique name. The first value in the table is the actor type, followed by the parameters specific for that actor type. For spheres, you save the position information (since the rotation matrix for a sphere is meaningless) and the color. GenericMeshObjects need to save the file that its mesh is loaded from, its effect file, transformation matrix, and color. Grids must save their color, transformation matrix, number of squares (for example, size), and their texture file. Teapots save their color and transformation matrix. After each parameter block, there is a function call to trigger a "request new actor" event with the parameters. When the LuaStateManager runs this file, it should trigger several "request new actor" events with the parameters for each actor.

ALWAYS USE RELATIVE PATH NAMES

Learning from someone else's mistakes is vastly better than learning from your own. Did you notice the file specification for XFile and FXFile in the previous code snippet? You should never do it this way in a commercial game editor, since it makes it impossible for you to move the game to a new directory or allow content developers to store editor files on different hard disks. Always store relative path names from your content root directory.

The purpose of the SaveLevel function is to construct this Lua file. It is declared in Source\Editor\EditorGlobalFunctions.cpp:

```
*void SaveLevel( char* fileName )
{
   FILE * pFile;
   pFile = fopen (fileName,"w");

   if (!pFile)
   {
      return;
   }

   EditorGame* pGame = (EditorGame*)g_pApp->m_pGame;
   if (!pGame)
   {
      return;
   }
   ActorMap::iterator itr;
   int actorArrayIndex;

   // To save out our level, we want to iterate through all the actors
   // and then write out information that will enable the editor to
   // recreate and reposition each actor when we want to reload this level
   for ( itr = pGame->GetActorMapBegin(), actorArrayIndex = 0;
      itr != pGame->GetActorMapEnd() &&
      actorArrayIndex < pGame->GetNumActors(); itr++, actorArrayIndex++ )
   {
      shared_ptr<IActor> pActor = itr->second;
      if (!pActor)
      {
         continue;
      }
```

```cpp
shared_ptr<ActorParams> pActorParams = pActor->VGetParams();
if (!pActorParams)
{
   continue;
}


ActorId actorId;
optional<ActorId> maybeID = pActor->VGetID();
if (maybeID.valid())
{
   actorId = *maybeID;
}
else
{
   continue;
}


switch (pActor->VGetType())
{
   case AT_Sphere:
   {
      // For the sphere, the relevant params we want to save are its
      // radius and segments. We don't care about its transform matrix
      // since, as a sphere, the only thing that really matters is its
      // position.
      WriteBeginningParamsBlock(pFile, "sphere", actorId);
      WritePosParams(pFile, pActor->VGetMat().GetPosition());
      shared_ptr<SphereParams> sphereParams =
         boost::static_pointer_cast<SphereParams>( pActorParams );
      fprintf(pFile, "   Radius = %f,\n", sphereParams->m_Radius);
      fprintf(pFile, "   Segments = %i,\n", sphereParams->m_Segments);
      WriteColorParams(pFile, sphereParams->m_Color);
      WriteEndParamsBlock(pFile, "sphere", actorId);
   }
   break;

   case AT_Teapot:
   {
      // We want to write out the matrix params for the teapot, since
      // we're interested in saving its position and rotation.
      WriteBeginningParamsBlock(pFile, "teapot", actorId);
      shared_ptr<TeapotParams> teapotParams =
         boost::static_pointer_cast<TeapotParams>( pActorParams );
      WriteColorParams(pFile, teapotParams->m_Color);
```

```
                    WriteMatrixParams(pFile, pActor->VGetMat());
                    WriteEndParamsBlock(pFile, "teapot", actorId);
                }
                break;

                case AT_Grid:
                {
                    // The grid contains some extra information, like its texture and
                    // number of squares.
                    WriteBeginningParamsBlock(pFile, "grid", actorId);
                    shared_ptr<GridParams> gridParams =
                        boost::static_pointer_cast<GridParams>( pActorParams );
                    WriteColorParams(pFile, gridParams->m_Color);
                    WriteMatrixParams(pFile, pActor->VGetMat());
                    fprintf(pFile, "   Texture = \"%s\",\n", gridParams->m_Texture);
                    fprintf(pFile, "   Squares = %i,\n", gridParams->m_Squares);
                    WriteEndParamsBlock(pFile, "grid", actorId);
                }
                break;

                case AT_GenericMeshObject:
                {
                    WriteBeginningParamsBlock(pFile, "genericMeshObject", actorId);
                    shared_ptr<GenericMeshObjectParams> genericMeshObjectParams =
                        boost::static_pointer_cast<GenericMeshObjectParams>(
                        pActorParams );
                    WriteColorParams(pFile, genericMeshObjectParams->m_Color);
                    WriteMatrixParams(pFile, pActor->VGetMat());
                    std::string meshFileName(genericMeshObjectParams->m_XFileName);
                    std::string effectFileName(genericMeshObjectParams->m_FXFileName);

                    ReplaceAllCharacters(meshFileName, "\\", "\\\\");
                    ReplaceAllCharacters(effectFileName, "\\", "\\\\");

                    fprintf(pFile, "   XFile = \"%s\",\n", meshFileName.c_str());
                    fprintf(pFile, "   FXFile = \"%s\",\n", effectFileName.c_str());
                    WriteEndParamsBlock(pFile, "genericMeshObject", actorId);
                }
                break;
            default:
                break;
            };
        }
        fclose (pFile);
    }
```

A new `File` object is created at the beginning of the function. The entire actor list is iterated, with each actor type having a custom bit of code to save its unique structure. `WriteBeginningParamsBlock()` is called for every actor type, since the beginning of each parameter block in the save file has the same format:

```
*void WriteBeginningParamsBlock(FILE* pFile, std::string paramType, ActorId
                                actorId)
{
   // Each param block in a lua file starts the same way. The only difference
   // is in the type of actor, and their id - which we add to make sure each
   // param block is unique.
   fprintf(pFile, "local %sParams%i=\n", paramType.c_str(), actorId);
   fprintf(pFile, "{\n");
   fprintf(pFile, "   ActorType = \"%s\",\n", paramType.c_str());
}
```

`WriteBeginningParamsBlock()` writes out the type of the parameters you are saving and appends the actor ID to the end. Each data type stored in the actor parameters gets its own method. The first two are for a `Mat4x4` object and a `Vec3` object:

```
void WriteMatrixParams( FILE* pFile, const Mat4x4 &mat )
{
   fprintf(pFile, "   Mat =\n");
   fprintf(pFile, "   {\n");
   for( int i = 0; i < 4; i++ )
   {
      for ( int j = 0; j < 4; j++ )
      {
         fprintf(pFile, "      _%i%i = %f,\n", i+1, j+1, mat.m[i][j]);
      }
   }
   fprintf(pFile, "   },\n");
}

void WritePosParams( FILE* pFile, const Vec3 &pos )
{
   fprintf(pFile, "   Pos =\n");
   fprintf(pFile, "   {\n");
   fprintf(pFile, "      %f,\n", pos.x);
   fprintf(pFile, "      %f,\n", pos.y);
   fprintf(pFile, "      %f,\n", pos.z);
   fprintf(pFile, "   },\n");
}
```

If this is an actor type that saves its transformation matrix, you call `WriteMatrixParams()`, which iterates through all the matrix values in the transformation matrix and writes it to your level file. If this is an actor type that saves its position, you call `WritePosParams()`, which writes the position information.

All the actor types have a color parameter, so that gets written to the save file using `WriteColorParams()`:

```
void WriteColorParams( FILE* pFile, const Color &color )
{
    fprintf(pFile, "   Color =\n");
    fprintf(pFile, "   {\n");
    fprintf(pFile, "       R = %f,\n", color.r);
    fprintf(pFile, "       G = %f,\n", color.g);
    fprintf(pFile, "       B = %f,\n", color.b);
    fprintf(pFile, "       A = %f,\n", color.a);
    fprintf(pFile, "   },\n");
}
```

A few of the actor types have very specific parameters, like radius or squares. For those parameters, you write those to file directly, rather than using any helper functions.

Some actors contain filenames in their parameter lists, such as the `GenericMeshObject`. Unfortunately, the filename contains single instances of the backslash character, \, which is interpreted as an escape character in Lua. The `ReplaceAllCharacters()` function can replace all instances of the single backslash with two backslashes, like this \\, which will create valid directory paths in Lua. This is a lot simpler to do in C#, where the replace function is built into the `std::string` class!

```
void ReplaceAllCharacters( std::string& origString, std::string subString,
    std::string newSubString )
{
    size_t subStringPos = origString.find(subString, 0);
    while (subStringPos != std::string.npos)
    {
        origString.replace( subStringPos, subString.length(), newSubString );
        subStringPos += newSubString.length();
        subStringPos = origString.find(subString, subStringPos);
    }
}
```

After saving all the parameters, `WriteEndParamsBlock()` closes off the parameter block in the save file:

```
void WriteEndParamsBlock(FILE* pFile, std::string paramType, ActorId actorId)
{
    // Each param block in a lua file ends the same way. We make sure to
    // get the actor id and the actor type, so we can add a final line at the
    // end of the param block that will cause the Lua Manager to trigger
    // a new event when this file is reloaded.
    fprintf(pFile, "}\n");
    fprintf(pFile, "EventManager:TriggerEvent( \"request_new_actor\",
        %sParams%i )\n", paramType.c_str(), actorId);
}
```

`WriteEndParamsBlock()` also writes the function call that will trigger the "request new actor" event.

FUTURE WORK

Well, that's it for our simple game editor! Woo! As I've mentioned throughout this chapter, this is by no means a complete set of features. If you feel compelled to take this code and tweak, you may want to add additional functionality. One thing you should do early on is integrate a real physics system into the level editor so you can see interactions between actors and the environment. You'll also want to be able to export an archive file that contains the resources used by the levels you create. This saves you the hassle of having to hunt for all the textures, meshes, and shaders you used in your level if you want to open your level on another machine. And you'll also want to add mouse-driven actor position and orientation, an undo/redo feature, an ability to launch a running game, simultaneous user configurable views, and about 10,000 other features. Like most chapters in this book, a few dozen pages is just not enough to really cover such a deep subject, but it is enough to get you started.

SPECIAL THANKS

I'd like to thank Mr. Mike for giving me the opportunity to write about level editors. Having been on both ends, as a level designer and as a tools programmer, it's been a real hoot being able to write about this subject.

FURTHER READING

Online

- **http://msdn.microsoft.com:** A lot of the reference material in MSDN is hair-rippingly frustrating, but they've got some good examples on how to set up C# projects.
- **http://blogs.msdn.com/csharpfaq/default.aspx:** And while we're talking about C#, this FAQ is a helpful guide to some common questions.
- **www.swig.org/:** It was sometimes frustrating getting the code to run in a managed environment. As you can see, I eventually went with exporting C-style functions, but ideally you'd want to be able to export entire classes. SWIG will take your C++ classes and wrap them in a manner that is usable from C#. Not only that, but it'll wrap your classes for other languages as well!
- **www.garagegames.com/:** The Torque Game Engine is one of the most inexpensive game engines you can find, and it comes with a level editor that enables you to script in game events.
- **www.unrealtechnology.com/:** I can't have a list of game editor resources and not mention Unreal. They probably have the most in-depth, feature-rich level editor out there. It comes at a pretty hefty cost if you're licensing Unreal to develop a game, but if you just want to use the editor itself, just pick up a copy of Unreal Tournament 3.

In This Chapter

By the end of any game development project, the programmers and their teammates spend all of their time fixing bugs and tweaking performance. As important as debugging is (especially in game development), techniques in debugging are rarely taught. They tend to just come from experience, or are traded around the programming team. Since I'm communicating to you through a book, we can't trade much, but since you bought the book, I think we can call it even.

Games are complicated pieces of software, and they push every piece of hardware in the system. Bugs are usually pilot error, but there are plenty of cases where bugs trace their roots to the compiler, operating system, drivers, and even specific pieces of hardware. Bugs also happen as a result of unexpected interactions between code written by different programmers; each module functions perfectly in a unit test but failures are seen after they are integrated. Programmers spend lots of time hunting down issues in code they didn't write.

If you are going to have a chance in hell of fixing broken code, whether you wrote it or not, you should have a few ideas and techniques in your toolbox. I've often considered myself a much better debugger than a programmer, which is lucky because I tend to find bugs caused by my own flawed code pretty fast. As I say, be careful of harping on other people's mistakes, because the next person to screw up could be you! This happened, I'm sure, because of how I learned to program. I programmed for years in BASIC on the old Apple][, which didn't have a debugger. When I went to college, I programmed in PASCAL on the VAX mini computer at the University of Houston. After four years of college, I noticed an odd-looking screen in the computer lab. I asked the person sitting there what I was seeing. "A debugger," he replied. "What's a debugger?" I asked. I got this blank stare back as if I'd asked what electricity was.

I'd spent my entire college experience coding programs without using a symbolic debugger. Needless to say, programming got a lot easier after I was introduced to my first debugger, but the experience I gained without one left me with some good programming practices and solution strategies that you can use whether you use debuggers or not.

I need to warn you up front that you're going to see some assembly code and other heavy metal in this chapter. You simply can't perform the task of debugging without a basic working knowledge of assembly code and how the CPU really works. This is not a gentle chapter, because we're not discussing a gentle problem. However, it's not brutally hard to learn assembly, and you have an excellent teacher—your debugger.

All debuggers, Visual Studio included, let you look at your source code at the same time as the assembly. Take some time to learn how each C++ statement is broken down into its assembly instructions, and you'll end up being a much better programmer for it. Fear not—I'm with you in spirit, and I wasn't born with a full knowledge of assembly. You can learn it the same way I did, which was playing with the debugger.

The Art of Handling Failure

If you are looking for some wisdom about handling personal failure, stop reading and call a shrink. My focus here is to discuss application failure, the situation where some defensive code has found an anomaly and needs to handle it. There's a great conversation you can start with a group of programmers about how to handle errors or failures in games. The subject has more gray area than you'd think, and therefore doesn't have a single best strategy. The debate starts when you ask if games should ignore failures or if they should stop execution immediately.

I'm talking about the release build, of course. The debug build should always report any oddity with an assert so that programmers can catch more bugs in the act. The release build strips asserts, so there's a good question about what should happen if the assert condition would have been satisfied in the release build. Does the game continue, or should it halt? As with many things, there's no right answer. Here's an example of two functions that handle the same error in two different ways:

```
void DetectFixAndContinue(int variable)
{
   if (variable < VARIABLE_MINIMUM)
   {
      variable = VARIABLE_MINIMUM;
      assert(0 && "Parameter is invalid");
   }

   // More code follows...
}


void DetectAndBail(int variable)
{
   if (variable < VARIABLE_MINIMUM)
   {
      throw ("Parameter is invalid");
   }

   // More code follows...
}
```

The first function resets the errant variable and calls an assert to alert a programmer that something has gone wrong. The execution continues, since the variable now has a legal value. The second function throws an exception, clearly not allowing the execution to continue.

USE TEXT STRINGS IN ASSERT STATEMENTS

Notice the assert statement in this example. It's a conditional that includes a text string. Since the conditional is always false, the assert will always fire. The text string will appear in the assert dialog box, and can give testers a clue about reporting the problem and even what to do about it. You might add, "You can always ignore this" to the text string so testers can continue playing.

The debate most programmers have goes something like this: If you ever reach code where an assert condition in debug mode evaluates to false, then something has gone horribly wrong. Since you can't predict the nature of the failure, you must assume a worst-case scenario and exit the program as elegantly as possible. After all, the failure could be bad enough to corrupt data, save game files, or worse.

The other side of the argument takes a kinder, gentler approach. Failures can and will happen, even in the shipping product. If the program can fix a bogus parameter or ignore corrupt data and continue running, it is in the best interests of the player to do so. After all, they might get a chance to save their game and reload it later without a problem. Since we're working on computer games, we have the freedom to fudge things a little; there are no human lives at stake, and there is no property at risk due to a program failure. Both arguments are valid. I tend to favor the second argument because computer games are frequently pushed into testing before they are ready and released way before testing is completed. Bugs will remain in the software, and if the game can recover from them it should.

That's not to say that games can't find themselves in an unrecoverable situation. If a computer game runs out of memory, you're hosed. You have no choice but to bring up a dialog and say, "Sorry dude. You're hosed," and start throwing exceptions. If you're lucky, your exit code might be able to save the game into a temporary file, much like Microsoft Word sometimes does when it crashes. When the game reloads, it can read the temporary file and attempt to begin again just

SOME BUGS ARE ACCEPTABLE, AREN'T THEY?

Never forget that your game's purpose is entertainment. You aren't keeping an airplane from getting lost, and you aren't reporting someone's heartbeat. Remember that games can get away with lots of things that other software can't. If you are relatively sure that you can make a choice to allow the game to continue instead of crash, I suggest you do it.

Of course, this is true unless you work on a massive multiplayer title, and you are working on anything server side. Bugs here affect everyone on the server, and can result in actual lost value for players, and in turn the company. In that case, you get to code and test every bit as carefully as the programmer down the street working on banking software.

before everything went down the toilet. If this fails, you can exit again and lose the temporary file. All hope is lost. If it succeeds, your players will worship the ground you walk on. Trust me, as many times as Microsoft Word has recovered pieces of this book after my portable's batteries ran out of electrons, I can appreciate a little data recovery.

BEST PRACTICE

USE @err,hr IN YOUR WATCH WINDOW

If a Win32 function fails, you must usually call GetLastError() *to determine the exact nature of the error. Instead, simply put* @err,hr *in your debugger's watch window. This will show you a string-formatted version of the error.*

DEBUGGING BASICS

Before you learn some debugging tricks, you should know a little about how the debugger works and how to use it. Almost every computer has special assembly language instructions or CPU features that enable debugging. The Intel platform is no exception. A debugger works by stopping execution of a target program and associating memory locations and values with variable names. This association is possible through symbolic information that is generated by the compiler. One human readable form of this information is a MAP file. Here's an example of a MAP file generated by the linker in Visual Studio:

```
Sample
 Timestamp is 3c0020f3 (Sat Nov 24 16:36:35 2001)
 Preferred load address is 00400000

 Start          Length       Name              Class
 0001:00000000 000ab634H .text                 CODE
 0001:000ab640 00008b5fH .text$AFX_AUX         CODE
 0001:000b41a0 0000eec3H .text$AFX_CMNCTL      CODE
 0002:00000000 000130caH .rdata                DATA
 0002:000130d0 00006971H .rdata$r              DATA
 0002:000275d0 00000000H .edata                DATA
 0003:00000000 00000104H .CRT$XCA              DATA
 0003:00000104 00000109H .CRT$XCC              DATA
 0003:00001120 00026e6aH .data                 DATA
 0003:00027f90 00011390H .bss                  DATA
 0004:00000000 00000168H .idata$2              DATA
 0004:00000168 00000014H .idata$3              DATA
 0005:00000000 00000370H .rsrc$01              DATA
```

Address	Publics by Value	Rva+Base	Lib:Object
0001:00000b80	??0GameApp@@QAE@XZ	00401b80 f	GameApp.obj
0001:00000ca0	??_EGameApp@@UAEPAXI@Z	00401ca0 f i	GameApp.obj
0001:00000ca0	??_GGameApp@@UAEPAXI@Z	00401ca0 f i	GameApp.obj
0001:00000d10	??1GameApp@@UAE@XZ	00401d10 f	GameApp.obj
0001:00000e20	?OnClose@GameApp@@UAEXXZ	00401e20 f	GameApp.obj
0001:00000ec0	?OnRun@GameApp@@UAE_NXZ	00401ec0 f	GameApp.obj
0001:00001a10	??0CFileStatus@@QAE@XZ	00402a10 f i	GameApp.obj
0001:00001d00	?OnIdle@GameApp@@UAEHJ@Z	00402d00 f	GameApp.obj
0001:00001e30	?Update@GameApp@@UAEXK@Z	00402e30 f	GameApp.obj

The file maps the entire contents of the process as it is loaded into memory. The first section describes global data. The second section, which is much more interesting and useful, describes the memory addresses of methods and functions in your game.

Notice first that the symbol names are "munged." These are the actual name of the methods after the C++ symbol manager incorporates the class names and variable types into the names. The number that appears right after the name is the actual memory address of the entry point of the code. For example, the last function in the MAP file is ?Update@GameApp@@UAEXK@Z and is loaded into memory address 0x00402e30. You can use that information to track down crashes.

Have you ever seen a crash that reports the register contents? Usually, you'll see the entire set of registers: EAX, EBX, and so on. You'll also see EIP, the extended instruction pointer. You may have thought that this dialog box was nothing more than an annoyance—a slap in the face that your program is flawed. Used with the MAP file, you can at least find the name of the function that caused the crash. Here's how to do it:

1. Assume the crash dialog reported an EIP of 0x00402d20.
2. Looking at the MAP file above, you'll see that GameApp::OnIdle has an entry point of 0x00402d00 and GameApp::Update has an entry point of 0x00402e30.
3. The crash thus happened somewhere inside GameApp::OnIdle, since it is located in between those two entry points.

A debugger uses a much more complete symbol table. For example, Visual Studio stores these symbols in a PDB file, or program database file. That's one of the reasons it's so huge because it stores symbolic information of every identifier in your program. The debugger can use this information to figure out how to display the contents of local and global variables and figure out what source code to display as you step through the code. This doesn't explain how the debugger stops the debugged application cold in its tracks, however. That trick requires a little help from the CPU and a special interrupt instruction. If you use Visual Studio and you are running on an Intel processor, you can try this little program:

```
void main()
{
    __asm int 3
}
```

You may never have seen a line of code that looks like this. It is a special line of code that allows inline assembly. The assembly statement evokes the breakpoint interrupt. Without dragging you through all the gory details of interrupt tables, it suffices to say that a program with sufficient privileges can "trap" interrupts so that when they are evoked, a special function is called. This is almost exactly like registering a callback function, but it happens at a hardware level. DOS-based games used to grab interrupts all the time to redirect functions such as the mouse or display system to their own evil ends. Debuggers trap the breakpoint interrupt, and whenever you set a breakpoint, the debugger overwrites the *opcodes*, or the machine level instructions, at the breakpoint location with those that correspond to __asm int 3. When the breakpoint is hit, control is passed to the debugger, and it puts the original instructions back. If you press the "Step into" or "Step over" commands, the debugger finds the right locations for a new breakpoint and simply puts it there without you ever being the wiser.

BEST
PRACTICE

HARD-CODED BREAKPOINTS ARE COOL

I've found it useful to add hard-coded breakpoints, like the one in the earlier code example, to functions in the game. It can be convenient to set one to make sure that if control ever passes through that section of code, the debugger will always trap it. If a debugger is not present, it has no effect whatsoever. Windows programmers on other processors can use SetDebugBreak().

So now you have the most basic understanding of how a debugger does its work. It has a mechanism to stop a running program in its tracks, and it uses a compiler and linker generated data file to present symbolic information to programmers.

Using the Debugger

When you debug your code, you usually set a few breakpoints and watch the contents of variables. You have a pretty good idea of what should happen, and you'll find bugs when you figure out why the effect of your logic isn't what you planned. This assumes a few things. First, you know where to set the breakpoints, and second, you can interpret the effect the logic has on the state of your game. These two things are by no means trivial in all cases. This problem is made difficult by the size and complexity of the logic.

WHERE IS THAT BUG ANYWAY?

It's not necessarily true that a screwed-up sound effect has anything at all to do with the sound system. It could be a problem with the code that loads the sound from the game data files, or it could be a random memory "trasher" that changed the sound effect after it was loaded. The problem might also be a bad sound driver, or it might even be a bogus sound effect file from the original recording. Knowing where to look first has more to do with gut feeling than anything else, but good debugger skills can certainly speed up the process of *traversing the fault tree*—a catch phrase NASA uses to describe all possible permutations of a possible systems failure.

Debuggers like the one in Visual Studio can present an amazing amount of information, as shown in Figure 21.1.

The debugger provides some important windows beyond the normal source code window you will use all of the time.

- **Call stack:** From bottom to top, this window shows the functions and parameters that were used to call them. The function at the top of the list is the one you are currently running. It's extremely useful to double-click on any row of the call stack window; the location of the function call will be reflected in the source code window. This helps you understand how control passes from the caller to the called.
- **Watch/Locals/etc:** These windows let you examine the contents of variables. Visual Studio has some convenient debug windows like "Locals" and "This" that keep track of specific variables so you don't have to type them in yourself.
- **Breakpoints:** This window shows the list of breakpoints. Sometimes you want to enable/disable every breakpoint in your game at once or perform other bits of homework.
- **Threads:** This is probably the best addition to the debug window set in Visual Studio. Most games run multiple threads to manage the sound system, resource caching, or perhaps the AI. If the debugger hits a breakpoint or is stopped, this window will show you what thread is running. This window is the only way to distinguish between different threads of execution, and it is critical to debugging multithreaded applications. If you double-click on any line in this window, the source window will change to show the current execution position of that thread.
- **Disassembly:** This is a window that shows the assembly code for the current function. Sometimes you need to break a C++ statement down into its components to debug it or perhaps skip over a portion of the statement. I'll have more to say about these techniques later.

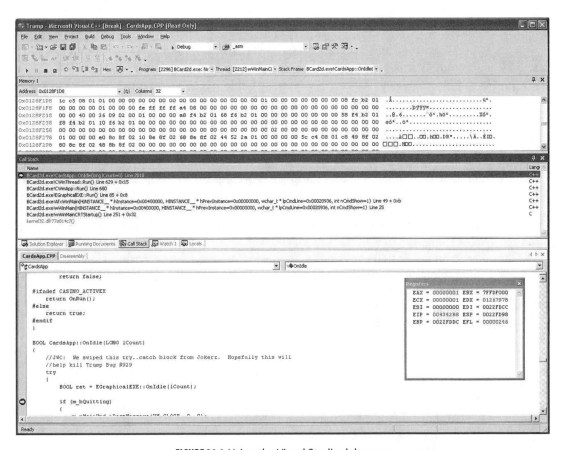

FIGURE 21.1 Using the Visual Studio debugger.

Beyond the windows, there are some actions that you'll need to know how to perform:

- **Set/Clear Breakpoints:** A basic debugging skill.
- **Stepping the Instruction Pointer:** These are usually controlled by hot keys because they are so frequently used. Debuggers will let you execute code one line at a time, and either trace into functions or skip over them (F11 and F10). There's also a really useful command that will let you step out of a current function (Shift-F11) without having to watch each line execute.
- **Setting the Instruction Pointer:** This takes a little care to use properly, since you can mess up the stack. I like to use it to skip over function calls or skip back to a previous line of code so that I can watch it execute again.

As we run through some debugging techniques I'll refer to these windows and actions. If you don't know how to do them in your debugger, now is a good time to read the docs and figure it out.

Installing Windows Symbol Files

If you've ever had a program crash deep in some Windows API call, your call stack might look like this:

```
ntdll.dll!77f60b6f()
ntdll.dll!77fb4dbd()
ntdll.dll!77f79b78()
ntdll.dll!77fb4dbd()
```

Useless, right? Yes, that call stack is useless, but only because you didn't install the Windows symbol files. Even though I write letters to Bill Gates every day, Microsoft still hasn't published the source code for pretty much anything they ever wrote. Yet they have, in their infinite wisdom, graciously supplied the next best thing.

You can install the debug symbols for your operating system, and that indecipherable call stack will turn into something you and I can read. Here's the same debug stack after the debug symbols have been installed:

```
ntdll.dll!_RtlDispatchException@8() + 0x6
ntdll.dll!_KiUserExceptionDispatcher@8() + 0xe
00031328()
ntdll.dll!ExecuteHandler@20() + 0x24
ntdll.dll!_KiUserExceptionDispatcher@8() + 0xe
000316f4()
ntdll.dll!ExecuteHandler@20() + 0x24
ntdll.dll!_KiUserExceptionDispatcher@8() + 0xe
00031ac0()
```

You might not know exactly what that call stack represents, but now you have a function name to help you, so you can search the Web or MSDN for help, whereas before you installed the debug symbols, you had nothing but a number.

There are a few ways to install debug symbols. You can install them from the Visual Studio CD-ROM, or you can download them from MSDN. Search for "System Debug Symbols," and you're sure to find them. The last time I downloaded them they were more than 170MB, so make sure you have reasonable bandwidth. Once you have the right symbols installed for your OS, the debugger will happily report the loaded symbols when you begin a debug session:

```
'BCard2d.exe': Loaded 'C:\WINDOWS\system32\ntdll.dll', Symbols loaded.
'BCard2d.exe': Loaded 'C:\WINDOWS\system32\kernel32.dll', Symbols loaded.
'BCard2d.exe': Loaded 'C:\WINDOWS\system32\gdi32.dll', Symbols loaded.
```

Etc., etc....

The problem with this solution is that the symbols you install will eventually become stale since they won't reflect any changes in your operating system as you update it with service packs. You can find out why symbols aren't loading for any EXE or DLL with the help of DUMPBIN.EXE, a utility included with Visual Studio. Use the /PDBPATH:VERBOSE switch as shown here:

```
Microsoft (R) COFF/PE Dumper Version 7.00.9466
Copyright (C) Microsoft Corporation.  All rights reserved.


Dump of file c:\windows\system32\user32.dll

File Type: DLL
  PDB file 'c:\windows\system32\user32.pdb' checked.  (File not found)
  PDB file 'user32.pdb' checked.  (File not found)
  PDB file 'C:\WINDOWS\symbols\dll\user32.pdb' checked.  (PDB signature
                                                          mismatch)
  PDB file 'C:\WINDOWS\dll\user32.pdb' checked.  (File not found)
  PDB file 'C:\WINDOWS\user32.pdb' checked.  (File not found)

  Summary

        2000 .data
        4000 .reloc
       2B000 .rsrc
       54000 .text
```

Do you see the "PDB signature mismatch" line about halfway down this output? That's what happens when the user32.pdb file is out of sync with the user32.dll image on your computer. It turns out this is easy to fix, mainly because Microsoft engineers had this problem multiplied by about 100,000. They have thousands of applications out there with sometimes hundreds of different builds. How could they ever hope to get the debug symbols straight for all these things? They came up with a neat solution called the *Microsoft Symbol Server*. It turns out you can use this server, too. Here's how to do it.

First, install the Microsoft Debugging Tools, which can be found at www.microsoft.com/ddk/debugging. Use the SYMCHK utility to pull the latest symbol information from Microsoft that matches a single EXE or DLL, or all of the ones in your Windows directory. Don't grab them all, though, if you can help it because you'll be checking and downloading hundreds of files. Here's how to grab an individual file:

```
C:\Program Files\Debugging Tools for Windows>symchk
                c:\windows\system32\user32.dll /s
                SRV*c:\windows\symbols*http://msdl.microsoft.com/download/
                symbols

SYMCHK: FAILED files = 0
SYMCHK: PASSED + IGNORED files = 1
```

This crazy utility doesn't actually put the new USER32.DLL where you asked. On a Windows XP system, it actually stuck it in *C:\WINDOWS\Symbols\ user32.pdb\3DB6D4ED1*, which Visual Studio will never find. The reason it does this is to keep all the USER32.PDB files from different operating systems or different service packs apart. If you installed the Windows symbols from MSDN into the default location, you'll want to copy it back into *C:\Windows\Symbols\dll* where Visual Studio will find it.

You can also set up your own symbol server, and even include symbols for your own applications. To find out how to do this, go up to http:// msdn.microsoft.com and search for "Microsoft Symbol Server."

Debugging Full-Screen Games

Back when I wrote the first edition of this book, multiple monitor setups were rare. Now I walk around my workplace and that's all I see. If you can afford it, a multiple monitor setup is the easiest way to debug full-screen applications, and it is the only way to develop console applications.

As much work as the Microsoft DirectX team has put into the effort of helping you debug full-screen games, this still doesn't work very well if you have a single monitor setup. This has nothing to do with the folks on DirectX; it has more to do with Visual Studio not overriding exclusive mode of the display. One manifestation of the problem occurs when your game hits a breakpoint while it's in full-screen mode. The game stops cold, but the computer doesn't switch focus to the debugger. Basically, the only thing you can do at this point is tap the F5 button to resume execution of the game.

If your game runs exclusively in full-screen mode, your only solution is a multimonitor setup. Every programmer should have two monitors: one for displaying the game screen and the other for displaying the debugger. DirectX will use the primary display for full-screen mode by default. It is possible to write code that enumerates the display devices so your game can choose the best display. This is a good idea because you can't count on players to set their display properties up in the way that benefits your game. If your game runs in windowed mode as well as full-screen mode, you have a few more options, even in a single monitor setup.

DEAL WITH DIRECTX LOST DEVICES AND RESOURCES

Most of the bugs in full-screen mode happen as a result of switching from full-screen to windowed mode or vice versa. This happens because DirectX features are lost and need to be restored after the switch, something that is easily forgotten by coders. Another problem that happens as a result of the switch is that surfaces can have the wrong pixel format. There's no guarantee that the full-screen pixel depth and format is identical to that of windowed mode. When the switch happens, lost or invalid surfaces refuse to draw and return errors. Your program might handle these errors by exiting or attempting to restore all the surfaces again. Of course, since the surface in question won't get restored in the first place, your game might get caught in a weird obsessive and repetitive attempt to fix something that can't be fixed.

It would be nice if you could simulate this problem entirely in windowed mode. To a large extent, you can. If you've followed the advice of the DirectX SDK, you always should check your display surfaces to see if they have been lost before you perform any action on them. It turns out that if you change your display settings while your game is running in windowed mode, you will essentially simulate the event of switching between windowed mode and full-screen mode. There are a few windows messages your game should handle to make this a little easier. You can see how to do this in the *Game Coding Complete* source code. Just look for "WM_" and you'll see how all these messages are handled. You'll need to handle WM_DISPLAYCHANGE, the message that is sent when the display changes, and WM_ACTIVATE, the message that signifies gain and loss of focus.

GOT FULL-SCREEN DISPLAY BUGS?

About 90 percent of all full-screen display bugs can be found and solved with a single monitor setup using windowed mode. Just start your game, change the bit depth, and see what happens. The other 10 percent can only be solved with a multimonitor setup or via remote debugging. It's much easier to debug these problems on a multimonitor rig, so make sure that at least one programmer has two monitors.

Remote Debugging

One solution for debugging full-screen-only games is remote debugging. The game runs on one computer and communicates to your development box via your network. One interesting thing about this setup is that it is as close to a pristine runtime environment as you can get (another way of saying it's very close to the environment people have when actually playing the game). I don't know about you, but people like my Mom don't have a copy of Visual Studio lying around. The presence of a debugger can subtly change the runtime environment, something that can make the hardest, nastiest bugs very difficult to find.

Remote debugging is a pain in the butt, not because it's hard to set up but because you have to make sure that the most recent version of your game executable is easily available for the remote machine. Most debuggers have a mechanism for remote debugging, and Visual Studio is no exception. The dirty secret is that Visual Studio doesn't run on Win9x architectures, which includes Windows 95, Windows 98, and Windows ME. Not that you'd want to run on these finicky operating systems, but it is a little surprising that remote debugging is your only choice if you want to find OS-specific bugs in a Visual Studio compiled application.

BEST PRACTICE

TO COPY OR TO SHARE, THAT IS THE QUESTION

Any wired or even a wireless network can allow you to share a directory on your development machine and have the Win9x machine read your game's executable and data files right where you develop. If your network is really slow or your game image is huge, it's going to be faster to copy the entire image of your game over to the test machine and run it from there. The only problem with this solution is that you have to constantly copy files from your development box over to the test machine, and it's easy to get confused regarding which files have been copied where. On a fast network, you can also eliminate file copying by sharing your development directory so the remote machine can directly access the most recent build.

On the remote system, you will run a little utility that serves as a communications conduit for your debugger. This utility for Visual Studio is called MSVS-MON.EXE. Run a search for this file where you installed Visual Studio and copy the contents of the entire directory to a shared folder on your primary development machine. The utility runs on the remote machine, and a convenient way to get it there is to place it in a shared spot on your development machine. MSVS-MON.EXE requires some of the DLLs in that directory and it's small enough to just copy the whole thing to the remote machine.

Since the methods for running the remote debugger change with updates to Visual Studio, the best way to learn how to do this is to go up to MSDN and search for "Set Up Remote Debugging." There are a few steps you need to follow. First, you share or copy your application to the remote machine. Next, run MSVS-MON.EXE on the remote machine to start the remote debugging monitor (see Figure 21.2). Back on your development machine, set your debugging properties to launch a remote debugger, and the remote debugging properties to find your remote machine. Make sure you have the right permissions or an administrator account on the remote machine, or you won't be able to connect. You'll also need to open ports in your firewall.

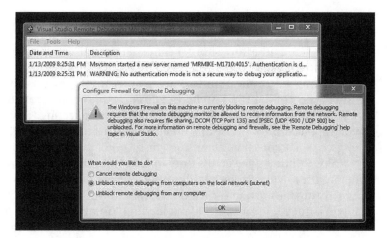

FIGURE 21.2 Running MSVSMON with the /noauth switch.

Once you get the connection madness out of the way, the remote machine is ready to start your game. Start the debugging session on your development machine (F5 in Visual Studio), and you'll see your game initialize on the remote machine. When you find a bug and rebuild your application, make sure that the remote machine has access to the most recent bits.

Debugging Minidumps

UNIX programmers have had a special advantage over Win32 programmers since the beginning of time because when a UNIX program crashes, the operating system copies the entire memory image of the crashed program to disk. This is called a *core dump*.

Needless to say, the core dump is usually quite large. UNIX debuggers can read the core dump and allow a programmer to look at the state of the process at the moment the crash occurred. Assuming the symbol files for the executable in question are available, they can see the entire call stack and even find the contents of local variables. This doesn't always expose the bug entirely, as some crashes can happen as a result of a bug's misbehavior in a completely separate part of the program, but this information is much better than a tester just telling you the game crashed.

Win32 dump files have been debuggable by a little known Windows debugger called WinDBG since the Windows NT days. These dump files were just as huge as the UNIX core dumps. It didn't matter very much, since most Windows developers didn't even know that WinDBG even existed—they always used the debugger in Visual Studio.

Since Windows XP applications don't just crash and burn, a little dialog box appears asking you if you want to send the crash information to Microsoft. One button click and a few short seconds later, and the dialog thanks you for your cooperation. What in the heck is going on here? Windows is sending a minidump of the crashed application to Microsoft. A minidump, as the name implies, is a tiny version of the UNIX style core dump. You can generate one yourself by going into the Debug menu under Visual Studio and selecting "Save Dump As…" when your application is sitting at a breakpoint. This tiny file stores enough information to give you some clues about the crash.

For Windows geeks, it's time to let you in on a little secret: Visual Studio can debug these very same minidump files. Here's how to reload it, because it isn't exactly obvious. Double-click on the minidump file in the Windows Explorer, and it will launch a surprisingly blank looking Visual Studio. The trick is to execute the minidump by hitting F5. Visual Studio will prompt you to save a solution file. Go ahead and save it alongside the minidump. Once you save, the last state of your debugged process will appear before your very eyes.

KEEP YOUR SOURCE TREE AND PDBS FOREVER

The minidump is really convenient, but there are a few gotchas to using minidumps. First, you must ensure that the minidump file matches exactly with the source code and symbol tables that were used to build the executable that crashed. This means that for any version of the executable that goes into your test department, you must save a complete build tree with source code and PDB files or the minidump will be useless. Second, the minidump's SLN file might need a hint about where to find the symbols. If the source window shows up with nothing but an assembler, it's likely that your source code tree can't be located. Open the properties page, and you'll see only one item under the Configuration tree: Debugging. Set the Symbol Path to the directory containing your PDB files, and you'll see the source tree.

The only thing left out of this discussion is how to have your game-generated minidump files when bad goes to worse. You'll need to call the `MiniDumpWriteDump()` in your general exception handler, which is one of the functions exported from DBGHELP.DLL. This call will generate a DMP file. You can add more information to the DMP file if you define a callback function that can insert more information into the dump file, such as some specific game state information that might give a programmer a leg up on investigating the crash.

MINIDUMPS ROCK

In 2001, Microsoft introduced our team to using minidumps. Microsoft's Dr. Watson team has established a huge database of minidumps for applications like Office and every OS release since XP. At first we were skeptical about using them. We thought that these dump files wouldn't provide enough information to diagnose crashes. We were wrong. After the first week, we were able to diagnose and solve some of the most elusive crashes in our game. Every Windows game should make use of this technology.

Here's a simple class you can use to write your own minidumps:

```cpp
#include "dbghelp.h"
class MiniDumper
{
protected:
    static MiniDumper *gpDumper;
    static LONG WINAPI Handler( struct _EXCEPTION_POINTERS *pExceptionInfo );

    _EXCEPTION_POINTERS *m_pExceptionInfo;
    TCHAR m_szDumpPath[_MAX_PATH];
    TCHAR m_szAppPath[_MAX_PATH];
    TCHAR m_szAppBaseName[_MAX_PATH];
    LONG WriteMiniDump(_EXCEPTION_POINTERS *pExceptionInfo );

    virtual void VSetDumpFileName(void);
    virtual MINIDUMP_USER_STREAM_INFORMATION *VGetUserStreamArray()
        { return NULL; }

public:
    MiniDumper(void);
};

// based on dbghelp.h
typedef BOOL (WINAPI *MINIDUMPWRITEDUMP)(HANDLE hProcess,
    DWORD dwPid, HANDLE hFile, MINIDUMP_TYPE DumpType,
    CONST PMINIDUMP_EXCEPTION_INFORMATION ExceptionParam,
    CONST PMINIDUMP_USER_STREAM_INFORMATION UserStreamParam,
    CONST PMINIDUMP_CALLBACK_INFORMATION CallbackParam);
```

```
MiniDumper *MiniDumper::gpDumper = NULL;

MiniDumper::MiniDumper( )
{
   // Detect if there is more than one MiniDumper.
   assert( !gpDumper );

   if (!gpDumper)
   {
      // set the trap for all your crashes
      ::SetUnhandledExceptionFilter( Handler );
      gpDumper = this;
   }
}

LONG MiniDumper::Handler( _EXCEPTION_POINTERS *pExceptionInfo )
{
   LONG retval = EXCEPTION_CONTINUE_SEARCH;

   if (!gpDumper)
   {
      return retval;
   }

   return gpDumper->WriteMiniDump(pExceptionInfo);
}

LONG MiniDumper::WriteMiniDump(_EXCEPTION_POINTERS *pExceptionInfo )
{
   LONG retval = EXCEPTION_CONTINUE_SEARCH;
   m_pExceptionInfo = pExceptionInfo;

   // You have to find the right dbghelp.dll.
   // Look next to the EXE first since the one in System32 might be old (Win2k)

   HMODULE hDll = NULL;
   TCHAR szDbgHelpPath[_MAX_PATH];

   if (GetModuleFileName( NULL, m_szAppPath, _MAX_PATH ))
   {
      TCHAR *pSlash = _tcsrchr( m_szAppPath, '\\' );
      if (pSlash)
      {
         _tcscpy( m_szAppBaseName, pSlash + 1);
```

```
         *(pSlash+1) = 0;
      }

      _tcscpy( szDbgHelpPath, m_szAppPath );
      _tcscat( szDbgHelpPath, _T("DBGHELP.DLL") );
      hDll = ::LoadLibrary( szDbgHelpPath );
   }

   if (hDll==NULL)
   {
      // If we haven't found it yet - try one more time.
      hDll = ::LoadLibrary( _T("DBGHELP.DLL") );
   }

   LPCTSTR szResult = NULL;

   if (hDll)
   {
      MINIDUMPWRITEDUMP pMiniDumpWriteDump =
         (MINIDUMPWRITEDUMP)::GetProcAddress( hDll, "MiniDumpWriteDump" );

      if (pMiniDumpWriteDump)
      {
         TCHAR szScratch [_MAX_PATH];

         VSetDumpFileName();

         // ask the user if they want to save a dump file
         if (::MessageBox( NULL, _T("There was an unexpected error, would you
                                     like to save a diagnostic file?"),
                                  NULL, MB_YESNO )==IDYES)
         {
            // create the file
            HANDLE hFile =
               ::CreateFile( m_szDumpPath, GENERIC_WRITE,
                  FILE_SHARE_WRITE, NULL, CREATE_ALWAYS,
                  FILE_ATTRIBUTE_NORMAL, NULL );

            if (hFile!=INVALID_HANDLE_VALUE)
            {
               _MINIDUMP_EXCEPTION_INFORMATION ExInfo;

               ExInfo.ThreadId = ::GetCurrentThreadId();
               ExInfo.ExceptionPointers = pExceptionInfo;
               ExInfo.ClientPointers = NULL;
```

```
                    // write the dump
                    BOOL bOK = pMiniDumpWriteDump(
                        GetCurrentProcess(), GetCurrentProcessId(),
                        hFile, MiniDumpNormal, &ExInfo,
                        VGetUserStreamArray(), NULL );

                    if (bOK)
                    {
                        szResult = NULL;
                        retval = EXCEPTION_EXECUTE_HANDLER;
                    }
                    else
                    {
                        sprintf( szScratch, _T("Failed to save dump file to '%s'
                                             (error %d)"), m_szDumpPath,
                                             GetLastError() );
                        szResult = szScratch;
                    }
                    ::CloseHandle(hFile);
                }
                else
                {
                    sprintf( szScratch, _T("Failed to create dump file '%s' (error
                                         %d)"), m_szDumpPath, GetLastError() );
                    szResult = szScratch;
                }
            }
        }
        else
        {
            szResult = _T("DBGHELP.DLL too old");
        }
    }
    else
    {
        szResult = _T("DBGHELP.DLL not found");
    }

    if (szResult)
        ::MessageBox( NULL, szResult, NULL, MB_OK );

    TerminateProcess(GetCurrentProcess(), 0);
    return retval;
}
```

```
void MiniDumper::VSetDumpFileName(void)
{
   _tcscpy( m_szDumpPath, m_szAppPath );
   _tcscat( m_szDumpPath, m_szAppBaseName );
   _tcscat( m_szDumpPath, _T(".dmp") );
}
```

If you want to save the minidump file with a different name, inherit from the MiniDump class and overload VSetDumpFileName. One thing you might consider doing is putting a timestamp in the dump filename so that one minidump file doesn't overwrite another. If you'd like to include your own data stream, overload VGetUserStreamArray().

Here's an example of this class at work:

```
MiniDumper gMiniDumper;
int main()
{
   *(int *)0 = 12;        // CRASH!!!!!
   return 0;
}
```

Just declare a global singleton of the MiniDumper, and when an unhandled exception comes along, your player will be asked if he or she wants to write out some diagnostic information. The minidump file will appear in the same directory as your executable, ready for debugging.

DEBUGGING TECHNIQUES

I think I could write an entire book about debugging. Certainly many people have, and for good reason. You can't be a good programmer unless you have at least passable debugging skills. Imagine for a moment that you are a programmer who never writes buggy code. Hey, stop laughing. I also want you to close your eyes and imagine that you have absolutely no skill at debugging. Why would you? Your code is always perfect! But the moment you are assigned to a team of programmers, your days are numbered. If you can't solve logic problems caused by another programmer's code, you are useless to a team.

If you have good debugging skills, you'll have much more fun programming. I've always looked at really tough bugs as a puzzle. Computers are deterministic, and they execute instructions without interpretation. That truth paves your way to solve every bug if you devote enough patience and skill to the problem.

Debugging Is an Experiment

When you begin a bug hunt, one implication is that you know how to recognize a properly running program. For any piece of code, you should be able to predict its behavior just by carefully reading each line. As an aggregate of modules, a large program should, in theory, accept user input and game data and act in a deterministic way.

Debugging a program requires that you figure out why the behavior of the program is different than what you expect. Certainly the computer's CPU isn't surprised. It executes exactly what you instructed. This delta is the cornerstone of debugging. As each instruction executes, the programmer tests the new state of the process against the predicted state by looking at memory and the contents of variables. The moment the prediction is different than the observed, the programmer has found the bug.

Clearly, you have to be able to predict the behavior of the system given certain stimuli, such as user input or a set of game data files. You should be able to repeat the steps to watch the behavior on your machine or anyone else's machine. When the bug manifests itself as a divergence from nominal operation, you should be able to use what you observed to locate the problem or at least narrow the source of the problem. Repeat these steps enough times, and you'll find the bug. What I've just described is the method any scientist uses to perform experiments.

It might seem odd to perform experiments on software, certainly odd when you wrote the software in question. Scientists perform experiments on complicated phenomena that they don't understand in the hopes that they will achieve knowledge. Why then must programmers perform experiments on systems that spawned from their own minds? The problem is that even the simplest, most deterministic systems can behave unpredictably given particular initial states. If you've never read Stephen Wolfram's book, *A New Kind of Science*, take a few months off and try to get through it. This book makes some surprising observations about complex behavior of simple systems. I'll warn you that once you read it, you may begin to wonder about the determinism of any system, no matter how simple!

Complex and unpredicted behavior in computer programs requires setting up good debugging experiments. If you fell asleep during the lecture in high school on the scientific method, now's a good time to refresh your memory. The examples listed in Table 21.1 show you how to run a successful experiment, but there's a lot more to good debugging than blindly running through the experimental method.

HYPOTHESIS, EXPERIMENTATION, AND ANALYSIS

Debugging is a serious scientific endeavor. If you approach each debugging task as an experiment, just like you were taught in high school, you'll find that debugging is more fun and less frustrating.

Table 21.1 How to Run a Successful Debugging Experiment

Scientific Method as It Applies to Software Systems	Example #1	Example #2
Step 1: Observe the behavior of a computer game.	Observation: A call to `OpenFile()` always fails.	Observation: The game crashes on the low-end machine when it tries to initialize.
Step 2: Attempt to explain the behavior that is consistent with your observations and your knowledge of the system.	Hypothesis: The input parameters to `OpenFile()` are incorrect, specifically the filename.	Hypothesis: The game is crashing because it is running out of video memory.
Step 3: Use your explanation to make predictions.	Predictions: If the proper filename is used, `OpenFile()` will execute successfully.	Predictions: If the amount of video memory were increased, the game would initialize properly. The game will crash when the original amount of video memory is restored.
Step 4: Test your predictions by performing experiments or making additional observations. Modify the hypothesis and predictions based on the results.	Experiment: Send the fully qualified path name of the file and try `OpenFile()` again.	Experiment: Switch the current video card with others that have more memory.
Step 5: Repeat steps three and four until there is no discrepancy between your explanations and the observations.	Results: `OpenFile()` executed successfully with a fully qualified path name.	Results: The game properly initializes with a better video card installed.
Step 6: Explain the results.	Explanation: The current working directory is different than the location of the file in question. The path name must be fully qualified.	Explanation: Video memory requirements have grown beyond expectations.

The first step seems easy: Observe the behavior of the system. Unfortunately, this is not so easy. The most experienced software testers I know do their very best to accurately observe the behavior of a game as it breaks. They record what keys they pressed, what options they turned off, and as best they can exactly what they did. In many cases, they leave out something innocuous. One of the first things I do when I don't observe the same problem a tester observed is go down to the test

BUGS IN GAMES ARE EXTREMELY TRICKY TO FIND

Unlike most software systems, games rely not only on random numbers but they also change vast amounts of data extremely quickly in seemingly unpredictable ways. The difficulty in finding game bugs lies in the simple fact that games run so much code so quickly that it's easy for a bug to appear to come from any of the many subsystems that manipulate the game state.

lab and watch them reproduce the bug myself. Sometimes I'll notice a little wiggle of the mouse or the fact that they're running in full-screen mode and have a "Eureka" moment.

The second step, attempt to explain the behavior, can be pretty hard if you don't know the software like the back of your hand. It's probably safe to say that you should know the software, the operating system, the CPU, video hardware, and audio hardware pretty well too. Sound tough? It is. It also helps to have a few years of game programming under your belt so that you've been exposed to the wacky behavior of broken games. This is probably one of the most frustrating aspects of programming in general: A lack of understanding and experience can leave you shaking your head in dismay when you see your game blow up in your face. Everybody gets through it, though, usually with the help of, dare I say, more experienced programmers.

Steps three through five represent the classic experimental phase of debugging. Your explanation will usually inspire some sort of test, input modification, or code change that should have predictable results. There's an important trick to this rinse and repeat cycle: Take detailed notes of everything you do. Inevitably, your notes will come in handy as you realize that you're chasing a dead-end hypothesis. They should send you back to the point where your predictions were accurate. This will put you back on track.

BEST

PRACTICE

CHANGE ONE THING AT A TIME—AND DON'T REWRITE ANYTHING—YET

Another critical aspect to the experiment-driven debugging process is that you should try to limit your changes to one small thing at a time. If you change too much during one experiment cycle, you won't be able to point to the exact change that fixed the problem. Change for change's sake is a horrible motivation to modify buggy code. Resist that temptation. Sometimes there is a desire to rip a subsystem out altogether and replace it without truly understanding the nature of the problem. This impulse is especially strong when the subsystem in question was written by a programmer that has less than, shall we say, stellar design and coding skills. The effect of this midnight remodeling is usually negative because it isn't guaranteed to fix the bug, and you'll demoralize your teammate at the same time.

Assuming that you follow Table 21.1, you'll eventually arrive at the source of the problem. If you're lucky, the bug can be fixed with a simple tweak of the code. Perhaps a loop exited too soon or a special case wasn't handled properly. You make your mod, rebuild the game, and perform your experiments one last time. Congratulations, your bug is fixed. Not every programmer is so lucky, and certainly I haven't been. Some bugs, once exposed in their full glory, tell you things about your game that you don't want to hear. I've seen bugs that told us we had to completely redesign the graphics system we were using. Other bugs enjoy conveying the message that some version of Windows can't be supported without sweeping modifications. Others make you wonder how the game ever worked in the first place.

If this ever happens to you, and I'm sure it will, I feel your pain. Grab some caffeine and your sleeping bag; it's going to be a long week.

Reproducing the Bug

A prerequisite of observing the behavior of a broken game is reproducing the bug. I've seen bug reports that say things like, "I was doing so-and-so, and the game crashed. I couldn't get it to happen again." In the light of an overwhelming number of reports of this kind, you might be able to figure out what's going on. Alone, these reports are nearly useless. *You cannot fix what you cannot observe.* After all, if you can't observe the broken system with certainty, how can you be sure you fixed the problem? You can't.

Most bugs can be reproduced easily by following a specific set of steps, usually observed and recorded by a tester. It's important that each step, however minor, is recorded from the moment the game is initialized. Anything missing might be important. Also, the state of the machine, including installed hardware and software, might be crucial to reproducing the bug's behavior.

REDUCE COMPLEXITY TO INCREASE PREDICTABILITY

Bugs are sometimes tough to nail down. They can be intermittent or disappear altogether as you attempt to create a specific series of steps that will always result in a manifestation of the problem. This can be explained in two ways: Either an important step or initial state has been left out, or the bug cannot be reproduced because the system being tested is too complex to be deterministic. Even if the bug can be reproduced exactly, it might be difficult to create an explanation of the problem. In both of these cases, you must find a way to reduce the complexity of the system; only then can the problem domain become small enough to understand.

Eliminating Complexity

A bug can only manifest itself if the code that contains it is executed. Eliminate the buggy code, and the bug will disappear. By the process of elimination, you can narrow your search over a series of steps to the exact line of code that is causing the problem. You can disable subsystems in your game, one by one. One of the first things to try is to disable the entire main loop and have your game initialize and exit without doing anything else. This is a good trick if the bug you're hunting is a memory leak. If the bug goes away, you can be sure that it only exists in the main loop somewhere.

DISABLE YOUR SOUND SYSTEM AS A FIRST STEP

Sound systems are usually multithreaded and can be a source of heinous problems. If you believe a bug is somewhere in the sound system, disable your sound system and rerun the game. If the bug disappears, turn the sound system back on, but eliminate only sound effects. Leave the music system on. Divide and conquer as necessary to find the problem. If the bug is in the sound system somewhere, you'll find it.

You should be able to creatively disable other systems as well, such as animation or AI. Once these systems are stubbed out, your game will probably act pretty strangely, and you don't want this strangeness to be interpreted as the bug you are looking for. You should have a pretty complete understanding of your game before you embark on excising large pieces of it from execution.

IT'S POSSIBLE, BUT TOUGH, TO STUB OUT AI SYSTEMS

If you can't simply stub out the AI of your game, replace the AI routines with the most trivial AI code you can write, and make triply sure it is bug free and will have limited, predictable side effects. An example of this is to replace the entire pathfind system with a simple teleport with calculated time delays. You can then slowly add the complex AI systems back in, one at a time, and rerun your tests to see when the bug pops back in.

If your game has options for sound, animation, and other subsystems, you can use these as debugging tools without having to resort to changing code. Turn everything off via your game options and try to reproduce the bug. Whether the bug continues to exist or disappears, the information you'll gain from the experiment is always valuable. As always, keep good records of what you try and try to change only one option at a time.

You can take this tactic to extremes and perform a binary search of sorts to locate a bug. Stub out half of your subsystems and see if the bug manifests itself. If it does, stub out half of what remains and repeat the experiment. Even in a large code base, you'll quickly locate the bug.

If the bug eludes this process, it might depend on the memory map of your application. Change the memory contents of your game, and the bug will change, too. Because this might be true, it's a good idea to stub out subsystems via a simple Boolean value, but leave their code and global data in place as much as possible. This is another example of making small changes rather than large ones.

Setting the Next Statement

Most debuggers give you the power to set the next statement to be executed, which is equivalent to setting the instruction pointer directly. This can be useful if you know what you are doing, but it can be a source of mayhem when applied indiscriminately. You might want to do this for a few reasons. You may want to skip some statements or rerun a section of code again with different parameters as a part of a debugging experiment. You might also be debugging through some assembler, and you want to avoid calling into other pieces of code.

You can set the next statement in Visual Studio by right-clicking on the target statement and selecting "Set Next Statement" from the pop-up menu. In other debuggers, you can bring up a register window and set the EIP register, also known as the *instruction pointer*, to the address of the target statement, which you can usually find by showing the disassembly window. You must be mindful of the code that you are skipping and the current state of your process. When you set the instruction pointer, it is equivalent to executing an assembly level JMP statement, which simply moves the execution path to a different statement.

In C++, objects can be declared inside local scopes such as `for` loops. In normal execution, these objects are destroyed when execution passes out of that scope. The C++ compiler inserts the appropriate code to do this, and you can't see it unless you look at a disassembly window. What do you suppose happens to C++ objects that go out of scope if you skip important lines of code? Let's look at an example:

```
class MyClass
{
public:
   int num;
   char *string;

   MyClass(int const n)
   {
      num = n;
      string = new char[128];
      sprintf(string, "%d  ", n);
   }

   ~MyClass() { delete string; }
};
```

```
void SetTheIP()
{
   char buffer[2048];
   buffer[0] = 0;

   for (int a=0; a<128; ++a)
   {
      MyClass m(a);
      strcat(buffer, m.string);    // START HERE...
   }
}                                  // JUMP TO HERE...
```

Normally, the MyClass object is created and destroyed once for each run of the for loop. If you jump out of the loop using "Set Next Statement," the destructor for MyClass never runs, leaking memory. The same thing would happen if you jumped backward to the line that initializes the buffer variable. The MyClass object in scope won't be destroyed properly.

Luckily, you don't have to worry about the stack pointer as long as you do all your jumping around within one function. Local scopes are creations of the compiler; they don't actually have stack frames. That's a good thing, because setting the next statement to a completely different function is sure to cause havoc with the stack. If you want to skip the rest of the current function and keep it from executing, just right-click on the last closing brace of the function and set the next statement to that point. The stack frame will be kept intact.

Assembly Level Debugging

Inevitably, you'll get to debug through some assembly code. You won't have source code or even symbols for every component of your application, so you should understand a little about the assembly window. Here's the assembly for the SetTheIP function we just talked about. Let's look at the debug version of this code:

```
void SetTheIP()
{
00411A10 55                       push      ebp
00411A11 8B EC                    mov       ebp,esp
00411A13 81 EC E8 08 00 00        sub       esp,8E8h
00411A19 53                       push      ebx
00411A1A 56                       push      esi
00411A1B 57                       push      edi
00411A1C 8D BD 18 F7 FF FF        lea       edi,[ebp-8E8h]
00411A22 B9 3A 02 00 00           mov       ecx,23Ah
00411A27 B8 CC CC CC CC           mov       eax,0CCCCCCCCh
```

```
00411A2C F3 AB                      rep stos    dword ptr [edi]
    char buffer[2048];
    buffer[0] = 0;
00411A2E C6 85 F8 F7 FF FF 00  mov              byte ptr [buffer],0


    for (int a=0; a<128; ++a)
00411A35 C7 85 EC F7 FF FF 00 00 00 00 mov      dword ptr [a],0
00411A3F EB 0F                      jmp         SetTheIP+40h (411A50h)
00411A41 8B 85 EC F7 FF FF      mov             eax,dword ptr [a]
00411A47 83 C0 01               add             eax,1
00411A4A 89 85 EC F7 FF FF      mov             dword ptr [a],eax
00411A50 81 BD EC F7 FF FF 80 00 00 00 cmp      dword ptr [a],80h
00411A5A 7D 35                  jge             SetTheIP+81h (411A91h)
    {
        MyClass m(a);
00411A5C 8B 85 EC F7 FF FF      mov             eax,dword ptr [a]
00411A62 50                     push            eax
00411A63 8D 8D DC F7 FF FF      lea             ecx,[m]
00411A69 E8 9C FA FF FF         call            MyClass::MyClass (41150Ah)
        strcat(buffer, m.string);
00411A6E 8B 85 E0 F7 FF FF      mov             eax,dword ptr [ebp-820h]
00411A74 50                     push            eax
00411A75 8D 8D F8 F7 FF FF      lea             ecx,[buffer]
00411A7B 51                     push            ecx
00411A7C E8 46 F7 FF FF         call            @ILT+450(_strcat) (4111C7h)
00411A81 83 C4 08               add             esp,8
    }
00411A84 8D 8D DC F7 FF FF      lea             ecx,[m]
00411A8A E8 76 FA FF FF         call            MyClass::~MyClass (411505h)
00411A8F EB B0                  jmp             SetTheIP+31h (411A41h)
}
00411A91 52                     push            edx
00411A92 8B CD                  mov             ecx,ebp
00411A94 50                     push            eax
00411A95 8D 15 B6 1A 41 00      lea             edx,[ (411AB6h)]
00411A9B E8 FA F6 FF FF         call            @ILT+405(@_RTC_CheckStackVars@8)
                                                (41119Ah)
00411AA0 58                     pop             eax
00411AA1 5A                     pop             edx
00411AA2 5F                     pop             edi
00411AA3 5E                     pop             esi
00411AA4 5B                     pop             ebx
00411AA5 81 C4 E8 08 00 00      add             esp,8E8h
00411AAB 3B EC                  cmp             ebp,esp
00411AAD E8 F0 F8 FF FF         call            @ILT+925(__RTC_CheckEsp) (4113A2h)
```

```
00411AB2 8B E5              mov      esp,ebp
00411AB4 5D                 pop      ebp
00411AB5 C3                 ret
```

One thing you'll realize immediately is that the disassembly window can be a big help in beginning to understand what assembly language is all about. I wish I had more time to go over each statement, addressing modes, and whatnot, but there are better resources for that anyway.

Notice first the structure of the disassembly window. The column of numbers on the left-hand side of the window is the memory address of each instruction. The list of one to 10 hexadecimal codes that follows each address represents the machine code bytes. Notice that the address of each line coincides with the number of machine code bytes. The more readable instruction on the far right is the assembler statement. Each group of assembler statements is preceded by the C++ statement that they compiled from, if the source is available. You can see that even a close brace can have assembly instructions, usually to return to the calling function or to destroy a C++ object.

The first lines of assembly, pushing various things onto the stack and messing with EBP and ESP, establish a local stack frame. The value 8E8h is the size of the stack frame, which is 2,280 bytes.

Check out the assembly code for the for loop. The beginning of the loop has seven lines of assembly code. The first two initialize the loop variable and jump over the lines that increment the loop variable. Skip over the guts of the loop for now and check out the last three assembly lines. Collectively, they call the destructor for the MyClass object and skip back to the beginning part of the loop that increments the loop variable and performs the exit comparison. If you've ever wondered why the debugger always skips back to the beginning of for loops when the exit condition is met, there's your answer. The exit comparison happens at the beginning.

The inside of the loop has two C++ statements: one to construct the MyClass object and another to call strcat(). Notice the assembly code that makes these calls work. In both cases, values are pushed onto the stack by the calling routine. The values are pushed from right to left, that is to say that the last variable in a function call is pushed first. What this means for you is that you should be mindful of setting the next statement. If you want to skip a call, make sure that you skip any assembly statements that push values onto the stack, or your program will lose its mind.

One last thing: Look at all the code that follows the closing brace of Set-TheIP(). There are two calls here to CheckStackVars() and CheckESP(). What the heck are those things? These are two functions inserted into the exit code of every function in debug builds that perform sanity checks on the integrity of the stack. You can perform a little experiment to see how these things work. Put a breakpoint on the very first line of SetTheIP(), skip over all the stack frame homework, and set the next statement to the one where the buffer gets initialized. The program will run fine until the sanity check code runs. You'll get a dialog box telling you that your stack has been corrupted.

It's nice to know that this check will keep you from chasing ghosts. If you mistakenly screw up the stack frame by moving the instruction pointer around, these sanity checks will catch the problem.

Peppering the Code

If you have an elusive bug that corrupts a data structure or even the memory system, you can hunt it down with a check routine. This assumes that the corruption is somewhat deterministic, and you can write a bit of code to see if it exists. Write this function and begin placing this code in strategic points throughout your game.

A good place to start this check is in your main loop and at the top and bottom of major components like your resource cache, draw code, AI, or sound manager. Place the check at the top and bottom to ensure that you can pinpoint a body of code that caused the corruption. If a check succeeds before a body of code and fails after it, you can begin to drill down into the system, placing more checks, until you nail the exact source of the problem. Here's an example:

```
void BigBuggySubsystem()
{
   BuggyObject crasher;

   CheckForTheBug("Enter BigBuggySubSystem.");

   DoSomething();

   CheckForTheBug("Calling DoSomethingElse");

   DoSomethingElse();

   CheckForTheBug("Calling CorruptEverything");

   CorruptEverything();

   CheckForTheBug("Leave BigBuggySubSystem");
}
```

In this example, CheckForTheBug() is a bit of code that will detect the corruption, and the other function calls are subsystems of the BigBuggySubsystem. It's a good idea to put a text string in your checking code so that it's quick and easy to identify the corruption location, even if the caller's stack is trashed.

Since there's plenty of C++ code that runs as a result of exiting a local scope, don't fret if your checking function finds a corruption on entry. You can target your search inside the destructors of any C++ objects used inside the previous scope. If the destructor for the `BuggyObject` code was wreaking some havoc, it won't be caught by your last call to your checking function. You wouldn't notice it until some other function called your checking code.

Draw Debug Information

This might seem incredibly obvious, but since I forget it all the time myself I figure it deserves mentioning. If you are having trouble with graphics- or physics-related bugs, it can be invaluable to draw additional information on your screen such as wireframes, direction vectors, or coordinate axes. This is especially true for 3D games, but any game can find visual debug helpers useful. Here are a few ideas:

- **Hot Areas:** If you are having trouble with user interface code, you can draw rectangles around your controls and change their color when they go active. You'll be able to see why one control is being activated when you didn't expect it.
- **Memory/Frame Rate:** In debug versions of your game, it can be very useful to draw current memory and frame rate information every few seconds. Don't do it every frame because you can't really see things that fast, and it will affect your frame rate.
- **Coordinate Axes:** A classic problem with 3D games is that the artist will create 3D models in the wrong coordinate system. Draw some additional debug geometry that shows the positive X-axis in red, the Y-axis in green, and the positive Z-axis in blue. You'll always know which way is up!
- **Wireframe:** You can apply wireframe drawing to collision geometry to see if they match up properly. A classic problem in 3D games is when these geometries are out of sync, and drawing the collision geometry in wireframe can help you figure out what's going on.
- **Targets:** If you have AI routines that select targets or destinations, it can be useful to draw them explicitly by using lines. Whether your game is 3D or 2D, line drawing can give you information about where the targets are. Use color information to convey additional information such as friend or foe.

BEST PRACTICE

EVERY 3D GAME NEEDS A TEST OBJECT

In 3D games, it's a good idea to construct a special test object that is asymmetrical on all three coordinate axes. Your game renderer and physics system can easily display things like cubes in a completely wrong way, but they will look right because a cube looks the same from many different angles. A good example of an asymmetrical object is a shoe, since there's no way you can slice it and get a mirror image from one side to another. In your 3D game, build something with similar properties, but make sure the shape is so asymmetrical that it will be obvious if any errors pop up.

Lint and Other Code Analyzers

These tools can be incredibly useful. Their best application is one where code is being checked often, perhaps each night. Dangerous bits of code are fixed as they are found, so they don't get the chance to exist in the system for any length of time. If you don't have Lint, make sure that you ramp up the warning level of the compiler as high as you can stand it. It will be able to make quite a few checks for you and catch problems as they happen.

A less useful approach involves using code analysis late in your project with the hope it will pinpoint a bug. You'll probably be inundated with warnings and errors, any of which could be perfectly benign for your game. The reason this isn't as useful at the end of your project is that you may have to make sweeping changes to your code to address every issue. This is not wise. It is much more likely that sweeping changes will create a vast set of additional issues, the aggregate of which could be worse than the original problem. It's best to perform these checks often and throughout the life of your project.

Nu-Mega's BoundsChecker and Runtime Analyzers

BoundsChecker is a great program, and every team should have at least one copy. In some configurations, it can run so slowly that your game will take three hours to display a single screen. Rather, use a targeted approach and filter out as many checks as you can and leave only the checks that will trap your problem.

Disappearing Bugs

The really nasty bug seems to actually possess intelligence, as well as awareness of itself and your attempts to destroy it. Just as you get close, the bug changes, and it can't be reproduced using your previously observed steps. It's likely that recent changes such as adding checking code have altered the memory map of your process. The bug might be corrupting memory that is simply unused. This is where your notes will really come in handy. It's time to backtrack, remove your recent changes one at a time, and repeat until the bug reappears. Begin again, but try a different approach in the hopes you can get closer.

BEST
PRACTICE

BUGS FIXING THEMSELVES?

Another version of the disappearing bug is one where a known failure simply disappears without any programmer actually addressing it. The bug might have been related to another issue that someone fixed—you hope. The safest thing to do is to analyze recent changes and attempt to perform an autopsy of sorts. Given the recent fixes, you might even be able to re-create the original conditions and code that made the bug happen, apply the fix again, and prove beyond a shadow of a doubt that a particular fix addressed more than one bug.

What's more likely is that the number of changes to the code will preclude the possibility of this examination, especially on a large team. Then you have a decision to make: Is the bug severe enough to justify a targeted search through all the changes to prove the bug is truly fixed? It depends on the seriousness of the bug.

Tweaking Values

A classic problem in programming is getting a constant value "just right." This is usually the case for things like the placement of a user interface object like a button or perhaps the velocity value of a particle stream. While you are experimenting with the value, put it in a static variable in your code:

```
void MyWeirdFountain::Update()
{
    static float dbgVelocity = 2.74f;
    SetParticleVelocity(dbgVelocity);

    // More code would follow….
}
```

It then becomes a trivial thing to set a breakpoint on the call to `SetParticleVelocity()` to let you play with the value of `dbgVelocity` in real time. This is much faster than recompiling, and even faster than making the value data driven, since you won't even have to reload the game data.

Once you find the values you're looking for, you can take the time to put them in a data file.

Caveman Debugging

If you can't use a debugger, or didn't even know they existed as I didn't in college, you get to do something I call *caveman debugging*. You might be curious as to why you wouldn't be able to use a debugger, and it's not because you work for someone so cheap that they won't buy one. Sometimes you'll see problems only in the release build of the application. These problems usually result from uninitialized variables or unexpected or even incorrect code generation. The problem simply goes away in the debug version. You might also be debugging a server application that fails intermittently, perhaps after hours of running nominally. It's useless to attempt debugging in that case.

BEST
PRACTICE

`OutputDebugString()` IS YOUR FRIEND

Make good use of `stderr` if you program in UNIX or `OutputDebugString()` if you program under Windows. These are your first and best tools for caveman debugging.

In both cases, you should resort to the caveman method. You'll write extra code to display variables or other important information on the screen, in the output window, or in a permanent log file. As the code runs, you'll watch the output for signs of misbehavior, or you'll pour over the log file to try to discern the nature of the bug. This is a slow process and takes a great deal of patience, but if you can't use a debugger, this method will work.

BEING HYPNOTIZED BY THE *ULTIMA ONLINE* LOGIN SERVERS...

When I was on *Ultima Online*, one of my tasks was to write the *UO* login servers. These servers were the main point of connection for the Linux game servers and the SQL server, so login was only a small portion of what the software actually did. An array of statistical information flowed from the game servers, was collated in the login server, and was written to the SQL database. The EA executives liked pretty charts and graphs, and we gave them what they wanted. Anyway, the login process was a Win32 console application, and to help me understand what was going on, I printed debug messages for logins, statistics data, and anything else that looked reasonable. When the login servers were running, these messages were scrolling by so fast that I certainly couldn't read them, but I could feel them. Imagine me sitting in the *UO* server room, staring blankly at three login server screens. I could tell just by the shape of the text flowing by whether or not a large number of logins were failing or a *UO* server was disconnected. It was very weird.

DEBUGGING WITH MUSIC

The best caveman debugging solution I ever saw was one that used the PC speaker. Herman was a programmer who worked on *Ultima V* through *Ultima IX*, and one of his talents was perfect pitch. He could tell you the difference between a B and a B flat and get it right every time. He used this to his advantage when he was searching for the nastiest crasher bugs of them all—they didn't even allow the debugger window to pop up. He wrote a special checker program that output specific tones through the PC speaker, and peppered the code with these checks. If you walked into his office while his spiced-up version of the game was running, it sounded a little like raw modem noise, until the game crashed. Because the PC speaker wasn't dependent on the CPU, it would remain emitting the tone of his last check. "Hmm...that's a D," he would say, and zero in on the line of code that caused the crash.

When All Else Fails

So you tried everything and hours later you are no closer to solving the problem than when you started. Your boss is probably making excuses to pass by your office and ask you cheerily, "How's it going?" You suppress the urge to jump up and make an example of his annoying behavior, but you still have no idea what to do. Here's a few last resort ideas.

First, go find another programmer and explain your problem. It doesn't really matter if you can find John Carmack or the greenest guy in your group, just find someone. Walk them through each step, explaining the behavior of the bug and each hypothesis you had—even it failed. Talk about your debugging experiments and step through the last one with him (or her) watching over your shoulder. For some odd reason, you'll find the solution to your problem without that person ever even speaking a single word. It will just come as if it were handed to you by the universe itself. I've never been able to explain that phenomenon, but it's real. This will solve half of the unsolvable bugs.

Another solution is static code analysis. You should have enough observations to guess at what is going on, you just can't figure out how the pieces of the puzzle fit together. Print out a suspect section of code on paper—the flat stuff you find in copy machines—and take it away from your desk. Study it and ask yourself how the code could fail. Getting away from your computer and the debugger helps to open your mind a bit, and removes your dependency on them.

If you get to this point and you still haven't solved the problem, you've probably been at it for a few solid hours, if not all night. It's time to walk away—not from the problem, but from your computer. Just leave. Do something to get your mind off the problem. Drive home. Eat dinner. Introduce yourself to your family. Take a shower.

The last one is particularly useful for me, not that I need any of you to visualize me in the shower. The combination of me being away from the office and in a relaxing environment frees a portion of my mind to continue working on the problem without adding to my stress level. Sometimes, a new approach to the problem or even better, a solution, will simply deposit itself in my consciousness. That odd event has never happened to me when I'm under pressure sitting at the computer. It's scary when you're at dinner, it dawns on you suddenly, and you've solved a bug just by getting away from it.

DIFFERENT KINDS OF BUGS

Tactics and technique are great, but that only describes debugging in the most generic sense. Everyone should build a taxonomy of bugs, a dictionary of bugs as it were, so that you can instantly recognize a type of bug and associate it with the beginning steps of a solution. One way to do this is to constantly trade "bug" stories with other programmers—a conversation that will bore nonprogrammers completely to death.

Memory Leaks and Heap Corruption

A memory leak is caused when a dynamically allocated memory block is "lost." The pointer that holds the address of the block is reassigned without freeing the block, and it will remain allocated until the application exits. This kind of bug is especially problematic if this happens frequently. The program will chew up physical and virtual memory over time, and eventually fail. Here's a classic example of a memory leak. This class allocates a block of memory in a constructor, but fails to declare a virtual destructor:

```
class LeakyMemory : public SomeBaseClass
{
protected:
   int *leaked;

   LeakyMemory() { leaked = new int[128]; }
   ~LeakyMemory() { delete leaked; }
};
```

This code might look fine but there's a potential memory leak in there. If this class is instantiated and is referenced by a pointer to SomeBaseClass, the destructor will never get called:

```
void main()
{
   LeakyMemory *ok = new LeakyMemory;
   SomeBaseClass *bad = new LeakyMemory;

   delete ok;
   delete bad;      // MEMORY LEAK RIGHT HERE!
}
```

You fix this problem by declaring the destructor in LeakyMemory as virtual. Memory leaks are easy to fix if the leaky code is staring you in the face. This isn't always the case. A few bytes leaked here and there as game objects are created and destroyed can go unnoticed for a long time until it is obvious that your game is chewing up memory without any valid reason.

Memory bugs and leaks are amazingly easy to fix, but tricky to find, if you use a memory allocator that doesn't have special code to give you a hand. Under Win32, the C runtime library lends a hand under the debug builds with the debug heap. The debug heap sets the value of uninitialized memory and freed memory.

- Uninitialized memory allocated on the heap is set to 0xCDCDCDCD.
- Uninitialized memory allocated on the stack is set to 0xCCCCCCCC. This is dependent on the /GX compiler option in Microsoft Visual Studio.

- Freed heap memory is set to 0xFEEEFEEE, before it has been reallocated. Sometimes, this freed memory is set to 0xDDDDDDDD, depending on how the memory was freed.
- The lead byte and trailing byte to any memory allocated on the heap is set to 0xFDFDFDFD.

Win32 programmers commit these values to memory. They'll come in handy when you are viewing memory windows in the debugger. You can tell what has happened to a block of dynamic memory.

The C-Runtime debug heap also provides many functions to help you examine the heap for problems. I'll tell you about three of them, and you can hunt for the rest in the Visual Studio help files or MSDN:

- `_CrtSetDbgFlag (int newFlag)`: Sets the behavior of the debug heap.
- `_CrtCheckMemory (void)`: Runs a check on the debug heap.
- `_CrtDumpMemoryLeaks (void)`: Reports any leaks to stdout.

Here's an example of how to put these functions into practice:

```
#include <crtdbg.h>
#if defined _DEBUG
   #define GCC_NEW new(_NORMAL_BLOCK,__FILE__, __LINE__)
#endif

int main()
{
   // get the current flags
   int tmpDbgFlag = _CrtSetDbgFlag(_CRTDBG_REPORT_FLAG);

   // don't actually free the blocks
   tmpDbgFlag |= _CRTDBG_DELAY_FREE_MEM_DF;

   // perform memory check for each alloc/dealloc
   tmpDbgFlag |= _CRTDBG_CHECK_ALWAYS_DF;
   _CrtSetDbgFlag(tmpDbgFlag);

   char *gonnaTrash = GCC_NEW char[15];

   _CrtCheckMemory();                       // everything is fine....

   strcpy(gonnaTrash, "Trash my memory!");   // overwrite the buffer

   _CrtCheckMemory();                       // everything is NOT fine!

   delete gonnaTrash;                       // This brings up a dialog box too...
```

```
    char *gonnaLeak = GCC_NEW char[100]; // Prepare to leak!

    _CrtDumpMemoryLeaks();                 // Reports leaks to stderr

    return 0;
}
```

Notice that the new operator is redefined. A debug version of new is included in the debug heap that records the file and line number of each allocation. This can go a long way toward detecting the cause of a leak.

The first few lines set the behavior of the debug heap. The first flag tells the debug heap to keep deallocated blocks around in a special list instead of recycling them back into the usable memory pool. You might use this flag to help you track a memory corruption or simply alter your processes' memory space in the hopes that a tricky bug will be easier to catch. The second flag tells the debug heap that you want to run a complete check on the debug heap's integrity each time memory is allocated or freed. This can be incredibly slow, so turn it on and off only when you are sure it will do you some good.

The output of the memory leak dump looks like this:

```
Detected memory leaks!
Dumping objects ->
c:\tricks\tricks.cpp(78) : {42} normal block at 0x00321100, 100 bytes long.
 Data: <              > CD CD CD CD CD CD CD CD CD CD CD CD CD CD CD CD
Object dump complete.
The program '[2940] Tricks.exe: Native' has exited with code 0 (0x0).
```

As you can see, the leak dump pinpoints the exact file and line of the leaked bits. What happens if you have a core system that allocates memory like crazy, such as a custom string class? Every leaked block of memory will look like it's coming from the same line of code, because it is. It doesn't tell you anything about who called it, which is the real perpetrator of the leak. If this is happening to you, tweak the redeclaration of new and store a self-incrementing counter instead of __LINE__:

```
#include <crtdbg.h>
#if defined _DEBUG
   static int counter = 0;
   #define GCC_NEW new(_NORMAL_BLOCK,__FILE__, counter++)
#endif
```

The memory dump report will tell you exactly when the leaky bits were allocated, and you can track the leak down easily. All you have to do is put a conditional breakpoint on GCC_NEW, and break when the counter reaches the value that leaked.

THE TASK MANGER LIES ABOUT MEMORY

You can't look at the Task Manager under Windows to determine if your game is leaking memory. The Task Manager is the process window you can show if you press Ctrl-Alt-Del and then click the Task Manager button. This window lies. For one thing, memory might be reported wrong if you have set the `_CRTDBG_DELAY_FREE_MEM_DF` flag. Even if you are running a release build, freed memory isn't reflected in the process window until the window is minimized and restored. Even the Microsoft test lab was stymied by this one. They wrote a bug telling us that our game was leaking memory like crazy, and we couldn't find it. It turned out that if you minimize the application window and restore it, the Task Manager will report the memory correctly, at least for a little while.

If you happen to write your own memory manager, make sure that you take the time to write some analogs to the C runtime debug heap functions. If you don't, you'll find chasing memory leaks and corruptions a full-time job.

DON'T IGNORE MEMORY LEAKS—EVER

Make sure that your debug build detects and reports memory leaks, and convince all programmers that they should fix all memory leaks before they check in their code. It's a lot harder to fix someone else's memory leak than your own.

COM objects can leak memory, too, and those leaks are also painful to find. If you fail to call `Release()` on a COM object when you're done with it, the object will remain allocated because its reference count will never drop to zero.

Here's a neat trick. First, put the following function somewhere in your code:

```
int Refs (IUnknown* pUnk)
{
    pUnk->AddRef();
    return pUnk->Release();
}
```

You can then put `Refs(myLeakingResourcePtr)` in the watch window in your debugger. This will usually return the current reference count for a COM object. Be warned, however, that COM doesn't require that `Release()` return the current reference count, but it usually does.

Game Data Corruption

Most memory corruptions are easy to diagnose. Your game crashes, and you find funky trash values where you were used to seeing valid data. The frustrating thing about memory corrupter bugs is that they can happen anywhere, anytime. Since the memory corruption is not trashing the heap, you can't use the debug heap functions, but you can use your own homegrown version of them. You need to write your own version of `_CrtCheckMemory()`, built especially for the data structures being vandalized. Hopefully, you'll have a reasonable set of steps you can use to reproduce the bug. Given those two things, the bug has only moments to live. If the trasher is intermittent, leave the data structure check code in the game. Perhaps someone will begin to notice a pattern of steps that cause the corruption to occur.

TALES FROM THE PIXEL MINES

THE BEST HACK I EVER SAW

I recall a truly excellent hack we encountered on *Savage Empire*, an *Ultima VI* spin-off that Origin shipped in late 1990. Origin was using Borland's 3.1 C Compiler, and the runtime module's exit code always checked memory location zero to see if a wayward piece of code accidentally overwrote that piece of memory, which was actually unused. If it detected the memory location was altered, it would print out "Error: (null) pointer assignment" at the top of the screen. Null pointer assignments were tough to find in those days since the CPU just happily assumed you knew what you were doing. *Savage Empire* programmers tried in vain to hunt down the null pointer assignment until the very last day of development. Origin's QA had signed off on the build, and Origin execs wanted to ship the product, since Christmas was right around the corner. Steve, one of the programmers, "fixed" the problem with an amazing hack. He hex edited the executable, savage.exe, and changed the text string "Error: (null) pointer assignment." to another string exactly the same length: "Thanks for playing *Savage Empire*."

If the memory corruption seems random—writing to memory locations here and there without any pattern—here's a useful but brute force trick: Declare an enormous block of memory and initialize it with an unusual pattern of bytes. Write a check routine that runs through the memory block and finds any bytes that don't match the original pattern, and you've got something that can detect your bug. I've been using this trick since *Ultima VII*.

A SAD TRICERATOPS

Ultima games classically stored their game data in large blocks of memory, and the data was organized as a linked list. If the object lists became corrupted, all manner of mayhem would result. If you ever played *Savage Empire,* you might have been one of the lucky people to see a triceratops walking across the opening screen—in two pieces.

Another example of this object corruption was a bug I saw in *Martian Dreams.* As I was walking my character across the alien landscape, all the plants turned into pocket watches and my character turned into a pair of boots. If I hadn't seen it with my own eyes, I wouldn't have believed it.

The worst of these bugs became something of a legend at Origin Systems— "The Barge Bug." The *Ultima VI* team found that the linked object lists could be used to create barges, a generic term for a bunch of linked objects that could move about the map as a group. This led to neat stuff like flying carpets, boats, and the barges of *Martian Dreams* that navigated the canals.

QA was observing a bug that made barges explode. The objects and their passengers would suddenly shatter into pieces, and if you attempted to move them one step in any direction that game would crash. I was assigned the task of fixing this bug. I tried again and again. Each time I was completely sure that the barge bug was dead. QA didn't share my optimism, and for four versions of the game I would see the bug report come back: "Not fixed."

The fourth time I saw the bug report, my exhausted mind simply snapped. I don't need to tell you what happened, because an artist friend of mine, Denis, drew this picture of me in Figure 21.3.

FIGURE 21.3 Artist's rendering of earwax blowing out of Mr. Mike's ears.

Stack Corruption

Stack corruption is evil because it wipes evidence from the scene of the crime. Take a look at this lovely code:

```
void StackTrasher()
{
    char hello[10];
    memset(hello, 0, 1000);
}
```

The call to memset() never returns, since it wipes the stack clean, including the return address. The most likely thing your computer will do is break into some crazy, codeless area—the debugger equivalent of shrugging its shoulders and leaving you to figure it out for yourself. Stack corruptions almost always happen as a result of sending bad data into an otherwise trusted function, like memset(). Again, you must have a reasonable set of steps you can follow to reproduce the error.

Begin your search by eliminating subsections of code, if you can. Set a breakpoint at the highest level of code in your main loop and step over each function call. Eventually, you should be able to find a case where stepping over a function call will cause the crash. Begin your experiment again, only this time step into the function and narrow the list of perpetrators. Repeat these steps until you've found the call that causes the crash.

Notice carefully with each step the call stack window. The moment it is trashed, the debugger will be unable to display the call stack. It is unlikely that you'll be able to continue or even set the next statement to a previous line for retesting, so if you missed the cause of the problem, you'll have to begin again. If the call that causes that stack to go south is something trusted like memset(), study each input parameter carefully. Your answer is there: one of those parameters is bogus.

Cut and Paste Bugs

This kind of bug doesn't have a specific morphology, an academic way of saying "pattern of behavior." It does have a common source, which is cutting and pasting code from one place to another. I know how it is; sometimes it's easier to cut and paste a little section of code rather than factor it out into a member of a class or utility function. I've done this myself many times to avoid a heinous recompile. I tell myself that I'll go back and factor the code later. Of course, I never get around to it. The danger of cutting and pasting code is pretty severe.

First, the original code segment could have a bug that doesn't show up until much later. The programmer who finds the bug will likely perform a debugging experiment where a tentative fix is applied to the first block of code, but he misses the second one. The bug may still occur exactly as it did before, convincing our hero that he has failed to find the problem, so he begins a completely different approach. Second, the cut-and-pasted code might be perfectly fine in its original location, but cause a subtle bug in the destination. You might have local variables stomping on each other or some such thing.

If you're like me at all, you feel a pang of guilt every time you hit Ctrl-V and you see more than two or three lines pop out of the clipboard. That guilt is there for a reason. Heed it and at least create a local free function while you get the logic straightened out. When you're done, you can refactor your work, make your change to game.h, and compile through the night.

There's another reason to feel guilty, too. If you have Visual Studio 2005 or later, you can use a free plug-in from Developer Express, Inc. called *Refactor!* It can extract functions from existing code, simplify expressions, and all manner of useful things. Cut-and-paste bugs might just become a thing of the past.

Running Out of Space

Everyone hates to run out of space. By space, I mean any consumable resource: memory, hard drive space, Windows handles, or memory blocks on a console's memory card. If you run out of space, your game is either leaking these resources or never had them to begin with.

TALES FROM THE PIXEL MINES

NINE DISKS IS WAY TOO MANY

In the final days of *Ultima VIII*, it took nine floppy disks to hold all of the install files. Origin execs had a hard limit on eight floppy disks, and we had to find some way of compressing what we had into one less disk. It made sense to concentrate on the largest file, SHAPES.FLX, which held all of the graphics for the game.

Zack, one of Origin's best programmers, came up with a great idea. The SHAPES.FLX file essentially held filmstrip animations for all the characters in *Ultima VIII*, and each frame was only slightly different from the previous frame. Before the install program compressed SHAPES.FLX, Zack wrote a program to delta-compress all of the animations. Each frame stored only the pixels that changed from the previous frame, and the blank space left over was run-length encoded. The whole shebang was compressed with a general compression algorithm for the install program.

It didn't make installation any faster, that's for sure, but Zack saved Origin a few tens of thousands of dollars with a little less than a week of hard-core programming.

We've already talked about the leaking problem, so let's talk about the other case. If your game needs certain resources to run properly, like a certain amount of hard drive space or memory blocks for save game files, then by all means check for the appropriate headroom when your game initializes. If any consumable is in short supply, you should bail right there or at least warn players that they won't be able to save games.

Release Mode Only Bugs

If you ever have a bug in the release build that doesn't happen in the debug build, most likely you have an uninitialized variable somewhere. The best way to find this type of bug is to use a runtime analyzer like BoundsChecker.

Another source of this problem can be a compiler problem, in that certain optimization settings or other project settings are causing bugs. If you suspect this, one possibility is to start changing the project settings one by one to look more like the debug build until the bug disappears. Once you have the exact setting that causes the bug, you may get some intuition about where to look next.

Multithreading Gone Bad

Multithreaded bugs are really nasty because they can be nigh impossible to reproduce accurately. The first clue that you may have a multithreaded issue is by a bug's unpredictable behavior. If you think you have a multithreaded bug on your hands, the first thing you should do is disable multithreading and try to reproduce the bug.

A good example of a classic multithreaded bug is a sound system crash. The sound system in most games runs in a separate thread, grabbing sound bits from the game every now and then as it needs them. It's these communication points where two threads need to synch up and communicate that most multithreading bugs occur.

Sound systems like Miles from RAD Game Tools are extremely well tested. It's much more likely that a sound system crash is due to your game deallocating some sound memory before its time or perhaps simply trashing the sound buffer. In fact, this is so likely, that my first course of action when I see a really strange, irreproducible bug is to turn off the sound system and see if I can get the problem to happen again.

The same is true for other multithreaded subsystems, such as AI or resource preloading. If your game uses multiple threads for these kinds of systems, make sure that you can turn them off easily for testing. Sure, the game will run in a jerky fashion since all the processing has to be performed in a linear fashion, but the added benefit is that you can eliminate the logic of those systems and focus on the communication and thread synchronization for the source of the problem.

THE PITCH DEBUGGER COMES TO THE RESCUE

Ultima VIII had an interrupt-driven multitasking system, which was something of a feat in DOS 5. A random crash was occurring in QA, and no one could figure out how to reproduce it, which meant there was little hope of it getting fixed. It was finally occurring once every 30 minutes or so—way too often to be ignored.

We set four or five programmers on the problem—each one attempting to reproduce the bug. Finally, the bug was reproduced by a convoluted path. We would walk the Avatar character around the map in a specific sequence, teleporting to one side of the map, then the other, and the crash would happen. We were getting close.

Herman, the guy with perfect pitch, turned on his pitch debugger. We followed the steps exactly, and when the crash happened, Herman called it: a B-flat meant that the bug was somewhere in the memory manager.

We eventually tracked it down to a lack of protection in the memory system—two threads were accessing the memory management system at the same time, and the result was a trashed section of memory. Since the bug was related to multithreading, it never corrupted the same piece of memory twice in a row.

Had we turned multithreading off, the bug would have disappeared, causing us to focus our effort on any shared data structure that could be corrupted by multiple thread access. In other words, we were extremely lucky to find this bug, and the only thing that saved us was a set of steps we could follow that made the bug happen.

Weird Ones

There are some bugs that are very strange, either by their behavior, intermittency, or the source of the problem. Driver-related issues are pretty common, not necessarily because there's a bug in the driver. It's more likely that you are assuming the hardware or driver can do something that it cannot. Your first clue that an issue is driver related is that it only occurs on specific hardware, such as a particular brand of video card. Video cards are sources of constant headaches in Windows games because each manufacturer wants to have some feature stand out from the pack, and do so in a manner that keeps costs down. More often than not, this will result in some odd limitations and behavior.

Weird bugs can also crop up in specific operating system versions, for exactly the same reasons. Windows 9x based operating systems are very different than Windows 2000 and Windows XP, based on the much beefier NT kernel. These different operating systems make different assumptions about parameters, return values, and even logic for the same API calls. If you don't believe me, just look at

HARDWARE LIMITATIONS CAN BE SURPRISING

A great example of an unruly video card was found on an old video card that was once made by the now defunct 3Dfx company. This card had a limitation that no video memory surface could have a width to height ratio greater than 8:1. A 256 × 32 surface would work just fine, but a 512 × 32 surface would fail in a very strange way. It would create a graphic effect not unlike a scrambled TV channel. If you weren't aware of this limitation, you would debug relentlessly through every line of code in your whole game, and you'd never find the problem. It turns out that problems like this are usually found through a targeted search of the Internet. Google groups (http://groups.google.com) is my personal favorite.

the bottom of the help files for any Win32 API like `GetPrivateProfileSection()`. That one royally screwed me.

Again, you diagnose the problem by attempting to reproduce the bug on a different operating system. Save yourself some time and try a system that is vastly different. If the bug appears in Windows 98, try it again in Windows XP. If the bug appears in both operating systems, it's extremely unlikely that your bug is OS specific.

A much rarer form of the weird bug is a specific hardware bug, one that seems to manifest as a result of a combination of hardware and operating systems, or even a specific piece of defective or incompatible hardware. These problems can manifest themselves most often in portable computers, oddly enough. If you've isolated the bug to something this specific, the first thing you should try is to update all the relevant drivers. This is a good thing to do in any case, since most driver-related bugs will disappear when the fresh drivers are installed.

BE CAREFUL OF THE BLEEDING EDGE

Be especially aware of new things. Back when MFC& was brand new, one of the latest changes to MFC7 was a complete restructuring of how it handled strings. The old code was thrown out in favor of an ATL-based system. MFC7 was distributed with Visual Studio, and we noticed immediately that our game was failing under Windows 98. After a painful remote debugging session, it seemed that the tried-and-true `CFileFind` class was corrupting memory. Go figure! One of the reasons it took me so long to find it was that I wasn't looking inside `CfileFind`, even though the source code was there right in front of me. I guess I'm just too trusting.

Finally, the duckbilled platypus of weird bugs are the ones generated by the compiler. It happens more often than anyone would care to admit. The bug will manifest itself most often in a release build with full optimizations. This is the most fragile section of the compiler. You'll be able to reproduce the bug on any platform, but it may disappear when release mode settings are tweaked. The only way to find this problem is to stare at the assembly code and figure out that the compiler-generated code is not semantically equal to the original source code. This is not that easy, especially in fully optimized assembly.

By the way, if you are wondering what you do if you don't know assembly, here's a clue: go find a programmer who knows assembly. Watch that person work, and learn something. Then convince yourself that maybe learning a little assembly is a good idea.

BEST

PRACTICE

REPORT EVERY COMPILER BUG YOU FIND

If you happen to be lucky (or unlucky) enough to find a weird compiler problem (especially one that could impact other game developers), do everyone a favor and write a tiny program that isolates the compiler bug and post it so everyone can watch out for the problem. You'll be held in high regard if you find a workaround and post that too. Be really sure that you are right about what you see. The Internet lasts forever, and it would be unfortunate if you blamed the compiler programmers for something they didn't do. In your posts, be gentle. Rather than say something like, "Those idiots who developed the xyz compiler really screwed up and put in this nasty bug …," try, "I think I found a tricky bug in the xyz compiler …"

PARTING THOUGHTS

An important thing to keep in mind when debugging is that computers are at their core *deterministic entities*. They don't do things unless instructions are loaded into the CPU. This should give you hope, since the bug you seek is always findable.

You know that with enough time and effort, you'll squash that bug. That thought alone can be a powerful motivating force.

FURTHER READING

Reversing: Secrets of Reverse Engineering, von Eldad Eilam

DRIVING TO THE FINISH

In This Chapter

- Finishing Issues
- Dealing with Big Trouble
- The Light—It's Not a Train After All

At some point in your schedule, you begin to realize that you're a lot closer to the end than the beginning. While the calendar might imply this harsh fact, your workload seems to increase exponentially. For every task that goes final, two or three seem to take its place. What's more, the team is likely working overtime, already exhausted, and somehow everyone has to pull together for another long weekend.

Sound familiar?

If you've ever worked on a game, it should. This phenomenon is pretty common in many project-oriented businesses, but games are especially susceptible because there's something games are required to deliver that doesn't exist anywhere else. Games have to be fun.

I've said it a few times in this book already, but it deserves another mention. You can't schedule fun, and you can't predict fun. Fun is the direct result of a few things: a great vision, lots of iteration, a mountain of effort, lots of playtesting and redesign, and a flexible plan. Any one of these things in abundance can make up something lacking in the other two. Most game companies simply rely on the effort component—a valiant but somewhat naive mistake.

If you've ever been in a sustained endurance sport like biking, you know that you start any event with lots of excitement and energy. Toward the end of the ride, you've probably suffered a few setbacks, like a flat tire or running out of water, making it hard to keep your rhythm. Your tired body begins to act robotically, almost as if your brain has checked out, and the highest thinking you are doing is working a few muscle groups. You refuse food and water, believing you don't need it. Then things really start to go wrong. You'll be lucky to cross the finish line.

The same thing happens to game development teams after a long stretch of overtime. Tired minds can't think, and not only do they make mistakes, but they don't even recognize them when they happen, and they attempt to solve the entire mess with even more mandatory overtime. This is not only tragic, but it is a choice doomed to fail.

Getting a project over the finish line is tough, and you'll be called upon to solve some sticky problems along the way. Some of these problems will happen fast, too fast for you to have a solution in your back pocket. You'll have to think on your feet—not unlike someone who happens upon an emergency situation. When you learn first aid, you are taught that you must be able to recognize a problem when you see it, have the skills to do something about it, and most importantly, you must decide to act.

I can give you the first two. The final one is up to you.

FINISHING ISSUES

If your project is going well, you'll likely only need a few tweaks here and there to make sure you "stick the landing," so to speak. You can recognize this on your project by looking for a few telltale signs:

- **Your bug count is under control.** Your developers have fewer than four active bugs to fix per day until the "zero bugs" date.
- **Everyone is in good spirits**.
- **The game is fun to play, performs well, and has only polishing issues remaining.**

If this describes your project, congratulations! But don't get too cocky, because there are some easy missteps you can make, even at this late stage.

Quality

Perhaps the two biggest questions you and everyone else on the team asks at this point are likely to be, "Is the game good enough? Is it fun?" If a bug comes out of the testing group, it's because they want something changed to make the game better. Anyone on the development team can motivate a change as well, and they should if they think the game will become better because of it.

The closer the project gets to the scheduled zero bugs milestone, the less likely minor, C level bugs will actually get fixed. This rule of thumb is directly related to the fact that any change in content or code induces some risk. I've seen a single bug fix create multiple new bugs. This implies that any high-risk change should either happen much earlier in the schedule, or there has to be some incredibly compelling reason, like there's no other choice and the project is in jeopardy if the change isn't made. These problems are usually elevated to the highest level severity in the bug database, and your game shouldn't ship if it hasn't been fixed.

Everyone on a project has his or her pet feature, something he or she really wants to see in the game. The best time to install these features is before the code complete milestone (some people call this *alpha*). There are a few good reasons for this. First, it gives the team a huge burst of energy. Everyone is working on their top-tier wish lists, and tons of important features make it into the game at a time where the risk of these changes is pretty tolerable. Second, it gives the team a message: either put your change in now or forever hold your peace. After code complete, nothing new code-wise should be installed into the game. For artists and other content folks, this rule is the same, just the milestone is different. They use the content complete milestone (or beta) as their drop-dead date for pet features. One more note about programmers and artists adding anything. If the game isn't reaching target performance goals, it's a bad idea to add anything. Adding things won't make your game any faster. Make sure the performance issues are completely taken care of before code complete, and monitor it closely until the project ships.

LORD BRITISH MUST DIE.

It's a common practice to put inside jokes or "Easter Eggs" into a game. On *Ultima VII,* the team installed a special way to kill Lord British, especially since Richard Garriott wanted Lord British to be completely invincible. You need a little background first.

Origin was in an office building in the west Austin hill country, and the building had those glass front doors secured with powerful magnets at the top of the door. One day, Richard and some other folks were headed out to lunch, and when Richard opened the door, the large block of metal that formed a part of the magnetic lock somehow became detached from the glass and fell right on Richard's head. Lord British must truly be unkillable, because that metal block weighed something like 10 pounds and had sharp edges....

The team decided to use that event as an inside way to kill the monarch of Britannia. At noon, the Lord British character's schedule took him into the courtyard of the castle. He would pause briefly under the doorway, right under a brass plaque that read, "Lord British's Throne Room." If you double-clicked the sign, it would fall on his head and kill him straightaway.

Perhaps the weirdest thing about this story is that a few weeks later the same metal block on the same door fell on Richard a second time, again with no permanent damage. The guy is truly protected by some supernatural force, but he did buy a hard-shell construction helmet, and he wasn't so speedy to be the first person to open the door anymore.

By the time the team is working solidly to zero bugs, all the code and content is installed, and there is nothing to do but fix bugs. It's a good idea to add a few steps to the bug-fixing protocol. Here's the usual way bugs get assigned and fixed:

1. A bug is written up in test and assigned to a team member to fix.
2. The bug is fixed and is sent back to test for verification.
3. The bug is closed when someone in test gets a new version and observes the game behaving properly.

Close to the zero bug date, a bit of sanity checking is in order. This sanity checking puts some safety valves on the scope of any change. By this time in the project, it usually takes two overworked human brains to equal the thinking power of one normal brain.

1. A bug is written up in test and discussed in a small group—usually, the team leads.
2. If the bug is serious enough, it is assigned to someone on the team to investigate a solution.

3. Someone investigates a potential solution. If a solution seems too risky, that person pulls the plug then and there and reports back that the bug should remain in its natural habitat.

4. The solution is coded and checked on the programmer's machine by a colleague.

5. The solution is presented to the leads, and a final decision to check in the code or abandon the change is made.

6. The bug is sent back to test for verification.

7. The bug is closed when someone in test gets a new version and observes the game behaving properly.

If you think that the bureaucracy is a little out of control, I'd understand your concerns. It does seem out of control, but it's out of control for a reason. Most bugs, about 70 percent to 80 percent, never make it out of step #1. Of those that remain, one-half to three-quarters of those are deemed too minor or too risky to fix, and never make it out of step #4.

TALES
FROM
THE
PIXEL
MINES

BUG MEETING ON *MARTIAN DREAMS*

My first experience with bugs in games was on *Martian Dreams* at Origin Systems. The whole team gathered in the conference room and each new bug from test was read aloud to the entire team. Sometimes the bugs were so funny the whole room was paralyzed with laughter, and while it wasn't the most efficient way to run a meeting, it sure took the edge off the day.

On *Ultima VII, Ultima VIII,* and *Ultima Online,* the teams were simply too big, and the bugs too numerous, to read aloud in a team meeting. Between the inevitable laughter and complaining about fixing the object lists again, we'd probably still be working on those games.

Even on smaller projects, like *Bicycle Casino* and *Magnadoodle,* we held bug meetings with the team leads. It turned out that the rest of the developers would rather spend their time making the game better and fixing as many bugs as they could than sitting in meetings. Outside of that, time away from the computer and sleep was a great diversion.

Of course, everything hinges on your active bug count. If you are two months away from your scheduled zero bug date, and you are already sitting at zero bugs (yeah, right!), then you have more options than a team skidding into their zero bug date with a high bug count. I hope you find yourself in the former situation someday. I've never seen it myself.

The only hard and fast rule is how many bugs your team can fix per day—this bug fix rate tends to be pretty predictable all through your testing period. It will be different for programmers than artists, because art bugs can be fixed faster and easier. Programmers tend to fix somewhere between three and 10 bugs per day per person, but your mileage may vary. The point is, measure how fast your bugs are dropping to zero and draw the line out to see when you'll actually reach zero. If the date looks grim, or doesn't even slope toward zero, you've got a serious problem on your hands. If things are looking good, loosen the screws a little and make your game better while you can.

You could just decide to fix fewer bugs, and while this will get you to zero bugs, it can create an overall game experience that seems sloppy. If you have no choice but to do this, make sure you focus on fixing bugs that materially affect the game experience. Minor graphical glitches you can ignore, but a repeatable crash on the common play path should get fixed no matter what.

Code

At the end of every game project, the programmers and scripters are the ones who are hammered the most. Artists, level builders, and audio are hit especially hard during the content complete milestone, but after that their work levels off, mostly because it is usually more predictable. If you don't believe me, just ask an artist how long it will take him to tweak the lighting on a model. Or ask a level designer how long it will take her to place a few more power-ups in a level, and she will not only give you a solid answer, but she will also be right about it.

Ask a programmer how long it will take to find the random memory trasher bug, and he will shrug and say something like, "I don't know—a few hours maybe?" You may find that same programmer, 48 hours later, bashing his head against the same bug, no closer to fixing it than when he started.

These setbacks happen all the time, and there's not much that can be done except to get as much caffeine into the programmer's bloodstream as he can stand, get the other programmers to take up the slack in the bug debt, and maybe lend a few more neurons to the problem. Don't forget about the advice earlier in the book: Any two programmers looking at the same problem are at least three times as smart as a lone programmer.

When the bug is eventually found, there is often a decision that has to be made about the nature of the solution. A simple hack may suffice, but a "real" solution exists that will touch a lot of code and perhaps induce more risk. At the very late stages of a project, I suggest hacking. Wonton, unabashed hacking.

Some of you may be reeling at this sacrilege, but I'm sure as many of you are cheering. The fact is that a well thought-out hack can be the best choice, especially if you can guarantee the safety and correctness of the change. "Hack" is probably a bad word to use to fully describe what I'm talking about, because it has somewhat negative connotations. Let me try to be specific in my definition:

Hack – n. *A piece of code written to solve a specific corner case of a specific problem, as opposed to code written to solve a problem in the general case.*

Let me put this in a different light. Everyone should be familiar with searching algorithms, where the choice of a particular search can achieve a "first solution" or a "best solution" criteria. At the beginning of a project, coding almost always follows the "best solution" path, because there is sufficient time to code a more complicated, albeit more general algorithm. At the end of the project, it is frequently the case that the best solution will lead a programmer down a complete reorganization of an entire subsystem, if not the entire code base.

Instead, games have a "get-out-of-jail-free" card, because the players don't generate the game data. Since the game inputs are predictable, or even static, the problem domain is reduced to a manageable level. A programmer can be relatively sure that a specific bit of code can be written to solve a specific problem, on a specific map level, with specific character attributes. It seems ugly, and to be honest, it is ugly. As a friend of mine at Microsoft taught me, shipping your game is its most important feature.

The hack doesn't have to live in the code base forever, although it frequently does. If your game is even mildly successful, and you get the chance to do a sequel, you might have time to rip out the hacks and install an upgraded algorithm. You'll then be able to sleep at night.

TALES FROM THE PIXEL MINES

HACKS IN *U7* AND *STRIKE COMMANDER*

At Origin it was common practice for programmers to add an appropriate comment if they had to install a hack to fix a bug. A couple of programmers were discussing which game had the most hacks—*Ultima VII* or *Strike Commander*. There was a certain pride in hacking in those days, since we were all young, somewhat arrogant, and enjoyed a good hack from time to time. The issue was settled with grep—a text file search utility. The *Strike Commander* team was the clear winner, with well over 500 hacks in their code. *Ultima VII* wasn't without some great comments, though. My favorite one was something like, "This hack must be removed before the game ships." It never was. What's more I think the same hack made it into *Ultima VIII*.

Commenting your code changes is a fantastic idea, especially late in the project. After the code complete milestone, the changes come so fast and furious that it's easy to lose track of what code changed, who changed it, and why. It's not uncommon for two programmers to make mutually exclusive changes to a piece of code, each change causing a bug in the other's code. You'll recognize this pretty fast, usually because you'll go into a piece of code and fix a bug, only to have the same bug reappear a few versions later. When you pop back into the code you fixed, you'll see the code has mysteriously reverted to the buggy version. This might not be a case of source code control gone haywire, as you would first suspect. It could be another programmer reverting your change because it caused another bug.

That situation is not nearly as rare as you think, but there is a more common scenario. Every now and then, I'll attempt a bug fix, only to have the testers throw it back to me saying that the bug still lives. By the time it comes back, I may have forgotten why I chose the solution, or what the original code looked like. Even better, I may look at the same block of code months later, and not have a clue what the fix was attempting to fix, or what test case exposed the bug.

The solution to the problem of short-term programmer memories is comments, as always, but comments in the late stages of development need some extra information to be especially useful. Here's an example of a late-stage comment structure we used on the Microsoft projects:

```
if  (CDisplay::m_iNumModals == 0)
{
    // ET - 04/10/02 - Begin
    // Jokerz #2107 - Close() here causes some errors,
    // instead use Quit() as it allows the app to shutdown
    // gracefully
    Quit(); // Close();
    // ET - 04/10/02 - End
}
```

The comment starts with the initials of the programmer and the date of the change. The entire change is bracketed with the same thing, the only difference between the two being a "begin" and "end" keyword. If the change is a trivial one-liner with an ultra short explanation, the comment can sit on the previous line or out to the right.

The explanation of the change is preceded with the code name for the project and the bug number that motivated the change. Code names are important because the bug might exist in code shared between multiple projects, which might be in parallel development or as a sequel. The explanation of the change follows, and where it makes sense, the old code is left in, but commented out.

Most programmers will instantly observe that the source code repository should be the designated keeper of all this trivia, and the code should be left clean. I respectfully disagree. I think it belongs in both places. Code reads like a story, and if you are constantly flipping from one application to another to find out what is going on, it is quite likely you'll miss the meaning of the change.

There are plenty of software companies that employ some form of code review in their process. The terms "code review" and "computer game development" don't seem to belong in the same universe, let alone the same book. This false impression comes from programmers who don't understand how a good code review process can turn a loose collection of individual programmers into a well-oiled team of coding machines.

EACH CHANGE GETS A BUG NUMBER

At the end of the project, it's a good idea, although somewhat draconian, to convince the team to attach an approved bug number with every change made to the code. This measure might seem extreme, but I've seen changes "snuck" into the code base at the last minute without any involvement from the rest of the team. The decision to do that shouldn't be made by a programmer at 3 a.m. on Sunday morning. If every change is required to have a bug number, it becomes a trivial matter to hunt down and revert any midnight changes made by well meaning but errant programmers.

When most programmers think of code reviews, they picture themselves standing in front of a bunch of people who laugh at every line of code they present. They think it will cramp their special programming style. Worst of all, they fear that a bad code review will kill their chances at a lead position or a raise.

I've been working with code reviews in a very informal sense for years, and while it probably won't stand up to NASA standards, I think it performs well in creative software, especially games. It turns out there are two primary points of process that make code reviews for games work well: who initiates the review, and who performs the review.

The person who writes the code that needs review should actually initiate the review. This has a few beneficial side effects. First, the code will definitely be ready to review, since the person needing it won't ask otherwise. Programmers hate surprises of the "someone just walked in my office and wants to see my code" kind. Because the code is ready, the programmer will be in a great state of mind to explain it. After all, they should take a little pride in their work, right? Even programmers are capable of craftsmanship, and there's not nearly enough opportunity to show it off. A code review should be one of those opportunities.

The person performing the review isn't the person you think it should be. Most of you reading this would probably say, "the lead programmer." This is especially true if you are the lead programmer. Well, you're wrong. Any programmer on the team should be able to perform a code review. Something that is a lot of fun is to have a junior programmer perform code reviews on the lead programmer's code. It's a great chance for everyone to share his or her tricks, experience, and double-check things that are critical to your project.

This implies that the programmers all trust each other, respect each other, and seek to learn more about their craft. I've had the privilege of working on a programming team that is exactly like that, and the hell of being on the other side as well. I'll choose the former, thank you very much. Find me a team that enjoys code reviews and performs them often, and I'll show you a programming team that will ship their games on time.

When I worked on the Microsoft casual games, the programmers performed code reviews for serious issues throughout the project, but they were done constantly after content complete, for each change, no matter how minor. Most of the time, a programmer would work all day on five or six bugs, and call someone who happened to be on his way back from the bathroom to do a quick code review before he checked everything in. This was pretty efficient, since the programmer doing the review was already away from his computer. Studies have shown that a programmer doesn't get back into the "zone" until 30 minutes after an interruption. I believe it, too.

Bottom line: The closer you get to zero bugs, the more checking and double-checking you do, on every semicolon. You even double-check the need to type a semicolon. This checking installs a governor on the number and the scope of every code change, and the governor is slowly throttled down to zero until the last bug is fixed. This increases the quality of every change and the quality of the whole game as a result. After that, the game is ready to ship.

Content

Programmers aren't immune to the inevitable discussions, usually late at night, about adding some extra content into the game at the eleventh hour. It could be something as innocuous as a few extra names in the credits, or it could be a completely new terrain system. You think I'm kidding, don't you?

Whether it is code, art, sounds, models, map levels, weapons, or whatever makes your game fun, you've got to be serious about finishing your game. You can't finish it if you keep screwing with it! If you are really lucky, you'll wind up at a company like Valve or id, who can pretty much release games when they're damn good and ready. The rest of us have to ship games when we get hungry, and the desire to make the best game can actually supersede basic survival. At some point, no matter how much you tweak it, your game is what it is, and even superhuman effort will only achieve a tiny amount of quality improvement. If you've ever heard of something called the "theory of diminishing returns," you know what I'm talking about. When this happens, you've already gone too far. Pack your game up and ship it, and hope it sells well enough for you to get a second try.

The problem most people have is recognizing when this happens—it's brutally difficult. If you're like me, you get pretty passionate about games, and sometimes you get so close to a project that you can't tell when it's time to throw in the towel.

BEST PRACTICE

FIND YOUR OWN BETA TESTERS

Microsoft employs late stage beta testers. These people work in other parts of Microsoft but play their latest games. Beta testers are different from playtesters because they don't play the game every day. They are always just distant enough and dispassionate enough to make a good judgment about when the game is fun, or when it's not. If you don't have Microsoft footing your development bills, find ad-hoc testers from just about anywhere. You don't need professional testing feedback. You just need to know if people would be willing to plunk down $60 for your game and keep it forever.

> ## A BUG BECOMES A FEATURE
>
> When I worked on the *Ultima* series, it wasn't uncommon for truly interesting things to be possible, code-wise, at a very late stage of development. On *Ultima VIII*, a particular magic spell had a bug that caused a huge wall of fire that destroyed everything in its path. It was so cool we decided to leave it in the game and replace one of the lamer spells. It wasn't exactly a low-risk move, completely replacing a known spell with a bug-turned-feature, but it was an awesome effect, and we all felt the game was better for it.

I'm trying my very best to give you some solid advice instead of some wishy-washy pabulum. The truth is there's no right answer regarding last-minute changes to your game. The only thing you can count on is 20-20 hindsight, and only the people that write the history books are the winners. In other words, when you are faced with a decision to make a big change late in the game, trust your experience, try to be at least a little bit conservative and responsible in your choices, and hope like hell that you are right.

> ## LET THE TEAM VOTE ON BUGS
>
> On *Mushroom Men: The Spore Wars*, we did something unusual. We had already established a "Bug Triage" room where all the team leads could discuss each bug as it came in from the testing team and either kill it or assign it to someone. A few weeks before we went into total lockdown mode, we gathered a list of 100 bugs that the team really wanted to see fixed, and let the entire team vote on them. This took a few rounds, but it was great to see things that were close to a developer's heart get fixed. We'll do this again.

DEALING WITH BIG TROUBLE

Murphy is alive and well in the computer game industry, and I'm sure he's been an invisible team member on most of my projects—some more than others, but most especially at Origin Systems, where Murphy had a corner office. I think his office was nicer than mine!

Big trouble on game projects comes in a few flavors: too much work and too little time, human beings under too much pressure, competing products in the target market, and dead-ends. There aren't necessarily standard solutions for these problems, but I can tell you what has been tried and how well it worked, or didn't work, as the case may be.

Projects Seriously Behind Schedule

Microsoft has a great way of describing a project behind schedule. They say it's "coming in hot and steep." I know because the first Microsoft *Casino* project was exactly like that. We had too much work to do, but too little time to do it in. There are a few solutions to this problem, such as working more overtime or throwing bodies at the problem. Each solution can work, but it can also have a dark side.

The Dreaded Crunch Mode—Working More Hours

It amazes me how much project managers choose to work their teams to death when the project falls behind schedule.

84-HOUR WORKWEEKS AT ORIGIN

On my very first day at Origin Systems, October 22, 1990, I walked by a white-board with an ominous message written in block letters: "84-Hour Workweeks—MANDATORY." With simple division, I realized that 84 divided by 7 is 12. Twelve hours per day, seven days per week was Origin's solution for shipping *Savage Empire* for the Christmas, 1990 season. To the *Savage Empire* team's credit, they shipped the game a few tortured weeks later, and this "success" translated into more mandatory overtime to solve problems.

   We were all young, mostly in our late 20s, and the amount of overtime that was worked was bragged about. There was a company award called the "100 Club," which was awarded to anyone who worked more than 100 hours in a single workweek. At Origin, this club wasn't very exclusive.

Humans are resilient creatures, and under extraordinary circumstances they can go long stretches with very little sleep or a break from work. Winston Churchill, during World War II, was famous for taking little catnaps in the Cabinet War Rooms lasting just a cumulative few hours per day, and he did this for years. Mr. Churchill had good reason to do this. He was trying to lead England in a war against Nazi Germany, and the cost of failure would have been catastrophic for his country and the entire world.

   Game companies consistently ask for a similar commitment on the part of their employees—to work long hours for months, even years on end. What a crime! It's one thing to save a nation from real tyranny, it's quite another to make a computer game. This is especially true when the culprit is overscoping the project, blind to the reality of a situation, and has a lack of skill in project management.

It is a known fact that under a normal working environment, projects can be artificially time-compressed up to 20 percent by working more hours. This is the equivalent of asking the entire team to work eight extra hours on Saturday. I define a normal working environment as one where people don't have their lives, liberty, or family at stake. This schedule can be kept up for months, if the team is well motivated.

TALES FROM THE PIXEL MINES

TAKE A BREAK—YOU'LL BE BETTER FOR IT

It was this schedule that compressed *Ultima VIII* after a last-minute feature addition: Origin asked the team to ship the game in two extra languages, German and French. The team bloated to nearly three times its original size, adding native German and French speakers to write the tens of thousands of lines of conversation and test the results. We worked overtime for five weeks—60 hours per week, and we took the sixth week and worked a normal workweek, which averaged 50 hours. This schedule went on from August to March, or eight months. Youth and energy went a long way, and in the end, we did ship the game when the team thought we were going to ship the game, but everyone was exhausted beyond their limits.

Weeks later, however, it was clear that the game wasn't all we wanted it to be. Our collective exhaustion at the end caused me and others to make some bad decisions about what we should fix. Reviews were coming in, and they weren't good. A few months down the road, the team got back together to fix many of the biggest problems, and we released a patch, which by all accounts was much better.

The moral of this story—it is possible to crunch like crazy, and it may seem like you are achieving your goals, but in the end, your game will suffer for it. Working overtime works only to solve short-term problems, not long-term disasters.

For short periods of time, perhaps a week or two weeks, truly extraordinary efforts are possible. Twelve-hour days for a short burst can make a huge difference in your game. Well managed and planned, it can even boost team morale. It feels a little like summer camp. A critical piece of this strategy is a well-formed goal such as the following:

- Fix 50 bugs per developer in one week.
- Finish integrating the major subsystems of the game.
- Achieve a playthrough of the entire game without cheating.

The goal should be something the team can see on the horizon, well within sprinting distance. They also have to be able to see their progress on a daily basis.

It can be quite demoralizing to sprint to a goal you can't see, because you have no idea how to gauge your level of effort.

RICHARD'S MIDNIGHT BBQ

On *Ultima VII*, Richard Garriott was always doing crazy things to support the development team. One night he brought in steaks to grill on Origin's BBQ pit. Another night, very late, he brought in his monster cappuccino machine from home and made everyone on the team some latte. One Saturday, he surprised the team and declared a day off, taking everyone sky diving. Richard was long past the time where he could jump into C++ and write some code, but his support of the team and simply being there during the wee hours made a huge difference.

There's a dark side to overtime in the extreme that many managers and producers can't see until it's too late. It happened at Origin, and it happens all the time in other companies. When people work enough hours to push their actual pay scale below minimum wage, they begin to expect something extraordinary in return, perhaps in the form of end-of-project bonuses, raises, promotions, and so on.

The evil truth is that the company usually cannot pay anything that will equal their level of effort. The crushing overtime is a result of a project in trouble, and that usually equates to a company in trouble. If it weren't so, company managers wouldn't push staggering overtime onto the shoulders of the team. At the end of the day, the project will ship, probably vastly over budget and most likely at a lower quality than was hoped. Unfortunately, these two things do *not* translate into huge amounts of money flowing into company coffers and subsequently into the pockets of the team.

A few months after these nightmare projects ship, the team begins to realize that all those hours amounted to nothing more than lost time away from home. Perhaps their firstborn took a few wobbling steps or spoke his or her first words, "Hey where in the hell is Daddy, anyway?" This frustration works into anger, and finally into people leaving the company for what they think are greener pastures. High turnover right after a project ships is pretty common in companies that require tons of overtime.

Someone once told me that you'll never find a tombstone with the following epitaph: "I wish I worked more weekends." As team member, you can translate that into a desire to predict your own schedule as best you can, and send up red flags when things begin to get off track. If you ever get to be a project lead, I hope you realize that there's a place for overtime, but it can't replace someone's life.

Pixel Fodder—Throw Warm Bodies at the Problem

Perhaps the second most common solution to projects seriously behind schedule is to throw more developers on the project. Well managed, this can have a positive effect, but it's never very cost effective, and there's a higher risk of mistakes. It turns out there's a sweet spot in the number of people who can work on any single project.

MORE PEOPLE MAKE WORK GO FASTER, RIGHT?

Ultima Online was the poster child of a bloated team. In December of 1996, the entire *Ultima IX* team was moved to *Ultima Online* in the hopes that throwing bodies at the problem would speed the project to completion. This ended up being something of a disaster, for a few reasons. First, the *Ultima IX* team really wanted to work on *Ultima IX*. Their motivation to work on another project was pretty low. Second, the *Ultima Online* team had a completely different culture and experience level, and there were clashes of philosophy and control. Third, *Ultima Online* didn't have a detailed project plan, somewhat due to the fact that no one had ever made a massive multiplayer game before. This made it difficult to deploy everyone in his or her area of expertise. I happened to find myself working with SQL servers, for example, and I didn't have a shred of experience!

Through a staggering amount of work—an Origin hallmark—on the part of the original *Ultima Online* team and the *Ultima IX* newcomers, the project went live less than nine months after the team was integrated. The cost was overwhelming, however, especially in terms of employee turnover in the old *Ultima IX* team. Virtually none of the programmers, managers, or designers of *Ultima IX* remained at Origin to see it completed.

One effect of overstaffing is an increased need to communicate and coordinate among the team members. It's a generally accepted fact that a manager's effectiveness falls sharply if he has any more than seven reports, and it is maximized at five reports. If you have a project team of 12 programmers, 14 artists, and 10 designers, you'll have two programming leads reporting to a technical director, and a similar structure for artists and designers. You'll likely have a project director as well, creating a project management staff of 10 people.

If your management staff is anything less than that, you'll probably run into issues like two artists working on the same model, or perhaps a programming task that falls completely through the cracks. To be honest, even with an experienced management team, you'll never be completely free of these issues.

TALES
FROM
THE
PIXEL
MINES

> ### WORKING IN PARALLEL ON *BICYCLE CARDS*
>
> Occasionally, you get lucky, and you can add people to a project simply because a project is planned and organized in the right way. A good example of this was the *Bicycle Cards* project, basically a bunch of little games packaged up in one product. When some of the games began to run behind schedule, we hired two contractors to take on a few games apiece. The development went completely smoothly with seven programmers in parallel. Their work was compartmentalized, communication of their tasks were covered nearly 100 percent by the design document, and this helped ease any problems.

They say that nine women can't make a baby in one month. That's true. There is also a documented case of a huge group of people who built an entire house from the ground up in three days due to an intricately coordinated plan, extremely skilled people, and very specialized building techniques. Your project could exist on either side of these extremes.

Slipping the Schedule

This solution seems de rigueur in the games industry, even with a coordinated application of crunch mode and bloating the team. There's a great poster of *Ultima VII* and *Strike Commander* that Origin published in 1992, in the style of movie posters that bragged "Coming this Christmas." It turns out that those posters got the season right, but they just had the wrong year.

There's a long list of games that shipped before their time, but perhaps the worst offender in my personal history was *Ultima Online*. There was even a lawsuit to that effect, where some subscribers filed a class action lawsuit against Electronic Arts for shipping a game that wasn't ready. Thankfully, it was thrown out of court. A case like that could have had drastic effects on the industry!

The pressure to ship on schedule is enormous. You might think that companies want to ship on time because of the additional costs of the development team, and while the weekly burn rate of a gigantic team can be many hundreds of thousands of dollars, it's not the main motivation. While I worked with Microsoft, I learned that the manufacturing schedule of our game was set in stone. We had to have master disks ready by such and such a date, or we would lose our slot in the manufacturing facility. Considering that the other Microsoft project coming out that particular year was Windows XP, I realized that losing my place in line meant a huge delay in getting the game out. Console games can have the same problem. If you miss your submission date to Nintendo, Sony, or Microsoft, you get to go on "standby," waiting for another empty slot so they can test your game for technical standards compliance.

While things like manufacturing and submission can usually be worked out, there's another, even bigger motivation for shipping on time. Months before the game is done, most companies begin spending huge money on marketing. Ads are bought in magazines or television, costing hundreds of thousands of dollars. You might not know this, but those special kiosks at the end of the shelves in retail stores, called *endcaps,* are bought and paid for like prime rental real estate, usually on a month-by-month basis. If your game isn't ready for the moment those ads are published or those kiosks are ready to show off your game, you lose the money. No refunds here!

This is one of the reasons you see the executives poking around your project six to eight months before you are scheduled to ship. It's because they are about to start writing big checks to media companies and game retail chains in the hopes that all this cash will drive up the sales of your game. The irony is, if the execs didn't believe you could finish on time, they wouldn't spend the big bucks on marketing, and your game would be buried somewhere on a bottom shelf in a dark corner of the store. Oh, and no ads either. Your best advertising will be by personal email to all your friends, and that just won't cut it. In other words, your game won't sell.

The difference between getting your marketing pressure at maximum and nothing at all may only be a matter of slipping a few weeks, or even a few days. What's worse, this judgment call is made months before you are at code complete—a time when your game is crashing every three minutes. Crazy, huh?

Probably the best advice I can give you is to make sure you establish a track record of hitting each and every milestone on time throughout the life of your project. Keep your bug count under control, too. These two things will convince the suits that you'll ship on time with all the features you promised. Whatever you do, don't choose schedule slippage at the last minute. If you must slip, slip it once and make sure you give the suits enough time to react to all the promises they made on your behalf. This is probably at least six months prior to your release date, but it could be even more.

Cutting Features and Postponing Bugs

Perhaps the most effective method of pulling a project out of the fire is reducing the scope of work. You can do it in two ways: nuke some features of the game and choose to leave some bugs in their natural habitat, perhaps to be fixed on the sequel. Unless you've been a bit arrogant in your project, the players and the media won't know about everything you wanted to install in the game. You might be able to shorten or remove a level from your game, reduce the number of characters or equipment, or live with a less accurate physics system.

Clearly, if you are going to cut something big, you have to do it as early in the project as you can. Game features tend to work themselves in to every corner of the project, and removing them wholesale can be tricky at best, impossible at worst. Also, you can't have already represented to the outside world that your game has 10,000 hours of gameplay when you're only going to have time for a fraction of that. It makes your team look young and a little stupid.

After code complete, the programmers are fixing bugs like crazy. One way to reduce the workload is to spirit away some of the less important bugs. As the ship date approaches, management's desire to "fix" bugs in this manner becomes somewhat ravenous, even to the point of leaving truly embarrassing bugs in the game, such as misspelled names in the credits or nasty crashes.

SHIPPING CHRISTMAS, 201?

Always give yourself some elbow room when making promises to anyone, but especially the game industry media. They love catching project teams in arrogant promises. It's great to tell them things about your game, but try to give them specifics in those features you are 100 percent sure are going be finished.

Anything can be bad in great quantities, and reducing your game's scope or quality is no exception. One thing is certainly true—your players won't miss what they never knew about in the first place.

THIS ONE MUST DIE SO THAT OTHERS MAY LIVE

Mushroom Men: The Spore Wars on the Wii was in late development, and one of the levels was falling behind. Art was unfinished, scripted events were still undone, and many other things left the team with the distinct impression that getting the level done was going to take a lot of work. After some serious soul searching, the team decided to cut the entire level and spend time making the other levels in the game better. It was a very hard decision, because so much work and care had already been spent on it—and had it been completed, it would have been one of the cooler parts of the game. In the end, it was the right decision.

It is incredibly difficult to step away from the guts of your project and look at it objectively from the outside. I've tried to do this many times, and it is one of the most difficult things to do, especially in those final days. Anyone who cares about his or her game won't want to leave a bug unfixed or cut a feature.

Ask yourself three serious questions when faced with this kind of decision: Will my decision sell more copies? Will the players really notice this change? Will it keep someone from returning the game? If your answer is yes, do what it takes. Otherwise, move on and get your game shipped.

Personnel-Related Problems

At the end of a project, everyone on the team is usually stretched to the limit. Good-natured and even-keeled people aren't immune to the stresses of overtime and the pressure of a mountain of tasks. Some game developers are far from good natured and even keeled! Remember always that whatever happens at the end of a project, it should be taken in the context of the stresses of the day, not necessarily as someone's habitual behavior. After all, if someone loses his cool at 3 a.m. after having worked 36 hours straight, I think a little slack is in order. If this same person loses his cool on a normal workday after a calm weekend, perhaps some professional adjustments are a good idea.

Exhaustion

The first and most obvious problem faced by teams is simple exhaustion. Long hours and missed weekends create pressure at home and a robotic sense of purpose at work. The team begins to make mistakes, and for every hour they work, the project slips back three hours. The only solution for this is a few days away from the project. Hopefully, you and your team won't let the problem get this bad. Sometimes, all it takes is for someone to stand up and point to the last three days of nonprogress and notice that the wheels are spinning, but the car isn't going anywhere. Everyone should go home for 48 hours, even if it's Tuesday. You'd be surprised how much energy people will bring back to the office.

One other thing: They may be away from their desks for 48 hours, but their minds will still have some background processes mulling over what they'll do when they get back to work. Oddly enough, these background thoughts can be amazingly productive, since they tend to concentrate on planning and the big picture rather than every curly brace. When they get back, the additional thought works to create an amazing burst of productivity.

TALES
FROM
THE
PIXEL
MINES

4 HOURS > 15 SECONDS

Late in the *Magnadoodle* project for Mattel Media, I was working hard on a graphics bug. I had been programming nearly 18 hours per day for the last week, and I was completely spent. At 3 a.m., I finally left the office, unsuccessful after four hours working on the same problem, and went to sleep. I specifically didn't set my alarm, and I unplugged all the telephones. I slept. The next morning, I awoke at a disgusting 11 a.m. and walked into the office with a fresh cup of Starbuck's in hand. I sat down in front of the code I was struggling with the night before and instantly solved the problem. The bug that had eluded me for four hours the day before was solved in less than 15 seconds. If that isn't a great advertisement for sleep gaining efficiency in a developer, I don't know what is.

Morale

Team morale is directly proportional to their progress toward their goal, and isn't related to their workload. This may seem somewhat counterintuitive, but it's true. One theory that has been proposed regarding the people that built the great pyramids of Egypt is that teams of movers actually competed with each other to see how many blocks they could move up the ramps in a single day. Their workload and effort was backbreaking and their project schedule spanned decades. The constant competition, as the theory suggests, created high productivity and increased morale at the same time.

Morale can slide under a few circumstances, all of which are completely controllable. As the previous paragraph suggests, the team must be convinced they are on track to achieve their goal. This implies that the goal shouldn't be a constantly moving target. If a project continually changes underneath the developers, they'll lose faith that it will ever be completed. The opposite is also true—a well designed project that is under control is a joy to work on, and developers will work amazingly hard to get to a finish line they can see.

There's also a lot to be said for installing a few creature comforts for the development team. If they are working long hours, you'll be surprised what a little effort toward team appreciation will accomplish.

SPEND A LITTLE MONEY—IT'S YOUR TEAM

Get out the company credit card and make sure people on the project are well cared for. Stock the refrigerator with drinks and snacks, buy decent dinners every night, and bring in donuts in the morning. Bring in good coffee and get rid of the cheap stuff. Every now and then, make sure the evening meal is a nice one, and send them home afterward instead of burning the midnight oil for the tenth night in a row.

Something I've seen in the past that affects morale is the relationship between the development team and the testing team. I've seen the entire range, from teams that wanted to beat each other with pipes to others that didn't even communicate verbally—they simply read each other's minds and made the game better. Someone needs to take this pulse every now and then, and apply a little rudder pressure when needed to keep things nice and friendly. Some warning signs to watch for include unfriendly japes in the bug commentary, discussion about the usefulness of an individual on either team or their apparent lack of skill, or the beginnings of disrespect for their leadership.

Perhaps the best insurance against this problem is forging personal relationships among the development leadership and testing leadership, and if possible, with individuals on the team. Make sure they get a chance to meet each other in person if at all possible, which can be difficult since most game developers are a few time zones away from their test team. Personal email, telephone conversations, conference calls, and face-to-face meetings can help forge these professional friendships and keep them going when discussions about bugs get heated.

This leads into something that may have the most serious affect on morale, both positive and negative. The developers need to feel like they are doing something worthwhile, and that they have the support of everyone. The moment they feel that their project isn't worth anything, due to something said in the media or perhaps an unfortunate comment by an executive, you can see the energy drain away to nothing. The opposite of this can be used to boost morale. Bring in a member of the press to see some kick-ass previews, or have a suit from the publisher shower the team with praise, and they'll redouble their effort. If you happen to work in a company with multiple projects, perhaps the best thing I've seen is one project team telling another that they have a great game. Praise from one's closest colleagues is far better than any other.

Other Stuff

Perhaps the darkest side of trouble on teams is when one person crosses the line and begins to behave in an unprofessional manner. I've seen everything from career blackmail to arrogant insubordination, and the project team has to keep this butthead on the team or risk losing their "genius." My suggestion here is to remember that the team is more important than any single individual. If someone leaves the team, even figuratively, during the project you should invite him/her to please leave in a more concrete manner.

Your Competition Beats You to the Punch

There's nothing that bursts your bubble quite as much as having someone walk into your office with a game in his hand, just released, that not only kicks butt but is exactly like your game in every way. You might think I'm crazy, but I'll tell you that you have nothing to worry about. The fact is that you can learn a lot from someone else's game simply by playing it, studying their graphics system, testing their user interface, and finding other chinks in their armor. After all, you can still compile your game, whereas they've burned theirs on optical media.

True, you won't be the first to market. Yes, you'd better be no later than second to market, and certainly you'd better make sure that you don't repeat their mistakes. At least you have the benefit of having a choice, and you also have the benefit of dissecting another competitor's product before you put your game on the shelf.

DON'T GIVE AWAY ALL YOUR SECRETS

They say that loose lips sink ships, right? This is certainly true in the game indus-try. *Strike Commander,* Origin's first 3D game, was due out in Christmas of 1992. In the summer of 1992, Origin took *Strike Commander* to the big industry trade show at the time, the Consumer Electronics Show, and made a big deal of *Strike Com-mander's* advanced 3D technology. They went so far as to give away technical details of the 3D engine, which the competition immediately researched and installed in their own games. Origin's competitive advantage was trumped by their own marketing department, and since the team had to slip the schedule past Christmas, the competition had more time to react. What a disaster!

The game industry tends to follow trends until they bleed out. That's because there's a surprisingly strong aversion to unique content on the part of game exec-utives. If a particular game is doing well, every company in the industry puts out a clone until there are 50 games out there that all look alike. Only the top two or three will sell worth a damn, so make sure you are in that top two or three.

There's No Way Out—or Is There?

Sometimes, you have to admit there's a grim reality—your game has coded itself into a corner. The testers say the game just isn't any fun. You might have gone down a dead-end technology track, such as coding your game for a dying plat-form.

What in the hell do you do now?

Mostly, you find a way to start over. If you're lucky, you might be able to recycle some code, art, map levels, or sounds. If you're really lucky, you might be able to replace a minor component and save the project. Either way, you have to find the courage to see the situation for what it is and act. Putting your head in the sand won't do any good.

One Last Word—Don't Panic

There are other things that can go terribly wrong on projects, such as when some-one deletes the entire project from the network or when the entire development team walks out the door to start their own company. Yes, I've seen both of these things happen, and no, the projects in question didn't instantly evaporate. Every problem can be fixed, but it does take something of a cool head. Panic and over-reaction—some might say these are hallmarks of your humble author—rarely lead to good decisions.

TALES FROM THE PIXEL MINES

I NEVER GAVE UP ON *ULTIMA IX*

After *Ultima IX* was put on ice, and I was working hard on the *Ultima Online* project, I secretly continued work on *Ultima IX* at my house in the evenings and on weekends. My goal wasn't so much to resurrect *Ultima IX* or try to finish it single-handedly. I just wanted to learn more about 3D hardware-accelerated polygon rasterization, which was pretty new at the time. I was playing around with Glide, a 3D API from 3DFx that worked on the VooDoo series of video cards. In a surprisingly little amount of work, I installed a Glide-compliant rasterizer into *Ultima IX*, complete with a basic, ultra stupid, texture cache.

What I saw was really amazing—*Ultima IX* running at over 40fps. The best frame rate I'd seen so far was barely 10fps using our best software rasterizer. I took my work into Origin to show it off a bit, and the old *Ultima IX* team just went wild. A few months later, the project was back in development with a new direction. *Ultima IX* would be the first Origin game that was solely written for hardware-accelerated video cards. A bold statement, but not out of character with the *Ultima* series. Each *Ultima* game pushed the limits of bleeding edge technology every time a new one was published, and *Ultima IX* was no exception.

Try to stay calm, and try to gather as much information about whatever tragedy is befalling you. Don't go on a witch hunt. You'll need every able-bodied programmer and artist to get you out of trouble. Whatever it is, your problem is only a finite string of 1s and 0s in the right order. Try to remember that, and you'll probably sleep better.

THE LIGHT—IT'S NOT A TRAIN AFTER ALL

It's a day you'll remember for every project. At some point, there will be a single approved bug in your bug database. It will be assigned to someone on the team, and likely it will be fixed in a crowded office with every team member watching. Someone will start the build machine, and after a short while, the new game will be sent to the testing folks. Then the wait begins for the final word the game has been signed off and sent to manufacturing. You may have to go through this process two or three times—something I find unnerving but inevitable. Eventually though, the phone will ring, and the lead tester will give you the good news. The final build has been accepted, and the game is going to be manufactured.

Your game is done. There will likely be a free flow of appropriate beverages. I keep a bottle of nice tequila or maybe a good single malt scotch in my office for just such an occasion. You have a few weeks to wait for the channel to push your game into every store and online site, so what do you do in the meantime?

Test the Archive

The first thing you do is take a snapshot of the build machine and the media files on your network. Your job is to rebuild the game from scratch, using all your build scripts, to make sure that if you ever need to, you can restore a backup of the game source and rebuild your game. Start with a completely clean machine and install the build machine backup. It should include all the build tools, such as your compiler and special tools that you used to create your game.

Restore a backup of the network files to a clean spot on your network. This may take some doing, since your network might be pretty full. It's a good idea to buy some extra hard drives to perform this task, since it is the only way you can be 100 percent sure your project backup will work.

After you have a duplicate of your build machine and a second copy of the network files, build your game again and compare it to the image that is signed off. If they compare bit for bit, make some copies of the backups and store them in a cool dark place, safe for all eternity. It is quite likely that your publisher will want a copy of the backup, too, so don't forget to make enough copies. If the files don't match, do your best to figure out why. It wouldn't be completely unusual for a few bits to be mysteriously different on the first attempt. The existence of a completely automated build process usually makes the archive perfectly accurate, which is a great reason to have it in the first place.

As a last resort, if your files don't match, the best thing you can do is document the delta and have your testers run the rebuilt archive through the testing process once more. This will ensure that at least the game is still in a shippable state, even though some of the bits are different.

ARCHIVE THE BUG DATABASE

Don't forget to back up the bug database in some readable format, such as an Excel spreadsheet or even a CSV file. Store it along with your project archive and if you ever want to start a sequel, the first thing you'll do is figure out which postponed bugs you'll fix.

The Patch Build or the Product Demo

It's not crazy to start working on a patch build or downloadable demo immediately after the project signs off. The patch build is something PC developers are somewhat well known for, and if you know you need to build one, there's no reason to wait. Console developers can work on patches too, now that they all connect to the Internet. A downloadable demo is always a good idea, and many game industry magazines can also place a demo in an included disc.

I suggest you leave the patch build in your main line of development in your source code repository. The patch build should simply be the next minor version of your game, and is exactly what you've been doing since your zero bug date. You can release the thumbscrews a little, and consider some slightly more radical solutions to problems that you wouldn't have considered just a few days ago—it all depends on your schedule for the patch.

It wouldn't be uncommon to wait for initial customer feedback for finalizing the features and fixes that you'll include in your patch. Your customer base can be tens of thousands, if not hundreds of thousands, of people. They will likely find something your testers missed, or you may discover that a known problem is a much bigger deal than anyone expected.

The downloadable demo should exist in a separate branch in your source code repository. This is especially true if you code the demo with `#ifdef _DEMO` blocks or some such mechanism to cut your game down to a tiny version of itself. It wouldn't be crazy for some programmers to work on the demo and the patch simultaneously, and a separate code branch will help keep everything organized.

The Post-Mortem

A good post-mortem should be held a few weeks after you sign off your game. There are tons of ways to handle it, but there are a few common goals. Every project is a chance to learn about game development, and the post mortem is a mechanism that formalizes those lessons, which will ultimately change the way you work. It isn't a forum to complain about things that went wrong and leave it at that. Instead, your post mortem should identify opportunities to improve your craft. It is a forum to recognize a job well done, whether on the part of individuals or as a group.

In post-mortems, it's really easy to get off track because everyone on the team wants to say his or her piece about nearly everything. That's good, but it can degenerate into a chaotic meeting. It's also not a crazy idea to split the team into their areas of expertise and have them conduct mini post-mortems in detail. For example, the programmers might get together to talk about aspects of the technology or their methodologies, surely stuff that will bore the artists to the point of chewing their own limbs off to escape the meeting. Each group, programmers, artists, designers, producers, and whomever, can submit their detailed report for any other similar group who wants to learn their lessons.

The team post-mortem should focus on the game design, the project schedule, lines of communication, and team process. If someone believes they have a good idea of how to improve things, he should speak up and if the group thinks the idea has merit, then they should act on the idea.

One thing that isn't immediately obvious is the fact that you won't learn everything in a public meeting. Some of the most important information might be better discussed in private, in the hopes that someone's feelings won't be bruised. If you get the chance to run a post-mortem, don't forget to follow the public meeting with private interviews with the team. It will take a long time, but it's a good idea.

What to Do with Your Time

When I reached the end of my longest project to date, *Ultima VIII*, my first act was to walk outside Origin's offices, sit down at a picnic table, and enjoy the light, smells, and sounds of a springtime Texas afternoon. I had been in a dark office working overtime for two years, and I'd forgotten what daytime was like. I went home and found a person there. After introductions, and reviewing surprising evidence in the form of a photo album, I realized that the person in my apartment was actually my wife for over three years. I asked her out on a date, and she accepted. Then I asked her to accompany me on a diving trip to Cozumel. She accepted that, too.

I suggest you follow my lead. If you don't have a spouse, go somewhere fun with a friend. See the world. Get away from your computer at all costs. It will do you some good, and may give you some fun ideas.

You won't be able to stay away from work forever. The paycheck is nice, but the desire to make another great game will soon overwhelm you. You may embark on a sequel to the game you just shipped, or you might get to do something entirely new. Either way, you'll be surprised at the energy level. People on the team who looked like the living dead just a few weeks ago will be ready to go around again.

There's nothing quite like starting a new project. You feel renewed, smarter, and if you're really lucky, you'll get to work with the same team. After what you've just been through, it's likely you'll have a good portion of mental telepathy worked out, and you won't need quite so many meetings.

One thing everyone will quietly do is make excuses to walk into computer game stores looking for the box. Eventually, you'll see it for the first time. There's nothing like it, holding a shrink-wrapped version of your game in your own hands. I sincerely hope you get the chance to do that someday. Everybody deserves that kind of reward for such a mammoth effort.

The game industry is a wacky place. The hours are long, and the money isn't that great. I know because I've been in it up to my neck since games ran on floppy disks. Somehow I find the energy to stay in the game. Am I just a glutton for punishment?

I guess there's a lot to be said for a profession that has one goal—fun. I learned in scouting that you should always leave a campsite better than you found it. I guess that working on computer games is a way to do that for much more than a campsite. My work in the computer game industry has hopefully had an effect on the people that enjoyed the games with my name somewhere in the credits. My work on this book has hopefully made working on the games themselves more fun and more enjoyable.

Only time will tell, eh?

INDEX